W9-CDC-943

India
a country study

Federal Research Division
Library of Congress
Edited by
James Heitzman and
Robert L. Worden
Research Completed
September 1995

On the cover: The peafowl, or peacock (*P. cristatus*), the national bird of India, is protected under the Indian Wild Life Protection Act of 1972. A traditional fixture in literature, folklore, legends, and art, the peafowl inhabits most of peninsular India, Jammu and Kashmir, eastern Assam, and southern Mizoram. Art of this type is found in parts of Uttar Pradesh and Rajasthan and is based on traditional paper stencil art (*sanzi khaka*) used on festive occasions for floor decorations employing marble dust and colored powders. From the Dover Pictorial Archive Series; used with permission of Dover Publications.

Fifth Edition, First Printing, 1996.

Library of Congress Cataloging-in-Publication Data

India : a country study / Federal Research Division, Library of Congress ; edited by James Heitzman and Robert L. Worden.—5th ed.

    p. cm. — (Area handbook series, ISSN 1057–5294) (DA Pam ; 550–21)

    "Supersedes the 1985 edition of India : a country study, edited by Richard F. Nyrop."—T.p. verso.

    "Research completed September 1995."

    Includes bibliographical references (pp. 671–785) and index.

    ISBN 0–8444–0833–6 (hardcover : alk. paper)

    1. India. I. Heitzman, James, 1950– . II. Worden, Robert L., 1945– . III. Library of Congress. Federal Research Division. IV. Series. V. Series: DA pam ; 550–21.

DS407.I4465 1996   96–19266

954—dc20   CIP

Headquarters, Department of the Army
DA Pam 550–21

Foreword

This volume is one in a continuing series of books prepared by the Federal Research Division of the Library of Congress under the Country Studies/Area Handbook Program sponsored by the Department of the Army. The last two pages of this book list the other published studies.

Most books in the series deal with a particular foreign country, describing and analyzing its political, economic, social, and national security systems and institutions, and examining the interrelationships of those systems and the ways they are shaped by historical and cultural factors. Each study is written by a multidisciplinary team of social scientists. The authors seek to provide a basic understanding of the observed society, striving for a dynamic rather than a static portrayal. Particular attention is devoted to the people who make up the society, their origins, dominant beliefs and values, their common interests and the issues on which they are divided, the nature and extent of their involvement with national institutions, and their attitudes toward each other and toward their social system and political order.

The books represent the analysis of the authors and should not be construed as an expression of an official United States government position, policy, or decision. The authors have sought to adhere to accepted standards of scholarly objectivity. Corrections, additions, and suggestions for changes from readers will be welcomed for use in future editions.

Louis R. Mortimer
Chief
Federal Research Division
Library of Congress
Washington, DC 20540–4840

Acknowledgments

The authors wish to thank individuals in various agencies of the Indian and United States governments and private institutions who gave their time, research materials, and special knowledge to provide information and perspective. These individuals include Hardeep Puri, Joint Secretary (America) of the Ministry of External Affairs; Madhukar Gupta, Joint Secretary (Kashmir) of the Ministry of Home Affairs; Bimla Bhalla, Director General of Advertising and Visual Publications, Ministry of Information and Broadcasting; Amulya Ratna Nanda, Registrar General of India; Ashok Jain, director of the National Institute of Science, Technology and Development Studies; T. Vishwanthan, director of the Indian National Scientific Documentation Centre; G.P. Phondke, director of the Publications and Information Directorate of the Council for Scientific and Industrial Research; Air Commander Jasjit Singh, director of the Institute for Defence Studies and Analyses; G. Madhavan, deputy executive secretary of the Indian Academy of Sciences; Sivaraj Ramaseshan, distinguished emeritus professor, Raman Research Institute; H.S. Nagaraja, public relations officer of the Indian Institute of Science; Virendra Singh, director of the Tata Institute of Fundamental Research; Bhabani Sen Gupta of the Centre for Policy Research; Pradeep Mehendiratta, Vice President and Executive Director, Indian Institute of American Studies; and Richard J. Crites, Chat Blakeman, Peter L.M. Heydemann, and Marcia S.B. Bernicat of the United States Embassy in New Delhi. Special thanks go to Lygia M. Ballantyne, director, and Alice Kniskern, deputy director, and the staff of the Library of Congress New Delhi Field Office, particularly Atish Chatterjee, for supplying bounteous amounts of valuable research materials on India and arranging interviews of Indian government officials.

Appreciation is also extended to Ralph K. Benesch, who formerly oversaw the Country Studies/Area Handbook Program for the Department of the Army, and to the desk officers in the Department of State and the Department of the Army who reviewed the chapters. Thanks also are offered to William A. Blanpied, Mavis Bowen, Ainslie T. Embree, Jerome Jacobson, Suzanne Hanchett, Barbara Leitch LePoer, Owen M. Lynch, and Sunalini Nayudu, who either assisted with substantive information or read parts of the manuscript or did both.

The authors also wish to thank those who contributed directly to the preparation of the manuscript. They include Sandra W. Meditz, who reviewed all textual and graphic materials, served as liaison with the Department of the Army, and provided numerous substantive and technical contributions; Sheila Ross, who edited the chapters; Andrea T. Merrill, who edited the tables and figures; Marilyn Majeska, who supervised editing and managed production; Alberta Jones King, who assisted with research, making wordprocessing corrections to various versions of the manuscript, and proofreading; Barbara Edgerton and Izella Watson, who performed the final wordprocessing; Marla D. Woodson, who assisted with proofreading; and Janie L. Gilchrist, David P. Cabitto, Barbara Edgerton, and Izella Watson, who prepared the camera-ready copy. Catherine Schwartzstein performed the final prepublication editorial review, and Joan C. Cook compiled the index.

Graphics support was provided by David P. Cabitto, who oversaw the production of maps and graphics and, with the assistance of Wayne Horne, designed the cover and the illustrations on the chapter title pages; and Harriet Blood and Maryland Mapping and Graphics, who assisted in the preparation of the maps and charts. Thanks also go to Gary L. Fitzpatrick and Christine M. Anderson, of the Library of Congress Geography and Map Division, for assistance in preparing early map drafts. A very special thank you goes to Janice L. Hyde, who did the research on and selection of cover and title-page illustrations and photographs, translated some of the photograph captions and textual references, and helped the editors on numerous matters of substance and analysis. Shantha S. Murthy of the Library of Congress Serial Record Division provided Indian language assistance. Clarence Maloney helped identify the subjects of some of the photographs.

Finally the authors acknowledge the generosity of individuals and public and private organizations who allowed their photographs to be used in this study. They have been acknowledged in the illustration captions.

Contents

Contributors.. 847

List of Figures

Preface

This edition supersedes the fourth edition of *India: A Country Study*, published in 1985 under the editorship of Richard F. Nyrop. The new edition provides updated information on the world's second most populous and fastest-growing nation. Although much of India's traditional behavior and organizational dynamics reported in 1985 have remained the same, internal and regional events have continued to shape Indian domestic and international policies.

To the extent possible, place-names used in the text conform to the United States Board on Geographic Names, but equal weight has been given to spellings provided by the official Survey of India. Selected acronyms and abbreviations are clarified in Table A, and a Chronology covering the long span of Indian history is given in Table B; both of these tables appear in the front of the book. Measurements are given in the metric system; a conversion table is provided to assist readers unfamiliar with metric measurements (see table 1, Appendix).

Users of this book are encouraged to consult the chapter bibliographies at the end of the book. They include several general and specialized bibliographies that will lead readers to further resources on India. Additionally, users may wish to consult the annual editions of the Association for Asian Studies' *Bibliography of Asian Studies*, as well as later editions of yearbooks listed in the bibliography of this volume. Other bibliographic sources of interest are N. Gerald Barrier's *India and America: American Publishing on India, 1930–1985* (New Delhi: American Institute of Indian Studies, 1986) and David Nelson's *Bibliography of South Asia* (Metuchen, New Jersey: Scarecrow, 1994). Those who read Indian classical and vernacular languages will find publications available in those languages in the Library of Congress and other major research libraries.

The illustrations on the cover and chapter title pages represent a variety of contemporary folk-art motifs from various parts of India.

The body of the text reflects information available as of September 1, 1995. Certain other portions of the text, however, have been updated. The Introduction discusses significant events that have occurred since the completion of research; the Country Profile includes updated information as available; and the Bibliography lists recently published sources thought to be particularly helpful to the reader.

Table A. Selected Acronyms, Abbreviations, and Full Party Names

Acronym or Abbreviation	Organization or Term
ABSU	All Bodo Students' Union
AGP	Asom Gana Parishad (Assam People's Assembly)
AIADMK	All-India Anna Dravida Munnetra Kazhagam (All-India Anna Dravidian Progressive Federation)
AIDS	acquired immune deficiency syndrome
ASEAN	Association of Southeast Asian Nations (see Glossary)
ASLV	Augmented Satellite Launch Vehicle
Arabsat	Arab Satellite Communication Organization
BAMCEF	All-India Backward, Scheduled Caste, Scheduled Tribe, Other Backward Classes, and Minority Communities Employees Federation
BJP	Bharatiya Janata Party (Indian People's Party)
BKD	Bharatiya Kranti Dal
BLD	Bharatiya Lok Dal (Indian People Party)
BPAC	Bodo People's Action Committee
BSP	Bahujan Samaj Party (Party of Society's Majority)
ca.	circa
CCN	Cable News Network
CFD	Congress for Democracy
Congress	Indian National Congress
Congress (I)	Congress (Indira)
Congress (O)	Congress (Organisation)
Congreess (R)	Congress (Requisition)
Congress (S)	Congress (Socialist and Secular)
Congress (U)	Congress (Urs)
CPI	Communist Party of India
CPI (M)	Communist Party of India (Marxist)
CPI (M-L)	Communist Party of India (Marxist-Leninist)
CSIR	Council of Scientific and Industrial Research
DK	Dravida Kazhagam (Dravidian Federation)
DMK	Dravida Munnetra Kazhagam (Dravidian Progressive Federation)
DMKP	Dalit Mazdoor Kisan Party (Oppressed Workers' and Peasants' Party)
DNA	deoxyribonucleic acid
DRDO	Defence Research and Development Organisation
ESCAP	Economic and Social Commission for Asia and the Pacific of the UN (*q.v.*)
FAO	Food and Agriculture Organization (see Glossary) of the UN (*q.v.*)
FY	fiscal year (see Glossary)
GATT	General Agreement on Tariffs and Trade
GDP	gross domestic product (see Glossary)

Table A. (Continued) Selected Acronyms, Abbreviations, and Full Party Names

Acronym or Abbreviation	Organization or Term
GNP	gross national product (see Glossary)
GSLV	Geostationary Launch Vehicle
HIV	human immunodeficiency virus
IIT	Indian Institute of Technology
IMF	International Monetary Fund (see Glossary)
INA	Indian National Army (Azad Hind Fauj)
INS	Indian Naval Ship
Insat	Indian National Satellite System
Intelsat	International Telecommunications Satellite Organization
IPF	Indian People's Front
IPKF	Indian Peace Keeping Force
ISRO	Indian Space Research Organisation
Jana Sangh	People's Union
Janata	Janata Party
Janata Dal	People's Party
Lok Dal	People Party
LTTE	Liberation Tigers of Tamil Eelam
NISTADS	National Institute of Science, Technology, and Development Studies
OPEC	Organization of the Petroleum Exporting Countries (see Glossary)
PSLV	polar satellite launch vehicle
PSP	Praja Socialist Party
r.	reigned
RSS	Rashtriya Swayamsevak Sangh (National Volunteer Organisation)
SAARC	South Asian Association for Regional Cooperation (see Glossary)
Samajwadi	Samajwadi Party (Socialist Party)
Samajwadi Janata	Socialist People's Party
SSP	Samyukta Socialist Party
Swatantra	Swatantra Party
Telugu Desam	Telugu National Party
ULFA	United Liberation Front of Assam
UN	United Nations
UNESCO	United Nations Educational, Scientific, and Cultural Organization
UNDP	United Nations Development Programme
VHP	Vishwa Hindu Parishad (World Hindu Council)
VSTOL	vertical and short takeoff and landing
WHO	World Health Organization

Table B. Chronology of Important Events

Period	Description
ANCIENT EMPIRES	
ca. 2500–1600 B.C.	Indus Valley culture.
ca. 1500–500 B.C.	Migrations of Aryan-speaking tribes; the Vedic Age.
ca. 1000 B.C.	Settlement of Bengal by Dravidian-speaking peoples.
ca. 563–ca. 483 B.C.	Life of Siddartha Gautama—the Buddha; founding of Buddhism.
ca. 326–184 B.C.	Mauryan Empire; reign of Ashoka (269–232 B.C.); spread of Buddhism.
ca. 180 B.C.–A.D. 150	Shaka dynasties in Indus Valley.
ca. A.D. 320–550	Gupta Empire; classical age in North India.
606–47	North Indian empire of Harsha.
711	Arab invaders conquer Sindh, establish Islamic presence in India.
750–1150	Pala Dynasty.
1150-1202	Sena Dynasty.
GROWTH OF ISLAM	
997–1027	Mahmud of Ghazni raids Indian subcontinent from Afghanistan.
1202	Turkish conquerors defeat Sena Dynasty and overrun Bengal.
1206–1398	Delhi Sultanate.
1398	Timur sacks Delhi.
1414–50	Sayyid Dynasty; renewal of Delhi Sultanate.
1451–1526	Lodi Dynasty.
THE MUGHAL PERIOD	
1526	Babur lays foundation of Mughal Empire; wins First Battle of Panipat.
1556–1605	Akbar expands and reforms the empire; Mughals win Second Battle of Panipat.
1605–27	Reign of Jahangir; in 1612 East India Company opens first trading post (factory).
1628–58	Reign of Shah Jahan.
1658–1707	Reign of Aurangzeb, last great Mughal ruler.
1707–1858	Lesser emperors; decline of the Mughal Empire.
BRITISH PERIOD	
1757	Battle of Plassey—British victory over Mughal forces in Bengal; British rule in India begins.
1835	Institution of British education and other reform measures.
1857–58	Revolt of Indian sepoys (soldiers) against East India Company.
1858	East India Company dissolved; rule of India under the British crown—the British Raj—begins with Government of India Act; formal end of Mughal Empire.
1885	Indian National Congress (Congress) formed.

Table B. (Continued) Chronology of Important Events

Period	Description
1905	Partition of Bengal into separate provinces of Eastern Bengal and Assam, West Bengal.
1906	All-India Muslim League (Muslim League) founded.
1909	Morley-Minto Reforms; separate electorates for Muslims.
1912	Partition of Bengal annulled; new province of Bihar and Orissa formed; plans to move capital from Calcutta to Delhi announced.
1916	Congress-League Scheme of Reforms (often referred to as Lucknow Pact) signed.
1919	Montagu-Chelmsford Reforms; Government of India Act.
1935	Government of India Act of 1935.
1940	Muslim League adopts Lahore Resolution; "Two Nations" theory articulated by Muslim League leader Mohammad Ali Jinnah and others.
August 16, 1946	"Direct Action Day" of Muslim League.
INDEPENDENT INDIA	
August 15, 1947	Partition of British India; India achieves independence and incorporates West Bengal and Assam; Jawaharlal Nehru becomes prime minister of India. Pakistan is created and incorporates East Bengal (the East Wing, or East Pakistan) and territory in the northwest (the West Wing, or West Pakistan); Jinnah becomes governor general of Pakistan.
August 15, 1947–May 27, 1964	Jawaharlal Nehru serves as prime minister and leader of Congress-controlled government.
October 22, 1947–January 1, 1949	Undeclared war with Pakistan; ends with United Nations-arranged ceasefire.
January 30, 1948	Mahatma Gandhi assassinated in New Delhi.
October 20–November 21, 1962	Border war with China.
June 9, 1964–January 11, 1966	Lal Bhadur Shastri serves as prime minister of Congress-led government.
August 5-September 23, 1965	Second war with Pakistan.
January 24, 1966–March 24, 1977	Indira Gandhi serves as prime minister for first time, head of government initially led by Congress, later Congress (R).
December 3–16, 1971	Third war with Pakistan; Bangladesh becomes independent following Indian invasion of East Pakistan.
June 25, 1975–January 18, 1977	State of Emergency proclaimed by Indira Gandhi.
March 24, 1977–July 28, 1979	Morarji Desai serves as prime minister as head of a multiparty front, Janata Party, India's first non-Congress government.
July 28, 1979–January 14, 1980	Chaudhury Charan Singh serves as prime minister as head of a Janata-led coalition government.
January 14, 1980–October 31, 1984	Indira Ganhdi serves as prime minister for second time, head of Congress (I) government.
October 31, 1984	Indira Gandhi assassinated in New Delhi.

Table B. (Continued) Chronology of Important Events

Period	Description
October 31, 1984–December 2, 1989	Rajiv Gandhi serves as prime minister of Congress (I)-led government.
December 2, 1989–November 7, 1990	Vishwanath Pratap Singh serves as prime minister of National Front-led coalition government.
November 10, 1990–June 20, 1991	Chandra Shekhar serves as prime minister, heading Samajwadi Janata Party government.
May 21, 1991	Rajiv Gandhi assassinated near Madras.
June 20, 1991–May 15, 1996	P.V. Narasimha Rao serves as prime minister of Congress (I)-led government.
December 6, 1992	Babri Masjid in Ayodhya, Uttar Pradesh, destroyed by Hindu activists.
January–March 1993	Communal violence in wake of Babri Masjid destruction wracks Indian cities, especially Bombay, which suffered from a series of bomb blasts in March.
May 1995	Unpopular Terrorist and Disruptive Activities (Prevention) Act of 1985 allowed to lapse
April 27–May 7, 1996	General elections for Lok Sabha oust Congress (I) government of P.V. Narasimha Rao.
May 15–28, 1996	Minority Bharatiya Janata Party (BJP) government led by Prime Minister Atal Bihari Vajpayee resigns after thirteen days.
June 1, 1996	Haradanahalli (H.D.) Deve Gowda, head of thirteen-party United Front, sworn in as India's eleventh prime minster.

Country Profile

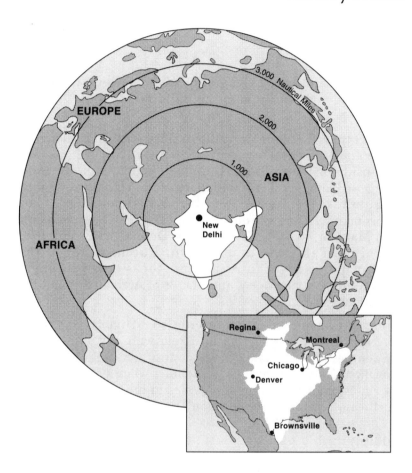

Country

Formal Name: Republic of India (The official, Sanskrit name for India is Bharat, the name of the legendary king in the *Mahabhrata*).

Short Form: India.

Term for Citizens: Indian(s).

Capital: New Delhi (National Capital Territory of Delhi).

Date of Independence: Proclaimed August 15, 1947, from

Britain.

National Holiday: Independence Day, August 15.

Geography

Size: Total land area 2,973,190 square kilometers. Total area, including territorial seas, claimed is 3,287,590 square kilometers.

Topography: Three main geological regions: Indo-Gangetic Plain and Himalayas, collectively known as North India; and Peninsula or South India. Ten physiological regions: Indo-Gangetic Plain, northern mountains of the Himalayas, Central Highlands, Deccan or Peninsular Plateau, East Coast (Coromandel Coast in south), West Coast (Konkan, Kankara, and Malabar coasts), Great Indian Desert (known as Thar Desert in Pakistan) and Rann of Kutch, valley of the Brahmaputra River in Assam, northeastern hill ranges surrounding Assam Valley, and islands of Arabian Sea and Bay of Bengal.

Climate: Climate varies significantly from Himalayas in north to tropical south. Four seasons: relatively dry, cool winter December to February; dry, hot summer March to May; southwest monsoon June to September when predominating southwest maritime winds bring rains to most of country; and northeast, or retreating, monsoon October and November.

Society

Population: 936,545,814 estimated in July 1995, with 1.8 percent annual growth rate. About 74 percent in rural areas in 1991; high population density—284 persons per square kilometer national average, major states more than 700 persons per square kilometer; 100 persons or fewer per square kilometer in some border states and insular territories. Bombay (officially renamed Mumbai in 1995) largest city, with 12.6 million in 1991; twenty-three other cities with populations of more than 1 million.

Health: In 1995 life expectancy for men 58.5 years, for women 59.6 years; infant mortality rate 76.3 per 1,000 live births. Malaria, filariasis, leprosy, cholera, pneumonic plague, tuberculosis, trachoma, goiter, and diarrheal diseases all occur.

In 1991 primary health centers, subcenters, and community health centers at local levels included more than 10,000 hospitals, 24,000 dispensaries, and 811,000 beds.

Education: Twelve-year education system; mandatory primary and middle levels, optional secondary education; high dropout rate even at compulsory levels. System supervised by Department of Education, part of Ministry of Human Resource Development. National adult literacy rate 52.2 percent in 1991 (male 63.9 percent, female 39.4 percent). More than 180 universities, some 500 teacher training colleges, and several thousand other colleges.

Religion: Most (82 percent) observe Hinduism; 12.1 percent Muslim, 2.3 percent Christian, 1.9 percent Sikh, 0.8 percent Buddhist, 0.4 percent Jains, 0.4 percent other, 0.1 percent not identified.

Language: Official language Hindi; English also has official status. For use in certain official capacities, constitution recognizes eighteen Scheduled Languages (see Glossary): Assamese, Bengali, Gujarati, Hindi, Kannada, Kashmiri, Konkani, Malayalam, Manipuri, Marathi, Nepali, Oriya, Punjabi, Sanskrit, Sindhi, Tamil, Telugu, and Urdu. Four major language families include officially 112 "mother tongues," each with 10,000 or more speakers; thirty-three languages spoken by 1 million or more persons. Total number of languages and dialects varies depending on source and how counted; between 179 and 188 languages and between forty-nine and 544 dialects have been tabulated; census respondents in 1961 provided names for 1,652 different "mother tongues."

Ethnic Groups: Indo-Aryan 72 percent, Dravidian 25 percent, Mongoloid and other 3 percent. Caste system, although no longer sanctioned by government, prevails. Some 16 percent listed as members of Scheduled Castes (see Glossary), 8 percent as members of Scheduled Tribes (see Glossary).

Economy

Salient Features: Economy transformed from primarily agriculture, forestry, fishing, and textile manufacturing in 1947 to major heavy industry, transportation, and telecommunications industries by late 1970s. Central government planning 1950 through late 1970s giving way to economic reforms and more private-sector initiatives in 1980s and 1990s.

Agriculture predominates and benefits from infusion of modern technology by government. World Bank Group and developed nations provide most aid; Japan largest donor. Major trade partners United States, Japan, European Union, and nations belonging to Organization of the Petroleum Exporting Countries (OPEC—see Glossary).

Currency and Exchange Rate: Rupee; US$1 = Rs35.67 (July 1996).

Fiscal Year (FY): April 1–March 31.

Gross Domestic Product (GDP): Rs36.7 trillion (nearly US$1.2 trillion) in 1994 (estimated). GDP annual average growth rate 3.8 percent in 1994.

Foreign Trade: Principal export trade with European Union, United States, and Japan. Main commodities agricultural and allied products, gems and jewelry, and ready-made garments. Iron ore, minerals, and leather and leather products also important. Exports 7.7 percent of GDP in FY 1992. Principal import trade with European Union, United States, and Japan. Major imports (28 percent of total) oil products from Middle East. Other major imports chemicals, dyes, plastics, pharmaceuticals, uncut precious stones, iron and steel, fertilizers, nonferrous metals, and pulp paper and paper products. Imports 9.3 percent of GDP in FY 1992.

Balance of Payments: Negative trade balance in late 1980s and early 1990s. In 1993 estimated exports US$22.7 billion versus US$23.9 billion imports.

Foreign Aid: Most aid provided by Aid-to-India Consortium, consisting of World Bank Group and Austria, Belgium, Britain, Canada, Denmark, Germany, France, Italy, Japan, Netherlands, Norway, Sweden, and United States. Japan largest aid granter and lender; US$337 million grants between 1984 and 1993, US$2.4 billion loans in same period. Indian aid program to Bhutan and Nepal; smaller programs assist Bangladesh and Vietnam.

Industry: Increasing share (27.4 percent in FY 1991) of GDP, but employed only about 9 percent of the work force in 1991. Basic industries: textiles, steel and aluminum, fertilizers and petrochemicals, and electronics and motor vehicles.

Energy: India importer of petroleum and natural gas but has abundant coal, hydroelectric power (especially in parts of

North India), and burgeoning nuclear power industry.

Minerals: Less than 2 percent share of GDP in FY 1990 and 1 percent of labor force involved in mining and quarrying in 1991. Basic minerals: iron, bauxite, copper, lead, zinc, mica, uranium ore, rare earths.

Services: Some 39.8 percent of GDP in FY 1991, then employing about 13 percent of work force. Large and diverse transportation system.

Agriculture: Declining share (32.8 percent) of GDP but employed majority of workers (67 percent of total labor force) in FY 1991. Around 45 percent (136 million hectares) of total land cultivated, 27 percent double cropped, effectively giving India 173 million hectares of cultivated land. Another 5 percent (15 million hectares) permanent pastureland or planted in tree crops or groves. Farming by smallholders; large landholders divested in 1970s. Rice, wheat, pulses, and oilseeds dominate production, but millet, corn (maize), and sorghum important; commercial crops—sugar (India world's largest producer), cotton, jute also important. Green Revolution technological advances and improved high-yielding variety seeds, and increased fertilizer production and irrigation between mid-1960s and early 1980s. Dairy farming, fishing, and forestry important parts of agricultural sector. Agricultural products around 18 percent of total exports.

Science and Technology: Major government investment (80 percent of total) in and control of science and technology sector; 200 national laboratories, 200 government-sector research and development institutions, and about 1,000 research and development units in industrial sector supported by both public and private funds. Substantial investments in research and development in defense, nuclear science, space, and agriculture.

Transportation and Telecommunications

Railroads: Track route length 62,458 in mid-1990s, fourth most heavily used system in world, both for passengers and freight; all government-owned and operated by Indian Railways. Some 14,600 kilometers double or multiple tracked; 11,000 kilometers electrified, 116,000 bridges; some high-speed routes; domestic production of most rolling stock and other components. Major government investment in modernization in 1990s. Full metro system in Calcutta, rapid transit system in Madras, and major system planned for New Delhi; Bombay served by suburban rail network.

Roads: Almost 2 million kilometers; 960,000 kilometers surfaced roads, and more than 1 million kilometers constructed of gravel, crushed stone, or earth. Fifty-three highways, almost 20,000 kilometers in total length, rated as national highways; carry about 40 percent of road traffic. Around 60 percent of all passenger traffic travels by road. Urban transit dominated by motor vehicles; increasing use of two- and three-wheel vehicles, automobiles, minibuses, buses, trucks. Large cities have major urban bus systems. Bullocks, camels, elephants, and other beasts of burden seen throughout India.

Maritime Transport: Eleven major ports and 139 minor ports. In 1995 three government-owned and between fifty and sixty privately owned shipping companies. Four major and three medium-sized shipyards, all government run, thirty-five smaller shipyards in private sector. Major coastal and ocean trade routes, more than 16,000 kilometers of inland waterways, more than 3,600 kilometers navigable by large vessels, although only about 2,000 kilometers used.

Airports: Two airlines (Air India and Indian Airlines) and one helicopter service (Pawan Hans) owned by government and six privately owned airlines; latter account for only 10 percent of domestic air traffic. Of 288 airports, 208 permanent-surface runways and two runways of more than 3,659 meters. Major international airports at Bombay (Mumbai), Delhi, Calcutta, Madras, and Thiruvananthapuram (Trivandrum). International service also from Mamargao (Goa), Bangalore, and Hyderabad. Major regional airports at Ahmadabad, Allahabad, Pune, Srinagar, Chandigarh, Kochi (Cochin), Nagpur, and Thiruvananthapuram.

Telecommunications: National system controlled by government, with public corporations running service in New Delhi and Bombay; some basic telephone services opened to private-sector competition in 1994; telephone line density only 0.7 per 100 persons in 1994, among lowest of major nations of Asia. Submarine cables link India to Malaysia and United Arab Emirates. Paging, cellular phone service, and electronic mail being introduced. Government-owned radio (Akashvani) and television (Doordarshan) networks with extensive national and local coverage; private-sector television networks via cable and satellite becoming prolific.

Government and Politics

Government: Federal republic based on separation of powers into executive, legislative, and judicial branches. Central government known as union government. Constitution of 1950 in force but much amended; power concentrated in Parliament with upper house—Rajya Sabha (Council of States)—appointed by president and elected by state and territory assemblies and lower house—Lok Sabha (House of the People)—popularly elected. Supreme Court highest court of land; high courts in states.

Administrative Divisions: Twenty-five states with 476 districts, one national capital territory, six union territories. State governors appointed by president, chief minister member of popularly elected state assembly; central-government agencies prevalent at local levels. Constitution allows central control of state government (President's Rule) during time of emergency on recommendation of governor. Districts subdivided into *taluqs* or *tehsils*, townships that contain from 200 to 600 villages. Small, centrally controlled union territories with lieutenant governor or chief commissioner appointed by president.

Politics: With 354 million voters, some 14,700 candidates, more than 500 parties, and nearly 595,000 polling stations in April–May 1996 elections, India often called "world's largest democracy." Since independence, dominated by Indian National Congress (Congress—see Glossary) and its factions; occasional rule by minority-party and coalition governments; Janata Party, Bharatiya Janata Party (BJP), communist parties, and several regional parties also important.

Foreign Relations: Member of United Nations (UN), South Asian Association for Regional Cooperation (SAARC), Nonaligned Movement, and numerous other international organizations. Relations with all major nations based on principles of nonalignment.

National Security

Armed Forces: Armed forces of India total active-duty personnel in 1994 approximately 1,104,000. Component services: army, 940,000; navy, 54,000, of which 5,000 naval aviation and 1,000 marines; air force, 110,000. Reserve forces personnel total 1,964,554; also twelve paramilitary forces under control of various ministries with total strength of 762,735 in 1994.

Military Units: Army structured as twelve corps (twenty-two infantry divisions) under central control, organized into five tactical area commands. Navy units in three area commands. Air Force units in five operational commands. Police commands coincide with state boundaries.

Military Equipment: Army main battle tanks, armored personnel carriers (APCs), towed and self-propelled artillery, helicopters. Navy: aircraft carriers, submarines, destroyers, frigates, fast-attack patrol craft, amphibious ships, fixed-wing aircraft, helicopters, and marine reconnaissance aircraft. Air Force: ground-attack fighters, transports, trainers, and helicopters. Emphasis on domestic production of most items; most imports from Britain, France, Germany, and Russia. Older equipment from Soviet Union.

Military Budget: Approximately US$6.9 billion, or less than 5 percent of gross national product in FY 1994.

Foreign Military Relations: Long-term ties with Soviet Union and, later, Russia. Occasional joint operations with Indian Ocean nations and United States. Peacekeeping forces sent to Sri Lanka and Maldives. Since 1950 Indian military and police contingents also have participated in UN peacekeeping forces in Korea, Suez Canal, Sinai Peninsula, Gaza, Congo, Lebanon, Yemen, West Irian, Iran-Iraq border, Costa Rica, El Salvador, Guatemala, Honduras, Nicaragua, Namibia, Angola, former Yugoslavia, Mozambique, Cambodia, and Somalia.

Internal Security Forces: Paramilitary forces guard coasts, borders, and sensitive military areas; paramilitary sent by central government to aid local police forces and against insurgencies. Provincial Armed Constabulary and Central Reserve Police Force handle police duties.

Introduction

INDIA IS A LAND of ancient civilization, with cities and villages, cultivated fields, and great works of art dating back 4,000 years. India's high population density and variety of social, economic, and cultural configurations are the products of a long process of regional expansion. In the last decade of the twentieth century, such expansion has led to the rapid erosion of India's forest and wilderness areas in the face of ever-increasing demands for resources and gigantic population pressures—India's population is projected to exceed 1 billion by the twenty-first century.

Such problems are a relatively recent phenomenon. Rhinoceros inhabited the North Indian plains as late as the sixteenth century. Historical records and literature of earlier periods reveal the motif of the forest everywhere. Stories of merchant caravans typically included travel through long stretches of jungle inhabited by wild beasts and strange people; royal adventures usually included a hunting expedition and meetings with unusual beings. In the *Mahabharata* and the *Ramayana*, early epics that reflect life in India before 1000 B.C. and 500 B.C., respectively, the forest begins at the edge of the city, and the heroes regularly spend periods of exile wandering far from civilization before returning to rid the world of evil. The formulaic rituals of the Vedas also reflect attempts to create a regulated, geometric space from the raw products of nature.

The country's past serves as a reminder that India today, with its overcrowding and scramble for material gain, its poverty and outstanding intellectual accomplishments, is a society in constant change. Human beings, mostly humble folk, have within a period of 200 generations turned the wilderness into one of the most complicated societies in the world. The process began in the northwest in the third millennium B.C., with the Indus Valley, or Harappan, civilization, when an agricultural economy gave rise to extensive urbanization and long-distance trade. The second stage occurred during the first millennium B.C., when the Ganga-Yamuna river basin and several southern river deltas experienced extensive agricultural expansion and population growth, leading to the rebirth of cities, trade, and a sophisticated urban culture.

By the seventh century A.D., a dozen core regions based on access to irrigation-supported kingdoms became tied to a pan-Indian cultural tradition and participated in increasing cross-cultural ties with other parts of Asia and the Middle East. India's inclusion within a global trading economy after the thirteenth century culminated in the arrival of Portuguese explorers, traders, and missionaries, beginning in 1498. Although there were ebbs and flows in the pattern, the overall tendency was for peasant cultivators and their overlords to expand agriculture and animal husbandry into new ecological zones, and to push hunting and gathering societies farther into the hills.

By the twentieth century, most such tribal (see Glossary) groups, although constituting a substantial minority within India, lived in restricted areas under severe pressure from the caste-based agricultural and trading societies pressing from the plains. Because this evolution took place over more than forty centuries and encompassed a wide range of ecological niches and peoples, the resulting social pattern is extremely complicated and alters constantly.

India had its share of conquerors who moved in from the northwest and overran the north or central parts of the country. These migrations began with the Aryan peoples of the second millennium B.C. and culminated in the unification of the entire country for the first time in the seventeenth century under the Mughals. Mostly these conquerors were nomadic or seminomadic people who adopted or expanded the agricultural economy and contributed new cultural forms or religions, such as Islam.

The Europeans, primarily the English, arrived in force in the early seventeenth century and by the eighteenth century had made a profound impact on India. India was forced, for the first time, into a subordinate role within a world system based on industrial production rather than agriculture. Many of the dynamic craft or cottage industries that had long attracted foreigners to India suffered extensively under competition with new modes of mass production fostered by the British. Modern institutions, such as universities, and technologies, such as railroads and mass communication, broke with Indian intellectual traditions and served British, rather than Indian, economic interests. A country that in the eighteenth century was a magnet for trade was, by the twentieth century, an underdeveloped and overpopulated land groaning under alien domination. Even at the end of the twentieth century, with the period of colonialism well in the past, Indians remain sensitive to foreign domination and are determined to prevent the country from coming under such domination again.

Through India's long history, religion has been the carrier and preserver of culture. One distinctive aspect of the evolution of civilization in India has been the importance of hereditary priesthoods, often Brahmans (see Glossary), who have functioned as intellectual elites. The heritage preserved by these groups had its origin in the Vedas and allied bodies of literature in the Sanskrit language, which evolved in North India during the second millennium B.C. This tradition always accepted a wide range of paths to ultimate truth, and thus encompassed numerous rituals and forms of divinity within a polytheistic system. Generally, Brahmans supported the phenomenon known as Sanskritization, or the inclusion of local or regional traditions within Sanskrit literary models and pan-Indian cultural motifs. In this way, there has been a steady spread of North Indian cultural and linguistic forms throughout the country. This process has not gone unopposed. Siddhartha Gautama (the Buddha) and Mahavira (founder of Jainism) in the fifth century B.C. represented alternative methods for truth-seekers; they renounced the importance of priesthoods in favor of monastic orders without reference to birth. The largest challenge came from Islam, which rests on Arabic rather than Sanskritic cultural traditions, and has served, especially since the eleventh century, as an important alternative religious path. The interaction of Brahmanical religious forms with local variations and with separate religions creates another level of complexity in Indian social life.

Closely allied with religious belief, and deeply rooted in history, caste remains an important feature of Indian society. Caste in many Indian languages is *jati,* or birth—a system of classifying and separating people from birth within thousands of different groups labeled by occupation, ritual status, social etiquette, and language. Scholars have long debated the origins of this system, and have suggested as the origin religious concepts of reincarnation, the incorporation of many ethnic groups within agricultural systems over the millennia, or occupational stratification within emerging class societies. What is certain is that nineteenth-century British administrators, in their drive to classify and regulate the many social groups they encountered in everyday administration, established lists or schedules of different caste groups. At that time, it seemed that the rules against intermarriage and interdining that defined caste boundaries tended to freeze these groups within unchanging little societies, a view that fit well with imperialistic models imposed on India as a whole. Experience during the twentieth century has demonstrated that the caste system is capable of radical change and adaptation.

Modernization and urbanization have led to a decline in the outward display of caste exclusiveness, so that issues of caste may never emerge directly on public transit or in the workplace. Entire castes have changed their status, claiming higher positions as they shed their traditional occupations or accumulate money and power. In many villages, however, the segregation of castes by neighborhood and through daily behavior still exists at the end of the twentieth century. In the cities, segregation takes more subtle forms, emerging directly at times of marriage but existing more often as an undercurrent of discrimination in educational opportunities, hiring, and promotion. The British schedules of different castes, especially those of very low or Untouchable (Dalit—see Glossary) groups, later became the basis for affirmative-action programs in independent India that allowed some members of the most oppressed caste groups access to good education and high-paying jobs. The reservation of positions for Backward Classes (see Glossary) has remained a sore point with higher-ranked groups and has contributed to numerous political confrontations. Meanwhile, attempts by low-ranking (and desperately poor) castes to organize and agitate against discrimination have been met with violence in most Indian states and territories. Caste, therefore, is a very live issue.

Religious, caste, and regional diversity exist in India against a background of poverty. At independence in 1947, the British left India in terrible condition. The country emerged from World War II with a rudimentary scientific and industrial base and a rapidly expanding population that lived primarily in villages and was divided by gross inequalities in status and wealth. Under the leadership of Jawaharlal Nehru, India's first prime minister (1947–64), India addressed its economic crisis through a combination of socialist planning and free enterprise. During the 1950s and 1960s, large government investments made India as a whole into one of the most industrialized nations in the world. Considerable expenditure on irrigation facilities and fertilizer plants, combined with the introduction of high-yield variety seeds in the 1960s, allowed the Green Revolution to banish famine. The abolition of princely states and large land holdings, combined with (mostly ineffective) land redistribution schemes, also eliminated some of the most glaring inequalities in the countryside and in some areas, such as Punjab, stimulated the growth of middle-sized entrepreneurial farms. Building on the education system bequeathed by the British, India established an infrastructure of universities, basic research institutes, and applied research facilities that trained one of the world's largest scientific and technical establishments.

The socialist model of development remained dominant in India through the 1970s, under the leadership of Prime Minister Indira Gandhi, Nehru's daughter. Government-owned firms controlled iron and steel, mining, electronics, cement, chemicals, and other major industries. Telecommunications media, railroads, and eventually the banking industry were nationalized. Import-substitution policies, designed to encourage Indian firms and push out multinational corporations, included strict and time-consuming procedures for obtaining licenses and laws that prohibited firms from operating in India without majority ownership by Indian citizens or corporations. These rules were instrumental, for example, in driving IBM from India in the 1970s, leading to the growth of an indigenous Indian computer industry. By the late 1980s, however, after Mrs. Gandhi's 1984 assassination, the disadvantages of the centrally planned economy began to outweigh its benefits. Inefficiency in public-sector firms, lack of entrepreneurial innovation, excessive bureaucracy, and the inability of the Indian scientific and technical apparatus to transfer technology to marketable goods kept many Indian firms from being competitive in international markets.

Under Prime Minister Rajiv Gandhi and his successors, the national and state-level (states, union territories, and the national capital territory) governments liberalized licensing requirements and eventually rescinded rules on foreign ownership, while taking steps to scale down government market share in a number of high-technology markets. Multinational firms began to reenter India in the late 1980s and the early 1990s, as the government encouraged private enterprise and international sales in its search for foreign exchange. India began to open its economy to the world.

Indian-style socialism was probably necessary in the years after independence to protect the nation from foreign economic domination, but its biggest problem was that it did not eliminate poverty. The vast majority of India's population continued to live in small agricultural villages with few public amenities. A significant minority of the population in the 1990s live below the Indian definition of the poverty line, surviving at subsistence level, unemployed or underemployed, with little education or opportunity for training, and suffering from a variety of curable health problems. There are also some 200 million people who live above the official poverty line, but whose lives remain precariously balanced on the border of destitution. The per capita income of India as a whole remains among the lowest in the world. One of the biggest issues facing India as its economy has changed direction is that free-market capitalism offers little help for this large mass of people, who lack the skills or opportunity to participate in the new economy.

The big social story of India in the 1980s and the 1990s is the emergence of the middle class. This group includes members of prosperous farming families, as well as the primarily urban-based professional, administrative, and business elites who benefited from forty years of government protection and training. By the mid-1990s, the drive toward modernization had transformed 26.1 percent of the country into urban areas, where, amid masses of impoverished citizens, a sizable class of consumers has arisen. The members of this increasingly vocal middle class chafe under the older, regulated economy and demand a loosening of economic controls to make consumer goods available on the free market. They want education for their children that prepares them for technical and professional careers, increasingly in the private sector instead of the traditional sinecures in government offices. They build their well-appointed brick houses in exclusive suburban neighborhoods or surround their lots with high walls amid urban squalor, driving their scooters or automobiles to work while their children attend private schools.

The result of these processes over the course of fifty years is a dynamic, modernizing India with major class cleavages. The upper 1 or 2 percent of the population includes some of the wealthiest people in the world, who can be seen at the racetrack in the latest fashions from Paris or Tokyo, who travel extensively outside India for business, pleasure, or advanced medical care, and whose children attend the most exclusive English-language schools within India and abroad. For the middle class, which makes up between 15 and 25 percent of the population, the end of the twentieth century is a time of relative prosperity: incomes generally keep pace with inflation and jobs may still be obtained through family connections. The increase in consumer goods, such as washing machines and electric kitchen appliances, makes life easier and reduces dependence on lower-class (and low-caste) servants. For the industrial working class, the 1990s are a period of transition as dynamic new industries grow, mostly in the private sector, while many large government-sponsored plants are in jeopardy. The trade union movement, closely connected in some states with communist parties, finds itself under considerable pressure during a period of structural change in the economy. For large numbers of peasants and dwellers in urban slums, a way out of poverty remains as elusive as it had seemed for their grandparents at independence.

The political system responsible for these gigantic successes and failures has been democratic; India has called itself "the world's largest democracy." Paradoxically, it was the autocratic rule of the British that gave birth to the rule of the people. Democratization started when a group of concerned British citizens in India and well-to-do Indian professionals gathered in Bombay in 1885 to form a political debating society, the Indian National Congress (Congress—see Glossary). Originally conceived as a lobbying group, the Congress after 1900 became radicalized and took the forefront in a drive for home rule that encompassed elected assemblies and parliamentary procedure. In the face of British intransigence, the Congress soon became the leading organization within a broad-based freedom struggle that finally forced the British out in 1947. Mohandas Karamchand Gandhi (the Mahatma or Great Soul) was a central figure in this struggle because he was able to turn the Congress from an elite pressure group into a mass movement that mobilized hundreds of millions of people against the immorality of a foreign, nondemocratic system.

Gandhi perfected nonviolent techniques for general strikes and civil disobedience, and coordinated demonstrations with mass publicity; the techniques that he popularized have played a part in later Indian and world politics (including the United States civil rights movement). He evolved a philosophy of political involvement as sacrifice for the good of the world and played the role of a holy man who was also a cagey politician—

an image that remained important for Indian political figures after independence.

In a move to undercut British industrial superiority, Gandhi encouraged a return to a communal, rustic life and village handicrafts as the most humane way of life. Finally, he railed against the segregation of the caste system and religious bigotry that reduced large minorities within India to second-class citizenship. Gandhi was thus able to unite European humanistic and democratic ideas with Indian concepts of an interdependent, responsible community to create a unique political philosophy complete with action plan. In the last years before his assassination in 1948, Gandhi's idiosyncratic program fell out of step with the modernization paradigm of Nehru and the leadership of an independent India, and his ideas became a background theme within Indian political economy. On a regular basis, however, Indian leaders continue to hearken back to his message and employ his organizational and media tactics on the independent Indian political scene.

The Congress remained the most important political organization in India after independence. Except for brief periods in the late 1970s and late 1980s and until the mid-1990s, the Congress always controlled Parliament and chose the prime minister. The political dynasty of Jawaharlal Nehru (1947–64), his daughter Indira Gandhi (1965–77, 1980–84), and her son Rajiv Gandhi (1984–89) was crucial in keeping the Congress in power and also providing continuity in leadership for the country. The party was able to appeal to a wide segment of the poor (including low castes and Muslims) through its ideology of social equality and welfare programs, while appealing to the more prosperous voters—usually from upper castes—by preserving private property and supporting village community leadership. Because it stayed in power so long, the Congress was able to dispense government benefits to a wide range of constituencies, which prompted charges of corruption and led to Congress reversals in the late 1980s. Because it affected a type of socialist policy, the Congress diffused or incorporated left-wing political rhetoric and prevented the growth of a communist-led insurrection that might have been expected under the difficult social conditions existing in India.

Although a vibrant communist movement remains a force in Indian politics, it manifests itself at the state level of government rather than in national political power or large-scale revolutionary turmoil. Challenges from the right were small as well until the early 1990s, when the Bharatiya Janata Party (BJP—Indian People's Party) emerged as a serious contender for national leadership. The BJP advocated a blend of Hindu nationalism that inserted religious issues into the heart of national political debates, unlike the secular ideology that officially dominated Indian political thought after independence. In the early 1990s, however, the Congress, after having entered its second century of dominance over the Indian political landscape, continued to hold on to power with a middle-of-the-road message and smaller majorities.

The federal structure of India, embodied in the constitution of 1951, attempts to strike a balance between a strong central government and the autonomous governments of the nation-sized states, each with a distinct culture and deep historical roots, that make up the union. A formidable array of powers at the center makes it possible for the central government to intervene in state issues; these powers include control over the military, the presence of an appointed governor to monitor affairs within each state, and the ability of the president to suspend state-level legislatures in times of internal disorder and declare direct President's Rule. In theory, these powers should come into play rarely because the regular administration of the states resides with elected assemblies and chief ministers appointed through parliamentary procedures. State governments have extensive powers over almost all of their internal affairs. The framers of the national constitution constructed a series of checks and balances among the legislative, executive, and judicial branches at the center, and between the center and the states, designed to provide national security while allowing a maximum of state autonomy within the diversified union.

The Indian political system has proven to be flexible and durable, but major internal conflicts have threatened the constitution. In practice, the elected office of the nation's president has gravitated toward the formal and ritual aspects of executive power, while the office of the prime minister, backed up by a majority in Parliament, the cabinet, national security forces, and the bureaucracy of the Indian Administrative Service, has wielded the actual power. The national Parliament has not developed an independent committee structure and critical tradition that could stand against the force of the executive branch. The judiciary, while remaining independent and at times crucial in determining national policy, has stayed in the background and is subject to future change through constitutional amendments. The constitution itself has been subject to numerous amendments since its adoption in 1950. By August 1996, the constitution had been amended eighty times.

National politics have become contests to set up the appointment of the prime minister, who then has considerable power to interfere directly or through a cooperative president in all aspects of national life. The most drastic example of this power occurred in 1975, when Indira Gandhi implemented the constitutional provision for a declaration of Emergency, suspending civil rights for eighteen months, using Parliament as a tool for eliminating opposition, and ruling with the aid of a small circle of advisers. The more common form of executive interference has been the suspension of state legislatures under a variety of pretexts and the implementation of President's Rule. This typically has occurred when opposition parties have captured state legislatures and set in motion policies unfavorable to the prime minister's party. After Indira Gandhi's assassination in 1984, her successors engaged in such overt acts of interference less often.

The main opposition to the national executive comes from the states, in a variety of legal and extralegal struggles for regional autonomy. Most of the states have developed specific political identities based on forms of ethnicity that claim a long historical past. The most common identifying characteristic is language. Agitation in what became the state of Andhra Pradesh led the way in the 1950s, resulting in the reorganization of state boundaries along linguistic lines. Agitations in the state of Tamil Nadu in the 1960s resulted in domination of the state by parties dedicated officially to Tamil nationalism.

In the northeast, regional struggles have coalesced around tribal identities, leading to the formation of a number of small states based on dominant tribal groupings. Farther south, in Kerala and West Bengal, communist parties have upheld the banner of regionalism by capturing state assemblies and implementing radical socialist programs against the wishes of the central government.

The regional movements most threatening to national integration have occurred in the northwest. The state of Punjab was divided by the Indian government twice after independence—Haryana and Himachal Pradesh were sliced off—before it achieved a Sikh majority population in what remained of Punjab. That majority allowed the Sikh-led Akali Dal (Eternal Party) to capture the state assembly in the early 1980s. By then radical separatist elements were determined to fight for an independent Sikh Punjab. The result was an army attack on Sikh militants occupying the Golden Temple in Amritsar, Indira Gandhi's assassination by her Sikh bodyguards, both in 1984, and a ten-year internal security struggle that has killed thousands. In India's state of Jammu and Kashmir (often referred to as Kashmir), where Muslims constitute the majority of the population, regional struggle takes a different religious form and has created intense security problems that keep bilateral relations with Pakistan, which also lays claim to Kashmir, in a tense mode.

The central government usually has been able to defuse regional agitations by agreeing to redefinition of state boundaries or by guaranteeing differing degrees of regional autonomy, including acquiescence in the control of the state government by regional political parties. This strategy defused the original linguistic agitations through the 1970s, and led to the resolution of the destructive political and ethnic crises in Assam in the mid-1980s. When national security interests came into play, however, as in Punjab and Jammu and Kashmir, the central government did not hesitate to use force.

In the mid-1990s, India remains a strong unified nation, with a long history of constitutional government and democracy, but at any moment there are half a dozen regional political agitations underway and a dozen guerrilla movements in different parts of the country advocating various types of official recognition or outright independence based on ethnic affiliation. The unity of the country as a whole has never been seriously threatened by these movements. Because the benefits of union within India have outweighed the advantages of independence for most people within each state, there have always been moderate elements within the states willing to make deals with the central government, and security forces have proven capable of repressing any armed struggle at the regional level. In addition, state-level opposition, whether in the legislatures or in the streets, has been an effective means of preventing massive interference from New Delhi in the day-to-day lives of citizens, and thus has provided a crucial check that has preserved the democratic system and the constitution.

One of the most serious challenges to India's internal security and democratic traditions has come from so-called communal disorders, or riots, based on ethnic cleavages. The most typical form is a religious riot, mostly between Hindus and Muslims, although some of these disturbances also occur between different castes or linguistic groups. Most of these struggles start with neighborhood squabbles of little significance, but rapidly escalate into mob looting and burning, street fighting, and violent intervention by the police or paramilitary forces.

Religious ideology has played only a small part in these events. Instead, the pressures of urban life in overcrowded, poorer neighborhoods, combined with competition for limited economic opportunities, create an environment in which ethnic differences become convenient labels for defining enemies, and criminal behavior becomes commonplace. Whether ignited by a street accident or a major political event, passions in these areas may be directed into mob action. However, after the catastrophe of independence (when hundreds of thousands in North India died during the partition of India and Pakistan and at least 12 million became refugees), and because the pattern of rioting has continued annually in various cities, a culture of distrust has grown up among a sizable minority of Hindus and Muslims. This distrust has manifested itself in the nationwide agitations fomented by elements of the BJP and communal Hindu parties in the early 1990s. It reached a peak in December 1992 with the dramatic destruction of the Babri Masjid, a mosque in Ayodhya (in Uttar Pradesh), and communal riots and bombings in major cities throughout India in early 1993. In this manner, the frictions of daily life in an overcrowded, poor nation have had a major impact on the national political agenda.

The internal conflict between Hindus and Muslims has received some of its stimulus since 1947 from the international conflict between India and Pakistan. One of the great tragedies of the freedom struggle was the relentless polarization of opinion between the Congress, which came to represent mostly Hindus, and the All-India Muslim League (Muslim League—see Glossary), which eventually stood behind a demand for a separate homeland for a Muslim majority. This division, encouraged under British rule by provisions for separate electorates for Muslims, led to the partition of Pakistan from India and the outbreak of hostilities over Kashmir. Warfare between India and Pakistan occurred in 1947, 1965, and 1971; the last conflict led to the independence of Bangladesh (formerly East Pakistan) and a major strategic victory by India.

The perception of Pakistan as an enemy nation has over-shadowed all other Indian foreign policy considerations because neither country has relinquished claims over Kashmir, and a series of border irritations continue to bedevil attempts at rapprochement. In the late 1980s, tensions over large-scale military maneuvers almost led to war, and regular fighting over glacial wastelands in Kashmir continues to keep the pressure high. An added dimension emerged in 1987 when Pakistan publicly admitted that it possessed nuclear weapons capability, matching Indian nuclear capabilities demonstrated in 1974. In the mid-1990s, both nations continue to devote a large percentage of their military budgets to developing or to purchasing advanced weaponry, which is mostly aimed at each other—a serious drain of resources needed for economic growth.

Nehru and the early leadership of independent India had envisioned a nation at peace with the rest of the world, in keeping with Gandhian ideals and socialist goals. Under Nehru's guidance, India distanced itself from Cold War politics and played a major part in the Nonaligned Movement (see Glossary). Until the early 1960s, India spent relatively little on national defense and enjoyed an excellent relationship with the United States, a relationship that peaked in John F. Kennedy's presidency. India's strategic position changed after China defeated the Indian army in the border war of 1962 and war with Pakistan occurred in 1965. During this period, the situation became more precarious because India had opponents on two fronts. In addition, Pakistan began to receive substantial amounts of military assistance from the United States, ostensibly to support anticommunism, but it was no secret that most of the weapons purchased with United States aid were a deterrent projected against India. Under these circumstances, India began to move closer to the Soviet Union, purchasing outright large amounts of military hardware or making agreements to produce it indigenously.

Relations between the United States and India reached a low point in 1971 during the Bangladesh war of independence, when a United States naval force entered the Bay of Bengal to show support for Pakistan although doing nothing to forestall its defeat. This display of force, which could not be opposed by India or the Soviet Union, served only to strain the relationship between India and the United States and heightened Cold War tensions in South Asia. During the 1970s, as the United States and China improved relations and China became closer in turn to Pakistan, India's strategic position became more entwined with Cold War issues, and the Soviet connection became even more important. These international postures contrasted dramatically with the increasing importance to India of American scientific and economic links, which were strengthened by the increasing emigration of Indian citizens to North America. The overall result, however, was India's weaker international situation in the view of some Americans.

During the 1980s, then, India was still officially a nonaligned nation but in fact found itself deeply embedded in Cold War strategy. India's reaction to the Soviet occupation of Afghanistan was a disquieting feature of Indian foreign policy, in that India decried the Soviet military presence but did nothing against it. Continued United States support for Pakistan, plus the buildup of United States strike forces on the small island of Diego Garcia in the Indian Ocean, heightened tensions. It was no coincidence, therefore, that the 1980s witnessed a major expansion of Indian naval forces, with the addition of two aircraft carriers, a submarine fleet, and major surface ships, including transport craft. But although the Indian buildup made the United States unhappy, India's technological capacities remained inferior to those of the United States Navy, and the Indian navy was never a large threat to United States interests. Instead, the growth of the Indian navy had major implications for the regional balance of power within South Asia. The Indian navy could potentially create a second front against Pakistan should major hostilities recur.

India's military buildup allowed it to intervene in low-intensity conflicts throughout South Asia. From 1987 to 1990, the Indian Peace Keeping Force of more than 60,000 personnel was active in Sri Lanka and became embroiled in a fruitless war against Tamil separatist guerrillas. And, in 1988 Indian forces briefly intervened in Maldives to prevent a coup. Regular border problems with Bangladesh after 1971, the Indian annexation of Sikkim in 1975, and the 1989 closure of the border with Nepal over economic disagreements all added up to the picture of a big country bullying its smaller neighbors, a vision Indian leaders took great pains to dispel. Thus, even though the country officially remained at peace during the 1980s, India's growing military power and the intersecting problems of regional dominance and Cold War ambivalence drove an ambitious foreign policy.

The Indian strategic position changed dramatically in the early 1990s. The end of the Cold War, and then the disintegration of the Soviet Union itself, deprived India of a great ally but also put a stop to many of the worldwide tensions that had relentlessly pulled India into global alignments. When the United States cut off military aid to Pakistan in 1990, it defused one of the most intractable barriers to good relations with India. Then, in 1992, the Persian Gulf War against Iraq brought India grudgingly into an alignment with both Pakistan and the United States, a connection strengthened in 1994 when troops from all three nations cooperated in Somalia under the aegis of the United Nations.

The possession of nuclear weapons by Pakistan and India immersed them in a familiar scenario of mutually assured destruction and made it more problematic for India, despite its military superiority, to overrun Pakistan. Thus, in the mid-1990s, despite continuing hostility over Kashmir, which intensified as the internal situation there disintegrated in the 1990s, the long-term possibilities for official peace between the two countries remained good. Threats from other South Asian nations were negligible. Issues with China were unresolved but not very significant. No other country in the world presented a strategic threat. As budgetary problems beset the government in the mid-1990s, therefore, the Indian military began cutbacks. The military also expanded contacts with a variety of other nations, including Russia and the United States. India hence has entered a period of relative security and multilateral contacts quite different from its twenty-five-year Cold War immersion.

India is a complex geographic, historical, religious, social, economic, and political entity. India is one of the oldest human civilizations and yet displays no cultural features common to all its members. It is one of the richest nations in history, but most of its people are among the poorest in the world. Its ideology rests on some of the most sublime concepts of humanism and nonviolence, but deep-seated discrimination and violent responses are daily news. It has one of the world's most stable political structures, but that structure is constantly in crisis. The nation is seeking a type of great power status, but no one is sure what that involves. India, in the end, defies easy analysis.

*   *   *

The most notable event that occurred in India after the manuscript for this book was completed in the summer of 1995 was the nationwide general elections for the Lok Sabha, the lower house of Parliament, held in April and May 1996. The elections were held in the wake of a US$18 million bribery scandal and resignations involving seven cabinet members and numerous others. Prime Minister P.V. Narasimha Rao, leader of the ruling Congress (I), was accused of accepting substantial bribes. Lal Krishna Advani, head of the BJP, the leading opposition party, was arrested for his alleged acceptance of bribes. For many voters, this scandal was the culmination of scandals and corruption associated for years with old-guard politicians.

The world's largest democracy went to the polls, except in Jammu and Kashmir, over three days between April 27 and May 7 with nearly 14,700 candidates from 522 parties running for 543 of the 545 Lok Sabha seats (the other two seats are filled with Anglo-Indians appointed by the president). Some 16,900 others vied for 914 seats in six state and union territory assembly elections. The candidates were as diverse as ever, with a plethora of Backward Class candidates rising to challenge high-caste hopefuls. Prominent among them was Janata Dal Party candidate Laloo Prasad Yadev, the chief minister of Bihar, who ran on an anti-Brahman caste platform. Phoolan Devi, a former convicted outlaw, who became world-famous as India's "Bandit Queen," also successfully ran for office. One highly favored potential candidate who decided not to run was Sonia Gandhi, widow of Rajiv Gandhi, daughter-in-law of Indira Gandhi, and granddaughter-in-law of Jawaharlal Nehru. She resisted the honor amidst tensions between herself and Rao and, in the minds of some observers, ended the Nehru-Gandhi dynasty while sealing the fate of the Congress (I).

Some 60 percent of India's 590 million voters turned out, but failed to elect a majority government. The BJP, which had tried to tone down its Hindu nationalist rhetoric, won with its allies 194, or 37 percent, of the seats announced on May 10. The Congress (I) won 136, or 25 percent, of the seats. The National Front-Left Front won 110 seats (21 percent), with the remaining ninety-four seats (17 percent) going to unaligned regional parties, independents, and others. The Congress, which had held national power for all but four years since 1947, received the lowest votes ever as many of its traditional Muslim and low-caste constituents defected to other parties and high-caste voters sided with the BJP.

1

After thirteen days in office as the head of a BJP minority government, Prime Minister Atal Bihari Vajpayee resigned on May 28, three days before a vote of no confidence would have brought down his government. He was succeeded as India's eleventh prime minister by the chief minister of Karnataka, the Janata Dal's Haradanahalli (H.D.) Deve Gowda, who headed a minority coalition with thirteen parties—the United Front—made up of some members of the National Front, the Left Front, and regional parties. Deve Gowda, a sixty-three-year-old civil engineer of middle-class, lower-caste farmer background, proclaimed the United Front as representative of India's great diversity and reaffirmed his commitment to modern India's secular heritage.

Although the Congress is not part of the left-center coalition, the United Front is dependent on it for survival. The United Front sought Congress and bipartisan support by declaring that the economic reforms started by the Congress were "irreversible" and committing itself to continued reforms and attracting foreign investment. Despite the Congress's electoral debacle, the party continued to be an important behind-the-scenes force in the new government. Former Prime Minister Rao's legal problems led him to resign as president of the Congress in September 1996. His successor, Sitaram Kesri, pledged to continue backing the coalition.

Because of continuing unrest in Jammu and Kashmir, long-awaited special elections for six Lok Sabha seats were held under tight security between May 7 and 30. The central government's Election Commission proclaimed that the elections were "relatively free and fair" despite the efforts of militants and separatists to sabotage them. There were widespread reports, however, that Indian security forces had coerced people into voting. In September state-level elections were held in Jammu and Kashmir for the first time in nine years. Farooq Abdullah's National Conference party won the violence-prone contest.

In foreign affairs, India and Pakistan continued to seek ways to reduce tensions between the two nations. Deve Gowda offered conciliatory signs to Benazir Bhutto, his counterpart in Islamabad, as the two sides moved toward high-level talks. Despite the opposition of the United States and the withdrawal of technical support from Russia, in April 1996 India completed its own design of a 7.5-ton cryogenic engine capable of launching rockets with 2,500-kilogram payloads. Such a development was a major technological advance for Indian science and gave India the potential to move into the company of the other space-exploring nations. India continued to maintain its stand in regard to nuclear weapons proliferation and in August 1996 refused to ratify the United Nations-sponsored Comprehensive Test Ban Treaty unless the treaty required the destruction of the world's existing nuclear weapons within a prescribed period. To concur with the treaty as it stood, some Indian observers felt, would limit the country's sovereignty. Meanwhile, several senior active-duty and retired military and foreign servicers proposed that India should formally declare itself a nuclear-weapons state and give a "no-first-use" assurance.

October 1, 1996   James Heitzman and Robert L. Worden

Chapter 1. Historical Setting

A leather puppet from Andhra Pradesh

THOSE "WHO WEAR COTTON CLOTHES, use the decimal system, enjoy the taste of [curried] chicken, play chess, or roll dice, and seek peace of mind or tranquility through meditation," writes historian Stanley Wolpert, "are indebted to India." India's deep-rooted civilization may appear exotic or even inscrutable to casual foreign observers, but a perceptive individual can see its evolution, shaped by a wide range of factors: extreme climatic conditions, a bewildering diversity of people, a host of competing political overlords (both local and outsiders), enduring religious and philosophical beliefs, and complex linguistic and literary developments that led to the flowering of regional and pan-Indian culture during the last three millennia. The interplay among a variety of political and socioeconomic forces has created a complex amalgam of cultures that continue amidst conflict; compromise, and adaptation. "Wherever we turn," says Wolpert, "we find . . . palaces, temples, mosques, Victorian railroad stations, Buddhist stupas, Mauryan pillars; each century has its unique testaments, often standing incongruously close to ruins of another era, sometimes juxtaposed one atop another, much like the ruins of Rome, or Bath."

India's "great cycle of history," as Professor Hugh Tinker put it, entails repeating themes that continue to add complexity and diversity to the cultural matrix. Throughout its history, India has undergone innumerable episodes involving military conquests and integration, cultural infusion and assimilation, political unification and fragmentation, religious toleration and conflict, and communal harmony and violence. A few other regions in the world also can claim such a vast and differentiated historical experience, but Indian civilization seems to have endured the trials of time the longest. India has proven its remarkable resilience and its innate ability to reconcile opposing elements from many indigenous and foreign cultures. Unlike the West, where modern political developments and industrialization have created a more secular worldview with redefined roles and values for individuals and families, India remains largely a traditional society, in which change seems only superficial. Although India is the world's largest democracy and the seventh-most industrialized country in the world, the underpinnings of India's civilization stem primarily from its own social structure, religious beliefs, philosophical outlook, and cultural values. The continuity of those time-honed traditional ways of life has provided unique and fascinating patterns in the tapestry of contemporary Indian civilization.

Antecedents

Harappan Culture

The earliest imprints of human activities in India go back to the Paleolithic Age, roughly between 400,000 and 200,000 B.C. Stone implements and cave paintings from this period have been discovered in many parts of the South Asia (see fig. 1). Evidence of domestication of animals, the adoption of agriculture, permanent village settlements, and wheel-turned pottery dating from the middle of the sixth millennium B.C. has been found in the foothills of Sindh and Baluchistan (or Balochistan in current Pakistani usage), both in present-day Pakistan. One of the first great civilizations—with a writing system, urban centers, and a diversified social and economic system—appeared around 3,000 B.C. along the Indus River valley in Punjab (see Glossary) and Sindh. It covered more than 800,000 square kilometers, from the borders of Baluchistan to the deserts of Rajasthan, from the Himalayan foothills to the southern tip of Gujarat (see fig. 2). The remnants of two major cities—Mohenjo-daro and Harappa—reveal remarkable engineering feats of uniform urban planning and carefully executed layout, water supply, and drainage. Excavations at these sites and later archaeological digs at about seventy other locations in India and Pakistan provide a composite picture of what is now generally known as Harappan culture (2500–1600 B.C.).

The major cities contained a few large buildings including a citadel, a large bath—perhaps for personal and communal ablution—differentiated living quarters, flat-roofed brick houses, and fortified administrative or religious centers enclosing meeting halls and granaries. Essentially a city culture, Harappan life was supported by extensive agricultural production and by commerce, which included trade with Sumer in southern Mesopotamia (modern Iraq). The people made tools and weapons from copper and bronze but not iron. Cotton was woven and dyed for clothing; wheat, rice, and a variety of vegetables and fruits were cultivated; and a number of animals, including the humped bull, were domesticated. Harappan culture was conservative and remained relatively unchanged for centuries; whenever cities were rebuilt after periodic flooding, the new level of construction closely followed the previous pattern. Although stability, regularity, and conservatism seem to have been the hallmarks of this people, it is unclear who wielded authority, whether an aristocratic, priestly, or commercial minority.

By far the most exquisite but most obscure Harappan artifacts unearthed to date are steatite seals found in abundance at Mohenjo-daro. These small, flat, and mostly square objects with human or animal motifs provide the most accurate picture there is of Harappan life. They also have inscriptions generally thought to be in the Harappan script, which has eluded scholarly attempts at deciphering it. Debate abounds as to whether the script represents numbers or an alphabet, and, if an alphabet, whether it is proto-Dravidian or proto-Sanskrit (see Languages of India, ch. 4).

The possible reasons for the decline of Harappan civilization have long troubled scholars. Invaders from central and western Asia are considered by some historians to have been the "destroyers" of Harappan cities, but this view is open to reinterpretation. More plausible explanations are recurrent floods caused by tectonic earth movement, soil salinity, and desertification.

Vedic Aryans

A series of migrations by Indo-European-speaking seminomads took place during the second millennium B.C. Known as Aryans, these preliterate pastoralists spoke an early form of Sanskrit, which has close philological similarities to other Indo-European languages, such as Avestan in Iran and ancient Greek and Latin. The term *Aryan* meant pure and implied the invaders' conscious attempts at retaining their tribal identity and roots while maintaining a social distance from earlier inhabitants.

Although archaeology has not yielded proof of the identity of the Aryans, the evolution and spread of their culture across the Indo-Gangetic Plain is generally undisputed (see Principal Regions, ch. 2). Modern knowledge of the early stages of this process rests on a body of sacred texts: the four Vedas (collections of hymns, prayers, and liturgy), the Brahmanas and the Upanishads (commentaries on Vedic rituals and philosophical treatises), and the Puranas (traditional mythic-historical works). The sanctity accorded to these texts and the manner of

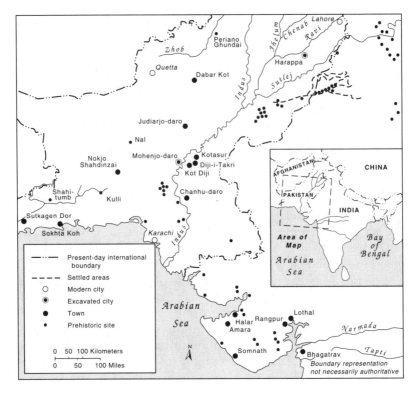

Source: Based on information from Joseph E. Schwartzberg, ed., *A Historical Atlas of South Asia*, New York, 1992, 9.

Figure 2. Indus Valley Culture Sites, ca. 2500–1600 B.C.

their preservation over several millennia—by an unbroken oral tradition—make them part of the living Hindu tradition (see Themes in Indian Society, ch. 5).

These sacred texts offer guidance in piecing together Aryan beliefs and activities. The Aryans were a pantheistic people, following their tribal chieftain or raja, engaging in wars with each other or with other alien ethnic groups, and slowly becoming settled agriculturalists with consolidated territories and differentiated occupations. Their skills in using horse-drawn chariots and their knowledge of astronomy and mathematics gave them a military and technological advantage that led others to accept their social customs and religious beliefs (see Science and Technology, ch. 6). By around 1,000 B.C., Aryan culture had spread over most of India north of the Vindhya Range and in the process assimilated much from other cultures that preceded it (see The Roots of Indian Religion, ch. 3).

The Aryans brought with them a new language, a new pantheon of anthropomorphic gods, a patrilineal and patriarchal family system, and a new social order, built on the religious and philosophical rationales of *varnashramadharma*. Although precise translation into English is difficult, the concept *varnashramadharma*, the bedrock of Indian traditional social organization, is built on three fundamental notions: *varna* (originally, "color," but later taken to mean social class—see Glossary), *ashrama* (stages of life such as youth, family life, detachment from the material world, and renunciation), and dharma (duty, righteousness, or sacred cosmic law). The underlying belief is that present happiness and future salvation are contingent upon one's ethical or moral conduct; therefore, both society and individuals are expected to pursue a diverse but righteous path deemed appropriate for everyone based on one's birth, age, and station in life (see Caste and Class, ch. 5). The original three-tiered society—Brahman (priest; see Glossary), Kshatriya (warrior), and Vaishya (commoner)—eventually expanded into four in order to absorb the subjugated people—Shudra (servant)—or even five, when the outcaste peoples are considered (see *Varna*, Caste, and Other Divisions, ch. 5).

The basic unit of Aryan society was the extended and patriarchal family. A cluster of related families constituted a village, while several villages formed a tribal unit. Child marriage, as practiced in later eras, was uncommon, but the partners' involvement in the selection of a mate and dowry and brideprice were customary. The birth of a son was welcome because he could later tend the herds, bring honor in battle, offer sacrifices to the gods, and inherit property and pass on the family name. Monogamy was widely accepted although polygamy was not unknown, and even polyandry is mentioned in later writings. Ritual suicide of widows was expected at a husband's death, and this might have been the beginning of the practice known as sati in later centuries, when the widow actually burnt herself on her husband's funeral pyre.

Permanent settlements and agriculture led to trade and other occupational differentiation. As lands along the Ganga (or Ganges) were cleared, the river became a trade route, the numerous settlements on its banks acting as markets. Trade was restricted initially to local areas, and barter was an essential component of trade, cattle being the unit of value in large-scale transactions, which further limited the geographical reach of the trader. Custom was law, and kings and chief priests were the arbiters, perhaps advised by certain elders of the community. An Aryan raja, or king, was primarily a military leader, who took a share from the booty after successful cattle raids or battles. Although the rajas had managed to assert their authority, they scrupulously avoided conflicts with priests as a group, whose knowledge and austere religious life surpassed others in the community, and the rajas compromised their own interests with those of the priests.

Kingdoms and Empires

From their original settlements in the Punjab region, the Aryans gradually began to penetrate eastward, clearing dense forests and establishing "tribal" settlements along the Ganga and Yamuna (Jamuna) plains between 1500 and ca. 800 B.C. By around 500 B.C., most of northern India was inhabited and had been brought under cultivation, facilitating the increasing knowledge of the use of iron implements, including ox-drawn plows, and spurred by the growing population that provided voluntary and forced labor. As riverine and inland trade flourished, many towns along the Ganga became centers of trade, culture, and luxurious living. Increasing population and surplus production provided the bases for the emergence of independent states with fluid territorial boundaries over which disputes frequently arose.

The rudimentary administrative system headed by tribal chieftains was transformed by a number of regional republics or hereditary monarchies that devised ways to appropriate revenue and to conscript labor for expanding the areas of settlement and agriculture farther east and south, beyond the Narmada River. These emergent states collected revenue through officials, maintained armies, and built new cities and highways. By 600 B.C., sixteen such territorial powers—including the Magadha, Kosala, Kuru, and Gandhara—stretched across the North India plains from modern-day Afghanistan to Bangladesh. The right of a king to his throne, no matter how it was gained, was usually legitimized through elaborate sacrifice rituals and genealogies concocted by priests who ascribed to the king divine or superhuman origins.

The victory of good over evil is epitomized in the epic *Ramayana* (The Travels of Rama, or Ram in the preferred modern form), while another epic, *Mahabharata* (Great Battle of the Descendants of Bharata), spells out the concept of dharma and duty. More than 2,500 years later, Mohandas Karamchand (Mahatma) Gandhi, the father of modern India, used these concepts in the fight for independence (see Mahatma Gandhi, this ch.). The *Mahabharata* records the feud between Aryan cousins that culminated in an epic battle in which both gods and mortals from many lands allegedly fought to the death, and the *Ramayana* recounts the kidnapping of Sita, Rama's wife, by Ravana, a demonic king of Lanka (Sri Lanka), her rescue by her husband (aided by his animal allies), and Rama's coronation, leading to a period of prosperity and justice. In the late twentieth century, these epics remain dear to the hearts of Hindus and are commonly read and enacted in many settings. In the 1980s and 1990s, Ram's story has been exploited by Hindu militants and politicians to gain power, and the much disputed Ramjanmabhumi, the birth site of Ram, has become an extremely sensitive communal issue, potentially pitting Hindu majority against Muslim minority (see Public Worship, ch. 3; Political Issues, ch. 8).

The Mauryan Empire

By the end of the sixth century B.C., India's northwest was integrated into the Persian Achaemenid Empire and became one of its satrapies. This integration marked the beginning of administrative contacts between Central Asia and India.

Although Indian accounts to a large extent ignored Alexander the Great's Indus campaign in 326 B.C., Greek writers recorded their impressions of the general conditions prevailing in South Asia during this period. Thus, the year 326 B.C. provides the first clear and historically verifiable date in Indian history. A two-way cultural fusion between several Indo-Greek elements—especially in art, architecture, and coinage—occurred in the next several hundred years. North India's political landscape was transformed by the emergence of Magadha in the eastern Indo-Gangetic Plain. In 322 B.C., Magadha, under the rule of Chandragupta Maurya, began to assert its hegemony over neighboring areas. Chandragupta, who ruled from 324 to 301 B.C., was the architect of the first Indian imperial power—the Mauryan Empire (326–184 B.C.)—whose capital was Pataliputra, near modern-day Patna, in Bihar.

Situated on rich alluvial soil and near mineral deposits, especially iron, Magadha was at the center of bustling commerce and trade. The capital was a city of magnificent palaces, temples, a university, a library, gardens, and parks, as reported by Megasthenes, the third-century B.C. Greek historian and ambassador to the Mauryan court. Legend states that Chandragupta's success was due in large measure to his adviser Kautilya, the Brahman author of the *Arthashastra* (Science of Material Gain), a textbook that outlined governmental administration and political strategy. There was a highly centralized and hierarchical government with a large staff, which regulated tax collection, trade and commerce, industrial arts, mining, vital statistics, welfare of foreigners, maintenance of public places including markets and temples, and prostitutes. A large standing army and a well-developed espionage system were maintained. The empire was divided into provinces, districts, and villages governed by a host of centrally appointed local officials, who replicated the functions of the central administration.

Ashoka, grandson of Chandragupta, ruled from 269 to 232 B.C. and was one of India's most illustrious rulers. Ashoka's inscriptions chiseled on rocks and stone pillars located at strategic locations throughout his empire—such as Lampaka (Laghman in modern Afghanistan), Mahastan (in modern Bangladesh), and Brahmagiri (in Karnataka)—constitute the second set of datable historical records. According to some of the inscriptions, in the aftermath of the carnage resulting from his campaign against the powerful kingdom of Kalinga (modern Orissa), Ashoka renounced bloodshed and pursued a policy of nonviolence or ahimsa, espousing a theory of rule by righteousness. His toleration for different religious beliefs and languages reflected the realities of India's regional pluralism although he personally seems to have followed Buddhism (see Buddhism, ch. 3). Early Buddhist stories assert that he convened a Buddhist council at his capital, regularly undertook tours within his realm, and sent Buddhist missionary ambassadors to Sri Lanka.

Contacts established with the Hellenistic world during the reign of Ashoka's predecessors served him well. He sent diplomatic-cum-religious missions to the rulers of Syria, Macedonia, and Epirus, who learned about India's religious traditions, especially Buddhism. India's northwest retained many Persian cultural elements, which might explain Ashoka's rock inscriptions—such inscriptions were commonly associated with Persian rulers. Ashoka's Greek and Aramaic inscriptions found in

Kandahar in Afghanistan may also reveal his desire to maintain ties with people outside of India.

After the disintegration of the Mauryan Empire in the second century B.C., South Asia became a collage of regional powers with overlapping boundaries. India's unguarded northwestern border again attracted a series of invaders between 200 B.C. and A.D. 300. As the Aryans had done, the invaders became "Indianized" in the process of their conquest and settlement. Also, this period witnessed remarkable intellectual and artistic achievements inspired by cultural diffusion and syncretism. The Indo-Greeks, or the Bactrians, of the northwest contributed to the development of numismatics; they were followed by another group, the Shakas (or Scythians), from the steppes of Central Asia, who settled in western India. Still other nomadic people, the Yuezhi, who were forced out of the Inner Asian steppes of Mongolia, drove the Shakas out of northwestern India and established the Kushana Kingdom (first century B.C.–third century A.D.). The Kushana Kingdom controlled parts of Afghanistan and Iran, and in India the realm stretched from Purushapura (modern Peshawar, Pakistan) in the northwest, to Varanasi (Uttar Pradesh) in the east, and to Sanchi (Madhya Pradesh) in the south. For a short period, the kingdom reached still farther east, to Pataliputra. The Kushana Kingdom was the crucible of trade among the Indian, Persian, Chinese, and Roman empires and controlled a critical part of the legendary Silk Road. Kanishka, who reigned for two decades starting around A.D. 78, was the most noteworthy Kushana ruler. He converted to Buddhism and convened a great Buddhist council in Kashmir. The Kushanas were patrons of Gandharan art, a synthesis between Greek and Indian styles, and Sanskrit literature. They initiated a new era called Shaka in A.D. 78, and their calendar, which was formally recognized by India for civil purposes starting on March 22, 1957, is still in use.

The Deccan and the South

During the Kushana Dynasty, an indigenous power, the Satavahana Kingdom (first century B.C.–third century A.D.), rose in the Deccan in southern India. The Satavahana, or Andhra, Kingdom was considerably influenced by the Mauryan political model, although power was decentralized in the hands of local chieftains, who used the symbols of Vedic religion and upheld the *varnashramadharma*. The rulers, however, were eclectic and patronized Buddhist monuments, such as those in Ellora (Maharashtra) and Amaravati (Andhra Pradesh). Thus, the Deccan served as a bridge through which politics, trade, and religious ideas could spread from the north to the south.

Farther south were three ancient Tamil kingdoms—Chera (on the west), Chola (on the east), and Pandya (in the south)—frequently involved in internecine warfare to gain regional supremacy. They are mentioned in Greek and Ashokan sources as lying at the fringes of the Mauryan Empire. A corpus of ancient Tamil literature, known as Sangam (academy) works, including *Tolkappiam*, a manual of Tamil grammar by Tolkappiyar, provides much useful information about their social life from 300 B.C. to A.D. 200. There is clear evidence of encroachment by Aryan traditions from the north into a predominantly indigenous Dravidian culture in transition.

Dravidian social order was based on different ecoregions rather than on the Aryan *varna* paradigm, although the Brahmans had a high status at a very early stage. Segments of society were characterized by matriarchy and matrilineal succession—which survived well into the nineteenth century—cross-cousin marriage, and strong regional identity. Tribal chieftains emerged as "kings" just as people moved from pastoralism toward agriculture, sustained by irrigation based on rivers, small-scale tanks (as man-made ponds are called in India) and wells, and brisk maritime trade with Rome and Southeast Asia.

Discoveries of Roman gold coins in various sites attest to extensive South Indian links with the outside world. As with Pataliputra in the northeast and Taxila in the northwest (in modern Pakistan), the city of Madurai, the Pandyan capital (in modern Tamil Nadu), was the center of intellectual and literary activities. Poets and bards assembled there under royal patronage at successive concourses and composed anthologies of poems, most of which have been lost. By the end of the first century B.C., South Asia was crisscrossed by overland trade routes, which facilitated the movements of Buddhist and Jain missionaries and other travelers and opened the area to a synthesis of many cultures (see Jainism, ch. 3).

The Classical Age

Gupta and Harsha

The Classical Age refers to the period when most of North India was reunited under the Gupta Empire (ca. A.D. 320–

550). Because of the relative peace, law and order, and extensive cultural achievements during this period, it has been described as a "golden age" that crystallized the elements of what is generally known as Hindu culture with all its variety, contradiction, and synthesis. The golden age was confined to the north, and the classical patterns began to spread south only after the Gupta Empire had vanished from the historical scene. The military exploits of the first three rulers—Chandragupta I (ca. 319–335), Samudragupta (ca. 335–376), and Chandragupta II (ca. 376–415)—brought all of North India under their leadership. From Pataliputra, their capital, they sought to retain political preeminence as much by pragmatism and judicious marriage alliances as by military strength. Despite their self-conferred titles, their overlordship was threatened and by 500 ultimately ruined by the Hunas (a branch of the White Huns emanating from Central Asia), who were yet another group in the long succession of ethnically and culturally different outsiders drawn into India and then woven into the hybrid Indian fabric.

Under Harsha Vardhana (or Harsha, r. 606–47), North India was reunited briefly, but neither the Guptas nor Harsha controlled a centralized state, and their administrative styles rested on the collaboration of regional and local officials for administering their rule rather than on centrally appointed personnel. The Gupta period marked a watershed of Indian culture: the Guptas performed Vedic sacrifices to legitimize their rule, but they also patronized Buddhism, which continued to provide an alternative to Brahmanical orthodoxy.

The most significant achievements of this period, however, were in religion, education, mathematics, art, and Sanskrit literature and drama. The religion that later developed into modern Hinduism witnessed a crystallization of its components: major sectarian deities, image worship, devotionalism, and the importance of the temple. Education included grammar, composition, logic, metaphysics, mathematics, medicine, and astronomy. These subjects became highly specialized and reached an advanced level. The Indian numeral system—sometimes erroneously attributed to the Arabs, who took it from India to Europe where it replaced the Roman system—and the decimal system are Indian inventions of this period. Aryabhatta's expositions on astronomy in 499, moreover, gave calculations of the solar year and the shape and movement of astral bodies with remarkable accuracy. In medicine, Charaka and

Sushruta wrote about a fully evolved system, resembling those of Hippocrates and Galen in Greece. Although progress in physiology and biology was hindered by religious injunctions against contact with dead bodies, which discouraged dissection and anatomy, Indian physicians excelled in pharmacopoeia, caesarean section, bone setting, and skin grafting (see Science and Technology, ch. 6).

The Southern Rivals

When Gupta disintegration was complete, the classical patterns of civilization continued to thrive not only in the middle Ganga Valley and the kingdoms that emerged on the heels of Gupta demise but also in the Deccan and in South India, which acquired a more prominent place in history. In fact, from the mid-seventh to the mid-thirteenth centuries, regionalism was the dominant theme of political or dynastic history of South Asia. Three features, as political scientist Radha Champakalakshmi has noted, commonly characterize the sociopolitical realities of this period. First, the spread of Brahmanical religions was a two-way process of Sanskritization of local cults and localization of Brahmanical social order. Second was the ascendancy of the Brahman priestly and landowning groups that later dominated regional institutions and political developments. Third, because of the seesawing of numerous dynasties that had a remarkable ability to survive perennial military attacks, regional kingdoms faced frequent defeats but seldom total annihilation.

Peninsular India was involved in an eighth-century tripartite power struggle among the Chalukyas (556–757) of Vatapi, the Pallavas (300–888) of Kanchipuram, and the Pandyas (seventh through the tenth centuries) of Madurai. The Chalukya rulers were overthrown by their subordinates, the Rashtrakutas, who ruled from 753 to 973. Although both the Pallava and Pandya kingdoms were enemies, the real struggle for political domination was between the Pallava and Chalukya realms.

Despite interregional conflicts, local autonomy was preserved to a far greater degree in the south where it had prevailed for centuries. The absence of a highly centralized government was associated with a corresponding local autonomy in the administration of villages and districts. Extensive and well-documented overland and maritime trade flourished with the Arabs on the west coast and with Southeast Asia. Trade facilitated cultural diffusion in Southeast Asia, where local elites selectively but willingly adopted Indian art, architecture, literature, and social customs.

The interdynastic rivalry and seasonal raids into each other's territory notwithstanding, the rulers in the Deccan and South India patronized all three religions—Buddhism, Hinduism, and Jainism. The religions vied with each other for royal favor, expressed in land grants but more importantly in the creation of monumental temples, which remain architectural wonders. The cave temples of Elephanta Island (near Bombay, or Mumbai in Marathi), Ajanta, and Ellora (in Maharashtra), and structural temples of Kanchipuram (in Tamil Nadu) are enduring legacies of otherwise warring regional rulers. By the mid-seventh century, Buddhism and Jainism began to decline as sectarian Hindu devotional cults of Shiva and Vishnu vigorously competed for popular support.

Although Sanskrit was the language of learning and theology in South India, as it was in the north, the growth of the *bhakti* (devotional) movements enhanced the crystallization of vernacular literature in all four major Dravidian languages: Tamil, Telugu, Malayalam, and Kannada; they often borrowed themes and vocabulary from Sanskrit but preserved much local cultural lore. Examples of Tamil literature include two major poems, *Cilappatikaram* (The Jewelled Anklet) and *Manimekalai* (The Jewelled Belt); the body of devotional literature of Shaivism and Vaishnavism—Hindu devotional movements; and the reworking of the *Ramayana* by Kamban in the twelfth century. A nationwide cultural synthesis had taken place with a minimum of common characteristics in the various regions of South Asia, but the process of cultural infusion and assimilation would continue to shape and influence India's history through the centuries.

The Delhi Sultanate

The Coming of Islam

Islam was propagated by the Prophet Muhammad during the early seventh century in the deserts of Arabia. Less than a century after its inception, Islam's presence was felt throughout the Middle East, North Africa, Spain, Iran, and Central Asia. Arab military forces conquered the Indus Delta region in Sindh in 711 and established an Indo-Muslim state there. Sindh became an Islamic outpost where Arabs established trade links with the Middle East and were later joined by teachers or sufis (see Glossary), but Arab influence was hardly felt in the rest of South Asia (see Islam, ch. 3). By the end of the tenth century, dramatic changes took place when the Central Asian Turkic tribes accepted both the message and mission of Islam. These warlike people first began to move into Afghanistan and Iran and later into India through the northwest. Mahmud of Ghazni (971–1030), who was also known as the "Sword of Islam," mounted seventeen plundering expeditions between 997 and 1027 into North India, annexing Punjab as his eastern province. The invaders' effective use of the crossbow while at a gallop gave them a decisive advantage over their Indian opponents, the Rajputs. Mahmud's conquest of Punjab foretold ominous consequences for the rest of India, but the Rajputs appear to have been both unprepared and unwilling to change their military tactics, which ultimately collapsed in the face of the swift and punitive cavalry of the Afghans and Turkic peoples.

In the thirteenth century, Shams-ud-Din Iletmish (or Iltutmish; r. 1211–36), a former slave-warrior, established a Turkic kingdom in Delhi, which enabled future sultans to push in every direction; within the next 100 years, the Delhi Sultanate extended its sway east to Bengal and south to the Deccan, while the sultanate itself experienced repeated threats from the northwest and internal revolts from displeased, independent-minded nobles. The sultanate was in constant flux as five dynasties rose and fell: Mamluk or Slave (1206–90), Khalji (1290–1320), Tughluq (1320–1413), Sayyid (1414–51), and Lodi (1451–1526). The Khalji Dynasty under Ala-ud-Din (r. 1296–1315) succeeded in bringing most of South India under its control for a time, although conquered areas broke away quickly. Power in Delhi was often gained by violence—nineteen of the thirty-five sultans were assassinated—and was legitimized by reward for tribal loyalty. Factional rivalries and court intrigues were as numerous as they were treacherous; territories controlled by the sultan expanded and shrank depending on his personality and fortunes.

Both the Quran and sharia (Islamic law) provided the basis for enforcing Islamic administration over the independent Hindu rulers, but the sultanate made only fitful progress in the beginning, when many campaigns were undertaken for plunder and temporary reduction of fortresses. The effective rule of a sultan depended largely on his ability to control the strategic places that dominated the military highways and trade routes, extract the annual land tax, and maintain personal

Wrought-iron pillar erected in honor of Vishnu by Gupta monarch Chandragupta II (ca. A.D. 376–415), located near the Qutb Minar, New Delhi
Courtesy Robert L. Worden

authority over military and provincial governors. Sultan Ala-ud-Din made an attempt to reassess, systematize, and unify land revenues and urban taxes and to institute a highly centralized system of administration over his realm, but his efforts were abortive. Although agriculture in North India improved as a result of new canal construction and irrigation methods, including what came to be known as the Persian wheel, prolonged political instability and parasitic methods of tax collection brutalized the peasantry. Yet trade and a market economy, encouraged by the free-spending habits of the aristocracy, acquired new impetus both inland and overseas. Experts in metalwork, stonework, and textile manufacture responded to the new patronage with enthusiasm.

Southern Dynasties

The sultans' failure to hold securely the Deccan and South India resulted in the rise of competing southern dynasties: the Muslim Bahmani Sultanate (1347–1527) and the Hindu Vijayanagar Empire (1336–1565). Zafar Khan, a former provincial governor under the Tughluqs, revolted against his Turkic overlord and proclaimed himself sultan, taking the title Ala-ud-Din Bahman Shah in 1347. The Bahmani Sultanate, located in the northern Deccan, lasted for almost two centuries, until it fragmented into five smaller states in 1527. The Bahmani Sultanate adopted the patterns established by the Delhi overlords in tax collection and administration, but its downfall was caused in large measure by the competition and hatred between *deccani* (domiciled Muslim immigrants and local converts) and *paradesi* (foreigners or officials in temporary service). The Bahmani Sultanate initiated a process of cultural synthesis visible in Hyderabad, where cultural flowering is still expressed in vigorous schools of *deccani* architecture and painting.

Founded in 1336, the empire of Vijayanagar (named for its capital Vijayanagar, "City of Victory," in present-day Karnataka) expanded rapidly toward Madurai in the south and Goa in the west and exerted intermittent control over the east coast and the extreme southwest. Vijayanagar rulers closely followed Chola precedents, especially in collecting agricultural and trade revenues, in giving encouragement to commercial guilds, and in honoring temples with lavish endowments. Added revenue needed for waging war against the Bahmani sultans was raised by introducing a set of taxes on commercial enterprises, professions, and industries. Political rivalry between the Bahmani and the Vijayanagar rulers involved control over the Krishna-Tunghabadhra river basin, which shifted hands depending on whose military was superior at any given time. The Vijayanagar rulers' capacity for gaining victory over their enemies was contingent on ensuring a constant supply of horses—initially through Arab traders but later through the Portuguese—and maintaining internal roads and communication networks. Merchant guilds enjoyed a wide sphere of operation and were able to offset the power of landlords and Brahmans in court politics. Commerce and shipping eventually passed largely into the hands of foreigners, and special facilities and tax concessions were provided for them by the ruler. Arabs and Portuguese competed for influence and control of west coast ports, and, in 1510, Goa passed into Portuguese possession.

The city of Vijayanagar itself contained numerous temples with rich ornamentation, especially the gateways, and a cluster of shrines for the deities. Most prominent among the temples was the one dedicated to Virupaksha, a manifestation of Shiva, the patron-deity of the Vijayanagar rulers. Temples continued to be the nuclei of diverse cultural and intellectual activities, but these activities were based more on tradition than on contemporary political realities. (However, the first Vijayanagar

Cow consuming left-over offerings in 1,000-pillared hall, an example
of the Vijayanagar style of architecture, Madurai, Tamil Nadu
Courtesy World Transportation Commission Collection,
Library of Congress

ruler—Harihara I—was a Hindu who converted to Islam and then reconverted to Hinduism for political expediency.) The temples sponsored no intellectual exchange with Islamic theologians because Muslims were generally assigned to an "impure" status and were thus excluded from entering temples. When the five rulers of what was once the Bahmani Sultanate combined their forces and attacked Vijayanagar in 1565, the empire crumbled at the Battle of Talikot.

The Mughal Era

The Mughals

In the early sixteenth century, descendants of the Mongol,

Turkish, Iranian, and Afghan invaders of South Asia—the Mughals—invaded India under the leadership of Zahir-ud-Din Babur. Babur was the great-grandson of Timur Lenk (Timur the Lame, from which the Western name Tamerlane is derived), who had invaded India and plundered Delhi in 1398 and then led a short-lived empire based in Samarkand (in modern-day Uzbekistan) that united Persian-based Mongols (Babur's maternal ancestors) and other West Asian peoples. Babur was driven from Samarkand and initially established his rule in Kabul in 1504; he later became the first Mughal ruler (1526–30). His determination was to expand eastward into Punjab, where he had made a number of forays. Then an invitation from an opportunistic Afghan chief in Punjab brought him to the very heart of the Delhi Sultanate, ruled by Ibrahim Lodi (1517–26). Babur, a seasoned military commander, entered India in 1526 with his well-trained veteran army of 12,000 to meet the sultan's huge but unwieldy and disunited force of more than 100,000 men. Babur defeated the Lodi sultan decisively at Panipat (in modern-day Haryana, about ninety kilometers north of Delhi). Employing gun carts, moveable artillery, and superior cavalry tactics, Babur achieved a resounding victory. A year later, he decisively defeated a Rajput confederacy led by Rana Sangha. In 1529 Babur routed the joint forces of Afghans and the sultan of Bengal but died in 1530 before he could consolidate his military gains. He left behind as legacies his memoirs (*Babur Namah*), several beautiful gardens in Kabul, Lahore, and Agra, and descendants who would fulfill his dream of establishing an empire in Hindustan.

When Babur died, his son Humayun (1530–56), also a soldier, inherited a difficult task. He was pressed from all sides by a reassertion of Afghan claims to the Delhi throne, by disputes over his own succession, and by the Afghan-Rajput march into Delhi in 1540. He fled to Persia, where he spent nearly ten years as an embarrassed guest at the Safavid court. In 1545 he gained a foothold in Kabul, reasserted his Indian claim, defeated Sher Khan Sur, the most powerful Afghan ruler, and took control of Delhi in 1555.

Humayun's untimely death in 1556 left the task of further imperial conquest and consolidation to his thirteen-year-old son, Jalal-ud-Din Akbar (r. 1556–1605). Following a decisive military victory at the Second Battle of Panipat in 1556, the regent Bayram Khan pursued a vigorous policy of expansion on Akbar's behalf. As soon as Akbar came of age, he began to free himself from the influences of overbearing ministers, court factions, and harem intrigues, and demonstrated his own capacity for judgment and leadership. A "workaholic" who seldom slept more than three hours a night, he personally oversaw the implementation of his administrative policies, which were to form the backbone of the Mughal Empire for more than 200 years. He continued to conquer, annex, and consolidate a far-flung territory bounded by Kabul in the northwest, Kashmir in the north, Bengal in the east, and beyond the Narmada River in the south—an area comparable in size to the Mauryan territory some 1,800 years earlier (see fig. 3).

Akbar built a walled capital called Fatehpur Sikri (Fatehpur means Fortress of Victory) near Agra, starting in 1571. Palaces for each of Akbar's senior queens, a huge artificial lake, and sumptuous water-filled courtyards were built there. The city, however, proved short-lived, perhaps because the water supply was insufficient or of poor quality, or, as some historians believe, Akbar had to attend to the northwest areas of his empire and simply moved his capital for political reasons. Whatever the reason, in 1585 the capital was relocated to Lahore and in 1599 to Agra.

Akbar adopted two distinct but effective approaches in administering a large territory and incorporating various ethnic groups into the service of his realm. In 1580 he obtained local revenue statistics for the previous decade in order to understand details of productivity and price fluctuation of different crops. Aided by Todar Mal, a Rajput king, Akbar issued a revenue schedule that the peasantry could tolerate while providing maximum profit for the state. Revenue demands, fixed according to local conventions of cultivation and quality of soil, ranged from one-third to one-half of the crop and were paid in cash. Akbar relied heavily on land-holding zamindars (see Glossary). They used their considerable local knowledge and influence to collect revenue and to transfer it to the treasury, keeping a portion in return for services rendered. Within his administrative system, the warrior aristocracy (*mansabdars*) held ranks (*mansabs*) expressed in numbers of troops, and indicating pay, armed contingents, and obligations. The warrior aristocracy was generally paid from revenues of nonhereditary and transferrable *jagirs* (revenue villages).

An astute ruler who genuinely appreciated the challenges of administering so vast an empire, Akbar introduced a policy of reconciliation and assimilation of Hindus (including Maryam

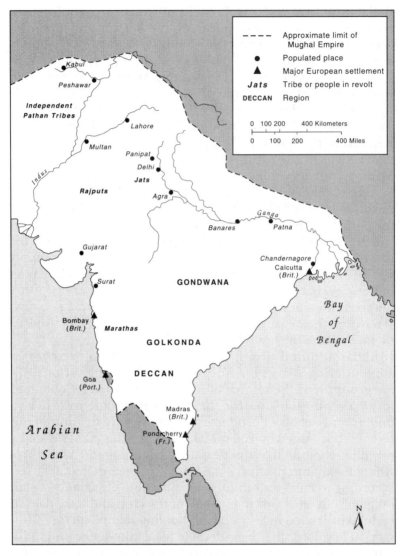

Source: Based on information from Joseph E. Schwartzberg, ed., *A Historical Atlas of
South Asia*, New York, 1992, 46.

Figure 3. Mughal Empire, Late Seventeenth Century

al-Zamani, the Hindu Rajput mother of his son and heir, Jahangir), who represented the majority of the population. He
recruited and rewarded Hindu chiefs with the highest ranks in
government; encouraged intermarriages between Mughal and
Rajput aristocracy; allowed new temples to be built; personally

participated in celebrating Hindu festivals such as Dipavali, or Diwali, the festival of lights; and abolished the *jizya* (poll tax) imposed on non-Muslims. Akbar came up with his own theory of "rulership as a divine illumination," enshrined in his new religion Din-i-Ilahi (Divine Faith), incorporating the principle of acceptance of all religions and sects. He encouraged widow marriage, discouraged child marriage, outlawed the practice of sati, and persuaded Delhi merchants to set up special market days for women, who otherwise were secluded at home (see Veiling and the Seclusion of Women, ch. 5). By the end of Akbar's reign, the Mughal Empire extended throughout most of India north of the Godavari River. The exceptions were Gondwana in central India, which paid tribute to the Mughals, and Assam, in the northeast.

Mughal rule under Jahangir (1605–27) and Shah Jahan (1628–58) was noted for political stability, brisk economic activity, beautiful paintings, and monumental buildings. Jahangir married the Persian princess whom he renamed Nur Jahan (Light of the World), who emerged as the most powerful individual in the court besides the emperor. As a result, Persian poets, artists, scholars, and officers—including her own family members—lured by the Mughal court's brilliance and luxury, found asylum in India. The number of unproductive, time-serving officers mushroomed, as did corruption, while the excessive Persian representation upset the delicate balance of impartiality at the court. Jahangir liked Hindu festivals but promoted mass conversion to Islam; he persecuted the followers of Jainism and even executed Guru (see Glossary) Arjun Das, the fifth saint-teacher of the Sikhs (see Sikhism, ch. 3). Nur Jahan's abortive schemes to secure the throne for the prince of her choice led Shah Jahan to rebel in 1622. In that same year, the Persians took over Kandahar in southern Afghanistan, an event that struck a serious blow to Mughal prestige.

Between 1636 and 1646, Shah Jahan sent Mughal armies to conquer the Deccan and the northwest beyond the Khyber Pass. Even though they demonstrated Mughal military strength, these campaigns consumed the imperial treasury. As the state became a huge military machine, whose nobles and their contingents multiplied almost fourfold, so did its demands for more revenue from the peasantry. Political unification and maintenance of law and order over wide areas encouraged the emergence of large centers of commerce and crafts—such as Lahore, Delhi, Agra, and Ahmadabad—linked by roads and waterways to distant places and ports. The world-famous Taj Mahal was built in Agra during Shah Jahan's reign as a tomb for his beloved wife, Mumtaz Mahal. It symbolizes both Mughal artistic achievement and excessive financial expenditures when resources were shrinking. The economic position of peasants and artisans did not improve because the administration failed to produce any lasting change in the existing social structure. There was no incentive for the reve-nue officials, whose concerns primarily were personal or famil-ial gain, to generate resources independent of dominant Hindu zamindars and village leaders, whose self-interest and local dominance prevented them from handing over the full amount of revenue to the imperial treasury. In their ever-greater dependence on land revenue, the Mughals unwittingly nurtured forces that eventually led to the break-up of their empire.

The last of the great Mughals was Aurangzeb (r. 1658–1707), who seized the throne by killing all his brothers and imprison-ing his own father. During his fifty-year reign, the empire reached its utmost physical limit but also witnessed the unmis-takable symptoms of decline. The bureaucracy had grown bloated and excessively corrupt, and the huge and unwieldy army demonstrated outdated weaponry and tactics. Aurangzeb was not the ruler to restore the dynasty's declining fortunes or glory. Awe-inspiring but lacking in the charisma needed to attract outstanding lieutenants, he was driven to extend Mughal rule over most of South Asia and to reestablish Islamic orthodoxy by adopting a reactionary attitude toward those Muslims whom he had suspected of compromising their faith.

Aurangzeb was involved in a series of protracted wars—against the Pathans in Afghanistan, the sultans of Bijapur and Golkonda in the Deccan, and the Marathas in Maharashtra. Peasant uprisings and revolts by local leaders became all too common, as did the conniving of the nobles to preserve their own status at the expense of a steadily weakening empire. The increasing association of his government with Islam further drove a wedge between the ruler and his Hindu subjects. Aurangzeb forbade the building of new temples, destroyed a number of them, and reimposed the *jizya*. A puritan and a cen-sor of morals, he banned music at court, abolished ceremonies, and persecuted the Sikhs in Punjab. These measures alienated so many that even before he died challenges for power had already begun to escalate. Contenders for the Mughal throne

Akbar, the third Mughal emperor, who reigned from
1556 to 1605
Courtesy Robert L. Worden

fought each other, and the short-lived reigns of Aurangzeb's successors were strife-filled. The Mughal Empire experienced dramatic reverses as regional governors broke away and founded independent kingdoms. The Mughals had to make peace with Maratha rebels, and Persian and Afghan armies invaded Delhi, carrying away many treasures, including the Peacock Throne in 1739.

The Marathas

The tale of the Marathas' rise to power and their eventual fall contains all the elements of a thriller: adventure, intrigue, and romanticism. Maratha chieftains were originally in the service of Bijapur sultans in the western Deccan, which was under siege by the Mughals. Shivaji Bhonsle (1627–80), a tenacious and fierce fighter recognized as the "father of the Maratha nation," took advantage of this conflict and carved out his own principality near Pune, which later became the Maratha capital. Adopting guerrilla tactics, he waylaid caravans in order to sustain and expand his army, which soon had money, arms, and horses. Shivaji led a series of successful assaults in the 1660s against Mughal strongholds, including the major port of Surat. In 1674 he assumed the title of "Lord of the Universe" at his elaborate coronation, which signaled his determination to challenge the Mughal forces as well as to reestablish a Hindu kingdom in Maharashtra, the land of his origin. Shivaji's battle cries were *swaraj* (translated variously as freedom, self-rule, independence), *swadharma* (religious freedom), and *goraksha* (cow protection). Aurangzeb relentlessly pursued Shivaji's successors between 1681 and 1705 but eventually retreated to the north as his treasury became depleted and as thousands of lives had been lost either on the battlefield or to natural calamities. In 1717 a Mughal emissary signed a treaty with the Marathas confirming their claims to rule in the Deccan in return for acknowledging the fictional Mughal suzerainty and remission of annual taxes. Yet the Marathas soon captured Malwa from Mughal control and later moved east into Orrisa and Bengal; southern India also came under their domain. Recognition of their political power finally came when the Mughal emperor invited them to act as auxiliaries in the internal affairs of the empire and still later to help the emperor in driving the Afghans out of Punjab.

The Marathas, despite their military prowess and leadership, were not equipped to administer the state or to undertake socioeconomic reform. Pursuing a policy characterized by plunder and indiscriminate raids, they antagonized the peasants. They were primarily suited for stirring the Maharashtrian regional pride rather than for attracting loyalty to an all-India confederacy. They were left virtually alone before the invading Afghan forces, headed by Ahmad Shah Abdali (later called Ahmad Shah Durrani), who routed them on the blood-drenched battlefield at Panipat in 1761. The shock of defeat hastened the break-up of their loosely knit confederacy into five independent states and extinguished the hope of Maratha dominance in India.

The Sikhs

The Afghan defeat of the Maratha armies accelerated the breakaway of Punjab from Delhi and helped the founding of Sikh overlordship in the northwest. Rooted in the *bhakti* movements that developed in the second century B.C. but swept across North India during the fifteenth and sixteenth centuries, the Sikh religion appealed to the hard-working peasants. The Sikh *khalsa* (army of the pure) rose up against the economic and political repressions in Punjab toward the end of Aurangzeb's rule. Guerrilla fighters took advantage of the political instability created by the Persian and Afghan onslaught against Delhi, enriching themselves and expanding territorial control. By the 1770s, Sikh hegemony extended from the Indus in the west to the Yamuna in the east, from Multan in the south to Jammu in the north. But the Sikhs, like the Marathas, were a loose, disunited, and quarrelsome conglomerate of twelve kin-groups. It took Ranjit Singh (1780–1839), an individual with modernizing vision and leadership, to achieve supremacy over the other kin-groups and establish his kingdom in which Sikhs, Hindus, and Muslims lived together in comparative equality and increasing prosperity. Ranjit Singh employed European officers and introduced strict military discipline into his army before expanding into Afghanistan, Kashmir, and Ladakh.

The Coming of the Europeans

The quest for wealth and power brought Europeans to Indian shores in 1498 when Vasco da Gama, the Portuguese voyager, arrived in Calicut (modern Kozhikode, Kerala) on the west coast. In their search for spices and Christian converts, the Portuguese challenged Arab supremacy in the Indian Ocean, and, with their galleons fitted with powerful cannons, set up a network of strategic trading posts along the Arabian Sea and the Persian Gulf. In 1510 the Portuguese took over the enclave of Goa, which became the center of their commercial and political power in India and which they controlled for nearly four and a half centuries.

Economic competition among the European nations led to the founding of commercial companies in England (the East

India Company, founded in 1600) and in the Netherlands (Verenigde Oost-Indische Compagnie—the United East India Company, founded in 1602), whose primary aim was to capture the spice trade by breaking the Portuguese monopoly in Asia. Although the Dutch, with a large supply of capital and support from their government, preempted and ultimately excluded the British from the heartland of spices in the East Indies (modern-day Indonesia), both companies managed to establish trading "factories" (actually warehouses) along the Indian coast. The Dutch, for example, used various ports on the Coromandel Coast in South India, especially Pulicat (about twenty kilometers north of Madras), as major sources for slaves for their plantations in the East Indies and for cotton cloth as early as 1609. (The English, however, established their first factory at what today is known as Madras only in 1639.) Indian rulers enthusiastically accommodated the newcomers in hopes of pitting them against the Portuguese. In 1619 Jahangir granted them permission to trade in his territories at Surat (in Gujarat) on the west coast and Hughli (in West Bengal) in the east. These and other locations on the peninsula became centers of international trade in spices, cotton, sugar, raw silk, saltpeter, calico, and indigo.

English company agents became familiar with Indian customs and languages, including Persian, the unifying official language under the Mughals. In many ways, the English agents of that period lived like Indians, intermarried willingly, and a large number of them never returned to their home country. The knowledge of India thus acquired and the mutual ties forged with Indian trading groups gave the English a competitive edge over other Europeans. The French commercial interest—Compagnie des Indes Orientales (East India Company, founded in 1664)—came late, but the French also established themselves in India, emulating the precedents set by their competitors as they founded their enclave at Pondicherry (Puduchcheri) on the Coramandel Coast.

In 1717 the Mughal emperor, Farrukh-siyar (r. 1713–19), gave the British—who by then had already established themselves in the south and the west—a grant of thirty-eight villages near Calcutta, acknowledging their importance to the continuity of international trade in the Bengal economy. As did the Dutch and the French, the British brought silver bullion and copper to pay for transactions, helping the smooth functioning of the Mughal revenue system and increasing the benefits to local artisans and traders. The fortified warehouses of the British brought extraterritorial status, which enabled them to administer their own civil and criminal laws and offered numerous employment opportunities as well as asylum to foreigners and Indians. The British factories successfully competed with their rivals as their size and population grew. The original clusters of fishing villages (Madras and Calcutta) or series of islands (Bombay) became headquarters of the British administrative zones, or presidencies as they generally came to be known. The factories and their immediate environs, known as the White-town, represented the actual and symbolic preeminence of the British—in terms of their political power—as well as their cultural values and social practices; meanwhile, their Indian collaborators lived in the Black-town, separated from the factories by several kilometers.

The British company employed sepoys—European-trained and European-led Indian soldiers—to protect its trade, but local rulers sought their services to settle scores in regional power struggles. South India witnessed the first open confrontation between the British and the French, whose forces were led by Robert Clive and François Dupleix, respectively. Both companies desired to place their own candidate as the nawab, or ruler, of Arcot, the area around Madras. At the end of a protracted struggle between 1744 and 1763, when the Peace of Paris was signed, the British gained an upper hand over the French and installed their man in power, supporting him further with arms and lending large sums as well. The French and the British also backed different factions in the succession struggle for Mughal viceroyalty in Bengal, but Clive intervened successfully and defeated Nawab Siraj-ud-daula in the Battle of Plassey (Palashi, about 150 kilometers north of Calcutta) in 1757. Clive found help from a combination of vested interests that opposed the existing nawab: disgruntled soldiers, landholders, and influential merchants whose commercial profits were closely linked to British fortunes.

Later, Clive defeated the Mughal forces at Buxar (Baksar, west of Patna in Bihar) in 1765, and the Mughal emperor (Shah Alam, r. 1759–1806) conferred on the company administrative rights over Bengal, Bihar, and Orissa, a region of roughly 25 million people with an annual revenue of 40 million rupees (for current value of the rupee—see Glossary). The imperial grant virtually established the company as a sovereign power, and Clive became the first British governor of Bengal.

Besides the presence of the Portuguese, Dutch, British, and French, there were two lesser but noteworthy colonial groups. Danish entrepreneurs established themselves at several ports on the Malabar and Coromandel coasts, in the vicinity of Calcutta and inland at Patna between 1695 and 1740. Austrian enterprises were set up in the 1720s on the vicinity of Surat in modern-day southeastern Gujarat. As with the other non-British enterprises, the Danish and Austrian enclaves were taken over by the British between 1765 and 1815.

The British Empire in India

Company Rule, 1757–1857

A multiplicity of motives underlay the British penetration into India: commerce, security, and a purported moral uplift of the people. The "expansive force" of private and company trade eventually led to the conquest or annexation of territories in which spices, cotton, and opium were produced. British investors ventured into the unfamiliar interior landscape in search of opportunities that promised substantial profits. British economic penetration was aided by Indian collaborators, such as the bankers and merchants who controlled intricate credit networks. British rule in India would have been a frustrated or half-realized dream had not Indian counterparts provided connections between rural and urban centers. External threats, both real and imagined, such as the Napoleonic Wars (1796–1815) and Russian expansion toward Afghanistan (in the 1830s), as well as the desire for internal stability, led to the annexation of more territory in India. Political analysts in Britain wavered initially as they were uncertain of the costs or the advantages in undertaking wars in India, but by the 1810s, as the territorial aggrandizement eventually paid off, opinion in London welcomed the absorption of new areas. Occasionally the British Parliament witnessed heated debates against expansion, but arguments justifying military operations for security reasons always won over even the most vehement critics.

The British soon forgot their own rivalry with the Portuguese and the French and permitted them to stay in their coastal enclaves, which they kept even after independence in 1947 (see National Integration, this ch.). The British, however, continued to expand vigorously well into the 1850s. A number of aggressive governors-general undertook relentless campaigns against several Hindu and Muslim rulers. Among them

Taj Mahal, a monumental white marble garden tomb built at Agra for Mumtaz Mahal, the beloved wife of Mughal emperor Shah Jahan
Courtesy Robert L. Worden

were Richard Colley Wellesley (1798–1805), William Pitt Amherst (1823–28), George Eden (1836–42), Edward Law (1842–44), and James Andrew Brown Ramsay (1848–56; also known as the Marquess of Dalhousie). Despite desperate efforts at salvaging their tottering power and keeping the British at bay, many Hindu and Muslim rulers lost their territories: Mysore (1799, but later restored), the Maratha Confederacy (1818), and Punjab (1849). The British success in large measure was the result not only of their superiority in tactics and weapons but also of their ingenious relations with Indian rulers through the "subsidiary alliance" system, introduced in the early nineteenth century. Many rulers bartered away their real responsibilities by agreeing to uphold British paramountcy in India, while they retained a fictional sovereignty under the rubric of Pax Britannica. Later, Dalhousie espoused the "doctrine of lapse" and annexed outright the estates of deceased princes of Satara (1848), Udaipur (1852), Jhansi (1853), Tanjore (1853), Nagpur (1854), and Oudh (1856).

European perceptions of India, and those of the British especially, shifted from unequivocal appreciation to sweeping condemnation of India's past achievements and customs. Imbued with an ethnocentric sense of superiority, British intellectuals, including Christian missionaries, spearheaded a movement that sought to bring Western intellectual and technological innovations to Indians. Interpretations of the causes of India's cultural and spiritual "backwardness" varied, as did the solutions. Many argued that it was Europe's mission to civilize India and hold it as a trust until Indians proved themselves competent for self-rule.

The immediate consequence of this sense of superiority was to open India to more aggressive missionary activity. The contributions of three missionaries based in Serampore (a Danish enclave in Bengal)—William Carey, Joshua Marshman, and William Ward—remained unequaled and have provided inspiration for future generations of their successors. The missionaries translated the Bible into the vernaculars, taught company officials local languages, and, after 1813, gained permission to proselytize in the company's territories. Although the actual number of converts remained negligible, except in rare instances when entire groups embraced Christianity, such as the Nayars in the south or the Nagas in the northeast, the missionary impact on India through publishing, schools, orphanages, vocational institutions, dispensaries, and hospitals was unmistakable.

The British Parliament enacted a series of laws, among which the Regulating Act of 1773 stood first, to curb the company traders' unrestrained commercial activities and to bring about some order in territories under company control. Limiting the company charter to periods of twenty years, subject to review upon renewal, the 1773 act gave the British government supervisory rights over the Bengal, Bombay, and Madras presidencies. Bengal was given preeminence over the rest because of its enormous commercial vitality and because it was the seat of British power in India (at Calcutta), whose governor was elevated to the new position of governor-general. Warren Hastings was the first incumbent (1773–85). The India Act of 1784, sometimes described as the "half-loaf system," as it sought to mediate between Parliament and the company directors, enhanced Parliament's control by establishing the Board of Control, whose members were selected from the cabinet. The Charter Act of 1813 recognized British moral responsibility by introducing just and humane laws in India, foreshadowing future social legislation, and outlawing a number of traditional practices such as sati and *thagi* (or thugee, robbery coupled with ritual murder).

As governor-general from 1786 to 1793, Charles Cornwallis (the Marquis of Cornwallis), professionalized, bureaucratized, and Europeanized the company's administration. He also outlawed private trade by company employees, separated the commercial and administrative functions, and remunerated company servants with generous graduated salaries. Because revenue collection became the company's most essential administrative function, Cornwallis made a compact with Bengali zamindars, who were perceived as the Indian counterparts to the British landed gentry. The Permanent Settlement system, also known as the zamindari system, fixed taxes in perpetuity in return for ownership of large estates; but the state was excluded from agricultural expansion, which came under the purview of the zamindars. In Madras and Bombay, however, the *ryotwari* (peasant) settlement system was set in motion, in which peasant cultivators had to pay annual taxes directly to the government.

Neither the zamindari nor the *ryotwari* systems proved effective in the long run because India was integrated into an international economic and pricing system over which it had no control, while increasing numbers of people subsisted on agriculture for lack of other employment. Millions of people involved in the heavily taxed Indian textile industry also lost their markets, as they were unable to compete successfully with cheaper textiles produced in Lancashire's mills from Indian raw materials.

Beginning with the Mayor's Court, established in 1727 for civil litigation in Bombay, Calcutta, and Madras, justice in the interior came under the company's jurisdiction. In 1772 an elaborate judicial system, known as *adalat*, established civil and criminal jurisdictions along with a complex set of codes or rules of procedure and evidence. Both Hindu pandits (see Glossary) and Muslim *qazis* (sharia court judges) were recruited to aid the presiding judges in interpreting their customary laws, but in other instances, British common and statutory laws became applicable. In extraordinary situations where none of these systems was applicable, the judges were enjoined to adjudicate on the basis of "justice, equity, and good conscience." The legal profession provided numerous opportunities for educated and talented Indians who were unable to secure positions in the company, and, as a result, Indian lawyers later dominated nationalist politics and reform movements.

Education for the most part was left to the charge of Indians or to private agents who imparted instruction in the vernaculars. But in 1813, the British became convinced of their "duty" to awaken the Indians from intellectual slumber by exposing them to British literary traditions, earmarking a paltry sum for the cause. Controversy between two groups of Europeans—the "Orientalists" and "Anglicists"—over how the money was to be spent prevented them from formulating any consistent policy until 1835 when William Cavendish Bentinck, the governor-general from 1828 to 1835, finally broke the impasse by resolving to introduce the English language as the medium of instruction. English replaced Persian in public administration and education.

The company's education policies in the 1830s tended to reinforce existing lines of socioeconomic division in society rather than bringing general liberation from ignorance and superstition. Whereas the Hindu English-educated minority spearheaded many social and religious reforms either in direct response to government policies or in reaction to them, Muslims as a group initially failed to do so, a position they endeavored to reverse. Western-educated Hindu elites sought to rid Hinduism of its much criticized social evils: idolatry, the caste system, child marriage, and sati. Religious and social activist Ram Mohan Roy (1772–1833), who founded the Brahmo Samaj (Society of Brahma) in 1828, displayed a readiness to synthesize themes taken from Christianity, Deism, and Indian monism, while other individuals in Bombay and Madras initiated literary and debating societies that gave them a forum for open discourse. The exemplary educational attainments and skillful use of the press by these early reformers enhanced the possibility of effecting broad reforms without compromising societal values or religious practices.

The 1850s witnessed the introduction of the three "engines of social improvement" that heightened the British illusion of permanence in India. They were the railroads, the telegraph, and the uniform postal service, inaugurated during the tenure of Dalhousie as governor-general. The first railroad lines were built in 1850 from Howrah (Haora, across the Hughli River from Calcutta) inland to the coalfields at Raniganj, Bihar, a distance of 240 kilometers. In 1851 the first electric telegraph line was laid in Bengal and soon linked Agra, Bombay, Calcutta, Lahore, Varanasi, and other cities. The three different presidency or regional postal systems merged in 1854 to facilitate uniform methods of communication at an all-India level. With uniform postal rates for letters and newspapers—one-half anna and one anna, respectively (sixteen annas equalled one rupee)—communication between the rural and the metropolitan areas became easier and faster. The increased ease of communication and the opening of highways and waterways accelerated the movement of troops, the transportation of raw materials and goods to and from the interior, and the exchange of commercial information.

The railroads did not break down the social or cultural distances between various groups but tended to create new categories in travel. Separate compartments in the trains were reserved exclusively for the ruling class, separating the educated and wealthy from ordinary people. Similarly, when the Sepoy Rebellion was quelled in 1858, a British official exclaimed that "the telegraph saved India." He envisaged, of course, that British interests in India would continue indefinitely.

The British Raj, 1858–1947

Sepoy Rebellion, 1857–59

On May 10, 1857, Indian soldiers of the British Indian Army, drawn mostly from Muslim units from Bengal, mutinied in Meerut, a cantonment eighty kilometers northeast of Delhi. The rebels marched to Delhi to offer their services to the Mughal emperor, and soon much of north and central India was plunged into a year-long insurrection against the British.

The uprising, which seriously threatened British rule in India, has been called many names by historians, including the Sepoy Rebellion, the Great Mutiny, and the Revolt of 1857; many people in South Asia, however, prefer to call it India's first war of independence. Undoubtedly, it was the culmination of mounting Indian resentment toward British economic and social policies over many decades. Until the rebellion, the British had succeeded in suppressing numerous riots and "tribal" wars or in accommodating them through concessions, but two events triggered the violent explosion of wrath in 1857. First, was the annexation in 1856 of Oudh, a wealthy princely state that generated huge revenue and represented a vestige of Mughal authority. The second was the British blunder in using cartridges for the Lee-Enfield rifle that were allegedly greased with animal fat, which was offensive to the religious beliefs of Muslim and Hindu sepoys. The rebellion soon engulfed much of North India, including Oudh and various areas once under the control of Maratha princes. Isolated mutinies also occurred at military posts in the center of the subcontinent. Initially, the rebels, although divided and uncoordinated, gained the upper hand, while the unprepared British were terrified, and even paralyzed, without replacements for the casualties. The civil war inflicted havoc on both Indians and British as each vented its fury on the other; each community suffered humiliation and triumph in battle as well, although the final outcome was victory for the British. The last major sepoy rebels surrendered on June 21, 1858, at Gwalior (Madhya Pradesh), one of the principal centers of the revolt. A final battle was fought at Sirwa Pass on May 21, 1859, and the defeated rebels fled into Nepal.

The spontaneous and widespread rebellion later fired the imagination of the nationalists who would debate the most effective method of protest against British rule. For them, the rebellion represented the first Indian attempt at gaining independence. This interpretation, however, is open to serious question.

Post-Rebellion Developments

The civil war was a major turning point in the history of modern India. In May 1858, the British exiled Emperor Bahadur Shah II (r. 1837–57) to Burma, thus formally liquidating the Mughal Empire. At the same time, they abolished the British East India Company and replaced it with direct rule under the British crown. In proclaiming the new direct-rule policy to "the Princes, Chiefs, and Peoples of India," Queen Victoria (who was given the title Empress of India in 1877) promised equal treatment under British law, but Indian mistrust of British rule had become a legacy of the 1857 rebellion. Many existing economic and revenue policies remained virtually unchanged in the post-1857 period, but several administrative modifications were introduced, beginning with the creation in London of a cabinet post, the secretary of state for India. The governor-general (called viceroy when acting as the direct representative of the British crown), headquartered in Calcutta, ran the administration in India, assisted by executive and legislative councils. Beneath the governor-general were the provincial governors, who held power over the district officials, who formed the lower rungs of the Indian Civil Service. For decades the Indian Civil Service was the exclusive preserve of the British-born, as were the superior ranks in such other professions as law and medicine. The British administrators were imbued with a sense of duty in ruling India and were rewarded with good salaries, high status, and opportunities for promotion. Not until the 1910s did the British reluctantly permit a few Indians into their cadre as the number of English-educated Indians rose steadily.

The viceroy announced in 1858 that the government would honor former treaties with princely states and renounced the "doctrine of lapse," whereby the East India Company had annexed territories of rulers who died without male heirs. About 40 percent of Indian territory and between 20 and 25 percent of the population remained under the control of 562 princes notable for their religious (Islamic, Sikh, Hindu, and other) and ethnic diversity. Their propensity for pomp and ceremony became proverbial, while their domains, varying in size and wealth, lagged behind sociopolitical transformations that took place elsewhere in British-controlled India.

A more thorough reorganization was effected in the constitution of army and government finances. Shocked by the extent of solidarity among Indian soldiers during the rebellion, the government separated the army into the three presidencies (see Company Armies, ch. 10).

British attitudes toward Indians shifted from relative openness to insularity and xenophobia, even against those with comparable background and achievement as well as loyalty. British families and their servants lived in cantonments at a distance from Indian settlements. Private clubs where the British gathered for social interaction became symbols of exclusivity and snobbery that refused to disappear decades after the British had left India. In 1883 the government of India attempted to remove race barriers in criminal jurisdictions by introducing a bill empowering Indian judges to adjudicate offenses committed by Europeans. Public protests and editorials in the British press, however, forced the viceroy, George Robinson, Marquis of Ripon (who served from 1880 to 1884), to capitulate and modify the bill drastically. The Bengali Hindu intelligentsia learned a valuable political lesson from this "white mutiny": the effectiveness of well-orchestrated agitation through demonstrations in the streets and publicity in the media when seeking redress for real and imagined grievances.

The Independence Movement

Origins of the Congress and the Muslim League

The decades following the Sepoy Rebellion were a period of growing political awareness, manifestation of Indian public opinion, and emergence of Indian leadership at national and provincial levels. Ominous economic uncertainties created by British colonial rule and the limited opportunities that awaited the ever-expanding number of Western-educated graduates began to dominate the rhetoric of leaders who had begun to think of themselves as a "nation," despite fissures along the lines of region, religion, language, and caste. Inspired by the suggestion made by A.O. Hume, a retired British civil servant, seventy-three Indian delegates met in Bombay in 1885 and founded the Indian National Congress (Congress—see Glossary). They were mostly members of the upwardly mobile and successful Western-educated provincial elites, engaged in professions such as law, teaching, and journalism. They had acquired political experience from regional competition in the professions and from their aspirations in securing nomination to various positions in legislative councils, universities, and special commissions.

At its inception, the Congress had no well-defined ideology and commanded few of the resources essential to a political organization. It functioned more as a debating society that met annually to express its loyalty to the Raj and passed numerous resolutions on less controversial issues such as civil rights or opportunities in government, especially the civil service. These resolutions were submitted to the viceroy's government and, occasionally, to the British Parliament, but the Congress's early gains were meager. Despite its claim to represent all India, the Congress voiced the interests of urban elites; the number of participants from other economic backgrounds remained negligible.

By 1900, although the Congress had emerged as an all-India political organization, its achievement was undermined by its singular failure to attract Muslims, who had by then begun to realize their inadequate education and underrepresentation in government service. Muslim leaders saw that their community had fallen behind the Hindus. Attacks by Hindu reformers against religious conversion, cow killing, and the preservation of Urdu in Arabic script deepened their fears of minority status and denial of their rights if the Congress alone were to represent the people of India. For many Muslims, loyalty to the British crown seemed preferable to cooperation with Congress leaders. Sir Sayyid Ahmad Khan (1817–98) launched a movement for Muslim regeneration that culminated in the founding in 1875 of the Muhammadan Anglo-Oriental College at Aligarh, Uttar Pradesh (renamed Aligarh Muslim University in 1921). Its objective was to educate wealthy students by emphasizing the compatibility of Islam with modern Western knowledge. The diversity among India's Muslims, however, made it impossible to bring about uniform cultural and intellectual regeneration.

Sir George Curzon, the governor-general (1899–1905), ordered the partition of Bengal in 1905. He wanted to improve administrative efficiency in that huge and populous region, where the Bengali Hindu intelligentsia exerted considerable influence on local and national politics. The partition created two provinces: Eastern Bengal and Assam, with its capital at Dhaka (then spelled Dacca), and West Bengal, with its capital at Calcutta (which also served as the capital of British India). An ill-conceived and hastily implemented action, the partition outraged Bengalis. Not only had the government failed to consult Indian public opinion but the action appeared to reflect the British resolve to "divide and rule." Widespread agitation ensued in the streets and in the press, and the Congress advocated boycotting British products under the banner of *swadeshi* (home-made—see Glossary).

The Congress-led boycott of British goods was so successful that it unleashed anti-British forces to an extent unknown since the Sepoy Rebellion. A cycle of violence, terrorism, and repression ensued in some parts of the country. The British tried to mitigate the situation by announcing a series of constitutional reforms in 1909 and by appointing a few moderates to the imperial and provincial councils. In 1906 a Muslim deputation met with the viceroy, Gilbert John Elliot (1905–10), seeking concessions from the impending constitutional reforms, including special considerations in government service and electorates. The All-India Muslim League (Muslim League—

see Glossary) was founded the same year to promote loyalty to the British and to advance Muslim political rights, which the British recognized by increasing the number of elective offices reserved for Muslims in the India Councils Act of 1909. The Muslim League insisted on its separateness from the Hindu-dominated Congress, as the voice of a "nation within a nation."

In what the British saw as an additional goodwill gesture, in 1911 King-Emperor George V (r. 1910–36) visited India for a durbar (a traditional court held for subjects to express fealty to their ruler), during which he announced the reversal of the partition of Bengal and the transfer of the capital from Calcutta to a newly planned city to be built immediately south of Delhi, which became New Delhi.

War, Reforms, and Agitation

World War I began with an unprecedented outpouring of loyalty and goodwill toward the British, contrary to initial British fears of an Indian revolt. India contributed generously to the British war effort, by providing men and resources. About 1.3 million Indian soldiers and laborers served in Europe, Africa, and the Middle East, while both the Indian government and the princes sent large supplies of food, money, and ammunition. But disillusionment set in early. High casualty rates, soaring inflation compounded by heavy taxation, a widespread influenza epidemic, and the disruption of trade during the war escalated human suffering in India. The prewar nationalist movement revived as moderate and extremist groups within the Congress submerged their differences in order to stand as a unified front. The Congress even succeeded in forging a temporary alliance with the Muslim League—the Lucknow Pact, or Congress-League Scheme of Reforms—in 1916, over the issues of devolution of political power and the future of Islam in the Middle East.

The British themselves adopted a "carrot and stick" approach in recognition of India's support during the war and in response to renewed nationalist demands. In August 1917, Edwin Montagu, the secretary of state for India, made the historic announcement in Parliament that the British policy for India was "increasing association of Indians in every branch of the administration and the gradual development of self-governing institutions with a view to the progressive realization of responsible government in India as an integral part of the British Empire." The means of achieving the proposed measure were later enshrined in the Government of India Act of 1919, which introduced the principle of a dual mode of administration, or dyarchy, in which both elected Indian legislators and appointed British officials shared power. The act also expanded the central and provincial legislatures and widened the franchise considerably. Dyarchy set in motion certain real changes at the provincial level: a number of noncontroversial or "transferred" portfolios—such as agriculture, local government, health, education, and public works—were handed over to Indians, while more sensitive matters such as finance, taxation, and maintaining law and order were retained by the provincial British administrators.

The positive impact of reform was seriously undermined in 1919 by the Rowlatt Acts, named after the recommendations made the previous year to the Imperial Legislative Council by the Rowlatt Commission, which had been appointed to investigate "seditious conspiracy." The Rowlatt Acts, also known as the Black Acts, vested the viceroy's government with extraordinary powers to quell sedition by silencing the press, detaining political activists without trial, and arresting any suspected individuals without a warrant. No sooner had the acts come into force in March 1919—despite opposition by Indian members on the Imperial Legislative Council—than a nationwide cessation of work (*hartal*) was called by Mohandas Karamchand Gandhi (1869–1948). Others took up his call, marking the beginning of widespread—although not nationwide—popular discontent. The agitation unleashed by the acts culminated on April 13, 1919, in Amritsar, Punjab. The British military commander, Brigadier Reginald E.H. Dyer, ordered his soldiers to fire at point-blank range into an unarmed and unsuspecting crowd of some 10,000 men, women, and children. They had assembled at Jallianwala Bagh, a walled garden, to celebrate a Hindu festival without prior knowledge of the imposition of martial law. A total of 1,650 rounds were fired, killing 379 persons and wounding 1,137 in the episode, which dispelled wartime hopes and goodwill in a frenzy of postwar reaction.

Mahatma Gandhi

That India opted for an entirely original path to solving this crisis and obtaining *swaraj* (independence) was due largely to Gandhi, commonly known as "Mahatma" (or Great Soul) or, as he himself preferred, "Gandhiji" (an honorific term for Gandhi). A native of Gujarat who had been educated in Britain, he was an obscure and unsuccessful provincial lawyer. Gandhi had accepted an invitation in 1893 to represent indentured Indian laborers in South Africa, where he stayed on for more than twenty years, emerging ultimately as the voice and conscience of thousands who had been subjected to blatant racial discrimination. He returned to India in 1915, virtually a stranger to public life but "fired with a religious vision of a new India, whose *swaraj* . . . would [be] a moral reformation of a whole people which would either convert the British also or render their Raj impossible by Indian withdrawal of support for it and its modern values," according to historian Judith M. Brown.

Gandhi's ideas and strategies of nonviolent civil disobedience (satyagraha—see Glossary), first applied during his South Africa days, initially appeared impractical to many educated Indians. In Gandhi's own words, "Civil disobedience is civil breach of unmoral statutory enactments," but as he viewed it, it had to be carried out nonviolently by withdrawing cooperation with the corrupt state. Observers realized Gandhi's political potential when he used the satyagraha during the anti-Rowlatt Acts protests in Punjab. In 1920, under Gandhi's leadership, the Congress was reorganized and given a new constitution, whose goal was *swaraj*. Membership in the party was opened to anyone prepared to pay a token fee, and a hierarchy of committees—from district, to province, to all-India—was established and made responsible for discipline and control over a hitherto amorphous and diffuse movement. During his first nationwide satyagraha, Gandhi urged the people to boycott British education institutions, law courts, and products (in favor of *swadeshi*); to resign from government employment; to refuse to pay taxes; and to forsake British titles and honors. The party was transformed from an elite organization to one of mass national appeal.

Although Gandhi's first nationwide satyagraha was too late to influence the framing of the new Government of India Act of 1919, the magnitude of disorder resulting from the movement was unparalleled and presented a new challenge to foreign rule. Gandhi was forced to call off the campaign in 1922 because of atrocities committed against police. However, the abortive campaign marked a milestone in India's political development. For his efforts, Gandhi was imprisoned until 1924. On his release from prison, he set up an ashram (a rural commune), established a newspaper, and inaugurated a series of reforms aimed at the socially disadvantaged within Hindu

Mahatma Gandhi spinning thread, 1925
Courtesy Biographic Collection, Library of Congress

society, the rural poor, and the Untouchables (see Changes in
the Caste System, ch. 5). His popularity soared in Indian politics as he reached the hearts and minds of ordinary people,
winning support for his causes as no one else had ever done
before. By his personal and eclectic piety, his asceticism, his
vegetarianism, his espousal of Hindu-Muslim unity, and his
firm belief in ahimsa, Gandhi appealed to the loftier Hindu
ideals. For Gandhi, moral regeneration, social progress, and
national freedom were inseparable.

Emerging leaders within the Congress—Jawaharlal Nehru,
Vallabhbhai Patel, Rajendra Prasad, C. Rajagopalachari, Mau-
lana Abdul Kalam Azad, Subhas Chandra Bose, and Jayaprakash (J.P.) Narayan—accepted Gandhi's leadership in articulating nationalist aspirations but disagreed on strategies for
wresting more concessions from the British. The Indian political spectrum was further broadened in the mid-1920s by the

emergence of both moderate and militant parties, such as the Swaraj Party (sometimes referred to as the Swarajist Party), the Mahasabha Party (literally, great council; an orthodox Hindu communal party), the Unionist Party, the Communist Party of India, and the Socialist Independence for India League. Regional political organizations also continued to represent the interests of non-Brahmans in Madras, Mahars in Maharashtra, and Sikhs in Punjab.

The Congress, however, kept itself aloof from competing in elections. As voices inside and outside the Congress became more strident, the British appointed a commission in 1927, under Sir John Simon, to recommend further measures in the constitutional devolution of power. The British failure to appoint an Indian member to the commission outraged the Congress and others, and, as a result, they boycotted it throughout India, carrying placards inscribed "Simon, Go Back." In 1929 the Congress responded by drafting its own constitution under the guidance of Motilal Nehru (Jawaharlal's father) demanding full independence (*purna swaraj*) by 1930; the Congress went so far as to observe January 26, 1930, as the first anniversary of the first year of independence.

Gandhi reemerged from his long seclusion by undertaking his most inspired campaign, a march of about 400 kilometers from his commune in Ahmadabad to Dandi, on the coast of Gujarat between March 12 and April 6, 1930. At Dandi, in protest against extortionate British taxes on salt, he and thousands of followers illegally but symbolically made their own salt from sea water. Their defiance reflected India's determination to be free, despite the imprisonment of thousands of protesters. For the next five years, the Congress and government were locked in conflict and negotiations until what became the Government of India Act of 1935 could be hammered out. But by then, the rift between the Congress and the Muslim League had become unbridgeable as each pointed the finger at the other acrimoniously. The Muslim League disputed the claim by the Congress to represent all people of India, while the Congress disputed the Muslim League's claim to voice the aspirations of all Muslims.

The 1935 act, the voluminous and final constitutional effort at governing British India, articulated three major goals: establishing a loose federal structure, achieving provincial autonomy, and safeguarding minority interests through separate electorates. The federal provisions, intended to unite princely states and British India at the center, were not implemented because of ambiguities in safeguarding the existing privileges of princes. In February 1937, however, provincial autonomy became a reality when elections were held; the Congress emerged as the dominant party with a clear majority in five provinces and held an upper hand in two, while the Muslim League performed poorly.

Political Impasse and Independence

The Congress neither acknowledged the Muslim League's performance, albeit poor, in the elections nor deigned to form a coalition government with the League, a situation that led to the collapse of negotiations and mutual trust between the leaders. Mohammad Ali Jinnah, a Western-educated Muslim lawyer, took over the presidency of the moribund Muslim League and galvanized it into a national force under the battle cry of "Islam in danger." Jinnah doubted the motives of Gandhi and Nehru and accused them of practicing Hindu chauvinism. He relentlessly attacked the Congress-led ministries, accusing them of casteism, corruption, and nepotism. Skillfully, he succeeded in unifying various regional Islamic organizations and factions in Punjab and Bengal under the umbrella of the Muslim League.

Electoral gains by the Congress in 1937 were rendered ephemeral as its leaders ordered provincial ministries to resign in November 1939, when the viceroy (Victor Alexander John Hope, Marquis of Linlithgow—1936–43) declared India's entrance into World War II without consulting Indian leaders. Jinnah and the Muslim League welcomed the Congress withdrawal from government as a timely opportunity and observed a day of thanksgiving on December 22, 1939. Jinnah persuaded the participants at the annual Muslim League session in Lahore in 1940 to adopt what later came to be known as the Pakistan Resolution, demanding the division of India into two separate sovereign states, one Muslim, the other Hindu. Although the idea of Pakistan had been introduced as early as 1930 at Allahabad, very few had responded to it. However, the volatile political climate, the personal hostilities between the leaders, and the opportunism of Jinnah transformed the idea of Pakistan into a popular demand.

Between 1940 and 1942, the Congress launched two abortive agitations against the British, and 60,000 Congress members were arrested, including Gandhi and Nehru. Unlike the uncooperative and belligerent Congress, the Muslim League supported the British during World War II (see The Indian Military under the British Raj, ch. 10). Belated but perhaps sincere British attempts to accommodate the demands of the two rival parties, while preserving the unitary state in India, seemed unacceptable to both as they alternately rejected whatever proposal was put forward during the war years. As a result, a three-way impasse settled in: the Congress and the Muslim League doubted British motives in handing over power to Indians, while the British struggled to retain some hold on India while offering to give greater autonomy.

The Congress wasted precious time denouncing the British rather than allaying Muslim fears during the highly charged election campaign of 1946. Even the more mature Congress leaders, especially Gandhi and Nehru, failed to see how genuinely afraid the Muslims were and how exhausted and weak the British had become in the aftermath of the war. When it appeared that the Congress had no desire to share power with the Muslim League at the center, Jinnah declared August 16, 1946, Direct Action Day, which brought communal rioting and massacre in many places in the north. Partition seemed preferable to civil war. On June 3, 1947, Viscount Louis Mountbatten, the viceroy (1947) and governor-general (1947–48), announced plans for partition of the British Indian Empire into the nations of India and Pakistan, which itself was divided into east and west wings on either side of India (see fig. 4). At midnight, on August 15, 1947, India strode to freedom amidst ecstatic shouting of *"Jai Hind"* (roughly, Long Live India), when Nehru delivered a memorable and moving speech on India's "tryst with destiny."

Independent India

National Integration

The euphoria of independence was short-lived as partition brought disastrous consequences for India in the wake of communal conflict. Partition unleashed untold misery and loss of lives and property as millions of Hindu and Muslim refugees fled either Pakistan or India. Both nations were also caught up in a number of conflicts involving the allocation of assets, demarcation of boundaries, equitable sharing of water resources, and control over Kashmir. At the same time, Indian leaders were faced with the stupendous task of national integration and economic development.

When the British relinquished their claims to paramountcy, the 562 independent princely states were given the option to join either of the two nations. A few princely states readily joined Pakistan, but the rest—except Hyderabad (the largest of the princely states with 132,000 square kilometers and a population of more than 14 million), Jammu and Kashmir (with 3 million inhabitants), and Junagadh (with a population of 545,000)—merged with India. India successfully annexed Hyderabad and Junagadh after "police actions" and promises of privileges to the rulers. The Hindu maharajah of predominantly Muslim Jammu and Kashmir remained uncommitted until armed tribesmen and regular troops from Pakistan infiltrated his domain, inducing him to sign the Instrument of Accession to India on October 27, 1947. Pakistan refused to accept the legality of the accession, and, as a result, war broke out (see The Experience of Wars, ch. 10). Kashmir remains a source of friction between the neighbors (see South Asia, ch. 9). The assassination of Mahatma Gandhi on January 30, 1948, in New Delhi, by a Hindu extremist opposed to Gandhi's openness to Muslims ended the tenuous celebration of independence and deepened the hatred and mutual suspicion in Hindu-Muslim relations.

Economic backwardness was one of the serious challenges that India faced at independence. Under three successive five-year plans, inaugurated between 1951 and 1964 under Nehru's leadership, India produced increasing amounts of food. Although food production did not allow self-sufficiency until fiscal year (FY—see Glossary) 1984, India has emerged as the nation with the seventh largest gross national product (GNP—see Glossary) in the world (see Industry, ch. 6; Production, ch. 7).

Linguistic regionalism eventually reached a crisis stage and undermined the Congress' attempts at nation building. Whereas in the early 1920s, the Congress had deemed that the use of regional vernaculars in education and administration would facilitate the governance of the country, partition made the leaders, especially Nehru, realize how quickly such provincial or subnational interests would dismantle India's fragile unity (see Diversity, Use, and Policy, ch. 4). However, in the face of widespread agitation for linguistic separation of states, beginning with the Telangana Movement in 1953, in 1956 Nehru reluctantly accepted the recommendations of the States Reorganisation Commission, and the number of states grew by reorganization along linguistic lines. The states became the loci for democratization of political processes at district levels, for expression of regional culture and popular demands against a national culture and unity, for economic development at strategic localities in the rural areas, and for proliferation of opposition parties that ended the possibility of a pan-Indian two-party system (see Political Parties, ch. 8).

Nehru's Legacy

Jawaharlal Nehru (1889–1964), India's first prime minister, was the chief architect of domestic and foreign policies between 1947 and 1964. Born into a wealthy Kashmiri Brahman family and educated at Oxford, Nehru embodied a synthesis of ideals: politically an ardent nationalist, ideologically a pragmatic socialist, and secular in religious outlook, Nehru possessed a rare combination of intellect, breadth of vision, and personal charisma that attracted support throughout India. Nehru's appreciation for parliamentary democracy coupled with concerns for the poor and underprivileged enabled him to formulate policies that often reflected his socialist leanings. Both as prime minister and as Congress president, Nehru pushed through the Indian Parliament, dominated by members of his own party, a series of legal reforms intended to emancipate Hindu women and bring equality. These reforms included raising the minimum marriageable age from twelve to fifteen, empowering women to divorce their husbands and inherit property, and declaring illegal the ruinous dowry system (see Life Passages, ch. 5).

The threat of escalating violence and the potential for "red revolution" across the country seemed daunting in the face of the country's growing population, unemployment, and economic inequality. Nehru induced Parliament to pass a number of laws abolishing absentee landlordism and conferring titles to land on the actual cultivators who could document their right to occupancy. Under his direction, the central Planning Commission allocated resources to heavy industries, such as steel plants and hydroelectric projects, and to revitalizing cottage industries. Whether producing sophisticated defense matériel or manufacturing everyday consumer goods, industrial complexes emerged across the country, accompanied by the expansion of scientific research and teaching at universities, institutes of technology, and research centers (see Education, ch. 2; Science and Technology, ch. 6).

Nehru demonstrated tremendous enthusiasm for India's moral leadership, especially among the newly independent Asian and African nations, in a world polarized by Cold War ideology and threatened by nuclear weapons. His guiding principles were nationalism, anticolonialism, internationalism, and nonalignment. He attained international prestige during his first decade in office, but after the Soviet invasion of Hungary in 1956—when New Delhi tilted toward Moscow—criticisms grew against his inconsistency in condemning Western but not communist aggression. In dealing with Pakistan, Nehru failed to formulate a consistent policy and was critical of the improving ties between Pakistan and the United States; mutual hostility and suspicion persisted as a result (see United States, ch. 9). Despite attempts at improving relations with China, based on his much-publicized five principles (Panch Shila—see Glossary)—territorial integrity and sovereignty, nonaggression, noninterference, equality and cooperation, and peaceful coexistence—war with China erupted in 1962. The war was a rude awakening for Nehru, as India proved ill-equipped and unprepared to defend its northern borders. At the conclusion of the conflict, the Chinese forces were partially withdrawn and an unofficial demilitarized zone was established, but India's prestige and self-esteem had suffered. Physically debilitated and mentally exhausted, Nehru suffered a stroke and died in office in May 1964. His legacy of a democratic, federal, and secular India continues to survive in spite of attempts by later leaders to establish either an autocratic or a theocratic state.

The Rise of Indira Gandhi

Nehru's long tenure in office gave continuity and cohesion to India's domestic and foreign policies, but as his health deteriorated, concerns over who might inherit his mantle or what might befall India after he left office frequently surfaced in political circles. After his death, the Congress Caucus, also known as the Syndicate, chose Lal Bahadur Shastri as prime minister in June 1964. A mild-mannered person, Shastri adhered to Gandhian principles of simplicity of life and dedication to the service of the country. His short period of leadership was beset with three major crises: widespread food shortages, violent anti-Hindi demonstrations in the state of Madras (as Tamil Nadu was then called) that were quelled by the army, and the second war with Pakistan over Kashmir. Shastri's premiership was cut short when he died of a heart attack on January 11, 1966, the day after having signed the Soviet-brokered Tashkent Declaration. The agreement required both sides to withdraw all armed personnel by February 26, 1966, to the positions they had held prior to August 5, 1965, and to observe the cease-fire line.

Indira Gandhi held a cabinet portfolio as minister of information and broadcasting in Shastri's government. She was the only child of Nehru, who was also her mentor in the nationalist movement. The Syndicate selected her as prime minister when Shastri died in 1966 even though her eligibility was challenged by Morarji Desai, a veteran nationalist and long-time aspirant to that office. The Congress "bosses" were apparently looking for a leading figure acceptable to the masses, who could command general support during the next general election but who would also acquiesce to their guidance. Hardly had Indira Gandhi begun in office than she encountered a series of problems that defied easy solutions: Mizo tribal uprisings in the northeast; famine, labor unrest, and misery among the poor in the wake of rupee devaluation; and agitation in Punjab for linguistic and religious separatism.

In the fourth general election in February 1967, the Congress majority was greatly reduced when it secured only 54 percent of the parliamentary seats, and non-Congress ministries were established in Bihar, Kerala, Orissa, Madras, Punjab, and West Bengal the next month. A Congress-led coalition government collapsed in Uttar Pradesh, while in April Rajasthan was brought under President's Rule—direct central government rule (see The Executive, ch. 8). Seeking to eradicate poverty, Mrs. Gandhi pursued a vigorous policy in 1969 of land reform and placed a ceiling on personal income, private property, and corporate profits. She also nationalized the major banks, a bold step amidst a growing rift between herself and the party elders. The Congress expelled her for "indiscipline" on November 12, 1969, an action that split the party into two factions: the Congress (O)—for Organisation—under Desai, and the Congress (R)—for Requisition—under Gandhi. She continued as prime minister with support from communists, Sikhs, and regional parties.

Gandhi campaigned fiercely on the platform "eliminate poverty" (*garibi hatao*) during the fifth general election in March 1971, and the Congress (R) gained a large majority in Parliament against her former party leaders whose slogan was "eliminate Indira" (*Indira hatao*). India's decisive victory over

The site of Mahatma Gandhi's last steps and assassination on January 30, 1948, New Delhi
Courtesy Robert L. Worden

Pakistan in the third war over Kashmir in December 1971, and Gandhi's insistence that the 10 million refugees from Bangladesh be sent back to their country generated a national surge in her popularity, later confirmed by her party's gains in state elections in 1972. She had firmly established herself at the pinnacle of power, overcoming challenges from the Congress (O), the Supreme Court, and the state chief ministers in the early 1970s. The more solidified her monopoly of power became, the more egregious was her intolerance of criticisms, even when they were deserved. As head of her party and the government, Gandhi nominated and removed the chief ministers at will and frequently reshuffled the portfolios of her own cabinet members. Ignoring their obligations to their constituencies, party members competed with each other in parading their loyalty to Gandhi, whose personal approval alone seemed crucial to their survival. In August 1971, Gandhi signed the twenty-year Treaty of Peace, Friendship, and Cooperation with the Soviet Union because ties with the United States, which had improved in Nehru's later years, had eroded (see Russia, ch. 9).

Neither Gandhi's consolidation of power, nor her imperious style of administration, nor even her rhetoric of radical reforms was enough to meet the deepening economic crisis spawned by the enormous cost of the 1971 war. A huge additional outlay was needed to manage the refugees, the crop failures in 1972 and 1973, the skyrocketing world oil prices in 1973–74, and the overall drop in industrial output despite a surplus of scientifically and technically trained personnel. No immediate sign of economic recovery or equity was visible despite a loan obtained from the International Monetary Fund (IMF—see Glossary) in 1974. Both Gandhi's office and character came under severe tests, beginning with railroad employee strikes, national civil disobedience advocated by J.P. Narayan, defeat of her party in Gujarat by a coalition of parties calling itself the Janata Morcha (People's Front), an all-party, no-confidence motion in Parliament, and, finally, a writ issued by the Allahabad High Court invalidating her 1971 election and making her ineligible to occupy her seat for six years.

What had once seemed a remote possibility took place on June 25, 1975: the president declared an Emergency and the government suspended civil rights. Because the nation's president, Fakhruddin Ali Ahmed (1974–77), and Gandhi's own party members in Parliament were amenable to her personal influence, Gandhi had little trouble in pushing through amendments to the constitution that exonerated her from any culpability, declaring President's Rule in Gujarat and Tamil Nadu where anti-Indira parties ruled, and jailing thousands of her opponents. In her need to trust and confide in someone during this extremely trying period, she turned to her younger son, Sanjay, who became an enthusiastic advocate of the Emergency. Under his watchful eyes, forced sterilization as a means of birth control was imposed on the poor, increased numbers of urban squatters and slum dwellers in Delhi were evicted in the name of beautification projects, and disgruntled workers were either disciplined or their wages frozen. The Reign of Terror, as some called it, continued until January 18, 1977, when Gandhi suddenly relaxed the Emergency, announced the next general election in March, and released her opponents from prison.

With elections only two months away, both J.P. Narayan and Morarji Desai reactivated the multiparty front, which campaigned as the Janata Party and rode anti-Emergency sentiment to secure a clear majority in the Lok Sabha (House of the People), the lower house of Parliament (see The Legislature, ch. 8). Desai, a conservative Brahman, became India's fourth prime minister (1977–79), but his government, from its inception, became notorious for its factionalism and furious internal competition. As it promised, the Janata government restored freedom and democracy, but its inability to effect sound reforms or ameliorate poverty left people disillusioned. Desai lost the support of Janata's left-wing parties by the early summer of 1979, and several secular and liberal politicians abandoned him altogether, leaving him without a parliamentary majority. A no-confidence motion was about to be introduced in Parliament in July 1979, but he resigned his office; Desai's government was replaced by a coalition led by Chaudhury Charan Singh (prime minister in 1979–80). Although Singh's lifelong ambition had been to become prime minister, his age and inefficiency were used against him, and his attempts at governing India proved futile; new elections were announced in January 1980.

Gandhi and her party, renamed Congress (I)—I for Indira—campaigned on the slogan "Elect a Government That Works!" and regained power. Sanjay Gandhi was elected to the Lok Sabha. Unlike during the Emergency, when India registered significant economic and industrial progress, Gandhi's return to power was hindered by a series of woes and tragedies, beginning with Sanjay's death in June 1980 while attempting to perform stunts in his private airplane. Secessionist forces in Punjab and in the northeast and the Soviet occupation of Afghanistan in December 1979 consumed her energy. She began to involve the armed forces in resolving violent domestic conflicts between 1980 and 1984. In May 1984, Sikh extremists occupied the Golden Temple in Amritsar, converting it into a haven for terrorists. Gandhi responded in early June when she launched Operation Bluestar, which killed and wounded hundreds of soldiers, insurgents, and civilians (see Insurgent Movements and External Subversion, ch. 10). Guarding against further challenges to her power, she removed the chief ministers of Jammu and Kashmir and Andhra Pradesh just months before her assassination by her Sikh bodyguards on October 31, 1984. The news of Indira Gandhi's assassination plunged New Delhi and other parts of India into anti-Sikh riots for three days; several thousand Sikhs were killed.

Rajiv Gandhi

When Rajiv Gandhi, Indira's eldest son, reluctantly consented to run for his brother's vacant Lok Sabha seat in 1980, and when he later took over the leadership of the Congress youth wing, becoming prime minister was the last thing on his mind; equally, his mother had her own misgivings about whether Rajiv would bravely "take the brutalities and the ruthlessness of politics." Yet on the day Indira was assassinated, Rajiv was sworn in as prime minister at the age of forty. He brought into politics energy, enthusiasm, and vision—qualities badly needed to lead the divided country. Moreover, his looks, personal charm, and reputation as "Mr. Clean" were assets that won him many friends in India and abroad, especially in the United States. Rajiv also had a clear mandate to rule the country with an overwhelming majority in Parliament.

Rajiv seemed to have understood the magnitude of the most critical and urgent problems that faced the nation when he assumed office. As Paul H. Kreisberg, a former United States foreign service officer, put it, Rajiv was faced with an unenviable four-pronged challenge: resolving political and religious violence in Punjab and the northeast; reforming the demoralized Congress (I), which was often identified with the interests of the upper and upper-middle classes; reenergizing the sagging economy in terms of productivity and budget control; and reducing tensions with neighbors, especially Pakistan and Sri Lanka. As Rajiv tackled these issues with singular determination, there was optimism and hope about the future of India. Between 1985 and 1987, temporary calm was restored by accommodating demands for regional control in the northeast and by granting more concessions to Punjab. Although Rajiv acknowledged the gradual attrition of the Congress, he was unwilling to relinquish control of the leadership, tolerate "cliques," or conduct new elections for offices at the state and district levels.

Economic reforms and incentives to private investors were introduced by easing government tax rates and licensing requirements, but officials manipulated the rules and frequently accepted bribes. These innovative measures also came under attack from business leaders, who for many years had controlled both markets and prices with little regard for quality. When the Ministry of Finance began its own investigation of tax and foreign-exchange evasion amounting to millions of dollars, many of India's leading families, including Rajiv's political allies, were found culpable. Despite these hindrances, Rajiv's fascination with electronics and telecommunications resulted in revamping the antiquated telephone systems to meet public demands. Collaboration with the United States and several

European governments and corporations brought more investment in research in electronics and computer software.

India's perennial, see-sawing tensions with Pakistan, whose potential nuclear-weapons capacity escalated concerns in the region, were ameliorated when the South Asian Association for Regional Cooperation (SAARC—see Glossary) was inaugurated in December 1985. Both nations signed an agreement in 1986 promising that neither would launch a first strike at the other's nuclear facilities. However, sporadic conflicts persist along the cease-fire line in Kashmir (see South Asia, ch. 9).

Relations with Sri Lanka degenerated because of unresolved Sinhalese-Tamil controversies and continued guerrilla warfare by Tamil militants, under the leadership of the Liberation Tigers of Tamil Eelam, who had bases in Tamil Nadu. Beginning in 1987, India's attempt to disarm and subdue the Tigers through intervention of the Indian Peace Keeping Force proved disastrous as thousands of Indian soldiers and Tamil militants were killed or wounded (see Peacekeeping Operations, ch. 10).

Rajiv Gandhi's performance in the middle of his term in office was best summed up, as Kreisberg put it, as "good intentions, some progress, frequently weak implementation, and poor politics." Two major scandals, the "Spy" and the "Bofors" affairs, tarnished his reputation. In January 1985, Gandhi confirmed in Parliament the involvement of top government officials, their assistants, and businessmen in "a wide-ranging espionage network." The ring reportedly infiltrated the prime minister's office as early as 1982 when Indira was in power and sold defense and economic intelligence to foreign diplomats at the embassies of France, Poland and other East European countries, and the Soviet Union. Although more than twenty-four arrests were made and the diplomats involved were expelled, the Spy scandal remained a lingering embarrassment to Rajiv's administration.

In 1986 India purchased US$1.3 billion worth of artillery pieces from the Swedish manufacturer A.B. Bofors, and months later a Swedish radio report remarked that Bofors had won the "biggest" export order by bribing Indian politicians and defense personnel. The revelation caught the nation's attention immediately because of the allegations that somehow Rajiv Gandhi and his friends were connected with the deal. When Vishwanath Pratap (V.P.) Singh, as minister of defence, investigated the alleged kickbacks, he was forced to resign, and he became Rajiv's Janata political rival. Despite relentless attacks and criticisms in the media as well as protests and resignations from cabinet members, Rajiv adamantly denied any role in the affair. But when he called parliamentary elections in November 1989, two months ahead of schedule, the opposition alliance, the National Front, vigorously campaigned on "removing corruption and restoring the dignity of national institutions," as did another opposition party, Janata Dal. Rajiv and his party won more seats in the election than any other party, but, being unable to form a government with a clear majority or a mandate, he resigned on November 29. Rajiv Gandhi was assassinated by Sri Lankan terrorists on May 21, 1991, near Madras. The Gandhi era, as future events would prove, was over, at least for the near term (see Political Parties, ch. 8).

*   *   *

The literature on Indian history in the English language alone is exhaustive as demonstrated in *South Asian Civilizations: A Bibliographic Synthesis* by Maureen L.P. Patterson. The most commonly used text is the two-volume *A History of India* by Romila Thapar (volume 1) and Percival Spear (volume 2). Monographs, such as Stanley Wolpert's *A New History of India* and Hermann Kulke and Dietmar Rothermund's *A History of India*, cover major epochs.

Critical works by Gregory L. Possehl (*The Harappan Civilization*), A.L. Basham (*The Wonder That Was India*), Kallidaikurchi Aiyah Nilakanta Sastri (*History of South India from Prehistoric Times to the Fall of Vijayanagar*), and Burton Stein (*Peasant, State, and Society in Medieval South India*) offer valuable insights as well as theoretical foundations for understanding India prior to Mughal rule. Essays in *The Cambridge Economic History of India*, edited by Tapan Raychaudhuri and Irfan Habib, provide a full account of life in India from the twelfth to the eighteenth centuries. *The Mughal Empire*, by John Richards, a volume in *The New Cambridge History of India*, reflects the current discussion on the dynamic nature and quality of the rulers; Irfan Habib's *An Atlas of Mughal Empire* and *The Agrarian System of Mughal India, 1556–1707* focus on the administrative and economic aspects of the empire. Bamber Gascoigne's *The Great Mughals* has photographs along with texts from original sources.

Several scholars have written about British activities from the mid-eighteenth century to independence and have incorporated new data garnered from various state archives and family histories as well as vernacular sources; their works reflect a deviation from the conventional approach of focusing on governor-generals or viceroys. They include C.A. Bayly's *Rulers, Townsmen, and Bazaars,* Robin Jeffrey's *People, Princes, and Paramount Power,* Judith M. Brown's *Modern India: The Origins of an Asian Democracy,* and Sumit Sarkar's *Modern India, 1885–1947.*

The nationalist movement also has generated numerous histories, both authoritative and controversial. Anil Seal's *The Emergence of Indian Nationalism* was followed by a group representing the "Cambridge School" whose critical examination of the background of personalities and the issues that dominated Indian politics has spawned much discussion. The literature on Mahatma Gandhi has increased over the decades. His *An Autobiography: The Story of My Experiments with Truth* is a leading source for the first half of his life, while Joan V. Bondurant's *The Conquest of Violence* and Erick H. Erikson's *Gandhi's Truth* offer probing insights into his strategies and personality.

Postindependence India has been portrayed variously depending on the writer's ideology, use of sources, and analysis. Sarvepalli Gopal's *Jawaharlal Nehru* and Zaheer Masani's *Indira Gandhi* provide lucid accounts of the period from the perspectives of the prime ministers. Scathing criticism from the view of the common man is found in Dilip Hiro's *Inside India Today* and Arun Shourie's *Symptoms of Fascism.* Pupul Jayakar's *Indira Gandhi: A Biography* presents a balanced view. Although a critical biography on Rajiv Gandhi has yet to appear, a number of works, such as *Rajiv Gandhi: Life and Message* by Arun Bhattacharjee and *Rajiv Gandhi and Parliament* edited by C.K. Jain, provide valuable insights. (For further information and complete citations, see Bibliography.)

Chapter 2. Geographic and Demographic Setting

Embroidered peacock depicted on a Rabari petticoat from Gujarat

INDIA IS A COUNTRY of great diversity with a wide range of landform types, including major mountain ranges, deserts, rich agricultural plains, and hilly jungle regions. Indeed, the term *Indian subcontinent* aptly describes the enormous extent of the earth's surface that India occupies, and any attempt to generalize about its physiography is inaccurate. Diversity is also evident in the geographical distribution of India's ethnic and linguistic groups. In ancient times, the major river valleys of the Indo-Gangetic Plain of South Asia were among the great cradles of civilization in Asia, as were the valleys of the Tigris and Euphrates rivers in West Asia and the Huang He (Yellow River) in East Asia. As a result of thousands of years of cultural and political expansion and amalgamation, contemporary India has come to include many different natural and cultural regions.

The Himalayas (and the nations of Nepal and Bhutan) form India's northern frontier with China. Pakistan borders India to the west and Bangladesh (formerly East Pakistan) to the east. Although both were formerly part of the British Indian Empire, India and Pakistan became separate countries in 1947 and East Pakistan became independent Bangladesh in 1971. The boundaries of the Indian polity are not fully demarcated because of regional ethnic and political disputes and are the source of occasional tensions.

When the 1991 national census was taken, India's population was approximately 846.3 million. The annual population growth rate from 1981 to 1991 was 2 percent. Accounting for only 2.4 percent of the world's landmass, India is home to 16 percent of the world's population. Every sixth person in the world in the early 1990s was an Indian. It is generally assumed that India's population will surpass the 1 billion mark some time before the next census in 2001. In July 1995, the population was estimated at 936.5 million.

Some 38 percent of all Indians were officially listed as living below the poverty line in fiscal year (FY—see Glossary) 1991. This number represented an increase from the low mark of 26 percent in FY 1989, but the rise was believed to be only temporary by some observers. Although government-sponsored health clinics are widely available in the mid-1990s, their emphasis is on curative techniques rather than preventive medicine. However, the lack of such basic amenities as safe, potable water for much of the population is indicative of the severity of health problems. This situation has traditionally led most Indians to have large families as their only form of insurance against sickness and for their care in old age. Although family planning programs are becoming integrated with the programs of urban and rural health clinics, no official birth control programs have widespread support. The severity of the acquired immune deficiency syndrome (AIDS) epidemic in India has become increasingly apparent to health specialists, but local awareness of the causes of and ways to prevent the spread of AIDS is growing slowly.

Although many public schools are inadequate, improvements to the education system overall have been substantial since 1947. In the mid-1990s, however, only about 50 percent of children between the ages of six and fourteen are enrolled in schools. The goal of compulsory and free primary and middle school education is embodied in the Indian constitution but has been elusive. The National Policy on Education of 1986 sought to institutionalize universal primary education by setting 1990 as a target date for the education of all children up to eleven years of age. The ability of India's education system to meet this goal has been constrained by lack of adequate financial resources. Important achievements have been made, however, with implementation of the nonformal education system and adult education programs. Whereas public education is generally below standard, education standards in private schools are very high. There also are high standards among the elite institutions in the higher education system.

Geography

Principal Regions

India's total land mass is 2,973,190 square kilometers and is divided into three main geological regions: the Indo-Gangetic Plain, the Himalayas, and the Peninsula region (see fig. 5). The Indo-Gangetic Plain and those portions of the Himalayas within India are collectively known as North India. South India consists of the peninsular region, often termed simply the Peninsula. On the basis of its physiography, India is divided into ten regions: the Indo-Gangetic Plain, the northern mountains of the Himalayas, the Central Highlands, the Deccan or Peninsular Plateau, the East Coast (Coromandel Coast in the south), the West Coast (Konkan, Kankara, and Malabar coasts), the

Great Indian Desert (a geographic feature known as the Thar Desert in Pakistan) and the Rann of Kutch, the valley of the Brahmaputra in Assam, the northeastern hill ranges surrounding the Assam Valley, and the islands of the Arabian Sea and the Bay of Bengal.

Indo-Gangetic Plain

In social and economic terms, the Indo-Gangetic Plain is the most important region of India. The plain is a great alluvial crescent stretching from the Indus River system in Pakistan to the Punjab Plain (in both Pakistan and India) and the Haryana Plain to the delta of the Ganga (or Ganges) in Bangladesh (where it is called the Padma). Topographically the plain is homogeneous, with only floodplain bluffs and other related features of river erosion and changes in river channels forming important natural features.

Two narrow terrain belts, collectively known as the Terai, constitute the northern boundary of the Indo-Gangetic Plain. Where the foothills of the Himalayas encounter the plain, small hills known locally as *ghar* (meaning house in Hindi) have been formed by coarse sands and pebbles deposited by mountain streams. Groundwater from these areas flows on the surface where the plains begin and converts large areas along the rivers into swamps. The southern boundary of the plain begins along the edge of the Great Indian Desert in the state of Rajasthan and continues east along the base of the hills of the Central Highlands to the Bay of Bengal (see fig. 1). The hills, varying in elevation from 300 to 1,200 meters, lie on a general east-west axis. The Central Highlands are divided into northern and southern parts. The northern part is centered on the Aravalli Range of eastern Rajasthan. In the northern part of the state of Madhya Pradesh, the Malwa Plateau comprises the southern part of the Central Highlands and merges with the Vindhya Range to the south. The main rivers that flow through the southern part of the plain—the Narmada, the Tapti, and the Mahanadi—delineate North India from South India (see Rivers, this ch.).

Some geographers subdivide the Indo-Gangetic Plain into three parts: the Indus Valley (mostly in Pakistan), the Punjab (divided between India and Pakistan) and Haryana plains, and the middle and lower Ganga. These regional distinctions are based primarily on the availability of water. By another definition, the Indo-Gangetic Plain is divided into two drainage basins by the Delhi Ridge; the western part consists of the Punjab Plain and the Haryana Plain, and the eastern part consists of the Ganga-Brahmaputra drainage systems. This divide is only 300 meters above sea level, contributing to the perception that the Indo-Gangetic Plain appears to be continuous between the two drainage basins. The Punjab Plain is centered in the land between five rivers: the Jhelum, the Chenab, the Ravi, the Beas, and the Sutlej. (The name *Punjab* comes from the Sanskrit *pancha ab*, meaning five waters or rivers.)

Both the Punjab and Haryana plains are irrigated with water from the Ravi, Beas, and Sutlej rivers. The irrigation projects emanating from these rivers have led to a decrease in the flow of water reaching the lower drainage areas in the state of Punjab in India and the Indus Valley in Pakistan. The benefits that increased irrigation has brought to farmers in the state of Haryana are controversial in light of the effects that irrigation has had on agricultural life in the Punjab areas of both India and Pakistan.

The middle Ganga extends from the Yamuna River in the west to the state of West Bengal in the east. The lower Ganga and the Assam Valley are more lush and verdant than the middle Ganga. The lower Ganga is centered in West Bengal from which it flows into Bangladesh and, after joining the Jamuna (as the lower reaches of the Brahmaputra are known in Bangladesh), forms the delta of the Ganga. The Brahmaputra (meaning son of Brahma) rises in Tibet (China's Xizang Autonomous Region) as the Yarlung Zangbo River, flows through Arunachal Pradesh and Assam, and then crosses into Bangladesh. Average annual rainfall increases moving west to east from approximately 600 millimeters in the Punjab Plain to 1,500 millimeters around the lower Ganga and Brahmaputra.

The Himalayas

The Himalayas, the highest mountain range in the world, extend along the northern frontiers of Pakistan, India, Nepal, Bhutan, and Burma. They were formed geologically as a result of the collision of the Indian subcontinent with Asia. This process of plate tectonics is ongoing, and the gradual northward drift of the Indian subcontinent still causes earthquakes (see Earthquakes, this ch.). Lesser ranges jut southward from the main body of the Himalayas at both the eastern and western ends. The Himalayan system, about 2,400 kilometers in length and varying in width from 240 to 330 kilometers, is made up of three parallel ranges—the Greater Himalayas, the Lesser Himalayas, and the Outer Himalayas—sometimes collectively called the Great Himalayan Range. The Greater Himalayas, or northern range, average approximately 6,000 meters in height and contain the three highest mountains on earth: Mount Everest (8,796 meters) on the China-Nepal border; K2 (8,611 meters, also known as Mount Godwin-Austen, and in China as Qogir Feng) in an area claimed by India, Pakistan, and China; and Kanchenjunga (8,598 meters) on the India-Nepal border. Many major mountains are located entirely within India, such as Nanda Devi (7,817 meters) in the state of Uttar Pradesh. The snow line averages 4,500 to 6,000 meters on the southern side of the Greater Himalayas and 5,500 to 6,000 on the northern side. Because of climatic conditions, the snow line in the eastern Himalayas averages 4,300 meters, while in the western Himalayas it averages 5,800 meters.

The Lesser Himalayas, located in northwestern India in the states of Himachal Pradesh and Uttar Pradesh, in north-central India in the state of Sikkim, and in northeastern India in the state of Arunachal Pradesh, range from 1,500 to 5,000 meters in height. Located in the Lesser Himalayas are the hill stations of Shimla (Simla) and Darjiling (Darjeeling). During the colonial period, these and other hill stations were used by the British as summer retreats to escape the intense heat of the plains. It is in this transitional vegetation zone that the contrasts between the bare southern slopes and the forested northern slopes become most noticeable.

The Outer or Southern Himalayas, averaging 900 to 1,200 meters in elevation, lie between the Lesser Himalayas and the Indo-Gangetic Plain. In Himachal Pradesh and Uttar Pradesh, this southernmost range is often referred to as the Siwalik Hills. It is possible to identify a fourth, and northernmost range, known as the Trans-Himalaya. This range is located entirely on the Qinghai-Xizang Plateau, north of the great west-to-east trending valley of the Yarlung Zangbo River. Although the Trans-Himalaya Range is divided from the Great Himalayan Range for most of its length, it merges with the Great Himalayan Range in the western section—the Karakoram Range—where India, Pakistan, and China meet.

The southern slopes of each of the Himalayan ranges are too steep to accumulate snow or support much tree life; the northern slopes generally are forested below the snow line. Between the ranges are extensive high plateaus, deep gorges, and fertile valleys, such as the vales of Kashmir and Kulu. The Himalayas serve a very important purpose. They provide a physical screen within which the monsoon system operates and are the source of the great river systems that water the alluvial plains below (see Climate, this ch.). As a result of erosion, the rivers coming from the mountains carry vast quantities of silt that enrich the plains.

The area of northeastern India adjacent to Burma and Bangladesh consists of numerous hill tracts, averaging between 1,000 and 2,000 meters in elevation, that are not associated with the eastern part of the Himalayas in Arunachal Pradesh. The Naga Hills, rising to heights of more than 3,000 meters, form the watershed between India and Burma. The Mizo Hills are the southern part of the northeastern ranges in India. The Garo, Khasi, and Jaintia hills are centered in the state of Meghalaya and, isolated from the northeastern ranges, divide the Assam Valley from Bangladesh to the south and west.

The Peninsula

The Peninsula proper is an old, geologically stable region with an average elevation between 300 and 1,800 meters. The Vindhya Range constitutes the main dividing line between the geological regions of the Indo-Gangetic Plain and the Peninsula. This range lies north of the Narmada River, and when viewed from there, it is possible to discern the prominent escarpments that rise between 800 and 1,400 meters. The Vindhya Range defines the north-central and northwestern boundary of the Peninsula, and the Chota Nagpur Plateau of southern Bihar forms the northeastern boundary. The uplifting of the plateau of the central Peninsula and its eastward tilt formed the Western Ghats, a line of hills running from the Tapti River south to the tip of the Peninsula. The Eastern Ghats mark the eastern end of the plateau; they begin in the hills of the Mahanadi River basin and converge with the Western Ghats at the Peninsula's southern tip.

The interior of the Peninsula, south of the Narmada River, often termed the Deccan Plateau or simply the Deccan (from the Sanskrit *daksina*, meaning south), is a series of plateaus topped by rolling hills and intersected by many rivers. The plateau averages roughly 300 to 750 meters in elevation. Its major rivers—the Godavari, the Krishna, and the Kaveri—rise in the Western Ghats and flow eastward into the Bay of Bengal.

The coastal plain borders the plateau. On the northwestern side, it is characterized by tidal marshes, drowned valleys, and estuaries; and in the south by lagoons, marshes, and beach ridges. Coastal plains on the eastern side are wider than those in the west; they are focused on large river deltas that serve as the centers of human settlement.

Offshore Islands

India's offshore islands, constituting roughly one-quarter of 1 percent of the nation's territory, lie in two groups located off the east and west coasts. The northernmost point of the union territory of the Andaman and Nicobar Islands lies 1,100 kilometers southeast of Calcutta. Situated in the Bay of Bengal in a chain stretching some 800 kilometers, the Andaman Islands comprise 204 islands and islets, and their topography is characterized by hills and narrow valleys. Although their location is tropical, the climate of the islands is tempered by sea breezes; rainfall is irregular. The Nicobar Islands, which are south of the Andaman Islands, comprise nineteen islands, some with flat, coral-covered surfaces and others with hills. The islands have a nearly equatorial climate, heavy rainfall, and high temperatures. The union territory of Lakshadweep (the name means 100,000 islands) in the Arabian Sea, comprises—from north to south—the Amindivi, Laccadive, Cannanore, and Minicoy islands. The islands, only ten of which are inhabited, are spread throughout an area of approximately 77,000 square kilometers. The islands are low-lying coral-based formations capable of limited cultivation.

Coasts and Borders

India has 7,000 kilometers of seacoast and shares 14,000 kilometers of land frontier with six nations: Pakistan, China, Nepal, Bhutan, Bangladesh, and Burma. India claims a twelve-nautical-mile territorial sea and an exclusive economic zone of 200 nautical miles. The territorial seas total 314,400 square kilometers.

In the mid-1990s, India had boundary disagreements with Pakistan, China, and Bangladesh; border distances are therefore approximations. The partition of India in 1947 established two India-Pakistan frontiers: one on the west and one on the east (East Pakistan became Bangladesh in 1971).

Disputes over the state of Jammu and Kashmir led to hostilities between India and Pakistan in 1947. The January 1, 1949, cease-fire arranged by the United Nations (UN) divided control of Kashmir. India controls Jammu, the Vale of Kashmir, and the capital, Srinagar, while Pakistan controls the mountainous area to the northwest. Neither side accepts a divided Kashmir as a permanent solution. India regards as illegal the 1963 China-Pakistan border agreement, which ceded to China a portion of Pakistani-controlled Kashmir. The two sides also dispute the Siachen Glacier near the Karakoram Pass. Further India-Pakistan hostilities in the 1965 war were settled through the Soviet-brokered Tashkent Declaration.

In 1968 an international tribunal settled the dispute over the Rann of Kutch, a region of salt flats that is submerged for six months of the year in the state of Gujarat. The following year, a new border was demarcated that recognized Pakistan's claim to about 10 percent of the area.

In 1992 India completed fencing most of the 547-kilometer-long section of the boundary between the Indian state of Punjab and the Pakistani province of Punjab. This measure was undertaken because of the continuing unrest in the region caused by both ethnic and religious disputes among the local Indian population and infiltrators from both sides of the frontier. The more rugged terrain north of Punjab along the entire cease-fire line between India and Pakistan in Jammu and Kashmir continues to be subject to infiltration and local strife (see Political Issues, ch. 8; South Asia, ch. 9; Insurgent Movements and External Subversion, ch. 10).

The 2,000-kilometer-long border with China has eastern, central, and western sections. In the western section, the border regions of Jammu and Kashmir have been the scene of conflicting claims since the nineteenth century. China has not accepted India's definitions of the boundary and has carried out defense and economic activities in parts of eastern Kashmir since the 1950s. In the 1960s, China finished construction of a motor road across Aksai Chin (a region under dispute between India and China), the main transportation route linking China's Xinjiang-Uygur Autonomous Region and Tibet.

In the eastern section, the China-India boundary follows the McMahon Line laid down in 1914 by Sir Arthur Henry McMahon, the British plenipotentiary to a conference of Indian, British, and Chinese representatives at Simla (now known as Shimla, Himachal Pradesh). The Simla Convention, as the agreement is known, set the boundary between India and Tibet. Although the British and Tibetan representatives signed

*Elephants bathing in the Gomati River, a tributary of the Ganga in
Uttar Pradesh
Courtesy Foreign Geography Collection, Library of Congress*

the agreement on July 3, 1914, the Chinese delegate declined
to sign. The line agreed to by Britain and Tibet generally follows the crest of the eastern Himalayas from Bhutan to Burma.
It serves as a legal boundary, although the Chinese have never
formally accepted it. China continued to claim roughly the
entire area of Arunachal Pradesh south of the McMahon Line
in the early 1990s. In 1962 China and India fought a brief border war in this region, and China occupied certain areas south
of the line for several months (see Nehru's Legacy, ch 1; The
Experience of Wars, ch. 10). India and China took a major step
toward resolving their border disputes in 1981 by opening
negotiations on the issue. Agreements and talks held in 1993
and 1995 eased tensions along the India-China border (see
China, ch. 9). Sikkim, which became an Indian state in 1975,
forms the small central section of India's northern border and
lies between Nepal and Bhutan.

India's border with Bangladesh is essentially the same as it
was before East Pakistan became Bangladesh in 1971. Some
minor disputes continued to occur over the size and number of
the numerous enclaves each country had on either side of the

border. These enclaves were established during the period from 1661 to 1712 during fighting between the Mughal Empire and the principality of Cooch Behar. This complex pattern of enclaves was preserved by the British administration and passed on intact to India and Pakistan.

The 1,300-kilometer frontier with Burma has been delimited but not completely demarcated. On March 10, 1967, the Indian and Burmese governments signed a bilateral treaty delimiting the boundary in detail. India also has a maritime boundary with Burma in the area of the northern Andaman Islands and Burma's Coco Islands in the Bay of Bengal. India's borders with Nepal and Bhutan have remained unchanged since the days of British rule. In 1977 India signed an accord with Indonesia demarcating the entire maritime boundary between the two countries. One year earlier, a similar accord was signed with the Maldives.

Rivers

The country's rivers are classified as Himalayan, peninsular, coastal, and inland-drainage basin rivers. Himalayan rivers are snow fed and maintain a high to medium rate of flow throughout the year. The heavy annual average rainfall levels in the Himalayan catchment areas further add to their rates of flow. During the monsoon months of June to September, the catchment areas are prone to flooding. The volume of the rain-fed peninsular rivers also increases. Coastal streams, especially in the west, are short and episodic. Rivers of the inland system, centered in western Rajasthan state, are few and frequently disappear in years of scant rainfall. The majority of the South Asia's major rivers flow through broad, shallow valleys and drain into the Bay of Bengal.

The Ganga River basin, India's largest, includes approximately 25 percent of the nation's area; it is bounded by the Himalayas in the north and the Vindhya Range to the south. The Ganga has its source in the glaciers of the Greater Himalayas, which form the frontier between India and Tibet in northwestern Uttar Pradesh. Many Indians believe that the legendary source of the Ganga, and several other important Asian rivers, lies in the sacred Mapam Yumco Lake (known to the Indians as Manasarowar Lake) of western Tibet located approximately 75 kilometers northeast of the India-China-Nepal tripoint. In the northern part of the Ganga River basin, practically all of the tributaries of the Ganga are perennial streams. However, in the southern part, located in the states of Rajasthan and Madhya Pradesh, many of the tributaries are not perennial.

The Brahmaputra has the greatest volume of water of all the rivers in India because of heavy annual rainfall levels in its catchment basin. At Dibrugarh the annual rainfall averages 2,800 millimeters, and at Shillong it averages 2,430 millimeters. Rising in Tibet, the Brahmaputra flows south into Arunachal Pradesh after breaking through the Great Himalayan Range and dropping rapidly in elevation. It continues to fall through gorges impassable by man in Arunachal Pradesh until finally entering the Assam Valley where it meanders westward on its way to joining the Ganga in Bangladesh.

The Mahanadi, rising in the state of Madhya Pradesh, is an important river in the state of Orissa. In the upper drainage basin of the Mahanadi, which is centered on the Chhattisgarh Plain, periodic droughts contrast with the situation in the delta region where floods may damage the crops in what is known as the rice bowl of Orissa. Hirakud Dam, constructed in the middle reaches of the Mahanadi, has helped in alleviating these adverse effects by creating a reservoir.

The source of the Godavari is northeast of Bombay (Mumbai in the local Marathi language) in the state of Maharashtra, and the river follows a southeasterly course for 1,400 kilometers to its mouth on the Andhra Pradesh coast. The Godavari River basin area is second in size only to the Ganga; its delta on the east coast is also one of the country's main rice-growing areas. It is known as the "Ganga of the South," but its discharge, despite the large catchment area, is moderate because of the medium levels of annual rainfall, for example, about 700 millimeters at Nasik and 1,000 millimeters at Nizamabad.

The Krishna rises in the Western Ghats and flows east into the Bay of Bengal. It has a poor flow because of low levels of rainfall in its catchment area—660 millimeters annually at Pune. Despite its low discharge, the Krishna is the third longest river in India.

The source of the Kaveri is in the state of Karnataka, and the river flows southeastward. The waters of the river have been a source of irrigation since antiquity; in the early 1990s, an estimated 95 percent of the Kaveri was diverted for agricultural use before emptying into the Bay of Bengal. The delta of the Kaveri is so mature that the main river has almost lost its link with the sea, as the Kollidam, the distributary of the Kaveri, bears most of the flow.

The Narmada and the Tapti are the only major rivers that flow into the Arabian Sea. The Narmada rises in Madhya Pradesh and crosses the state, passing swiftly through a narrow valley between the Vindhya Range and spurs of the Satpura Range. It flows into the Gulf of Khambhat (or Cambay). The shorter Tapti follows a generally parallel course, between eighty kilometers and 160 kilometers to the south of the Narmada, flowing through the states of Maharashtra and Gujarat on its way into the Gulf of Khambhat.

Harnessing the waters of the major rivers that flow from the Himalayas is an issue of great concern in Nepal, India, and Bangladesh. Issues of flood control, drought prevention, hydroelectric power generation, job creation, and environmental quality—but also traditional lifestyles and cultural continuities—are at stake as these countries grapple with the political realities, both domestic and international, of altering the flow of the Ganga and Brahmaputra. Although India, Nepal, and Bangladesh seek to alleviate problems through cooperation over Himalayan rivers, irrigation projects altering the flow of Punjab-area rivers are likely to continue to be an irritant between India and Pakistan—countries between which cooperation is less likely to occur—in the second half of the 1990s. Internally, large dam projects, such as one on the Narmada River, are also controversial (see Development Programs, ch. 7).

Climate

The Himalayas isolate South Asia from the rest of Asia. South of these mountains, the climate, like the terrain, is highly diverse, but some geographers give it an overall, one-word characterization—violent. What geographers have in mind is the abruptness of change and the intensity of effect when change occurs—the onset of the monsoon rains, sudden flooding, rapid erosion, extremes of temperature, tropical storms, and unpredictable fluctuations in rainfall. Broadly speaking, agriculture in India is constantly challenged by weather uncertainty.

It is possible to identify seasons, although these do not occur uniformly throughout South Asia. The Indian Meteorological Service divides the year into four seasons: the relatively dry, cool winter from December through February; the dry, hot summer from March through May; the southwest monsoon from June through September when the predominating southwest maritime winds bring rains to most of the country; and the northeast, or retreating, monsoon of October and November.

The southwest monsoon blows in from sea to land. The southwest monsoon usually breaks on the west coast early in June and reaches most of South Asia by the first week in July (see fig. 6). Because of the critical importance of monsoon rainfall to agricultural production, predictions of the monsoon's arrival date are eagerly watched by government planners and agronomists who need to determine the optimal dates for plantings.

Theories about why monsoons occur vary. Conventionally, scientists have attributed monsoons to thermal changes in the Asian landmass. Contemporary theory cites other factors—the barrier of the Himalayas and the sun's northward tilt (which shifts the jet stream north). The hot air that rises over South Asia during April and May creates low-pressure areas into which the cooler, moisture-bearing winds from the Indian Ocean flow.These circumstances set off a rush of moisture-rich air from the southern seas over South Asia.

The southwest monsoon occurs in two branches. After breaking on the southern part of the Peninsula in early June, the branch known as the Arabian Sea monsoon reaches Bombay around June 10, and it has settled over most of South Asia by late June, bringing cooler but more humid weather. The other branch, known as the Bay of Bengal monsoon, moves northward in the Bay of Bengal and spreads over most of Assam by the first week of June. On encountering the barrier of the Great Himalayan Range, it is deflected westward along the Indo-Gangetic Plain toward New Delhi. Thereafter the two branches merge as a single current bringing rains to the remaining parts of North India in July.

The withdrawal of the monsoon is a far more gradual process than its onset. It usually withdraws from northwest India by the beginning of October and from the remaining parts of the country by the end of November. During this period, the northeast winds contribute to the formation of the northeast monsoon over the southern half of the Peninsula in October. It is also known as the retreating monsoon because it follows in the wake of the southwest monsoon. The states of Tamil Nadu, Karnataka, and Kerala receive most of their rainfall from the northeast monsoon during November and December. However, 80 percent of the country receives most of its rainfall from the southwest monsoon from June to September.

South Asia is subject to a wide range of climates—from the subfreezing Himalayan winters to the tropical climate of the Coromandel Coast and from the damp, rainy climate in the states of Assam and West Bengal to the arid Great Indian Desert. Based on precipitation and temperature, experts define seven climatic regions: the Himalayas, Assam and West Bengal, the Indo-Gangetic Plain, the Western Ghats and coast, the Deccan (the interior of the Peninsula south of the Narmada River), and the Eastern Ghats and coast (see fig. 7).

In the Himalayan region, climate varies with altitude. At about 2,000 meters, the average summer temperature is near 18°C; at 4,500 meters, it is rarely above 0°C. In the valleys, summer temperatures reach between 32°C and 38°C. The eastern Himalayas receive as much as 1,000 to 2,000 millimeters more precipitation than do the Western Himalayas, and floods are common.

Assam and West Bengal are extremely wet and humid. The southeastern part of the state of Meghalaya has the world's highest average annual rainfall, some 10,900 millimeters.

The Indo-Gangetic Plain has a varied climatic pattern. Rainfall and temperature ranges vary significantly between the eastern and western extremes (see table 2, Appendix). In the Peninsula region, the Western Ghats and the adjoining coast receive heavy rains during the southwest monsoon. Rainfall in the peninsular interior averages about 650 millimeters a year, although there is considerable variation in different localities and from year to year. The Eastern Ghats receive less rainfall than the western coast. Rainfall there ranges between 900 and 1,300 millimeters annually.

The northern Deccan region, bounded by the Western Ghats, the Vindhya Range and the Narmada River to the north, and the Eastern Ghats, receives most of its annual rainfall during the summer monsoon season. The southern Deccan area is in a "rain shadow" and receives only fifty to 1,000 millimeters of rainfall a year. Temperature ranges are wide—from some 15°C to 38°C—making this one of India's most comfortable climatic areas.

Throughout most of non-Himalayan India, the heat can be oppressive and sometimes, such as was experienced in 1994 and 1995, literally can be a killer. Hot, relatively dry weather is the norm before the southwest monsoons, which, along with heavy rains and high humidity, bring cloud cover that lowers temperatures slightly. Temperatures reach the upper 30s°C and can reach as high as 48°C during the day in the premonsoon months.

Earthquakes

India has experienced some of the world's most devastating earthquakes. Some 19,000 people died in Kangra District, northeastern Himachal Pradesh, in April 1905, and more than 30,000 died in Maharashtra and Andhra Pradesh in September 1993. Although resulting in less extensive loss of life, major earthquakes occurred in Assam in 1950 (more than 1,500 killed) and in Uttarkashi District, Uttar Pradesh, in 1991 (1,600 killed).

Population

Structure and Dynamics

The 1991 final census count gave India a total population of 846,302,688. However, estimates of India's population vary widely. According to the Population Division of the United Nations Department of International Economic and Social Affairs, the population had already reached 866 million in 1991. The Population Division of the United Nations Economic and Social Commission for Asia and the Pacific (ESCAP) projected 896.5 million by mid-1993 with a 1.9 percent annual growth rate. The United States Bureau of the Census, assuming an annual population growth rate of 1.8 percent, put India's population in July 1995 at 936,545,814. These higher projections merit attention in light of the fact that the Planning Commission had estimated a figure of 844 million for 1991 while preparing the Eighth Five-Year Plan (FY 1992–96; see Population Projections, this ch.).

India accounts for some 2.4 percent of the world's landmass but is home to about 16 percent of the global population. The magnitude of the annual increase in population can be seen in the fact that India adds almost the total population of Australia or Sri Lanka every year. A 1992 study of India's population notes that India has more people than all of Africa and also more than North America and South America together. Between 1947 and 1991, India's population more than doubled.

Throughout the twentieth century, India has been in the midst of a demographic transition. At the beginning of the century, endemic disease, periodic epidemics, and famines kept the death rate high enough to balance out the high birth rate. Between 1911 and 1920, the birth and death rates were virtually equal—about forty-eight births and forty-eight deaths per 1,000 population. The increasing impact of curative and preventive medicine (especially mass inoculations) brought a steady decline in the death rate. By the mid-1990s, the estimated birth rate had fallen to twenty-eight per 1,000, and the estimated death rate had fallen to ten per 1,000. Clearly, the future configuration of India's population (indeed the future of India itself) depends on what happens to the birth rate (see fig. 8). Even the most optimistic projections do not suggest that the birth rate could drop below twenty per 1,000 before the year 2000. India's population is likely to exceed the 1 billion mark before the 2001 census.

The upward population spiral began in the 1920s and is reflected in intercensal growth increments. South Asia's population increased roughly 5 percent between 1901 and 1911 and actually declined slightly in the next decade. Population increased some 10 percent in the period from 1921 to 1931 and 13 to 14 percent in the 1930s and 1940s. Between 1951 and 1961, the population rose 21.5 percent. Between 1961 and 1971, the country's population increased by 24.8 percent. Thereafter a slight slowing of the increase was experienced: from 1971 to 1981, the population increased by 24.7 percent, and from 1981 to 1991, by 23.9 percent (see table 3, Appendix).

Population density has risen concomitantly with the massive increases in population. In 1901 India counted some seventy-seven persons per square kilometer; in 1981 there were 216 persons per square kilometer; by 1991 there were 267 persons per square kilometer—up almost 25 percent from the 1981 population density (see table 4, Appendix). India's average population density is higher than that of any other nation of comparable size. The highest densities are not only in heavily urbanized regions but also in areas that are mostly agricultural.

Population growth in the years between 1950 and 1970 centered on areas of new irrigation projects, areas subject to refugee resettlement, and regions of urban expansion. Areas where population did not increase at a rate approaching the national average were those facing the most severe economic hardships, overpopulated rural areas, and regions with low levels of urbanization.

The 1991 census, which was carried out under the direction of the Registrar General and Census Commissioner of India (part of the Ministry of Home Affairs), in keeping with the previous two censuses, used the term *urban agglomerations*. An urban agglomeration forms a continuous urban spread and consists of a city or town and its urban outgrowth outside the statutory limits. Or, an urban agglomerate may be two or more adjoining cities or towns and their outgrowths. A university campus or military base located on the outskirts of a city or town, which often increases the actual urban area of that city or town, is an example of an urban agglomeration. In India urban agglomerations with a population of 1 million or more—there were twenty-four in 1991—are referred to as metropolitan areas. Places with a population of 100,000 or more are termed "cities" as compared with "towns," which have a population of less than 100,000. Including the metropolitan areas, there were 299 urban agglomerations with more than 100,000 population in 1991. These large urban agglomerations are designated as Class I urban units. There were five other classes of urban agglomerations, towns, and villages based on the size of their populations: Class II (50,000 to 99,999), Class III (20,000 to 49,999), Class IV (10,000 to 19,999), Class V (5,000 to 9,999), and Class VI (villages of less than 5,000; see table 5, Appendix).

The results of the 1991 census revealed that around 221 million, or 26.1 percent, of Indian's population lived in urban areas. Of this total, about 138 million people, or 16 percent, lived in the 299 urban agglomerations. In 1991 the twenty-four metropolitan cities accounted for 51 percent of India's total population living in Class I urban centers, with Bombay and Calcutta the largest at 12.6 million and 10.9 million, respectively (see table 6, Appendix).

In the early 1990s, growth was the most dramatic in the cities of central and southern India. About twenty cities in those two regions experienced a growth rate of more than 100 percent between 1981 and 1991. Areas subject to an influx of refugees also experienced noticeable demographic changes. Refugees from Bangladesh, Burma, and Sri Lanka contributed substantially to population growth in the regions in which they settled. Less dramatic population increases occurred in areas where Tibetan refugee settlements were founded after the Chinese annexation of Tibet in the 1950s.

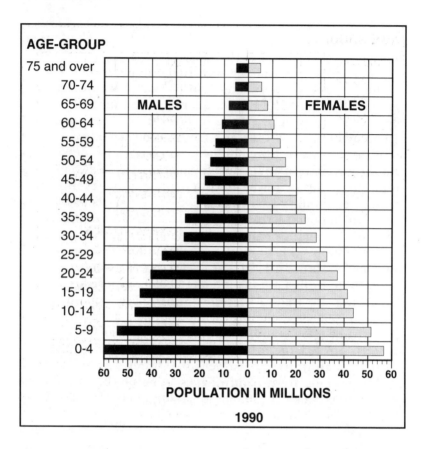

AGE-GROUP

MALES · FEMALES

POPULATION IN MILLIONS

1990

Source: Based on information from Eduard Bos, My T. Vu, Ann Levin, and Rodolfo A. Bulatao, *World Population Projections, 1992–93 Edition*, Baltimore, 1992, 266.

Figure 8. Population by Age and Sex, 1990 and 2000

The majority of districts had urban populations ranging on average from 15 to 40 percent in 1991. According to the 1991 census, urban clusters predominated in the upper part of the Indo-Gangetic Plain; in the Punjab and Haryana plains, and in part of western Uttar Pradesh. The lower part of the Indo-Gangetic Plain in southeastern Bihar, southern West Bengal, and northern Orissa also experienced increased urbanization. Similar increases occurred in the western coastal state of Gujarat and the union territory of Daman and Diu. In the Central Highlands in Madhya Pradesh and Maharashtra, urbanization was most noticeable in the river basins and adjacent plateau regions of the Mahanadi, Narmada, and Tapti rivers.

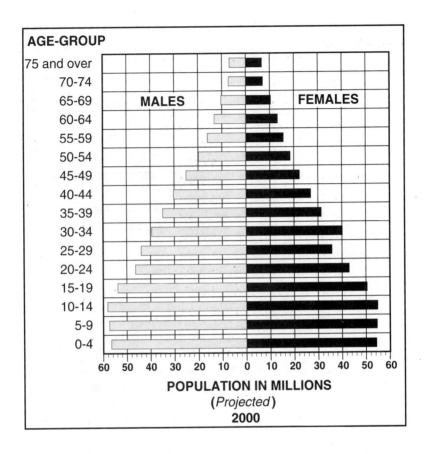

AGE-GROUP

| | MALES | FEMALES |

POPULATION IN MILLIONS
(*Projected*)
2000

The coastal plains and river deltas of the east and west coasts also showed increased levels of urbanization.

The hilly, inaccessible regions of the Peninsular Plateau, the northeast, and the Himalayas remain sparsely settled. As a general rule, the lower the population density and the more remote the region, the more likely it is to count a substantial portion of tribal (see Glossary) people among its population (see Tribes, ch. 4). Urbanization in some sparsely settled regions is more developed than would seem warranted at first glance at their limited natural resources. Areas of western India that were formerly princely states (in Gujarat and the desert regions of Rajasthan) have substantial urban centers that originated as political-administrative centers and since independence have continued to exercise hegemony over their hinterlands.

The vast majority of Indians, nearly 625 million, or 73.9 percent, in 1991 lived in what are called villages of less than 5,000 people or in scattered hamlets and other rural settlements (see The Village Community, ch. 5). The states with proportionately the greatest rural populations in 1991 were the states of Assam (88.9 percent), Sikkim (90.9 percent) and Himachal Pradesh (91.3 percent), and the tiny union territory of Dadra and Nagar Haveli (91.5 percent). Those with the smallest rural populations proportionately were the states of Gujarat (65.5 percent), Maharashtra (61.3 percent), Goa (58.9 percent), and Mizoram (53.9 percent). Most of the other states and the union territory of the Andaman and Nicobar Islands were near the national average.

Two other categories of population that are closely scrutinized by the national census are the Scheduled Castes (see Glossary) and Scheduled Tribes (see Glossary). The greatest concentrations of Scheduled Caste members in 1991 lived in the states of Andhra Pradesh (10.5 million, or nearly 16 percent of the state's population), Tamil Nadu (10.7 million, or 19 percent), Bihar (12.5 million, or 14 percent), West Bengal (16 million, or 24 percent), and Uttar Pradesh (29.3 million, or 21 percent). Together, these and other Scheduled Caste members comprised about 139 million people, or more than 16 percent of the total population of India. Scheduled Tribe members represented only 8 percent of the total population (about 68 million). They were found in 1991 in the greatest numbers in Orissa (7 million, or 23 percent of the state's population), Maharashtra (7.3 million, or 9 percent), and Madhya Pradesh (15.3 million, or 23 percent). In proportion, however, the populations of states in the northeast had the greatest concentrations of Scheduled Tribe members. For example, 31 percent of the population of Tripura, 34 percent of Manipur, 64 percent of Arunachal Pradesh, 86 percent of Meghalaya, 88 percent of Nagaland, and 95 percent of Mizoram were Scheduled Tribe members. Other heavy concentrations were found in Dadra and Nagar Haveli, 79 percent of which was composed of Scheduled Tribe members, and Lakshadweep, with 94 percent of its population being Scheduled Tribe members.

Population Projections

The Registrar General and Census Commissioner of India (both positions are held by the same person) oversees an ongoing intercensal effort to help maintain accurate annual estimates of population. The projection method used in the mid-1980s to predict the 1991 population, which was accurate enough to come within 3 million (843 million) of the official, final census count in 1991 (846 million), was based on the Sample Registration System. The system employed birth and death rates from each of the twenty-five states, six union territories, and one national capital territory plus statistical data on effective contraceptive use. Assuming a 1.7 percent error rate, India's projection for 1991 was close to those made by the World Bank and the UN.

Projections of future population growth prepared by the Registrar General, assuming the highest level of fertility, show decreasing growth rates: 1.8 percent by 2001, 1.3 percent by 2011, and 0.9 percent by 2021. These rates of growth, however, will put India's population above 1.0 billion in 2001, at 1.2 billion in 2011, and at 1.3 billion in 2021. ESCAP projections published in 1993 were close to those made by India: nearly 1.2 billion by 2010, still considerably less than the 2010 population projection for China of 1.4 billion. In 1992 the Washington-based Population Reference Bureau had a similar projection to ESCAP's for India's population in 2010 and projected nearly 1.4 billion by 2025 (nearly the same as projected for 2025 by the United Nations Department of International Economic and Social Affairs). According to other UN projections, India's population may stabilize at around 1.7 billion by 2060.

Such projections also show an increasingly aging population, with 76 million (8 percent of the population) age sixty and above in 2001, 102 million (9 percent) in 2011, and 137 million (11 percent) in 2021. These figures coincide closely with those estimated by the United States Bureau of the Census, which also projected that whereas the median age was twenty-two in 1992, it was expected to increase to twenty-nine by 2020, placing the median age in India well above all of its South Asian neighbors except Sri Lanka.

Population and Family Planning Policy

Population growth has long been a concern of the government, and India has a lengthy history of explicit population policy. In the 1950s, the government began, in a modest way, one of the earliest national, government-sponsored family planning efforts in the developing world. The annual population growth rate in the previous decade (1941 to 1951) had been below 1.3 percent, and government planners optimistically believed that the population would continue to grow at roughly the same rate.

Implicitly, the government believed that India could repeat the experience of the developed nations where industrialization and a rise in the standard of living had been accompanied by a drop in the population growth rate. In the 1950s, existing hospitals and health care facilities made birth control information available, but there was no aggressive effort to encourage the use of contraceptives and limitation of family size. By the late 1960s, many policy makers believed that the high rate of population growth was the greatest obstacle to economic development. The government began a massive program to lower the birth rate from forty-one per 1,000 to a target of twenty to twenty-five per 1,000 by the mid-1970s. The National Population Policy adopted in 1976 reflected the growing consensus among policy makers that family planning would enjoy only limited success unless it was part of an integrated program aimed at improving the general welfare of the population. The policy makers assumed that excessive family size was part and parcel of poverty and had to be dealt with as integral to a general development strategy. Education about the population problem became part of school curriculum under the Fifth Five-Year Plan (FY 1974–78). Cases of government-enforced sterilization made many question the propriety of state-sponsored birth control measures, however.

During the 1980s, an increased number of family planning programs were implemented through the state governments with financial assistance from the central government. In rural areas, the programs were further extended through a network of primary health centers and subcenters. By 1991, India had more than 150,000 public health facilities through which family planning programs were offered (see Health Care, this ch.). Four special family planning projects were implemented under the Seventh Five-Year Plan (FY 1985–89). One was the All-India Hospitals Post-partum Programme at district- and subdistrict-level hospitals. Another program involved the reorganization of primary health care facilities in urban slum areas, while another project reserved a specified number of hospital beds for tubal ligature operations. The final program called for the renovation or remodelling of intrauterine device (IUD) rooms in rural family welfare centers attached to primary health care facilities.

Despite these developments in promoting family planning, the 1991 census results showed that India continued to have one of the most rapidly growing populations in the world.

A family planning billboard exhorting "Fewer children, Happy people" and "2 or 3 children, that's all"
Courtesy Doranne Jacobson

Between 1981 and 1991, the annual rate of population growth was estimated at about 2 percent. The crude birth rate in 1992 was thirty per 1,000, only a small change over the 1981 level of thirty-four per 1,000. However, some demographers credit this slight lowering of the 1981–91 population growth rate to moderate successes of the family planning program. In FY 1986, the number of reproductive-age couples was 132.6 million, of whom only 37.5 percent were estimated to be protected effectively by some form of contraception. A goal of the seventh plan was to achieve an effective couple protection rate of 42 percent, requiring an annual increase of 2 percent in effective use of contraceptives.

The heavy centralization of India's family planning programs often prevents due consideration from being given to regional differences. Centralization is encouraged to a large extent by reliance on central government funding. As a result, many of the goals and assumptions of national population control programs do not correspond exactly with local attitudes toward birth control. At the Jamkhed Project in Maharashtra, which has been in operation since the late 1970s and covers approximately 175 villages, the local project directors noted that it required three to four years of education through direct contact with a couple for the idea of family planning to gain acceptance. Such a timetable was not compatible with targets. However, much was learned about policy and practice from the Jamkhed Project. The successful use of women's clubs as a means of involving women in community-wide family planning activities impressed the state government to the degree that it set about organizing such clubs in every village in the state. The project also serves as a pilot to test ideas that the government wants to incorporate into its programs. Government medical staff members have been sent to Jamkhed for training, and the government has proposed that the project assume the task of selecting and training government health workers for an area of 2.5 million people.

Another important family planning program is the Project for Community Action in Family Planning. Located in Karnataka, the project operates in 154 project villages and 255 control villages. All project villages are of sufficient size to have a health subcenter, although this advantage is offset by the fact that those villages are the most distant from the area's primary health centers. As at Jamkhed, the project is much assisted by local voluntary groups, such as the women's clubs. The local voluntary groups either provide or secure sites suitable as distribution depots for condoms and birth control pills and also make arrangements for the operation of sterilization camps. Data provided by the Project for Community Action in Family Planning show that important achievements have been realized in the field of population control. By the mid-1980s, for example, 43 percent of couples were using family planning, a full 14 percent above the state average. The project has significantly improved the status of women, involving them and empowering them to bring about change in their communities. This contribution is important because of the way in which the deeply entrenched inferior status of women in many communities in India negates official efforts to decrease the fertility rate.

Studies have found that most couples in fact regard family planning positively. However, the common fertility pattern in India diverges from the two-child family that policy makers hold as ideal. Women continue to marry young; in the mid-1990s, they average just over eighteen years of age at marriage. When women choose to be sterilized, financial inducements, although helpful, are not the principal incentives. On average, those accepting sterilization already have four living children, of whom two are sons.

The strong preference for sons is a deeply held cultural ideal based on economic roots. Sons not only assist with farm labor as they are growing up (as do daughters) but they provide labor in times of illness and unemployment and serve as their parents' only security in old age. Surveys done by the New Delhi Operations Research Group in 1991 indicated that as many as 72 percent of rural parents continue to have children until at least two sons are born; the preference for more than one son among urban parents was tabulated at 53 percent. Once these goals have been achieved, birth control may be used or, especially in agricultural areas, it may not if additional child labor, later adult labor for the family, is deemed desirable.

A significant result of this eagerness for sons is that the Indian population has a deficiency of females. Slightly higher female infant mortality rates (seventy-nine per 1,000 versus seventy-eight per 1,000 for males) can be attributed to poor health care, abortions of female fetuses, and female infanticide. Human rights activists have estimated that there are at least 10,000 cases of female infanticide annually throughout India. The cost of theoretically illegal dowries and the loss of daughters to their in-laws' families are further disincentives for some parents to have daughters. Sons, of course continue to carry on the family line (see Family Ideals, ch. 5). The 1991 census revealed that the national sex ratio had declined from 934 females to 1,000 males in 1981 to 927 to 1,000 in 1991. In only one state—Kerala, a state with low fertility and mortality rates and the nation's highest literacy—did females exceed males. The census found, however, that female life expectancy at birth had for the first time exceeded that for males.

India's high infant mortality and elevated mortality in early childhood remain significant stumbling blocks to population control (see Health Conditions, this ch.). India's fertility rate is decreasing, however, and, at 3.4 in 1994, it is lower than those of its immediate neighbors (Bangladesh had a rate of 4.5 and Pakistan had 6.7). The rate is projected to decrease to 3.0 by 2000, 2.6 by 2010, and 2.3 by 2020.

During the 1960s, 1970s, and 1980s, the growth rate had formed a sort of plateau. Some states, such as Kerala, Tamil Nadu, and, to a lesser extent, Punjab, Maharashtra, and Karnataka, had made progress in lowering their growth rates, but most did not. Under such conditions, India's population may not stabilize until 2060.

Health

Health Conditions

Life Expectancy and Mortality

The average Indian male born in the 1990s can expect to live 58.5 years; women can expect to live only slightly longer (59.6 years), according to 1995 estimates. Life expectancy has risen dramatically throughout the century from a scant twenty years in the 1911–20 period. Although men enjoyed a slightly longer life expectancy throughout the first part of the twentieth century, by 1990 women had slightly surpassed men. The death rate declined from 48.6 per 1,000 in the 1910–20 period to fifteen per 1,000 in the 1970s, and improved thereafter, reaching ten per 1,000 by 1990, a rate that held steady through the mid-1990s. India's high infant mortality rate was estimated to exceed 76 per 1,000 live births in 1995 (see table 7, Appendix). Thirty percent of infants had low birth weights, and the death rate for children aged one to four years was around ten per 1,000 of the population.

According to a 1989 National Nutrition Monitoring Bureau report, less than 15 percent of the population was adequately nourished, although 96 percent received an adequate number of calories per day. In 1986 daily average intake was 2,238 calories as compared with 2,630 calories in China. According to UN findings, caloric intake per day in India had fallen slightly to 2,229 in 1989, lending credence to the concerns of some experts who claimed that annual nutritional standards statistics cannot be relied on to show whether poverty is actually being reduced. Instead, such studies may actually pick up short-term amelioration of poverty as the result of a period of good crops rather than a long-term trend.

Official Indian estimates of the poverty level are based on a person's income and corresponding access to minimum nutritional needs (see Growth since 1980, ch. 6). There were 332 million people at or below the poverty level in FY 1991, most of whom lived in rural areas.

Communicable and Noncommunicable Diseases

A number of endemic communicable diseases present a serious public health hazard in India. Over the years, the government has set up a variety of national programs aimed at controlling or eradicating these diseases, including the

National Malaria Eradication Programme and the National Filaria Control Programme. Other initiatives seek to limit the incidence of respiratory infections, cholera, diarrheal diseases, trachoma, goiter, and sexually transmitted diseases.

Smallpox, formerly a significant source of mortality, was eradicated as part of the worldwide effort to eliminate that disease. India was declared smallpox-free in 1975. Malaria remains a serious health hazard; although the incidence of the disease declined sharply in the postindependence period, India remains one of the most heavily malarial countries in the world. Only the Himalaya region above 1,500 meters is spared. In 1965 government sources registered only 150,000 cases, a notable drop from the 75 million cases in the early postindependence years. This success was short-lived, however, as the malarial parasites became increasingly resistant to the insecticides and drugs used to combat the disease. By the mid-1970s, there were nearly 6.5 million cases on record. The situation again improved because of more conscientious efforts; by 1982 the number of cases had fallen by roughly two-thirds. This downward trend continued, and in 1987 slightly fewer than 1.7 million cases of malaria were reported.

In the early 1990s, about 389 million people were at risk of infection from filaria parasites; 19 million showed symptoms of filariasis, and 25 million were deemed to be hosts to the parasites. Efforts at control, under the National Filaria Control Programme, which was established in 1955, have focused on eliminating the filaria larvae in urban locales, and by the early 1990s there were more than 200 filaria control units in operation.

Leprosy, a major public health and social problem, is endemic, with all the states and union territories reporting cases. However, the prevalence of the disease varies. About 3 million leprosy cases are estimated to exist nationally, of which 15 to 20 percent are infectious. The National Leprosy Control Programme was started in 1955, but it only received high priority after 1980. In FY 1982, it was redesignated as the National Leprosy Eradication Programme. Its goal was to achieve eradication of the disease by 2000. To that end, 758 leprosy control units, 900 urban leprosy centers, 291 temporary hospitalization wards, 285 district leprosy units, and some 6,000 lower-level centers had been established by March 1990. By March 1992, nearly 1.7 million patients were receiving regular multidrug treatment, which is more effective than the standard single drug therapy (Dapsone monotherapy).

India is subject to outbreaks of various diseases. Among them is pneumonic plague, an episode of which spread quickly throughout India in 1994 killing hundreds before being brought under control. Tuberculosis, trachoma, and goiter are endemic. In the early 1980s, there were an estimated 10 million cases of tuberculosis, of which about 25 percent were infectious. During 1991 nearly 1.6 million new tuberculosis cases were detected. The functions of the Trachoma Control Programme, which started in 1968, have been subsumed by the National Programme for the Control of Blindness. Approximately 45 million Indians are vision-impaired; roughly 12 million are blind. The incidence of goiter is dominant throughout the sub-Himalayan states from Jammu and Kashmir to the northeast. There are some 170 million people who are exposed to iodine deficiency disorders. Starting in the late 1980s, the central government began a salt iodinization program for all edible salt, and by 1991 record production—2.5 million tons—of iodized salt had been achieved. There are as well anemias related to poor nutrition, a variety of diseases caused by vitamin and mineral deficiencies—beriberi, scurvy, osteomalacia, and rickets—and a high incidence of parasitic infection.

Diarrheal diseases, the primary cause of early childhood mortality, are linked to inadequate sewage disposal and lack of safe drinking water. Roughly 50 percent of all illness is attributed to poor sanitation; in rural areas, about 80 percent of all children are infected by parasitic worms. Estimates in the early 1980s suggested that although more than 80 percent of the urban population had access to reasonably safe water, fewer than 5 percent of rural dwellers did. Waterborne sewage systems were woefully overburdened; only around 30 percent of urban populations had adequate sewage disposal, but scarcely any populations outside cities did. In 1990, according to United States sources, only 3 percent of the rural population and 44 percent of the urban population had access to sanitation services, a level relatively low by developing nation standards. There were better findings for access to potable water: 69 percent in the rural areas and 86 percent in urban areas, relatively high percentages by developing nation standards. In the mid-1990s, about 1 million people die each year of diseases associated with diarrhea.

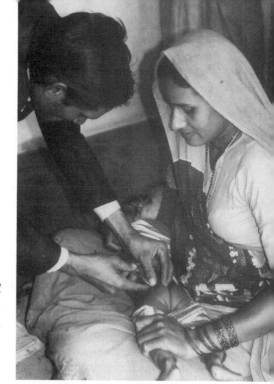

Infant vaccination, rural
Madhya Pradesh
Courtesy Doranne Jacobson

India has an estimated 1.5 million to 2 million cases of cancer, with 500,000 new cases added each year. Annual deaths from cancer total around 300,000. The most common malignancies are cancer of the oral cavity (mostly relating to tobacco use and pan chewing—about 35 percent of all cases), cervix, and breast. Cardiovascular diseases are a major health problem; men and women suffer from them in almost equal numbers (14 million versus 13 million in FY 1990).

Acquired Immune Deficiency Syndrome

The incidence of AIDS cases in India is steadily rising amidst concerns that the nation faces the prospect of an AIDS epidemic. By June 1991, out of a total of more than 900,000 screened, some 5,130 people tested positive for the human immunodeficiency virus (HIV). However, the total number infected with HIV in 1992 was estimated by a New Delhi-based official of the World Health Organization (WHO) at 500,000, and more pessimistic estimates by the World Bank in 1995 suggested a figure of 2 million, the highest in Asia. Confirmed cases of AIDS numbered only 102 by 1991 but had jumped to 885 by 1994, the second highest reported number in Asia after Thailand. Suspected AIDS cases, according to WHO and the Indian government, may be in the area of 80,000 in 1995.

The main factors cited in the spread of the virus are hetero-sexual transmission, primarily by urban prostitutes and migrant workers, such as long-distance truck drivers; the use of unsteril-ized needles and syringes by physicians and intravenous drug users; and transfusions of blood from infected donors. Based on the HIV infection rate in 1991, and India's position as the second most populated country in the world, it was projected that by 1995 India would have more HIV and AIDS cases than any other country in the world. This prediction appeared true. By mid-1995 India had been labeled by the media as "ground zero" in the global AIDS epidemic, and new predictions for 2000 were that India would have 1 million AIDS cases and 5 million HIV-positive.

In 1987 the newly formed National AIDS Control Pro-gramme began limited screening of the blood supply and mon-itoring of high-risk groups. A national education program aimed at AIDS prevention and control began in 1990. The first AIDS prevention television campaign began in 1991. By the mid-1990s, AIDS awareness signs on public streets, condoms for sale near brothels, and media announcements were more in evidence. There was very negative publicity as well. Posters with the names and photographs of known HIV-positive per-sons have been seen in New Delhi, and there have been reports of HIV patients chained in medical facilities and deprived of treatment.

Fear and ignorance have continued to compound the diffi-culty of controlling the spread of the virus, and discrimination against AIDS sufferers has surfaced. For example, in 1990 the All-India Institute of Medical Sciences, New Delhi's leading medical facility, reportedly turned away two people infected with HIV because its staff were too scared to treat them.

A new program to control the spread of AIDS was launched in 1991 by the Indian Council of Medical Research. The coun-cil looked to ancient scriptures and religious books for tradi-tional messages that preach moderation in sex and describe prostitution as a sin. The council considered that the great extent to which Indian life-styles are shaped by religion rather than by science would cause many people to be confused by foreign-modeled educational campaigns relying on television and printed booklets.

The severity of the growing AIDS crisis in India is clear, according to statistics compiled during the mid-1990s. In Bom-bay, a city of 12.6 million inhabitants in 1991, the HIV infection rate among the estimated 80,000 prostitutes jumped from 1 percent in 1987 to 30 percent in 1991 to 53 percent in 1993. Migrant workers engaging in promiscuous and unprotected sexual relations in the big city carry the infection to other sexual partners on the road and then to their homes and families.

India's blood supply, despite official blood screening efforts, continues to become infected. In 1991 donated blood was screened for HIV in only four major cities: New Delhi, Calcutta, Madras, and Bombay. One of the leading factors in the contamination of the blood supply is that 30 percent of the blood required comes from private, profit-making banks whose practices are difficult to regulate. Furthermore, professional donors are an integral part of the Indian blood supply network, providing about 30 percent of the annual requirement nationally. These donors are generally poor and tend to engage in high-risk sex and use intravenous drugs more than the general population. Professional donors also tend to donate frequently at different centers and, in many cases, under different names. Reuse of improperly sterilized needles in health care and blood-collection facilities also is a factor. India's minister of health and family welfare reported in 1992 that only 138 out of 608 blood banks were equipped for HIV screening. A 1992 study conducted by the Indian Health Organisation revealed that 86 percent of commercial blood donors surveyed were HIV-positive.

Health Care

Role of the Government

The Indian constitution charges the states with "the raising of the level of nutrition and the standard of living of its people and the improvement of public health" (see The Constitutional Framework, ch. 8). However, many critics of India's National Health Policy, endorsed by Parliament in 1983, point out that the policy lacks specific measures to achieve broad stated goals. Particular problems include the failure to integrate health services with wider economic and social development, the lack of nutritional support and sanitation, and the poor participatory involvement at the local level.

Central government efforts at influencing public health have focused on the five-year plans, on coordinated planning with the states, and on sponsoring major health programs. Government expenditures are jointly shared by the central and state governments. Goals and strategies are set through central-state government consultations of the Central Council of Health and Family Welfare. Central government efforts are administered by the Ministry of Health and Family Welfare, which provides both administrative and technical services and manages medical education. States provide public services and health education.

The 1983 National Health Policy is committed to providing health services to all by 2000 (see table 8, Appendix; The Legislature, ch. 8). In 1983 health care expenditures varied greatly among the states and union territories, from Rs13 per capita in Bihar to Rs60 per capita in Himachal Pradesh (for value of the rupee—see Glossary), and Indian per capita expenditure was low when compared with other Asian countries outside of South Asia. Although government health care spending progressively grew throughout the 1980s, such spending as a percentage of the gross national product (GNP—see Glossary) remained fairly constant. In the meantime, health care spending as a share of total government spending decreased. During the same period, private-sector spending on health care was about 1.5 times as much as government spending.

Expenditures

In the mid-1990s, health spending amounts to 6 percent of GDP, one of the highest levels among developing nations. The established per capita spending is around Rs320 per year with the major input from private households (75 percent). State governments contribute 15.2 percent, the central government 5.2 percent, third-party insurance and employers 3.3 percent, and municipal government and foreign donors about 1.3, according to a 1995 World Bank study. Of these proportions, 58.7 percent goes toward primary health care (curative, preventive, and promotive) and 38.8 percent is spent on secondary and tertiary inpatient care. The rest goes for nonservice costs.

The fifth and sixth five-year plans (FY 1974–78 and FY 1980–84, respectively) included programs to assist delivery of preventive medicine and improve the health status of the rural population. Supplemental nutrition programs and increasing the supply of safe drinking water were high priorities. The sixth plan aimed at training more community health workers and increasing efforts to control communicable diseases. There

The Mysore Plateau from Chamundi Hill, Karnataka Courtesy Robert L. Worden

were also efforts to improve regional imbalances in the distribution of health care resources.

The Seventh Five-Year Plan (FY 1985–89) budgeted Rs33.9 billion for health, an amount roughly double the outlay of the sixth plan. Health spending as a portion of total plan outlays, however, had declined over the years since the first plan in 1951, from a high of 3.3 percent of the total plan spending in FY 1951–55 to 1.9 percent of the total for the seventh plan. Mid-way through the Eighth Five-Year Plan (FY 1992–96), however, health and family welfare was budgeted at Rs20 billion, or 4.3 percent of the total plan spending for FY 1994, with an additional Rs3.6 billion in the nonplan budget.

Primary Services

Health care facilities and personnel increased substantially between the early 1950s and early 1980s, but because of fast population growth, the number of licensed medical practitioners per 10,000 individuals had fallen by the late 1980s to three per 10,000 from the 1981 level of four per 10,000. In 1991 there were approximately ten hospital beds per 10,000 individuals.

Primary health centers are the cornerstone of the rural health care system. By 1991, India had about 22,400 primary health centers, 11,200 hospitals, and 27,400 dispensaries. These facilities are part of a tiered health care system that funnels more difficult cases into urban hospitals while attempting to provide routine medical care to the vast majority in the countryside. Primary health centers and subcenters rely on trained paramedics to meet most of their needs. The main problems affecting the success of primary health centers are the predominance of clinical and curative concerns over the intended emphasis on preventive work and the reluctance of staff to work in rural areas. In addition, the integration of health services with family planning programs often causes the local population to perceive the primary health centers as hostile to their traditional preference for large families. Therefore, primary health centers often play an adversarial role in local efforts to implement national health policies.

According to data provided in 1989 by the Ministry of Health and Family Welfare, the total number of civilian hospitals for all states and union territories combined was 10,157. In 1991 there was a total of 811,000 hospital and health care facilities beds. The geographical distribution of hospitals varied according to local socioeconomic conditions. In India's most populous state, Uttar Pradesh, with a 1991 population of more than 139 million, there were 735 hospitals as of 1990. In Kerala, with a 1991 population of 29 million occupying an area only one-seventh the size of Uttar Pradesh, there were 2,053 hospitals. In light of the central government's goal of health care for all by 2000, the uneven distribution of hospitals needs to be reexamined. Private studies of India's total number of hospitals in the early 1990s were more conservative than official Indian data, estimating that in 1992 there were 7,300 hospitals. Of this total, nearly 4,000 were owned and managed by central, state, or local governments. Another 2,000, owned and managed by charitable trusts, received partial support from the government, and the remaining 1,300 hospitals, many of which were relatively small facilities, were owned and managed by the private sector. The use of state-of-the-art medical equipment, often imported from Western countries, was primarily limited to urban centers in the early 1990s. A network of regional cancer diagnostic and treatment facilities was being established in the early 1990s in major hospitals that were part of government medical colleges. By 1992 twenty-two such centers were in operation. Most of the 1,300 private hospitals lacked sophisticated medical facilities, although in 1992 approximately 12 percent possessed state-of-the-art equipment for diagnosis and treatment of all major diseases, including cancer. The fast pace of development of the private medical sector and the burgeoning middle class in the 1990s have led to the emergence of the new concept in India of establishing hospitals and health care facilities on a for-profit basis.

By the late 1980s, there were approximately 128 medical colleges—roughly three times more than in 1950. These medical colleges in 1987 accepted a combined annual class of 14,166 students. Data for 1987 show that there were 320,000 registered medical practitioners and 219,300 registered nurses. Various studies have shown that in both urban and rural areas people preferred to pay and seek the more sophisticated services provided by private physicians rather than use free treatment at public health centers.

Indigenous or traditional medical practitioners continue to practice throughout the country. The two main forms of traditional medicine practiced are the *ayurvedic* (meaning science of life) system, which deals with causes, symptoms, diagnoses, and treatment based on all aspects of well-being (mental, physical, and spiritual), and the *unani* (so-called Galenic medicine) herbal medical practice. A *vaidya* is a practitioner of the *ayurvedic* tradition, and a hakim (Arabic for a Muslim physician) is a practitioner of the *unani* tradition. These professions are frequently hereditary. A variety of institutions offer training in indigenous medical practice. Only in the late 1970s did official health policy refer to any form of integration between Western-oriented medical personnel and indigenous medical practitioners. In the early 1990s, there were ninety-eight *ayurvedic* colleges and seventeen *unani* colleges operating in both the governmental and nongovernmental sectors.

Education

Administration and Funding

Education is divided into preprimary, primary, middle (or intermediate), secondary (or high school), and higher levels. Primary school includes children of ages six to eleven, organized into classes one through five. Middle school pupils aged eleven through fourteen are organized into classes six through eight, and high school students ages fourteen through seventeen are enrolled in classes nine through twelve. Higher education includes technical schools, colleges, and universities.

Article 42 of the constitution, an amendment added in 1976, transferred education from the state list of responsibilities to the central government. Prior to this assumption of direct responsibility for promoting educational facilities for all parts of society, the central government had responsibility only for the education of minorities. Article 43 of the constitution set the goal of free and compulsory education for all children through age fourteen and gave the states the power to set standards for education within their jurisdictions. Despite this joint responsibility for education by state and central governments, the central government has the preponderant role because it drafts the five-year plans, which include education policy and some funding for education. Moreover, in 1986 the implementation of the National Policy on Education initiated a long-term series of programs aimed at improving India's education system by ensuring that all children through the primary level have access to education of comparable quality irrespective of caste, creed, location, or sex. The 1986 policy set a goal that, by 1990, all children by age eleven were to have five years of schooling or its equivalent in nonformal education. By 1995 all children up to age fourteen were to have been provided free and compulsory education. The 1990 target was not achieved, but by setting such goals, the central government was seen as expressing its commitment to the ideal of universal education.

The Department of Education, part of the Ministry of Human Resource Development, implements the central government's responsibilities in educational matters. The ministry coordinates planning with the states, provides funding for experimental programs, and acts through the University Grants Commission and the National Council of Educational Research and Training. These organizations seek to improve education standards, develop and introduce instructional materials, and design textbooks in the country's numerous languages (see The Social Context of Language, ch. 4). The National Council of Educational Research and Training collects data about education and conducts educational research.

State-level ministries of education coordinate education programs at local levels. City school boards are under the supervision of both the state education ministry and the municipal government. In rural areas, either the district board or the *panchayat* (village council—see Glossary) oversees the school board (see Local Government, ch. 8). The significant role the *panchayats* play in education often means the politicization of

A primary school class, Dharmsala, Himachal Pradesh
Courtesy Karl E. Ryavek

elementary education because the appointment and transfer of teachers often become emotional political issues.

State governments provide most educational funding, although since independence the central government increasingly has assumed the cost of educational development as outlined under the five-year plans. India spends an average 3 percent of its GNP on education. Spending for education ranged between 4.6 and 7.7 percent of total central government expenditures from the 1950s through the 1970s. In the early 1980s, about 10 percent of central and state funds went to education, a proportion well below the average of seventy-nine other developing countries. More than 90 percent of the expenditure was for teachers' salaries and administration. Per capita budget expenditures increased from Rs36.5 in FY 1977 to Rs112.7 in FY 1986, with highest expenditures found in the union territories. Nevertheless, total expenditure per student per year by the central and state governments declined in real terms.

Primary and Secondary Education

Several factors work against universal education in India. Although Indian law prohibits the employment of children in factories, the law allows them to work in cottage industries, family households, restaurants, or in agriculture. Primary and middle school education is compulsory. However, only slightly more than 50 percent of children between the ages of six and fourteen actually attend school, although a far higher percentage is enrolled. School attendance patterns for children vary from region to region and according to gender. But it is noteworthy that national literacy rates increased from 43.7 percent in 1981 to 52.2 percent in 1991 (male 63.9 percent, female 39.4 percent), passing the 50 percent mark for the first time. There are wide regional and gender variations in the literacy rates, however; for example, the southern state of Kerala, with a 1991 literacy rate of about 89.8 percent, ranked first in India in terms of both male and female literacy. Bihar, a northern state, ranked lowest with a literacy rate of only 39 percent (53 percent for males and 23 percent for females). School enrollment rates also vary greatly according to age (see table 9, Appendix).

To improve national literacy, the central government launched a wide-reaching literacy campaign in July 1993. Using a volunteer teaching force of some 10 million people, the government hoped to have reached around 100 million Indians by 1997. A special focus was placed on improving literacy among women.

A report in 1985 by the Ministry of Education, entitled *Challenge of Education: A Policy Perspective*, showed that nearly 60 percent of children dropped out between grades one and five. (The Ministry of Education was incorporated into the Ministry of Human Resources in 1985 as the Department of Education. In 1988 the Ministry of Human Resources was renamed the Ministry of Human Resource Development.) Of 100 children enrolled in grade one, only twenty-three reached grade eight. Although many children lived within one kilometer of a primary school, nearly 20 percent of all habitations did not have schools nearby. Forty percent of primary schools were not of masonry construction. Sixty percent had no drinking water facilities, 70 percent had no library facilities, and 89 percent lacked toilet facilities. Single-teacher primary schools were commonplace, and it was not unusual for the teacher to be absent or even to subcontract the teaching work to unqualified substitutes (see table 10, Appendix).

The improvements that India has made in education since independence are nevertheless substantial. From the first plan until the beginning of the sixth (1951–80), the percentage of the primary school-age population attending classes more than doubled. The number of schools and teachers increased dramatically. Middle schools and high schools registered the steepest rates of growth. The number of primary schools increased by more than 230 percent between 1951 and 1980. During the same period, however, the number of middle schools increased about tenfold. The numbers of teachers showed similar rates of increase. The proportion of trained teachers among those working in primary and middle schools, fewer than 60 percent in 1950, was more than 90 percent in 1987 (see table 11, Appendix). However, there was considerable variation in the geographical distribution of trained teachers in the states and union territories in the 1986–87 school year. Arunachal Pradesh had the highest percentage (60 percent) of untrained teachers in primary schools, and Assam had the highest percentage (72 percent) of untrained teachers in middle schools. Gujarat, Tamil Nadu, Chandigarh, and Pondicherry (Puduchcheri) reportedly had no untrained teachers at either kind of school.

Various forms of private schooling are common; many schools are strictly private, whereas others enjoy government grants-in-aid but are run privately. Schools run by church and missionary societies are common forms of private schools. Among India's Muslim population, the *madrasa*, a school attached to a mosque, plays an important role in education (see Islamic Traditions in South Asia, ch. 3). Some 10 percent of all children who enter the first grade are enrolled in private schools. The dropout rate in these schools is practically nonexistent.

Traditional notions of social rank and hierarchy have greatly influenced India's primary school system. A dual system existed in the early 1990s, in which middle-class families sent their children to private schools while lower-class families sent their children to underfinanced and underequipped municipal and village schools. Evolving middle-class values have made even nursery school education in the private sector a stressful event for children and parents alike. Tough entrance interviews for admission, long classroom hours, heavy homework assignments, and high tuition rates in the mid-1990s led to charges of "lost childhood" for preschool children and acknowledgment of both the social costs and enhanced social benefits for the families involved.

The government encourages the study of classical, modern, and tribal languages with a view toward the gradual switch from English to regional languages and to teaching Hindi in non-Hindi speaking states. As a result, there are schools conducted in various languages at all levels. Classical and foreign language training most commonly occurs at the postsecondary level, although English is also taught at the lower levels (see Diversity, Use, and Policy; Hindi and English, ch. 4).

Colleges and Universities

Receiving higher education, once the nearly exclusive domain of the wealthy and privileged, since independence has become the aspiration of almost every student completing high school. In the 1950–51 school year, there were some 360,000 students enrolled in colleges and universities; by the 1990–91 school year, the number had risen to nearly 4 million, a more than tenfold increase in four decades. At that time, there were 177 universities and university-level institutions (more than six times the number at independence), some 500 teacher training colleges, and several thousand other colleges.

There are three kinds of colleges in India. The first type, government colleges, are found only in those states where private enterprise is weak or which were at one time controlled by princes (see Company Rule, 1757–1857, ch. 1). The second kind are colleges managed by religious organizations and the private sector. Many of the latter institutions were founded after 1947 by wealthy business owners and politicians wishing to gain local fame and importance. Professional colleges comprise the third kind and consist mostly of medical, teacher-training, engineering, law, and agricultural colleges. More than 50 percent of them are sponsored and managed by the government. However, about 5 percent of these colleges are privately run without government grant support. They charge fees of ten to twelve times the amount of the government-run colleges. The profusion of new engineering colleges in India in the late 1980s and early 1990s caused concern in official education circles that the overall quality and reputation of India's higher education system would be threatened by these new schools, which operated mainly on a for-profit basis. As the government tightened its support to higher education in the early 1990s, colleges and universities came under considerable financial stress.

The All-India Council of Technical Education is empowered to regulate the establishment of any new private professional colleges to limit their proliferation. In 1992 the Karnataka High Court directed the state government to rescind permission to nine organizations to start new engineering and medical colleges in the state.

Gaining admission to a nonprofessional college is not unduly difficult except in the case of some select colleges that are particularly competitive. Students encounter greater difficulties in gaining admission to professional colleges in such fields as architecture, business, medicine, and dentistry.

There are four categories of universities. The largest number are teaching universities that maintain and run a large number of colleges. Unitary institutions, such as Allahabad University and Lucknow University, make up the second kind. The third kind are the twenty-six agricultural universities, each managed by the state in which it is located. Technical universities constitute the fourth kind. In the late 1980s, more technical universities, such as the Jawaharlal Nehru Technological University in the state of Hyderabad, were founded. There were also proposals to found medical universities in some states. By 1990 Andhra Pradesh and Tamil Nadu already had established such universities. Out of the 177 universities in the country, only ten are funded by the central government. The majority of universities are managed by the states, which establish them and provide funding.

There was a high rate of attrition among students in higher education in the 1980s. A substantial portion failed their examinations more than once, and large numbers dropped out; only about one out of four students successfully completed the full course of studies. Even those students who were successful could not count on a university degree to assure them employment. In the early postindependence years, a bachelor's degree often provided entrance to the elite, but in contemporary India, it provides a chance to become a white-collar worker at a relatively modest salary. The government traditionally has been the principal employer of educated manpower.

State governments play a powerful role in the running of all but the national universities. Political considerations, if not outright political patronage, play a significant part in appointments. The state governor is usually the university chancellor, and the vice chancellor, who actually runs the institution, is usually a political appointee. Appointments are subject to political jockeying, and state governments have control over grants and other forms of recognition. Caste affiliation and regional background are recognized criteria for admission and appointments in many colleges. To offset the inequities implicit in such practices, a certain number of places are reserved for members of Scheduled Castes and Scheduled Tribes.

Education and Society

Historically, Indian education has been elitist. Traditional Hindu education was tailored to the needs of Brahman (see Glossary) boys who were taught to read and write by a Brahman teacher (see The Roots of Indian Religion, ch. 3). During Mughal rule (1526–1858), Muslim education was similarly elitist, although its orientation reflected economic factors rather than those of caste background. Under British company and crown rule (1757–1947), official education policies reinforced the preexisting elitist tendencies of South Asian education. By tying entrance and advancement in government service to academic education, colonial rule contributed to the legacy of an education system geared to preserving the position and prerogatives of the more privileged. Education served as a "gatekeeper," permitting an avenue of upward mobility to those few able to muster sufficient resources.

Even the efforts of the nationalistic Indian National Congress (the Congress—see Glossary) faltered in the face of the entrenched interests defending the existing system of education (see Origins of the Congress and the Muslim League, ch. 1). Early in the 1900s, the Congress called for national education, placing an emphasis on technical and vocational training. In 1920 the Congress initiated a boycott of government-aided and government-controlled schools; it founded several "national" schools and colleges, but to little avail. The rewards of British-style education were so great that the boycott was largely ignored, and the Congress schools temporarily disappeared.

Postprimary education has traditionally catered to the interests of the higher and upwardly mobile castes (see Changes in the Caste System, ch. 5). Despite substantial increases in the spread of middle schools and high schools' growth in enrollment, secondary schooling is necessary for those bent on social status and mobility through acquisition of an office job.

In the nineteenth century, postprimary students were disproportionately Brahmans; their traditional concern with

A young student learning to write Hindi in rural central India
Courtesy Doranne Jacobson

learning gave them an advantage under British education policies. By the early twentieth century, several powerful cultivator castes had realized the advantages of education as a passport to political power and had organized to acquire formal learning. "Backward" castes (usually economically disadvantaged Shudras) who had acquired some wealth took advantage of their status to secure educational privilege. In the mid-1980s, the vast majority of students making it through middle school to high school continued to be from high-level castes and middle-to upper-class families living in urban areas (see Varna, Caste, and Other Divisions, ch. 5). A region's three or four most powerful castes typically dominated the school system. In addition, the widespread role of private education and the payment of fees even at government-run schools discriminated against the poor.

The goals of the 1986 National Policy on Education demanded vastly increased enrollment. In order to have attained universal elementary education in 1995, the 1981 enrollment level of 72.7 million would have had to increase to 160 million in 1995. Although the seventh plan suggested the adoption of new education methods to meet these goals, such as the promotion of television and correspondence courses (often referred to as "distance learning") and open school systems, the actual extended coverage of children was not very great. Many critics of India's education policy argue that total school enrollment is not actually a goal of the government considering the extent of society's vested interest in child labor. In this context, education can be seen as a tool that one social class uses to prevent the rise of another. Middle-class Indians frequently distinguish between the children of the poor as "hands," or children who must be taught to work, and their own children as "minds," or children who must be taught to learn. The upgraded curriculum with increased requirements in English and in the sciences appears to be causing difficulties for many children. Although all the states have recognized that curriculum reform is needed, no comprehensive plan to link curricular changes with new ways of teaching, learning, teacher training, and examination methods has been implemented.

The government instituted an important program for improving physical facilities through a phased drive in all primary schools in the country called Operation Blackboard. Under Operation Blackboard, Rs1 billion was allocated—but not spent—in 1987 to pay for basic amenities for village schools, such as toys and games, classroom materials, blackboards, and maps. This financial allotment averaged Rs2,200 for each government-run primary school. Additional goals of Operation Blackboard included construction of classrooms that would be usable in all weather, and an additional teacher, preferably a woman, in all single-teacher schools.

The nonformal education system implemented in 1979 was the major government effort to educate dropouts and other unenrolled children. Special emphasis was given to the nonformal education system in the nine states regarded by the government as having deficient education systems: Andhra Pradesh, Assam, Bihar, Jammu and Kashmir, Madhya Pradesh, Orissa, Rajasthan, Uttar Pradesh, and West Bengal. A large number of children who resided in these states could not attend formal schools because they were employed, either with or without wages. Seventy-five percent of the country's children who were not enrolled in school resided in these states in the 1980s.

The 1986 National Policy on Education gave new impetus to the nonformal education system. Revised and expanded programs focused on involving voluntary organizations and training talented and dedicated young men and women in local communities as instructors. The results of a late 1980s integrated pilot project for nonformal and adult education for

*Temple complex dedicated to Jagannath—one of the names of
Vishnu—viewed from the monastery library opposite,
at Puri, Orissa*
Courtesy Bernice Huffman Collection, Library of Congress

women and girls in the Lucknow district of Uttar Pradesh provide important data for analyzing recent implementation trends and initial results of both the nonformal education system and adult education in India. Under this project, 300 centers were opened in rural parts of the district with the approval of the Department of Education, the central government, and the state government of Uttar Pradesh with financial and advisory support from the United Nations Educational, Scientific, and Cultural Organization (UNESCO).

Because of the shortage of women teachers in rural areas of Uttar Pradesh, in the pilot project nonformal education for girls aged six to fourteen was integrated with the adult education program for women aged fifteen to thirty-five, so that the same staff and infrastructure could be used. Most of the families of the project participants were in subsistence farming or engaged as farmhands, clerical workers, and petty merchants. Often the brothers of female participants attended a formal school situated about one or two kilometers from their homes. Most of the 300 instructors for the 300 centers were young women between the ages of eighteen and thirty-five. Each center averaged twenty-five women and twenty girl participants. The physical facilities of the centers varied from village to village. Classes might be held on the balcony of a brick house, within a temple, in a room of a mud-walled house, or under open thatch-roof structures. Besides focusing on the acquisition of literacy skills, the project increased participant motivation by also offering instruction in household work, such as sewing, knitting, and preserving food. In 1987 a UNESCO mission to evaluate progress in this project in the areas of functional literacy, vocational skills, and civic awareness observed that randomly chosen participants in both nonformal and adult education classes effectively demonstrated their reading and writing skills at appropriate levels. As a result of many such local programs, literacy rates improved between 1981 and 1991. Male literacy increased from 56.5 percent in 1981 to 64.2 percent in 1991 while women's literacy rate increased from 29.9 percent in 1981 to 39.2 percent in 1991.

Understanding India's health care and education systems contributes to the larger understanding of this complex nation's diverse society. General trends and averages concerning social conditions on a national level may not adequately describe how human activity is expressed spatially and temporally in specific areas. The great variations in local environmental and social conditions require that national and state or union territory programs aimed at improving the quality of life not adhere too strictly to any one standard plan. Local climate, topography, and drainage patterns all need to be considered in terms of how they relate to local forms of land use and ethnic and linguistic groupings. Increasing urbanization in India also complicates efforts at monitoring local conditions. Only with the full support and understanding of India's many rural and urban residents will new ways of focusing India's immense human resources toward the goals of developing and conserving renewable natural resources, limiting population growth, providing increased health care, and achieving education for all be successful.

*   *   *

Indian atlases useful for gaining a basic understanding of India's physical, political, and cultural geography include *A Social and Economic Atlas of India* edited by S. Muthiah and the *River Basin Atlas* of India prepared by the Central Board for the Prevention and Control of Water Pollution. V.S. Katiyar's *The Indian Monsoon and Its Frontiers* provides a good description and analysis of one of the major facets of South Asian climatology. A standard work on postpartition Indian boundaries in terms of their political status is John Robert Victor Prescott's *Map of Mainland Asia by Treaty*. A *Historical Atlas of South Asia* edited by Joseph E. Schwartzberg, is another extremely useful resource.

Official information on India's demography can be found in the *Census of India 1991, Final Population Totals*. These results also provide useful data on literacy levels in India. Additional insight into the contemporary field of Indian population policy is given in G. Narayana and J.F. Kantner's *Doing the Needful: The Dilemma of India's Population Policy*. Concise official data on health care are listed in the Ministry of Planning's annual *Statistical Abstract*. An informed outsider's view of the health situation in India is presented in Roger Jeffery's *The Politics of Health in India*.

Contemporary official education plans and goals are outlined in J.C. Aggarwal's *National Policy on Education: Agenda for India 2001*. A more critical account of India's education system has been compiled by UNESCO's Asia-Pacific Program of Education for All and published in *National Studies: India*. Detailed field results of a recent UNESCO project to provide nonformal and adult education for women and girls can be found in *Simultaneous Education for Women and Girls: Report of a Project.* Myron Weiner's *The Child and State in India* has useful analysis of education policy. (For further information and complete citations, see Bibliography.)

Chapter 3. Religious Life

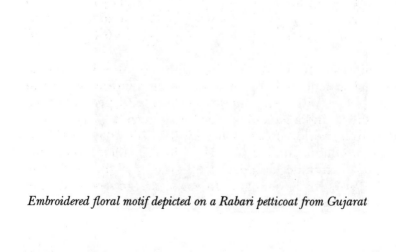

Embroidered floral motif depicted on a Rabari petticoat from Gujarat

IT IS IMPOSSIBLE TO KNOW INDIA without understanding its religious beliefs and practices, which have a large impact on the personal lives of most Indians and influence public life on a daily basis. Indian religions have deep historical roots that are recollected by contemporary Indians. The ancient culture of South Asia, going back at least 4,500 years, has come down to India primarily in the form of religious texts. The artistic heritage, as well as intellectual and philosophical contributions, has always owed much to religious thought and symbolism. Contacts between India and other cultures have led to the spread of Indian religions throughout the world, resulting in the extensive influence of Indian thought and practice on Southeast and East Asia in ancient times and, more recently, in the diffusion of Indian religions to Europe and North America. Within India, on a day-to-day basis, the vast majority of people engage in ritual actions that are motivated by religious systems that owe much to the past but are continuously evolving. Religion, then, is one of the most important facets of Indian history and contemporary life.

A number of world religions originated in India, and others that started elsewhere found fertile ground for growth there. Devotees of Hinduism, a varied grouping of philosophical and devotional traditions, officially numbered 687.6 million people, or 82 percent of the population in the 1991 census (see table 13, Appendix). Buddhism and Jainism, ancient monastic traditions, have had a major influence on Indian art, philosophy, and society and remain important minority religions in the late twentieth century. Buddhists represented 0.8 percent of the total population while Jains represented 0.4 percent in 1991.

Islam spread from the West throughout South Asia, from the early eighth century, to become the largest minority religion in India. In fact, with 101.5 million Muslims (12.1 percent of the population), India has at least the fourth largest Muslim population in the world (after Indonesia with 174.3 million, Pakistan with 124 million, and Bangladesh with 103 million; some analysts put the number of Indian Muslims even higher—128 million in 1994, which would give India the second largest Muslim population in the world).

Sikhism, which started in Punjab in the sixteenth century, has spread throughout India and the world since the mid-nineteenth century. With nearly 16.3 million adherents, Sikhs represent 1.9 percent of India's population.

Christianity, represented by almost all denominations, traces its history in India back to the time of the apostles and counted 19.6 million members in India in 1991. Judaism and Zoroastrianism, arriving originally with traders and exiles from the West, are represented by small populations, mostly concentrated on India's west coast. A variety of independent tribal religious groups also are lively carriers of unique ethnic traditions.

The listing of the major belief systems only scratches the surface of the remarkable diversity in Indian religious life. The complex doctrines and institutions of the great traditions, preserved through written documents, are divided into numerous schools of thought, sects, and paths of devotion. In many cases, these divisions stem from the teachings of great masters, who arise continually to lead bands of followers with a new revelation or path to salvation. In contemporary India, the migration of large numbers of people to urban centers and the impact of modernization have led to the emergence of new religions, revivals, and reforms within the great traditions that create original bodies of teaching and kinds of practice. In other cases, diversity appears through the integration or acculturation of entire social groups—each with its own vision of the divine—within the world of village farming communities that base their culture on literary and ritual traditions preserved in Sanskrit or in regional languages. The local interaction between great traditions and local forms of worship and belief, based on village, caste, tribal, and linguistic differences, creates a range of ritual forms and mythology that varies widely throughout the country. Within this range of differences, Indian religions have demonstrated for many centuries a considerable degree of tolerance for alternate visions of the divine and of salvation.

Religious tolerance in India finds expression in the definition of the nation as a secular state, within which the government since independence has officially remained separate from any one religion, allowing all forms of belief equal status before the law. In practice it has proven difficult to divide religious affiliation from public life. In states where the majority of the population embrace one religion, the boundary between government and religion becomes permeable; in Tamil Nadu, for example, the state government manages Hindu temples, while in Punjab an avowedly Sikh political party usually controls the state assembly. One of the most notable features of Indian politics, particularly since the 1960s, has been the steady growth of militant ideologies that see in only one religious tradition the way toward salvation and demand that public institutions conform to their interpretations of scripture. The vitality of religious fundamentalism and its impact on public life in the form of riots and religion-based political parties have been among the greatest challenges to Indian political institutions in the 1990s.

The Roots of Indian Religion

The Vedas and Polytheism

Hinduism in India traces its source to the Vedas, ancient hymns composed and recited in Punjab as early as 1500 B.C. Three main collections of the Vedas—the Rig, Sama, and Yajur—consist of chants that were originally recited by priests while offering plant and animal sacrifices in sacred fires. A fourth collection, the Atharva Veda, contains a number of formulas for requirements as varied as medical cures and love magic. The majority of modern Hindus revere these hymns as sacred sounds passed down to humanity from the greatest antiquity and as the source of Hindu tradition.

The vast majority of Vedic hymns are addressed to a pantheon of deities who are attracted, generated, and nourished by the offerings into the sacred flames and the precisely chanted mantras (mystical formulas of invocation) based on the hymns. Each of these deities may appear to be the supreme god in his or her own hymns, but some gods stand out as most significant. Indra, god of the firmament and lord of the weather, is the supreme deity of the Vedas. Indra also is a god of war who, accompanied by a host of storm gods, uses thunderbolts as weapons to slay the serpent demon Vritra (the name means storm cloud), thus releasing the rains for the earth. Agni, the god of fire, accepts the sacrificial offerings and transmits them to all the gods. Varuna passes judgment, lays down the law, and protects the cosmic order. Yama, the god of death, sends earthly dwellers signs of old age, sickness, and approaching mortality as exhortations to lead a moral life. Surya is the sun god, Chandra the moon god, Vayu the wind god, and Usha the dawn goddess.

121

Some of the later hymns of the Rig Veda contain speculations that form the basis for much of Indian religious and philosophical thought. From one perspective, the universe originates through the evolution of an impersonal force manifested as male and female principles. Other hymns describe a personal creator, Prajapati, the Lord of creatures, from whom came the heavens and the earth and all the other gods. One hymn describes the universe as emerging from the sacrifice of a cosmic man (*purusha*) who was the source of all things but who was in turn offered into the fire by gods. Within the Vedic accounts of the origin of things, there is a tension between visions of the highest reality as an impersonal force, or as a creator god, or as a group of gods with different jobs to do in the universe. Much of Hinduism tends to accept all these visions simultaneously, claiming that they are all valid as different facets of a single truth, or ranks them as explanations with different levels of sophistication. It is possible, however, to follow only one of these explanations, such as believing in a single personal god while rejecting all others, and still claim to be following the Vedas. In sum, Hinduism does not exist as a single belief system with one textual explanation of the origin of the universe or the nature of God, and a wide range of philosophies and practices can trace their beginnings somewhere in the hymns of the Vedas.

By the sixth century B.C., the Vedic gods were in decline among the people, and few people care much for Indra, Agni, or Varuna in contemporary India. These gods might appear as background characters in myths and stories about more important deities, such as Shiva or Vishnu; in some Hindu temples, there also are small statues of Vedic deities. Sacrificial fire, which once accompanied major political activities, such as the crowning of kings or the conquest of territory, still forms the heart of household rituals for many Hindus, and some Brahman (see Glossary) families pass down the skill of memorizing the hymns and make a living as professional reciters of the Vedas (see Domestic Worship, this ch.). One of the main legacies of Brahmanical sacrifice, seen even among traditions that later denied its usefulness, was a concentration on precise ritual actions and a belief in sacred sound as a powerful tool for manifesting the sacred in daily life.

Karma and Liberation

The Upanishads, originating as commentaries on the Vedas

First century B.C. Buddhist stupa at Sanchi, Madhya Pradesh
Courtesy American Institute of Indian Studies

between about 800 and 200 B.C., contain speculations on the meaning of existence that have greatly influenced Indian religious traditions. Most important is the concept of *atman* (the human soul), which is an individual manifestation of *brahman* (see Glossary). *Atman* is of the same nature as *brahman*, characterized either as an impersonal force or as God, and has as its goal the recognition of identity with *brahman*. This fusion is not possible, however, as long as the individual remains bound to the world of the flesh and desires. In fact, the deathless *atman* that is so bound will not join with *brahman* after the death of the body but will experience continuous rebirth. This fundamental concept of the transmigration of *atman*, or reincarnation after death, lies at the heart of the religions emerging from India.

Indian religious tradition sees karma (see Glossary) as the source of the problem of transmigration. While associated with physical form, for example, in a human body, beings experience the universe through their senses and their minds and attach themselves to the people and things around them and constantly lose sight of their true existence as *atman,* which is of the same nature as *brahman.* As the time comes for the dropping of the body, the fruits of good and evil actions in the past remain with *atman,* clinging to it, causing a tendency to continue experience in other existences after death. Good deeds in this life may lead to a happy rebirth in a better life, and evil deeds may lead to a lower existence, but eventually the consequences of past deeds will be worked out, and the individual will seek more experiences in a physical world. In this manner, the bound or ignorant *atman* wanders from life to life, in heavens and hells and in many different bodies. The universe may expand and be destroyed numerous times, but the bound *atman* will not achieve release.

The true goal of *atman* is liberation, or release (*moksha*), from the limited world of experience and realization of oneness with God or the cosmos. In order to achieve release, the individual must pursue a kind of discipline (yoga, a "tying," related to the English word yoke) that is appropriate to one's abilities and station in life. For most people, this goal means a course of action that keeps them rather closely tied to the world and its ways, including the enjoyment of love (*kama*), the attainment of wealth and power (*artha*), and the following of socially acceptable ethical principles (dharma—see Glossary). From this perspective, even manuals on sexual love, such as the *Kama Sutra* (Book of Love), or collections of ideas on politics and governance, such as the *Arthashastra* (Science of Material Gain), are part of a religious tradition that values action in the world as long as it is performed with understanding, a *karma-yoga* or selfless discipline of action in which every action is offered as a sacrifice to God. Some people, however, may be interested in breaking the cycle of rebirth in this life or soon thereafter. For them, a wide range of techniques has evolved over the thousands of years that gives Indian religion its great diversity. The discipline that involves physical positioning of the body (hatha-yoga), which is most commonly equated with yoga outside of India, sees the human body as a series of spiritual centers that can be awakened through meditation and exercise, leading eventually to a oneness with the universe. Tantrism is the belief in the Tantra (from the Sanskrit, context or continuum), a collection of texts that stress the usefulness of rituals, carried out with a strict discipline, as a means for attaining understanding and spiritual awakening. These rituals include chanting powerful mantras; meditating on complicated or auspicious diagrams (mandalas); and, for one school of advanced practitioners, deliberately violating social norms on food, drink, and sexual relations.

A central aspect of all religious discipline, regardless of its emphasis, is the importance of the guru, or teacher. Indian religion may accept the sacredness of specific texts and rituals but stresses interpretation by a living practitioner who has personal experience of liberation and can pass down successful techniques to devoted followers. In fact, since Vedic times, it has never been possible, and has rarely been desired, to unite all people in India under one concept of orthodoxy with a single authority that could be presented to everyone. Instead, there has been a tendency to accept religious innovation and diversity as the natural result of personal experience by successive generations of gurus, who have tailored their messages to particular times, places, and peoples, and then passed down their knowledge to lines of disciples and social groups. As a result, Indian religion is a mass of ancient and modern traditions, some always preserved and some constantly changing, and the individual is relatively free to stress in his or her life the beliefs and religious behaviors that seem most effective on the path to deliverance.

The Monastic Path

By about 500 B.C., some teachers had moved so far down the path of liberation that they no longer viewed the standard perception of life in the social world as valid for the dedicated spiritual devotee. They formed communities of religious renunciants (*shramanas*) who withdrew from the world and evolved a full-time monastic discipline. The most successful of these early communities, the Jains (or, in Sanskrit, Jaina) and the Buddhists, rejected the value of the Vedas and created independent textual traditions based on the words and examples of their early teachers, eventually evolving entirely new ways for interacting with the lay community.

Jainism

The oldest continuous monastic tradition in India is Jainism, the path of the Jinas, or victors. This tradition is traced to Vardhamana Mahavira (The Great Hero; ca. 599–527 B.C.), the twenty-fourth and last of the Tirthankaras (Sanskrit for ford-makers). According to legend, Mahavira was born to a ruling family in the town of Vaishali, located in the modern state of Bihar. At the age of thirty, he renounced his wealthy life and devoted himself to fasting and self-mortification in order to purify his consciousness and discover the meaning of existence. He never again dwelt in a house, owned property, or wore clothing of any sort. Following the example of the teacher Parshvanatha (ninth century B.C.), he attained enlightenment and spent the rest of his life meditating and teaching a dedicated group of disciples who formed a monastic order following rules he laid down. His life's work complete, he entered a final fast and deliberately died of starvation.

The ancient belief system of the Jains rests on a concrete understanding of the working of karma, its effects on the living soul (*jiva*), and the conditions for extinguishing action and the soul's release. According to the Jain view, the soul is a living substance that combines with various kinds of nonliving matter and through action accumulates particles of matter that adhere to it and determine its fate. Most of the matter perceptible to human senses, including all animals and plants, is attached in various degrees to living souls and is in this sense alive. Any action has consequences that necessarily follow the embodied soul, but the worst accumulations of matter come from violence against other living beings. The ultimate Jain discipline, therefore, rests on complete inactivity and absolute nonviolence (ahimsa) against any living beings. Some Jain monks and nuns wear face masks to avoid accidently inhaling small organisms, and all practicing believers try to remain vegetarians. Extreme renunciation, including the refusal of all food, lies at the heart of a discipline that purges the mind and body of all desires and actions and, in the process, burns off the consequences of actions performed in the past. In this sense, Jain renunciants may recognize or revere deities, but they do not view the Vedas as sacred texts and instead concentrate on the atheistic, individual quest for purification and removal of karma. The final goal is the extinguishing of self, a "blowing out" (nirvana) of the individual self.

By the first century A.D., the Jain community evolved into two main divisions based on monastic discipline: the Digambara or "sky-clad" monks who wear no clothes, own nothing, and collect donated food in their hands; and the Svetambara

The mid-nineteenth-century Paresnath Jain Temple, Calcutta
Courtesy Bernice Huffman Collection, Library of Congress

or "white-clad" monks and nuns who wear white robes and carry bowls for donated food. The Digambara do not accept the possibility of women achieving liberation, while the Svetambara do. Western and southern India have been Jain strongholds for many centuries; laypersons have typically formed minority communities concentrated primarily in urban areas and in mercantile occupations. In the mid-1990s, there were about 7 million Jains, the majority of whom live in the states of Maharashtra (mostly the city of Bombay, or Mumbai in Marathi), Rajasthan, and Gujarat (see Structure and Dynamics, ch. 2). Karnataka, traditionally a stronghold of Digambaras, has a sizable Jain community.

The Jain laity engage in a number of ritual activities that resemble those of the Hindus around them (see The Ceremonies of Hinduism, this ch.). Special shrines in residences or in public temples include images of the Tirthankaras, who are not worshiped but remembered and revered; other shrines house the gods who are more properly invoked to intercede with worldly problems. Daily rituals may include meditation and bathing; bathing the images; offering food, flowers, and lighted lamps for the images; and reciting mantras in Ardhamagadhi, an ancient language of northeast India related to Sanskrit. Many Jain laity engage in sacramental ceremonies during life-cycle rituals, such as the first taking of solid food, marriage, and death, resembling those enacted by Hindus. Jains may also worship local gods and participate in local Hindu or Muslim celebrations without compromising their fundamental devotion to the path of the Jinas. The most important festivals of Jainism celebrate the five major events in the life of Mahavira: conception, birth, renunciation, enlightenment, and final release at death.

At a number of pilgrimage sites associated with great teachers of Jainism, the gifts of wealthy donors made possible the building of architectural wonders. Shatrunjaya Hills (Siddhagiri) in Gujarat is a major Svetambara site, an entire city of about 3,500 temples. Mount Abu in Rajasthan, with one Digambara and five Svetambara temples, is the site of some of India's greatest architecture, dating from the eleventh through thirteenth centuries A.D. In Karnataka, on the hill of Sravana Belgola, stands the monolithic seventeen-meter-high statue of the naked Bhagwan Bahubali (Gomateshvara), the first person in the world believed by the faithful to have attained enlightenment, so deep in meditation that vines are growing around his legs. At this site every twelve years, a major concourse of Jain ascetics and laity participate in a purification ceremony in which the statue is anointed from head to toe. Carved in 981, the statue is considered the holiest Jain shrine. In addition to its lavish patronage of shrines, the Jain community, with its long scriptural tradition and wealth gained from trade, has always been known for its philanthropy and especially for its support of education and learning. Prestigious Jain schools are located in most major cities. The largest concentrations of Jains are in Maharashtra (more than 965,000) and Rajasthan (nearly 563,000), with sizable numbers also in Gujarat and Madhya Pradesh.

Buddhism

Buddhism began with the life of Siddhartha Gautama (ca. 563–483 B.C.), a prince from the small Shakya Kingdom

Itinerant Jain nuns along a road in Rajasthan
Courtesy Doranne Jacobson

located in the foothills of the Himalayas in Nepal. Brought up
in luxury, the prince abandoned his home and wandered forth
as a religious beggar, searching for the meaning of existence.
The stories of his search presuppose the Jain tradition, as
Gautama was for a time a practitioner of intense austerity, at
one point almost starving himself to death. He decided, however, that self-torture weakened his mind while failing to
advance him to enlightenment and therefore turned to a
milder style of renunciation and concentrated on advanced
meditation techniques. Eventually, under a tree in the forests
of Gaya (in modern Bihar), he resolved to stir no farther until
he had solved the mystery of existence. Breaking through the
final barriers, he achieved the knowledge that he later
expressed as the Four Noble Truths: all of life is suffering; the
cause of suffering is desire; the end of desire leads to the end of
suffering; and the means to end desire is a path of discipline

and meditation. Gautama was now the Buddha, or the awakened one, and he spent the remainder of his life traveling about northeast India converting large numbers of disciples. At the age of eighty, the Buddha achieved his final passing away (*parinirvana*) and died, leaving a thriving monastic order and a dedicated lay community to continue his work.

By the third century B.C., the still-young religion based on the Buddha's teachings was being spread throughout South Asia through the agency of the Mauryan Empire (ca. 326–184 B.C.; see The Mauryan Empire, ch. 1). By the seventh century A.D., having spread throughout East Asia and Southeast Asia, Buddhism probably had the largest religious following in the world.

For centuries Indian royalty and merchants patronized Buddhist monasteries and raised beautiful, hemispherical stone structures called stupas over the relics of the Buddha in reverence to his memory. Since the 1840s, archaeology has revealed the huge impact of Buddhist art, iconography, and architecture in India. The monastery complex at Nalanda in Bihar, in ruins in 1993, was a world center for Buddhist philosophy and religion until the thirteenth century. But by the thirteenth century, when Turkic invaders destroyed the remaining monasteries on the plains, Buddhism as an organized religion had practically disappeared from India. It survived only in Bhutan and Sikkim, both of which were then independent Himalayan kingdoms; among tribal groups in the mountains of northeast India; and in Sri Lanka. The reasons for this disappearance are unclear, and they are many: shifts in royal patronage from Buddhist to Hindu religious institutions; a constant intellectual struggle with dynamic Hindu intellectual schools, which eventually triumphed; and slow adoption of popular religious forms by Buddhists while Hindu monastic communities grew up with the same style of discipline as the Buddhists, leading to the slow but steady amalgamation of ideas and trends in the two religions.

Buddhism began a steady and dramatic comeback in India during the early twentieth century, spurred on originally by a combination of European antiquarian and philosophical interest and the dedicated activities of a few Indian devotees. The foundation of the Mahabodhi Society (Society of Great Enlightenment) in 1891, originally as a force to wrest control of the Buddhist shrine at Gaya from the hands of Hindu managers, gave a large stimulus to the popularization of Buddhist philosophy and the importance of the religion in India's past.

A major breakthrough occurred in 1956 after some thirty years of Untouchable, or Dalit (see Glossary), agitation when Bhimrao Ramji (B.R.) Ambedkar, leader of the Untouchable wing within the Congress (see Glossary), announced that he was converting to Buddhism as a way to escape from the impediments of the Hindu caste system (see Varna, Caste, and Other Divisions, ch. 5). He brought with him masses of Untouchables—also known as Harijans (see Glossary) or Dalits—and members of Scheduled Castes (see Glossary), who mostly came from Maharashtra and border areas of neighboring states and from the Agra area in Uttar Pradesh. By the early 1990s, there were more than 5 million Buddhists in Maharashtra, or 79 percent of the entire Buddhist community in India, almost all recent converts from low castes. When added to longtime Buddhist populations in hill areas of northeast India (West Bengal, Assam, Sikkim, Mizoram, and Tripura) and high Himalayan valleys (Ladakh District in Jammu and Kashmir, Himachal Pradesh, and northern Uttar Pradesh), and to the influx of Tibetan Buddhist refugees who fled from Tibet with the Dalai Lama in 1959 and thereafter, the recent converts raised the number of Buddhists in India to 6.4 million by 1991. This was a 35.9 percent increase since 1981 and made Buddhism the fifth largest religious group in the country.

The forms of Buddhism practiced by Himalayan communities and Tibetan refugees are part of the Vajrayana, or "Way of the Lightning Bolt," that developed after the seventh century A.D. as part of Mahayana (Great Path) Buddhism. Although retaining the fundamental importance of individual spiritual advancement, the Vajrayana stresses the intercession of bodhisattvas, or enlightened beings, who remain in this world to aid others on the path. Until the twentieth century, the Himalayan kingdoms supported a hierarchy in which Buddhist monks, some identified from birth as bodhisattvas, occupied the highest positions in society.

Most other Buddhists in India follow Theravada Buddhism, the "Doctrine of the Elders," which traces its origin through Sri Lankan and Burmese traditions to scriptures in the Pali language, a Sanskritic dialect in eastern India. Although replete with miraculous events and legends, these scriptures stress a more human Buddha and a democratic path toward enlightenment for everyone. Ambedkar's plan for the expanding Buddhist congregation in India visualized Buddhist monks and nuns developing themselves through service to others. Convert communities, by embracing Buddhism, have embarked on social transformations, including a decline in alcoholism, a simplification of marriage ceremonies and abolition of ruinous marriage expenses, a greater emphasis on education, and a heightened sense of identity and self-worth.

The Tradition of the Enlightened Master

A number of avowedly Hindu monastic communities have grown up over time and adopted some of the characteristics associated with early Buddhism and Jainism, while remaining dedicated to the Hindu philosophical traditions. One of the oldest and most respected of the Hindu orders traces its origin to the teacher Shankara (788–820), believed by many devotees to have lived hundreds of years earlier. Shankara's philosophy is a primary source of Vedanta, or the "End of the Veda," the final commentary on revealed truth, which is one of the most influential trends in modern Hinduism. His interpretation of the Upanishads portrays *brahman* as absolutely one and without qualities. The phenomenal world is illusion (*maya*), which the embodied soul must transcend in order to achieve oneness with *brahman*. As a wandering monk, Shankara traveled throughout India, combating Buddhist atheism and founding five seats of learning at Badrinath (Uttar Pradesh), Dwaraka (Gujarat), Puri (Orissa), Sringeri (Karnataka), and Kanchipuram (Tamil Nadu). In the 1990s, those seats are still held by successors to Shankara's philosophy (Shankara Acharyas), who head an order of orange-clad monks that is highly respected by the Hindu community throughout India. Activities of the *acharyas*, including their periodic trips away from their home monasteries to visit and preach to devotees, receive exposure in regional and national media. Their conservative viewpoints and pronouncements on a variety of topics, although not binding on most believers, attract considerable public attention.

The initiation of a renunciant usually depends on the judgment of an *acharya* who determines whether a candidate is dedicated and prepared or not; he then gives to the disciple training and instructions including the initiate's own secret formula or mantra. After initiation, the disciple may remain with his teacher or in a monastery for an indefinite period or may wander forth in a variety of careers. The Ramanandi order in

North India, for example, includes holy men (sadhus) who practice ascetic disciplines, militant members of fortified temples, and priests in charge of temple administration and ritual.

There are other orders of renunciants who lead still more austere existences, including naked ascetics who wander begging for their food and assemble for spectacular parades at major festivals. A few dedicated seekers still withdraw to the fastness of the Himalayas or other remote spots and work on their meditation and yoga in total obscurity. Others beg in populated areas, sometimes engaging in fierce austerities such as piercing their bodies with pins and knives. They are a reminder to all people that the path of renunciation waits for anyone who has the dedication and the courage to leave the world behind.

Another kind of renunciation appears in the cult of Sai Baba, who achieved national and international fame in the twentieth century. The first person known by this name was a holy man—Sai Baba (died 1918)—who appeared in 1872 in Maharashtra and lived a humble life that blended meditation and devotional techniques from a variety of sources. This saint has a small but dedicated following throughout India. A later incarnation was Satya Sai Baba (*satya* means true), born in 1926 in Andhra Pradesh. At age thirteen, he experienced the first of several seizures that resulted in a changed personality and intense devotional activity, leading to his statement that he is the second incarnation of Sai Baba. By 1950 he had set up a retreat at Puttaparti in what later became Andhra Pradesh and was accepting disciples. His fame spread along with numerous apocryphal stories of his ability to perform miracles, including the manifestation of sacred ash and, according to some accounts, watches or other objects, from thin air or from his own body. The cult has expanded to include publishing, social service, and education institutions and includes an international association of thousands of believers. Devotion to Satya Sai Baba does not preclude attachment to other religious observances but concentrates instead on worship and veneration of the holy man himself, often in the form of a photograph. Thousands of pilgrims have traveled to his retreat annually to participate in group activities, obtain mementos, and perhaps a view of the teacher himself.

The Worship of Personal Gods

For the vast majority of Hindus, the most important religious path is *bhakti* (devotion) to personal gods. There are a wide variety of gods to choose from, and although sectarian adherence to particular deities is often strong, there is a widespread acceptance of choice in the desired god (*ishta devata*) as the most appropriate focus for any particular person. Most devotees are therefore polytheists, worshiping all or part of the vast pantheon of deities, some of whom have come down from Vedic times. In practice, a worshiper tends to concentrate prayers on one deity or on a small group of deities with whom there is a close personal relationship.

Puja (worship) of the gods consists of a range of ritual offerings and prayers typically performed either daily or on special days before an image of the deity, which may be in the form of a person or a symbol of the sacred presence. In its more developed forms, *puja* consists of a series of ritual stages beginning with personal purification and invocation of the god, followed by offerings of flowers, food, or other objects such as clothing, accompanied by fervent prayers. Some dedicated worshipers perform these ceremonies daily at their home shrines; others travel to one or more temples to perform *puja*, alone or with the aid of temple priests who receive offerings and present these offerings to the gods. The gifts given to the gods become sacred through contact with their images or with their shrines, and may be received and used by worshipers as the grace (*prasada*) of the divine. Sacred ash or saffron powder, for example, is often distributed after *puja* and smeared on the foreheads of devotees. In the absence of any of these ritual objects, however, *puja* may take the form of a simple prayer sent toward the image of the divine, and it is common to see people stop for a moment before roadside shrines to fold their hands and offer short invocations to the gods.

Since at least the seventh century A.D., the devotional path has spread from the south throughout India through the literary and musical activities of saints who have been some of the most important representatives of regional languages and traditions. The hymns of these saints and their successors, mostly in vernacular forms, are memorized and performed at all levels of society. Every state in India has its own *bhakti* tradition and poets who are studied and revered. In Tamil Nadu, groups called Nayanmars (devotees of Shiva) and Alvars (devotees of Vishnu) were composing beautiful poetry in the Tamil language as early as the sixth century. In Bengal one of the greatest poets was Chaitanya (1485–1536), who spent much of his

A sadhu with sacred rudraksha beads, Varanasi. The writing on his shawl says Om Ram, *a phrase invoking the name of the Lord Ram. Courtesy Doranne Jacobson*

life in a state of mystical ecstasy. One of the greatest North Indian saints was Kabir (ca. 1440–1518), a common leather-worker who stressed faith in God without devotion to images, rituals, or scriptures. Among female poets, Princess Mirabai (ca. 1498–1546) from Rajasthan stands out as one whose love for Krishna was so intense that she suffered persecution for her public singing and dancing for the lord.

A recurring motif that emerges from the poetry and the hagiographies of these saints is the equality of all men and women before God and the ability of people from all castes and occupations to find their way to union with God if they have enough faith and devotion. In this sense, the *bhakti* tradition serves as one of the equalizing forces in Indian society and culture.

Vishnu

As one of the most important gods in the Hindu pantheon, Vishnu is surrounded by a number of extremely popular and well-known stories and is the focus of a number of sects devoted entirely to his worship. Vishnu contains a number of personalities, often represented as ten major descents (avatars) in which the god has taken on physical forms in order to save earthly creatures from destruction. In one story, the earth was drowning in a huge flood, so to save it Vishnu took on the body of a giant turtle and lifted the earth on his back out of the waters. A tale found in the Vedas describes a demon who could not be conquered. Responding to the pleas of the gods, Vishnu appeared before the demon as a dwarf. The demon, in a classic instance of pride, underestimated this dwarf and granted him as much of the world as he could tread in three steps. Vishnu then assumed his universal form and in three strides spanned the entire universe and beyond, crushing the demon in the process.

The incarnation of Vishnu known to almost everyone in India is his life as Ram (Rama in Sanskrit), a prince from the ancient north Indian kingdom of Ayodhya, in the cycle of stories known as the *Ramayana* (The Travels of Ram). On one level, this is a classic adventure story, as Ram is exiled from the kingdom and has to wander in the forests of southern India with his beautiful wife Sita and his loyal younger brother Lakshman. After many adventures, during which Ram befriends the king of the monkey kingdom and joins forces with the great monkey hero Hanuman, the demon king Ravana kidnaps Sita and takes her to his fortress on the island of Lanka (modern Sri Lanka). A huge war then ensues, as Ram with his animal allies attacks the demons, destroys them all, and returns in triumph to North India to occupy his lawful throne. Village storytellers, street theater players, the movies, and the national television network all have their versions of this story. In many parts of the country, but especially in North India, the annual festival of Dussehra celebrates Ram's adventures and his final triumph and includes the public burning of huge effigies of Ravana at the end of several days of parties. Everyone knows that Ram is really Vishnu, who came down to rid the earth of the demons and set up an ideal kingdom of righteousness— Ram Raj—which stands as an ideal in contemporary India. Sita is in reality his consort, the goddess Lakshmi, the ideal of feminine beauty and devotion to her husband. Lakshmi, also known as Shri, eventually became the goddess of fortune, surplus, and happiness. Hanuman, as the faithful sidekick with great physical and magical powers, is one of the most beloved images in the Hindu pantheon with temples of his own throughout the country.

Another widely known incarnation is Krishna. In the *Mahabharata* (Great Battle of the Descendants of Bharata), the gigantic, multivolume epic of ancient North Indian kingdoms,

Krishna appears as the ruler of one of the many states allied either with the heroic Pandava brothers or with their treacherous cousins, the Kauravas. Bharata was an ancient king whose achievements are celebrated in the *Mahabharata* and from whose name derives one of the names for modern India, that is Bharat. During the final battle, Krishna serves as charioteer for the hero Arjuna, and before the fighting starts he bolsters Arjuna's faltering will to fight against his kin. Krishna reveals himself as Vishnu, the supreme godhead, who has set up the entire conflict to cleanse the earth of evildoers according to his inscrutable will. This section of the epic, the *Bhagavad Gita,* or Song of the Lord, is one of the great jewels of world religious literature and of central importance in modern Hinduism. One of its main themes is *karma-yoga,* or selfless discipline in offering all of one's allotted tasks in life as a devotion to God and without attachment to consequences. The true reality is the soul that neither slays nor is slain and that can rejoin God through selfless dedication and through Krishna's saving grace.

A completely different cycle of stories portrays Krishna as a young cowherd, growing up in the country after he was saved from an evil uncle who coveted his kingdom. In this incarnation, Krishna often appears as a happy, roly-poly infant, well known for his pranks and thefts of butter. Although his enemies send evil agents to destroy him, the baby miraculously survives their attacks and kills his demonic assailants. Later, as he grows into an adolescent, he continues to perform miracles such as saving the cowherds and their flocks from a dangerous storm by holding up a mountain over their heads until the weather clears. His most striking exploits, however, are his affairs as a young adult with the *gopis* (cowherding maidens), all of whom are in love with him because of his good looks and talent with the flute.

These explicitly sexual activities, including stealing the clothes of the maidens while they are bathing, are the basis for a wide range of poetry and songs to Krishna as a lover; the devotee of the god takes on a female role and directs toward the beloved lord the heartfelt longing for union with the divine. Krishna's relationship with Radha, his favorite among the *gopis,* has served as a model for male and female love in a variety of art forms, and since the sixteenth century appears prominently as a motif in North Indian paintings. Unlike many other deities, who are depicted as very fair in color, Krishna appears in all these adventures as a dark lord, either black or blue in color.

In this sense, he is a figure who constantly overturns accepted conventions of order, hierarchy, and propriety, and introduces a playful and mischievous aspect of a god who hides from his worshipers but saves them in the end. The festival of Holi at the spring equinox, in which people of all backgrounds play in the streets and squirt each other with colored water, is associated with Krishna.

In iconography Vishnu may appear as any of his ten incarnations but often stands in sculpture as a princely male with four arms that bear a club, discus, conch, and lotus flower. He may also appear lying on his back on the thousand-headed king of the serpents, Shesha-Naga, in the milk ocean at the center of time, with his feet massaged by Lakshmi, and with a lotus growing from his navel giving birth to the god Brahma, a four-headed representation of the creative principle. Vishnu in this representation is the ultimate source of the universe that he causes to expand and contract at regular cosmic intervals measuring millions of years. On a more concrete level, Vishnu may become incarnate at any moment on earth in order to continue to bring sentient creatures back to himself, and a number of great religious teachers (including, for example, Chaitanya in Bengal) are identified by their followers as incarnations of Vishnu.

Shiva

The god Shiva is the other great figure in the modern pantheon. In contrast to the regal attributes of Vishnu, Shiva is a figure of renunciation. A favorite image portrays him as an ascetic, performing meditation alone in the fastness of the Himalayas. There he sits on a tiger skin, clad only in a loincloth, covered with sacred ash that gives his skin a gray color. His trident is stuck into the ground next to him. Around his neck is a snake. From his matted hair, tied in a topknot, the river Ganga (Ganges) descends to the earth. His neck is blue, a reminder of the time he drank the poison that emerged while gods and demons competed to churn the milk ocean. Shiva often appears in this image as an antisocial being, who once burned up Kama, the god of love, with a glance. But behind this image is the cosmic lord who, through the very power of his meditating consciousness, expands the entire universe and all beings in it. Although he appears to be hard to attain, in reality Shiva is a loving deity who saves those devotees who are wholeheartedly dedicated to him.

The *bhakti* literature of South India, where Shiva has long been important, describes the numerous instances of pure-hearted devotion to the beautiful lord and the final revelation of himself as Shiva after testing his devotees. Shiva often appears on earth in disguise, perhaps as a wandering Brahman priest, to challenge the charity or belief of a suffering servant, only to appear eventually in his true nature. Many of these divine plays are connected directly with specific people and specific sites, and almost every ancient Shiva temple can claim a famous poem or a famous miracle in its history. The hundreds of medieval temples in Tamil Nadu, almost all dedicated to Shiva, contain sculptured panels depicting the god in a variety of guises: Bhikshatana, the begging lord; Bhairava, a horrible, destructive image; or Nataraja, the lord of the dance, beating a drum that keeps time while he manifests the universe.

Because he withholds his sexual urges and controls them, Shiva is able to transmute sexual energy into creative power, by generating intense heat. It is, in fact, the heat generated from discipline and austerity (*tapas*) that is seen as the source for the generative power of all renunciants, and in this sense Shiva is often connected with wandering orders of monks in modern India. For the average worshiper, the sexual power of Shiva is seen in the most common image that represents him, the lingam. This is typically a cylindrical stone several feet tall, with a rounded top, standing in a circular base. On one level, this is the most basic image of divinity, providing a focus for worship with a minimum of artistic embellishment, attempting to represent the infinite. The addition of carved anatomical details on many lingams, however, leaves no doubt for the worshiper that this is an erect male sexual organ, showing the procreative power of God at the origin of all things. The concept of reality as the complex interplay of opposite principles, male and female, thus finds its highest form in the mythology of Shiva and his consort Parvati (also known as Shakti, Kali, or Durga), the daughter of the mountains. This most controlled deity, the meditating Shiva, then has still another form, as the erotic lover of Parvati, embracing her passionately.

Shiva and Parvati have two sons, who have entire cycles of myths and legends and *bhakti* cults in their own right. One son is called variously Karttikeya (identified with the planet Mars) or Skanda (the god of war or Subrahmanya). He is extremely handsome, carries a spear, and rides a peacock. According to some traditions, he emerged motherless from Shiva when the gods needed a great warrior to conquer an indestructible demon. In southern India, where he is called Murugan, he is a lord of mountain places and a great friend of those who dedicate themselves to him. Some devotees vow to carry on their shoulders specially carved objects of wood for a determined number of weeks, never putting them down during that time. Others may go further, and insert knives or long pins into their bodies for extended periods.

Another son of Shiva and Parvati is Ganesh, or Ganapati, the Lord of the Ganas (the hosts of Shiva), who has a male human's body with four arms and the head of an elephant. One myth claims that he originated directly from Parvati's body and entered into a quarrel with Shiva, who cut off his human head and replaced it later with the head of the first animal he found, which happened to be an elephant. For most worshipers, Ganesh is the first deity invoked during any ceremony because he is the god of wisdom and remover of obstacles. People worship Ganesh when beginning anything, for example, at the start of a trip or the first day of the new school year. He is often pictured next to his mount, the rat, symbol of the ability to get in anywhere. Ganesh is therefore a clever figure, a trickster in many stories, who presents a benevolent and friendly image to those worshipers who placate him. His image is perhaps the most widespread and public in India, visible in streets and transportation terminals everywhere. The antics of Ganesh and Karttikeya and the interactions of Shiva and Parvati have generated a series of entertaining myths of Shiva as a henpecked husband, who would prefer to keep meditating but instead is drawn into family problems, providing a series of morality tales in households throughout India.

Brahma and the Hindu Trinity

It is often said that the Hindu pantheon has three gods at its head: Brahma, the creator of the universe; Vishnu, the preserver of life; and Shiva, the destroyer of ignorance. Brahma is a representation of the impersonal *brahman* in a human form, usually with four faces facing the cardinal directions and four arms (see Karma and Liberation, this ch.). In reality, Brahma receives little devotion from worshipers, who may mention him in passing while giving their attention to the other main gods. There are few temples in India dedicated to him; instead, his image may stand in niches on the walls of temples built for

Lavishly decorated mid-seventh-century A.D. Parasuramesvar temple, dedicated to Shiva, Bhubaneshwar, Orissa
Courtesy Bernice Huffman Collection, Library of Congress

other deities. Religious stories usually place Brahma as an intermediate authority who cannot handle a problem and passes it on to either Vishnu or Shiva. The concept of the trinity (*trimurti*), expressed in beautiful art works or invoked even by believers, is in practice a philosophical construct that unites all deistic traditions within Hinduism into one overarching symbol.

The Goddess

Philosophical musings as far back as the Rig Veda contemplated the universe as the result of an interplay between the male principle (*purusha*), the prime source of generative power but quiescent, and a female principle that came to be known as *prakriti*, an active principle that manifests reality, or power (*shakti*), at work in the world. On a philosophical level, this female principle ultimately rests in the oneness of the male, but on a practical level it is the female that is most significant in the world. The vast array of iconography and mythology that surround the gods such as Vishnu and Shiva is a backdrop for the worship of their female consorts, and the male deities fade into the background. Thus it is that the divine is often female in India.

Vishnu's consort, Lakshmi, has a number of well-known incarnations that are the center of cults in their own right. In

141

the *Ramayana,* for example, female characters are responsible for most of the important events, and the dutiful Sita, who resists the advances of lustful Ravana, is a much beloved figure of devotion. Lakshmi receives direct worship along with Ram during the big national festival of Dipavali (Diwali), celebrated with massive fireworks demonstrations, when people pray for success and wealth during the coming year. The *Mahabharata* is equally packed with tales of male and female relationships in which women hold their own, and the beautiful Draupadi, wife of the five Pandava heroes, has her own cult in scattered locations throughout India.

Parvati, in a variety of forms, is the most common focus of devotion in India. She presents two main facets to her worshipers: a benign and accepting personality that provides assistance and a powerful and dangerous personality that must be placated. The benign vision exists in many temples to Shiva throughout the country, where the goddess has her own shrine that is in practice the most frequented site of heartfelt devotion. During annual festivals in which the god and goddess emerge from their shrines and travel in processions, it is often the goddess who is most eagerly anticipated. In North India, for example, life-like statues of the loving goddess Kali, who is ultimately a manifestation of Parvati, are carried through huge crowds that line village and city streets. In South India, where gigantic temples are the physical and social centers of town life, the shrines and their annual festivals are often known by the names of their goddesses. One of the more famous is the sixteenth- and seventeenth-century Minakshi Temple in Madurai, Tamil Nadu. The temple is named after the "fish-eyed goddess" Minakshi, described in myths as a dark queen born with three breasts, who set out to conquer the universe. After overrunning the world and vanquishing the gods, Minakshi finally met Shiva and, when her third breast disappeared, accepted him as her lord. This motif of physical power and energy appears in many stories where the goddess is a warrior or conqueror of demons who in the end joins with Shiva.

Alternative visions, however, portray a goddess on the loose, with the potential for causing havoc in the world unless appeased. The goddess Durga is a great warrior who carries swords and a shield, rides a tiger, and destroys demons when the gods prove incapable; in this incarnation, she never submits, but remains capable of terrible deeds of war. The goddess Kali often appears as an even more horrific vision of the divine, with garlands of human skulls around her neck and a severed head in her hand; her bloody tongue hangs from her mouth, and the weapons in her arms drip gore. This image attempts to capture the destructive capacity of the divine, the suffering in the world, and the ultimate return of all things to the goddess at death.

In many small shrines throughout India, in marked contrast to the large and ornate temples dominated by Brahmanical principles and the philosophy of nonviolence, the female divinity receives regular gifts of blood sacrifices, usually chickens and goats. In addition, the goddess may manifest herself as the bearer of a number of diseases. The goddess of smallpox, known as Shitala in North India and Mariamman in South India, remains a feared and worshiped figure even after the official elimination of the disease, for she is still capable of afflicting people with a number of fevers and poxes. Many more localized forms of goddesses, known by different names in different regions, are the focus for prayers and vows that lead worshipers to undertake acts of austerity and pilgrimages in return for favors.

Local Deities

Along many paths in the countryside, and in some urban neighborhoods, there are sacred spots at the base of trees, or small stones set in niches, or simply made statues with flowers or a small flame burning in front of them. These are shrines for deities who are locally honored for protecting the people from harm caused by natural disasters or evil influences. Worshipers often portray these protectors as warriors, and, in some cases, they may be traced back to great human fighters who died for their village and later became immortalized. In South India, there are thousands of hero stones, simple representations of warriors on slabs of stone, found in and around agricultural settlements, in memory of nameless local fighters who may have died while protecting their communities hundreds of years ago. At one time, these stones may have received regular signs of devotion, but they are mostly ignored in contemporary India. In the fields on the outskirts of many villages, there are large, multicolored, terra-cotta figures of warriors with raised swords or figures of war horses; these are open-air shrines of the god Aiyanar, who serves as the village protector and who has very few connections with the great tradition of Hinduism.

Local deities may begin to attract the attention of worshipers from a wide geographical area, which may include many villages or neighborhoods, or from a large percentage of the members of particular castes, who come to the deity seeking protection or boons. These deities have their own shrines, which may be simple, independent enclosures with pillared halls or may stand as separate establishments attached to temples of Shiva, Vishnu, or any other great god. Deities at this level attract expressive and ecstatic forms of worship and tend to possess special devotees on a regular basis or enter into their believers during festivals. People who are possessed by the god may speak to their families and friends concerning important personal or social problems, predicting the future or clarifying mysteries. These local gods often expect offerings of animals, usually goats or chickens, which are killed in the vicinity of the shrines and then consumed in communal meals by families and friends.

In the twentieth century, there has been an increase in the number of new, regional gods attracting worshipers from many different groups, spurred by vast improvements in transport and communication. For example, in the hills bordering the states of Tamil Nadu and Kerala is a shrine for the god Ayyappan, whose origin is uncertain but who is sometimes called the offspring of Shiva and Vishnu in his female form. Ayyappan's annual festival is a time of pilgrimage for ever-growing numbers of men from throughout South India. These devotees fast and engage in austerities under the leadership of a teacher for weeks beforehand and then travel in groups to the shrine for a glimpse of the god. Bus tickets are hard to obtain for several weeks as masses of elated men, clad in distinctive ritual dhotis of various colors, throng public transportation during their trip to the shrine. In northwestern India, the popularity of the goddess Vaishno Devi has risen meteorically since independence. Vaishno Devi, who combines elements of Lakshmi and Durga, is an extremely benevolent manifestation of the eternal virgin who gives material well-being to her worshipers. One million pilgrims travel annually to her cave shrine in the foothills of the Himalayas, about fifty kilometers north of the city of Jammu.

Since the 1950s, the most spectacular example of a deity's increasing influence throughout northern and central India is the cult of Santoshi Ma (Mother of Contentment). Her myths recount the sufferings of a young woman left alone by her working husband and abused by her in-laws, who nevertheless remains loving and faithful to her man and, by performing simple vows to the goddess (fasting one day every week), eventually sees the return of her now-rich husband and moves with him into her own house. Santoshi Ma, thought to be the daughter of Ganesh, is worshiped mostly by lower middle-class women who also pray for material goods. In the 1980s and early 1990s, her shrines were spreading everywhere and even taking over older temples, aided by the release in the 1970s of an extremely popular film version of her story, *Jay Santoshi Ma.*

The Ceremonies of Hinduism

The ritual world of Hinduism, manifestations of which differ greatly among regions, villages, and individuals, offers a number of common features that link all Hindus into a greater Indian religious system and influence other religions as well. The most notable feature in religious ritual is the division between purity and pollution. Religious acts presuppose some degree of impurity or defilement for the practitioner, which must be overcome or neutralized before or during ritual procedures. Purification, usually with water, is thus a typical feature of most religious action. Avoidance of the impure—taking animal life, eating flesh, associating with dead things, or body fluids—is another feature of Hindu ritual and is important for repressing pollution. In a social context, those individuals or groups who manage to avoid the impure are accorded increased respect. Still another feature is a belief in the efficacy of sacrifice, including survivals of Vedic sacrifice. Thus, sacrifices may include the performance of offerings in a regulated manner, with the preparation of sacred space, recitation of texts, and manipulation of objects. A third feature is the concept of merit, gained through the performance of charity or good works, that will accumulate over time and reduce sufferings in the next world.

Domestic Worship

The home is the place where most Hindus conduct their worship and religious rituals. The most important times of day for performance of household rituals are dawn and dusk, although especially devout families may engage in devotion more often. For many households, the day begins when the women in the house draw auspicious geometric designs in chalk or rice flour on the floor or the doorstep. For orthodox Hindus, dawn and dusk are greeted with recitation from the Rig Veda of the Gayatri Mantra for the sun—for many people, the only Sanskrit prayer they know. After a bath, there is personal worship of the gods at a family shrine, which typically includes lighting a lamp and offering foodstuffs before the images, while prayers in Sanskrit or a regional language are recited. In the evenings, especially in rural areas, mostly female devotees may gather together for long sessions of singing hymns in praise of one or more of the gods.

Minor acts of charity punctuate the day. During daily baths, there are offerings of a little water in memory of the ancestors. At each meal, families may set aside a handful of grain to be donated to beggars or needy persons, and daily gifts of small amounts of grain to birds or other animals serve to accumulate merit for the family through their self-sacrifice.

Life-Cycle Rituals

A detailed series of life-cycle rituals (*samskara*, or refinements) mark major transitions in the life of the individual. Especially orthodox Hindu families may invite Brahman priests to their homes to officiate at these rituals, complete with sacred fire and recitations of mantras. Most of these rituals, however, do not occur in the presence of such priests, and among many groups who do not revere the Vedas or respect Brahmans, there may be other officiants or variations in the rites.

Ceremonies may be performed during pregnancy to ensure the health of the mother and growing child. The father may part the hair of the mother three times upward from the front to the back, to assure the ripening of the embryo. Charms may serve to ward off the evil eye and witches or demons. At birth, before the umbilical cord is severed, the father may touch the baby's lips with a gold spoon or ring dipped in honey, curds, and ghee. The word *vak* (speech) is whispered three times into the right ear, and mantras are chanted to ensure a long life. A number of rituals for the infant include the first visit outside to a temple, the first feeding with solid food (usually cooked rice), an ear-piercing ceremony, and the first haircut (shaving the head) that often occurs at a temple or during a festival when the hair is offered to a deity.

A crucial event in the life of the orthodox, upper-caste Hindu male is an initiation (*upanayana*) ceremony, which takes place for some young males between the ages of six and twelve to mark the transition to awareness and adult religious responsibilities. At the ceremony itself, the family priest invests the boy with a sacred thread to be worn always over the left shoulder, and the parents instruct him in pronouncing the Gayatri Mantra. The initiation ceremony is seen as a new birth; those groups entitled to wear the sacred thread are called the twice-born (see Glossary). In the ancient categorization of society associated with the Vedas, only the three highest groups—Brahman, warrior (Kshatriya), and commoner or merchant (Vaishya)—were allowed to wear the thread, to make them distinct from the fourth group of servants (Shudra). Many individuals and groups who are only hazily associated with the old "twice-born" elites perform the *upanayana* ceremony and claim the higher status it bestows. For young Hindu women in South India, a different ritual and celebration occurs at the first menses.

The next important transition in life is marriage. For most people in India, the betrothal of the young couple and the exact date and time of the wedding are matters decided by the parents in consultation with astrologers. At Hindu weddings, the bride and bridegroom represent the god and the goddess, although there is a parallel tradition that sees the groom as a prince coming to wed his princess. The groom, decked in all his finery, often travels to the wedding site on a caparisoned white horse or in an open limousine, accompanied by a procession of relatives, musicians, and bearers of ornate electrified lamps. The actual ceremonies in many cases become extremely elaborate, but orthodox Hindu marriages typically have at their center the recitation of mantras by priests. In a crucial rite, the new couple take seven steps northward from a sacred household fire, turn, and make offerings into the flames. Independent traditions in regional languages and among different caste groups support wide variations in ritual (see Life Passages, ch. 5).

After the death of a family member, the relatives become involved in ceremonies for preparation of the body and a procession to the burning or burial ground. For most Hindus, cremation is the ideal method for dealing with the dead, although many groups practice burial instead; infants are buried rather than cremated. At the funeral site, in the presence of the male mourners, the closest relative of the deceased (usually the eldest son) takes charge of the final rite and, if it is cremation, lights the funeral pyre. After a cremation, ashes and fragments of bone are collected and eventually immersed in a holy river. After a funeral, everyone undergoes a purifying bath. The immediate family remains in a state of intense pollution for a set number of days (sometimes ten, eleven, or thirteen). At the end of that period, close family members meet for a ceremonial meal and often give gifts to the poor or to charities. A particular feature of the Hindu ritual is the preparation of rice balls (*pinda*) offered to the spirit of the dead person during memorial services. In part these ceremonies are seen as contributing to the merit of the deceased, but they also pacify the soul so that it will not linger in this world as a ghost but will pass through the realm of Yama, the god of death.

Public Worship

Temples

The basic form of the temple in India is a square cell, oriented to the four cardinal directions, containing a platform with an image of the deity in the center, a flat roof overhead, and a doorway on the east side. In front of the doorway is a porch or platform, shaded by a roof supported by pillars, where worshipers gather before and after approaching the god. At the founding of the temple, priests establish a sanctified area in the center of the shrine and, while praying and performing rituals, set up the image of the god. The deity is then said to be one with the image, which contains or manifests the power of the god on earth. Every Hindu temple in India, then, exists as the center of the universe, where the god overlooks his or her domain and aids devotees.

Worship at the temple is not congregational. Instead, individuals or small groups of devotees approach the sanctum in order to obtain a vision (*darshana*) of the god, say prayers, and perform devotional worship. Because the god exists in totality in the shrine, any objects that touch the image or even enter the sanctum are filled with power and, when returned to their givers, confer the grace of the divine on the human world. Only persons of requisite purity who have been specially trained are able to handle the power of the deity, and most temple sanctums are operated by priests who take the offerings from worshipers, present them directly to the image of the deity, and then return most of the gifts to the devotees for use or consumption later at home.

Since the sixth century, after the decline of Buddhism as the main focus of religious patronage, temples have been accumulating generous donations from kings, nobles, and the wealthy. The result is a huge number of shrines throughout the country, many of which, especially in South India, date back hundreds of years. The statuary and embellishment in some of the ancient shrines constitute one of the world's greatest artistic heritages. The layout of major temples has expanded into gigantic architectural complexes.

Along with architectural elaboration has come a complex administrative system to manage the many gifts bestowed by wealthy donors in the past and continually replenished by the piety of devotees in the present. The gods are legal landholders and command substantial investment portfolios throughout the country. The management of these fortunes in many states lies in the hands of private religious endowments, although in some states, such as Tamil Nadu, the state government manages most of the temples directly. Struggles over the control of temple administration have clogged the courts for several hundred years, and the news media readily report on the drama of these battles. Several cases have had an impact on religious, or communal, affairs. The most spectacular case involved ownership of a site in Ayodhya, Uttar Pradesh, claimed by Hindus as the site of Ram's birth but taken over by Muslims as the site for a mosque, the Babri Masjid, built in 1528. After much posturing by the conservative Bharatiya Janata Party (BJP—Indian People's Party) and its nationalist parent organization, the Rashtriya Swayamsevak Sangh (RSS—National Volunteer Organisation), matters came to a head in December 1992 (see Modern Transformations, this ch.; Political Parties, ch. 8). Some 200,000 militant Hindus, under the direction of RSS marshals, descended on Ayodhya, razing the Babri Masjid to the ground on December 6, 1992. Reprisals and communal violence occurred throughout India and in neighboring Pakistan and Bangladesh (see Political Issues, ch. 8).

Pilgrimage

India is covered with holy sites associated with the exploits of the gods, the waters of a sacred river, or the presence of holy men. Texts called the Puranas (ancient lore in Sanskrit) contain lengthy sections that describe numerous sacred places and the merit gained by traveling to them in a devout manner. Bathing at such sites is a specially meritorious act. With the

Ghats on the banks of the Ganga at Varanasi, Uttar Pradesh
Courtesy Bernice Huffman Collection, Library of Congress

expansion of public transportation in the twentieth century, there has been a vast increase in the numbers of people who visit these spots to partake of the divine and visit new places. In fact, for many Indians pilgrimage is the preferred form of tourism, involving family and community groups in enjoyable and uplifting vacations.

Certain important sites are well-known throughout India and attract hundreds of thousands of pilgrims annually. Probably the most significant is Varanasi (also known as Banaras, Benares, or Kashi) in southeastern Uttar Pradesh on the north bank of the Ganga. It is sacred to Hindus, Buddhists, and Jains, who flock to the ghats, or steps, leading from temples down to the banks of the sacred Ganga in their search for an auspicious site for death, cremation, or immersion of ashes. Hardwar, in northwestern Uttar Pradesh, far up the Ganga in the foothills of the Himalayas, is theVaranasi of northwest India for Hindus living there and is a favorite spot for ritual bathing. There are numerous destinations in the Himalayas, including Badrinath and Kedarnath, isolated sites in northern Uttar Pradesh that once required a long journey on foot. In southern India, the rivers Kaveri, Krishna, and Godavari attract pilgrims to a large number of bathing sites, and the coastline features major temples such as the Ramalingesvara Temple in Ramesvaram, Tamil Nadu, where Ram and his army crossed over to Lanka to rescue Sita. Pandharpur, in Maharashtra, is the destination for many thousands of devotees of Vitthala, an incarnation of Vishnu, whose tradition goes back at least to the thirteenth century and was written about by the great Marathi *bhakti* poets Namdev, Tukaram, and Eknath. There are smaller sites near almost every river or scenic hilltop.

For many pilgrims, the process of getting to their destination involves preliminary vows and fasting, intensive cooperative efforts among different families and groups, extensive traveling on foot, and the constant singing of devotional songs. On arrival, groups of pilgrims often make contact with priests who specialize in the pilgrim trade and for a fee plan the group's schedule and ritual activity. At some of the major sites, the families of the priests have served as hereditary guides for groups of pilgrims over many generations. Where a shrine is the focus, the devotee may circumambulate the buildings and wait in line for long hours just for a glimpse of the deity's image as security personnel move the crowds along. At auspicious bathing sites, pilgrims may have to wade through the crush of other devotees to dip into the sacred waters of a river or a tank. Worshipers engaged in special vows or in praying for the cure of a loved one may purchase shrine amulets to give to the god (which are circulated back to the shrine's shop) or purchase foodstuffs, sanctified by the god's presence, to take to friends and family. Nearby, souvenir hawkers and shopkeepers and sometimes even amusement parks contribute to a lively atmosphere that is certainly part of the attraction of many pilgrimage sites.

Festivals

A vast number of local Hindu festivals revolve around the worship of gods at the neighborhood, village, or caste level. All over India, at least once a year the images of the gods are taken from their shrines to travel in processions around their domains. The images are carried on palanquins that require human bearers or on human-drawn, large-wheeled carts. The images may be intricately made up in order for the stone or wooden statues to appear lifelike. They may wear costly vestments, and flower garlands may surround their necks or entire shrines. The gods move down village or city streets in parades that may include multiple palanquins and, at sites of major temples, even elephants decked out in traditional vestments. As the parade passes, throngs of worshipers pray and make vows to the gods while the community as a whole looks on and participates in the spectacle. In many locations, these public parades go on for a number of days and include special events where the gods engage in "play" (*lila*) that may include mock battles and the defeat of demons. The ceremonial bathing of the images and displays of the gods in all their finery in public halls also occur. In the south, where temples stand at the geographic and psychological heart of village and town, some "chariots" of the gods stand many stories tall and require the concerted effort of dozens of men to pull them through the streets.

There are a number of Hindu religious festivals that are officially recognized by the government as "closed holidays," on which work stops throughout the country. The biggest of these occur within two blocks of time after the end of the southwest monsoon. The first comes at the end of the ten-day festival of Dussehra, late in the month of Asvina (September–October) according to the Shaka calendar, India's official calendar (see table 14, Appendix). This festival commemorates Ram's victory over Ravana and the rescue of his wife Sita (see Vishnu, this ch.). On the ninth day of Dusshera, people bless with sandalwood paste the "weapons" of their business life, including everything from plows to computers. On the final day of Dussehra, in North India celebrating crowds set fire to huge paper effigies of Ravana. Several weeks later comes Dipavali (Diwali), or the Festival of Lights, in the month of Kartika (October–November). This is officially a one-day holiday, but in reality it becomes a week-long event when many people take vacations. One tradition links this festival to the victory of Krishna over the demon Naraka, but for most devotees the holiday is a recreation of Ram's triumphant return with Sita, his wife, from his adventures. People light rows of lamps and place them on sills around their houses, set off gigantic amounts of fireworks, pray for wealth and good fortune, distribute sweets, and send greeting cards to friends and business associates.

The other closed holidays associated with Hindu festivals include Mahashivaratri, or the great night of Shiva, during the month of Magha (January–February). This festival celebrates Shiva's emanation of the universe through his cosmic dance, and is a day of fasting, visiting temples, and in many places staying up all night to sing devotional songs. On the fourth day in the month of Bhadra (August–September) comes the festival of Ganesh Chaturthi. Families and businesses prepare for this festival by purchasing brightly painted images of Ganesh and worshiping them for a number of days. On the festival itself, with great celebration, participants bathe the images (and in most cases permanently dump them) in nearby rivers, lakes, or seas. Janmashtami, the birthday of Krishna, also occurs in the month of Bhadra.

There are a large number of "restricted holidays" celebrated by the vast majority of the population and resulting in closures of business establishments. Major Hindu events include Ramanavami, the birthday of Ram in the month of Chaitra (March–April), and Holi, celebrated at the end of the month of Phalguna (February–March), when people engage in cross-dressing, play tricks on each other, and squirt colored water or powder on each other. These primarily northern festivals receive varying amounts of attention in other parts of the country. A separate series of restricted holidays allow regional cultures to celebrate their own feasts, such as the harvest festival of Pongal in Tamil Nadu in mid-January, which celebrates the harvest and the sun's entrance into Capricorn.

Islam

Islam is India's largest minority religion, with Muslims officially comprising 12.1 percent of the country's population, or 101.6 million people as of the 1991 census. The largest concentrations—about 52 percent of all Muslims in India—live in the states of Bihar (12 million), West Bengal (16 million), and Uttar Pradesh (24 million), according to the 1991 census. Muslims represent a majority of the local populations only in Jammu and Kashmir (not tabulated in 1991 but 65 percent in 1981) and Lakshadweep (94 percent). As a faith with its roots outside South Asia, Islam also offers some striking contrasts to those religions that originated in India.

Origins and Tenets

Islam began with the ministry of the Prophet Muhammad (570–632), who belonged to a merchant family in the trading town of Mecca in Arabia. In his middle age, Muhammad received visions in which the Archangel Gabriel revealed the word of God to him. After 620 he publicly preached the message of these visions, stressing the oneness of God (Allah), denouncing the polytheism of his fellow Arabs, and calling for moral uplift of the population. He attracted a dedicated band of followers, but there was intense opposition from the leaders of the city, who profited from pilgrimage trade to the shrine called the Kaaba. In 622 Muhammad and his closest supporters migrated to the town of Yathrib (now renamed Medina) to the north and set up a new center of preaching and opposition to the leadership of Mecca. This move, the hijrah or hegira, marks the beginning of the Islamic calendar and the origin of the new religion of Islam. After a series of military engagements, Muhammad and his followers were able to defeat the authorities in Mecca and return to take control of the city. Before his death in 632, Muhammad was able to bring most of the tribes of Arabia into the fold of Islam. Soon after his death, the united Arabs conquered present-day Syria, Iraq, Egypt, and Iran, making Islam into a world religion by the end of the seventh century.

Islam means submission to God, and a Muslim is one who has submitted to the will of God. At the center of the religion is an intense concentration on the unity of God and the separation between God and his creatures. No physical representation of God is allowed. There are no other gods. The duty of humanity is to profess the simple testimony: "There is no god but God (Allah), and Muhammad is his Prophet." Obedience to God's will rests on following the example of the Prophet in one's own life and faithfulness to the revelations collected into the most sacred text, the Quran. The Five Pillars of Islam are reciting the profession of faith; praying five times a day; almsgiving to the poor; fasting (abstaining from dawn to dusk from food, drink, sexual relations, and smoking) during the month of Ramazan (the ninth month of the Islamic calendar, known as Ramadan in Arab countries), the holy month when God's revelations were received by Muhammad; and making the pilgrimage (hajj) to Mecca at least once during one's life if possible. People who obey God's commandments and live a good life will go to heaven after death; those who disobey will go to hell. All souls will be resurrected for a last judgment at the end of the world. Muslims view themselves as followers of the same tradition preserved in the Judaic and Christian scriptures, accept the prophetic roles of Ibrahim (Abraham), Musa (Moses), and Isa (Jesus), and view Islam as the final statement of revealed truth for the entire world.

Regulation of the Muslim community rests primarily on rules in the Quran, then on authenticated tales of the conduct (*sunna*) of the Prophet Muhammad, then on reasoning, and finally on the consensus of opinion. By the end of the eighth century, four main schools of Muslim jurisprudence had emerged in Sunni (see Glossary) Islam to interpret the sharia (Islamic law). Prominent among these groups was the Hanafi school, which dominated most of India, and the Shafii school, which was more prevalent in South India. Because Islam has no ordained priesthood, direction of the Muslim community rests on the learning of religious scholars (ulama) who are expert in understanding the Quran and its appended body of commentaries.

Early leadership controversies within the Muslim community led to divisions that still have an impact on the body of believers. When Muhammad died, leadership fell to his father-in-law, Abu Bakr, who became the first caliph (*khalifa*, or successor), a position that combined spiritual and secular power. A separate group advocated the leadership of Ali, the cousin and son-in-law of the Prophet, who had married his daughter Fatima. Leadership could have fallen to Ali's son Husayn, but, in the power struggle that followed, in 680 Husayn and seventy-two followers were murdered at Karbala (now in modern Iraq).

This leadership dispute formed the most crucial dividing point in Islamic history: the victorious party went on to found the Umayyad Dynasty (661–750), which had its headquarters at Damascus, leading the majority of Muslims in the Sunni path. The disaffected Shiat Ali (or Party of Ali) viewed only his line as legitimate and continued to follow descendants of Husayn as their leader (imam—see Glossary). Among the followers of this Shia (see Glossary) path, there is a party of "Seveners" who trace the lineage of imams down to Ismail (d. 762), the Seventh Imam and eldest son of the Sixth Imam. The Ismailis are the largest Shia group in India, and are concentrated in Maharashtra and Gujarat. A second group, the "Twelvers" (the most numerous Shia group worldwide), traces the lineage of imams through twelve generations, believing that the last or Twelfth Imam became "hidden" and will reappear in the world as a savior, or Mahdi, at some time in the future.

The division between Sunni and Shia dates back to purely political struggles in the seventh century, but over time between the two major communities many divisive differences in ritual and legal interpretations have evolved. The vast majority of Muslims are Sunni, and in contemporary India 90 percent of Muslims follow this path. Sunnis have recognized no legitimate caliph after the position was abolished in Turkey in 1924, placing the direction of the community clearly with the ulama.

Public worship for the average Muslim consists of going to a mosque (*masjid*)—normally on Fridays, although mosques are well attended throughout the week—for congregational prayers led by a local imam, following the public call to prayer, which may be intoned from the top of a minaret (*minar*) at the mosque. After leaving their footwear at the door, men and women separate; men usually sit in front, women in back, either inside the mosque or in an open courtyard. The prayer leader gives a sermon in the local regional language, perhaps interspersed with Arabic or Farsi (sometimes called Persian or Parsi) quotations, depending on his learning and the sophistication of the audience. Announcements of events of interest that may include political commentary are often included. Then follow common prayers that involve responses from the worshipers who stand, bow, and kneel in unison during devotions.

Islamic Traditions in South Asia

Muslims practice a series of life-cycle rituals that differ from those of Hindus, Jains, or Buddhists. The newborn baby has the call to prayer whispered into the left ear, the profession of faith whispered into the right ear, honey or date paste placed in the mouth, and a name selected. On the sixth day after birth, the first bath occurs. On the seventh day or a multiple of the seventh, the head is shaved, and alms are distributed, ideally in silver weighing as much as the hair; a sacrifice of animals imitates the sheep sacrificed instead of Ishmael (Ismail) in biblical times. Religious instruction starts at age four years, four months, and four days, beginning with the standard phrase: "In the name of God, the Beneficent, the Merciful." Male circumcision takes place between the ages of seven and twelve. Marriage requires a payment by the husband to the wife and the solemnization of a marital contract in a social gathering. Marriage ceremonies include the donning of a nose ring by the bride, or in South India a wedding necklace, and the procession of the bridegroom. In a traditional wedding, males and females attend ceremonies in different rooms, in keeping with the segregation of sexes in most social settings. After death the family members wash and enshroud the body, after which it is buried as prayers from the Quran are recited. On the third day, friends and relatives come to console the bereaved, read the Quran, and pray for the soul of the deceased. The family observe a mourning period of up to forty days.

The annual festivals of Islam are based on a lunar calendar of 354 days, which makes the Islamic holy year independent of the Gregorian calendar. Muslim festivals make a complete circuit of the solar year every thirty-three years.

The beginning of the Islamic calendar is the month of Muharram, the tenth day of which is Ashura, the anniversary of the death of Husayn, the son of Ali. Ashura, a major holiday, is of supreme importance for the Shia. Devotees engage in ritualized mourning that may include processions of colorful replicas of Husayn's tomb at Karbala and standards with palms on top, which are carried by barefoot mourners and buried at an imitation Karbala. In many areas of India, these parades provide a dramatic spectacle that draws large numbers of non-Muslim onlookers. Demonstrations of grief may include bouts of self-flagellation that can draw blood and may take place in public streets, although many families retain personal mourning houses. Sunni Muslims may also commemorate

*A late nineteenth-century view of the Jama Masjid (Friday Mosque),
India's largest mosque, built in the seventeenth century, Delhi
Courtesy Stereograph Collection, Library of Congress*

Husayn's death but in a less demonstrative manner, concentrating instead on the redemptive aspect of his martyrdom.

The last day of Ramazan is Id al Fitr (Feast of Breaking the Fast), another national holiday, which ends the month of fasting with almsgiving, services in mosques, and visits to friends and neighbors. Bakr Id, or Id al Zuha (Feast of Sacrifice), begins on the tenth day of the Islamic month of Dhul Hijjah and is a major holiday. Prescribed in the Quran, Id al Zuha commemorates Ibrahim's willingness to sacrifice Ishmael (rather than Ishaq—Isaac—as in the Judeo-Christian tradition) according to God's command, but it is also the high point of the pilgrim's ritual cycle while on the hajj in Mecca. All of these festivals involve large feasts, gifts given to family and neighbors, and the distribution of food for charitable purposes.

A significant aspect of Islam in India is the importance of

shrines attached to the memory of great Sufi saints. Sufism is a mystical path (*tariqat*) as distinct from the path of the sharia. A Sufi attains a direct vision of oneness with God, often on the edges of orthodox behavior, and can thus become a *pir* (living saint) who may take on disciples (*murids*) and set up a spiritual lineage that can last for generations. Orders of Sufis became important in India during the thirteenth century following the ministry of Muinuddin Chishti (1142–1236), who settled in Ajmer, Rajasthan, and attracted large numbers of converts to Islam because of his holiness. His Chishtiyya order went on to become the most influential Sufi lineage in India, although other orders from Central Asia and Southwest Asia also reached to India and played a large role in the spread of Islam. Many Sufis were well known for weaving music, dance, intoxicants, and local folktales into their songs and lectures. In this way, they created a large literature in regional languages that embedded Islamic culture deeply into older South Asian traditions.

In the case of many great teachers, the memory of their holiness has been so intense that they are still viewed as active intercessors with God, and their tombs have become the site of rites and prayers by disciples and lay people alike. Tales of miraculous deeds associated with the tombs of great saints have attracted large numbers of pilgrims attempting to gain cures for physical maladies or solutions to personal problems. The tomb of the *pir* thus becomes a *dargah* (gateway) to God and the focus for a wide range of rituals, such as daily washing and decoration by professional attendants, touching or kissing the tomb or contact with the water that has washed it, hanging petitions on the walls of the shrine surrounding the tomb, lighting incense, and giving money.

The descendants of the original *pir* are sometimes seen as inheritors of his spiritual energy, and, as *pirs* in their own right, they might dispense amulets sanctified by contact with them or with the tomb. The annual celebration of the *pir's* death is a major event at important shrines, attracting hundreds of thousands of devotees for celebrations that may last for days. Free communal kitchens and distribution of sweets are also big attractions of these festivals, at which Muslim fakirs, or wandering ascetics, sometimes appear and where public demonstrations of self-mortification, such as miraculous piercing of the body and spiritual possession of devotees, sometimes occur. Every region of India can boast of at least one major Sufi shrine

*A Muslim bride, Madhya
Pradesh
Courtesy Doranne Jacobson*

that attracts expressive devotion, which remains important, especially for Muslim women.

The leadership of the Muslim community has pursued various directions in the evolution of Indian Islam during the twentieth century. The most conservative wing has typically rested on the education system provided by the hundreds of religious training institutes (*madrasa*) throughout the country, which have tended to stress the study of the Quran and Islamic texts in Arabic and Persian, and have focused little on modern managerial and technical skills (see Education and Society, ch. 2). Several national movements have emerged from this sector of the Muslim community. The Jamaati Islami (Islamic Party), founded in 1941, advocates the establishment of an overtly Islamic government through peaceful, democratic, and non-missionary activities. It had about 3,000 active members and 40,000 sympathizers in the mid-1980s. The Tablighi Jamaat (Outreach Society) became active after the 1940s as a movement, primarily among the ulama, stressing personal renewal, prayer, a missionary and cooperative spirit, and attention to orthodoxy. It has been highly critical of the kind of activities that occur in and around Sufi shrines and remains a minor if respected force in the training of the ulama. Other ulama have upheld the legitimacy of mass religion, including exaltation of *pirs* and the memory of the Prophet. A powerful secularizing drive led to the founding of Aligarh Muslim University (founded in 1875 as the Muhammadan Anglo-Oriental College)—with its modern curriculum—and other major Muslim universities. This educational drive has remained the most dominant force in guiding the Muslim community.

Sikhism

Sikhism has about 20 million believers worldwide but has an importance far beyond those numbers because Sikhs have played a disproportionately large role in the armed forces and public affairs in India for the last 400 years. Although most Indian Sikhs (79 percent) remain concentrated in the state of Punjab, nearly 3.5 million Sikhs live outside the state, while about 4 million live abroad. This Sikh diaspora, driven by ambition and economic success, has made Sikhism a world religion as well as a significant minority force within the country.

Early History and Tenets

Sikhism began with Guru Nanak (1469–1539), a member of a trading caste in Punjab who seems to have been employed for some time as a government servant, was married and had two sons, and at age forty-five became a religious teacher. At the heart of his message was a philosophy of universal love, devotion to God, and the equality of all men and women before God. He set up congregations of believers who ate together in free communal kitchens in an overt attempt to break down caste boundaries based on food prohibitions. As a poet, musician, and enlightened master, Nanak's reputation spread, and by the time he died he had founded a new religion of "disciples" (*shiksha* or sikh) that followed his example.

Nanak's son, Baba Sri Chand, founded the Udasi sect of celibate ascetics, which continued in the 1990s. However, Nanak chose as his successor not his son but Angad (1504–52), his chief disciple, to carry on the work as the second guru. Thus began a lineage of teachers that lasted until 1708 and amounted to ten gurus in the Sikh tradition, each of whom is viewed as an enlightened master who propounded directly the word of God. The third guru, Amar Das (1479–1574), established missionary centers to spread the message and was so well respected that the Mughal emperor Akbar visited him (see The

Mughals, ch. 1). Amar Das appointed his son-in-law Ram Das (1534–81) to succeed him, establishing a hereditary succession for the position of guru. He also built a tank for water at Amritsar in Punjab, which, after his death, became the holiest center of Sikhism.

By the late sixteenth century, the influence of the Sikh religion on Punjabi society was coming to the notice of political authorities. The fifth guru, Arjun Das (1563–1606), was executed in Lahore by the Mughal emperor Jahangir (r. 1605–27) for alleged complicity in a rebellion. In response, the next guru, Hargobind (d. 1644), militarized and politicized his position and fought three battles with Mughal forces. Hargobind established a militant tradition of resistance to persecution by the central government in Delhi that remains an important motif in Sikh consciousness. Hargobind also established at Amritsar, in front of the Golden Temple, the central shrine devoted to Sikhism, the Throne of the Eternal God (Akal Takht) from which the guru dispensed justice and administered the secular affairs of the community, clearly establishing the tradition of a religious state that remains a major issue. The ninth guru, Tegh Bahadur (1621–75), because he refused Mughal emperor Aurangzeb's order to convert to Islam, was brought to Delhi and beheaded on a site that later became an important *gurdwara* (abode of the guru, a Sikh temple) on Chandni Chauk, one of the old city's main thoroughfares.

These events led the tenth guru, Gobind Singh (1666–1708), to transform the Sikhs into a militant brotherhood dedicated to defense of their faith at all times. He instituted a baptism ceremony involving the immersion of a sword in sugared water that initiates Sikhs into the Khalsa (*khalsa*, from the Persian term for "the king's own," often taken to mean army of the pure) of dedicated devotion. The outward signs of this new order were the "Five Ks" to be observed at all times: uncut hair (*kesh*), a long knife (*kirpan*), a comb (*kangha*), a steel bangle (*kara*), and a special kind of breeches not reaching below the knee (*kachha*). Male Sikhs took on the surname Singh (meaning lion), and women took the surname Kaur (princess). All made vows to purify their personal behavior by avoiding intoxicants, including alcohol and tobacco. In modern India, male Sikhs who have dedicated themselves to the Khalsa do not cut their beards and keep their long hair tied up under turbans, preserving a distinctive personal appearance recognized throughout the world.

Much of Guru Gobind Singh's later life was spent on the move, in guerrilla campaigns against the Mughal Empire, which was entering the last days of its effective authority under Aurangzeb (1658–1707). After Gobind Singh's death, the line of gurus ended, and their message continued through the *Adi Granth* (Original Book), which dates from 1604 and later became known as the *Guru Granth Sahib* (Holy Book of the Gurus). The *Guru Granth Sahib* is revered as a continuation of the line of gurus and as the living word of God by all Sikhs and stands at the heart of all ceremonies.

Most of the Sikh gurus were excellent musicians, who composed songs that conveyed their message to the masses in the saints' own language, which combined variants of Punjabi with Hindi and Braj and also contained Arabic and Persian vocabulary. Written in Gurmukhi script, these songs are one of the main sources of early Punjabi language and literature. There are 5,894 hymns in all, arranged according to the musical measure in which they are sung. An interesting feature of this literature is that 937 songs and poems are by well-known *bhakti* saints who were not members of the lineage of Sikh gurus, including the North Indian saint Kabir and five Muslim devotees. In the *Guru Granth Sahib,* God is called by all the Hindu names and by Allah as well. From its beginnings, then, Sikhism was an inclusive faith that attempted to encompass and enrich other Indian religious traditions.

The belief system propounded by the gurus has its origins in the philosophy and devotions of Hinduism and Islam, but the formulation of Sikhism is unique. God is the creator of the universe and is without qualities or differentiation in himself. The universe (*samsar*) is not sinful in its origin but is covered with impurities; it is not suffering, but a transitory opportunity for the soul to recognize its true nature and break the cycle of rebirth. The unregenerate person is dominated by self-interest and remains immersed in illusion (*maya*), leading to bad karma. Meanwhile, God desires that his creatures escape and achieve enlightenment (nirvana) by recognizing his order in the universe. He does this by manifesting his grace as a holy word, attainable through recognition and recitation of God's holy name (*nam*). The role of the guru, who is the manifestation of God in the world, is to teach the means for prayer through the *Guru Granth Sahib* and the community of believers. The guru in this system, and by extension the *Guru Granth*

*The Golden Temple of the Sikhs, Amritsar, Punjab, in a late
nineteenth-century photograph
Courtesy Stereograph Collection, Library of Congress*

Sahib, are coexistent with the divine and play a decisive role in
saving the world.

Where the *Guru Granth Sahib* is present, that place becomes
a *gurdwara.* Many Sikh homes contain separate rooms or designated areas where a copy of the book stands as the center of
devotional ceremonies. Throughout Punjab, or anywhere there
is a substantial body of believers, there are special shrines
where the *Guru Granth Sahib* is displayed permanently or is
installed daily in a ceremonial manner. These public *gurdwaras*
are the centers of Sikh community life and the scene of periodic assemblies for worship. The typical assembly involves
group singing from the *Guru Granth Sahib,* led by distinguished
believers or professional singers attached to the shrine, distribution of holy food, and perhaps a sermon delivered by the
custodian of the shrine.

As for domestic and life-cycle rituals, well into the twentieth century many Sikhs followed Hindu customs for birth, marriage, and death ceremonies, including readings from Hindu scriptures and the employment of Brahmans as officiants. Reform movements within the Sikh community have purged many of these customs, substituting instead readings from the *Guru Granth Sahib* as the focus for rituals and the employment of Sikh ritual specialists. At major public events—weddings, funerals, or opening a new business—patrons may fund a reading of the entire *Guru Granth Sahib* by special reciters.

Twentieth-Century Developments

The existence of the Khalsa creates a potential division within the Sikh community between those who have undergone the baptism ceremony and those who practice the system laid down in the *Guru Granth Sahib* but who do not adopt the distinctive life-style of the Khalsa. Among the latter is a sect of believers founded by Baba Dayal (d. 1853) named the Nirankaris, who concentrate on the formless quality of God and his revelation purely through the guru and the *Guru Granth Sahib*, and who accept the existence of a living, enlightened teacher as essential for spiritual development. The dominant tendency among the Sikhs since the late nineteenth century has been to stress the importance of the Khalsa and its outward signs.

Revivalist movements of the late nineteenth century centered on the activities of the Singh Sabha (Assembly of Lions), who successfully moved much of the Sikh community toward their own ritual systems and away from Hindu customs, and culminated in the Akali (eternal) mass movement in the 1920s to take control of *gurdwaras* away from Hindu managers and invest it in an organization representing the Sikhs. The result was passage of the Sikh Gurdwara Act of 1925, which established the Central Gurdwara Management Committee to manage all Sikh shrines in Punjab, Haryana, and Himachal Pradesh through an assembly of elected Sikhs. The combined revenues of hundreds of shrines, which collected regular contributions and income from endowments, gave the committee a large operating budget and considerable authority over the religious life of the community. A simultaneous process led to the Akali Dal (Eternal Party), a political organization that originally coordinated nonviolent agitations to gain control over *gurdwaras*, then participated in the independence struggle, and since 1947 has competed for control over the Punjab state government. The ideology of the Akali Dal is simple—single-minded devotion to the guru and preservation of the Sikh faith through political power—and the party has served to mobilize a majority of Sikhs in Punjab around issues that stress Sikh separatism.

There is no official priesthood within Sikhism or any widely accepted institutional mechanism for policy making for the entire faith. Instead, decisions are made by communities of believers (*sangat*) based on the *Guru Granth Sahib*—a tradition dating back to the eighteenth century when scattered bodies of believers had to fight against persecution and manage their own affairs. Anyone may study the scriptures intensively and become a "knower" (*giani*) who is recognized by fellow believers, and there is a variety of training institutes with full-time students and teachers.

Leaders of sects and sectarian training institutions may feel free to issue their own orders. When these orders are combined with the prestige and power of the Central Gurdwara Management Committee and the Akali Dal, which have explicitly narrow administrative goals and are often faction-ridden, a mixture of images and authority emerges that often leaves the religion as a whole without clear leadership. Thus it became possible for Sant Jarnail Singh Bhindranwale, head of a training institution, to stand forth as a leading authority on the direction of Sikhism; initiate reforms of personal morality; participate in the persecution of Nirankaris; and take effective control of the holiest Sikh shrine, the Golden Temple in Amritsar, Punjab, in the early 1980s. His takeover of the Golden Temple led to a violent siege and culminated in the devastation of the shrine by the army in 1984 (see The Rise of Indira Gandhi, ch. 1; Insurgent Movements and External Subversion, ch. 10). Later terrorist activities in Punjab, carried out in the name of Sikhism, were performed by a wide range of organizations claiming to represent an authoritative vision of the nature and direction of the community as a whole.

Other Minority Religions

Tribal Religions

Among the 68 million citizens of India who are members of tribal groups, the religious concepts, terminologies, and practices are as varied as the hundreds of tribes, but members of these groups have one thing in common: they are under constant pressure from the major organized religions. Some of this pressure is intentional, as outside missionaries work among tribal groups to gain converts. Most of the pressure, however, comes from the process of integration within a national political and economic system that brings tribes into increasing contact with other groups and different, prestigious belief systems. In general, those tribes that remain geographically isolated in desert, hill, and forest regions or on islands are able to retain their traditional cultures and religions longer. Those tribes that make the transition away from hunting and gathering and toward sedentary agriculture, usually as low-status laborers, find their ancient religious forms in decay and their place filled by practices of Hinduism, Islam, Christianity, or Buddhism.

One of the most studied tribal religions is that of the Santal of Orissa, Bihar, and West Bengal, one of the largest tribes in India, having a population estimated at 4.2 million. According to the 1991 census, however, only 23,645 people listed Santal as their religious belief.

According to the Santal religion, the supreme deity, who ultimately controls the entire universe, is Thakurji. The weight of belief, however, falls on a court of spirits (*bonga*), who handle different aspects of the world and who must be placated with prayers and offerings in order to ward off evil influences. These spirits operate at the village, household, ancestor, and subclan level, along with evil spirits that cause disease, and can inhabit village boundaries, mountains, water, tigers, and the forest. A characteristic feature of the Santal village is a sacred grove on the edge of the settlement where many spirits live and where a series of annual festivals take place.

The most important spirit is Maran Buru (Great Mountain), who is invoked whenever offerings are made and who instructed the first Santals in sex and brewing of rice beer. Maran Buru's consort is the benevolent Jaher Era (Lady of the Grove).

A yearly round of rituals connected with the agricultural cycle, along with life-cycle rituals for birth, marriage and burial at death, involves petitions to the spirits and offerings that include the sacrifice of animals, usually birds. Religious leaders are male specialists in medical cures who practice divination and witchcraft. Similar beliefs are common among other tribes of northeast and central India such as the Kharia, Munda, and Oraon.

Smaller and more isolated tribes often demonstrate less articulated classification systems of the spiritual hierarchy, described as animism or a generalized worship of spiritual energies connected with locations, activities, and social groups. Religious concepts are intricately entwined with ideas about nature and interaction with local ecological systems. As in Santal religion, religious specialists are drawn from the village or family and serve a wide range of spiritual functions that focus on placating potentially dangerous spirits and coordinating rituals.

Unlike the Santal, who have a large population long accustomed to agriculture and a distinguished history of resistance to outsiders, many smaller tribal groups are quite sensitive to ecological degradation caused by modernization, and their unique religious beliefs are under constant threat. Even among the Santal, there are 300,000 Christians who are alienated from traditional festivals, although even among converts the belief in the spirits remains strong. Among the Munda and Oraon in Bihar, about 25 percent of the population are Christians. Among the Kharia of Bihar (population about 130,000), about 60 percent are Christians, but all are heavily influenced by Hindu concepts of major deities and the annual Hindu cycle of festivals. Tribal groups in the Himalayas were similarly affected by both Hinduism and Buddhism in the late twentieth century. Even the small hunting-and-gathering groups in the union territory of Andaman and Nicobar Islands have been under severe pressure because of immigration to this area and the resulting reduction of their hunting area.

Christianity

The first Christians in India, according to tradition and legend, were converted by Saint Thomas the Apostle, who arrived on the Malabar Coast of India in A.D. 52. After evangelizing and performing miracles in Kerala and Tamil Nadu, he is believed to have been martyred in Madras and buried on the site of San Thomé Cathedral. Members of the Syro-Malabar Church, an eastern rite of the Roman Catholic Church, adopted the Syriac liturgy dating from fourth century Antioch. They practiced what is also known as the Malabar rite until the arrival of the Portuguese in the late fifteenth century. Soon thereafter, the Portuguese attempted to latinize the Malabar rite, an action which, by the mid-sixteenth century, led to charges of heresy against the Syro-Malabar Church and a lengthy round of political machinations. By the middle of the next century, a schism occurred when the adherents of the Malankar rite (or Syro-Malankara Church) broke away from the Syro-Malabar Church. Fragmentation continued within the Syro-Malabar Church up through the early twentieth century when a large contingent left to join the Nestorian Church, which had had its own roots in India since the sixth or seventh century. By 1887, however, the leaders of the Syro-Malabar Church had reconciled with Rome, which formally recognized the legitimacy of the Malabar rite. The Syro-Malankara Church was reconciled with Rome in 1930 and, while retaining the Syriac liturgy, adopted the Malayalam language instead of the ancient Syriac language.

Throughout this period, foreign missionaries made numerous converts to Christianity. Early Roman Catholic missionaries, particularly the Portuguese, led by the Jesuit Saint Francis Xavier (1506–52), expanded from their bases on the west coast making many converts, especially among lower castes and outcastes. The miraculously undecayed body of Saint Francis Xavier is still on public view in a glass coffin at the Basilica of Bom Jesus in Goa. Beginning in the eighteenth century, Protestant missionaries began to work throughout India, leading to the growth of Christian communities of many varieties.

The total number of Christians in India according to the 1991 census was 19.6 million, or 2.3 percent of the population. About 13.8 million of these Christians were Roman Catholics, including 300,000 members of the Syro-Malankara Church. The remainder of Roman Catholics were under the Catholic Bishops' Conference of India. In January 1993, after centuries of self-government, the 3.5-million-strong Latin-rite Syro-Malabar Church was raised to archepiscopate status as part of the Roman Catholic Church. In total, there were nineteen archbishops, 103 bishops, and about 15,000 priests in India in 1995.

Most Protestant denominations are represented in India, the result of missionary activities throughout the country, starting with the onset of British rule. Most denominations, however, are almost exclusively staffed by Indians, and the role of foreign missionaries is limited. The largest Protestant denomination in the country is the Church of South India, since 1947 a union of Presbyterian, Reformed, Congregational, Methodist, and Anglican congregations with approximately 2.2 million members. A similar Church of North India has 1 million members. There are 473,000 Methodists, 425,000 Baptists, and about 1.3 million Lutherans. Orthodox churches of the Malankara and Malabar rites total 2 million and 700,000 members, respectively.

All Christian churches have found the most fertile ground for expansion among Dalits, Scheduled Castes, and Scheduled Tribe groups (see Tribes, ch. 4). During the twentieth century, the fastest growing Christian communities have been located in the northeast, among the Khasis, Mizos, Nagas, and other hill tribes. Christianity offers a non-Hindu mode of acculturation during a period when the state and modern economy have been radically transforming the life-styles of the hill peoples. Missionaries have led the way in the development of written languages and literature for many tribal groups. Christian churches have provided a focus for unity among different ethnic groups and have brought with them a variety of charitable services.

Zoroastrianism

According to the 1991 census, there were 79,382 members of the Zoroastrian faith. Some 79 percent lived in Maharashtra (primarily in Bombay) and most of the rest in Gujarat. Zoroastrians are primarily descendants of tenth-century immigrants from Persia who preserved the religion of Zoroaster, a prophet of Iran who taught probably in the sixth century B.C. Although the number of Parsis steadily declined during the twentieth century as a result of emigration and low birth rates, their religion is significant because of the financial influence wielded by this mostly trading community and because they represent the world's largest surviving group of believers in this ancient faith.

Originally, the Parsis were shipbuilders and traders located in the ports and towns of Gujarat. Their freedom from food or occupational restrictions based on caste affiliation enabled them to take advantage of the numerous commercial opportunities that accompanied the colonial expansion of trade and control. Substantial numbers moved to Bombay, which served as a base for expanding their business activities throughout India and abroad. A combination of Western commercial contacts and English-language education during the colonial period made the Parsis arguably the most cosmopolitan community in India. Socially, they were equally at home with Indians and Westerners; Parsi women enjoyed freedom of movement earlier than most high-caste Hindu or upper-class

Muslim women. In contemporary India, Parsis are the most urban, elite, and wealthy of any of the nation's religious groups. Their role in the development of trade, industry, finance, and philanthropy has earned them an important place in the country's social and economic life, and several have achieved high rank in government.

The source of Parsi religion is a body of texts called the *Avesta*, which includes a number of sections in archaic language attributed to Zoroaster himself, and which preserve the cult of the fire sacrifice as the focus of ritual life. The supreme spirit is Ahura Mazda (or Ohrmazd), whose will is manifest in the world through the actions of bountiful immortals or good spiritual attributes that support life and love. Opposing the supreme spirit is the force of evil, Angra Mainyu (or Ahriman), which is the cause of all destruction and corruption in the world. Equipped with free will, humans can choose sides in this struggle and after death will appear at the bridge of judgment. People who choose to do good deeds go to heaven, those who commit evil go to hell. The opposed cosmic forces battle through the history of the universe, until at the end of time there will be a final judgment and a resurrection of the dead to a perfect world.

The extensive ritual life of devout Parsis revolves around sacred fires, of which there are three grades dependent on extensive ceremonial preparation. The highest two grades can only be maintained in fire temples by hereditary priests, who undergo extensive purificatory rites and wear special face masks to prevent polluting the flames with breath or saliva, while the third grade of fire can exist in the household. The most important rite for most lay people is the Navjote, which occurs between the seventh and fifteenth year of life, and initiates the young person into the adult community. The ceremony involves purifying bathing, reciting *Avesta*-based scriptures, and being invested with a sacred shirt (*sudrah*) and waist thread (*kusti*) that should always be worn thereafter. Marriage is also an important rite, complete with scriptural recitations. At death, great care is taken to avoid pollution from the body, and funeral services usually take place within twenty-four hours. The dead are then disposed of by exposure to vultures on large, circular "towers of silence" (*dakhma*). Most rituals take place in the home or in special pavilions; congregational worship at fire temples is limited to spring and autumn festivals.

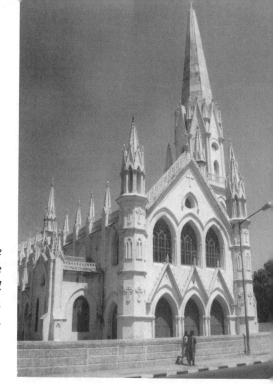

San Thomé Cathedral, the burial place of Saint Thomas the Apostle, in Madras, Tamil Nadu
Courtesy Robert L. Worden

The towns of Sanjan, Nausari, and Udvada in Gujarat are of prime importance to Parsis, having long served as community centers before mass migration to Bombay in the nineteenth century. Bombay is home to 70 percent of India's Parsis, where the management of Parsi affairs rests in the hands of a *panchayat* (see Glossary), the assembly that serves as a charitable and educational organization providing a comprehensive social welfare system at the local level.

Judaism

Trade contacts between the Mediterranean region and the west coast of India probably led to the presence of small Jewish settlements in India as long ago as the early first millennium B.C. In Kerala a community of Jews tracing its origin to the fall of Jerusalem in A.D. 70 has remained associated with the cities of Cranganore and Kochi (formerly known as Cochin) for at least 1,000 years. The Pardesi Synagogue in Kochi, rebuilt in 1568, is in the architectural style of Kerala but preserves the archaic ritual style of the Sephardic rite, with Babylonian and Yemenite influence as well. The Jews of Kochi, concentrated mostly in the old "Jew Town," were completely integrated into local culture, speaking Malayalam and taking local names while preserving their knowledge of Hebrew and contacts with

Southwest Asia. A separate community of Jews, called the Bene Israel, had lived along the Konkan Coast in and around Bombay, Pune, and Ahmadabad for almost 2,000 years. Unlike the Kochi Jews, they became a village-based society and maintained little contact with other Jewish communities. They always remained within the orthodox Jewish fold, practicing the Sephardic rite without rabbis, with the synagogue as the center of religious and cultural life. A third group of Jews immigrated to India, beginning at the end of the eighteenth century, following the trade contacts established by the British Empire. These Baghdad Jews came mostly from the area of modern Iraq and settled in Bombay and Calcutta, where many of them became wealthy and participated in the economic leadership of these growing cities.

The population of the Kochi Jews, always small, had decreased from 5,000 in 1951 to about fifty in the early 1990s. During the same period, the Bene Israel decreased from about 20,000 to 5,000, while the Baghdad Jews declined from 5,000 to 250. Emigration to Australia, Israel, Britain, and North America accounts for most of this decline. According to the 1981 Indian census, there were 5,618 Jews in India, down from 5,825 in 1971. The 1991 census showed a further decline to 5,271, most of whom lived in Maharashtra and Mizoram.

Modern Transformations

The process of modernization in India, well under way during the British colonial period (1757–1947), has brought with it major changes in the organizational forms of all religions. The missionary societies that came with the British in the early nineteenth century imported, along with modern concepts of print media and propaganda, an ideology of intellectual competition and religious conversion. Instead of the customary interpretation of rituals and texts along received sectarian lines, Indian religious leaders began devising intellectual syntheses that could encompass the varied beliefs and practices of their traditions within a framework that could withstand Christian arguments.

One of the most important reactions was the Arya Samaj (Arya Society), founded in 1875 by Swami Dayananda (1824–83), which went back to the Vedas as the ultimate revealed source of truth and attempted to purge Hinduism of more recent accretions that had no basis in the scriptures. Originally active in Punjab, this small society still works to purify Hindu rituals, converts tribal people, and runs centers throughout India. Other responses include the Ramakrishna order of renunciants established by Swami Vivekananda (1863–1902), which set forth a unifying philosophy that followed the Vedanta teacher Shankara and other teachers by accepting all paths as ultimately leading toward union with the undifferentiated *brahman* (see The Tradition of the Enlightened Master, this ch.). One of the primary goals of the Ramakrishna movement has been to educate Hindus about their own scriptures; the movement also runs book stores and study centers in all major cities. Both of these paths are directly modeled on the institutional and intellectual forms used by European missionaries and religious leaders.

During the 1930s and 1940s, again responding to institutional models from Europe, the more activist Rashtriya Swayamsevak Sangh (RSS—National Volunteer Organisation) emerged to protect Hinduism. The RSS had been founded in 1925 by Keshav Baliram Hedgewar (1889–1944), a native of Maharashtra who was concerned that Hinduism was in danger of extinction from its external foes and needed a strong, militant force of devotees to protect it. Members believe that the Indian nation is the divine mother to whom the citizen devotes mind and body through *karma-yoga*, or disciplined service. Training consists of daily early morning meetings at which the saffron, white, and green Indian flag and the swallow-tailed, red-ocher RSS banner are raised as rows of members salute silently. There are then group drills in gymnastic exercises, sports, discussions of patriotic themes from a primarily Hindu viewpoint, group singing of nationalist songs, and a final assembly with saluting. Throughout India in the early 1990s, there were cells (*shakha*) of fifty to 100 members from all walks of life (the RSS rejects class differences) who were devoted to the nation. Although it has attracted hundreds of thousands of members from all over India, the RSS has never projected itself as a political party, always remaining a national club that is ready to send its members to trouble spots for the defense of the nation and the national culture, embodied in Hinduism. The Jana Sangh, established in 1951, was the RSS's political arm until it joined the Janata Party in 1977 and its membership split away in 1980 to form the BJP.

Another activist organization is the Vishwa Hindu Parishad (VHP—World Hindu Council), founded in 1964. The VHP runs schools, medical centers, hostels, orphanages, and mass movements to support Hinduism wherever it is perceived as threatened. This ultraconservative organization played a role in the extensive agitation for the demolition of a mosque in Ayodhya, leading to the destruction of the structure during a huge demonstration in 1992. As a result of the VHP's complicity in the affair, the Ministry of Home Affairs imposed a two-year ban on the Vishwa Hindu Parishad under the Unlawful Activities Act. When the ban expired in December 1994, the government reimposed it for two additional years.

The spread of Hindu "communal" (that is, religious) sentiment parallels a similar rise in religious chauvinism and "fundamentalist" ideologies among religious minorities, including Muslims and Sikhs. Against this background of agitation, the periodic outbreak of communal riots in urban areas throughout India contributes to an atmosphere of religious tension that has been a hallmark of the national political scene during the twentieth century. Hindu-Muslim riots, especially in North India, reached a peak during the partition of India in 1947 and periodically escalated in urban areas in the early 1990s (see Political Impasse and Independence, ch. 1). This strife typically involves low-income groups from both communities in struggles over land, jobs, or local resources that coalesced around a religious focus after seemingly trivial incidents polarized the two communities. In practice, although members of other religious communities are the victims of violence, rioters are rarely motivated by religious instructors, although fundamentalist agitators are often implicated. The situation in North India became complicated during the 1980s by Sikh terrorism connected with the crisis in Punjab, the widespread anti-Sikh riots after Prime Minister Indira Gandhi's assassination in November 1984 by her Sikh bodyguards, and a series of terrorist or counterterrorist actions lasting into the 1990s. In all of these cases, many observers believe that religion has appeared as a cover for political and economic struggles.

The perception that one's religion is in danger receives periodic reinforcement from the phenomenon of public mass religious conversion that receives coverage from the news media. Many of these events feature groups of Scheduled Caste members who attempt to escape social disabilities through conversion to alternative religions, usually Islam, Buddhism, or Christianity. These occasions attract the attention of fundamentalist organizations from all sides and heighten public consciousness of religious divisions. The most conspicuous movement of this sort occurred during the 1950s during the mass conversions of Mahars to Buddhism (see Buddhism, this ch.). In the early 1980s, the primary example was the conversion of Dalits to Islam in Meenakshipuram, Tamil Nadu, an event that resulted in considerable discussion in the media and an escalation of agitation in South India. Meanwhile, conversions to Christianity among tribal groups continue, with growing opposition from Hindu revivalist organizations.

Alongside the more publicized violent outbreaks, there have been major nonviolent changes, as new sectarian movements continue to grow and as established movements change. For example, the Radhasoami Satsang movement of North India, which includes adherents in Punjab and Uttar Pradesh, encompasses yogic ideas on the relationship between humans and the universe, the *bhakti* saint tradition including select Sikh influences, and the veneration of the enlightened guru. The dominant tendency of these new religions, following the example of the great teachers of the past that was reiterated by Mahatma Gandhi and most modern gurus, remains nonviolence to all living beings and acceptance of the remarkable diversity of Indian religion.

*   *   *

Introductory sources on Hinduism include David R. Kinsley's *Hinduism: A Cultural Perspective* and David M. Knipe's *Hinduism: Experiments in the Sacred*. For a deeper immersion into the classical textual tradition, a number of books by Wendy Doniger O'Flaherty, including *Hindu Myths: A Source Book Translated from the Sanskrit*, provide excellent translations and straightforward commentary. David Shulman has prepared a number of up-to-date translations of Tamil literature, including *Songs of the Harsh Devotee*. Lawrence A. Babb has written several introductions to modern Hinduism, such as *The Divine Hierarchy*, which deals with rural life, and *Redemptive Encounters*, which discusses recent innovations, mostly among urbanites. A good study of pilgrimage and modern devotion, in this case in Maharashtra, is *Palkhi: An Indian Pilgrimage* by D.B. Mokashi. A short study of temples as architectural and social institutions is George Michell's *The Hindu Temple*.

For Jainism, a good survey is Padmanabh S. Jaini's *The Jaina Path of Purification*. Historical introductions to Buddhism include Edward J. Thomas's *The Life of Buddha as Legend and*

History, Richard H. Robinson and Willard J. Johnson's *The Buddhist Religion,* and Peter Harvey's *An Introduction to Buddhism.*

For Islam, *The Muslims of India: Beliefs and Practices* edited by Paul Jackson provides a good overview. More detailed studies include *Shias and Shia Islam in India,* by Nadeem Nasnain and Abrar Husain, and *Muslim Shrines in India,* edited by Christian W. Troll. An excellent short study of modern Sufi shrines is Peter Van der Veer's article, "Playing or Praying: A Sufi Saint's Day in Surat" in the *Journal of Asian Studies.*

A good starting point for Sikhism is the *Sri Guru Granth Sahib: An Anthology* translated and introduced by Gopal Singh. Another helpful book is W.H. McLeod's *The Sikhs: History, Religion, and Society.* More recent studies of the situation in Punjab include *Tragedy of Punjab* by Kuldip Nayar and Kushwant Singh and *Agony of Punjab* by V.D. Chopra, R.K. Mishra, and Nirmal Singh.

Tribal belief and practice are described in R.S. Mann and Vijoy S. Sahay's *Nature-Man-Spirit Complex in Tribal India,* J. Troisi's *Tribal Religion,* Abdesh Prasad Sinha's *Religious Life in Tribal India,* and Christoph von Fürer-Haimendorf's *Tribal Populations and Cultures of the Indian Subcontinent.* The Catholic Bishop's Conference of India's *Catholic Directory of India* describes the modern organization of Christianity in detail, Lionel Caplan presents a case study of Christianity in *Class and Culture in Urban India,* and Frederick S. Downs, in *Christianity in North East India,* describes proselytization among tribal groups. Introductions to Zoroastrianism in India are Eckehard Kulke's *The Parsees in India* and Cyrus R. Pangborn's *Zoroastrianism: A Beleaguered Faith.* For Judaism, see Thomas A. Timberg's *Jews in India.*

An exhaustive survey of writings on Indian religion until the 1980s can be found in Maureen L.P. Patterson's *Bibliography of South Asia* and more recent updates in the annual *Bibliography of Asian Studies* published by the Association for Asian Studies. (For further information and complete citations, see Bibliography.)

Chapter 4. Language, Ethnicity, and Regionalism

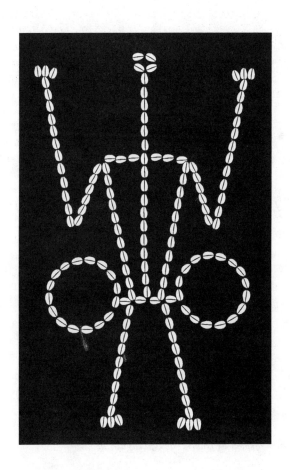

A human figure formed by cowrie shells, Nagaland

INDIA'S ETHNIC, LINGUISTIC, AND REGIONAL complexity sets it apart from other nations. To gain even a superficial understanding of the relationships governing the huge number of ethnic, linguistic, and regional groups, the country should be visualized not as a nation-state but as the seat of a major world civilization on the scale of Europe. The population—estimated at 936.5 million in 1995—is not only immense but also has been highly varied throughout recorded history; its systems of values have always encouraged diversity. The linguistic requirements of numerous former empires, an independent nation, and modern communication are superimposed on a heterogeneous sociocultural base. Almost 8 percent of the population, approaching 65 million people at the time of the 1991 census, belongs to social groups recognized by the government as Scheduled Tribes (see Glossary), with social structures somewhat different from the mainstream of society. Powerful trends of "regionalism"—both in the sense of an increasing attachment to the states as opposed to the central government, and in the sense of movements for separation from the present states or greater autonomy for regions within them—threaten the current distribution of power and delineation of political divisions of territory.

Linguistic Relations

Diversity, Use, and Policy

The languages of India belong to four major families: Indo-Aryan (a branch of the Indo-European family), Dravidian, Austroasiatic (Austric), and Sino-Tibetan, with the overwhelming majority of the population speaking languages belonging to the first two families. (A fifth family, Andamanese, is spoken by at most a few hundred among the indigenous tribal peoples in the Andaman Islands, and has no agreed upon connections with families outside them.) The four major families are as different in their form and construction as are, for example, the Indo-European and Semitic families. A variety of scripts are employed in writing the different languages. Furthermore, most of the more widely used Indian languages exist in a number of different forms or dialects influenced by complex geographic and social patterns.

Sir George Grierson's twelve-volume *Linguistic Survey of India*, published between 1903 and 1923, identified 179 languages and 544 dialects. The 1921 census listed 188 languages and forty-nine dialects. The 1961 census listed 184 "mother tongues," including those with fewer than 10,000 speakers. This census also gave a list of all the names of mother tongues provided by the respondents themselves; the list totals 1,652 names. The 1981 census—the last census to tabulate languages—reported 112 mother tongues with more than 10,000 speakers and almost 1 million people speaking other languages. The encyclopedic *People of India* series, published by the government's Anthropological Survey of India in the 1980s and early 1990s, identified seventy-five "major languages" within a total of 325 languages used in Indian households. In the early 1990s, there were thirty-two languages with 1 million or more speakers (see table 15, Appendix).

The Indian constitution recognizes official languages (see The Constitutional Framework, ch. 8). Articles 343 through 351 address the use of Hindi, English, and regional languages for official purposes, with the aim of a nationwide use of Hindi while guaranteeing the use of minority languages at the state and local levels. Hindi has been designated India's official language, although many impediments to its official use exist.

The constitution's Eighth Schedule, as amended by Parliament in 1992, lists eighteen official or Scheduled Languages (see Glossary). They are Assamese, Bengali, Gujarati, Hindi, Kannada, Kashmiri, Konkani, Malayalam, Manipuri, Marathi, Nepali, Oriya, Punjabi, Sanskrit, Sindhi, Tamil, Telugu, and Urdu. (Precise numbers of speakers of these languages are not known. They were not reported in the 1991 census, and estimates are subject to considerable variation because of the use of multiple languages by individual speakers.) Of the official languages, approximately 403 million people, or about 43 percent of the estimated total 1995 population, speak Hindi as their mother tongue. Telugu, Bengali, Marathi, and Tamil rank next, each the mother tongue of about 4 to 5 percent (about 37 million to 47 million people); Urdu, Gujarati, Malayalam, Kannada, and Oriya are claimed by between 2 and 3 percent (roughly 19 million to 28 million people); Bhojpuri, Punjabi, and Assamese by 1 to 2 percent (9 million to 19 million people); and all other languages by less than 1 percent (less than 9 million speakers) each.

Since independence in 1947, linguistic affinity has served as a basis for organizing interest groups; the "language question" itself has become an increasingly sensitive political issue. Efforts to reach a consensus on a single national language that transcends the myriad linguistic regions and is acceptable to diverse language communities have been largely unsuccessful.

Many Indian nationalists originally intended that Hindi would replace English—the language of British rule (1757–1947)—as a medium of common communication. Both Hindi and English are extensively used, and each has its own supporters. Native speakers of Hindi, who are concentrated in North India, contend that English, as a relic from the colonial past and spoken by only a small fraction of the population, is hopelessly elitist and unsuitable as the nation's official language. Proponents of English argue, in contrast, that the use of Hindi is unfair because it is a liability for those Indians who do not speak it as their native tongue. English, they say, at least represents an equal handicap for Indians of every region.

English continues to serve as the language of prestige. Efforts to switch to Hindi or other regional tongues encounter stiff opposition both from those who know English well and whose privileged position requires proficiency in that tongue and from those who see it as a means of upward mobility. Partisans of English also maintain it is useful and indeed necessary as a link to the rest of the world, that India is lucky that the colonial period left a language that is now the world's predominant international language in the fields of culture, science, technology, and commerce. They hold, too, that widespread knowledge of English is necessary for technological and economic progress and that reducing its role would leave India a backwater in world affairs.

Linguistic diversity is apparent on a variety of levels. Major regional languages have stylized literary forms, often with an extensive body of literature, which may date back from a few centuries to two millennia ago. These literary languages differ markedly from the spoken forms and village dialects that coexist with a plethora of caste idioms and regional lingua francas (see Village Unity and Divisiveness, ch. 5). Part of the reason for such linguistic diversity lies in the complex social realities of South Asia. India's languages reflect the intricate levels of social hierarchy and caste. Individuals have in their speech repertoire a variety of styles and dialects appropriate to various social situations. In general, the higher the speaker's status, the more speech forms there are at his or her disposal. Speech is adapted in countless ways to reflect the specific social context and the relative standing of the speakers.

Determining what should be called a language or a dialect is more a political than a linguistic question. Sometimes the word *language* is applied to a standardized and prestigious form, recognized as such over a large geographic area, whereas the word *dialect* is used for the various forms of speech that lack prestige or that are restricted to certain regions or castes but are still regarded as forms of the same language. Sometimes mutual intelligibility is the criterion: if the speakers can understand each other, even though with some difficulty, they are speaking the same language, although they may speak different dialects. However, speakers of Hindi, Urdu, and Punjabi can often understand each other, yet they are regarded as speakers of different languages. Whether or not one thinks Konkani—spoken in Goa, Karnataka, and the Konkan region of Maharashtra—is a distinct language or a dialect of Marathi has tended to be linked with whether or not one thinks Goa ought to be merged with Maharashtra. The question has been settled from the central government's point of view by making Goa a state and Konkani a Scheduled Language. Moreover, the fact that the Latin script is predominantly used for Konkani separates it further from Marathi, which uses the Devanagari (see Glossary) script. However, Konkani is also sometimes written in Devanagari and Kannada scripts.

Regional languages are an issue in the politically charged atmosphere surrounding language policy. Throughout the 1950s and 1960s, attempts were made to redraw state boundaries to coincide with linguistic usage. Such efforts have had mixed results. Linguistic affinity has often failed to overcome other social and economic differences. In addition, most states have linguistic minorities, and questions surrounding the definition and use of the official language in those regions are fraught with controversy.

States have been accused of failure to fulfill their obligations under the national constitution to provide for the education of linguistic minorities in their mother tongues, even when the minority language is a Scheduled Language. Although the constitution requires that legal documents and petitions may be submitted in any of the Scheduled Languages to any government authority, this right is rarely exercised. Under such circumstances, members of linguistic minorities may feel they and their language are oppressed by the majority, while people who are among linguistic majorities may feel threatened by what some might consider minor concessions. Thus, attempts to make seemingly minor accommodations for social diversity may have extensive and volatile ramifications. For example, in 1994 a proposal in Bangalore to introduce an Urdu-language television news segment (aimed primarily at Muslim viewers) led to a week of urban riots that left dozens dead and millions of dollars in property damage.

Languages of India

About 80 percent of all Indians—nearly 750 million people based on 1995 population estimates—speak one of the Indo-Aryan group of languages. Persian and the languages of Afghanistan are close relatives, belonging, like the Indo-Aryan languages, to the Indo-Iranian branch of the Indo-European family. Brought into India from the northwest during the second millennium B.C., the Indo-Aryan tongues spread throughout the north, gradually displacing the earlier languages of the area.

Modern linguistic knowledge of this process of assimilation comes through the Sanskrit language employed in the sacred literature known as the Vedas (see The Vedas and Polytheism, ch. 3). Over a period of centuries, Indo-Aryan languages came to predominate in the northern and central portions of South Asia (see Antecedents, ch. 1).

As Indo-Aryan speakers spread across northern and central India, their languages experienced constant change and development. By about 500 B.C., Prakrits, or "common" forms of speech, were widespread throughout the north. By about the same time, the "sacred," "polished," or "pure" tongue—Sanskrit—used in religious rites had also developed along independent lines, changing significantly from the form used in the Vedas. However, its use in ritual settings encouraged the retention of archaic forms lost in the Prakrits. Concerns for the purity and correctness of Sanskrit gave rise to an elaborate science of grammar and phonetics and an alphabetical system seen by some scholars as superior to the Roman system. By the fourth century B.C., these trends had culminated in the work of Panini, whose Sanskrit grammar, the *Ashtadhyayi* (Eight Chapters), set the basic form of Sanskrit for subsequent generations. Panini's work is often compared to Euclid's as an intellectual feat of systematization.

The Prakrits continued to evolve through everyday use. One of these dialects was Pali, which was spoken in the western portion of peninsular India. Pali became the language of Theravada Buddhism; eventually it came to be identified exclusively with religious contexts. By around A.D. 500, the Prakrits had changed further into Apabhramshas, or the "decayed" speech; it is from these dialects that the contemporary Indo-Aryan languages of South Asia developed. The rudiments of modern Indo-Aryan vernaculars were in place by about A.D. 1000 to 1300.

It would be misleading, however, to call Sanskrit a dead language because for many centuries huge numbers of works in all genres and on all subjects continued to be written in Sanskrit. Original works are still written in it, although in much smaller numbers than formerly. Many students still learn Sanskrit as a second or third language, classical music concerts regularly feature Sanskrit vocal compositions, and there are even television programs conducted entirely in Sanskrit.

Around 18 percent of the Indian populace (about 169 million people in 1995) speak Dravidian languages. Most Dravidian speakers reside in South India, where Indo-Aryan influence was less extensive than in the north. Only a few isolated groups of Dravidian speakers, such as the Gonds in Madhya Pradesh and Orissa, and the Kurukhs in Madhya Pradesh and Bihar, remain in the north as representatives of the Dravidian speakers who presumably once dominated much more of South Asia. (The only other significant population of Dravidian speakers are the Brahuis in Pakistan.)

The oldest documented Dravidian language is Tamil, with a substantial body of literature, particularly the Cankam poetry, going back to the first century A.D. Kannada and Telugu developed extensive bodies of literature after the sixth century, while Malayalam split from Tamil as a literary language by the twelfth century. In spite of the profound influence of the Sanskrit language and Sanskritic culture on the Dravidian languages, a strong consciousness of the distinctness of Dravidian languages from Sanskrit remained. All four major Dravidian languages had consciously differentiated styles varying in the amount of Sanskrit they contained. In the twentieth century, as part of an anti-Brahman movement in Tamil Nadu, a strong movement arose to "purify" Tamil of its Sanskrit elements, with mixed success. The other three Dravidian languages were not much affected by this trend.

There are smaller groups, mostly tribal peoples, who speak Sino-Tibetan and Austroasiatic languages. Sino-Tibetan speakers live along the Himalayan fringe from Jammu and Kashmir to eastern Assam (see fig. 9). They comprise about 1.3 percent, or 12 million, of India's 1995 population. The Austroasiatic languages, composed of the Munda tongues and others thought to be related to them, are spoken by groups of tribal peoples from West Bengal through Bihar and Orissa and into Madhya Pradesh. These groups make up approximately 0.7 percent (about 6.5 million people) of the population.

Despite the extensive linguistic diversity in India, many scholars treat South Asia as a single linguistic area because the various language families share a number of features not found together outside South Asia. Languages entering South Asia were "Indianized." Scholars cite the presence of retroflex consonants, characteristic structures in verb formations, and a significant amount of vocabulary in Sanskrit with Dravidian or Austroasiatic origin as indications of mutual borrowing, influences, and counterinfluences. Retroflex consonants, for example, which are formed with the tongue curled back to the hard palate, appear to have been incorporated into Sanskrit and other Indo-Aryan languages through the medium of borrowed Dravidian words.

Hindi and English

For the speakers of the country's myriad tongues to function within a single administrative unit requires some medium of common communication. The choice of this tongue, known in India as the "link" language, has been a point of significant controversy since independence. Central government policy on the question has been necessarily equivocal. The vested interests proposing a number of language policies have made a decisive resolution of the "language question" all but impossible.

The central issue in the link-language controversy has been and remains whether Hindi should replace English. Proponents of Hindi as the link language assert that English is a foreign tongue left over from the British Raj (see Glossary). English is used fluently only by a small, privileged segment of the population; the role of English in public life and governmental affairs constitutes an effective bar to social mobility and further democratization. Hindi, in this view, is not only already spoken by a sizable minority of all Indians but also would be easier to spread because it would be more congenial to the cultural habits of the people. On the other hand, Dravidian-speaking southerners in particular feel that a switch to Hindi in the well-paid, nationwide bureaucracies, such as the Indian Administrative Service, the military, and other forms of national service would give northerners an unfair advantage in government examinations (see The Civil Service, ch. 8). If the learning of English is burdensome, they argue, at least the burden weighs equally on Indians from all parts of the country. In the meantime, an increasing percentage of Indians send their children to private English-medium schools, to help assure their offspring a chance at high-privilege positions in business, education, the professions, and government.

Hindi

The development of Hindi and Urdu gives a glimpse of the processes at work in language evolution in South Asia.

Hindi and Urdu are essentially one language with two scripts, Devanagari and Persian-Arabic, respectively. In their most formal literary forms, the two languages have two vocabularies (Hindi taking words by preference from Sanskrit, Urdu from Persian and Arabic) and tend to be culturally connected with Hindu and Islamic culture, respectively. Hindi-Urdu developed from the Khari Boli dialect of Delhi, the capital city of the Delhi Sultanate, and it was the speech of the classes and neighborhoods most closely connected with the Mughal court (1556–1858). In time, the language spread even into South India because it served as a common medium of communication for trade, administration, and military purposes. Classical Urdu appropriated a large number of words from Persian, the official language of the Mughal Empire, and through Persian from Arabic.

By the late seventeenth and early eighteenth centuries, Urdu had developed into a highly stylized form written in a Persian-Arabic script. After the British took over from the Mughals, whose language of administration was Persian, Urdu began to serve as the language of administration in lower courts in the north. British administrators and missionaries, however, felt that the high literary form of Urdu was too remote from everyday life and was suffused by a Persian vocabulary unintelligible to the masses. Therefore, they instigated the development of modern standard Hindi in Devanagari script. Hindi now predominates in a number of states, including Uttar Pradesh,

Bihar, Madhya Pradesh, Rajasthan, Haryana, and Himachal Pradesh, and in the National Capital Territory of Delhi. Urdu is the majority language in no large region but is more commonly spoken in North India and is the official administrative language of the state of Jammu and Kashmir. In South India, people in urban Muslim communities in former administrative capitals, such as Hyderabad or Bangalore, may regularly use Urdu at home or in their workplace.

Hindi has spread throughout North India as a contemporary lingua franca. Its speakers range from illiterate workers in large cities to highly educated civil servants. Many city dwellers learn Hindi as a second or third language even if they speak another regional language, such as Marathi, Bengali, or Gujarati. As professionals have become increasingly mobile, they rely more heavily on Hindi as a means of communication; those aspiring to career advancement need to learn standard Hindi. Speakers of other Indo-Aryan languages tend to chose Hindi for their third language in school because of similarities in grammar, vocabulary, or script with their own mother tongue and because it has a wider use than another regional language.

Hindi, especially in the less highly Sanskritized form used in everyday speech, is barely distinct from everyday Urdu, which before independence was called Hindustani. However, Hindi has long had pan-Indian uses extending beyond the regions where it is the majority language. Hindi is the lingua franca at pilgrimage sites in all regions and is used to deal with devotees from all parts of the country. It is also the common means of communication of wandering Hindu holy men in their discussions with each other and is used frequently in preaching. Many publishers issue Sanskrit classics on religion, astrology, medicine, and other subjects with Hindi translations, cribs, or commentaries to help purchasers who may not be confident of their Sanskrit ability. Purchasers appear to find those aids useful, even though Hindi may not be their primary spoken or written language. Although there are major cinema industries in several other languages, the Hindi cinema (centered in Bombay, also known as Mumbai in the Marathi language) dominates the Indian motion picture market, and Hindi films (the songs tend to be in Urdu) are shown around the country without subtitles or dubbing (see The Media, ch. 8).

A number of former literary languages with established and major bodies of literature, such as Braj, Avadhi, and Maithili, have been essentially subsumed under the rubric of Hindi.

Maithili, spoken in northern Bihar, has a body of literature and its own grammar. Proponents of its use insist that it is a language in its own right and that it is related more closely to eastern Indo-Aryan tongues than to Hindi. Nonetheless, efforts to revive Maithili have had minimal success beyond its use in elementary education. Other regional tongues that lack literary forms, such as Marwari (in Rajasthan) and Magadhi (in southern Bihar), are considered variants of Hindi. Some of them differ from Hindi considerably more than does Urdu. In general, religious affiliation is the distinguishing characteristic of Hindi and Urdu speakers; Muslims speak Urdu, and Hindus speak Hindi, although what they actually say in informal situations is likely to be about the same. The use of two radically different scripts is a statement of cultural identity. However, there are still Hindu religious periodicals published in Urdu, and Urdu writers who are Hindu by religion.

English

There is little information on the extent of knowledge of English in India. Books and articles abound on the place of English in the Indian education system, job competition, and culture; and on its sociolinguistic aspects, pronunciation and grammar, its effect on Indian languages, and Indian literature in English. Little information is available, however, on the number of people who "know" English and the extent of their knowledge, or even how many people study English in school. In the 1981 census, 202,400 persons (0.3 percent of the population) gave English as their first language. Fewer than 1 percent gave English as their second language while 14 percent were reported as bilingual in two of India's many languages. However, the census did not allow for recording more than one second language and is suspected of having significantly underrepresented bilingualism and multilingualism.

The 1981 census reported 13.3 percent of the population as bilingual. The People of India project of the Anthropological Survey of India, which assembled statistics on communities rather than on individuals, found that only 34 percent of communities reported themselves as monolingual. An Assamese who also knew Bengali, or someone from a Marathi-speaking family living in Delhi who attended a Hindi-medium school, might give Bengali or Hindi as his or her second language but also know English from formal school instruction or picking it up on the street. It is suspected that many people identify lan-

A temple entrance sign, Thanjavur, Tamil Nadu. It includes instructions in Tamil, English, Hindi, Telugu, Kannada, and Malayalam. Courtesy Doranne Jacobson

guage with literacy and hence will not describe themselves as knowing a language unless they can read it and, conversely, may say they know a language if they can make out its alphabet. Thus people who speak English but are unable to read or write it may say they do not know the language.

English-language daily newspapers have a circulation of 3.1 million copies per day, but each copy is probably read by several people. There are estimates of about 3 percent (some 27 million people) for the number of literates in English, but even if this percentage is valid, the number of people with a speaking knowledge is certainly higher than of those who read it. And, the figure of 3 percent for English literacy may be low. According to one set of figures, 17.6 million people were enrolled in English classes in 1977, which would be 3.2 percent of the population of India according to the 1971 census. Taking the most conservative evaluation of how much of the instruction would "stick," this still leaves a larger part of the population than 3 percent with some English literacy.

Some idea of the possibilities of studying English can be found in the 1992 Fifth All-India Education Survey. According to the survey, only 1.3 percent of primary schools, 3.4 percent of upper primary schools, 3.9 percent of middle schools, and 13.2 percent of high schools use English as a medium of instruction. Schools treating English as the first language (requiring ten years of study) are only 0.6 percent of rural primary schools, 2.8 percent of rural high schools, and 9.9 percent of urban high schools. English is offered as a second language (six years of study) in 51 percent of rural primary schools, 55 percent of urban primary schools, 57 percent of rural high schools, and 51 percent of urban high schools. As a third language (three years of study), English is offered in 5 percent of rural primary schools, 21 percent of urban primary schools, 44 percent of rural high schools, and 41 percent of urban high schools. These statistics show a considerable desire to study English among people receiving a mostly vernacular education, even in the countryside.

In higher education, English continues to be the premier prestige language. Careers in business and commerce, government positions of high rank (regardless of stated policy), and science and technology (attracting many of the brightest) continue to require fluency in English. It is also necessary for the many students who contemplate study overseas.

English as a prestige language and the tongue of first choice continues to serve as the medium of instruction in elite schools at every level without apology. All large cities and many smaller cities have private, English-language middle schools and high schools (see Education, ch. 2). Even government schools run for the benefit of senior civil service officers are conducted in English because only that language is an acceptable medium of communication throughout the nation.

Working-class parents, themselves rural-urban migrants and perhaps bilingual in their village dialect and the regional standard language, perceive English as the tool their children need in order to advance. Schools in which English is the medium of instruction are a "growth industry." Facility in English enhances a young woman's chances in the marriage market—no small advantage in the often protracted marriage negotiations between families (see Life Passages, ch. 5). The English speaker also encounters more courteous responses in some situations than does a speaker of an indigenous language.

Linguistic States

The constitution and various other government documents are purposely vague in defining such terms as national languages and official languages and in distinguishing either one from officially adopted regional languages. States are free to adopt their own language of administration and educational instruction from among the country's officially recognized languages, the Scheduled Languages. Further, all citizens have the right to primary education in their native tongue, although the constitution does not stipulate how this objective is to be accomplished.

As drafted, the constitution provided that Hindi and English were to be the languages of communication for the central government until 1965, when the switch to Hindi was mandated. The Official Languages Act of 1963, pursuing this mandate, said that Hindi would become the sole official national language in 1965. English, however, would continue as an "associate additional official language." After ten years, a parliamentary committee was to consider the situation and whether the status of English should continue if the knowledge of Hindi among peoples of other native languages had not progressed sufficiently. The act, however, was ambiguous about whether Hindi could be imposed on unwilling states by 1975. In 1964 the Ministry of Home Affairs requested all central ministries to state their progress on the switch to Hindi and their plans for the period after the transition date in 1965. The news of this directive led to massive riots and self-immolations in Tamil Nadu in late 1964 and early 1965, leading the central government, then run by the Congress (see Glossary), to back away from its stand. A conference of Congress leaders, cabinet ministers, and chief ministers of all the states was held in New Delhi in June 1965. Non-Hindi-speaking states were assured that Hindi would not be imposed as the sole language of communication between the central government and the states as long as even one state objected. In addition any of the Scheduled Languages could be used in taking examinations for entry into the central government services.

Before independence in 1947, the Congress was committed to redrawing state boundaries to correspond with linguistics. The States Reorganisation Commission, which was formed in 1953 to study the problems involved in redrawing state boundaries, viewed language as an important, although by no means the sole, factor. Other factors, such as economic viability and geographic realities, had to be taken into account. The commission issued its report in 1955; the government's request for comments from the populace generated a flood of petitions and letters. The final bill, passed in 1956 and amended several times in the 1960s, by no means resolved even the individual states' linguistic problems.

Even regions with a long history of agitation for a linguistic state sometimes have found the actual transition less than smooth. For example, proponents began lobbying for a Telugu-speaking state in the early twentieth century. In 1956 the central government formed a single state, Andhra Pradesh, composed of the predominantly Telugu-speaking parts of what in British India had been the Madras Presidency and the large polyglot princely state of Hyderabad. Although more than 80 percent of the residents (some 53 million people as of 1991) of Andhra Pradesh speak Telugu, like most linguistic states it has a sizable linguistic minority. In this case, the minority consists of Urdu speakers centered in the state's capital, Hyderabad, where nearly 40 percent (some 1.7 million people in 1991) of the population speak that language. Linguistic affinity did not form a firm basis for unity between the two regions from which the state had been formed because they were separated by cultural and economic differences. Although there were riots in the late 1960s and early 1970s in support of the formation of two separate states, the separation did not occur.

The violence that broke out in the state of Assam in the early 1980s reflected the complexities of linguistic and ethnic politics in South Asia (see Political Issues, ch. 8). The state has a significant number of Bengali-speaking Muslims—immigrants and their descendants who began settling the region in the late nineteenth and early twentieth centuries. The Muslims came in response to a British-initiated colonization plan to bring under cultivation land left fallow by the Assamese. By the 1931 census, the Assamese not only had lost a hefty portion of their land but also had become a disadvantaged minority in their traditional homeland. They represented less than 33 percent of the total population of Assam, and the Muslim immigrants (who accounted for roughly 25 percent of the population) dominated commerce and the government bureaucracy.

Assamese-Bengali rioting started in 1950, and in the 1951 census many Bengalis listed Assamese as their native tongue in an effort to placate the Assamese. Further immigration of Bengali speakers after the formation of Bangladesh in 1971 and a resurgence of pro-Bengali feeling among earlier immigrants and their descendants reawakened Assamese fears of being outnumbered. Renewed violence in the early and mid-1980s was sufficiently serious for the central government to avoid holding general elections in Assam during December 1984 (see Insurgent Movements and External Subversion, ch. 10).

The Social Context of Language

Contemporary languages and dialects, as they figure in the lives of most Indians, are a far cry from the stylized literary forms of Indo-Aryan or Dravidian languages. North India especially can be viewed as a continuum of village dialects. As a proverb has it, "Every two miles the water changes, every four miles the speech." Spoken dialects of more distant villages will be less and less mutually understandable and finally become simply mutually unintelligible outside the immediate region. In some cases, a variety of caste dialects coexist in the same village or region. In addition, there are numerous regional dialects that villagers use when doing business in nearby towns or bazaars.

Since the late eighteenth and early nineteenth centuries, regional languages, such as Bengali, Punjabi, and Marathi, have become relatively standardized and are now used throughout their respective states for most levels of administration, business, and social intercourse. Each is associated with a body of literature. British rule was an impetus for the official codification of these regional tongues. British colonial administrators and missionaries learned regional languages and often studied their literatures, and their translations of English-language materials and the Bible encouraged the development of written, standard languages. To provide teaching materials, prose compositions, grammars, and textbooks were often commissioned and, in some cases, were closer to everyday speech than was the standard literary language. Industrialization, modernization, and printing gave a major boost to the vocabulary and standardization of regional tongues, especially by making possible the wide dissemination of dictionaries.

Such written forms still often differ widely from spoken vernaculars and village dialects. Diglossia—the coexistence of a highly elaborate, formal language alongside a more colloquial form of the same tongue—occurs in many instances. For example, spoken Bengali is so divergent from written Bengali as to be nearly another tongue. Similarly, Telugu scholars waged a bitter battle in the early twentieth century over proper language style. Reformers favored a simplified prose format for written Telugu, while traditional classicists wished to continue using a classical literary poetic form. In the end, the classicists won, although a more colloquial written form eventually began to appear in the mass media. Diglossia reinforces social barriers because only a fraction of the populace is sufficiently educated to master the more literary form of the language.

The standard regional language may be the household tongue of only a small group of educated inhabitants of the region's major urban center that has long exercised politico-economic hegemony in a region. Even literate villagers may have difficulty understanding it. The more socially isolated—women and Dalits (see Glossary)—tend to be more parochial in their speech than people of higher caste, who are often able to use a colloquial form of the regional dialect, the caste patois, and the regional standard dialect. An educated person may master several different speech forms that are often so different as to be considered separate languages. Western-educated scholars may well use the regional standard language mixed with English vocabulary with their colleagues at work. At home, a man may switch to a more colloquial vernacular, particularly if his wife is uneducated. Even the highly educated frequently communicate in their village dialects at home.

Only around 3 percent of the population (about 28 million people in 1995) is truly fluent in both English and an Indian language. By necessity, a substantial minority are able to speak two Indian languages; even in the so-called linguistic states, there are minorities who do not speak the official language as their native tongue and must therefore learn it as a second language. Many tribal people are bilingual. Rural-urban migrants are frequently bilingual in the regional standard language as well as in their village dialect. In Bombay, for example, many migrants speak Hindi or Marathi in addition to their native tongue. Religious celebrations, popular festivals, and political meetings are typically carried on in the regional language, which may be unintelligible to many attendees. Bilingualism in India, however, is inextricably linked to social context. South Asia's long history of foreign rule has fostered what Clarence Maloney terms "the linguistic flight of the elite." Language—either Sanskrit, Persian, or English—has formed a barrier to advancement that only a few have been fortunate enough to overcome.

Throughout the twentieth century, radio, television, and the print media have fostered standardization of regional dialects, if only to facilitate communication. Linguistic standardization has contributed to ethnic or regional differentiation insofar as language has served as a cultural marker. Mass communication forces the adoption of a single standard regional tongue; typi-

Graffiti protesting the use of Hindi, Madras, Tamil Nadu
Courtesy Robert L. Worden

cally, the choice is the dialect of the majority in the region or of the region's preeminent business or cultural center. The use of less standard forms clearly labels speakers outside their immediate home base. To fulfill its purposes, the regional language must be standardized and taught to an increasing percentage of the population, thereby encroaching both on its own dialects and the minority languages of the region. The language of instruction and administration affects the economic and career interests and the self-respect of an ever-greater proportion of the population.

Ethnic Minorities

Tribes

Composition and Location

Tribal peoples constitute roughly 8 percent of the nation's total population, nearly 68 million people according to the 1991 census. One concentration lives in a belt along the Himalayas stretching through Jammu and Kashmir, Himachal Pradesh, and Uttar Pradesh in the west, to Assam, Meghalaya, Tripura, Arunachal Pradesh, Mizoram, Manipur, and Nagaland in the northeast (see fig. 1). Another concentration lives in the hilly areas of central India (Madhya Pradesh, Orissa, and, to a lesser extent, Andhra Pradesh); in this belt, which is bounded by the Narmada River to the north and the Godavari River to the southeast, tribal peoples occupy the slopes of the region's mountains. Other tribals, the Santals, live in Bihar and West Bengal. There are smaller numbers of tribal people in Karnataka, Tamil Nadu, and Kerala, in western India in Gujarat and Rajasthan, and in the union territories of Lakshadweep and the Andaman and Nicobar Islands.

The extent to which a state's population is tribal varies considerably. In the northeastern states of Arunachal Pradesh, Meghalaya, Mizoram, and Nagaland, upward of 90 percent of the population is tribal. However, in the remaining northeast states of Assam, Manipur, Sikkim, and Tripura, tribal peoples form between 20 and 30 percent of the population. The largest tribes are found in central India, although the tribal population there accounts for only around 10 percent of the region's total population. Major concentrations of tribal people live in Maharashtra, Orissa, and West Bengal. In the south, about 1 percent of the populations of Kerala and Tamil Nadu are tribal, whereas about 6 percent in Andhra Pradesh and Karnataka are members of tribes.

There are some 573 communities recognized by the government as Scheduled Tribes and therefore eligible to receive special benefits and to compete for reserved seats in legislatures and schools. They range in size from the Gonds (roughly 7.4 million) and the Santals (approximately 4.2 million) to only eighteen Chaimals in the Andaman Islands. Central Indian states have the country's largest tribes, and, taken as a whole, roughly 75 percent of the total tribal population live there.

Apart from the use of strictly legal criteria, however, the problem of determining which groups and individuals are tribal is both subtle and complex. Because it concerns economic interests and the size and location of voting blocs, the question of who are members of Scheduled Tribes rather than Backward Classes (see Glossary) or Scheduled Castes (see Glossary) is often controversial (see The Fringes of Society, ch. 5). The apparently wide fluctuation in estimates of South Asia's tribal population through the twentieth century gives a sense of how unclear the distinction between tribal and nontribal can be. India's 1931 census enumerated 22 million tribal people, in 1941 only 10 million were counted, but by 1961 some 30 million and in 1991 nearly 68 million tribal members were included. The differences among the figures reflect changing census criteria and the economic incentives individuals have to maintain or reject classification as a tribal member.

These gyrations of census data serve to underline the complex relationship between caste and tribe. Although, in theory, these terms represent different ways of life and ideal types, in reality they stand for a continuum of social groups. In areas of substantial contact between tribes and castes, social and cultural pressures have often tended to move tribes in the direction of becoming castes over a period of years. Tribal peoples with ambitions for social advancement in Indian society at large have tried to gain the classification of caste for their tribes; such efforts conform to the ancient Indian traditions of caste mobility (see Caste and Class, ch. 5). Where tribal leaders prospered, they could hire Brahman priests to construct credible pedigrees and thereby join reasonably high-status castes. On occasion, an entire tribe or part of a tribe joined a Hindu sect and thus entered the caste system en masse. If a specific tribe engaged in practices that Hindus deemed polluting, the tribe's status when it was assimilated into the caste hierarchy would be affected.

Since independence, however, the special benefits available to Scheduled Tribes have convinced many groups, even Hindus and Muslims, that they will enjoy greater advantages if so designated. The schedule gives tribal people incentives to maintain their identity. By the same token, the schedule also includes a number of groups whose "tribal" status, in cultural terms, is dubious at best; in various districts, the list includes Muslims and a congeries of Hindu castes whose main claim seems to be their ability to deliver votes to the party that arranges their listing among the Scheduled Tribes.

A number of traits have customarily been seen as establishing tribal rather than caste identity. These include language, social organization, religious affiliation, economic patterns, geographic location, and self-identification. Recognized tribes typically live in hilly regions somewhat remote from caste settlements; they generally speak a language recognized as tribal.

Unlike castes, which are part of a complex and interrelated local economic exchange system, tribes tend to form self-sufficient economic units. Often they practice swidden farming—clearing a field by slash-and-burn methods, planting it for a number of seasons, and then abandoning it for a lengthy fallow period—rather than the intensive farming typical of most of rural India (see Land Use, ch. 7). For most tribal people, land-use rights traditionally derive simply from tribal membership. Tribal society tends to be egalitarian, its leadership being based on ties of kinship and personality rather than on hereditary status. Tribes typically consist of segmentary lineages whose extended families provide the basis for social organization and control. Unlike caste religion, which recognizes the hegemony of Brahman priests, tribal religion recognizes no authority outside the tribe.

Any of these criteria can be called into question in specific instances. Language is not always an accurate indicator of tribal or caste status. Especially in regions of mixed population, many tribal groups have lost their mother tongues and simply speak local or regional languages. Linguistic assimilation is an ongoing process of considerable complexity. In the highlands of Orissa, for example, the Bondos—a Munda-language-speaking tribe—use their own tongue among themselves. Oriya, however, serves as a lingua franca in dealings with Hindu neighbors. Oriya as a prestige language (in the Bondo view), however, has also supplanted the native tongue as the language of ritual. In parts of Assam, historically divided into warring tribes and villages, increased contact among villagers began during the colonial period and has accelerated since independence. A pidgin Assamese developed while educated tribal members learned Hindi and, in the late twentieth century, English.

Self-identification and group loyalty are not unfailing markers of tribal identity either. In the case of stratified tribes, the loyalties of clan, kin, and family may well predominate over those of tribe. In addition, tribes cannot always be viewed as people living apart; the degree of isolation of various tribes has varied tremendously. The Gonds, Santals, and Bhils traditionally have dominated the regions in which they have lived. Moreover, tribal society is not always more egalitarian than the rest of the rural populace; some of the larger tribes, such as the Gonds, are highly stratified.

Economic and Political Conditions

Most tribes are concentrated in heavily forested areas that combine inaccessibility with limited political or economic significance. Historically, the economy of most tribes was subsistence agriculture or hunting and gathering. Tribal members

*A painter of the Warli tribe,
Maharashtra
Courtesy Doranne Jacobson*

traded with outsiders for the few necessities they lacked, such as salt and iron. A few local Hindu craftsmen might provide such items as cooking utensils. The twentieth century, however, has seen far-reaching changes in the relationship between tribals and the larger society and, by extension, traditional tribal economies. Improved transportation and communications have brought ever deeper intrusions into tribal lands; merchants and a variety of government policies have involved tribal peoples more thoroughly in the cash economy, although by no means on the most favorable of terms. Large areas fell into the hands of nontribals around 1900, when many regions were opened by the government to homestead-style settlement. Immigrants received free land in return for cultivating it. Tribal people, too, could apply for land titles, although even title to the portion of land they happened to be planting that season could not guarantee their ability to continue swidden cultivation. More important, the notion of permanent, individual ownership of land was foreign to most tribals. Land, if seen in terms of ownership at all, was viewed as a communal resource, free to whoever needed it. By the time tribals accepted the necessity of obtaining formal land titles, they had lost the opportunity to lay claim to lands that might rightfully have been considered theirs. Generally, tribals were severely disadvantaged in dealing with government officials who granted land titles. Albeit belatedly, the colonial regime realized the necessity of protecting tribals from the predations of outsiders and prohibited the sale of tribal lands. Although an important loophole in the form of land leases was left open, tribes made some gains in the mid-twentieth century. Despite considerable obstruction by local police and land officials, who were slow to delineate tribal holdings and slower still to offer police protection, some land was returned to tribal peoples.

In the 1970s, the gains tribal peoples had made in earlier decades were eroded in many regions, especially in central India. Migration into tribal lands increased dramatically, and the deadly combination of constabulary and revenue officers uninterested in tribal welfare and sophisticated nontribals willing and able to bribe local officials was sufficient to deprive many tribals of their landholdings. The means of subverting protective legislation were legion: local officials could be persuaded to ignore land acquisition by nontribal people, alter land registry records, lease plots of land for short periods and then simply refuse to relinquish them, or induce tribal members to become indebted and attach their lands. Whatever the means, the result was that many tribal members became landless laborers in the 1960s and 1970s, and regions that a few years earlier had been the exclusive domain of tribes had an increasingly heterogeneous population. Unlike previous eras in which tribal people were shunted into more remote forests, by the 1960s relatively little unoccupied land was available. Government efforts to evict nontribal members from illegal occupation have proceeded slowly; when evictions occur at all, those ejected are usually members of poor, lower castes. In a 1985 publication, anthropologist Christoph von Fürer-Haimendorf describes this process in Andhra Pradesh: on average only 25 to 33 percent of the tribal families in such villages had managed to keep even a portion of their holdings. Outsiders had paid about 5 percent of the market value of the lands they took.

Improved communications, roads with motorized traffic, and more frequent government intervention figured in the increased contact that tribal peoples had with outsiders. Tribes fared best where there was little to induce nontribals to settle; cash crops and commercial highways frequently signaled the dismemberment of the tribes. Merchants have long been a link to the outside world, but in the past they were generally petty traders, and the contact they had with tribal people was transient. By the 1960s and 1970s, the resident nontribal shop-keeper was a permanent feature of many villages. Shopkeepers often sold liquor on credit, enticing tribal members into debt and into mortgaging their land. In the past, tribes made up shortages before harvest by foraging from the surrounding for-est. More recently shopkeepers have offered ready credit—with the proviso that loans be repaid in kind with 50 to 100 percent interest after harvest. Repaying one bag of millet with two bags has set up a cycle of indebtedness from which many have been unable to break loose.

The possibility of cultivators growing a profitable cash crop, such as cotton or castor-oil plants, continues to draw merchants into tribal areas. Nontribal traders frequently establish an extensive network of relatives and associates as shopkeepers to serve as agents in a number of villages. Cultivators who grow a cash crop often sell to the same merchants, who provide con-sumption credit throughout the year. The credit carries a high-interest price tag, whereas the tribal peoples' crops are bought at a fraction of the market rate. Cash crops offer a further dis-advantage in that they decrease the supply of available food-stuffs and increase tribal dependence on economic forces beyond their control. This transformation has meant a decline in both the tribes' security and their standard of living.

In previous generations, families might have purchased sil-ver jewelry as a form of security; contemporary tribal people are more likely to buy minor consumer goods. Whereas jewelry could serve as collateral in critical emergencies, current pur-chases simply increase indebtedness. In areas where gathering forest products is remunerative, merchants exchange their products for tribal labor. Indebtedness is so extensive that although such transactions are illegal, traders sometimes "sell" their debtors to other merchants, much like indentured ser-vants.

In some instances, tribes have managed to hold their own in contacts with outsiders. Some Chenchus, a hunting and gather-ing tribe of the central hill regions of Andhra Pradesh, have continued to specialize in collecting forest products for sale. Caste Hindus living among them rent land from the Chenchus and pay a portion of the harvest. The Chenchus themselves have responded unenthusiastically to government efforts to induce them to take up farming. Their relationship to non-tribal people has been one of symbiosis, although there were indications in the early 1980s that other groups were beginning to compete with the Chenchus in gathering forest products. A large paper mill was cutting bamboo in their territory in a manner that did not allow regeneration, and two groups had begun to collect for sale the same products the Chenchus sell. Dalits settled among them with the help of the Chenchus and learned agriculture from them. The nomadic Banjara herders who graze their cattle in the forest also have been allotted land there. The Chenchus have a certain advantage in dealing with caste Hindus; because of their long association with Hindu hermits and their refusal to eat beef, they are considered an unpolluted caste. Other tribes, particularly in South India, have cultural practices that are offensive to Hindus and, when they are assimilated, are often considered Dalits.

The final blow for some tribes has come when nontribals, through political jockeying, have managed to gain legal tribal status, that is, to be listed as a Scheduled Tribe. The Gonds of Andhra Pradesh effectively lost their only advantage in trying to protect their lands when the Banjaras, a group that had been settling in Gond territory, were classified as a Scheduled Tribe in 1977. Their newly acquired tribal status made the Banjaras eligible to acquire Gond land "legally" and to compete with Gonds for reserved political seats, places in education institutions, and other benefits. Because the Banjaras are not scheduled in neighboring Maharashtra, there has been an influx of Banjara emigrants from that state into Andhra Pradesh in search of better opportunities.

Tribes in the Himalayan foothills have not been as hard-pressed by the intrusions of nontribals. Historically, their political status was always distinct from the rest of India. Until the British colonial period, there was little effective control by any of the empires centered in peninsular India; the region was populated by autonomous feuding tribes. The British, in efforts to protect the sensitive northeast frontier, followed a policy dubbed the "Inner Line"; nontribal people were allowed into the areas only with special permission. Postindependence governments have continued the policy, protecting the Himalayan tribes as part of the strategy to secure the border with China (see Principal Regions, ch. 2).

This policy has generally saved the northern tribes from the kind of exploitation that those elsewhere in South Asia have suffered. In Arunachal Pradesh (formerly part of the North-East Frontier Agency), for example, tribal members control commerce and most lower-level administrative posts. Govern-

Young Khond tribal women, Orissa
Courtesy Doranne Jacobson

ment construction projects in the region have provided tribes
with a significant source of cash—both for setting up businesses and for providing paying customers. Some tribes have
made rapid progress through the education system. Instruction
was begun in Assamese but was eventually changed to Hindi; by
the early 1980s, English was taught at most levels. Both education and the increase in ready cash from government spending
have permitted tribal people a significant measure of social
mobility. The role of early missionaries in providing education
was also crucial in Assam.

Government policies on forest reserves have affected tribal
peoples profoundly. Wherever the state has chosen to exploit
forests, it has seriously undermined the tribes' way of life. Government efforts to reserve forests have precipitated armed (if
futile) resistance on the part of the tribal peoples involved.
Intensive exploitation of forests has often meant allowing outsiders to cut large areas of trees (while the original tribal inhabitants were restricted from cutting), and ultimately replacing
mixed forests capable of sustaining tribal life with single-prod-
uct plantations. Where forests are reserved, nontribals have
proved far more sophisticated than their forest counterparts at
bribing the necessary local officials to secure effective (if extra-

legal) use of forestlands. The system of bribing local officials charged with enforcing the reserves is so well established that the rates of bribery are reasonably fixed (by the number of plows a farmer uses or the amount of grain harvested). Tribal people often end up doing unpaid work for Hindus simply because a caste Hindu, who has paid the requisite bribe, can at least ensure a tribal member that he or she will not be evicted from forestlands. The final irony, notes von Fürer-Haimendorf, is that the swidden cultivation many tribes practiced had maintained South Asia's forests, whereas the intensive cultivating and commercial interests that replaced the tribal way of life have destroyed the forests (see Forestry, ch. 7).

Extending the system of primary education into tribal areas and reserving places for tribal children in middle and high schools and higher education institutions are central to government policy, but efforts to improve a tribe's educational status have had mixed results (see Education, ch. 2). Recruitment of qualified teachers and determination of the appropriate language of instruction also remain troublesome. Commission after commission on the "language question" has called for instruction, at least at the primary level, in the students' native tongue. In some regions, tribal children entering school must begin by learning the official regional language, often one completely unrelated to their tribal tongue. The experiences of the Gonds of Andhra Pradesh provide an example. Primary schooling began there in the 1940s and 1950s. The government selected a group of Gonds who had managed to become semiliterate in Telugu and taught them the basics of written script. These individuals became teachers who taught in Gondi, and their efforts enjoyed a measure of success until the 1970s, when state policy demanded instruction in Telugu. The switch in the language of instruction both made the Gond teachers superfluous because they could not teach in Telugu and also presented the government with the problem of finding reasonably qualified teachers willing to teach in outlying tribal schools.

The commitment of tribes to acquiring a formal education for their children varies considerably. Tribes differ in the extent to which they view education positively. Gonds and Pardhans, two groups in the central hill region, are a case in point. The Gonds are cultivators, and they frequently are reluctant to send their children to school, needing them, they say, to work in the fields. The Pardhans were traditionally bards and ritual specialists, and they have taken to education with enthusiasm. The effectiveness of educational policy likewise varies by region. In those parts of the northeast where tribes have generally been spared the wholesale onslaught of outsiders, schooling has helped tribal people to secure political and economic benefits. The education system there has provided a corps of highly trained tribal members in the professions and high-ranking administrative posts.

Many tribal schools are plagued by high dropout rates. Children attend for the first three to four years of primary school and gain a smattering of knowledge, only to lapse into illiteracy later. Few who enter continue up to the tenth grade; of those who do, few manage to finish high school. Therefore, very few are eligible to attend institutions of higher education, where the high rate of attrition continues.

Practices

The influx of newcomers disinclined to follow tribal ways has had a massive impact on social relations and tribal belief systems. In many communities, the immigrants have brought on nothing less than the total disintegration of the communities they entered. Even where outsiders are not residents in villages, traditional forms of social control and authority are less effective because tribal people are patently dependent on politico-economic forces beyond their control. In general, traditional headmen no longer have official backing for their role in village affairs, although many continue to exercise considerable influence. Headmen can no longer control the allocation of land or decide who has the right to settle in the village, a loss of power that has had an insidious effect on village solidarity.

Some headmen have taken to leasing village land to outsiders, thus enriching themselves at the expense of the rest of the tribes. Conflict over land rights has introduced a point of cleavage into village social relations; increased factional conflict has seriously eroded the ability of tribes to ward off the intrusion of outsiders. In some villages, tribal schoolteachers have emerged as a new political force, a counterbalance to the traditional headman. Changes in landholding patterns have also altered the role of the joint family. More and more couples set up separate households as soon as they marry. Because land is no longer held and farmed in common and has grown more scarce, inheritance disputes have increased.

Hunters and gatherers are particularly vulnerable to these far-reaching changes. The lack of strong authority figures in most hunting and gathering groups handicaps these tribes in organizing to negotiate with the government. In addition, these tribes are too small to have much political leverage. Forced settlement schemes also have had a deleterious impact on the tribes and their environment. Government-organized villages are typically larger than traditional hunting and gathering settlements. Forest reserves limit the amount of territory over which tribes can range freely. Larger villages and smaller territories have led, in some instances, to an increase in crime and violence. Traditionally, hunters and gatherers "settled" their disputes by arranging for the antagonists simply to avoid one another; new, more circumscribed villages preclude this arrangement.

Tribal beliefs and rituals have altered in the face of increased contact with Hindus and missionaries of a variety of persuasions (see Tribal Religions, ch. 3). Among groups in more intense contact with the Hindu majority, there have been various transformations. The Gonds, for example, traditionally worshiped clan gods through elaborate rites, with Pardhans organizing and performing the necessary rituals. The increasing impoverishment of large sections of the Gond tribe has made it difficult, if not impossible, to support the Pardhans as a class of ritual specialists. At the same time, many Gonds have concluded that the tribal gods were losing their power and efficacy. Gonds have tended to seek the assistance of other deities, and thus there has been widespread Hinduization of Gondi belief and practice. Some tribes have adopted the Hindu practice of having costly elaborate weddings—a custom that contributes to indebtedness (as it has in many rural Indian families) and subjects them to the cash economy on the most deleterious of terms. Some families have adapted a traditional marriage pattern—that of capturing a bride—to modern conditions, using the custom to avoid the costly outlays associated with a formal wedding.

Christian missionaries have been active among sundry tribes since the mid-nineteenth century. Conversion to Christianity offers a number of advantages, not the least of which is education. It was through the efforts of various Christian sects to translate the Bible into tribal languages that those tongues acquired a written script. Christian proselytizing has served to preserve tribal lore and language in written form at the same time that it has tended to change drastically the tribe's cultural heritage and belief systems. In some instances, the introduction of Christianity has driven a wedge between converts and their fellow tribal members who continue to adhere to traditional beliefs and practices (see Christianity, ch. 3).

Descendants of Foreign Groups

Jews and Parsis

There are several groups descended from ancient settlers in India. These groups include the Jews, the first group of whom are said to have migrated from West Asia and to have settled in Cranganore (also the traditional first site where Muslims later arrived in India) on the Malabar Coast of Kerala in the first century A.D., a second group of Jews who fled the Arabian Peninsula in the face of Muslim ascendancy in the seventh century, and the Parsis, who came to India in the eighth century A.D. to escape Muslim persecution in Persia (see Zoroastrianism; Judaism, ch. 3).

Portuguese

The European powers left a small ethnic imprint on India. The Portuguese came first and left last, but at no time had they extensive dominions such as the Indian kingdoms and empires or the lands of the British in India. The Austrians, Danish, Dutch, and French had yet smaller territories for shorter periods. By the time truly large numbers of Europeans came to spend their working lives in India as part of the British Raj, racist prejudices that were largely absent in earlier centuries had developed in the Europeans. Improvements in transportation (the steamship and the Suez Canal) also had made travel swifter and safer so at least the more prosperous classes could return to Europe on leave to marry or choose brides coming on the so-called "fishing fleets" for tourism and husband-hunting.

There are around 730,000 Portuguese Indians, commonly known as Goans or Goanese, about half of whom live in the state of Goa and the others elsewhere in India. They are descended from Indians in the former Portuguese colony who assimilated to Portuguese culture and in many cases are the descendants of Indo-Portuguese marriages, which the Portuguese civil and religious authorities encouraged.

Anglo-Indians

The largest group of European Indians, however, are descendants of British men, generally from the colonial service and the military, and lower-caste Hindu or Muslim women. From some time in the nineteenth century, both the British and the Indian societies rejected the offspring of these unions, and so the Anglo-Indians, as they became known, sought marriage partners among other Anglo-Indians. Over time this group developed a number of caste-like features and acquired a special occupational niche in the railroad, postal, and customs services. A number of factors fostered a strong sense of community among Anglo-Indians. The school system focused on English language and culture and was virtually segregated, as were Anglo-Indian social clubs; the group's adherence to Christianity also set members apart from most other Indians; and distinctive manners, diet, dress, and speech contributed to their segregation.

During the independence movement, many Anglo-Indians identified (or were assumed to identify) with British rule, and, therefore, incurred the distrust and hostility of Indian nationalists. Their position at independence was difficult. They felt a loyalty to a British "home" that most had never seen and where they would gain little social acceptance. They felt insecure in an India that put a premium on participation in the independence movement as a prerequisite for important government positions. Some Anglo-Indians left the country in 1947, hoping to make a new life in Britain or elsewhere in the Commonwealth of Nations, such as Australia or Canada. Many of these people returned to India after unsuccessful attempts to find a place in "alien" societies. Most Anglo-Indians, however, opted to stay in India and made whatever adjustments they deemed necessary.

Like the Parsis, the Anglo-Indians are essentially urban dwellers. Unlike the Parsis, relatively few have attained high levels of education, amassed great wealth, or achieved more than subordinate government positions. In the 1990s, Anglo-Indians remained scattered throughout the country in the larger cities and those smaller towns serving as railroad junctions and communications centers.

Constitutional guarantees of the rights of communities and religious and linguistic minorities permit Anglo-Indians to maintain their own schools and to use English as the medium of instruction. In order to encourage the integration of the

*A Bhil tribal woman at the
Baneshwar Fair, Rajasthan
Courtesy Doranne Jacobson*

community into the larger society, the government stipulates
that a certain percentage of the student body come from other
Indian communities. There is no evident official discrimination against Anglo-Indians in terms of current government
employment. A few have risen to high posts; some are high-
ranking officers in the military, and a few are judges. In occupational terms, at least, the assimilation of Anglo-Indians into
the mainstream of Indian life was well under way by the 1990s.
Nevertheless, the group will probably remain socially distinct as
long as its members marry only other Anglo-Indians and its
European descent continues to be noted.

Africans

Still another foreign-origin group, usually known collectively
as Siddhis, are the descendants of Africans brought to India as
slaves. Although most African-origin Indians are descendants
of the large influx of slaves brought to western India in the seventeenth century, the first Africans reportedly arrived on the
Konkani Coast in the first century A.D. as a result of the Arab
slave trade, and there was an important African presence,
including several short-term rulers, in Bengal in the fifteenth
century. Siddhis (the name means lord or prince in African
usage) sometimes rose to prominent—even ruling—govern-

mental and military positions during the Mughal and British periods.

Most modern-day Siddhis are Muslims and are engaged in agricultural pursuits. They are found in Gujarat, Daman and Diu, Maharashtra, Karnataka, Andhra Pradesh, and other states and union territories, where they are designated as Scheduled Tribe members.

Regionalism

The formation of states along linguistic and ethnic lines has occurred in India in numerous instances since independence in 1947 (see Linguistic States, this ch.). There have been demands, however, to form units within states based not only along linguistic, ethnic, and religious lines but also, in some cases, on a feeling of the distinctness of a geographical region and its culture and economic interests. The most volatile movements are those ongoing in Jammu and Kashmir and Punjab (see Political Issues, ch. 8; Insurgent Movements and External Subversion, ch. 9). How the central government responds to these demands will be an area of scrutiny through the late 1990s and beyond. It is believed by some officials that conceding regional autonomy is less arduous and takes less time and fewer resources than does meeting agitation, violence, and demands for concessions.

Telangana Movement

An early manifestation of regionalism was the Telangana movement in what became the state of Andhra Pradesh. The princely ruler of Hyderabad, the nizam, had attempted unsuccessfully to maintain Hyderabad as an independent state separate from India in 1947. His efforts were simultaneous with the largest agrarian armed rebellion in modern Indian history. Starting in July 1946, communist-led guerrilla squads began overthrowing local feudal village regimes and organizing land reform in Telugu-speaking areas of Hyderabad, collectively known as Telangana (an ancient name for the region dating from the Vijayanagar period). In time, about 3,000 villages and some 41,000 square kilometers of territory were involved in the revolt. Faced with the refusal of the nizam of Hyderabad to accede his territory to India and the violence of the communist-led rebellion, the central government sent in the army in September 1948. By November 1949, Hyderabad had been forced to accede to the Indian union, and, by October 1951, the violent phase of the Telangana movement had been suppressed. The effect of the 1946–51 rebellion and communist electoral victories in 1952 had led to the destruction of Hyderabad and set the scene for the establishment of a new state along linguistic lines. In 1953, based on the recommendation of the States Reorganisation Commission, Telugu-speaking areas were separated from the former Madras States to form Andhra, India's first state established along linguistic lines. The commission also contemplated establishing Telangana as a separate state, but instead Telangana was merged with Andhra to form the new state of Andhra Pradesh in 1956.

The concerns about Telangana were manifold. The region had a less developed economy than Andhra, but a larger revenue base (mostly because it taxed rather than prohibited alcoholic beverages), which Telanganas feared might be diverted for use in Andhra. They also feared that planned dam projects on the Krishna and Godavari rivers would not benefit Telangana proportionately even though Telanganas controlled the headwaters of the rivers. Telanganas feared too that the people of Andhra would have the advantage in jobs, particularly in government and education.

The central government decided to ignore the recommendation to establish a separate Telangana state and, instead, merged the two regions into a unified Andhra Pradesh. However, a "gentlemen's agreement" provided reassurances to the Telangana people. For at least five years, revenue was to be spent in the regions proportionately to the amount they contributed. Education institutions in Telangana were to be expanded and reserved for local students. Recruitment to the civil service and other areas of government employment such as education and medicine was to be proportional. The use of Urdu was to continue in the administration and the judiciary for five years. The state cabinet was to have proportional membership from both regions and a deputy chief minister from Telangana if the chief minister was from Andhra and vice versa. Finally, the Regional Council for Telangana was to be responsible for economic development, and its members were to be elected by the members of the state legislative assembly from the region.

In the following years, however, the Telangana people had a number of complaints about how the agreements and guarantees were implemented. The deputy chief minister position was never filled. Education institutions in the region were greatly expanded, but Telanganas felt that their enrollment was not proportionate to their numbers. The selection of the city of Hyderabad as the state capital led to massive migration of people from Andhra into Telangana. Telanganas felt discriminated against in education employment but were told by the state government that most non-Telanganas had been hired on the grounds that qualified local people were unavailable. In addition, the unification of pay scales between the two regions appeared to disadvantage Telangana civil servants. In the atmosphere of discontent, professional associations that earlier had amalgamated broke apart by region.

Discontent with the 1956 gentlemen's agreement intensified in January 1969 when the guarantees that had been agreed on were supposed to lapse. Student agitation for the continuation of the agreement began at Osmania University in Hyderabad and spread to other parts of the region. Government employees and opposition members of the state legislative assembly swiftly threatened "direct action" in support of the students. The Congress-controlled state and central governments offered assurances that non-Telangana civil servants in the region would be replaced by Mulkis, disadvantaged local people, and that revenue surpluses from Telangana would be returned to the region. The protestors, however, were dissatisfied, and severe violence, including mob attacks on railroads, road transport, and government facilities, spread over the region. In addition, seventy-nine police firings resulted in twenty-three deaths according to official figures, the education system was shut down, and examinations were cancelled. Calls for a separate Telangana state came in the midst of counter violence in Andhra areas bordering Telangana. In the meantime, the Andhra Pradesh High Court decreed that a central government law mandating replacement of non-Telangana government employees with Mulkis was beyond Parliament's constitutional powers.

Although the Congress faced dissension within its ranks, its leadership stood against additional linguistic states, which were regarded as "antinational." As a result, defectors from the Congress, led by M. Chenna Reddy, founded the Telangana People's Association (Telangana Praja Samithi). Despite electoral successes, however, some of the new party leaders gave up their agitation in September 1971 and, much to the disgust of many

*A Kuruvikkaran tribal forest
dweller south of Madras,
Tamil Nadu
Courtesy Doranne Jacobson*

separatists, rejoined the safer political haven of the Congress ranks.

In 1972 the Supreme Court reversed the Andhra Pradesh High Court's ruling that the Mulki rules were unconstitutional. This decision triggered agitation in the Andhra region that produced six months of violence.

Throughout the 1970s, Andhra Pradesh settled into a pattern of continuous domination by Congress (R) and later Congress (I), with much instability and dissidence within the state party and constant interference from Indira Gandhi and the national party. Chenna Reddy, the erstwhile opposition leader, was for a time the Congress (I) state chief minister. Congress domination was only ended by the founding of the Telugu National Party by N.T. Rama Rao in 1982 and its overwhelming victory in the state elections in 1983.

Polls taken after the end of the Telangana movement showed a certain lack of enthusiasm for it, and for the idea of a separate state. Although urban groups (students and civil servants) had been most active in the movement, its support was stronger in rural areas. Its supporters were mixed: low and middle castes, the young and the not so young, women, illiterates and the poorly educated, and rural gentry. Speakers of several other languages than Telugu were heavily involved. The movement had no element of religious communalism, but some observers thought Muslims were particularly involved in the movement. Other researchers found the Muslims were unenthusiastic about the movement and noted a feeling that migration from Andhra to Telangana was creating opportunities that were helping non-Telanganas. On the other hand, of the two locally prominent Muslim political groups, only one supported a separate state; the other opposed the idea while demanding full implementation of the regional safeguards. Although Urdu speakers were appealed to in the agitation (e.g., speeches were given in Urdu as well as Telugu), in the aftermath Urdu disappeared from the schools and the administration.

The Telangana movement grew out of a sense of regional identity as such, rather than out of a sense of ethnic identity, language, religion, or caste. The movement demanded redress for economic grievances, the writing of a separate history, and establishment of a sense of cultural distinctness. The emotions and forces generated by the movement were not strong enough, however, for a continuing drive for a separate state. In the late 1980s and early 1990s, the People's War Group, an element of the Communist Party of India (Marxist-Leninist), renewed violence in Andhra Pradesh but was dealt with by state police forces. The Telangana movement was never directed against the territorial integrity of India, unlike the insurrections in Jammu and Kashmir and some of the unrest in northeastern India.

Jharkhand Movement

The word *Jharkhand*, meaning "forest region," applies to a forested mountainous plateau region in eastern India, south of the Indo-Gangetic Plain and west of the Ganga's delta in Bangladesh. The term dates at least to the sixteenth century. In the more extensive claims of the movement, Jharkhand comprises seven districts in Bihar, three in West Bengal, four in Orissa, and two in Madhya Pradesh. Ninety percent of the Scheduled Tribes in Jharkhand live in the Bihar districts. The tribal peoples, who are from two groups, the Chotanagpurs and the Santals, have been the main agitators for the movement.

Jharkhand is mountainous and heavily forested and, therefore, easy to defend. As a result, it was traditionally autonomous from the central government until the seventeenth century when its riches attracted the Mughal rulers. Mughal administration eventually led to more outside interference and a

A Kuruvikkaran tribal girl with a chipmunk on her shoulder, Mahabalipuram, Tamil Nadu Courtesy Doranne Jacobson

change from the traditional collective system of land ownership to one of private landholders.

These trends intensified under British colonial rule, leading to more land being transferred to the local tribes' creditors and the development of a system of "bonded labor," which meant permanent and often hereditary debt slavery to one employer. Unable to make effective use of the British court system, tribal peoples resorted to rebellion starting in the late eighteenth century. In response, the British government passed a number of laws in the nineteenth and twentieth centuries to restrict alienation of tribal lands and to protect the interests of tribal cultivators.

The advent of Christian missions in the region in 1845 led to major cultural changes, which were later to be important in the Jharkhand movement. A significant proportion of the tribes converted to Christianity, and schools were founded for both sexes, including higher institutions to train tribal people as teachers.

Jharkhand's mineral wealth also has been a problem for the tribes. The region is India's primary source of coal and iron. Bauxite, copper, limestone, asbestos, and graphite also are found there. Coal mining began in 1856, and the Tata Iron and Steel Factory was established in Jamshedpur in 1907.

The modern Jharkhand movement dates to the early part of the twentieth century; activity was initially among Christian tribal students but later also among non-Christians and even some nontribals. Rivalries developed among the various Protestant churches and with the Roman Catholic Church, but most of the groups coalesced in the electoral arena and achieved some successes on the local level in the 1930s. The movement at this period was directed more at Indian *dikus* (outsiders) than at the British. Jharkhand spokesmen made representations to British constitutional commissions requesting a separate state and redress of grievances, but without much success.

Independence in 1947 brought emphasis on planned industrialization centering on heavy industries, including a large expansion of mining. A measure of the economic importance of the Jharkhand mines is that the region produces more than 75 percent of the revenue of Bihar, a large state. The socialist pattern of development pursued by the central government led to forced sales of tribal lands to the government, with the usual problem of perceived inadequate compensation. On the other hand, government authorities felt that because the soils of the region are poor, industrialization was particularly necessary for the local people, not just for the national good. However, industrial development brought about further influx of outsiders, and local people considered that they were not being hired in sufficient numbers. The nationalization of the mines in 1971 allegedly was followed by the firing of almost 50,000 miners from Jharkhand and their replacement by outsiders.

Land was also acquired by the government for building dams and their reservoirs. However, some observers thought that very little of the electricity and water produced by the dams was going to the region. In addition, government forestry favored the replacement of species of trees that had multiple uses to the forest dwellers with others useful only for commercial sales. Traditional shifting cultivation and forest grazing were restricted, and the local people felt that the prices paid by the government for forest products they gathered for sale were too low. In the decades since independence, these problems have persisted and intensified.

On the political front, in 1949 the Jharkhand Party, under the leadership of Jaipal Singh, swept the tribal districts in the first general elections. When the States Reorganisation Commission was formed, a memorandum was submitted to it asking for an extensive region to be established as Jharkhand, which would have exceeded West Bengal in area and Orissa in population. The commission rejected the idea of a Jharkhand state, however, on the grounds that it lacked a common language. In the 1950s, the Jharkhand Party continued as the largest opposition party in the Bihar legislative assembly, but it gradually declined in strength. The worst blow came in 1963 when Jaipal Singh merged the party into the Congress without consulting the membership. In the wake of this move, several splinter Jharkhand parties were formed, with varying degrees of electoral success. These parties were largely divided along tribal lines, which the movement previously had not seen.

There also has been dissention between Christian and non-Christian tribal people because of differences in level of education and economic development. Non-Christian tribals formed separate organizations to promote their interests in the 1940s and again in the 1960s. In 1968 a parliamentary study team visited Ranchi investigating the removal of groups from the official list of Scheduled Tribes (thereby depriving these groups of various compensatory privileges). Mass meetings were held and petitions submitted to the study team maintaining that Christians had ceased to be tribals by conversion from tribal religions, and that they benefitted unfairly both from mission schooling and from government protection as members of Scheduled Tribes. In the following years, there were accusations that the missionaries were foreign outside agitators.

In August 1995, the state government of Bihar established the 180-member Provisional Jharkhand Area Autonomous Council. The council has 162 elected members (two each from eighty-one assembly constituencies in the Jharkhand area) and eighteen appointed members.

Uttarakhand

The term *Uttarakhand,* meaning "northern tract" or "higher tract," refers to the Himalayan districts of Uttar Pradesh, between the state of Himachal Pradesh to the west and Nepal to the east. It contains the eight districts of the Kumaon and Garhwal divisions. The main local languages are Kumaoni, Garhwali, and Pahari ("mountain"), a language of the Indo-Aryan family. The language of the elite, business, and administration is Hindi.

The Uttarakhand movement is motivated by regional factors along with economic factors stemming from its particular geography. There is no protest against the dominance of Hindi in education and administration in the state. As regards religion, the population of the hills is almost entirely Hindu, like the large majority of Uttar Pradesh. The influx of outsiders has not become an issue; indeed, the problem has rather been the need for natives of the region to leave it.

The residents of hill districts have felt themselves lost in the large state of Uttar Pradesh and their needs ignored by the politicians more concerned with wider regional issues. There has been almost no development of industry or higher education, although the 1962 border war with China resulted in some infrastructure development, particularly roads, which also were extended to make the more remote pilgrimage sites more accessible.

Men of the region are forced to leave their families in the hills and seek employment in the plains, where they mostly find menial positions as domestic servants, which they consider undignified and inappropriate to their caste. Students must also go to the plains for higher education. All find the heat of the lowlands very oppressive.

The major potential in Uttarakhand for hydroelectric power from the Ganga and Yamuna rivers and for tourism has not been developed, locals feel. Springs, which are essential for drinking and irrigation water, have been allowed to dry up. The particular needs of hill agriculture have been ignored. The plains produce grain primarily, whereas fruit growing is more promising in the hills. On the other hand, adjacent Himachal Pradesh, which consists of Himalayan districts formerly in Punjab or in associated princely states, became a state in 1948. Himachal Pradesh is geographically and culturally quite similar to Uttarakhand and has enjoyed satisfying progress in power generation, tourism, and cultivation. Some administrators observe that small states such as Himachal Pradesh can make more rapid progress just by virtue of being smaller, so that the problems are less overwhelming and local needs are not lost.

The first demand for a separate Uttarakhand state was voiced by P.C. Joshi, a member of the Communist Party of India (CPI), in 1952. However, a movement did not develop in earnest until 1979 when the Uttarakhand Kranti Dal (Uttarakhand Revolutionary Front) was formed to fight for separation. In 1991 the Uttar Pradesh legislative assembly passed a resolution supporting the idea, but nothing came of it. In 1994 student agitation against the state's implementation of the

Mandal Commission (see Glossary) report increasing the number of reserved government positions and university places for lower caste people (the largest caste of Kumaon and Garhwal is the high-ranking Rajput Kshatriya group) expanded into a struggle for statehood. Violence spread on both sides, with attacks on police, police firing on demonstrators, and rapes of female Uttarakhand activists. In 1995 the agitation was renewed, mostly peacefully, under the leadership of the Uttarakhand Samyukta Sangharsh Samiti (Uttarakhand United Struggle Association), a coalition headed by the Uttarakhand Kranti Dal. The Bharatiya Janata Party (BJP), seeing the appeal of statehood to its high-caste constituencies, also supported the movement, but wanted to act on its own. To distinguish its activities, the BJP wanted the new state to be called Uttaranchal, meaning "northern border or region," essentially a synonym for Uttarakhand. In 1995 various marches and demonstrations of the Uttarakhand movement were tense with the possibility of conflict not just with the authorities, but also between the two main political groups. Actual violence, however, was rare. A march to New Delhi in support of statehood was being planned later in the year. An interesting development was that women were playing an active leadership role in the agitation.

Gorkhaland

The Gorkhaland movement grew from the demand of Nepalis living in Darjiling District of West Bengal for a separate state for themselves. The Gorkhaland National Liberation Front led the movement, which disrupted the district with massive violence between 1986 and 1988. The issue was resolved, at least temporarily, in 1988 with the establishment of the Darjiling Gorkha Hill Council within West Bengal.

Historically, Darjiling belonged to the kingdom of Sikkim, which had lost it several times since the eighteenth century. The ethnic identity "Gorkha" comes from the kingdom with that name that united Nepal in the late eighteenth century and was the focal point of Nepalese in the British army.

Immigration from Nepal expanded with British rule in India, and some 34 percent of the population of Darjiling in 1876 was of Gorkha (also seen as Gurkha) ethnicity. By the start of the twentieth century, Nepalese immigrants made a modest socioeconomic advance through government service, and a small anglicized elite developed among them. In 1917 the Hillmen's Association came into being and petitioned for the administrative separation of Darjiling in 1917 and again in 1928 and 1942. In 1928 the Akhil Bharatiya Gorkha League (All India Gorkha League) was formed. It gained additional support after World War II with the influx of ex-soldiers from the Gurkha regiments who had been exposed to nationalist movements in Southeast Asia during service there.

During the 1940s, the CPI organized Gorkha tea workers. In presentations to the States Reorganisation Commission in 1954, the CPI favored regional autonomy for Darjiling within West Bengal, with recognition of Nepali as a Scheduled Language. The All India Gorkha League preferred making the area a union territory under the national government (see Local Government, ch. 8).

The state of West Bengal nominally has been supportive of the use of the Nepali language. The West Bengal Official Language Act of 1961 made Nepali the official language of the hill subdivisions of Darjiling, Kalimpong, and Kurseong, where Nepalese are a majority. The state legislative assembly passed a resolution in 1977 that led Parliament to amend the national constitution to include Nepali as a Scheduled Language. However, the Gorkhaland National Liberation Front has accused the state government of failure to actually implement use of the language.

The Gorkhaland movement distinguished Darjiling Gorkhas from nationals of Nepal legally resident in India, from Nepali-speaking Indian citizens from other parts of the country, and even from the majority in neighboring Sikkim, where Nepali is the official language. The movement was emphatic that it had no desire to separate from India, only from the state of West Bengal. Gorkhaland supporters therefore preferred to call the Gorkhas' language Gorkhali rather than Nepali, although they did not attempt to claim there is any linguistic difference from what other people call Nepali. The 1981 census of India, whether in deference to this sentiment or for some other reason, called the language *Gorkhali/Nepali*. However, when the Eighth Schedule of the constitution was amended in 1992 to make it a Scheduled Language, the term *Nepali* alone was used.

In 1986 the Gorkhaland National Liberation Front, having failed to obtain a separate regional administrative identity from Parliament, again demanded a separate state of Gorkhaland. The party's leader, Subhash Ghising, headed a demonstration that turned violent and was severely repressed by the state gov-

Young Pathan Muslim woman
in gold and pearl jewelry,
Bhopal, Madhya Pradesh
Courtesy Doranne Jacobson

ernment. The disturbances almost totally shut down the districts' economic mainstays of tea, tourism, and timber. The Left Front government of West Bengal, which earlier had supported some form of autonomy, now opposed it as "antinational." The state government claimed that Darjiling was no worse off than the state in general and was richer than many districts. Ghising made lavish promises to his followers, including the recruitment of 40,000 Indian Gorkhas into the army and paying Rs100,000 (for value of the rupee—see Glossary) for every Gorkha writer. After two years of fighting and the loss of at least 200 lives, the government of West Bengal and the central government finally agreed on an autonomous hill district. In July 1988, the Gorkhaland National Liberation Front gave up the demand for a separate state, and in August the Darjiling Gorkha Hill Council came into being with Ghising as chairman. The council had authority over economic development programs, education, and culture.

However, difficulties soon arose over the *panchayat* (see Glossary) elections. Ghising wanted the hill council excluded from the national law on *panchayat* elections. Rajiv Gandhi's government was initially favorable to his request and introduced a constitutional amendment in 1989 to exclude the Darjiling Gorkha Hill Council, along with several other northeast hill states and regions (Nagaland, Meghalaya, Mizoram, and the

225

hill regions of Manipur), but it did not pass. However, in 1992 Parliament passed the Seventy-third Amendment, which seemed to show a newly serious commitment to the idea of local self-government by *panchayats*. The amendment excluded all the hill areas just mentioned except Darjiling. Ghising insisted this omission was a machination of West Bengal and threatened to revive militant agitation for a Gorkhaland state. He also said the Gorkhaland National Liberation Front would boycott the village *panchayat* elections mandated by the amendment. A large portion of his party, however, refused to accept the boycott and split off under the leadership of Chiten Sherpa to form the All India Gorkha League, which won a sizable number of *panchayat* seats.

In 1995 it was unclear whether the region would remain content with autonomy rather than statehood. In August 1995, Sherpa complained to the state government that Ghising's government had misused hill council funds, and West Bengal chief minister Jyoti Basu promised to investigate. Both Gorkha parties showed willingness to use general shutdowns to forward their ends. The fact that so many people were willing to follow Sherpa instead of the hitherto unchallenged Ghising may indicate that they will be satisfied with regional autonomy.

Ladakh

The region of Ladakh is isolated in the Himalayas next to Tibet and differs radically from the rest of the state in that the majority of the population is culturally, ethnically, religiously, and linguistically close to Tibet. There also is a Muslim minority. The region has no interest in the separatist and Islamicist sentiments of the Vale of Kashmir.

Following several years of discontent and agitation about the position of Ladakh District in the state of Jammu and Kashmir, the central government passed the Ladakh Autonomous Hill Development Councils Act in May 1995. The 1995 act established councils for the Leh and Kargil subdistricts and allotted them powers for economic development, land use, and taxation. Elections for the Leh council were held in August 1995. Congress (I) won all twenty-two elective seats unopposed; the governor of Jammu and Kashmir was authorized to appoint four members from among minorities and women.

The Northeast

Northeastern India is made up of the states of Assam,

Meghalaya, Tripura, Arunachal Pradesh, Mizoram, Manipur, and Nagaland. Certain tensions exist between these states and a relatively distant central government and between the tribal peoples, who are natives of these states, and migrant peoples from other parts of India. These tensions have led the natives of these states to seek a greater participation in their own governance, control of their states' economies, and their role in society. Emerging from these desires for greater self-governance are new regional political parties and continued insurgent movements (see Political Parties, ch. 8; Insurgent Movements and External Subversion, ch. 10). In addition to the more frequently analyzed regional movements in Jammu and Kashmir, Punjab, and states such as Assam and Nagaland in the northeast, there are other regional movements, such as those in the Tripura and Miso tribal areas.

In May 1995, the state government of Tripura extended the area covered by the Tripura Tribal Areas Autonomous District Council, a result of the tripartite accord among the central government, the state government, and the Tripura National Volunteers movement concluded in 1988. In the elections in July 1995, the Left Front, led by the Communist Party of India (Marxist), defeated the alliance of the Congress (I) and the local Tripura Tribal Youth Association (Tripura Upajati Juba Samiti), which had controlled the council since 1990. The new council proceeded to dissolve the more than 400 development committees at various levels under its jurisdiction for corruption and inaction and promised to constitute new ones swiftly.

In June 1995, the Assam government signed an agreement with two organizations of the Mising tribe, the Mising Autonomous Demand Committee and the Mising Greater Council (Mising Bane Kebang), to set up an autonomous council for the Misings. The council will include villages with majority tribal populations in four districts of Assam, with a total population expected to be about 315,000. However, villages in so-called Reserve Forest Areas will be included only with the approval of the central minister of state with independent charge of environment and forests. This decision is a possible source of discontent because tribals frequently feel themselves hampered by restrictions on the use of forests by the government. However, in July 1995 the Mising Bane Kebang boycotted the swearing in of the interim council because it said the Mising Autonomous Demand Committee had kept it out of its formation.

Outlook

In the 1990s, the central government has seemed far more willing than previously to grant demands for regional political entities within states, acceding to more demands and doing so after less agitation. This change may be part of a wider willingness to decentralize manifested in the recent trend of serious support of *panchayati raj*, granting more taxing, legislative, and development powers to *panchayats* at various levels and holding long-delayed elections to them. The demands on money, time, and military and police personnel caused by the disturbances in Jammu and Kashmir, Punjab, and the northeastern states, and other military actions, such as that in Sri Lanka, may have made the central authorities more reluctant to resist demands if resistance might require military suppression. This trend to concede substate entities presages a number of possible outcomes for the Indian polity.

It should be noted that any of these regional changes, from the purely legal point of view, could be reversed by the central government on its own accord. Most constitutional amendments require only a two-thirds vote of Parliament. However, once in place, the various regional entities create a heavy self-interest among their office-holders and employees, in addition to those who feel served by their creation. An attempt to reverse the delegation of power could arouse agitations at least as intense as the original movements to force the issue.

The traditional worry about further divisions of or within states was that they would be "antinational," weakening national unity. Although the reorganization of states on linguistic lines was initially resisted as a challenge to national unity, once established, new states were not regarded as a threat, perhaps because they just had to be accepted as a fait accompli, and no attempt to reverse the organization of states on linguistic grounds has been suggested. This attitude prevails in spite of the secessionist sentiment that used to exist in Tamil Nadu and still does in Punjab and Jammu and Kashmir. Once the substate entities are operational, their continued existence may be regarded as similarly inevitable. However, as has been observed, the regionalist movements have mostly preached, with apparent sincerity, their attachment to the nation; their complaints have rather been with state apparatuses. Anyone concerned about the possibility of secession from India might consider that a process granting more regional government bodies might in fact strengthen national unity. The regional governments within linguistic states could serve as additional centers of loyalty, benefits, and patronage in competition with the linguistic states, weakening a state's ability to attract an exclusive attachment and be seen as a candidate to be an independent national entity.

Whereas regional sentiment is partly linguistic, promotion of the local languages may provide a counterweight to the tendencies of states to insist on the spread of the state language at the expense of all others, a spread which, to the extent that it succeeds, makes the state something more nearly approaching a nation-state. The substate regions have been granted financial and other political powers, which, if they wish, they can use to encourage the formation or intensification of ethnic consciousness, as the states also can. But, since the regions are smaller bodies, they are less likely to contemplate independence or to concur with a move toward independence if the states should do so.

Apart from the reduction of threats to national unity, the recognition of regionalism may have further political benefits. First is the reduction of the violence that ensues from regional movements and their repression. It is hoped that intermediate governments also will be able to reduce political violence by allowing the swifter expression and solution of the woes of discontented peoples. Such action cannot be guaranteed; it depends in part on which politicians get elected. Resolution of problems neglected by central and state authorities and that originally motivated the movements is also possible. Moreover, such resolution may result in greater participation in democratic government by those voting or holding office in organizations closer to local concerns and groups than is the national Parliament or even the state legislatures. In this way, there is a continuation of the political mobilization started in the course of the movements.

If substate regions proliferate, including regional entities within regional entities, the process will resemble traditional Indian polities with imperial powers, feudatory monarchies, subinfeudation within those, and real political power at the local level. Arguably, this situation would accommodate the true nature of the society better than the quite centralized system India has had since independence and provide scope for real democracy.

* * *

Michael Shapiro and Harold Schiffmann's *Language and Society in South Asia* is the best summation of research on the languages of the region and their place in social life. Among somewhat older works, *Language and Civilization Change in South Asia,* edited by Clarence Maloney, remains useful, and in particular the introduction by the editor gives a good general overview. An excellent summary of the history and current state of research on the linguistics, sociolinguistics, and history of Indo-Aryan languages is found in Colin P. Masica's *The Indo-Aryan Languages.*

Language statistics, as well as lists of languages, are found in the decennial Indian census. Useful statistics gathered on different principles, counting communities (Scheduled Castes, Scheduled Tribes, and other categories) rather than individuals, gathered by the Anthropological Survey of India are found in the volumes edited by Kumar Suresh Singh, in the series *People of India.* Particularly useful on tribes are K.S. Singh's *An Anthropological Atlas,* which includes maps covering culture, language, physical anthropology, and other useful categories; his *The Scheduled Tribes* is a thorough encyclopedia of all the tribes.

On the construction of linguistic and other identities, Paul R. Brass's *Language, Religion and Politics in North India* remains basic to an understanding of the subject. Themes in it are updated in his *The Politics of India since Independence.*

All of Christoph von Fürer-Haimendorf's works on India's tribal people are useful. His *Tribal Populations and Cultures of the Indian Subcontinent* provides a contemporary view of some of the country's larger tribes. Moonis Raza and Aijazuddin Ahmad's *An Atlas of Tribal India* is also useful.

Bernard S. Cohn's *India: The Social Anthropology of a Civilization* and David G. Mandelbaum's two-volume *Society in India* remain essential background works. (For further information and complete citations, see Bibliography.)

Chapter 5. Social Systems

Wedding scene from a drawing, Madhubani, Bihar

INDIA IS JUSTLY FAMOUS for its complex social systems. Indian society is multifaceted to an extent perhaps unknown in any other of the world's great civilizations. Virtually no generalization made about Indian society is valid for all of the nation's multifarious groups. Comprehending the complexities of Indian social structure has challenged scholars and other observers over many decades.

The ethnic and linguistic diversity of Indian civilization is more like the diversity of an area as variable as Europe than like that of any other single nation-state. Living within the embrace of the Indian nation are vast numbers of different regional, social, and economic groups, each with different cultural practices. Particularly noteworthy are differences between social structures in the north and the south, especially in the realm of kinship systems. Throughout the country, religious differences can be significant, especially between the Hindu majority and the large Muslim minority; and other Indian groups—Buddhists, Christians, Jains, Jews, Parsis, Sikhs, and practitioners of tribal religions—all pride themselves on being unlike members of other faiths.

Access to wealth and power varies considerably, and vast differences in socioeconomic status are evident everywhere. The poor and the wealthy live side by side in urban and rural areas. It is common in city life to see a prosperous, well-fed man or woman chauffeured in a fine car pass gaunt street dwellers huddled beneath burlap shelters along the roadway. In many villages, solid cement houses of landowners rise not far from the flimsy thatched shacks of landless laborers. Even when not so obvious, distinctions of class are found in almost every settlement in India.

Urban-rural differences can be immense. Nearly 74 percent of India's population dwells in villages, with agriculture providing support for most of these rural residents. In villages, mud-plastered walls ornamented with traditional designs, dusty lanes, herds of grazing cattle, and the songs of birds at sunset provide typical settings for the social lives of most Indians. In India's great cities, however, millions of people live amidst cacophony—roaring vehicles, surging crowds, jammed apartment buildings, busy commercial establishments, loudspeakers blaring movie tunes—while breathing the poisons of industrial and automotive pollution.

Gender distinctions are pronounced. The behavior expected of men and women can be quite different, especially in villages, but also in urban centers. Prescribed ideal gender roles help shape the actions of both sexes as they move between family and the world outside the home.

Crosscutting and pervading all of these differences of region, language, wealth, status, religion, urbanity, and gender is the special feature of Indian society that has received most attention from observers: caste. The people of India belong to thousands of castes and castelike groups—hierarchically ordered, named groups into which members are born. Caste members are expected to marry within the group and follow caste rules pertaining to diet, avoidance of ritual pollution, and many other aspects of life.

Given the vast diversity of Indian society, any observation must be tempered with the understanding that it cannot apply to all Indians. Still, certain themes or underlying principles of life are widely accepted in India.

Themes in Indian Society

Hierarchy

India is a hierarchical society. Within Indian culture, whether in the north or the south, Hindu or Muslim, urban or village, virtually all things, people, and groups of people are ranked according to various essential qualities. If one is attuned to the theme of hierarchy in India, one can discern it everywhere. Although India is a political democracy, in daily life there is little advocacy of or adherence to notions of equality.

Castes and castelike groups—those quintessential groups with which almost all Indians are associated—are ranked. Within most villages or towns, everyone knows the relative rankings of each locally represented caste, and people's behavior toward one another is constantly shaped by this knowledge. Between the extremes of the very high and very low castes, however, there is sometimes disagreement on the exact relative ranking of castes clustered in the middle.

Castes are primarily associated with Hinduism but also exist among other Indian religious groups. Muslims sometimes expressly deny that they have castes—they state that all Muslims are brothers under God—but observation of Muslim life in various parts of India reveals the existence of castelike groups and clear concern with social hierarchy. Among Indian Christians, too, differences in caste are acknowledged and maintained.

Throughout India, individuals are also ranked according to their wealth and power. For example, there are "big men" (*bare admi,* in Hindi) and "little men" (*chhote admi*) everywhere. "Big men" sit confidently on chairs, while "little men" come before them to make requests, either standing or crouching down on their haunches, certainly not presuming to sit beside a man of high status as an equal. Even men of nearly equal status who might share a string cot to sit on take their places carefully—the higher-ranking man at the head of the cot, the lower-ranking man at the foot.

Within families and kinship groupings, there are many distinctions of hierarchy. Men outrank women of the same or similar age, and senior relatives outrank junior relatives. Several other kinship relations involve formal respect. For example, in northern India, a daughter-in-law of a household shows deference to a daughter of a household. Even among young siblings in a household, there is constant acknowledgment of age differences: younger siblings never address an older sibling by name, but rather by respectful terms for elder brother or elder sister. However, an older sibling may address the younger by name (see Linguistic Relations, ch. 4).

Even in a business or academic setting, where colleagues may not openly espouse traditional observance of caste or class ranking behavior, they may set up fictive kinship relations, addressing one another by kinship terms reflecting family or village-style hierarchy. For example, a younger colleague might respectfully address an older colleague as *chachaji* (respected father's younger brother), gracefully acknowledging the superior position of the older colleague.

Purity and Pollution

Many status differences in Indian society are expressed in terms of ritual purity and pollution. Notions of purity and pollution are extremely complex and vary greatly among different castes, religious groups, and regions. However, broadly speaking, high status is associated with purity and low status with pollution. Some kinds of purity are inherent, or inborn; for example, gold is purer than copper by its very nature, and, similarly, a member of a high-ranking Brahman (see Glossary), or priestly, caste is born with more inherent purity than a member of a low-ranking Sweeper (Mehtar, in Hindi) caste. Unless the Brahman defiles himself in some extraordinary way, throughout his life he will always be purer than a Sweeper. Other kinds of purity are more transitory—a Brahman who has just taken a bath is more ritually pure than a Brahman who has not bathed for a day. This situation could easily reverse itself temporarily, depending on bath schedules, participation in polluting activities, or contact with temporarily polluting substances.

Purity is associated with ritual cleanliness—daily bathing in flowing water, dressing in properly laundered clothes of approved materials, eating only the foods appropriate for one's caste, refraining from physical contact with people of lower rank, and avoiding involvement with ritually impure substances. The latter include body wastes and excretions, most especially those of another adult person. Contact with the products of death or violence are typically polluting and threatening to ritual purity.

During her menstrual period, a woman is considered polluted and refrains from cooking, worshiping, or touching anyone older than an infant. In much of the south, a woman spends this time "sitting outside," resting in an isolated room or shed. During her period, a Muslim woman does not touch the Quran. At the end of the period, purity is restored with a complete bath. Pollution also attaches to birth, both for the mother and the infant's close kin, and to death, for close relatives of the deceased (see The Ceremonies of Hinduism; Islam, ch. 3).

Members of the highest priestly castes, the Brahmans, are generally vegetarians (although some Bengali and Maharashtrian Brahmans eat fish) and avoid eating meat, the product of violence and death. High-ranking Warrior castes (Kshatriyas), however, typically consume nonvegetarian diets, considered appropriate for their traditions of valor and physical strength.

A Brahman born of proper Brahman parents retains his inherent purity if he bathes and dresses himself properly, adheres to a vegetarian diet, eats meals prepared only by persons of appropriate rank, and keeps his person away from the bodily exuviae of others (except for necessary contact with the secretions of family infants and small children).

If a Brahman happens to come into bodily contact with a polluting substance, he can remove this pollution by bathing and changing his clothing. However, if he were to eat meat or commit other transgressions of the rigid dietary codes of his particular caste, he would be considered more deeply polluted and would have to undergo various purifying rites and payment of fines imposed by his caste council in order to restore his inherent purity.

In sharp contrast to the purity of a Brahman, a Sweeper born of Sweeper parents is considered to be born inherently polluted. The touch of his body is polluting to those higher on the caste hierarchy than he, and they will shrink from his touch, whether or not he has bathed recently. Sweepers are associated with the traditional occupation of cleaning human feces from latrines and sweeping public lanes of all kinds of dirt. Traditionally, Sweepers remove these polluting materials in baskets carried atop the head and dumped out in a garbage pile at the edge of the village or neighborhood. The involvement of Sweepers with such filth accords with their low-status position at the bottom of the Hindu caste hierarchy, even as their services allow high-status people, such as Brahmans, to maintain their ritual purity.

Members of the Leatherworker (Chamar) caste are ascribed a very low status consonant with their association with the caste occupation of skinning dead animals and tanning the leather. Butchers (Khatiks, in Hindi), who kill and cut up the bodies of animals, also rank low on the caste hierarchy because of their association with violence and death.

However, castes associated with ruling and warfare—and the killing and deaths of human beings—are typically accorded high rank on the caste hierarchy. In these instances, political power and wealth outrank association with violence as the key determinant of caste rank.

Maintenance of purity is associated with the intake of food and drink, not only in terms of the nature of the food itself, but also in terms of who has prepared it or touched it. This requirement is especially true for Hindus, but other religious groups hold to these principles to varying degrees. Generally, a person risks pollution—and lowering his own status—if he accepts beverages or cooked foods from the hands of people of lower caste status than his own. His status will remain intact if he accepts food or beverages from people of higher caste rank. Usually, for an observant Hindu of any but the very lowest castes to accept cooked food from a Muslim or Christian is regarded as highly polluting.

In a clear example of pollution associated with dining, a Brahman who consumed a drink of water and a meal of wheat bread with boiled vegetables from the hands of a Sweeper would immediately become polluted and could expect social rejection by his caste fellows. From that moment, fellow Brahmans following traditional pollution rules would refuse food touched by him and would abstain from the usual social interaction with him. He would not be welcome inside Brahman homes—most especially in the ritually pure kitchens—nor would he or his close relatives be considered eligible marriage partners for other Brahmans.

Generally, the acceptance of water and ordinary foods cooked in water from members of lower-ranking castes incurs the greatest pollution. In North India, such foods are known as *kaccha khana*, as contrasted with fine foods cooked in butter or oils, which are known as *pakka khana*. Fine foods can be accepted from members of a few castes slightly lower than one's own. Local hierarchies differ on the specific details of these rules.

Completely raw foods, such as uncooked grains, fresh unpeeled bananas, mangoes, and uncooked vegetables can be accepted by anyone from anyone else, regardless of relative status. Toasted or parched foods, such as roasted peanuts, can also be accepted from anyone without ritual or social repercussions. (Thus, a Brahman may accept gifts of grain from lower-caste patrons for eventual preparation by members of his own caste, or he may purchase and consume roasted peanuts or tangerines from street vendors of unknown caste without worry.)

Water served from an earthen pot may be accepted only from the hands of someone of higher or equal caste ranking, but water served from a brass pot may be accepted even from someone slightly lower on the caste scale. Exceptions to this rule are members of the Waterbearer (Bhoi, in Hindi) caste, who are employed to carry water from wells to the homes of the prosperous and from whose hands members of all castes may drink water without becoming polluted, even though Waterbearers are not ranked high on the caste scale.

These and a great many other traditional rules pertaining to purity and pollution constantly impinge upon interaction between people of different castes and ranks in India. Although to the non-Indian these rules may seem irrational and bizarre, to most of the people of India they are a ubiquitous and accepted part of life. Thinking about and following purity and pollution rules make it necessary for people to be constantly aware of differences in status. With every drink of

Woman operating a hand pump
Courtesy Doranne Jacobson

water, with every meal, and with every contact with another person, people must ratify the social hierarchy of which they are a part and within which their every act is carried out. The fact that expressions of social status are intricately bound up with events that happen to everyone every day—eating, drinking, bathing, touching, talking—and that transgressions of these rules, whether deliberate or accidental, are seen as having immediately polluting effects on the person of the transgressor, means that every ordinary act of human life serves as a constant reminder of the importance of hierarchy in Indian society.

There are many Indians, particularly among the educated urban elite, who do not follow traditional purity and pollution practices. Dining in each others' homes and in restaurants is common among well-educated people of diverse backgrounds, particularly when they belong to the same economic class. For these people, guarding the family's earthen water pot from inadvertent touch by a low-ranking servant is not the concern it is for a more traditional villager. However, even among those people whose words and actions denigrate traditional purity rules, there is often a reluctance to completely abolish consciousness of purity and pollution from their thinking. It is surely rare for a Sweeper, however well-educated, to invite a

Brahman to dinner in his home and have his invitation unself-consciously accepted. It is less rare, however, for educated urban colleagues of vastly different caste and religious heritage to enjoy a cup of tea together. Some high-caste liberals pride themselves on being free of "casteism" and seek to accept food from the hands of very low-caste people, or even deliberately set out to marry someone from a significantly lower caste or a different religion. Thus, even as they deny it, these progressives affirm the continuing significance of traditional rules of purity, pollution, and hierarchy in Indian society.

Social Interdependence

One of the great themes pervading Indian life is social interdependence. People are born into groups—families, clans, subcastes, castes, and religious communities—and live with a constant sense of being part of and inseparable from these groups. A corollary is the notion that everything a person does properly involves interaction with other people. A person's greatest dread, perhaps, is the possibility of being left alone, without social support, to face the necessary challenges of life. This sense of interdependence is extended into the theological realm: the very shape of a person's life is seen as being greatly influenced by divine beings with whom an ongoing relationship must be maintained.

Social interaction is regarded as being of the highest priority, and social bonds are expected to be long lasting. Even economic activities that might in Western culture involve impersonal interactions are in India deeply imbedded in a social nexus. All social interaction involves constant attention to hierarchy, respect, honor, the feelings of others, rights and obligations, hospitality, and gifts of food, clothing, and other desirable items. Finely tuned rules of etiquette help facilitate each individual's many social relationships. ·

Western visitors to India are sometimes startled to find that important government and business officials have left their posts—often for many days at a time—to attend a cousin's wedding or participate in religious activities in a distant part of the country. "He is out of station and will be back in a week or two," the absent official's officemates blandly explain to the frustrated visitor. What is going on is not laziness or hedonistic recreation, but is the official's proper recognition of his need to continually maintain his social ties with relatives, caste fellows, other associates, and God. Without being enmeshed in such ties throughout life, a person cannot hope to maintain long-term efficacy in either economic or social endeavors. Social bonds with relatives must be reinforced at family events or at rites crucial to the religious community. If this is not done, people who could offer vital support in many phases of life would be alienated.

In every activity, there is an assumption that social ties can help a person and that their absence can bring failure. Seldom do people carry out even the simplest task on their own. From birth onward, a child learns that his "fate" has been "written" by divine forces and that his life will be shaped by a plan decided by more powerful beings. When a small child eats, his mother puts the mouthfuls of food into his mouth with her own hand. When a boy climbs a tree to pluck mangoes, another stands below with a basket to receive them. When a girl fetches water from the well in pots on her head, someone at her home helps her unload the pots. When a farmer stacks sheaves of grain onto his bullock cart, he stands atop the cart, catching the sheaves tossed up to him by his son.

A student applying to a college hopes that he has an influential relative or family friend who can put in a good word for him with the director of admissions. At the age of marriage, a young person expects that parents will take care of finding the appropriate bride or groom and arranging all the formalities. At the birth of a child, the new mother is assured that the child's kin will help her attend to the infant's needs. A businessman seeking to arrange a contract relies not only on his own abilities but also on the assistance of well-connected friends and relatives to help finalize the deal. And finally, when facing death, a person is confident that offspring and other relatives will carry out the appropriate funeral rites, including a commemorative feast when, through gifts of clothing and food, continuing social ties are reaffirmed by all in attendance.

Family and Kinship

Family Ideals

In India, people learn the essential themes of cultural life within the bosom of a family. In most of the country, the basic units of society are the patrilineal family unit and wider kinship groupings. The most widely desired residential unit is the joint family, ideally consisting of three or four patrilineally related generations, all living under one roof, working, eating, worshiping, and cooperating together in mutually beneficial social and economic activities. Patrilineal joint families include men related through the male line, along with their wives and children. Most young women expect to live with their husband's relatives after marriage, but they retain important bonds with their natal families.

Despite the continuous and growing impact of urbanization, secularization, and Westernization, the traditional joint household, both in ideal and in practice, remains the primary social force in the lives of most Indians. Loyalty to family is a deeply held ideal for almost everyone.

Large families tend to be flexible and well-suited to modern Indian life, especially for the 67 percent of Indians who are farmers or agricultural workers or work in related activities (see Size and Composition of the Workforce, ch. 6). As in most primarily agricultural societies, few individuals can hope to achieve economic security without being part of a cooperating group of kinsmen. The joint family is also common in cities, where kinship ties can be crucial to obtaining scarce jobs or financial assistance. Numerous prominent Indian families, such as the Tatas, Birlas, and Sarabhais, retain joint family arrangements even as they work together to control some of the country's largest financial empires.

The joint family is an ancient Indian institution, but it has undergone some change in the late twentieth century. Although several generations living together is the ideal, actual living arrangements vary widely depending on region, social status, and economic circumstance. Many Indians live in joint families that deviate in various ways from the ideal, and many live in nuclear families—a couple with their unmarried children—as is the most common pattern in the West. However, even where the ideal joint family is seldom found (as, for example, in certain regions and among impoverished agricultural laborers and urban squatters), there are often strong networks of kinship ties through which economic assistance and other benefits are obtained. Not infrequently, clusters of relatives live very near each other, easily available to respond to the give and take of kinship obligations. Even when relatives cannot actually live in close proximity, they typically maintain strong bonds of kinship and attempt to provide each other with economic help, emotional support, and other benefits.

As joint families grow ever larger, they inevitably divide into smaller units, passing through a predictable cycle over time.

The breakup of a joint family into smaller units does not necessarily represent the rejection of the joint family ideal. Rather, it is usually a response to a variety of conditions, including the need for some members to move from village to city, or from one city to another to take advantage of employment opportunities. Splitting of the family is often blamed on quarrelling women—typically, the wives of coresident brothers. Although women's disputes may, in fact, lead to family division, men's disagreements do so as well. Despite cultural ideals of brotherly harmony, adult brothers frequently quarrel over land and other matters, leading them to decide to live under separate roofs and divide their property. Frequently, a large joint family divides after the demise of elderly parents, when there is no longer a single authority figure to hold the family factions together. After division, each new residential unit, in its turn, usually becomes joint when sons of the family marry and bring their wives to live in the family home.

Variations in Family Structure

Some family types bear special mention because of their unique qualities. In the sub-Himalayan region of Uttar Pradesh, polygyny is commonly practiced. There, among Hindus, a simple polygynous family is composed of a man, his two wives, and their unmarried children. Various other family types occur there, including the supplemented subpolygynous household—a woman whose husband lives elsewhere (perhaps with his other wife), her children, plus other adult relatives. Polygyny is also practiced in other parts of India by a tiny minority of the population, especially in families in which the first wife has not been able to bear children.

Among the Buddhist people of the mountainous Ladakh District of Jammu and Kashmir, who have cultural ties to Tibet, fraternal polyandry is practiced, and a household may include a set of brothers with their common wife or wives. This family type, in which brothers also share land, is almost certainly linked to the extreme scarcity of cultivable land in the Himalayan region, because it discourages fragmentation of holdings.

The peoples of the northeastern hill areas are known for their matriliny, tracing descent and inheritance in the female line rather than the male line. One of the largest of these groups, the Khasis—an ethnic or tribal people in the state of Meghalaya—are divided into matrilineal clans; the youngest daughter receives almost all of the inheritance including the house. A Khasi husband goes to live in his wife's house. Khasis, many of whom have become Christian, have the highest literacy rate in India, and Khasi women maintain notable authority in the family and community.

Perhaps the best known of India's unusual family types is the traditional Nayar *taravad*, or great house. The Nayars are a cluster of castes in Kerala. High-ranking and prosperous, the Nayars maintained matrilineal households in which sisters and brothers and their children were the permanent residents. After an official prepuberty marriage, each woman received a series of visiting husbands in her room in the *taravad* at night. Her children were all legitimate members of the *taravad*. Property, matrilineally inherited, was managed by the eldest brother of the senior woman. This system, the focus of much anthropological interest, has been disintegrating in the twentieth century, and in the 1990s probably fewer than 5 percent of the Nayars live in matrilineal *taravads*. Like the Khasis, Nayar women are known for being well-educated and powerful within the family.

Malabar rite Christians, an ancient community in Kerala, adopted many practices of their powerful Nayar neighbors, including naming their sons for matrilineal forebears. Their kinship system, however, is patrilineal. Kerala Christians have a very high literacy rate, as do most Indian Christian groups (see Christianity, ch. 3).

Large Kinship Groups

In most of Hindu India, people belong not only to coresident family groups but to larger aggregates of kin as well. Subsuming the family is the patrilineage (known in northern and central India as the *khandan, kutumb,* or *kul*), a locally based set of males who trace their ancestry to a common progenitor a few generations back, plus their wives and unmarried daughters. Larger than the patrilineage is the clan, commonly known as the *gotra* or *got*, a much larger group of patrilineally related males and their wives and daughters, who often trace common ancestry to a mythological figure. In some regions, particularly among the high-ranking Rajputs of western India, clans are hierarchically ordered. Some people also claim membership in larger, more amorphous groupings known as *vansh* and *sakha*.

Hindu lineages and clans are strictly exogamous—that is, a person may not marry or have a sexual alliance with a member of his own lineage or clan; such an arrangement would be considered incestuous. In North India, rules further prohibit marriage between a person and his mother's lineage members as well. Among some high-ranking castes of the north, exogamy is also extended to the mother's, father's mother's, and mother's mother's clans. In contrast, in South India, marriage to a member of the mother's kin group is often encouraged.

Muslims also recognize kinship groupings larger than the family. These include the *khandan*, or patrilineage, and the *azizdar*, or kindred. The *azizdar* group differs slightly for each individual and includes all relatives linked to a person by blood or marriage. Muslims throughout India encourage marriage within the lineage and kindred, and marriages between the children of siblings are common.

Within a village or urban neighborhood, members of a lineage recognize their kinship in a variety of ways. Mutual assistance in daily work, in emergencies, and in factional struggles is expected. For Hindus, cooperation in specific annual rituals helps define the kin group. For example, in many areas, at the worship of the goddess deemed responsible for the welfare of the lineage, patrilineally related males and their wives join in the rites and consume specially consecrated fried breads or other foods. Unmarried daughters of the lineage are only spectators at the rites and do not share in the special foods. Upon marriage, a woman becomes a member of her husband's lineage and then participates regularly in the worship of her husband's lineage goddess. Lineage bonds are also evident at life-cycle observances, when kin join together in celebrating births, marriages, and religious initiations. Upon the death of a lineage member, other lineage members observe ritual death pollution rules for a prescribed number of days and carry out appropriate funeral rites and feasts.

For some castes, especially in the north, careful records of lineage ties are kept by a professional genealogist, a member of a caste whose traditional task is maintaining genealogical tomes. These itinerant bards make their rounds from village to village over the course of a year or more, recording births, deaths, and glorious accomplishments of the patrilineal descent group. These genealogical services have been especially crucial among Rajputs, Jats, and similar groups whose lineages own land and where power can depend on fine calculations of pedigree and inheritance rights.

Some important kinship linkages are not traced through men but through women. These linkages involve those related to an individual by blood and marriage through a mother, married sisters, or married daughters, and for a man, through his wife. Anthropologist David Mandelbaum has termed these "feminal kin." Key relationships are those between a brother and sister, parents and daughters, and a person and his or her mother's brother. Through bonds with these close kin, a person has links with several households and lineages in many settlements. Throughout most of India, there are continuous visits—some of which may last for months and include the exchange of gifts at visits, life-cycle rites, and holidays, and many other key interactions between such relatives. These relationships are often characterized by deep affection and willingly offered support.

These ties cut across the countryside, linking each person with kin in villages and towns near and far. Almost everywhere a villager goes—especially in the north, where marriage networks cover wide distances—he can find some kind of relative. Moral support, a place to stay, economic assistance, and political backing are all available through these kinship networks.

The multitude of kinship ties is further extended through the device of fictive kinship. Residents of a single village usually use kinship terms for one another, and especially strong ties of fictive kinship can be ceremonially created with fellow religious initiates or fellow pilgrims of one's village or neighborhood. In the villages and cities of the north, on the festival of Raksha Bandhan (the Tying of the Protective Thread, during which sisters tie sacred threads on their brothers' wrists to symbolize the continuing bond between them), a female may tie a thread on the wrist of an otherwise unrelated male and "make him her brother." Fictive kinship bonds cut across caste and class lines and involve obligations of hospitality, gift-giving, and variable levels of cooperation and assistance.

Neighbors and friends may also create fictive kinship ties by informal agreement. Actually, any strong friendship between otherwise unrelated people is typically imbued with kinship-like qualities. In such friendships, kinship terms are adopted for address, and the give and take of kinship may develop. Such bonds commonly evolve between neighbors in urban apartment buildings, between special friends at school, and between close associates at work. The use of kinship terms enhances affection in the relationship. In Gujarat, personal names usually include the word for "sister" and "brother," so that the use of someone's personal name automatically sounds affectionate and caring.

Family Authority and Harmony

In the Indian household, lines of hierarchy and authority are clearly drawn, shaping structurally and psychologically complex family relationships. Ideals of conduct are aimed at creating and maintaining family harmony.

All family members are socialized to accept the authority of those ranked above them in the hierarchy. In general, elders rank above juniors, and among people of similar age, males outrank females. Daughters of a family command the formal respect of their brothers' wives, and the mother of a household is in charge of her daughters-in-law. Among adults in a joint family, a newly arrived daughter-in-law has the least authority. Males learn to command others within the household but expect to accept the direction of senior males. Ideally, even a mature adult man living in his father's household acknowledges his father's authority on both minor and major matters. Women are especially strongly socialized to accept a position subservient to males, to control their sexual impulses, and to subordinate their personal preferences to the needs of the family and kin group. Reciprocally, those in authority accept responsibility for meeting the needs of others in the family group.

There is tremendous emphasis on the unity of the family grouping, especially as differentiated from persons outside the kinship circle. Internally, efforts are made to deemphasize ties between spouses and between parents and their own children in order to enhance a wider sense of harmony within the entire household. Husbands and wives are discouraged from openly displaying affection for one another, and in strictly traditional households, they may not even properly speak to one another in the presence of anyone else, even their own children. Young parents are inhibited by "shame" from ostentatiously dandling their own young children but are encouraged to play with the children of siblings.

Psychologically, family members feel an intense emotional interdependence with each other and the family as an almost organic unit. Ego boundaries are permeable to others in the family, and any notion of a separate self is often dominated by a sense of what psychoanalyst Alan Roland has termed a more inclusive "familial self." Interpersonal empathy, closeness, loyalty, and interdependency are all crucial to life within the family.

Family resources, particularly land or businesses, have traditionally been controlled by family males, especially in high-status groups. Customarily, according to traditional schools of Hindu law, women did not inherit land or buildings and were thus beholden to their male kin who controlled these vital resources. Under Muslim customary law, women are entitled to inherit real estate and often do so, but their shares have typically been smaller than those of similarly situated males. Under modern law, all Indian women can inherit land.

Veiling and the Seclusion of Women

A particularly interesting aspect of Indian family life is purdah (from the Hindi *parda*, literally, curtain), or the veiling and seclusion of women. In much of northern and central India, particularly in rural areas, Hindu and Muslim women follow complex rules of veiling the body and avoidance of public appearance, especially in the presence of relatives linked by marriage and before strange men. Purdah practices are inextricably linked to patterns of authority and harmony within the family. Rules of Hindu and Muslim purdah differ in certain key ways, but female modesty and decorum as well as concepts of family honor are essential to the various forms of purdah. In most areas, purdah restrictions are stronger for women of high-status families.

The importance of purdah is not limited to family life; rather, these practices all involve restrictions on female activity and access to power and the control of vital resources in a male-dominated society. Restriction and restraint for women in virtually every aspect of life are the basic essentials of purdah. In India, both males and females are circumscribed in their actions by economic disabilities, hierarchical rules of deference in kinship groups, castes, and the larger society. But for women who observe purdah, there are additional constraints.

For almost all women, modest dress and behavior are important. Clothing covering most of the body is common; only in tribal groups and among a few castes do women publicly bare their legs or upper bodies. In most of the northern half of India, traditionally dressed women cover the tops of their heads with the end of the sari or scarf (*dupatta*). Generally, females are expected to associate only with kin or companions approved by their families and to remain sexually chaste.

Women are not encouraged to roam about on pleasure junkets, but rather travel only for explicit family-sanctioned purposes. In North India, women do relatively little shopping; most shopping is done by men. In contrast to females, males have much more freedom of movement and observe much less body modesty.

For both males and females, free association with the opposite sex is limited, and dating in the Western sense is essentially limited to members of the educated urban elite. In all areas, illicit liaisons do occur. Although the male may escape social repudiation if such liaisons become known, the female may suffer lasting damage to her own reputation and bring dishonor to her family. Further, if a woman is sexually linked with a man of lower caste status, the woman is regarded as being irremediably polluted, "like an earthen pot." A male so sullied can be cleansed of his temporary pollution, "like a brass pot," with a ritual bath.

Such rules of feminine modesty are not considered purdah but merely proper female behavior. For traditional Hindus of northern and central India, purdah observances begin at marriage, when a woman acquires a husband and in-laws. Although she almost never observes purdah in her natal home or before her natal relatives, a woman does observe purdah in her husband's home and before his relatives. As a young woman, she remains inside her husband's house much of the time (rather than going out into lanes or fields), absents herself or covers her face with her sari in the presence of senior males and females related by marriage, and, when she does leave the house in her marital village, covers her face with her sari.

Through use of the end of the sari as a face veil and deference of manner, a married woman shows respect to her affinal kin who are older than or equal to her husband in age, as well as certain other relatives. She may speak to the women before whom she veils, but she usually does not converse with the men. Exceptions to this are her husband's younger brothers, before whom she may veil her face, but with whom she has a warm joking relationship involving verbal banter.

Initially almost faceless and voiceless in her marital home, a married woman matures and gradually relaxes some of these practices, especially as elder in-laws become senescent or die and she herself assumes senior status. In fact, after some years, a wife may neglect to veil her face in front of her husband when others are present and may even speak to her husband in public.

Such practices help shield women from unwanted male advances and control women's sexuality but also express relations within and between groups of kin. Familial prestige, household harmony, social distance, affinal respect, property ownership, and local political power are all linked to purdah.

Restricting women to household endeavors rather than involving them in tasks in fields and markets is associated with prestige and high rank in northern India. There the wealthiest families employ servants to carry water from the well and to work in the fields alongside family males. Mature women of these families may make rare appearances in the fields to bring lunch to the family males working there and sometimes to supervise laborers. Thus elitism is expressed in women's exclusive domesticity, with men providing economic necessities for the family.

Only women of poor and low-ranking groups engage in heavy manual labor outside the home, especially for pay. Such women work long hours in the fields, on construction gangs, and at many other tasks, often veiling their faces as they work.

For Muslim women, purdah practices involve less emphasis on veiling from in-laws and more emphasis on protecting women from contact with strangers outside the sphere of kinship. Because Muslims often marry cousins, a woman's in-laws may also be her natal relatives, so veiling her face within the marital home is often inappropriate. Unlike Hindus, Muslim women do not veil from other women as do Hindus. Traditional Muslim women and even unmarried girls, however, often refrain from appearing in public, or if they do go out, they wear an all-covering garment known as a *burka*, with a full face covering. A *burka* protects a woman—and her family—from undue familiarity with unknown outsiders, thus emphasizing the unity of the family vis-à-vis the outside world. Because Muslim women are entitled to a share in the family real estate, controlling their relationships with males outside the family can be crucial to the maintenance of family property and prestige.

In rural communities and in older sections of cities, purdah observances remain vital, although they are gradually diminishing in intensity. Among the educated urban and rural elite, purdah practices are rapidly vanishing and for many have all but disappeared. Chastity and female modesty are still highly valued, but, for the elite, face-veiling and the *burka* are consid-

Rajasthani village women and children participate in a wedding ritual.
Courtesy Janice Hyde

ered unsophisticated. As girls and women become more widely and more highly educated, female employment outside the home is commonplace, even for women of elite families.

Life Passages

In India, the ideal stages of life have been most clearly articulated by Hindus. The ancient Hindu ideal rests on childhood, followed by four stages: undergoing religious initiation and becoming a celibate student of religious texts, getting married and becoming a householder, leaving home to become a forest hermit after becoming a grandparent, and becoming a homeless wanderer free of desire for all material things. Although few actually follow this scheme, it serves as a guide for those attempting to live according to valued standards. For Hindus,

251

dharma (a divinely ordained code of proper conduct), karma (the sum of one's deeds in this life and in past lives), and *kismat* (fate) are considered relevant to the course of life (see The Roots of Indian Religion, ch. 3). Crucial transitions from one phase of life to another are marked by sometimes elaborate rites of passage.

Children and Childhood

Throughout much of India, a baby's birth is celebrated with rites of welcome and blessing—songs, drums, happy distribution of sweets, auspicious unguents, gifts for infant and mother, preparation of horoscopes, and inscriptions in the genealogist's record books. In general, children are deeply desired and welcomed, their presence regarded as a blessing on the household. Babies are often treated like small deities, pampered and coddled, adorned with makeup and trinkets, and carried about and fed with the finest foods available to the family. Young girls are worshiped as personifications of Hindu goddesses, and little boys are adulated as scions of the clan.

In their children, parents see the future of the lineage and wider kin group, helpers in daily tasks, and providers of security in the parents' old age. These delightful ideals are articulated and enacted over and over again; yet, a coexisting harsher reality emerges from a close examination of events and statistics. Many children lead lives of striking hardship, and many die premature deaths. In general, conditions are significantly worse for girls than for boys.

Birth celebrations for baby daughters are more muted than for sons and are sometimes absent altogether. Although India was once led by a woman prime minister, Indira Gandhi, and Indian women currently hold a wide range of powerful positions in every walk of life, there is a strong cultural bias toward males. Girls are frequently victims of underfeeding, medical neglect, sex-selective abortion, and outright infanticide. According to the 1991 census final population totals, there were 927 females per 1,000 males in India—a figure that has gradually declined from 972 females per 1,000 males in 1901 and from 934 just since 1981. Much of this imbalance is attained through neglecting the nutritional and health needs of female children, and much is also the result of inadequate health care for women of childbearing years. The sex ratio is even more imbalanced in urban areas (894 per 1,000 in 1991) than in rural areas (938 per 1,000 in 1991), partially because a large number of village men go to work in cities, leaving their wives and children behind in their rural homes (see Structure and Dynamics, ch. 2).

That girls are victims of fatal neglect and murder has been thoroughly discussed in the Indian press and in scholarly investigations. It has been noted that infant girls are killed with potions of opium in Rajasthan and pastes of poisonous oleander in Tamil Nadu—most especially girls preceded by the birth of several sisters. Clinics offering ultrasound and amniocentesis in order to detect and abort female fetuses have become popular in various parts of the country, and many thousands of female fetuses have been so destroyed. In Maharashtra, Rajasthan, and Punjab such selective abortions have been outlawed because of pressure from feminist groups. More usually, girls are simply fed and cared for less well than their brothers.

The sex ratio is particularly unfavorable to females in the central northern section of the country. For example, in Uttar Pradesh there are only eighty-eight females per 100 males; in Haryana, eighty-seven per 100; and in Rajasthan ninety-one per 100. By contrast, in Kerala, on the southwest coast, a region traditionally noted for matriliny, the sex ratio is reversed, with females outnumbering males 104 to 100. In Andhra Pradesh and Tamil Nadu, two large southern states, there are ninety-seven females per 100 males.

Parents favor boys for various reasons. In the north, a boy's value in agricultural endeavors is higher than a girl's, and after marriage a boy continues to live with his parents, ideally supporting them in their old age. Political scientist Philip Oldenburg notes that in some violence-prone regions of the north, having sons may enhance families' capacity to defend themselves and to exercise power. A girl, however, moves away to live with her husband's relatives, and with her goes a dowry. In the late twentieth century, the values of dowries have been increasing, and, furthermore, groups that never gave dowries in the past are being pressured to do so. Thus, a girl child can represent a significant economic liability to her parents. In rice-growing areas, especially in the south, girls receive better treatment, and there is some evidence that the better treatment is related to the value of women as field workers in wet-rice cultivation. Throughout most of India, for Hindus it is important to have a son conduct funeral rites for his parents; a daughter, as a member of her husband's lineage, has not traditionally been able to do so.

For both boys and girls, infant mortality rates tend to be high, and in the absence of confidence that their infants will live, parents tend to produce numerous offspring in the hope that at least two sons will survive to adulthood. Family planning measures are used to a modest degree in India; perhaps 37.5 percent of couples use contraceptives at least occasionally (see Population and Family Planning Policy, ch. 2). Abortion is legal, condoms are advertised on colorful billboards, and government health services offer small bounties for patients undergoing vasectomies and tubal ligations. In some regions, most notably Kerala, better health care and higher infant survival rates are associated with lowered fertility rates (see Health Conditions, ch. 2).

Most children survive infancy and do not fall victim to the cultural and economic pressures alluded to above. The majority of children grow up as valued members of a family, treasured by their parents and encouraged to participate in appropriate activities. Although relative ages of children are always known and reflected in linguistic and deference behavior, there is little age-grading in daily life. Children of all ages associate with each other and with adults, unlike the situation in the West, where age-grading is common.

Studies of Indian psychology by Sudhir Kakar, Alan Roland, and others stress that the young Indian child grows up in intimate emotional contact with the mother and other mothering persons. Because conjugal marital relationships are deemphasized in the joint household, a woman looks to her children to satisfy some of her intimacy needs. Her bond to her children, especially her sons but also her daughters, becomes enormously strong and lasting. A child is suckled on demand, sometimes for years, sleeps with a parent or grandparent, is bathed by doting relatives, and is rarely left alone. Massaged with oil, carried about, gently toilet-trained, and gratified with treats, the young child develops an inner core of well-being and a profound sense of expectation of protection from others. Such indulgent and close relationships produce a symbiotic mode of relating to others and effect the development of a person with a deeply held sense of involvement with relatives, so vital to the Indian family situation.

The young child learns early about hierarchy within the family, as he watches affectionate and respectful relationships between seniors and juniors, males and females. A young child is often carried about by an older sibling, and strong and close sibling bonds usually develop. Bickering among siblings is not as common as it is in the West; rather, most siblings learn to think of themselves as part of a family unit that must work together as it meets the challenges of the outside world.

Young children are encouraged to participate in the numerous rituals that emphasize family ties. The power of sibling relationships is recognized, for example, when a brother touches his sister's feet, honoring in her the principle of feminine divinity, which, if treated appropriately, can bring him prosperity. In calendrical and life-cycle rituals in both the north and the south, sisters bless their brothers and also symbolically request their protection throughout life.

After about four or five years of indulgence, children typically experience greater demands from family members. In villages, children learn the rudiments of agricultural labor, and young children often help with weeding, harvesting, threshing, and the like. Girls learn domestic chores, and boys are encouraged to take cattle for grazing, learn plowing, and begin to drive bullock carts and ride bicycles. City children also learn household duties, and children of poor families often work as servants in the homes of the prosperous. Some even pick through garbage piles to find shreds of food and fuel.

In some areas, children work as exploited laborers in factories, where they weave carpets for the export market and make matches, glass bangles, and other products. At Sivakasi, in Tamil Nadu, some 45,000 children work in the match, fireworks, and printing industries, comprising perhaps the largest single concentration of child labor in the world. Children reportedly as young as four years old work long hours each day.

Education in a school setting is available for most of India's children, and many young people attend school (see Primary and Secondary Education, ch. 2). Officials state that education is "compulsory," but the reality is that a significant percentage of children—especially girls—fail to become literate and instead carry out many other tasks in order to contribute to family income. More than half of India's children between the ages of six and fourteen—82.2 million—are not in school. Instead they participate in the labor force, even as more privileged children study at government and private schools and prepare for more prestigious jobs. Thus children learn early the realities of socioeconomic and urban-rural differentiation and grow up to perpetuate India's hierarchical society.

For many children, especially boys, an important event of young adolescence is religious initiation. Initiation rituals vary among different regions, religious communities, and castes (see Life-Cycle Rituals, ch. 3). In the north, girls reach puberty without public notice and in an atmosphere of shyness, whereas in much of the south, puberty celebrations joyously announce to the family and community that a young girl has grown to maturity.

Marriage

In India there is no greater event in a family than a wedding, dramatically evoking every possible social obligation, kinship bond, traditional value, impassioned sentiment, and economic resource. In the arranging and conducting of weddings, the complex permutations of Indian social systems best display themselves.

Marriage is deemed essential for virtually everyone in India. For the individual, marriage is the great watershed in life, marking the transition to adulthood. Generally, this transition, like everything else in India, depends little upon individual volition but instead occurs as a result of the efforts of many people. Even as one is born into a particular family without the exercise of any personal choice, so is one given a spouse without any personal preference involved. Arranging a marriage is a critical responsibility for parents and other relatives of both bride and groom. Marriage alliances entail some redistribution of wealth as well as building and restructuring social realignments, and, of course, result in the biological reproduction of families.

Some parents begin marriage arrangements on the birth of a child, but most wait until later. In the past, the age of marriage was quite young, and in a few small groups, especially in Rajasthan, children under the age of five are still united in marriage. In rural communities, prepuberty marriage for girls traditionally was the rule. In the late twentieth century, the age of marriage is rising in villages, almost to the levels that obtain in cities. Legislation mandating minimum marriage ages has been passed in various forms over the past decades, but such laws have little effect on actual marriage practices.

Essentially, India is divided into two large regions with regard to Hindu kinship and marriage practices, the north and the south. Additionally, various ethnic and tribal groups of the central, mountainous north, and eastern regions follow a variety of other practices. These variations have been extensively described and analyzed by anthropologists, especially Irawati Karve, David G. Mandelbaum, and Clarence Maloney.

Broadly, in the Indo-Aryan-speaking north, a family seeks marriage alliances with people to whom it is not already linked by ties of blood. Marriage arrangements often involve looking far afield. In the Dravidian-speaking south, a family seeks to strengthen existing kin ties through marriage, preferably with blood relatives. Kinship terminology reflects this basic pattern. In the north, every kinship term clearly indicates whether the person referred to is a blood relation or an affinal relation; all blood relatives are forbidden as marriage mates to a person or a person's children. In the south, there is no clear-cut distinction between the family of birth and the family of marriage. Because marriage in the south commonly involves a continuing exchange of daughters among a few families, for the married couple all relatives are ultimately blood kin. Dravidian terminology stresses the principle of relative age: all relatives are arranged according to whether they are older or younger than each other without reference to generation.

On the Indo-Gangetic Plain, marriages are contracted outside the village, sometimes even outside of large groups of villages, with members of the same caste beyond any traceable consanguineal ties. In much of the area, daughters should not be given into villages where daughters of the family or even of the natal village have previously been given. In most of the region, brother-sister exchange marriages (marriages linking a brother and sister of one household with the sister and brother of another) are shunned. The entire emphasis is on casting the marriage net ever-wider, creating new alliances. The residents of a single village may have in-laws in hundreds of other villages.

In most of North India, the Hindu bride goes to live with strangers in a home she has never visited. There she is sequestered and veiled, an outsider who must learn to conform to new ways. Her natal family is often geographically distant, and her ties with her consanguineal kin undergo attenuation to varying degrees.

In central India, the basic North Indian pattern prevails, with some modifications. For example, in Madhya Pradesh, village exogamy is preferred, but marriages within a village are not uncommon. Marriages between caste-fellows in neighboring villages are frequent. Brother-sister exchange marriages are sometimes arranged, and daughters are often given in marriage to lineages where other daughters of their lineage or village have previously been wed.

In South India, in sharp contrast, marriages are preferred between cousins (especially cross-cousins, that is, the children of a brother and sister) and even between uncles and nieces (especially a man and his elder sister's daughter). The principle involved is that of return—the family that gives a daughter expects one in return, if not now, then in the next generation. The effect of such marriages is to bind people together in relatively small, tight-knit kin groups. A bride moves to her in-laws' home—the home of her grandmother or aunt—and is often comfortable among these familiar faces. Her husband may well be the cousin she has known all her life that she would marry.

Many South Indian marriages are contracted outside of such close kin groups when no suitable mates exist among close relatives, or when other options appear more advantageous. Some sophisticated South Indians, for example, consider cousin marriage and uncle-niece marriage outmoded.

Rules for the remarriage of widows differ from one group to another. Generally, lower-ranking groups allow widow remarriage, particularly if the woman is relatively young, but the highest-ranking castes discourage or forbid such remarriage. The most strict adherents to the nonremarriage of widows are Brahmans. Almost all groups allow widowers to remarry. Many groups encourage a widower to marry his deceased wife's younger sister (but never her older sister).

Among Muslims of both the north and the south, marriage between cousins is encouraged, both cross-cousins (the children of a brother and sister) and parallel cousins (the children of two same-sex siblings). In the north, such cousins grow up calling each other "brother" and "sister", yet they may marry. Even when cousin marriage does not occur, spouses can often trace between them other kinship linkages.

Some tribal people of central India practice an interesting permutation of the southern pattern. Among the Murias of Bastar in southeastern Madhya Pradesh, as described by anthropologist Verrier Elwin, teenagers live together in a dormitory (*ghotul*), sharing life and love with one another for several blissful years. Ultimately, their parents arrange their marriages, usually with cross-cousins, and the delights of teenage romance are replaced with the serious responsibilities of adulthood. In his survey of some 2,000 marriages, Elwin found

*Jain wedding ceremony, with
bride, groom, and sacred fire,
Jodhpur, Rajasthan
Courtesy Doranne Jacobson*

only seventy-seven cases of *ghotul* partners eloping together
and very few cases of divorce. Among the Muria and Gond
tribal groups, cross-cousin marriage is called "bringing back
the milk," alluding to the gift of a girl in one generation being
returned by the gift of a girl in the next.

Finding the perfect partner for one's child can be a challenging task. People use their social networks to locate potential brides and grooms of appropriate social and economic
status. Increasingly, urban dwellers use classified matrimonial
advertisements in newspapers. The advertisements usually
announce religion, caste, and educational qualifications, stress
female beauty and male (and in the contemporary era, sometimes female) earning capacity, and may hint at dowry size.

In rural areas, matches between strangers are usually
arranged without the couple meeting each other. Rather, parents and other relatives come to an agreement on behalf of the
couple. In cities, however, especially among the educated
classes, photographs are exchanged, and sometimes the couple
are allowed to meet under heavily chaperoned circumstances,
such as going out for tea with a group of people or meeting in
the parlor of the girl's home, with her relatives standing by.
Young professional men and their families may receive inquir-
ies and photographs from representatives of several girls' families. They may send their relatives to meet the most promising

259

candidates and then go on tour themselves to meet the young women and make a final choice. In the early 1990s, increasing numbers of marriages arranged in this way link brides and grooms from India with spouses of Indian parentage resident in Europe, North America, and the Middle East.

Almost all Indian children are raised with the expectation that their parents will arrange their marriages, but an increasing number of young people, especially among the college-educated, are finding their own spouses. So-called love marriages are deemed a slightly scandalous alternative to properly arranged marriages. Some young people convince their parents to "arrange" their marriages to people with whom they have fallen in love. This process has long been possible for Indians from the south and for Muslims who want to marry a particular cousin of the appropriate marriageable category. In the upper classes, these semi-arranged love marriages increasingly occur between young people who are from castes of slightly different rank but who are educationally or professionally equal. If there are vast differences to overcome, such as is the case with love marriages between Hindus and Muslims or between Hindus of very different caste status, parents are usually much less agreeable, and serious family disruptions can result.

In much of India, especially in the north, a marriage establishes a structural opposition between the kin groups of the bride and groom—bride-givers and bride-takers. Within this relationship, bride-givers are considered inferior to bride-takers and are forever expected to give gifts to the bride-takers. The one-way flow of gifts begins at engagement and continues for a generation or two. The most dramatic aspect of this asymmetrical relationship is the giving of dowry.

In many communities throughout India, a dowry has traditionally been given by a bride's kin at the time of her marriage. In ancient times, the dowry was considered a woman's wealth—property due a beloved daughter who had no claim on her natal family's real estate—and typically included portable valuables such as jewelry and household goods that a bride could control throughout her life. However, over time, the larger proportion of the dowry has come to consist of goods and cash payments that go straight into the hands of the groom's family. In the late twentieth century, throughout much of India, dowry payments have escalated, and a groom's parents sometimes insist on compensation for their son's higher education and even for his future earnings, to which the bride will presumably have access. Some of the dowries demanded are quite oppressive, amounting to several years' salary in cash as well as items such as motorcycles, air conditioners, and fancy cars. Among some lower-status groups, large dowries are currently replacing traditional bride-price payments. Even among Muslims, previously not given to demanding large dowries, reports of exorbitant dowries are increasing.

The dowry is becoming an increasingly onerous burden for the bride's family. Antidowry laws exist but are largely ignored, and a bride's treatment in her marital home is often affected by the value of her dowry. Increasingly frequent are horrible incidents, particularly in urban areas, where a groom's family makes excessive demands on the bride's family—even after marriage—and when the demands are not met, murder the bride, typically by setting her clothes on fire in a cooking "accident." The groom is then free to remarry and collect another sumptuous dowry. The male and female in-laws implicated in these murders have seldom been punished.

Such dowry deaths have been the subject of numerous media reports in India and other countries and have mobilized feminist groups to action. In some of the worst areas, such as the National Capital Territory of Delhi, where hundreds of such deaths are reported annually and the numbers are increasing yearly, the law now requires that all suspicious deaths of new brides be investigated. Official government figures report 1,786 registered dowry deaths nationwide in 1987; there is also an estimate of some 5,000 dowry deaths in 1991. Women's groups sometimes picket the homes of the in-laws of burned brides. Some analysts have related the growth of this phenomenon to the growth of consumerism in Indian society.

Fears of impoverishing their parents have led some urban middle-class young women, married and unmarried, to commit suicide. However, through the giving of large dowries, the newly wealthy are often able to marry their treasured daughters up the status hierarchy so reified in Indian society.

After marriage arrangements are completed, a rich panoply of wedding rituals begins. Each religious group, region, and caste has a slightly different set of rites. Generally, all weddings involve as many kin and associates of the bride and groom as possible. The bride's family usually hosts most of the ceremonies and pays for all the arrangements for large numbers of guests for several days, including accommodation, feasting, decorations, and gifts for the groom's party. These arrangements are often extremely elaborate and expensive and are intended to enhance the status of the bride's family. The groom's party usually hires a band and brings fine gifts for the bride, such as jewelry and clothing, but these are typically far outweighed in value by the presents received from the bride's side.

After the bride and groom are united in sacred rites attended by colorful ceremony, the new bride may be carried away to her in-laws' home, or, if she is very young, she may remain with her parents until they deem her old enough to depart. A prepubescent bride usually stays in her natal home until puberty, after which a separate consummation ceremony is held to mark her departure for her conjugal home and married life. The poignancy of the bride's weeping departure for her new home is prominent in personal memory, folklore, literature, song, and drama throughout India.

Adulthood

In their new status, a young married couple begin to accept adult responsibilities. These include work inside and outside of the home, childbearing and childrearing, developing and maintaining social relationships, fulfilling religious obligations, and enhancing family prosperity and prestige as much as possible.

The young husband usually remains resident with his natal family, surrounded by well-known relatives and neighbors. The young bride, however, is typically thrust into a strange household, where she is expected to follow ideal patterns of chaste and cheerfully obedient behavior.

Ideally, the Hindu wife should honor her husband as if he were her personal god. Through her marriage, a woman becomes an auspicious wife (*suhagan*), adorned with bangles and amulets designed to protect her husband's life and imbued with ritual powers to influence prosperity and procreation. At her wedding, the Hindu bride is likened to Lakshmi, the Goddess of Wealth, in symbolic recognition of the fact that the groom's patrilineage can increase and prosper only through her fertility and labors. Despite this simile, elegantly stated in the nuptial ritual, the young wife is pressed into service as the most subordinate member of her husband's family. If any misfortunes happen to befall her affinal family after her arrival, she may be blamed as the bearer of bad luck. Not surprisingly, some young women find adjusting to these new circumstances extremely upsetting. A small percentage experience psychological distress so severe that they seem to be possessed by outspoken ghosts and spirits.

In these difficult early days of a marriage, and later on throughout her life, a woman looks to her natal kin for moral and often economic support. Although she has become part of another household and lineage, she depends on her natal relatives—especially her brothers—to back her up in a variety of circumstances. A wide range of long visits home, ritual obligations, gifts, folklore, and songs reflect the significance of a woman's lifelong ties to her blood relatives.

By producing children, especially highly valued sons, and, ultimately, becoming a mother-in-law herself, a woman gradually improves her position within the conjugal household. In motherhood the married woman finds social approval, economic security, and emotional satisfaction.

A man and his wife owe respect and obedience to his parents and other senior relatives. Ideally, all cooperate in the joint family enterprise. Gradually, as the years pass, members of the younger generation take the place of the older generation and become figures of authority and respect. As this transition occurs, it is generally assumed that younger family members will physically care for and support elders until their demise.

In their adult years, men and women engage in a wide variety of tasks and occupations strongly linked to socioeconomic status, including caste membership, wealth, place of residence, and many other factors. In general, the higher the status of a family, the less likely its members are to engage in manual labor and the more likely its members are to be served by employees of lower status. Although educated women are increasingly working outside the home, even in urbane circles some negative stigma is still attached to women's employment. In addition, students from high-status families do not work at temporary menial jobs as they do in many Western countries.

People of low status work at the many menial tasks that high-status people disdain. Poor women cannot afford to abstain from paid labor, and they work alongside their menfolk in the fields and at construction projects. In low-status families, women are less likely than high-status women to unquestioningly accept the authority of men and even of elders because they are directly responsible for providing income for the family. Among Sweepers, very low-status latrine cleaners, women carry out more of the traditional tasks than do men and hold a relatively less subordinate position in their families than do women of traditional high-status families. Such women are, nonetheless, less powerful in the society at large than are women of economically prosperous high-status families, who control and influence the control of more assets than do poor women.

Along with economically supporting themselves, their elders, and their children, adults must maintain and add to the elaborate social networks upon which life depends. Offering gracious hospitality to guests is a key ingredient of proper adult behavior. Adults must also attend to religious matters, carrying out rites intended to protect their families and communities. In these efforts, men and women constantly work for the benefit of their kin groups, castes, and other social units.

Death and Beyond

The death of an infant or young child—a common event in India—causes sorrow but usually not major social disruption. The death of a married adult has wider repercussions. Among Hindus, the demise of a lineage member immediately ritually pollutes the entire lineage for a period of several days. As part of the mourning process, closely related male mourners have their heads and facial hair shaved, thus publicly declaring their close links to the deceased. Various funeral rites, feasts, and mourning practices affirm kinship ties with the deceased and among survivors. Crucial social bonds become visible to all concerned.

Although a man may grieve for his deceased wife, a widow may face not only a personal loss but a major restructuring of her life. Becoming a widow in India is not a benign or neutral event. A man's death, particularly if it occurs when he is young, may be attributed to ill fortune brought upon him by his wife, possibly because of her sins in a past life.

With the death of her husband, a woman's auspicious wifehood ends, and she is plunged into dreaded widowhood. The very word *widow* is used as an epithet. As a widow, a woman is devoid of reason to adorn herself. If she follows tradition, she may shave her head, shed her jewelry, and wear only plain white or dark clothing.

Widows of low-ranking groups have always been allowed to remarry, but widows of high rank have been expected to remain unmarried and chaste until death. In earlier times, for

Street vendor, Jaipur, Rajasthan
Courtesy Sandra Day O'Connor

child brides married to older men and widowed young, these strictures caused great hardship and inspired reform movements in some parts of the country.

In past centuries, the ultimate rejection of widowhood occurred in the burning of the Hindu widow on her husband's funeral pyre, a practice known as sati (meaning, literally, true or virtuous one). Women who so perished in the funeral flames were posthumously adulated, and even in the late twentieth century are worshiped at memorial tablets and temples erected in their honor. In western India, Rajput lineages proudly point to satis in their history. Sati was never widespread, and it has been illegal since 1829, but a few cases of sati still occur in India every year. In choosing to die with her husband, a woman evinces great merit and power and is considered able to bring boons to her husband's patrilineage and to others who honor her. Thus, through her meritorious death, a widow avoids disdain and achieves glory, not only for herself, but for all of her kin as well.

By restricting widow remarriage, high-status groups limit restructuring of the lineage on the death of a male member. An unmarried widow remains a member of her husband's lineage, with no competing ties to other groups of in-laws. Her rights to her husband's property, traditionally limited though they are to management rather than outright inheritance, remain uncomplicated by remarriage to a man from another lineage. It is among lower-ranking groups with lesser amounts of property and prestige that widow remarriage is most frequent.

Most Indians see their present lifetimes as but a prelude to an afterlife, the quality of which depends on their behavior in this life. Muslims envision heaven and hell, but Hindus conceptualize a series of rebirths ideally culminating in union with the divine (see The Monastic Path, ch. 3). Some Hindus believe they are destined to marry the same person in each of their lifetimes. Thus people feel connected with different permutations of themselves and others over cosmic cycles of time.

Caste and Class

Varna, Caste, and Other Divisions

Although many other nations are characterized by social inequality, perhaps nowhere else in the world has inequality been so elaborately constructed as in the Indian institution of caste. Caste has long existed in India, but in the modern period it has been severely criticized by both Indian and foreign observers. Although some educated Indians tell non-Indians that caste has been abolished or that "no one pays attention to caste anymore," such statements do not reflect reality.

Caste has undergone significant change since independence, but it still involves hundreds of millions of people. In its preamble,* India's constitution forbids negative public discrimination on the basis of caste. However, caste ranking and caste-based interaction have occurred for centuries and will continue to do so well into the foreseeable future, more in the countryside than in urban settings and more in the realms of kinship and marriage than in less personal interactions.

Castes are ranked, named, endogamous (in-marrying) groups, membership in which is achieved by birth. There are thousands of castes and subcastes in India, and these large kinship-based groups are fundamental to South Asian social structure. Each caste is part of a locally based system of interdependence with other groups, involving occupational specialization, and is linked in complex ways with networks that stretch across regions and throughout the nation.

The word *caste* derives from the Portuguese *casta,* meaning breed, race, or kind. Among the Indian terms that are sometimes translated as caste are *varna* (see Glossary), *jati* (see Glossary), *jat, biradri,* and *samaj.* All of these terms refer to ranked groups of various sizes and breadth. *Varna,* or color, actually refers to large divisions that include various castes; the other terms include castes and subdivisions of castes sometimes called subcastes.

Many castes are traditionally associated with an occupation, such as high-ranking Brahmans; middle-ranking farmer and artisan groups, such as potters, barbers, and carpenters; and very low-ranking "Untouchable" leatherworkers, butchers, launderers, and latrine cleaners. There is some correlation between ritual rank on the caste hierarchy and economic prosperity. Members of higher-ranking castes tend, on the whole, to be more prosperous than members of lower-ranking castes. Many lower-caste people live in conditions of great poverty and social disadvantage.

According to the Rig Veda, sacred texts that date back to oral traditions of more than 3,000 years ago, progenitors of the four ranked *varna* groups sprang from various parts of the body of the primordial man, which Brahma created from clay (see The Vedas and Polytheism, ch. 3). Each group had a function in sustaining the life of society—the social body. Brahmans, or priests, were created from the mouth. They were to provide for the intellectual and spiritual needs of the community. Kshatriyas, warriors and rulers, were derived from the arms. Their role was to rule and to protect others. Vaishyas—landowners and merchants—sprang from the thighs, and were entrusted with the care of commerce and agriculture. Shudras—artisans and servants—came from the feet. Their task was to perform all manual labor.

Later conceptualized was a fifth category, "Untouchable" menials, relegated to carrying out very menial and polluting work related to bodily decay and dirt. Since 1935 "Untouchables" have been known as Scheduled Castes, referring to their listing on government rosters, or schedules. They are also often called by Mohandas Karamchand (Mahatma) Gandhi's term

Harijans, or "Children of God." Although the term *Untouchable* appears in literature produced by these low-ranking castes, in the 1990s, many politically conscious members of these groups prefer to refer to themselves as Dalit (see Glossary), a Hindi word meaning oppressed or downtrodden. According to the 1991 census, there were 138 million Scheduled Caste members in India, approximately 16 percent of the total population.

The first four *varnas* apparently existed in the ancient Aryan society of northern India. Some historians say that these categories were originally somewhat fluid functional groups, not castes. A greater degree of fixity gradually developed, resulting in the complex ranking systems of medieval India that essentially continue in the late twentieth century.

Although a *varna* is not a caste, when directly asked for their caste affiliation, particularly when the questioner is a Westerner, many Indians will reply with a *varna* name. Pressed further, they may respond with a much more specific name of a caste, or *jati*, which falls within that *varna*. For example, a Brahman may specify that he is a member of a named caste group, such as a Jijotiya Brahman, or a Smartha Brahman, and so on. Within such castes, people may further belong to smaller sub-caste categories and to specific clans and lineages. These finer designations are particularly relevant when marriages are being arranged and often appear in newspaper matrimonial advertisements.

Members of a caste are typically spread out over a region, with representatives living in hundreds of settlements. In any small village, there may be representatives of a few or even a score or more castes.

Numerous groups usually called tribes (often referred to as Scheduled Tribes) are also integrated into the caste system to varying degrees. Some tribes live separately from others—particularly in the far northeast and in the forested center of the country, where tribes are more like ethnic groups than castes. Some tribes are themselves divided into groups similar to sub-castes. In regions where members of tribes live in peasant villages with nontribal peoples, they are usually considered members of separate castes ranking low on the hierarchical scale.

Inequalities among castes are considered by the Hindu faithful to be part of the divinely ordained natural order and are expressed in terms of purity and pollution. Within a village, relative rank is most graphically expressed at a wedding or death

A Potter (Kumhar) caste woman painting ceramic pots, Madhya Pradesh Courtesy Doranne Jacobson

feast, when all residents of the village are invited. At the home of a high-ranking caste member, food is prepared by a member of a caste from whom all can accept cooked food (usually by a Brahman). Diners are seated in lines; members of a single caste sit next to each other in a row, and members of other castes sit in perpendicular or parallel rows at some distance. Members of Dalit castes, such as Leatherworkers and Sweepers, may be seated far from the other diners—even out in an alley. Farther away, at the edge of the feeding area, a Sweeper may wait with a large basket to receive discarded leavings tossed in by other diners. Eating food contaminated by contact with the saliva of others not of the same family is considered far too polluting to be practiced by members of any other castes. Generally, feasts and ceremonies given by Dalits are not attended by higher-ranking castes.

Among Muslims, although status differences prevail, brotherhood may be stressed. A Muslim feast usually includes a cloth laid either on clean ground or on a table, with all Muslims, rich and poor, dining from plates placed on the same cloth. Muslims who wish to provide hospitality to observant Hindus, however, must make separate arrangements for a high-caste Hindu cook and ritually pure foods and dining area.

Castes that fall within the top four ranked *varnas* are sometimes referred to as the "clean castes," with Dalits considered "unclean." Castes of the top three ranked *varnas* are often designated "twice-born," in reference to the ritual initiation undergone by male members, in which investiture with the Hindu sacred thread constitutes a kind of ritual rebirth. Non-Hindu castelike groups generally fall outside these designations.

Each caste is believed by devout Hindus to have its own dharma, or divinely ordained code of proper conduct. Accordingly, there is often a high degree of tolerance for divergent lifestyles among different castes. Brahmans are usually expected to be nonviolent and spiritual, according with their traditional roles as vegetarian teetotaler priests. Kshatriyas are supposed to be strong, as fighters and rulers should be, with a taste for aggression, eating meat, and drinking alcohol. Vaishyas are stereotyped as adept businessmen, in accord with their traditional activities in commerce. Shudras are often described by others as tolerably pleasant but expectably somewhat base in behavior, whereas Dalits—especially Sweepers—are often regarded by others as followers of vulgar life-styles. Conversely, lower-caste people often view people of high rank as haughty and unfeeling.

The chastity of women is strongly related to caste status. Generally, the higher ranking the caste, the more sexual control its women are expected to exhibit. Brahman brides should be virginal, faithful to one husband, and celibate in widowhood. By contrast, a Sweeper bride may or may not be a virgin, extramarital affairs may be tolerated, and, if widowed or divorced, the woman is encouraged to remarry. For the higher castes, such control of female sexuality helps ensure purity of lineage—of crucial importance to maintenance of high status. Among Muslims, too, high status is strongly correlated with female chastity.

Within castes explicit standards are maintained. Transgressions may be dealt with by a caste council (*panchayat*—see Glossary), meeting periodically to adjudicate issues relevant to the caste. Such councils are usually formed of groups of elders, almost always males. Punishments such as fines and outcasting, either temporary or permanent, can be enforced. In rare cases, a person is excommunicated from the caste for gross infractions of caste rules. An example of such an infraction might be marrying or openly cohabiting with a mate of a caste lower than one's own; such behavior would usually result in the higher-caste person dropping to the status of the lower-caste person.

Activities such as farming or trading can be carried out by anyone, but usually only members of the appropriate castes act as priests, barbers, potters, weavers, and other skilled artisans, whose occupational skills are handed down in families from one generation to another. As with other key features of Indian social structure, occupational specialization is believed to be in accord with the divinely ordained order of the universe.

The existence of rigid ranking is supernaturally validated through the idea of rebirth according to a person's karma, the sum of an individual's deeds in this life and in past lives. After death, a person's life is judged by divine forces, and rebirth is assigned in a high or a low place, depending upon what is deserved. This supernatural sanction can never be neglected, because it brings a person to his or her position in the caste hierarchy, relevant to every transaction involving food or drink, speaking, or touching.

In past decades, Dalits in certain areas (especially in parts of the south) had to display extreme deference to high-status people, physically keeping their distance—lest their touch or even their shadow pollute others—wearing neither shoes nor any upper body covering (even for women) in the presence of the upper castes. The lowest-ranking had to jingle a little bell in warning of their polluting approach. In much of India, Dalits were prohibited from entering temples, using wells from which the "clean" castes drew their water, or even attending schools. In past centuries, dire punishments were prescribed for Dalits who read or even heard sacred texts.

Such degrading discrimination was made illegal under legislation passed during British rule and was protested against by preindependence reform movements led by Mahatma Gandhi and Bhimrao Ramji (B.R.) Ambedkar, a Dalit leader. Dalits agitated for the right to enter Hindu temples and to use village wells and effectively pressed for the enactment of stronger laws opposing disabilities imposed on them. After independence, Ambedkar almost singlehandedly wrote India's constitution, including key provisions barring caste-based discrimination. Nonetheless, discriminatory treatment of Dalits remains a factor in daily life, especially in villages, as the end of the twentieth century approaches.

In modern times, as in the past, it is virtually impossible for an individual to raise his own status by falsely claiming to be a member of a higher-ranked caste. Such a ruse might work for a time in a place where the person is unknown, but no one would dine with or intermarry with such a person or his off-spring until the claim was validated through kinship networks. Rising on the ritual hierarchy can only be achieved by a caste as a group, over a long period of time, principally by adopting behavior patterns of higher-ranked groups. This process, known as Sanskritization, has been described by M.N. Srinivas and others. An example of such behavior is that of some Leatherworker castes adopting a policy of not eating beef, in the hope that abstaining from the defiling practice of consuming the flesh of sacred bovines would enhance their castes' status. Increased economic prosperity for much of a caste greatly aids in the process of improving rank.

Intercaste Relations

In a village, members of different castes are often linked in what has been called the *jajmani* system, after the word *jajman*, which in some regions means patron. Members of various service castes perform tasks for their patrons, usually members of the dominant, that is, most powerful landowning caste of the village (commonly castes of the Kshatriya *varna*). Households of service castes are linked through hereditary bonds to a household of patrons, with the lower-caste members providing services according to traditional occupational specializations. Thus, client families of launderers, barbers, shoemakers, carpenters, potters, tailors, and priests provide customary services to their patrons, in return for which they receive customary seasonal payments of grain, clothing, and money. Ideally, from generation to generation, clients owe their patrons political allegiance in addition to their labors, while patrons owe their clients protection and security.

The harmonious qualities of the *jajmani* system have been overidealized and variations of the system overlooked by many observers. Further, the economic interdependence of the system has weakened since the 1960s. Nevertheless, it is clear that members of different castes customarily perform a number of functions for one another in rural India that emphasize cooperation rather than competition. This cooperation is revealed in economic arrangements, in visits to farmers' threshing floors by service caste members to claim traditional payments, and in rituals emphasizing interdependence at life crises and calendrical festivals all over South Asia. For example, in rural Karnataka, in an event described by anthropologist Suzanne Hanchett, the annual procession of the village temple cart bearing images of the deities responsible for the welfare of the village cannot go forward without the combined efforts of representatives of all castes. It is believed that the sacred cart will literally not move unless all work together to move it, some pushing and some pulling.

Some observers feel that the caste system must be viewed as a system of exploitation of poor low-ranking groups by more prosperous high-ranking groups. In many parts of India, land is largely held by dominant castes—high-ranking owners of property—that economically exploit low-ranking landless laborers and poor artisans, all the while degrading them with ritual emphases on their so-called god-given inferior status. In the early 1990s, blatant subjugation of low-caste laborers in the northern state of Bihar and in eastern Uttar Pradesh was the subject of many news reports. In this region, scores of Dalits who have attempted to unite to protest low wages have been the victims of lynchings and mass killings by high-caste landowners and their hired assassins.

In 1991 the news magazine *India Today* reported that in an ostensibly prosperous village about 160 kilometers southeast of Delhi, when it became known that a rural Dalit laborer dared to have a love affair with the daughter of a high-caste landlord, the lovers and their Dalit go-between were tortured, publicly hanged, and burnt by agents of the girl's family in the presence of some 500 villagers. A similar incident occurred in 1994, when a Dalit musician who had secretly married a woman of the Kurmi cultivating caste was beaten to death by outraged Kurmis, possibly instigated by the young woman's family. The terrified bride was stripped and branded as punishment for her transgression. Dalit women also have been the victims of gang rapes by the police. Many other atrocities, as well as urban riots resulting in the deaths of Dalits, have occurred in recent years. Such extreme injustices are infrequent enough to be reported in outraged articles in the Indian press, while much more common daily discrimination and exploitation are considered virtually routine.

Changes in the Caste System

Despite many problems, the caste system has operated successfully for centuries, providing goods and services to India's many millions of citizens. The system continues to operate, but changes are occurring. India's constitution guarantees basic rights to all its citizens, including the right to equality and equal protection before the law. The practice of untouchability, as well as discrimination on the basis of caste, race, sex, or religion, has been legally abolished. All citizens have the right to vote, and political competition is lively. Voters from every stratum of society have formed interest groups, overlapping and crosscutting castes, creating an evolving new style of integrating Indian society.

Castes themselves, however, far from being abolished, have certain rights under Indian law. As described by anthropologist Owen M. Lynch and other scholars, in the expanding political arena caste groups are becoming more politicized and forced to compete with other interest groups for social and economic benefits. In the growing cities, traditional intercaste interdependencies are negligible.

Independent India has built on earlier British efforts to remedy problems suffered by Dalits by granting them some benefits of protective discrimination. Scheduled Castes are entitled to reserved electoral offices, reserved jobs in central and state governments, and special educational benefits. The constitution mandates that one-seventh of state and national legislative seats be reserved for members of Scheduled Castes in order to guarantee their voice in government. Reserving seats has proven useful because few, if any, Scheduled Caste candidates have ever been elected in nonreserved constituencies.

Educationally, Dalit students have benefited from scholarships, and Scheduled Caste literacy increased (from 10.3 percent in 1961 to 21.4 percent in 1981, the last year for which such figures are available), although not as rapidly as among the general population. Improved access to education has resulted in the emergence of a substantial group of educated Dalits able to take up white-collar occupations and fight for their rights.

There has been tremendous resistance among non-Dalits to this protective discrimination for the Scheduled Castes, who constitute some 16 percent of the total population, and efforts have been made to provide similar advantages to the so-called Backward Classes (see Glossary), who constitute an estimated 52 percent of the population. In August 1990, Prime Minister Vishwanath Pratap (V.P.) Singh announced his intention to enforce the recommendations of the Backward Classes Commission (Mandal Commission—see Glossary), issued in December 1980 and largely ignored for a decade. The report, which urged special advantages for obtaining civil service positions and admission to higher education for the Backward Classes, resulted in riots and self-immolations and contributed to the fall of the prime minister. The upper castes have been particularly adamant against these policies because unemployment is a major problem in India, and many feel that they are being unjustly excluded from posts for which they are better qualified than lower-caste applicants.

As an act of protest, many Dalits have rejected Hinduism with its rigid ranking system. Following the example of their revered leader, Dr. Ambedkar, who converted to Buddhism four years before his death in 1956, millions of Dalits have embraced the faith of the Buddha (see Buddhism, ch. 3). Over the past few centuries, many Dalits have also converted to Christianity and have often by this means raised their socioeconomic status. However, Christians of Dalit origin still often suffer from discrimination by Christians—and others—of higher caste backgrounds.

Despite improvements in some aspects of Dalit status, 90 percent of them live in rural areas in the mid-1990s, where an increasing proportion—more than 50 percent—work as landless agricultural laborers. State and national governments have attempted to secure more just distribution of land by creating land ceilings and abolishing absentee landlordism, but evasive tactics by landowners have successfully prevented more than minimal redistribution of land to tenant farmers and laborers. In contemporary India, field hands face increased competition from tractors and harvesting machines. Similarly, artisans are being challenged by expanding commercial markets in mass-produced factory goods, undercutting traditional mutual obligations between patrons and clients. The spread of the Green Revolution has tended to increase the gap between the prosperous and the poor—most of whom are low-caste (see The Green Revolution, ch. 7).

The growth of urbanization (an estimated 26 percent of the population now lives in cities) is having a far-reaching effect on caste practices, not only in cities but in villages. Among anonymous crowds in urban public spaces and on public transportation, caste affiliations are unknown, and observance of purity and pollution rules is negligible. Distinctive caste costumes have all but vanished, and low-caste names have been modified, although castes remain endogamous, and access to employment often occurs through intracaste connections. Restrictions on interactions with other castes are becoming more relaxed, and, at the same time, observance of other pollution rules is declining—especially those concerning birth, death, and menstruation. Several growing Hindu sects draw members from many castes and regions, and communication between cities and villages is expanding dramatically. Kin in town and country visit one another frequently, and television programs available to huge numbers of villagers vividly portray new lifestyles. As new occupations open up in urban areas, the correlation of caste with occupation is declining.

Caste associations have expanded their areas of concern beyond traditional elite emulation and local politics into the wider political arenas of state and national politics. Finding power in numbers within India's democratic system, caste groups are pulling together closely allied subcastes in their quest for political influence. In efforts to solidify caste bonds, some caste associations have organized marriage fairs where families can make matches for their children. Traditional hierarchical concerns are being minimized in favor of strengthening horizontal unity. Thus, while pollution observances are declining, caste consciousness is not.

Education and election to political office have advanced the status of many Dalits, but the overall picture remains one of great inequity. In recent decades, Dalit anger has been expressed in writings, demonstrations, strikes, and the activities of such groups as the Dalit Panthers, a radical political party demanding revolutionary change. A wider Dalit movement, including political parties, educational activities, self-help centers, and labor organizations, has spread to many areas of the country.

In a 1982 Dalit publication, Dilip Hiro wrote, "It is one of the great modern Indian tragedies and dangers that even well meaning Indians still find it so difficult to accept Untouchable mobility as being legitimate in fact as well as in theory. . . ." Still, against all odds, a small intelligentsia has worked for many years toward the goal of freeing India of caste consciousness.

Classes

In village India, where nearly 74 percent of the population resides, caste and class affiliations overlap. According to anthropologist Miriam Sharma, "Large landholders who employ hired labour are overwhelmingly from the upper castes, while the agricultural workers themselves come from the ranks of the lowest—predominantly Untouchable—castes."

A member of a Weaver caste at work, Rajasthan
Courtesy Doranne Jacobson

She also points out that household-labor-using proprietors come from the ranks of the middle agricultural castes. Distribution of other resources and access to political control follow the same pattern of caste-cum-class distinctions. Although this congruence is strong, there is a tendency for class formation to occur despite the importance of caste, especially in the cities, but also in rural areas.

In an analysis of class formation in India, anthropologist Harold A. Gould points out that a three-level system of stratification is taking shape across rural India. He calls the three levels Forward Classes (higher castes), Backward Classes (middle and lower castes), and Harijans (very low castes). Members of these groups share common concerns because they stand in approximately the same relationship to land and production—that is, they are large-scale farmers, small-scale farmers, and landless laborers. Some of these groups are drawing together within regions across caste lines in order to work for political power and access to desirable resources. For example, since the late 1960s, some of the middle-ranking cultivating castes of northern India have increasingly cooperated in the political arena in order to advance their common agrarian and market-oriented interests. Their efforts have been spurred by competition with higher-caste landed elites.

In cities other groups have vested interests that crosscut caste boundaries, suggesting the possibility of forming classes in the future. These groups include prosperous industrialists and entrepreneurs, who have made successful efforts to push the central government toward a probusiness stance; bureaucrats, who depend upon higher education rather than land to preserve their positions as civil servants; political officeholders, who enjoy good salaries and perquisites of all kinds; and the military, who constitute one of the most powerful armed forces in the developing world (see Organization and Equipment of the Armed Forces, ch. 10).

Economically far below such groups are members of the menial underclass, which is taking shape in both villages and urban areas. As the privileged elites move ahead, low-ranking menial workers remain economically insecure. Were they to join together to mobilize politically across lines of class and religion in recognition of their common interests, Gould observes, they might find power in their sheer numbers.

India's rapidly expanding economy has provided the basis for a fundamental change—the emergence of what eminent journalist Suman Dubey calls a "new vanguard" increasingly dictating India's political and economic direction. This group is India's new middle class—mobile, driven, consumer-oriented, and, to some extent, forward-looking. Hard to define precisely, it is not a single stratum of society, but straddles town and countryside, making its voice heard everywhere. It encompasses prosperous farmers, white-collar workers, business people, military personnel, and myriad others, all actively working toward a prosperous life. Ownership of cars, televisions, and other consumer goods, reasonable earnings, substantial savings, and educated children (often fluent in English) typify this diverse group. Many have ties to kinsmen living abroad who have done very well.

The new middle class is booming, at least partially in response to a doubling of the salaries of some 4 million central government employees in 1986, followed by similar increases for state and district officers. Unprecedented liberalization and opening up of the economy in the 1980s and 1990s have been part of the picture (see Growth since 1980, ch. 6).

There is no single set of criteria defining the middle class, and estimates of its numbers vary widely. The mid-range of figures presented in a 1992 survey article by analyst Suman Dubey is approximately 150 to 175 million—some 20 percent of the population—although other observers suggest alternative figures. The middle class appears to be increasing rapidly. Once primarily urban and largely Hindu, the phenomenon of the consuming middle class is burgeoning among Muslims and prosperous villagers as well. According to V.A. Pai Panandikar, director of the Centre for Policy Research, New Delhi, cited by Dubey, by the end of the twentieth century 30 percent—some 300 million—of India's population will be middle class.

The middle class is bracketed on either side by the upper and lower echelons. Members of the upper class—around 1 percent of the population—are owners of large properties, members of exclusive clubs, and vacationers in foreign lands, and include industrialists, former maharajas, and top executives. Below the middle class is perhaps a third of the population—ordinary farmers, tradespeople, artisans, and workers. At the bottom of the economic scale are the poor—estimated at 320 million, some 45 percent of the population in 1988—who live in inadequate homes without adequate food, work for pittances, have undereducated and often sickly children, and are the victims of numerous social inequities.

The Fringes of Society

India's complex society includes some unique members—sadhus (holy men) and *hijras* (transvestite-eunuchs). Such people have voluntarily stepped outside the usual bonds of kinship and caste to join with others in castelike groups based upon personal—yet culturally shaped—inclinations.

In India of the 1990s, several hundred thousand Hindu and Jain sadhus and a few thousand holy women (*sadhvis*) live an ascetic life. They have chosen to wear ocher robes, or perhaps no clothing at all, to daub their skin with holy ash, to pray and meditate, and to wander from place to place, depending on the charity of others. Most have given up affiliation with their caste and kin and have undergone a funeral ceremony for themselves, followed by a ritual rebirth into their new ascetic life. They come from all walks of life, and range from illiterate villagers to well-educated professionals. In their new lives as renunciants, they are devoted to spiritual concerns, yet each is affiliated with an ascetic order or subsect demanding strict adherence to rules of dress, itinerancy, diet, worship, and ritual pollution. Within each order, hierarchical concerns are exhibited in the subservience novitiates display to revered gurus (see The Tradition of the Enlightened Master, ch. 3). Further, at pilgrimage sites, different orders take precedence in accordance with an accepted hierarchy. Thus, although sadhus have foresworn many of the trappings of ordinary life, they have not given up the hierarchy and interdependence so pervasive in Indian society.

The most extreme sadhus, the *aghoris*, turn normal rules of conduct completely upside down. Rajesh and Ramesh Bedi, who have studied sadhus for decades, estimate that there may be fewer than fifteen *aghoris* in contemporary India. In the quest for great spiritual attainment, the *aghori* lives alone, like Lord Shiva, at cremation grounds, supping from a human skull bowl. He eats food provided only by low-ranking Sweepers and prostitutes, and in moments of religious fervor devours his own bodily wastes and pieces of human flesh torn from burning corpses. In violating the most basic taboos of the ordinary Hindu householder, the *aghori sadhu* graphically reminds himself and others of the correct rules of social behavior.

Hijras are males who have become "neither man nor woman," transsexual transvestites who are usually castrated and are attributed with certain ritual powers of blessing. As described by anthropologist Serena Nanda, they are distinct from ordinary male homosexuals (known as *zenana*, woman, or *anmarad*, un-man), who retain their identity as males and continue to live in ordinary society. Most *hijras* derive from a middle- or lower-status Hindu or Muslim background and have experienced male impotency or effeminacy. A few originally had ambiguous or hermaphroditic sexual organs. An estimated 50,000 *hijras* live throughout India, predominantly in cities of the north. They are united in the worship of the Hindu goddess Bahuchara Mata.

Hijras voluntarily leave their families of birth, renounce male sexuality, and assume a female identity, name, and dress. A *hijra* undergoes a surgical emasculation in which he is transformed from an impotent male into a potentially powerful new person. Like Shiva—attributed with breaking off his phallus and throwing it to earth, thereby extending his sexual power to the universe (recognized in Hindu worship of the lingam)—the emasculated *hijra* has the power to bless others with fertility (see Shiva, ch. 3). Groups of *hijras* go about together, dancing and singing at the homes of new baby boys, blessing them with virility and the ability to continue the family line. *Hijras* are also attributed with the power to bring rain in times of drought. *Hijras* receive alms and respect for their powers, yet they are also ridiculed and abused because of their unusual sexual condition and because some act as male prostitutes.

The *hijra* community functions much like a caste. They have communal households; newly formed fictive kinship bonds, marriage-like arrangements; and seven nationwide "houses," or symbolic descent groups, with regional and national leaders, and a council. There is a hierarchy of gurus and disciples, with expulsion from the community a possible punishment for failure to obey group rules. Thus, although living on the margins of society, *hijras* are empowered by their special relationship with their goddess and each other and occupy an accepted and meaningful place in India's social world.

The Village Community

Settlement and Structure

Scattered throughout India are approximately 500,000 villages. The Census of India regards most settlements of fewer than 5,000 as a village. These settlements range from tiny hamlets of thatched huts to larger settlements of tile-roofed stone and brick houses (see Structure and Dynamics, ch. 2). Most villages are small; nearly 80 percent have fewer than 1,000 inhabitants, according to the 1991 census. Most are nucleated settlements, while others are more dispersed. It is in villages that India's most basic business—agriculture—takes place. Here, in the face of vicissitudes of all kinds, farmers follow time-tested as well as innovative methods of growing wheat, rice, lentils, vegetables, fruits, and many other crops in order to accomplish the challenging task of feeding themselves and the nation. Here, too, flourish many of India's most valued cultural forms.

Viewed from a distance, an Indian village may appear deceptively simple. A cluster of mud-plastered walls shaded by a few trees, set among a stretch of green or dun-colored fields, with a few people slowly coming or going, oxcarts creaking, cattle lowing, and birds singing—all present an image of harmonious simplicity. Indian city dwellers often refer nostalgically to "simple village life." City artists portray colorfully garbed village women gracefully carrying water pots on their heads, and writers describe isolated rural settlements unsullied by the complexities of modern urban civilization. Social scientists of the past wrote of Indian villages as virtually self-sufficient communities with few ties to the outside world.

In actuality, Indian village life is far from simple. Each village is connected through a variety of crucial horizontal linkages with other villages and with urban areas both near and far. Most villages are characterized by a multiplicity of economic, caste, kinship, occupational, and even religious groups linked vertically within each settlement. Factionalism is a typical feature of village politics. In one of the first of the modern anthropological studies of Indian village life, anthropologist Oscar Lewis called this complexity "rural cosmopolitanism."

Throughout most of India, village dwellings are built very close to one another in a nucleated settlement, with small lanes for passage of people and sometimes carts. Village fields surround the settlement and are generally within easy walking distance. In hilly tracts of central, eastern, and far northern India, dwellings are more spread out, reflecting the nature of the topography. In the wet states of West Bengal and Kerala, houses are more dispersed; in some parts of Kerala, they are constructed in continuous lines, with divisions between villages not obvious to visitors.

In northern and central India, neighborhood boundaries can be vague. The houses of Dalits are generally located in separate neighborhoods or on the outskirts of the nucleated settlement, but there are seldom distinct Dalit hamlets. By contrast, in the south, where socioeconomic contrasts and caste pollution observances tend to be stronger than in the north, Brahman homes may be set apart from those of non-Brahmans, and Dalit hamlets are set at a little distance from the homes of other castes.

The number of castes resident in a single village can vary widely, from one to more than forty. Typically, a village is dominated by one or a very few castes that essentially control the village land and on whose patronage members of weaker groups must rely. In the village of about 1,100 population near Delhi studied by Lewis in the 1950s, the Jat caste (the largest cultivating caste in northwestern India) comprised 60 percent of the residents and owned all of the village land, including the house sites. In Nimkhera, Madhya Pradesh, Hindu Thakurs and Brahmans, and Muslim Pathans own substantial land, while lower-ranking Weaver (Koli) and Barber (Khawas) caste members and others own smaller farms. In many areas of the south, Brahmans are major landowners, along with some other relatively high-ranking castes. Generally, land, prosperity, and power go together.

In some regions, landowners refrain from using plows themselves but hire tenant farmers and laborers to do this work. In other regions, landowners till the soil with the aid of laborers, usually resident in the same village. Fellow villagers typically include representatives of various service and artisan castes to supply the needs of the villagers—priests, carpenters, blacksmiths, barbers, weavers, potters, oilpressers, leatherworkers, sweepers, waterbearers, toddy-tappers, and so on. Artisanry in pottery, wood, cloth, metal, and leather, although diminishing, continues in many contemporary Indian villages as it did in centuries past. Village religious observances and weddings are occasions for members of various castes to provide customary ritual goods and services in order for the events to proceed according to proper tradition.

Aside from caste-associated occupations, villages often include people who practice nontraditional occupations. For example, Brahmans or Thakurs may be shopkeepers, teachers, truckers, or clerks, in addition to their caste-associated occupations of priest and farmer. In villages near urban areas, an increasing number of people commute to the cities to take up jobs, and many migrate. Some migrants leave their families in the village and go to the cities to work for months at a time. Many people from Kerala, as well as other regions, have temporarily migrated to the Persian Gulf states for employment and send remittances back to their village families, to which they will eventually return.

At slack seasons, village life can appear to be sleepy, but usually villages are humming with activity. The work ethic is strong, with little time out for relaxation, except for numerous divinely sanctioned festivals and rite-of-passage celebrations. Residents are quick to judge each other, and improper work or social habits receive strong criticism. Villagers feel a sense of village pride and honor, and the reputation of a village depends upon the behavior of all of its residents.

Village Unity and Divisiveness

Villagers manifest a deep loyalty to their village, identifying themselves to strangers as residents of a particular village, harking back to family residence in the village that typically extends into the distant past. A family rooted in a particular village does not easily move to another, and even people who have lived in a city for a generation or two refer to their ancestral village as "our village."

Villagers share use of common village facilities—the village pond (known in India as a tank), grazing grounds, temples and shrines, cremation grounds, schools, sitting spaces under large shade trees, wells, and wastelands. Perhaps equally important, fellow villagers share knowledge of their common origin in a locale and of each other's secrets, often going back generations. Interdependence in rural life provides a sense of unity among residents of a village.

A great many observances emphasize village unity. Typically, each village recognizes a deity deemed the village protector or protectress, and villagers unite in regular worship of this deity, considered essential to village prosperity. They may cooperate in constructing temples and shrines important to the village as a whole. Hindu festivals such as Holi, Dipavali (Diwali), and Durga Puja bring villagers together (see Public Worship, ch.3). In the north, even Muslims may join in the friendly splashing of colored water on fellow villagers in Spring Holi revelries, which involve villagewide singing, dancing, and joking. People of all castes within a village address each other by kinship terms, reflecting the fictive kinship relationships recognized within each settlement. In the north, where village exogamy is important, the concept of a village as a significant unit is clear. When the all-male groom's party arrives from another village, residents of the bride's village in North India treat the visitors with the appropriate behavior due to them as bride-takers—men greet them with ostentatious respect, while women cover their faces and sing bawdy songs at them. A woman born in a village is known as a daughter of the village while an in-married bride is considered a daughter-in-law of the village. In her conjugal home in North India, a bride is often known by the name of her natal village; for example, Sanchiwali (woman from Sanchi). A man who chooses to live in his wife's natal village—usually for reasons of land inheritance—is known by the name of his birth village, such as Sankheriwala (man from Sankheri).

Traditionally, villages often recognized a headman and listened with respect to the decisions of the *panchayat*, composed of important men from the village's major castes, who had the power to levy fines and exclude transgressors from village social life. Disputes were decided within the village precincts as much as possible, with infrequent recourse to the police or court system. In present-day India, the government supports an elective *panchayat* and headman system, which is distinct from the traditional council and headman, and, in many instances, even includes women and very low-caste members. As older systems of authority are challenged, villagers are less reluctant to take disputes to court.

The solidarity of a village is always riven by conflicts, rivalries, and factionalism. Living together in intensely close relationships over generations, struggling to wrest a livelihood from the same limited area of land and water sources, closely watching some grow fat and powerful while others remain weak and dependent, fellow villagers are prone to disputes, strategic contests, and even violence. Most villages include what villagers call "big fish," prosperous, powerful people, fed and serviced through the labors of the struggling "little fish." Villagers commonly view gains as possible only at the expense of neighbors. Further, the increased involvement of villagers with the wider economic and political world outside the village via travel, work, education, and television; expanding government influence in rural areas; and increased pressure on land and resources as village populations grow seem to have resulted in increased factionalism and competitiveness in many parts of rural India.

Urban Life

The Growth of Cities

Accelerating urbanization is powerfully affecting the transformation of Indian society. Slightly more than 26 percent of the country's population is urban, and in 1991 more than half of urban dwellers lived in 299 urban agglomerates or cities of more than 100,000 people. By 1991 India had twenty-four cities with populations of at least 1 million. By that year, among cities of the world, Bombay (or Mumbai, in Marathi), in Maharashtra, ranked seventh in the world at 12.6 million, and Calcutta, in West Bengal, ranked eighth at almost 11 million. In the 1990s, India's larger cities have been growing at twice the rate of smaller towns and villages. Between the 1960s and 1991, the population of the Union Territory of Delhi quadrupled, to 8.4 million, and Madras, in Tamil Nadu, grew to 5.4 million. Bangalore, in Karnataka; Hyderabad, in Andhra Pradesh; and many other cities are expanding rapidly. About half of these increases are the result of rural-urban migration, as villagers seek better lives for themselves in the cities.

Most Indian cities are very densely populated. New Delhi, for example, had 6,352 people per square kilometer in 1991.

Congestion, noise, traffic jams, air pollution, and major shortages of key necessities characterize urban life. Every major city of India faces the same proliferating problems of grossly inadequate housing, transportation, sewerage, electric power, water supplies, schools, and hospitals. Slums and jumbles of pavement dwellers' lean-tos constantly multiply. An increasing number of trucks, buses, cars, three-wheel autorickshaws, motorcycles, and motorscooters, all spewing uncontrolled fumes, surge in sometimes haphazard patterns over city streets jammed with jaywalking pedestrians, cattle, and goats. Accident rates are high (India's fatality rate from road accidents, the most common cause of accidental death, is said to be twenty times higher than United States rates), and it is a daily occurrence for a city dweller to witness a crash or the running down of a pedestrian. In 1984 the citizens of Bhopal suffered the nightmare of India's largest industrial accident, when poisonous gas leaking from a Union Carbide plant killed and injured thousands of city dwellers. Less spectacularly, on a daily basis, uncontrolled pollutants from factories all over India damage the urban environments in which millions live.

Urban Inequities

Major socioeconomic differences are much on display in cities. The fine homes—often a walled compound with a garden, servants' quarters, and garage—and gleaming automobiles of the super wealthy stand in stark contrast to the burlap-covered huts of the barefoot poor. Shops filled with elegant silk saris and air-conditioned restaurants cater to the privileged, while ragged dust-covered children with outstretched hands wait outside in hopes of receiving a few coins. The wealthy and the middle class employ servants and workers of various kinds, but *jajmani*-like ties are essentially lacking, and the rich and the poor live much more separate lives than in villages. At the same time, casual interaction and physical contact among people of all castes is constant, on public streets and in buses, trains, and movie theaters.

As would-be urbanites stream into the cities, they often seek out people from their village, caste, or region who have gone before them and receive enough hospitality to tide them over until they can settle in themselves. They find accommodation wherever they can, even if only on a quiet corner of a sidewalk, or inside a concrete sewer pipe waiting to be laid. Some are fortunate enough to find shelter in decrepit tenements or in open

A busy street in Jaipur, Rajasthan
Courtesy Sandra Day O'Connor

areas where they can throw up flimsy structures of mud, tin
sheeting, or burlap. In such slum settlements, a single out-
house may be shared by literally thousands of people, or, more
usually, there are no sanitary facilities at all. Ditches are awash
in raw sewage, and byways are strewn with the refuse of people
and animals with nowhere else to go.

Despite the exterior appearance of chaos, slum life is highly
structured, with many economic, religious, caste, and political
interests expressed in daily activity. Living conditions are
extremely difficult, and slum dwellers fear the constant threat
of having their homes bulldozed in municipal "slum clearance"
efforts; nonetheless, slum life is animated by a strong sense of
joie de vivre.

In many sections of Indian cities, scavenging pigs, often
owned by Sweepers, along with stray dogs, help to recycle fecal

287

material. Piles of less noxious vegetal and paper garbage are sorted through by the poorest people, who seek usable or salable bits of things. Cattle and goats, owned by entrepreneurial folk, graze on these piles, turning otherwise useless garbage into valuable milk, dung (used for cooking fuel), and meat. These domestic animals roam even in neighborhoods of fine homes, outside the compound walls that protect the privileged and their gardener-tended rose bushes from needy animals and people.

Finding employment in the urban setting can be extremely challenging, and, whenever possible, networks of relatives and friends are used to help seek jobs. Millions of Indians are unemployed or underemployed. Ingenuity and tenacity are the hallmarks of urban workers, who carry out a remarkable multitude of tasks and sell an incredible variety of foods, trinkets, and services, all under difficult conditions. Many of the urban poor are migrant laborers carrying headloads of bricks and earth up rickety bamboo scaffolding at construction sites, while their small children play about at the edge of excavations or huddle on mounds of gravel in the blazing sun. Nursing mothers must take time out periodically to suckle their babies at the edge of construction sites; such "recesses" are considered reason to pay a woman less for a day's work than a man earns (male construction workers earned about US$1 a day in 1994). Moreover, women are seen as physically weaker by some employers and thus not deserving of equal wages with men.

These construction projects are financed by governments and by business enterprises, which are run by cadres of well-educated, healthy, well-dressed men and, increasingly, women, who occupy positions of power and make decisions affecting many people. India's major cities have long been headquarters for the country's highest socioeconomic groups, people with transnational and international connections whose choices are taking India into new realms of economic development and social change. Among these well-placed people, intercaste marriages raise few eyebrows, as long as marital unions link people of similar upper- or upper-middle-class backgrounds. Such marriages, sometimes even across religious lines, help knit India's most powerful people together.

Increasingly conspicuous in India's cities are the growing ranks of the middle class. In carefully laundered clothes, they emerge from modest and semiprosperous homes to ride buses and motorscooters to their jobs in offices, hospitals, courts, and

An urban street scene in Delhi
Courtesy Robert L. Worden

commercial establishments. Their well-tended children are educated in properly organized schools. Family groups go out together to places of worship, social events, snack shops, and to bazaars bustling with consumers eager to buy the necessities of a comfortable life. Members of the middle class cluster around small stock-market outlets in cities all over the country. Even in Calcutta, notorious for slums and street dwellers, the dominant image is of office workers in pressed white garments riding crowded buses—or Calcutta's world-class subway line—to their jobs as office workers and professionals (see Transportation, ch. 6).

For nearly everyone within the highly challenging urban environment, ties to family and kin remain crucial to prosperity. Even in the harshest urban conditions, families show remarkable resilience. Neighborhoods, too, take on impor-

289

tance, and neighbors from various backgrounds develop cooperative ties with one another. Neighborhood solidarity is expressed at such annual Hindu festivals as Ganesh's Birthday (Ganesh Chaturthi) in Bombay and Durga Puja in Calcutta, when neighborhood associations create elaborate images of the deities and take them out in grand processions.

Cities as Centers

Cosmopolitan cities are the great hubs of commerce and government upon which the nation's functioning depends. Bombay, India's largest city and port, is India's economic powerhouse and locus of the nation's atomic research. The National Capital Territory of Delhi, where a series of seven cities was built over centuries, is the site of the capital—New Delhi—and political nerve center of the world's largest democracy. Calcutta and Madras fill major roles in the country's economic life, as do high-tech Bangalore and Ahmadabad (in Gujarat), famous for textiles. Great markets in foods, manufactured goods, and a host of key commodities are centered in urban trading and distribution points. Most eminent institutions of higher learning, cradles of intellectual development and scientific investigation, are situated in cities. The visual arts, music, classical dancing, poetry, and literature all flourish in the urban setting. Critical political and social commentary appears in urban newspapers and periodicals. Creative new trends in architecture and design are conceptualized and brought to reality in cities.

Cities are the source of television broadcasts and those great favorites of the Indian public, movies. Bombay, sometimes called "Bollywood," and Madras are major centers of film production, bringing depictions of urban lifestyles before the eyes of small-town dwellers and villagers all over the nation. With the continuing national proliferation of television sets, videocassette recorders, and movie videocassettes, the influence of such productions should not be underestimated.

Social revolutions, too, receive the support of urban visionaries. Among the more important social developments in contemporary India is the growing women's movement, largely led by educated urban women. Seeking to restructure society and gender relations, activists, scholars, and workers in the women's movement have come together in numerous loosely allied and highly diverse organizations focusing on issues of rights and equality, empowerment, and justice for women.

Bombay's skyline
Courtesy Robert L. Worden

Some of these groups exist in rural areas, but most are city based.

The escalating issues of dowry-related murder and suicide are most pressing in New Delhi, where groups such as Saheli (Woman Friend) provide essential support to troubled women. The pathbreaking feminist publication *Manushi* is published in New Delhi and distributed throughout the country. The overwhelming economic needs of self-employed poor female workers in Ahmadabad inspired Ela Bhatt and her coworkers in the Self-Employed Women's Association, which has been highly successful in helping poor women improve their own lives.

Urban women have initiated protests challenging female feticide, child marriage, child prostitution, domestic violence, polygyny, sati, sexual harassment, police rape of female plaintiffs, and other gender-related injustices. Their efforts have brought new ways of thinking out of elite, educated circles into the broader public arena of India's multilevel society.

In 1994, two attractive urban Indian women won the most prominent international beauty contests, the Miss Universe and the Miss World competitions. Thousands of young Indian women idolized the glamorous beauties and many newspapers gushed about the victories, but women's groups and feminist commentators decried this adulation. They pointed out that the deprivations and injustices experienced by a high proportion of Indian women were being given short shrift. While the beauty contest winners were being paraded about in crowns and white chariots before admiring throngs, almost ignored by the public and the media were the torture-slaying of a village

291

woman accused of theft by a soothsayer and the historic qualification of six women as the Indian air force's first female pilots (see The Air Force, ch. 10). In 1995, the All India Democratic Women's Association and other groups protested in New Delhi against the Miss India contest.

Future Trends

By the twenty-first century, India's population will be more than 1 billion. Approximately one-third of this enormous population will live in urban areas, which means adding the population of another Calcutta, Bombay, or Madras to India's already overburdened cities each year into the foreseeable future. In rural areas, pressures on land and other resources will continue to intensify.

In India's democracy, ideas are often vociferously expressed, and members of different groups are increasingly demanding what they consider a fair share of resources and benefits. Tolerance for inequity is diminishing among the less privileged, even as inequity is increasing in both rural and urban areas. As competition for scarce resources and benefits grows, some political leaders have been encouraging the populace to blame these problems on religious differences.

Prosperity is available to many, and access to education and an expanding range of consumer goods is possible for an ever-increasing number of people. At the same time, the sheer numbers of the poor and less privileged are increasing as they are left behind, inadequately educated, and forced by circumstance to labor under insecure conditions. Class and gender justice, widely sought by a significant number of people, remains an elusive goal.

India is part of a much wider community of nations facing these and other problems, so it will not be alone in seeking solutions. In this endeavor, the great structural principles of hierarchy and interdependence that have held Indian society together over the millennia will be brought to the fore. Creating manageable order from complexity, bringing together widely disparate groups in structured efforts to benefit the wider society, encouraging harmony among people with divergent interests, knowing that close family and friends can rely on each other in times of stress, allocating different tasks to those with different skills, and striving to do what is morally right in the eyes of the divine and the human community—

these are some of the great strengths upon which Indian society can rely as it meets the challenges of the future.

*   *   *

The English-language literature on Indian society is enormous. Many of the most highly regarded works have been published in both India and the United States. Among these are David G. Mandelbaum's two-volume *Society in India,* a classic synthesis of sociological and anthropological research; historian Stanley Wolpert's *India,* a highly readable introduction to many aspects of Indian culture and history; Owen M. Lynch's *The Politics of Untouchability;* Sudhir Kakar's *The Inner World;* M.N. Srinivas's *Social Change in Modern India;* Pauline M. Kolenda's *Caste in Contemporary India;* Miriam Sharma's *The Politics of Inequality;* and V.S. Naipaul's *India: A Million Mutinies Now.*

Works published in the United States, which may also be available in India, include Maureen L.P. Patterson's comprehensive *South Asian Civilizations: A Bibliographic Synthesis,* an essential reference; Clarence Maloney's *Peoples of South Asia,* an extremely useful overview; Robert W. Stern's *Changing India,* an introduction to India's modern history and social institutions; and Myron Weiner's *The Child and the State in India,* a thought-provoking examination of children's place in Indian social structure. To stay abreast of current events, it is worthwhile to read the fortnightly news magazine *India Today,* published in both Indian and American editions. (For further information and complete citations, see Bibliography.)

Chapter 6. Character and Structure of the Economy

A traditional-style printer using a wood block to print designs on fabric

INDIA'S ECONOMY HAS MADE great strides in the years since independence. In 1947 the country was poor and shattered by the violence and economic and physical disruption involved in the partition from Pakistan. The economy had stagnated since the late nineteenth century, and industrial development had been restrained to preserve the area as a market for British manufacturers. In fiscal year (FY—see Glossary) 1950, agriculture, forestry, and fishing accounted for 58.9 percent of the gross domestic product (GDP—see Glossary) and for a much larger proportion of employment. Manufacturing, which was dominated by the jute and cotton textile industries, accounted for only 10.3 percent of GDP at that time.

India's new leaders sought to use the power of the state to direct economic growth and reduce widespread poverty. The public sector came to dominate heavy industry, transportation, and telecommunications. The private sector produced most consumer goods but was controlled directly by a variety of government regulations and financial institutions that provided major financing for large private-sector projects. Government emphasized self-sufficiency rather than foreign trade and imposed strict controls on imports and exports. In the 1950s, there was steady economic growth, but results in the 1960s and 1970s were less encouraging.

Beginning in the late 1970s, successive Indian governments sought to reduce state control of the economy. Progress toward that goal was slow but steady, and many analysts attributed the stronger growth of the 1980s to those efforts. In the late 1980s, however, India relied on foreign borrowing to finance development plans to a greater extent than before. As a result, when the price of oil rose sharply in August 1990, the nation faced a balance of payments crisis. The need for emergency loans led the government to make a greater commitment to economic liberalization than it had up to this time. In the early 1990s, India's postindependence development pattern of strong centralized planning, regulation and control of private enterprise, state ownership of many large units of production, trade protectionism, and strict limits on foreign capital was increasingly questioned not only by policy makers but also by most of the intelligentsia.

As India moved into the mid-1990s, the economic outlook was mixed. Most analysts believed that economic liberalization would continue, although there was disagreement about the speed and scale of the measures that would be implemented. It seemed likely that India would come close to or equal the relatively impressive rate of economic growth attained in the 1980s, but that the poorest sections of the population might not benefit.

Structure of the Economy

Independence to 1979

At independence the economy was predominantly agrarian. Most of the population was employed in agriculture, and most of those people were very poor, existing by cropping their own small plots or supplying labor to other farms. Landownership, land rental, and sharecropping rights were complex, involving layers of intermediaries (see Land Use, ch. 7). Moreover, the structural economic problems inherited at independence were exacerbated by the costs associated with the partition of British India, which had resulted in about 12 million to 14 million refugees fleeing past each other across the new borders between India and Pakistan (see National Integration, ch. 1). The settlement of refugees was a considerable financial strain. Partition also divided complementary economic zones. Under the British, jute and cotton were grown in the eastern part of Bengal, the area that became East Pakistan (after 1971, Bangladesh), but processing took place mostly in the western part of Bengal, which became the Indian state of West Bengal in 1947. As a result, after independence India had to employ land previously used for food production to cultivate cotton and jute for its mills.

India's leaders—especially the first prime minister, Jawaharlal Nehru, who introduced the five-year plans—agreed that strong economic growth and measures to increase incomes and consumption among the poorest groups were necessary goals for the new nation. Government was assigned an important role in this process, and since 1951 a series of plans have guided the country's economic development. Although there was considerable growth in the 1950s, the long-term rates of growth were less positive than India's politicians desired and less than those of many other Asian countries. From FY 1951 to FY 1979, the economy grew at an average rate of about 3.1 percent a year in constant prices, or at an annual rate of 1.0 percent per capita (see table 16, Appendix). During this period, industry grew at an average rate of 4.5 percent a year, compared with an annual average of 3.0 percent for agriculture. Many factors contributed to the slowdown of the economy after the mid-1960s, but economists differ over the relative importance of those factors. Structural deficiencies, such as the need for institutional changes in agriculture and the inefficiency of much of the industrial sector, also contributed to economic stagnation. Wars with China in 1962 and with Pakistan in 1965 and 1971; a flood of refugees from East Pakistan in 1971; droughts in 1965, 1966, 1971, and 1972; currency devaluation in 1966; and the first world oil crisis, in 1973–74, all jolted the economy.

Growth since 1980

The rate of growth improved in the 1980s. From FY 1980 to FY 1989, the economy grew at an annual rate of 5.5 percent, or 3.3 percent on a per capita basis. Industry grew at an annual rate of 6.6 percent and agriculture at a rate of 3.6 percent. A high rate of investment was a major factor in improved economic growth. Investment went from about 19 percent of GDP in the early 1970s to nearly 25 percent in the early 1980s. India, however, required a higher rate of investment to attain comparable economic growth than did most other low-income developing countries, indicating a lower rate of return on investments. Part of the adverse Indian experience was explained by investment in large, long-gestating, capital-intensive projects, such as electric power, irrigation, and infrastructure. However, delayed completions, cost overruns, and underuse of capacity were contributing factors.

Private savings financed most of India's investment, but by the mid-1980s further growth in private savings was difficult because they were already at quite a high level. As a result, during the late 1980s India relied increasingly on borrowing from foreign sources (see Aid, this ch.). This trend led to a balance of payments crisis in 1990; in order to receive new loans, the government had no choice but to agree to further measures of economic liberalization. This commitment to economic reform was reaffirmed by the government that came to power in June 1991.

India's primary sector, including agriculture, forestry, fishing, mining, and quarrying, accounted for 32.8 percent of GDP in FY 1991 (see table 17, Appendix). The size of the agricultural sector and its vulnerability to the vagaries of the monsoon cause relatively large fluctuations in the sector's contribution to GDP from one year to another (see Crop Output, ch. 7).

In FY 1991, the contribution to GDP of industry, including manufacturing, construction, and utilities, was 27.4 percent; services, including trade, transportation, communications, real estate and finance, and public- and private-sector services, contributed 39.8 percent. The steady increase in the proportion of services in the national economy reflects increased market-determined processes, such as the spread of rural banking, and government activities, such as defense spending (see Agricultural Credit, ch. 7; Defense Spending, ch. 10).

Despite a sometimes disappointing rate of growth, the Indian economy was transformed between 1947 and the early 1990s. The number of kilowatt-hours of electricity generated, for example, increased more than fiftyfold. Steel production rose from 1.5 million tons a year to 14.7 million tons a year. The country produced space satellites and nuclear-power plants, and its scientists and engineers produced an atomic explosive device (see Major Research Organizations, this ch.; Space and Nuclear Programs, ch. 10). Life expectancy increased from twenty-seven years to fifty-nine years. Although the population increased by 485 million between 1951 and 1991, the availability of food grains per capita rose from 395 grams per day in FY 1950 to 466 grams in FY 1992 (see Structure and Dynamics, ch. 2).

However, considerable dualism remains in the Indian economy. Officials and economists make an important distinction between the formal and informal sectors of the economy. The informal, or unorganized, economy is largely rural and encompasses farming, fishing, forestry, and cottage industries. It also includes petty vendors and some small-scale mechanized industry in both rural and urban areas. The bulk of the population is employed in the informal economy, which contributes more than 50 percent of GDP. The formal economy consists of large units in the modern sector for which statistical data are relatively good. The modern sector includes large-scale manufacturing and mining, major financial and commercial businesses, and such public-sector enterprises as railroads, telecommunications, utilities, and government itself.

The greatest disappointment of economic development is the failure to reduce more substantially India's widespread poverty. Studies have suggested that income distribution changed little between independence and the early 1990s, although it is possible that the poorer half of the population improved its position slightly. Official estimates of the proportion of the population that lives below the poverty line tend to vary sharply from year to year because adverse economic conditions, especially rises in food prices, are capable of lowering the standard of living of many families who normally live just above the subsistence level. The Indian government's poverty line is based on an income sufficient to ensure access to minimum nutritional standards, and even most persons above the poverty line have low levels of consumption compared with much of the world.

Estimates in the late 1970s put the number of people who lived in poverty at 300 million, or nearly 50 percent of the population at the time. Poverty was reduced during the 1980s, and in FY 1989 it was estimated that about 26 percent of the population, or 220 million people, lived below the poverty line. Slower economic growth and higher inflation in FY 1990 and FY 1991 reversed this trend. In FY 1991, it was estimated that 332 million people, or 38 percent of the population, lived below the poverty line.

Farmers and other rural residents make up the large majority of India's poor. Some own very small amounts of land while others are field hands, seminomadic shepherds, or migrant workers. The urban poor include many construction workers and petty vendors. The bulk of the poor work, but low productivity and intermittent employment keep incomes low. Poverty is most prevalent in the states of Orissa, Bihar, Uttar Pradesh, and Madhya Pradesh, and least prevalent in Haryana, Punjab, Himachal Pradesh, and Jammu and Kashmir.

By the early 1990s, economic changes led to the growth in the number of Indians with significant economic resources. About 10 million Indians are considered upper class, and roughly 300 million are part of the rapidly increasing middle class. Typical middle-class occupations include owning a small business or being a corporate executive, lawyer, physician, white-collar worker, or land-owning farmer. In the 1980s, the growth of the middle class was reflected in the increased consumption of consumer durables, such as televisions, refrigerators, motorcycles, and automobiles. In the early 1990s, domestic and foreign businesses hoped to take advantage of

India's economic liberalization to increase the range of consumer products offered to this market.

Housing and the ancillary utilities of sewer and water systems lag considerably behind the population's needs. India's cities have large shantytowns built of scrap or readily available natural materials erected on whatever space is available, including sidewalks. Such dwellings lack piped water, sewerage, and electricity. The government has attempted to build housing facilities and utilities for urban development, but the efforts have fallen far short of demand. Administrative controls and other aspects of government policy have discouraged many private investors from constructing housing units.

Liberalization in the Early 1990s

Increased borrowing from foreign sources in the late 1980s, which helped fuel economic growth, led to pressure on the balance of payments. The problem came to a head in August 1990 when Iraq invaded Kuwait, and the price of oil soon doubled. In addition, many Indian workers resident in Persian Gulf states either lost their jobs or returned home out of fear for their safety, thus reducing the flow of remittances (see Size and Composition of the Work Force, this ch.). The direct economic impact of the Persian Gulf conflict was exacerbated by domestic social and political developments. In the early 1990s, there was violence over two domestic issues: the reservation of a proportion of public-sector jobs for members of Scheduled Castes (see Glossary) and the Hindu-Muslim conflict at Ayodhya (see Public Worship, ch. 3; Political Issues, ch. 8). The central government fell in November 1990 and was succeeded by a minority government. The cumulative impact of these events shook international confidence in India's economic viability, and the country found it increasingly difficult to borrow internationally. As a result, India made various agreements with the International Monetary Fund (IMF—see Glossary) and other organizations that included commitments to speed up liberalization (see United Nations, ch. 9).

In the early 1990s, considerable progress was made in loosening government regulations, especially in the area of foreign trade. Many restrictions on private companies were lifted, and new areas were opened to private capital. However, India remains one of the world's most tightly regulated major economies. Many powerful vested interests, including private firms that have benefited from protectionism, labor unions, and

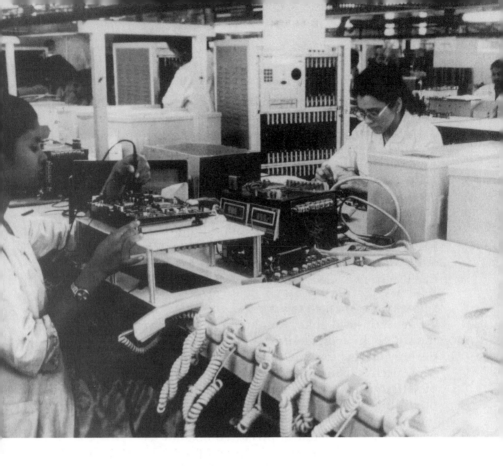

Telephone manufacturing factory, Maharashtra
Courtesy India Abroad News Service

much of the bureaucracy, oppose liberalization. There is also considerable concern that liberalization will reinforce class and regional economic disparities.

The balance of payments crisis of 1990 and subsequent policy changes led to a temporary decline in the GDP growth rate, which fell from 6.9 percent in FY 1989 to 4.9 percent in FY 1990 to 1.1 percent in FY 1991. In March 1995, the estimated growth rate for FY 1994 was 5.3 percent. Inflation peaked at 17 percent in FY 1991, fell to 9.5 percent in FY 1993, and then accelerated again, reaching 11 percent in late FY 1994. This increase was attributed to a sharp increase in prices and a shortfall in such critical sectors as sugar, cotton, and oilseeds. Many analysts agree that the poor suffer most from the increased inflation rate and reduced growth rate.

The Role of Government

Early Policy Developments

Many early postindependence leaders, such as Nehru, were influenced by socialist ideas and advocated government intervention to guide the economy, including state ownership of key industries. The objective was to achieve high and balanced economic development in the general interest while particular programs and measures helped the poor. India's leaders also believed that industrialization was the key to economic development. This belief was all the more convincing in India because of the country's large size, substantial natural resources, and desire to develop its own defense industries.

The Industrial Policy Resolution of 1948 gave government a monopoly in armaments, atomic energy, and railroads, and exclusive rights to develop minerals, the iron and steel industries, aircraft manufacturing, shipbuilding, and manufacturing of telephone and telegraph equipment. Private companies operating in those fields were guaranteed at least ten years more of ownership before the government could take them over. Some still operate as private companies.

The Industrial Policy Resolution of 1956 greatly extended the preserve of government. There were seventeen industries exclusively in the public sector. The government took the lead in another twelve industries, but private companies could also engage in production. This resolution covered industries producing capital and intermediate goods. As a result, the private sector was relegated primarily to production of consumer goods. The public sector also expanded into more services. In 1956 the life insurance business was nationalized, and in 1973 the general insurance business was also acquired by the public sector. Most large commercial banks were nationalized in 1969. Over the years, the central and state governments formed agencies, and companies engaged in finance, trading, mineral exploitation, manufacturing, utilities, and transportation. The public sector was extensive and influential throughout the economy, although the value of its assets was small relative to the private sector.

Controls over prices, production, and the use of foreign exchange, which were imposed by the British during World War II, were reinstated soon after independence. The Industries (Development and Regulation) Act of 1951 and the Essential Commodities Act of 1955 (with subsequent additions) provided the legal framework for the government to extend price controls that eventually included steel, cement, drugs, nonferrous metals, chemicals, fertilizer, coal, automobiles, tires and tubes, cotton textiles, food grains, bread, butter, vegetable oils, and other commodities. By the late 1950s, controls were pervasive, regulating investment in industry, prices of many commodities, imports and exports, and the flow of foreign exchange.

Export growth was long ignored. The government's extensive controls and pervasive licensing requirements created imbalances and structural problems in many parts of the economy. Controls were usually imposed to correct specific problems but often without adequate consideration of their effect on other parts of the economy. For example, the government set low prices for basic foods, transportation, and other commodities and services, a policy designed to protect the living standards of the poor. However, the policy proved counterproductive when the government also limited the output of needed goods and services. Price ceilings were implemented during shortages, but the ceiling frequently contributed to black markets in those commodities and to tax evasion by black-market participants. Import controls and tariff policy stimulated local manufacturers toward production of import-substitution goods, but under conditions devoid of sufficient competition or pressure to be efficient.

Private trading and industrial conglomerates (the so-called large houses) existed under the British and continued after independence. The government viewed the conglomerates with suspicion, believing that they often manipulated markets and prices for their own profit. After independence the government instituted licensing controls on new businesses, especially in manufacturing, and on expanding capacity in existing businesses. In the 1960s, when shortages of goods were extensive, considerable criticism was leveled at traders for manipulating markets and prices. The result was the 1970 Monopolies and Restrictive Practices Act, which was designed to provide the government with additional information on the structure and investments of all firms that had assets of more than Rs200 million (for value of the rupee—see Glossary), to strengthen the licensing system in order to decrease the concentration of private economic power, and to place restraints on certain business practices considered contrary to the public interest. The act emphasized the government's aversion to large companies in the private sector, but critics contended that the act resulted from political motives and not from a strong case against big firms. The act and subsequent enforcement restrained private investment.

The extensive controls, the large public sector, and the many government programs contributed to a substantial growth in the administrative structure of government. The government also sought to take on many of the unemployed. The result was a swollen, inefficient bureaucracy that took inordinate amounts of time to process applications and forms. Business leaders complained that they spent more time getting government approval than running their companies. Many observers also reported extensive corruption in the huge bureaucracy. One consequence was the development of a large underground economy in small-scale enterprises and the services sector.

India's current economic reforms began in 1985 when the government abolished some of its licensing regulations and other competition-inhibiting controls. Since 1991 more "new economic policies" or reforms have been introduced. Reforms include currency devaluations and making currency partially convertible, reduced quantitative restrictions on imports, reduced import duties on capital goods, decreases in subsidies, liberalized interest rates, abolition of licenses for most industries, the sale of shares in selected public enterprises, and tax reforms. Although many observers welcomed these changes and attributed the faster growth rate of the economy in the late 1980s to them, others feared that these changes would create more problems than they solved. The growing dependence of the economy on imports, greater vulnerability of its balance of payments, reliance on debt, and the consequent susceptibility to outside pressures on economic policy directions caused concern. The increase in consumerism and the display of conspicuous wealth by the elite exacerbated these fears.

The pace of liberalization increased after 1991. By the mid-1990s, the number of sectors reserved for public ownership was slashed, and private-sector investment was encouraged in areas such as energy, steel, oil refining and exploration, road building, air transportation, and telecommunications. An area still closed to the private sector in the mid-1990s was defense industry. Foreign-exchange regulations were liberalized, foreign investment was encouraged, and import regulations were simplified. The average import-weighted tariff was reduced from

87 percent in FY 1991 to 33 percent in FY 1994. Despite these changes, the economy remained highly regulated by international standards. The import of many consumer goods was banned, and the production of 838 items, mostly consumer goods, was reserved for companies with total investment of less than Rs6 million. Although the government had sold off minority stakes in public-sector companies, it had not in 1995 given up control of any enterprises, nor had any of the loss-making public companies been closed down. Moreover, although import duties had been lowered substantially, they were still high compared to most other countries.

Political successes in the mid-1990s by nationalist-oriented political parties led to some backlash against foreign investment in some parts of India (see Political Parties, ch. 8). In early 1995, official charges of serving adulterated products were made against a KFC outlet in Bangalore, and Pepsi-Cola products were smashed and advertisements defaced in New Delhi. The most serious backlash occurred in Maharashtra in August 1995 when the Bharatiya Janata Party (BJP—Indian People's Party)-led state government halted construction of a US$2.8 million 2,015-megawatt gas-fired electric-power plant being built near Bombay (Mumbai in the Marathi language) by another United States company, Enron Corporation.

Antipoverty Programs

The government has initiated, sustained, and refined many programs since independence to help the poor attain self sufficiency in food production. Probably the most important initiative has been the supply of basic commodities, particularly food at controlled prices, available throughout the country. The poor spend about 80 percent of their income on food while the rest of the population spends more than 60 percent. The price of food is a major determinant of wage scales. Often when food prices rise sharply, rioting and looting follow. Until the late 1970s, the government frequently had difficulty obtaining adequate grain supplies in years of poor harvests. During those times, states with surpluses of grain were cordoned off to force partial sales to public agencies and to keep private traders from shipping grain to deficit areas to secure very high prices; state governments in surplus-grain areas were often less than cooperative. After the late 1970s, the central government, by holding reserve stocks and importing grain adequately and early, maintained sufficient supplies to meet the increased demand during drought years. It also provided more remunerative prices to farmers.

In rural areas, the government has undertaken programs to mitigate the worst effects of adverse monsoon rainfall, which affects not only farmers but village artisans and traders when the price of grain rises. The government has supplied water by financing well digging and, since the early 1980s, by power-assisted well drilling; rescinded land taxes for drought areas; tried to maintain stable food prices; and provided food through a food-for-work program. The actual work accomplished through food-for-work programs is often a secondary consideration, but useful projects sometimes result. Employment is offered at a low daily wage, usually paid in grain, the rationale being that only the truly needy will take jobs at such low pay.

In the 1980s and early 1990s, Indian government programs attempted to provide basic needs at stable, low prices; to increase income through pricing and regulations, such as supplying water from irrigation works, fertilizer, and other inputs; to foster location of industry in backward areas; to increase access to basic social services, such as education, health, and potable water supply; and to help needy groups and deprived areas. The total money spent on such programs for the poor was not discernible from the budget data, but probably exceeded 10 percent of planned budget outlays.

India has had a number of antipoverty programs since the early 1960s. These include, among others, the National Rural Employment Programme and the Rural Landless Employment Guarantee Programme. The National Rural Employment Programme evolved in FY 1980 from the earlier Food for Work Programme to use unemployed and underemployed workers to build productive community assets. The Rural Landless Employment Guarantee Programme was instituted in FY 1983 to address the plight of the hard-core rural poor by expanding employment opportunities and building the rural infrastructure as a means of encouraging rapid economic growth. There were many problems with the implementation of these and otherschemes, but observers credit them with helping reduce poverty. To improve the effectiveness of the National Rural Employment Programme, in 1989 it was combined with the Rural Landless Employment Guarantee Programme and renamed Jawahar Rozgar Yojana, or Jawahar Employment Plan (see Development Programs, ch. 7).

State governments are important participants in antipoverty programs. The constitution assigns responsibility to the states in a number of matters, including ownership, redistribution, improvement, and taxation of land (see The Constitutional Framework, ch. 8). State governments implement most central government programs concerned with land reform and the situation of small landless farmers. The central government tries to establish programs and norms among the states and union territories, but implementation has often remained at the lower bureaucratic levels. In some matters concerning subsoil rights and irrigation projects, the central government exerts political and financial leverage to obtain its objectives, but the states sometimes modify or retard the impact of central government policies and programs.

Development Planning

Planning in India dates back to the 1930s. Even before independence, the colonial government had established a planning board that lasted from 1944 to 1946. Private industrialists and economists published three development plans in 1944. India's leaders adopted the principle of formal economic planning soon after independence as an effective way to intervene in the economy to foster growth and social justice.

The Planning Commission was established in 1950. Responsible only to the prime minister, the commission is independent of the cabinet. The prime minister is chairperson of the commission, and the minister of state with independent charge for planning and program implementation serves as deputy chairperson. A staff drafts national plans under the guidance of the commission; draft plans are presented for approval to the National Development Council, which consists of the Planning Commission and the chief ministers of the states. The council can make changes in the draft plan. After council approval, the draft is presented to the cabinet and subsequently to Parliament, whose approval makes the plan an operating document for central and state governments (see The Legislature; Local Government, ch. 8).

The First Five-Year Plan (FY 1951–55) attempted to stimulate balanced economic development while correcting imbalances caused by World War II and partition. Agriculture, including projects that combined irrigation and power generation, received priority. By contrast, the Second Five-Year Plan (FY 1956–60) emphasized industrialization, particularly basic, heavy industries in the public sector, and improvement of the economic infrastructure. The plan also stressed social goals, such as more equal distribution of income and extension of the benefits of economic development to the large number of disadvantaged people. The Third Five-Year Plan (FY 1961–65) aimed at a substantial rise in national and per capita income while expanding the industrial base and rectifying the neglect of agriculture in the previous plan. The third plan called for national income to grow at a rate of more than 5 percent a year; self-sufficiency in food grains was anticipated in the mid-1960s.

Economic difficulties disrupted the planning process in the mid–1960s. In 1962, when a brief war was fought with China on the Himalayan frontier, agricultural output was stagnating, industrial production was considerably below expectations, and the economy was growing at about half of the planned rate (see Nehru's Legacy, ch. 1). Defense expenditures increased sharply, and the increased foreign aid needed to maintain development expenditures eventually provided 28 percent of public development spending. Midway through the third plan, it was clear that its goals could not be achieved. Food prices rose in 1963, causing rioting and looting of grain warehouses in 1964. War with Pakistan in 1965 sharply reduced the foreign aid available. Successive severe droughts in 1965 and 1966 further disrupted the economy and planning. Three annual plans guided development between FY 1966 and FY 1968 while plan policies and strategies were reevaluated. Immediate attention centered on increasing agricultural growth, stimulating exports, and searching for efficient uses of industrial assets. Agriculture was to be expanded, largely through the supply of inputs to take advantage of new high-yield seeds becoming available for food grains. The rupee was substantially devalued in 1966, and export incentives were adjusted to promote exports. Controls affecting industry were simplified, and greater reliance was placed on the price mechanism to achieve industrial efficiency.

The Fourth Five-Year Plan (FY 1969–73) called for a 24 percent increase over the third plan in real terms of public development expenditures. The public sector accounted for 60 percent of plan expenditures, and foreign aid contributed 13 percent of plan financing. Agriculture, including irrigation, received 23 percent of public outlays; the rest was mostly spent on electric power, industry, and transportation. Although the plan projected national income growth at 5.7 percent a year, the realized rate was only 3.3 percent.

The Fifth Five-Year Plan (FY 1974–78) was drafted in late 1973 when crude oil prices were rising rapidly; the rising prices quickly forced a series of revisions. The plan was subsequently approved in late 1976 but was terminated at the end of FY 1977 because a new government wanted different priorities and programs. The fifth plan was in effect only one year, although it provided some guidance to investments throughout the five-year period. The economy operated under annual plans in FY 1978 and FY 1979.

The Sixth Five-Year Plan (FY 1980–84) was intended to be flexible and was based on the principle of annual "rolling" plans. It called for development expenditures of nearly Rs1.9 trillion (in FY 1979 prices), of which 90 percent would be financed from domestic sources, 57 percent of which would come from the public sector. Public-sector development spending would be concentrated in energy (29 percent); agriculture and irrigation (24 percent); industry including mining (16 percent); transportation (16 percent); and social services (14 percent). In practice, slightly more was spent on social services at the expense of transportation and energy. The plan called for GDP growth to increase by 5.1 percent a year, a target that was surpassed by 0.3 percent. A major objective of the plan was to increase employment, especially in rural areas, in order to reduce the level of poverty. Poor people were given cows, bullock carts, and handlooms; however, subsequent studies indicated that the income of only about 10 percent of the poor rose above the poverty level.

The Seventh Five-Year Plan (FY 1985–89) envisioned a greater emphasis on the allocation of resources to energy and social spending at the expense of industry and agriculture. In practice, the main increase was in transportation and communications, which took up 17 percent of public-sector expenditure during this period. Total spending was targeted at nearly Rs3.9 trillion, of which 94 percent would be financed from domestic resources, including 48 percent from the public sector. The planners assumed that public savings would increase and help finance government spending. In practice that increase did not occur; instead, the government relied on foreign borrowing for a greater share of resources than expected.

The schedule for the Eighth Five-Year Plan (FY 1992–96) was affected by changes of government and by growing uncertainty over what role planning could usefully perform in a more liberal economy. Two annual plans were in effect in FY 1990 and FY 1991. The eighth plan was finally launched in April 1992 and emphasized market-based policy reform rather than quantitative targets. Total spending was planned at Rs8.7 trillion, of which 94 percent would be financed from domestic resources, 45 percent of which would come from the public sector. The eighth plan included three general goals. First, it sought to cut back the public sector by selling off failing and inessential industries while encouraging private investment in such sectors as power, steel, and transport. Second, it proposed that agriculture and rural development have priority. Third, it sought to renew the assault on illiteracy and improve other aspects of social infrastructure, such as the provision of fresh drinking water. Government documents issued in 1992 indicated that GDP growth was expected to increase from around 5 percent a year during the seventh plan to 5.6 percent a year during the eighth plan. However, in 1994 economists expected annual growth to be around 4 percent during the period of the eighth plan.

Four decades of planning show that India's economy, a mix of public and private enterprise, is too large and diverse to be wholly predictable or responsive to directions of the planning authorities. Actual results usually differ in important respects from plan targets. Major shortcomings include insufficient improvement in income distribution and alleviation of poverty, delayed completions and cost overruns on many public-sector projects, and far too small a return on many public-sector investments. Even though the plans have turned out to be less effective than expected, they help guide investment priorities, policy recommendations, and financial mobilization.

Finance

The early governments after independence operated with only modest budget deficits, but in the 1970s and 1980s the amount of the budget deficit as a proportion of GDP increased gradually, reaching 8.4 percent in FY 1990. Following economic reforms, the deficit declined to 6.7 percent by FY 1994. More than 80 percent of the public debt was financed from domestic sources, but the proportion of foreign debt rose steadily in the late 1980s. However, although foreign aid to India was substantial, it was much lower than most other developing countries when calculated on a per capita basis. Banking and credit were dominated by government-controlled institutions, but the importance of the private sector in financial services was increasing slowly.

Budget

India's public finance system follows the British pattern. The constitution establishes the supremacy of the bicameral Parliament—specifically the Lok Sabha (House of the People)—in financial matters. No central government taxes are levied and no government expenditure from public funds disbursed without an act of Parliament, which also scrutinizes and audits all government accounts to ensure that expenditures are legally authorized and properly spent. Proposals for taxation or expenditures, however, may be initiated only within the Council of Ministers—specifically by the minister of finance. The minister of finance is required to submit to Parliament, usually on the last day of February, a financial statement detailing the estimated receipts and expenditures of the central government for the forthcoming fiscal year and a financial review of the current fiscal year.

The Lok Sabha has one month to review and modify the government's budget proposals. If by April 1, the beginning of the fiscal year, the parliamentary discussion of the budget has not been completed, the budget as proposed by the minister of finance goes into effect, subject to retroactive modifications after the parliamentary review. On completion of its budget discussions, the Lok Sabha passes the annual appropriations act, authorizing the executive to spend money, and the finance act, authorizing the executive to impose and collect taxes. Supplemental requests for funds are presented during the course of the fiscal year to cover emergencies, such as war or other catastrophes. The bills are forwarded to the Rajya Sabha (Council of States—the upper house of Parliament) for comment. The Lok Sabha, however, is not bound by the comments, and the Rajya Sabha cannot delay passage of money bills. When signed by the president, the bills become law. The Lok Sabha cannot increase the request for funds submitted by the executive, nor can it authorize new expenditures. Taxes passed by Parliament may be retroactive.

Each state government maintains its own budget, prepared by the state's minister of finance in consultation with appropriate officials of the central government. Primary control over state finances rests with the state legislature in the same man-

313

ner as at the central government level. State finances are supervised by the central government, however, through the comptroller and the auditor general; the latter reviews state government accounts annually and reports the findings to the appropriate state governor for submission to the state's legislature. The central and state budgets consist of a budget for current expenditures, known as the budget on revenue account, and a capital budget for economic and social development expenditures.

The national railroad (Indian Railways), the largest public-sector enterprise, and the Department of Posts and Telegraph have their own budgets, funds, and accounts (see Railroads; Telecommunications, this ch.). The appropriations and disbursements under their budgets are subject to the same form of parliamentary and audit control as other government revenues and expenditures. Dividends accrue to the central government, and deficits are subsidized by it, a pattern that holds true also, directly or indirectly, for other government enterprises.

During the eighth plan, the states were expected to spend nearly Rs1.9 trillion, or 42.9 percent of the public outlay. Because of its greater revenue sources, the central government shared with the states its receipts from personal income taxes and certain excise taxes. It also collected other minor taxes, the total proceeds of which were transferred to the states. The division of the shared taxes is determined by financial commissions established by the president, usually at five-year intervals. In the early 1990s, the states received 75 percent of the revenue collected from income taxes and around 43 percent of the excise taxes. The central government also provided the states with grants to meet their commitments. In FY 1991, these grants and the states' share of taxes collected by the central government amounted to 40.9 percent of the total revenue of state governments.

The states' share of total public revenue collected declined from 48 percent in FY 1955 to about 42 percent in the late 1970s, and to about 33 percent in the early 1990s. An important cause of the decline was the diminished importance of the land revenue tax, which traditionally had been the main direct tax on agriculture. This tax declined from 8 percent of all state and central tax revenues in FY 1950 to less than 1 percent in the 1980s and early 1990s. The states have jurisdiction over taxes levied on land and agricultural income, and vested interests exerted pressure on the states not to raise agricultural taxation. As a result, in the 1980s and early 1990s agriculture largely escaped significant taxation, although there has long been nationwide discussion about increasing land taxes or instituting some sort of tax on incomes of the richer portion of the farm community. The share of direct taxes in GDP increased from 2.1 percent in FY 1991 to 2.8 percent in FY 1994.

Since independence government has favored more politically palatable indirect taxes—customs and excise duties—over direct taxes. In the 1980s and early 1990s, indirect taxes accounted for around 75 percent of all tax revenue collected by the central government. State governments relied heavily on sales taxes. Overall, indirect taxes accounted for 84.1 percent of all government tax revenues in FY 1990. Total government tax revenues amounted to 17.1 percent of GDP in that year, up from 9.0 percent in FY 1960, 11.5 percent in FY 1970, and 14.9 percent in FY 1980. In FY 1990, the share of the public sector in GDP was 26.4 percent. In terms of rupees (in current prices), total government income rose from Rs259.8 billion in FY 1981 to Rs1.3 trillion in FY 1992 (see table 18, Appendix).

Comprehensive tax reforms were implemented with the FY 1985 budget. Corporate tax was cut, income taxes simplified and lowered for high-income groups, and wealth taxes reduced. Tax receipts in FY 1985 rose by 20 percent over FY 1984 as a result of tightened enforcement, and taxpayers responded to lower taxes with greater compliance. In FY 1986, another major change was made with the launching of a long-term program of tax reform designed to eliminate annual changes, which had produced uncertainty. However, in FY 1987, when the monsoon failed, the government raised taxes on higher income groups. The emergency budget of FY 1991, designed to cope with the nation's 1990 balance of payments crisis, increased indirect and corporate taxes, but the budgets for FY 1992 and FY 1993 reflected the policy of economic liberalization. They reduced and simplified direct taxes, removed the wealth tax from financial investments, and indexed the capital gains tax. The highest marginal rate of personal income tax was 42.5 percent in FY 1992.

Fiscal Administration

Historically, the Indian government has pursued a cautious policy with regard to financing budgets, allowing only small amounts of deficit spending. Budget deficits increased in the late 1980s, and the necessity of financing these deficits from foreign borrowing contributed to the 1990 balance of payments crisis. The central government budget deficit reached 8.4 percent of GDP in FY 1990, up from 2.6 percent in FY 1970, 5.9 percent in FY 1980, and 7.8 percent in FY 1989. The deficit was cut to 5.9 percent in FY 1991 and 5.2 percent in FY 1992, but widened to 7.4 percent in FY 1993. It was expected to recede to 6.2 percent in FY 1995.

The central government's budget deficits during the 1980s increased the total public debt rapidly until in FY 1991 it stood at Rs3.9 trillion. The bulk of this debt was owed to citizens and domestic institutions and firms, particularly the central bank. Readers of Indian monetary statistics should be alert to the use of the terms *lakh* (see Glossary) and *crore* (see Glossary), which are used to express higher numbers.

Monetary Process

The basic elements of the financial system were established during British rule (1757–1947). The national currency, the rupee, had long been used domestically before independence and even circulated abroad, for example, in the Persian Gulf region. Foreign banks, mainly British and including some from such other parts of the empire as Hong Kong, provided banking and other services. The Reserve Bank of India was formed in 1935 as a private bank, but it also carried out some central bank functions. This colonial banking system, however, was geared to foreign trade and short-term loans. Banking was concentrated in the major port cities.

The Reserve Bank was nationalized on January 1, 1949, and given broader powers. It was the bank of issue for all rupee notes higher than the one-rupee denomination; the agent of the Ministry of Finance in controlling foreign exchange; and the banker to the central and state governments, commercial banks, state cooperative banks, and other financial institutions. The Reserve Bank formulated and administered monetary policy to promote stable prices and higher production. It was given increasing responsibilities for the development of banking and credit and to coordinate banking and credit with the five-year plans. The Reserve Bank had a number of tools with which to affect commercial bank credit.

After independence the government sought to adapt the banking system to promote development and formed a number of specialized institutions to provide credit to industry, agriculture, and small businesses. Banking penetrated rural areas, and agricultural and industrial credit cooperatives were promoted. Deposit insurance and a system of postal savings banks and offices fostered use by small savers. Subsidized credit was provided to particular groups or activities considered in need and which deserved such help. A credit guarantee corporation covered loans by commercial banks to small traders, transport operators, self-employed persons, and other borrowers not otherwise effectively covered by major institutions. The system effectively reached all kinds of savers and provided credit to many different customers.

The government nationalized fourteen major private commercial banks in 1969 and six more in 1980. Nationalization forced commercial banks increasingly to meet the credit requirements of the weaker sections of the nation and to eliminate monopolization by vested interests of large industry, trade, and agriculture.

The banking system expanded rapidly after nationalization. The number of bank branches, for instance, increased from about 7,000 in 1969 to more than 60,000 in 1994, two-thirds of which were in rural areas. The deposit base rose from Rs50 billion in 1969 to around Rs3.5 trillion in 1994. Nevertheless, currency accounted for well over 50 percent of all the money supply circulating among the public. In 1992 the nationalized banks held 93 percent of all deposits.

In FY 1990, twenty-three foreign banks operated in India. The most important were ANZ Grindlays Bank, Citibank, the Hongkong and Shanghai Banking Corporation, and Standard Chartered Bank.

Public-sector banks are required to reserve their lending based on 40 percent of their deposits for priority sectors, especially agriculture, at favorable rates. In addition, 35 percent of their deposits have to be held in liquid form to satisfy statutory liquidity requirements, and 15 percent are needed to meet the cash reserve requirements of the Reserve Bank. Both these percentages represent an easing of earlier requirements, but only a small proportion of public-sector banks' resources can be deployed freely. In late 1994, the rate of interest on bank loans was deregulated, but deposit rates were still subject to ceilings.

More than 50 percent of bank lending is to the government sector. With the onset of economic reform, India's banks were experiencing major financial losses as the result of low productivity, bad loans, and poor capitalization. Seeking to stabilize the banking industry, the Reserve Bank of India developed new reporting formats and has initiated takeovers and mergers of smaller banks that were operating with financial losses.

India has a rapidly expanding stock market that in 1993 listed around 5,000 companies in fourteen stock exchanges, although only the stocks of about 400 of these companies were actively traded. Financial institutions and government bodies controlled an estimated 45 percent of all listed capital. In April 1992, the Bombay stock market, the nation's largest with a market capital of US$65.1 billion, collapsed, in part because of revelations about financial malpractice amounting to US$2 billion. Afterward, the Securities and Exchange Board of India, the government's capital market regulator, implemented reforms designed to strengthen investor confidence in the stock market. In the mid-1990s, foreign institutional investors took greater interest than ever before in the Indian stock markets, investing around US$2 billion in FY 1993 alone.

Despite increases in energy costs and other pressures from the world economy, for most of the period since independence India has not experienced severe inflation. The underlying average rate of inflation, however, has tended to rise. Consumer prices rose at an annual average of 2.1 percent in the 1950s, 6.3 percent in the 1960s, 7.8 percent in the 1970s, and 8.5 percent in the 1980s.

Three factors lay behind India's relative price stability. First, the government has intervened, either directly or indirectly, to keep stable the price of certain staples, including wheat, rice, cloth, and sugar. Second, monetary regulation has restricted growth in the money supply. Third, the overall influence of the labor unions on wages has been small because of the weakness of the unions in India's labor surplus economy.

Foreign Economic Relations

Aid

Since independence India has had to draw on foreign investments to finance part of its economic development. Although the government has attempted to be as self-reliant as possible, the absolute amount of foreign aid received has been high. In per capita terms, however, it has been much less than most other developing countries receive.

Two of the many modes of transportation found in India
Courtesy Robert L. Worden

In August 1958, the World Bank (see Glossary) organized the Aid-to-India Consortium, consisting of the World Bank Group and thirteen countries: Austria, Belgium, Britain, Canada, Denmark, the Federal Republic of Germany (at that time, West Germany), France, Italy, Japan, the Netherlands, Norway, Sweden, and the United States. The consortium was formed to coordinate aid and establish priorities among India's major sources of foreign assistance and to simplify India's requests for aid based on its plans for development. Consortium aid was bilateral government-to-government aid from the thirteen consortium countries, and almost all of the aid, including that from the World Bank Group, was for specific projects judged to be valuable contributions to India's development. Of the Rs630 billion in aid authorized by all aid donors between FY 1974 and FY 1989, more than 60 percent was provided by the consortium.

Collectively, the Western nations have donated a substantial amount of aid to India. In 1980 this aid totaled nearly US$1.5 billion and reached US$2.5 billion in 1990. In 1992 Western aid reached a new height: US$3.9 billion, which represented 49.8 percent of all Western multilateral and bilateral aid given to South Asian nations that year. The largest bilateral donor is Japan. Between 1984 and 1993, Japan's official development assistance grants to India totaled US$337 million. Much greater than the outright grants has been Japan's large-scale loan program, which supports economic infrastructure development (power plants and delivery systems, and road improvement) and environmental protection. Between 1984 and 1993, Japanese loans to India totaled nearly US$2.4 billion. A ¥125 billion (US$1.2 billion) loan financing major projects was granted in December 1994, bringing Japanese loans to India since 1957 to a total of ¥1.6 trillion.

United States assistance was significant in the late 1950s and 1960s but, because of strained India-United States relations, fell off sharply in the 1970s (see United States, ch. 9). The United States accounted for 8.6 percent of all of the aid India received from independence through FY 1988, but for only 0.7 percent in FY 1989 and 0.6 percent in FY 1990. United States aid to India remained relatively insignificant in the early 1990s when it took the form of grants for food aid and consultants in a wide variety of economic growth areas, such as computers, steel, telecommunications, and energy production. In FY 1993, actual United States obligations through the United States Agency for International Development totaled almost US$161 million. The bulk of this aid was provided as United States Public Law 480 food aid grants with lesser amounts for development assistance (including energy and the environment, population control, child survival, acquired immune deficiency syndrome (AIDS) prevention, and economic growth) and housing guaranty loans. Germany and Britain also have substantial aid-to-India programs.

Among countries not in the World Bank consortium, the Soviet Union was the most important contributor, providing more than 16 percent of all aid between 1947 and FY 1988. Since 1991, however, Russia has provided little aid.

About 90 percent of all aid received by India has been in the form of loans. Aid disbursements from all providers for FY 1990 were Rs67 billion.

India maintains a small but well-established foreign aid program of its own. In FY 1990, Rs1.6 billion of aid was authorized, of which Rs582 million was for Bhutan and Rs578 million for Nepal. Bangladesh and Vietnam received significant amounts of aid during the 1980s, but, as the result of changing world political and economic conditions, these programs were small by the early 1990s (see South Asia; Southeast Asia, ch. 9).

Trade

Despite its size, India plays a relatively small role in the world economy. Until the 1980s, the government did not make exports a priority. In the 1950s and 1960s, Indian officials believed that trade was biased against developing countries and that prospects for exports were severely limited. Therefore, the government aimed at self-sufficiency in most products through import substitution, with exports covering the cost of residual import requirements. Foreign trade was subjected to strict government controls, which consisted of an all-inclusive system of foreign exchange and direct controls over imports and exports. As a result, India's share of world trade shrank from 2.4 percent in FY 1951 to 0.4 percent in FY 1980. Largely because of oil price increases in the 1970s, which contributed to balance of payments difficulties, governments in the 1970s and 1980s placed more emphasis on the promotion of exports. They hoped exports would provide foreign exchange needed for the import of oil and high-technology capital goods. Nevertheless, in the early 1990s India's share of world trade stood at only 0.5 percent. In FY 1992, imports accounted for 9.3 percent of GDP and exports for 7.7 percent of GDP.

Based on trends throughout the 1980s and early 1990s, it appears likely that the balance of trade will remain negative for the foreseeable future (see table 19, Appendix). The 1979 increase in the price of oil produced a Rs58.4 billion deficit in FY 1980, close to 5 percent of GNP. The deficit was barely reduced in nominal rupee terms over the next five years, although it improved considerably as a share of GNP (to 2.3 percent in FY 1984) and in dollar terms (from US$7.4 billion in FY 1980 to US$4.3 billion in FY 1984). Pressure on the balance of trade continued through the late 1980s and worsened with the attempted annexation of Kuwait by Iraq in August 1990, which led to a temporary but sharp increase in the price of oil. In FY 1990, the balance of trade deficit reached a record level in rupees (Rs106.5 billion) and in dollars (US$6 billion).

Import controls and devaluation of the rupee allowed the trade deficit to fall to US$1.6 billion in FY 1991. However, it widened to US$3.3 billion in FY 1992 before falling to an estimated US$1 billion in FY 1993. However, one optimistic sign, noted by India's minister of finance in March 1995, was that exports had come to finance 90 percent of India's imports, compared with only 60 percent in the mid-1980s.

No one product dominates India's exports. In FY 1993, handicrafts, gems, and jewelry formed the most important sector and accounted for an estimated US$4.9 billion (22.2 percent) of exports. Since the early 1990s, India has become the world's largest processor of diamonds (imported in the rough from South Africa and then fabricated into jewelry for export). Along with other semiprecious commodities, such as gold, India's gems and jewelry accounted for 11 percent of its foreign-exchange receipts in early 1993. Textiles and ready-made garments combined were also an important category, accounting for an estimated US$4.1 billion (18.5 percent) of exports. Other significant exports include industrial machinery, leather products, chemicals and related products (see table 20, Appendix).

The dominant imports are petroleum products, valued in FY 1993 at nearly US$5.8 billion, or 24.7 percent of principal imports, and capital goods, amounting to US$4.2 billion, or 21.8 percent of principal imports. Other important import categories are chemicals, dyes, plastics, pharmaceuticals, uncut precious stones, iron and steel, fertilizers, nonferrous metals, and pulp paper and paper products (see table 21, Appendix).

India's most important trading partners are the United States, Japan, the European Union, and nations belonging to the Organization of the Petroleum Exporting Countries (OPEC). From the 1950s until 1991, India also had close trade links with the Soviet Union, but the breakup of that nation into fifteen independent states led to a decline of trade with the region. In FY 1993, some 30 percent of all imports came from the European Union, 22.4 percent from OPEC nations, 11.7 percent from the United States, and 6.6 percent from Japan. In that same year, 26 percent of all exports were to the European Union, 18 percent to the United States, 7.8 percent to Japan, and 10.7 to the OPEC nations (see table 22, Appendix).

Trade and investment with the United States seemed likely to experience an upswing following a January 1995 trade mission from the United States led by Secretary of Commerce

Ronald H. Brown and including top executives from twenty-six United States companies. During the weeklong visit, some US$7 billion in business deals were agreed on, mostly in the areas of infrastructure development, transportation, power and communication systems, food processing, health care services, insurance and financing projects, and automotive catalytic converters. In turn, greater access for Indian goods in United States markets was sought by Indian officials.

In February 1995, in a bid to improve commercial prospects in Southeast Asia, India signed a four-part agreement with the Association of Southeast Asian Nations (ASEAN—see Glossary). The pact covers trade, investment, science and technology, and tourism, and there are prospects for further agreements on joint ventures, banks, and civil aviation.

India's balance of payments position is closely related to the balance of trade. Foreign aid and remittances from Indians employed overseas, however, make the balance of payments more favorable than the balance of trade (see Size and Composition of the Work Force, this ch.).

Foreign-Exchange System

The central government has wide powers to control transactions in foreign exchange. Until 1992 all foreign investments and the repatriation of foreign capital required prior approval of the government. The Foreign-Exchange Regulation Act, which governs foreign investment, rarely allowed foreign majority holdings. However, a new foreign investment policy announced in July 1991 prescribed automatic approval for foreign investments in thirty-four industries designated high priority, up to an equity limit of 51 percent. Initially the government required that a company's automatic approval must rely on matching exports and dividend repatriation, but in May 1992 this requirement was lifted, except for low-priority sectors. In 1994 foreign and nonresident Indian investors were allowed to repatriate not only their profits but also their capital. Indian exporters are also free to use their export earnings as they see fit. However, transfer of capital abroad by Indian nationals is only permitted in special circumstances, such as emigration. Foreign exchange is automatically made available for imports for which import licenses are issued.

Because foreign-exchange transactions are so tightly controlled, Indian authorities are able to manage the exchange rate, and from 1975 to 1992 the rupee was tied to a trade-weighted basket of currencies. In February 1992, the government began moves to make the rupee convertible, and in March 1993 a single floating exchange rate was implemented. In July 1995, Rs31.81 were worth US$1, compared with Rs7.86 in 1980, Rs12.37 in 1985, and Rs17.50 in 1990.

External Debt

India has frequently encountered balance of payments difficulties (see table 23, Appendix). The usual recourse has been to contract imports, thereby reducing production and economic growth, although the amount of foreign aid available has been an important factor in how harsh the restrictions have become. Following the first round of oil price increases in 1973–74, increased foreign aid and some belt-tightening overcame the country's balance of payments problems. The growth of exports and the increased remittances from Indians working abroad in the late 1970s permitted a buildup of substantial foreign-currency reserves. Toward the end of the 1970s, the country's external payments situation was more favorable than it had been for many years.

The second large oil price increase, in the 1979–80 period, quickly altered India's terms of trade and balance of payments situation. Between FY 1978 and FY 1980, India's oil bill increased threefold, by about US$4.6 billion. The deficit on the balance of trade rose from US$1.5 billion in FY 1979 to US$7.7 billion in FY 1980. Officials negotiated a substantial loan from the IMF, which, along with the foreign-exchange reserves, foreign aid, and export possibilities, made adjustments possible. The intent was to keep annual economic growth at 5 percent or more to reduce poverty, while making structural adjustments in the economy to compensate for the change in the external environment. Nonetheless, the external debt rose from US$20.6 billion in 1980 to nearly US$70.2 billion in 1990. In FY 1990, commercial loans accounted for 26.3 percent of the external debt; loans from international institutions, especially the World Bank, made up 45.2 percent; borrowing from foreign governments accounted for 28.5 percent. The largest sums were owed to Japan, Germany, and the United States. At the time of the economic crisis of 1990, external debt was increasing at around US$8 billion a year. By 1993–94, the annual increase had been cut to less than US$1 billion and was expected to be further reduced. India's foreign currency reserves, which stood at US$1 billion in June 1991, had reached a record level of US$20 billion by March 1995.

Labor

Size and Composition of the Work Force

Based on the 1991 census, the government estimated that the labor force had grown by more than 65 million since 1981 and that the total number of "main workers"—the "economically active population"—had reached 285.9 million people. This total did not include Jammu and Kashmir, which was not enumerated in the 1991 census. Labor force statistics for 1991 covered nine main-worker "industrial" categories: cultivators (39 percent of the main-worker force); agricultural laborers (26 percent); livestock, forestry, fishing, hunting, plantations, orchards, and allied activities (2 percent); mining and quarrying (1 percent); manufacturing (household 2 percent, other than household 7 percent); construction (2 percent); trade and commerce (8 percent); transportation, storage, and communications (3 percent); and "other services" (10 percent). Another 28.2 million "marginal workers" were also counted in the census but not tabulated among the nine categories even though unpaid farm and family enterprise workers were counted among the nine categories. Of the total work force—both main and marginal workers—29 percent were women, and nearly 78 percent worked in rural areas.

Included in the labor force are some 55 million children, other than those working directly for their parents. The Ministry of Labour and nongovernmental organizations estimate that there are 25 million children employed in the agricultural sector, 20 million in service jobs (hotels, shops, and as servants in homes), and 5 million in the handloom, carpet-making, gem-cutting, and match-making industries. With mixed success, nongovernmental organizations monitor the child labor market for abuse and conformity to child labor laws.

In government organizations throughout the nation and in nonagricultural enterprises with twenty-five persons or more in 1991, the public sector employed nearly 19 million people compared with about 8 million people employed in the private sector. Most of the growth in the organized work force between 1970 and 1990 was in the public sector. Observers expected that this trend might be reversed if the government's policy of economic liberalization continued. Labor law makes it very difficult for companies to lay off workers. Some observers feel that this restriction deters companies from hiring because they fear carrying a bloated workforce in case of an economic turndown.

A new source of employment appeared after OPEC sharply increased crude oil prices in 1974. The Middle East oil-exporting countries quickly undertook massive development programs based on their large oil revenues. Most of these countries required the importation of labor, both skilled and unskilled, and India became one of many nations supplying the labor. Because some labor agents and employers took advantage of expatriate workers, especially those with little education or few skills, in 1983 India enacted a law governing workers going abroad. In general, the new legislation provided more protection and required fairer treatment of Indians employed outside the country. By 1983 some 900,000 Indian workers were registered as temporary residents in the Middle East. In the mid-1980s, there was a shift in the kinds of skills needed. Fewer laborers, metalworkers, and engineers, for example, were required for construction projects, but the need for maintenance workers and operating staff in power plants, hospitals, and offices increased. In 1990 it was estimated that more than 1 million Indians were resident in the Middle East. India benefited not only from the opening of job opportunities but also from the remittances the workers sent back, which amounted to around US$4.3 billion of foreign exchange in FY 1988. Both employment and remittances suffered as a result of the 1991 Persian Gulf War, when about 180,000 Indian workers were displaced. In the mid-1990s, the outlook for Indian employment in the Middle East was only fair.

India's labor force exhibits extremes ranging from large numbers of illiterate workers unaccustomed to machinery or routine, to a sizable pool of highly educated scientists, technicians, and engineers, capable of working anywhere in the world. A substantial number of skilled people have left India to work abroad; the country has suffered a brain drain since independence. Nonetheless, many remain in India working alongside a trained industrial and commercial work force. Administrative skills, particularly necessary in large projects or programs, are in short supply, however. In the mid-1990s, salaries for top administrators and technical staff rose sharply, partly in response to the arrival of foreign companies in India.

Indian Oil Corporation refinery in Guwahati, Assam
Courtesy Indian Ministry of External Affairs

Labor Relations

The Trade Unions Act of 1926 provided recognition and
protection for a nascent Indian labor union movement. The
number of unions grew considerably after independence, but
most unions are small and usually active in only one firm.
Union membership is concentrated in the organized sector,
and in the early 1990s total membership was about 9 million.
Many unions are affiliated with regional or national federations, the most important of which are the Indian National
Trade Union Congress, the All-India Trade Union Congress,
the Centre of Indian Trade Unions, the Indian Workers' Association, and the United Trade Union Congress. Politicians have
often been union leaders, and some analysts believe that strikes
and other labor protests are called primarily to further the
interests of political parties rather than to promote the interests of the work force.

The government recorded 1,825 strikes and lockouts in 1990. As a result, 24.1 million workdays were lost, 10.6 million to strikes and 13.5 million to lockouts. More than 1.3 million workers were involved in these labor disputes. The number and seriousness of strikes and lockouts have varied from year to year. However, the figures for 1990 and preliminary data from 1991 indicate declines from levels reached in the 1980s, when in some years as many as 35 million workdays were lost because of labor disputes.

The isolated, insecure, and exploited laborers in rural areas and in the urban unorganized sectors present a stark contrast to the position of unionized workers in many modern enterprises. In the early 1990s, there were estimates that between 10 percent and 20 percent of agricultural workers were bonded laborers. The International Commission of Jurists, studying India's bonded labor, defines such a person as one who works for a creditor or someone in the creditor's family against nominal wages in cash or kind until the creditor, who keeps the books and sets the prices, declares the loan repaid, often with usurious rates of interest. The system sometimes extends to a debtor's wife and children, who are employed in appalling working conditions and exposed to sexual abuse. The constitution, as interpreted by India's Supreme Court, and a 1976 law prohibit bonded labor. Implementation of the prohibition, however, has been inconsistent in many rural areas.

Many in the urban unorganized sector are self-employed laborers, street vendors, petty traders, and other services providers who receive little income. Along with the unemployed, they have no unemployment insurance or other benefits.

Industry

At independence, industrialization was viewed as the engine of growth for the rest of the economy and the supplier of jobs to reduce poverty. By the early 1990s, substantial progress had been made, but industrial growth had failed to live up to expectations. Industrial production rose an average of 6.1 percent in the 1950s, 5.3 percent in the 1960s, and 4.2 percent in the 1970s. Although this increase was respectable, it was less than the rate achieved by some other developing countries and less than what the planners expected and the economy needed to bring about a large reduction in poverty. The emphasis on large-scale, capital-intensive industries created far fewer jobs than the estimated 10 million annual entrants into the labor force required. Hence unemployment and underemployment remained growing problems. In the 1980s, however, industrial production rose at an average rate of 6.6 percent. Observers believed that this increase was largely a response to economic liberalization, which led to increased investment and competition.

Government Policies

Government has played an important role in industry since independence. The government has both owned a large proportion of industrial establishments and has tightly regulated the private sector. From the late 1970s, the government sought to reduce its role, but progress remained slow throughout the 1980s. The Congress (I) government that came to power in June 1991 had a renewed commitment to cutting back the role of government, and in the mid-1990s the liberalization program made progress, although many uncertainties remained about its implementation.

The Industrial Policy Resolution of 1948 gave the government the go-ahead to build and operate key industries, which largely meant those producing capital and intermediate goods (see Early Policy Developments, this ch.). This policy partly reflected socialist ideas then current in India. It was believed that public ownership of basic industry was necessary to ensure development in the interest of the whole population. The decision also reflected the belief that private industrialists would find establishment of many of the basic industries on the scale that the country needed either unattractive or beyond their financial capabilities. Moreover, there was concern that private industrialists could enlarge their profits by dominating markets in key commodities. The industrial policy resolutions of 1948 and 1956 delineated the lines between the public and private sectors and stressed the need for a large degree of self-sufficiency in manufacturing, the basic strategy that guided industrialization until the mid-1980s.

Another early decision on industrial policy mandated that defense industries would be developed by the public sector. Building defense industries for a modern military force required the concomitant development of heavy industries, including metallurgy and machine tools. Production often started under foreign licensing, but as much as possible, design and production became Indianized. India was one of only a few developing countries to produce a variety of high-technology military equipment to supply its own needs.

Before independence there was a strong tendency for ownership or control of much of the large-scale private industrial economy to be concentrated in managing agencies, which became powerful under the British because they had access to London money markets. Through diversified investments and interlocking directorates, the individuals who controlled the managing agencies controlled much of the preindependence economy. After independence Parliament passed legislation to restrain further concentration, used the development of the stock market to induce the sale of stock in tightly held companies to the public, and applied high corporate tax rates to such companies. It also attempted to offset the monopoly effects of the managing agencies by fixing prices on a number of basic commodities, including cement, steel, and coal, and assumed considerable control of their distribution. The government eventually abolished some of the managing agencies in 1969 and the remainder in 1971. In 1970 the Monopolies and Restrictive Practices Act supplied the government with additional authority to diminish concentrations of private economic power and to restrict business practices contrary to the public interest. This act was strengthened in 1984.

Industrialization occurred in a protected environment, which led to distortions that, after the mid-1960s, contributed to the sagging industrial growth rate. Tariffs and quantitative controls largely kept foreign competition out of the domestic market, and most Indian manufacturers looked on exports only as a residual possibility. Industry paid insufficient attention to the quality of products, technological development elsewhere, and economies of scale. Management was weak in many private and public plants. Shortfalls in reaching plan goals in public enterprises, moreover, denied the rest of the industrial sector key inputs, such as coal and electricity.

In the 1980s and early 1990s, India began increasingly to remove some of the controls on industry. Nevertheless, in the mid-1990s, there were state monopolies for most energy and communications production and services, and the state dominated the steel, nonferrous metal, machine tool, shipbuilding, chemical, fertilizer, paper, and coal industries. In FY 1992, public enterprises had a turnover of Rs1.7 trillion (see table 24, Appendix). Well over 50 percent of this total was accounted for by ten enterprises, the most important of which were the oil, steel, and coal companies. Public enterprises in aggregate made a net profit after tax of 2.4 percent on capital in FY 1992, but the three oil companies earned 95 percent of these net profits. In fact, 106 of the 233 public companies sustained losses. Some analysts believed that the inefficiency of the public sector was concealed by passing on to consumers the high costs of monopoly products.

Manufacturing

Textiles

Cotton textiles is a well-established manufacturing industry and employs more workers than any other sector. Production in FY 1992 was 19 billion square meters of cloth (see table 25, Appendix). In Indian textile mills, yarn is spun, woven into fabrics, and processed under one roof. Production as a share of the manufacturing industry fell from 79 percent in 1951 to under 30 percent in the early 1990s as a result of curbs on capacity expansion and new equipment and differential excise duties. The main export market is Russia and other former Soviet republics. The power-loom sector forms the largest portion of the decentralized part of the textile industry. It expanded from 24,000 units in 1951 to 800,000 units in 1989. Power-loom fabric dominates India's garment export industry. There is also a substantial handloom sector, which provides employment in rural areas (see fig. 10).

Steel and Aluminum

After independence, successive governments placed great emphasis on the development of a steel industry. In FY 1991, the six major plants, of which five were in the public sector, produced 10 million tons. The rest of the steel production, 4.7 million tons, came from 180 small plants, almost all of which were in the private sector. Steel production more than doubled during the 1980s but still did not meet demand in FY 1991, when 2.7 million tons were imported. In the mid-1990s, the government is seeking private-sector investment in new steel plants. Production is projected to increase substantially as the result of plans to set up a 1 million ton steel plant and three pig-iron plants totalling 600,000 tons capacity in West Bengal, with Chinese technical assistance and financial investment.

The aluminum industry grew from 5,000 tons a year at independence to 483,000 tons in FY 1992, of which 113,000 tons were exported. Analysts believe the industry has a good long-term future because of India's abundant supply of bauxite.

Fertilizer and Petrochemicals

The fertilizer industry is another major industrial sector. In FY 1991, production reached 7.4 million tons of nitrogen and 2.6 million tons of phosphate. In the early 1990s, an increasing share of fertilizer production came from private-sector plants. Substantial imports were necessary in FY 1990, but the prospects for expansion of domestic production are good.

In the early 1990s, the petrochemical industry was expanding rapidly. It produces a wide variety of thermoplastics, elastomers, synthetic fibers, and chemicals. Substantial imports, however, are required to meet domestic demand. Analysts forecast a major expansion in production during the 1990s.

Electronics and Motor Vehicles

The engineering sector is large and varied and provides around 12 percent of India's exports in the mid-1990s. Two subsectors, electronics and motor vehicles, are the most dynamic.

Electronics companies benefited from the economic liberalization policies of the 1980s, including the loosening of restrictions on technology and component imports, delicensing, foreign investment, and reduction of excise duties. Output from electronics plants grew from Rs1.8 billion in FY 1970 to Rs8.1 billion in FY 1980 and to Rs123 billion in FY 1992. Most of the expansion took place in the production of computers and consumer electronics.

Computer production rose from 7,500 units in 1985 to 60,000 units in 1988 and to an estimated 200,000 units in 1992. During this period, major advances were made in the domestic computer industry that led to further sales.

Consumer electronics account for about 30 percent of total electronics production. In FY 1990, production included 5 million television sets, 6 million radios, 5 million tape recorders, 5 million electronic watches, and 140,000 video cassette recorders.

A similar expansion occurred in the motor vehicle industry. Until the 1980s, the government considered automobiles an unnecessary luxury and discouraged their production and use.

Production rose from 30,000 cars in FY 1980 to 181,000 cars in FY 1990.

The largest company, Maruti, which is publicly owned, exports some automobiles to Eastern Europe and to France and became a net foreign-exchange earner in FY 1991. The production of other motor vehicles is also expanding. In FY 1990, India produced 176,000 commercial vehicles, such as trucks and buses, and 1.8 million two-wheeled motor vehicles. Following the government's abolition of the manufacturing licensing system in March 1993, British, French, German, Italian, and United States manufacturers and firms in the Republic of Korea (South Korea) announced they would join Japanese and other South Korean companies already operating in India in joint-venture passenger car production in 1995. The growth of the Indian middle class sustains such industrial expansion and is forcing old-line domestic companies, such as Hindustan Motors, to become more competitive.

Construction

Construction contributes 5 to 6 percent of GDP and employs a similar proportion of the organized labor force plus large numbers of people in the informal sector. In the early 1990s, construction absorbed around 40 percent of public-sector plan outlays, and more than 1 million workers were engaged in public-sector construction projects. Indian firms also won many construction contracts in the Middle East during the 1980s and early 1990s. Most companies are small and lack access to modern equipment.

House building has not been a priority of the government, and a housing shortage persists in both urban and rural areas. Analysts believe that one-third of the population of big cities live in areas officially regarded as slums.

Energy

India produces nearly 90 percent of its energy requirements, 65 percent of which are met by coal. Although commercial energy production has expanded substantially since independence, an inadequate supply of energy remains a constraint on industrial growth. Overall growth in the demand for energy was rapid in the early 1990s, but commercial energy consumption was among the lowest in the world. Much energy use in the subsistence sector, such as the use of firewood and cattle dung, is unrecorded. Analysts believe that the share of noncommercial energy fell from around 65 percent in the early 1950s to 23 percent in 1991, and they expect this proportion to fall further during the 1990s. Most commercial energy production and distribution are in the public sector, but in the mid-1990s, the government was moving slowly to encourage the entry of private capital.

Coal

The coal industry is a key segment of the economy. Reserves are estimated at 192 billion tons, 78 billion tons of which are proven reserves. Additional coal exists in small seams, at great depths, and in undiscovered locations. The bulk of the coal found has been in Bihar, Madhya Pradesh, Orissa, and West Bengal. Known reserves should last well into the twenty-first century. In the 1980s, development of strip mines was stressed over underground mines because of the speed with which they could be exploited. Most of the industry was nationalized in the early 1970s. Coal India Limited was established in 1975 as the government's holding company for several operating subsidiaries. Production stagnated in the second half of the 1970s at around 105 million tons after an initial surge in production following nationalization. In the late 1970s and throughout the 1980s, the industry was plagued by the flooding of mines, serious power outages, delays in commissioning new mines, labor unrest, lack of explosives, poor transportation, and environmental problems. Government-set coal prices did not cover operating expenses of the more technically difficult mines. The central government was the main source of investment funds.

Throughout the late 1970s and 1980s, the coal industry—along with the electric power and transportation sectors—was a critical bottleneck in the economy and particularly handicapped industrial growth. The Seventh Five-Year Plan (1985–89) set a target of 226 million tons for coal production in FY 1989, but actual production reached only 214 million tons. Production rose to 241 million tons in FY 1991 and to 251 million tons in FY 1992. The annual demand for coal in the mid-1990s was around 320 million tons, a level that appeared to be out of reach without a significant leap in efficiency and large-scale investment. Subsurface mine fires in Bihar, some of which have been burning since 1916, have consumed some 37 million tons of coal and make another 2 billion tons inaccessible.

Oil and Natural Gas

India has significant amounts of oil and natural gas, and four of India's top six revenue-generating companies are in the oil and natural gas business. India has indigenous sources for around 60 percent of its oil needs and has worked diligently to use substitute forms of energy to fulfill the other 40 percent. Oil in commercial quantities was first discovered in Assam in 1889. The Oil and Natural Gas Commission was established in 1954 as a department of the Geological Survey of India, but a 1959 act of Parliament made it, in effect, the country's national oil company. Oil India Limited, at one time one-third government owned, was also established in 1959 and developed an oil field that had been discovered by the Burmah Oil Company. By 1981 the government had purchased all of the Burmah Oil Company's assets in India and completely owned Oil India Limited. The Oil and Natural Gas Commission discovered oil in Gujarat in 1959 and opened other fields in the 1960s and 1970s.

The early oil fields discovered in India were of modest size. Oil production amounted to 200,000 tons in 1950 and 400,000 tons in 1960. By the early 1970s, production had increased to more than 8 million tons. In 1974 the Oil and Natural Gas Commission discovered a large field—called the Bombay High—offshore from Bombay. Production from that field was responsible for the rapid growth of the country's total crude oil production in the late 1970s and throughout the 1980s. In FY 1989, oil production peaked at 34 million tons, of which Bombay High accounted for 22 million tons. In the early 1990s, wells were shut in offshore fields that had been inefficiently exploited, and production fell to 27 million tons in FY 1993. That amount did not meet India's needs, and 30.7 million tons of crude oil were imported in FY 1993.

India has thirty-five major fields onshore (primarily in Assam and Gujarat) and four major offshore oil fields (near Bombay, south of Pondicherry, and in the Palk Strait). Of the 4,828 wells, in 1990 2,514 were producing at a rate of 664,582 barrels per day. The oil field with the greatest output is Bombay High, with 402,797 barrels per day production in 1990, about fifteen times the amount produced by the next largest fields. Total reserves are estimated at 6.1 billion barrels.

The government has sanctioned ambitious exploration plans to raise production in line with demand and to exploit new discoveries as rapidly as possible. In the late 1980s and early 1990s, there were encouraging finds in Tamil Nadu, Gujarat, Andhra Pradesh, and Assam; many of these discoveries were made offshore. Officials estimated that by the mid-1990s these new fields could contribute as much as 15 million to 20 million tons in new production and that total crude oil production could increase to 51 million tons in FY 1994. In the early 1990s, the government renewed attempts, which had begun in the early 1980s, to interest foreign oil companies in purchasing exploration and production leases. These efforts drew only a modest response because the terms offered were difficult, and foreign companies remained suspicious of India's investment climate. One response, agreed on in January 1995, was an Indian-Kuwaiti joint venture to invest in a new oil refinery to be built on the east coast of India.

Substantial quantities of natural gas are produced in association with crude oil production. Until the 1980s, most of this gas was flared off because there were no pipelines or processing facilities to bring it to customers. In the early 1980s, large investments were made to bring gases from Bombay High and other offshore fields ashore for use as fuel and to supply feedstock to fertilizer and petrochemical plants, which also had to be constructed or converted to use gas. By the mid-1980s, natural gas could be delivered to facilities near Bombay and near Kandla in Gujarat. In the mid-1990s, a 1,700-kilometer trans-India pipeline was being built; the pipeline will link the facilities near Bombay and Kandla to a series of gas-based fertilizer plants and power stations. Officials envisage a grid system covering 11,500 kilometers by FY 2004, which will supply 120 million cubic meters of gas a day. Total production in FY 1992 was 18.1 billion cubic meters.

India's need for oil and petroleum-based products—about 40 million tons per year—far exceeded its domestic production capabilities of 28 million tons per year in the early 1990s. Given India's dependency on Persian Gulf resources, proposals were made in the early 1990s to develop natural gas pipelines from Iran, Qatar, and Oman that would run under the Arabian Sea to one or more west coast terminals. To assist with oil and natural gas production, in 1992 the government decided to open reserves to private offshore developers. In February 1994, contracts were awarded for three offshore fields in the Arabian Sea to an Indian-United States consortium and one in the Bay of Bengal to an Indian-Australian-Japanese consortium. In June

1995, an agreement was reached to set a joint-venture company to construct the first leg of the pipeline, from Iran to Pakistan.

Electric Power

The electric power industry is both a supplier and a consumer of primary energy, depending on the kind of energy used to turn the generators. Hydroelectric and nuclear power plants add to the country's supply of primary energy. The total installed electricity capacity in public utilities in 1992 was 69,100 megawatts, of which 70 percent was thermal, 27 percent hydropower, and 3 percent nuclear. The total installed capacity was programmed to reach around 100,000 megawatts by FY 1996 through a package of government-supported incentives to the private sector.

Because they cannot always depend on public utilities, many larger industrial enterprises have developed their own power generation systems. In 1992 there was a capacity of 9,000 megawatts outside the public utility system. Overall, the generation and transmission of power—with an average 57 percent plant load factor in FY 1992 in thermal plants and transmission losses of 22 percent—were inefficient. About 322 billion kilowatt-hours of power were generated by utilities in FY 1992, approximately 8.5 percent shy of demand. The resulting deficit led to acute shortages in some states. This trend continued the next year when 315 billion kilowatt-hours were produced. Many factors contributed to the shortfall of electric power, including slow completion of new installations, low use of installed capacity because of insufficient maintenance and coal, and poor management. In FY 1990, industry accounted for 45 percent of electricity consumed, agriculture 26 percent, and domestic use 16.5 percent. Other sectors, including commerce and railroads, accounted for the remaining 12.5 percent.

Rural electrification made great progress in the 1980s; more than 200,000 villages received electricity for the first time. In 1990 around 84 percent of India's villages had access to electricity. Most of the villages without electricity were in Bihar, Orissa, Rajasthan, Uttar Pradesh, and West Bengal. Villagers complain that government figures on electrification of villages are artificially inflated. Actually, although lines have been run to most villages, electricity is provided only sporadically (for example, only nine to twelve hours per day), and villagers feel they cannot depend on electricity to operate pumps and other equipment. Electricity to cities also is sporadic; blackouts occur every day in most cities.

India's first hydroelectric station was constructed in 1897 in Darjiling (then Darjeeling). In FY 1990, installed capacity for hydroelectric power was 18,000 megawatts. The country has a large economically exploitable hydroelectric potential, especially in the foothills of the Himalayas, but no large increase in capacity is predicted for the mid-1990s. Hydroelectric facilities have to be coordinated with other sources of electricity because seasonal and annual variations in rainfall affect the amount of water needed to turn the generators and consequently the amount of electricity that can be produced.

Hydroelectric power projects have not been without controversy. Dams for irrigation and power generation have displaced people and raised the specter of ecological problems.

Nuclear Power

Nuclear-power developments are under the purview of the Nuclear Power Corporation of India, a government-owned entity under the Department of Atomic Energy. The corporation is responsible for designing, constructing, and operating nuclear-power plants. In 1995 there were nine operational plants with a potential total capacity of 1,800 megawatts, about 3 percent of India's total power generation. There are two units each in Tarapur, north of Bombay in Maharashtra; in Rawatbhata in Rajasthan; in Kalpakkam near Madras in Tamil Nadu; and in Narora in Uttar Pradesh; and one unit in Kakrapur in southeastern Gujarat. However, of the nine plants, all have been faced with safety problems that have shut down reactors for periods ranging from months to years. The Rajasthan Atomic Power Station in Rawatbhata was closed indefinitely, as of February 1995. Moreover, environmental problems, caused by radiation leaks, have cropped up in communities near Rawatbhata. Other plants operate at only a fraction of their capacity, and some foreign experts consider them the most inefficient nuclear-power plants in the world.

In addition to the nine established plants, seven reactors are under construction in the mid-1990s: one at Kakrapur and two each at Kaiga, on the coast of Karnataka, Rawatbhata, and Tarapur, which, when finished, will bring an additional 2,320 megawatts of energy online. Construction of ten additional reactors is in the planning stage for Kaiga, Rawatbhata, and Kudangulam in Tamil Nadu, which, when combined, will supply 4,800 megawatts capacity. The overall plan is to increase nuclear-generation capacity to 10,000 megawatts by FY 2000, but work has been slowed because of financial shortages. India partially overcame its shortage of enriched uranium—needed to fuel the Tarapur units—by imports from China, starting in 1995.

Mining and Quarrying

For a country of its size, India does not have a great deal of mineral wealth (see fig. 11). Mining accounted for less than 2 percent of GDP in FY 1990. Nonetheless, iron and bauxite are found in sufficient quantities to base industries on their extraction and processing. Assessment of the country's resources by the Geological Survey of India is still far from complete in the mid-1990s, and observers do not rule out the possibility of important new finds.

In 1992 reserves of iron ore were estimated at among the world's largest—at 19.2 billion tons. Extraction capacity is 67 million tons of ore per year, but only 53 million tons were produced in FY 1992. About 60 percent of output is exported, mainly to the South Korea and Japan. The largest iron ore mining project is at Kudremukh, Chikmagalore District, Karnataka. India also has abundant bauxite, the main mineral source for aluminum. Reserves are estimated at about 2.7 billion tons, or 8 percent of the world total. In FY 1991, 512,000 tons of aluminum were produced, of which 61,000 tons were exported. Most bauxite mines are in Bihar and Karnataka. India is the world's third largest producer of manganese, and its mines extracted around 1.4 million tons of manganese ore per year in the early 1990s from a total estimated reserve of 180 million tons. India also has significant reserves of copper, estimated at 422 million tons. However, the production of copper, at 46,000 tons in FY 1991, fell well short of domestic demand. Most copper mines are in Bihar and Rajasthan. Smaller amounts of lead, zinc, and mica are also produced.

Ownership and the power to grant mineral concessions generally have rested with the state governments. The central government, however, has exerted considerable influence over such leases, particularly in cases of important and strategic minerals. In fact, most mining of important and strategic minerals is undertaken by central government enterprises in which states sometimes hold part ownership. In the early 1990s, uranium ore was mined, milled, and processed only in Bihar; rare earths—including mineral sands, monazite, ilmenite, rutile, zircon, rare earths chloride, and others—were mined in Tamil Nadu, Kerala, and Orissa. During this period, the central government was attempting to increase the private sector's share of this industry.

Transportation

Transportation is a large and varied sector of the economy. Modes of conveyance for goods range from people's heads (on which loads are balanced) and bicycle rickshaws to trucks and railroad cars. The national railroad was the major freight hauler at independence, but road transport grew rapidly after 1947. Both rail and road transport remain important.

The share of transportation investments in total public investment declined during the period from the early 1950s to the early 1980s; real public transportation investment also declined during much of that period because of the need for funds in the rest of the economy. As a consequence, by the early 1980s the transportation system was barely meeting the needs of the nation or preparing for future economic growth. Many roads, for example, were breaking up because of overuse and lack of maintenance; railroads required new track and rolling stock. Ports needed equipment and facilities, particularly for bulk and container cargo; and at many airports the national civil airlines needed supporting equipment, including provision for instrument landings. The government planned to devote 19 percent of the Eighth Five-Year Plan (1992–96) budget to transportation and communications, up from the 16 percent devoted to the sector during the seventh plan.

Although there is a large private-sector involvement in transportation, government plays a large regulatory and developmental role. The central government has ministries to handle civil aviation, railroads, and surface transportation. Counterpart agencies are found at the state and union territory level. Critical to improving the entire transportation sector in the late 1990s is the ability of the sector to adjust to the central government's national reform initiatives, including privatization, deregulation, and reduced subsidies. The sector must also adjust to foreign trade expansion, demographic pressures and increasing urbanization, technological change and obsolescence, energy availability, and environmental and public safety concerns.

Railroads

India's railroad system is the government's largest public enterprise (see fig. 12). Its route length extends 62,458 kilometers. The railroads of India are the fourth most heavily used system in the world, which suggests the large investment made in rail transportation. In the mid-1990s, the railroad system employed 1.7 million people and carried around 66 percent of India's goods traffic (some 350 million tons in FY 1992) and 40 percent of passenger traffic (3.7 billion passenger journeys in FY 1992).

Indian Railways is administered and managed by the Railway Board, which is subordinate to the Ministry of Railways. The minister of railways is assisted by the minister of state for railways. Indian Railways is Asia's largest railroad system and the second largest state-owned system under a single management in the world. The 62,458 kilometers of route-length track run in three gauges: narrow gauge (610 and 762 millimeters), meter gauge (1,000 millimeters), and broad gauge (1,676 millimeters). Around 17 percent, or about 11,000 kilometers, of all gauges is electrified, and about 27 percent, or 10,859 kilometers, of the broad-gauge track is electrified. Some 14,600 kilometers are double or multiple tracked. As of FY 1991, there were some 116,000 railroad bridges and some 7,100 railroad stations.

The railroad system is divided into nine zones: central, eastern, northern, northeastern, northeast frontier, southern, south-central, southeastern, and western. As of FY 1993, Indian Railways had 1,725 steam, 4,069 diesel, and 2,012 electric locomotives; 3,444 electric multiple-unit coaches; 30,298 conventional passenger coaches; 6,163 other passenger cars (including luggage and mail cars in which passengers sometimes travel); and 337,562 freight cars of all kinds.

The Eighth Five-Year Plan provided for a Rs45 trillion investment in railroad development. Priority was to be given to track and roadbed renovation, additional electrification, conversion of high-use meter-gauge lines to broad-gauge track, the replacement of all steam locomotives, and improved signalling and telecommunications. By 1992, however, the funds actually approved by the government were only 80 percent of the eighth plan's amount, and only 42 percent would be covered by the central government budget. Indian Railways was expected to come up with the balance. Thus, in FY 1994, the outlay was set at Rs65.1 billion; Rs11.5 billion was to come from central government revenues, Rs43.1 billion from internal railroad resources, and Rs10.5 billion from loans. Some of the investment funds, as in the past, were expected from the World Bank. The only way to cover these outlays with such low budgetary support was with drastic increases in fares and rates in passenger service. In FY 1993, Indian Railways made capital expenditures amounting to US$2 billion for items such as new rolling stock, new line construction, track renewal, and electrification.

An example of the scale of new rail line construction is the new broad-gauge high-speed Konkan Railway, a 760-kilometer coastal connection between Bombay and Mangalore featuring fifty-five stations, seventy-three tunnels, 143 major bridges, and some 1,670 minor bridges. The line crosses several mountain ranges and runs some 380 kilometers through an earthquake-prone zone. Besides opening up an all-weather transportation infrastructure between two important cities, it cuts the distance by rail between them by 1,127 circuitous kilometers.

India has a major railroad-equipment production industry. Although some state-of-the-art electrical components and equipment are imported, India is developing sufficient industrial capacity to meet most of its standard locomotive and passenger-car and ancillary equipment needs and has made plans to export locomotives. The Research, Design, and Standards Organisation of Indian Railways engages in research and simulations aimed at further improving the quality of domestic achievements, which have included high-speed passenger trains (up to 140 kilometers per hour) and freight trains (up to 80 kilometers per hour) and solid-state signalling equipment. Because some two-thirds of the nation's freight is carried by train, there is a serious freight car shortage. To overcome this and other industry-related rail transportation problems, Indian Railways envisions having to import up to 5,000 freight cars a year.

Rapid Transit

India also has two rapid-rail systems and a third in the planning stage. The most advanced is the world-class metro system in Calcutta that opened in 1984 and carried 50,000 passengers daily in 1992–93. It uses Indian-made subway cars that run on the initial ten kilometers of what will be a 16.5 kilometer-long, seventeen-station (eleven stations were in service in 1995) route scheduled for completion in 1995. Plans for more than

Passenger train arriving in New Delhi
Courtesy Robert L. Worden

bay Port, was established in 1982 under the administration of the Jawaharlal Nehru Port Trust as a separate port rather than an adjunct to Bombay. The eleven ports are the responsibility of the Ministry of State for Surface Transport but are managed by semi-independent port trusts overseen by boards appointed by the ministry from government departments, including the navy, port labor and industry, and ship owners and shipping companies.

In order of gross weight tonnage conveyed annually, Bombay, Vishakhapatnam, Madras, and Marmagao are the most important ports. In addition, there are some 139 minor working ports along the two coasts and on offshore islands administered by local, state, or union territory maritime administrations. Total traffic at the eleven major ports increased from 107 million tons in FY 1984 to 179 million tons in FY 1993. In FY 1993, some US$250 million in profits were earned, an achievement that attracted some US$4.5 billion in foreign investments in the ports in FY 1992–FY 1993.

In 1995 there were three government-owned shipping corporations, the most important of which was the Shipping Corporation of India. There were also between fifty and sixty private companies operating a total of 443 vessels amounting to

6.3 million gross registered tons, more than 300 of which were 1,000 gross registered tons or more. Indian tonnage represented 1.7 percent of the world total. Overall, the share of Indian vessels in total Indian trade is around 35 percent. Approximately 40 to 50 percent of capacity is underused. As a result of the global slump of the late 1980s, shipping companies experienced financial difficulties; the leading private shipping company, Scindia Steam Navigation Company, collapsed in 1987. The collapse left most Indian shipping under public ownership. The government's director general of shipping provides oversight for all aspects of shipping.

India has four major and three medium-sized shipyards, all government run. The Cochin Shipyards in Kochi, Hindustan Shipyard in Vishakhapatnam, and Hooghly Dock and Port Engineers in Calcutta are the most important shipbuilding enterprises in India. Thirty-five smaller shipyards are in the private sector. Drydocks at Kochi and Vishakhapatnam accommodate the nation's major ship repair needs.

In addition to its coastal and ocean trade routes, India has more than 16,000 kilometers of inland waterways. Of that number, more than 3,600 kilometers are navigable by large vessels, although in practice only about 2,000 kilometers are used. Inland waters are regulated by the Inland Waterways Authority of India, which was established in 1986 to develop, maintain, and regulate the nation's waterways and to advise the central and state governments on inland waterway development.

Civil Aviation

Air transportation is under the purview of the Department of Civil Aviation, a part of the Ministry of Civil Aviation and Tourism. In 1995 the government owned two airlines and one helicopter service, and private companies owned six airlines.

The government-owned airlines dominated India's air transportation in the mid-1990s. Air India is the international carrier; it carried more than 2.2 million passengers in FY 1992. Indian Airlines is the major domestic carrier and also runs international flights to nearby countries. It carried 9.8 million passengers in FY 1989, when it had a load factor of more than 80 percent in its fifty-nine airplanes. Analysts, however, attributed this high load factor to a shortage of capacity rather than efficiency of operation. A major expansion was planned for the 1990s, but an airplane crash in 1990 and a pilots' strike in 1991 damaged the airline, which carried only 7.8 million passengers

A bus in rural Rajasthan
Courtesy Janice Hyde
Semi-articulated double-decker bus, Bangalore, Karnataka
Courtesy Robert L. Worden

in FY 1992. Two other accidents in 1993, plus several hijackings, put constraints on the growth of both airlines.

A third government-owned airline, Vayudoot, was also a domestic carrier in the early 1990s. It provided feeder service between smaller cities and the larger places served by Air India and Indian Airlines. By 1994 Indian Airlines had taken over Vayudoot. Another publicly owned company, Pawan Hans, runs helicopter service, mostly to offshore locations and other areas that cannot be served by fixed-wing aircraft.

In 1995 India's six private airlines accounted for more than 10 percent of domestic air traffic. Both the number of carriers and their market share are expected to rise in the mid-1990s. The four major private airlines are East West Airlines, Jagsons Airlines, Continental Aviation, and Damania Airways.

In addition to the Indian-owned airlines, many foreign airlines provide international service. In 1995 forty-two airlines operated air services to, from, and through India.

In the mid-1990s, India had 288 usable airports. Of these, 208 had permanent-surface runways and two had runways of more than 3,659 meters, fifty-nine had runways of between 2,400 and 3,659 meters, and ninety-two had runways between 1,200 and 2,439 meters. There are major international airports at Bombay, Delhi, Calcutta, Madras, and Thiruvananthapuram (Trivandrum), under the management of the International Airport Authority of India. International service also operates from Marmagao, Bangalore, and Hyderabad. A consortium of Indian and British companies signed a memorandum of understanding with the state government of Maharashtra in June 1995 to build a new international airport for Bombay, across the harbor from the main city and to be linked by a cross-harbor roadway. Major regional airports are located at Ahmadabad, Allahabad, Pune, Srinagar, Chandigarh, Kochi, and Nagpur.

Telecommunications

National Policy

In 1994 the government issued its National Telecommunications Policy. The policy was issued in recognition of the "urgent need" to provide universal access to basic telecommunications services by 1997 and offers guidelines for entry of the private sector into basic telecommunications services. To facilitate private-sector participation, licensing procedures were established in the Department of Telecommunications, and equity participation for companies registered in India (with 51 or more percent Indian ownership) was anticipated. Private-sector licenses, however, were to be granted only for local (versus long-distance) telecommunications networks. An autonomous body, the Telecommunications Authority of India, was established to regulate private-sector activity.

Telephone

The telephone system, like many other aspects of telecommunications, is in the government sector, under the control of the Ministry of Information and Broadcasting. The modernization of the telephone system has been underway since 1986 when Mahanagar Telephone Nigam, a government corporation, was established to operate systems in Bombay and New Delhi, and Videsh Sanchar Nigam, also government owned, was set up as the overseas carrier. Progress was slow, however; the rest of the nation's service continued as a civil-service-run operation under the Department of Telecommunications until 1994 when basic telephone services were opened to private-sector competition.

The number of telephone connections rose from 800,000 in FY 1968 to 8 million in FY 1994. The system remains substandard by international standards, however, and there is a waiting list for connections of 2.8 million people. Sometimes several years elapse between application and installation of a telephone line. Close to 1 million new connections a year are being established in the mid-1990s. Plans for increasing the capacity of the system to handle more directly dialed calls were being implemented in the early 1990s, and 20 million lines should be in operation by FY 2000. This number is very low for a population that by then will probably exceed 1 billion. Telephone line density was less than 0.7 per 100 persons in 1994, one of the lowest densities among the major nations of Asia.

There also are submarine telecommunications cables linking India with Malaysia and the United Arab Emirates. Although the government is a major manufacturer of telephone equipment, the private sector—especially foreign ventures—is becoming increasingly involved in manufacturing in the mid-1990s and paging, cellular phone service, and electronic mail are being introduced.

Radio

Radio broadcasting is a government monopoly under the Directorate General of All India Radio—established in 1936 and since 1957 also known as Akashvani—a government-owned, semicommercial operation of the Ministry of Information and Broadcasting. From only six stations at the time of independence, All India Radio's network had expanded by the mid-1990s to 146 AM stations plus a National Channel, the Integrated North-East Service (aimed at tribal groups in northeast India), and the External Service. There are five regional headquarters for All India Radio: the North Zone in New Delhi; the North-East Zone in Guwahati, Assam; the East Zone in Calcutta; the West Zone in Bombay; and the South Zone in Madras.

The government-owned network provides both national and local programs in Hindi, English, and sixteen regional languages. Commercial services, which were inaugurated in 1967, are provided by Vividh Bharati Service, headquartered in Bombay. Vividh Bharati, which accepts advertisements, broadcasts from thirty-one AM and FM stations in the mid-1990s.

India has an extensive network of mediumwave and shortwave stations. In 1994 there were eighty-five FM stations and seventy-three shortwave stations that covered the entire country. The broadcasting equipment is mostly Indian made and reaches special audiences, such as farmers needing agroclimatic, plant protection, and other agriculture-related information. The number of radio receivers increased almost fivefold between 1970 and 1994, from around 14 million to nearly 65 million. Most radios are also produced within India.

The foreign broadcast service is a function of the External Services Division of All India Radio. In 1994 seventy hours of news, features, and entertainment programs were broadcast daily in twenty-five languages using thirty-two shortwave transmitters. The principal target audiences are listeners in neighboring countries and the large overseas Indian community.

Television

Television service is available throughout the country. Broadcasting is a central government monopoly under the Ministry of Information and Broadcasting, but the only network system, Doordarshan, also known as TV1, accepts advertisements for some programs. Doordarshan, established in

1959 and a part of All India Radio until 1976, consists of one national network and seven regional networks. In 1992 there were sixty-three high-power television transmitters, 369 medium-power transmitters, seventy-six low-power transmitters, and twenty-three transposers. Regular satellite transmissions began in 1982 (the same year color transmission began).

By 1994 some 6 million people were receiving television broadcasts via satellite, and the number was expected to increase rapidly throughout the rest of the decade. Cable television was even more prolific, with an estimated 12 to 15 million subscribers in 1994. Besides Doordarshan, Zee TV—an independent station broadcasting from Bombay since 1992—uses satellite transmissions. In fact, because Doordarshan is the only network that is permitted to broadcast television signals domestically, Zee TV and other entrepreneurs broadcast their Indian-made videotapes via foreign transmitters. Other networks joining the fray are Cable News Network (CNN—starting in 1990); Asia Television Network (1991); Hong Kong-based Star TV (1991); Jain TV, near Bombay (1994); EL TV, a spinoff of Zee TV in Bombay (1994); HTV, an affiliate of the *Hindustan Times* in New Delhi (1994); and Sun TV, a Tamil-language service in Madras (1994) (see Broadcast Media, ch. 8). In a communications breakthrough in July 1995, Doordarshan agreed, for a US$1.5 million annual fee and 50 percent of advertising revenue when it exceeds US$1.5 million, to allow CNN to broadcast twenty-four hours a day via an Indian satellite.

Doordarshan offers national, regional, and local service. The number of television sets increased from around 500,000 in 1976 to 9 million in early 1987 and to around 47 million in 1994; increases are expected to continue at around 6 million sets per year. More than 75 percent of television sets were black and white models in 1992, but the proportion of color sets is increasing annually. Most television sets are produced in India.

Tourism

Tourism has not been a government priority, but it nonetheless provides around 6 percent of foreign-exchange earnings. The total number of visitors to India was estimated at nearly 1.8 million in FY 1992. The Eighth Five-Year Plan estimated an annual increase of 6 to 7 percent in visitor arrivals; tourists from Europe and North America were targeted. In the mid-1990s, the government offered special tax incentives to the industry to help alleviate a shortage of hotel rooms. Estimated gross export earnings from tourism were Rs24 billion and net earnings Rs17 billion, making the industry an important foreign-exchange earner. With under 0.3 percent of the world's tourists and around 1 percent of world tourism spending, India, however, has barely tapped its tourism potential.

Science and Technology

Origin and Development

Indian scientific research and technological developments since independence in 1947 have received substantial political support and most of their funding from the government. Science and technology initiatives have been important aspects of the government's five-year plans and usually are based on fulfilling short-term needs, while aiming to provide the institutional base needed to achieve long-term goals. As India has striven to develop leading scientists and world-class research institutes, government-sponsored scientific and technical developments have aided diverse areas such as agriculture, biotechnology, cold regions research, communications, environment, industry, mining, nuclear power, space, and transportation. As a result, India has experts in such fields as astronomy and astrophysics, liquid crystals, condensed matter physics, molecular biology, virology, and crystallography. Observers have pointed out, however, that India's emphasis on basic and theoretical research rather than on applied research and technical applications has diminished the social and economic effects of the government's investments. In the mid-1990s, government funds supported nearly 80 percent of India's research and development activities, but, as elsewhere in the economic sector, emphasis increasingly was being put on independent, nongovernmental sources of support (see Liberalization in the Early 1990s; Resource Allocation, this ch.).

India has a long and proud scientific tradition. Nehru, in his *Discovery of India* published in 1946, praised the mathematical achievements of Indian scholars, who are said to have developed geometric theorems before Pythagoras did in the sixth century B.C. and were using advanced methods of determining the number of mathematical combinations by the second century B.C. By the fifth century A.D., Indian mathematicians were using ten numerals and by the seventh century were treating zero as a number. These breakthroughs, Nehru said, "liberated the human mind . . . and threw a flood of light on the behavior of numbers." The conceptualization of squares, rectangles, circles, triangles, fractions, the ability to express the number ten to the twelfth power, algebraic formulas, and astronomy had even more ancient origins in Vedic literature, some of which was compiled as early as 1500 B.C. The concepts of astronomy, metaphysics, and perennial movement are all embodied in the Rig Veda (see The Vedas and Polytheism, ch. 3). Although such abstract concepts were further developed by the ancient Greeks and the Indian numeral system was popularized in the first millennium A.D. by the Arabs (the Arabic word for number, Nehru pointed out, is *hindsah*, meaning "from Hind (India)"), their Indian origins are a source of national pride.

Technological discoveries have been made relating to pharmacology, brain surgery, medicine, artificial colors and glazes, metallurgy, recrystalization, chemistry, the decimal system, geometry, astronomy, and language and linguistics (systematic linguistic analysis having originated in India with Panini's fourth-century B.C. Sanskrit grammar, the *Ashtadhyayi*). These discoveries have led to practical applications in brick and pottery making, metal casting, distillation, surveying, town planning, hydraulics, the development of a lunar calendar, and the means of recording these discoveries as early as the era of Harappan culture (ca. 2500–1500 B.C.; see Harappan Culture, ch. 1).

Written information on scientific developments from the Harrapan period to the eleventh century A.D. (when the first permanent Muslim settlements were established in India) is found in Sanskrit, Pali, Arabic, Persian, Tamil, Malayalam, and other classical languages that were intimately connected to Indian religious and philosophical traditions. Archaeological evidence and written accounts from other cultures with which India has had contact have also been used to corroborate the evidence of Indian scientific and technological developments. The technology of textile production, hydraulic engineering, water-powered devices, medicine, and other innovations, as well as mathematics and other theoretical sciences, continued to develop and be influenced by techniques brought in from the Muslim world by the Mughals after the fifteenth century.

The practical applications of scientific and technical developments are witnessed, for example, by the proliferation of hundreds of thousands of water tanks for irrigation in South India by the eighteenth and nineteenth centuries. Although each tank was built through local efforts, together, in effect, they created a closely integrated network supplying water throughout the region. The science of metallurgy led to the construction of numerous small but sophisticated furnaces for producing iron and steel. By the late eighteenth century, it is estimated that production capability may have reached 200,000 tons per year. High levels of textile production—making India the world's leading producer and exporter of textiles before 1800—were the result of refinements in spinning technology.

Several millennia of interest in astronomy in India eventually resulted in the invention and construction of a network of sophisticated, large-scale astronomical observatories—the Jantar Mantars (meaning "house of instruments")—in the early eighteenth century. Constructed of stone, brick, stucco, and marble, the Jantar Mantar complexes were used to determine the seasons, phases of the moon and sun, and locations of stars and planets from points in Delhi, Mathura, Jaipur, Varanasi, and Ujjain. The Jantar Mantars were designed and built by a renowned astronomer and city planner, Sawai Jai Singh II, the Hindu maharajah of Amber, between 1725 and 1734, after he been asked by Mohammad Shah, the tenth Mughal emperor, to reform the calendar. These complexes had the patronage of the Mughal emperors and have long attracted the attention of Western scholars and travelers, some of whom have found them anachronistic in light of the use of telescopes in Europe and China more than a century before Jai Singh's projects. As United States scientist William A. Blanpied has pointed out, Jai Singh, who subscribed to Hindu cosmology, was aware of Western developments but preferred to perfect his naked-eye observations rather than concentrate on precise calculational astronomy.

The arrival of the British in India in the early seventeenth century—the Portuguese, Dutch, and French also had a presence, although it was much less pervasive—led eventually to new scientific developments that added to the indigenous achievements of the previous millennia (see The Coming of the Europeans, ch. 1). Although colonization subverted much of Indian culture, turning the region into a source of raw materials for the factories of England and France and leaving only low-technology production to local entrepreneurs, a new organization was brought to science in the form of the British education system. Science education under British rule (by the East India Company from 1757 to 1857 and by the British government from 1858 to 1947) initially involved only rudimentary mathematics, but as greater exploitation of India took place, there was more need for surveying and medical schools to train indigenous people to assist Europeans in their explorations and research. What new technologies were implemented were imported rather than developed indigenously, however, and it was only during the immediate preindependence period that Indian scientists came to enjoy political patronage and support for their work (see The Independence Movement, ch. 1).

Western education and techniques of scientific inquiry were added to the already established Indian base, making way for later developments. The major result of these developments was the establishment of a large and sophisticated educational infrastructure that placed India as the leader in science and technology in Asia at the time of independence in 1947. Thereafter, as other Asian nations emerged, India lost its primacy in science, a situation much lamented by India's leaders and scientists. However, the infrastructure was in place and has continued to produce generations of top scientists.

One of the most famous scientists of the pre- and postindependence era was Indian-trained Chandrasekhara Venkata (C.V.) Raman, an ardent nationalist, prolific researcher, and writer of scientific treatises on the molecular scattering of light and other subjects of quantum mechanics. In 1930 Raman was awarded the Nobel prize in physics for his 1928 discovery of the Raman Effect, which demonstrates that the energy of a photon can undergo partial transformation within matter. In 1934–36, with his colleague Nagendra Nath, Raman propounded the Raman-Nath Theory on the diffraction of light by ultrasonic waves. He was a director of the Indian Institute of Science and founded the Indian Academy of Sciences in 1934 and the Raman Research Institute in 1948.

Another leading scientist was Homi Jehangir Bhabha, an eminent physicist internationally recognized for his contributions to the fields of positron theory, cosmic rays, and muon physics at the University of Cambridge in Britain. In 1945, with financial assistance from the Sir Dorabji Tata Trust, Bhabha established the Tata Institute of Fundamental Research in Bombay (see Major Research Organizations, this ch.).

Other eminent preindependence scientists include Sir Jagadish Chandra (J.C.) Bose, a Cambridge-educated Bengali physicist who discovered the application of electromagnetic waves to wireless telegraphy in 1895 and then went on to a second notable career in biophysical research. Meghnad Saha, also from Bengal, was trained in India, Britain, and Germany and became an internationally recognized nuclear physicist whose mathematical equations and ionization theory gave new insight into the functions of stellar spectra. In the late 1930s, Saha began promoting the importance of science to national economic modernization, a concept fully embraced by Nehru and several generations of government planners. The Bose-Einstein Statistics, used in quantum physics, and Boson particles are named after another leading scientist, mathematician Satyendranath (S.N.) Bose. S.N. Bose was trained in India, and his research discoveries gave him international fame and an opportunity for advanced studies in France and Germany. In 1924 he sent the results of his research on radiation as a form of gas to Albert Einstein. Einstein extended Bose's statistical methods to ordinary atoms, which led him to predict a new state of matter—called the Bose-Einstein Condensation—that was scientifically proved in United States laboratory experiments in 1995. Prafulla Chandra Ray, another Bengali, earned a doctorate in inorganic chemistry from the University of Edinburgh in 1887 and went on to a devoted career of teaching and research. His work was instrumental in establishing the chemical industry in Bengal in the early twentieth century.

At the onset of independence, Nehru called science "the very texture of life" and optimistically declared that "science alone . . . can solve problems of hunger and poverty, of insanitation and illiteracy, of superstition and deadening customs." Under his leadership, the government set out to cure numerous societal problems. The Green Revolution, educational improvement, establishment of hundreds of scientific laboratories, industrial and military research, massive hydraulic projects, and entry into the frontiers of space all evolved from this early decision to embrace high technology (see The Green Revolution, ch. 7).

One of the early planning documents was the Scientific Policy Resolution of 1958, which called for embracing "by all appropriate means, the cultivation of science and scientific research in all its aspects—pure, applied, and educational" and encouraged individual initiatives. In 1983 the government issued a similar statement, which, while stressing the importance of international cooperation and the diffusion of scientific knowledge, put considerable emphasis on self-reliance and

Part of the eighteenth-century Jantar Mantar observatory, New Delhi
Courtesy Robert L. Worden

the development of indigenous technology. This goal is still in place in the mid-1990s.

Infrastructure and Government Role

Science and technology policy and research have largely been the domains of government since 1947 and are largely patterned after the structure left behind by the British. Within the central government, there are a top-down apparatus and a plethora of ministries, departments, lower-level agencies, and institutions involved in the science and technology infrastructure.

Government-administered science and technology emanate from the Office of the Prime Minister, to which a chief science adviser and the Science Advisory Council, when they are appointed, have direct input. The prime minister de jure controls the science and technology sector through the National Council on Science and Technology, the minister of state for science and technology (who has control over day-to-day operations of the science and technology infrastructure), and ministers responsible for ocean development, atomic energy, electronics, and space. Other ministries and departments also have significant science and technology components and answer to the prime minister through their respective ministers. Among them are agriculture, chemicals and fertilizers, civil aviation and tourism, coal, defence, environment, food, civil supplies, forests and wildlife, health and family welfare, home affairs, human resource development, nonconventional energy sources, petrochemicals, and petroleum and natural gas, as well as other governmental entities.

The Ministry of Science and Technology was established in 1971 to formulate science and technology policies and implement, identify, and promote "frontline" research throughout the science and technology infrastructure. The ministry, through its subordinate Department of Science and Technology, also coordinates intragovernmental and international cooperation and provides funding for domestic institutions and research programs. The Department of Scientific and Industrial Research, a technology transfer organization, and the Department of Biotechnology, which runs a number of developmental laboratories, are the ministry's other administrative elements. Indicative of the level of importance placed on science and technology is the fact that Prime Minister P.V. Narasimha Rao held the portfolio for this ministry in the early and mid-1990s. Some argued, however, that Rao could truly strengthen the sector by appointing, as his predecessors did, a chief science adviser and a committee of leading scientists to provide high-level advice and delegate the running of these ministries to others.

The National Council on Science and Technology is at the apex of the science and technology infrastructure and is chaired by the prime minister. The integration of science and technology planning with national socioeconomic planning is carried out by the Planning Commission (see Development Planning, this ch.). Scientific advisory committees in individual socioeconomic ministries formulate long-term programs and identify applicable technologies for their particular area of responsibility. The rest of the infrastructure has seven major components. The national-level component includes government organizations that provide hands-on research and development, such as the ministries of atomic energy and space, the Council of Scientific and Industrial Research (CSIR—a component of the Ministry of Science and Technology), and the Indian Council of Agricultural Research. The second component, organizations that support research and development, includes the departments or ministries of biotechnology, nonconventional energy sources, ocean development, and science and technology. The third-echelon component includes state government research and development agencies, which are usually involved with agriculture, animal husbandry, irrigation, public health, and the like and that also are part of the national infrastructure. The four other major components are the university system, private research organizations, public-sector research and development establishments, and research and development centers within private industries. Almost all internationally recognized university-level research is carried out in government-controlled or government-supported institutions. The results of government-sponsored research are transferred to public- and private-sector industries through the National Research and Development Corporation. This corporation is part of the Ministry of Science and Technology and has as its purpose the commercialization of scientific and technical know-how, the promotion of research through grants and loans, promotion of government and industry joint projects, and the export of Indian technology.

Resource Allocation

Central government financial support of research and development—including subsidies to public-sector industries—was 75.7 percent of total financial support in FY 1992. State governments provided an additional 9.3 percent. However, even when combined with the private-sector contribution (15.0 percent), research and development expenditures were only just over 0.8 percent of the GDP in FY 1992. Although there was growth in research and development expenditures during the 1980s and early 1990s, the rate of growth was less than the GNP rate of growth during the same period and was a cause of concern for government planners. Moreover, the bulk of government research and development expenditures (80 percent in FY 1992) goes to only five agencies: the Defence Research and Development Organisation (DRDO), the Ministry of Space, the Indian Council of Agricultural Research, the Ministry of Atomic Energy, and CSIR, and to their constituent organizations.

Despite long-term government commitment to research and development, India compares poorly with other major Asian countries. In Japan, for example, nearly 3 percent of GDP goes to research and development; in South Korea and Taiwan, the figure is nearly 2 percent. In India, research and development receives only 0.8 percent of GDP; only China among the major players spends less (0.7 percent). However, India's share of GDP expenditure on research and development has increased slightly: in 1975 it stood at 0.5 percent, in 1980 at 0.6 percent, and in 1985 at 0.8, where it has become static.

Because of the allocation of financial inputs, India has been more successful at promoting security-oriented and large-scale scientific endeavors, such as space and nuclear science programs, than at promoting industrial technology. Part of the latter lack of achievement has been attributed to the limited role of universities in the research and development system. Instead, India has concentrated on government-sponsored specialized institutes and provided minimal funding to university research programs. The low funding level has encouraged university scientists to find jobs in the more liberally funded public-sector national laboratories. Moreover, private industry in India plays a relatively minor role in the science and technology system (15 percent of the total investment compared with Japan's 80 percent and slightly more than 50 percent in the United States). This low level of private-sector investment has been attributed to a number of factors, including the preponderance of trade-oriented rather than technology-oriented industries, protectionist tariffs, and rigid regulation of foreign investment. The largest private-sector research and development expenditures during the FY 1990–FY 1992 period were in the areas of engineering and technology, particularly in the industrial development, transportation, communications, and health services sectors. Nonetheless, they were relatively small expenditures when compared with government and public-sector inputs in the same fields. The key element for Indian industry to benefit from the greater government and public-sector efforts in the 1990s is the ability of the government and public-sector laboratories to develop technologies with broad applications and to transfer these technologies—as is done by the National Research and Development Corporation—to private-sector industries able to apply them with maximum efficiency.

India ranks eleventh in the world in its number of active scientific and technical personnel. Including medical personnel, they were estimated at around 188,000 in 1950, 450,000 in 1960, 1.2 million in 1970, 1.8 million in 1980, and 3.8 million in 1990. India's universities, university-level institutions, and colleges have produced more than 200,000 science and technology graduates per year since 1985. Doctorates are awarded each year to about 3,000 people in science, between 500 and 600 in engineering, around 800 in agricultural sciences, and close to 6,000 in medicine. However, in 1990 India had the lowest number of scientific and engineering personnel (3.3) per 10,000 persons in the national labor force of the major Asian nations. For example, Japan, had nearly seventy-five per 10,000, South Korea had more than thirty-seven per 10,000, and China had 5.6 per 10,000.

The quality of higher education in the sciences has not improved as quickly as desired since independence because of the flight of many top scientists from academia to higher-paying jobs in government-funded research laboratories. Foreign aid, aimed at counteracting university faculty shortages, has produced top-rate graduates as intended. However, because of limited job prospects at home, many of the brightest physicians, scientists, and engineers have been attracted by opportunities abroad, particularly in Western nations. Since the early 1990s, this trend has appeared to be changing as more high-technology jobs, especially in fields requiring computer science skills, have begun to open in India as a result of economic liberalization. The "brain bank" network of Indian scientists abroad that was seen as a potential source of talent by some observers in the 1980s has proven to be a valuable resource in the 1990s.

Using imported technology, scientists made major advances in microprocessors during the 1980s that brought the country to only one generation (three to four years) behind international leaders. A sign of how much microcomputer use has developed could be seen in sales: from US$93 million in FY 1983 to US$488 million in FY 1988. Facilitating the use of automation has been a counterpart to the expansion of the data communication field. The development of the "Param 9000" supercomputer prototype, reportedly capable of billions of floating point operations per second, was completed in December 1994 and was announced by the state-owned Centre for Development of Advanced Computing as ready for sale to operational users in March 1995. Earlier Param models, using parallel processing technologies to achieve near-supercomputer performance, were produced in sufficient quantity for export in the early 1990s.

DRDO developed its own parallel processing computer, which was unveiled by Prime Minister Rao in April 1995. Developed by DRDO's Advanced Numerical Research and Analysis

Group in Hyderabad, the supercomputer is capable of 1 billion points per second speed and can be used for geophysics, image processing, and molecular modeling.

Major Research Organizations

Agriculture

The Indian Council of Agricultural Research was established in 1929 as an autonomous clearinghouse-type organization charged with conducting, aiding, promoting, and coordinating agricultural and animal husbandry research. It has seventy-six institutes, bureaus, centers, and project directorates and seventy-one nationwide coordinated research projects. Education programs are mostly operated through India's twenty-six agricultural universities. The council has administrative links to the Department of Agricultural Research and Education of the Ministry of Agriculture (see Development Programs, ch. 7).

The council supports numerous research institutes throughout the states and union territories. They include laboratories doing research on arid zones, birds, aquaculture, cattle, agroengineering, horticulture, wool, salinity, soils, veterinary science, animal and plant genetics, land use, dairy production, and a variety of crops, including rice, jute, cotton, tobacco, oilseeds, potatoes, and others.

Biotechnology

India has placed considerable effort on biotechnology. At the national level, the Department of Biotechnology, established in 1986 as part of the Ministry of Science and Technology, is responsible for biotechnology research and development and biotechnology-related manufacturing, including bio-safety regulation. It also acts as the government's agent for biotechnology imports. The department supports two autonomous laboratories, the National Institute of Immunobiology in New Delhi and the National Facility for Animal Tissue and Cell Culture in Pune, Maharashtra. Research and development takes place in the areas of burn, heart, and cornea treatment; germplasma banks for plants, animals, algae, and microbes; viral vaccine; animal embryo technology; animal and human fertility control; communicable and genetic disease prevention; and biofertilizer, biocontrol, and biomass agents. The department also controls two state-owned enterprises involved in vaccine production, the Bharat Immunologicals

and Biologicals Corporation and the Indian Vaccines Corporation, both in New Delhi.

CSIR oversees numerous subnational biotechnology institutions. These include the Central Drug Research Institute in Lucknow, Uttar Pradesh; the Centre for Cellular and Molecular Biology in Hyderabad, Andhra Pradesh; the Indian Institute of Chemical Biology in Calcutta; and the Institute of Microbial Technology in Chandigarh among others.

Defense

DRDO is subordinate to the Ministry of Defence, and its director general is the chief scientific adviser to the minister of defence. DRDO, which was established in 1958, has forty-five research laboratories and institutes serving the research and development needs of the armed forces. Its significant achievements include the development of light combat aircraft, aircraft engines, light field artillery, ballistic bomb fuses, smoke and incendiary devices, combat vehicles, satellite communications terminals, encryption devices, sonar systems, torpedo propulsion devices, high-performance inertial guidance systems, target acquisition and ground electronics, and various rocket and missile systems.

Education Institutions

The Indian Institute of Science is a university-level organization that has contributed much to Bangalore's development as a technology capital. The institute was founded in 1909 on land in Bangalore donated by the maharajah of Mysore, using an endowment provided by one of the major benefactors of modern Indian science, Jamsetji Nusserwanji (J.N.) Tata, for the development of experimental science. Before independence and for some years after independence, the institute had a primarily British and British-trained faculty committed to raising India's scientific levels. In 1956 the institute was given university status.

The Indian Institute of Science has more than forty departments, centers, laboratories, and education programs organized for the study of biological, chemical, electrical, mathematical, mechanical, and physical sciences. It also has a major library, the National Centre for Science Information, and a fee-based Centre for Scientific and Industrial Consultancy.

The Indian Academy of Sciences is also located in Bangalore. The academy was founded by C.V. Raman in 1934 "to promote the progress and uphold the cause of science, both in the pure and applied branches." Although the academy is not a research institute, it provides scholarships and fellowships, publishes research results, and bestows honors on deserving scientists, both Indian and foreign. The academy is half funded by the Department of Science and Technology, and the remainder of the budget is met through subscriptions to its publications. Raman also founded the Raman Research Institute in 1948 as an independent, private science laboratory at which he and others continued to conduct ground-breaking research on the campus of the Indian Institute of Science.

The Indian Institute of Technology (IIT) is a university-level entity providing undergraduate and graduate education in engineering and technology. The five autonomous IIT campuses listed in order of their founding, are located in Kharagpur (West Bengal; 1950), Bombay (1958), Madras (1959), Kanpur (Uttar Pradesh; 1960), and New Delhi (1961). The IIT system was founded by the central government in 1950 and raised to an "institution of national importance" by Parliament by means of the Indian Institute of Technology Act of 1956 and its subsequent amendments. Besides receiving central government support in the early years, IIT received assistance from West Germany, the Soviet Union, Britain, the United Nations Educational, Scientific, and Cultural Organization (UNESCO), and the United States. Instructional and research departments range from agricultural engineering to aeronautical engineering and from earth sciences and postharvest technology to naval architecture and ocean engineering. To round out students' education, the IIT system also offers humanities and social science courses. For example, the Madras campus of IIT teaches economics, history, English, psychology, and business at the undergraduate level in support of other departments and at the graduate level leading to a master's degree in industrial management. While each campus has departments in the basic physical sciences, there are unique departments and specializations at each of the five sites. Admission to IIT is highly competitive; some 100,000 applicants take placement examinations for 2,000 student positions each year.

Although most important research is done in government- and industry-sponsored laboratories, several universities, in addition to the Indian Institute of Science and the five IIT campuses, are involved in significant research. Those with notable science programs are Delhi University, Benares Hindu University in Varanasi, Uttar Pradesh, Aligarh Muslim University in Aligarh, Uttar Pradesh, and Shanti Niketan University in Shanti Niketan, West Bengal.

Information Science

The Indian National Scientific Documentation Centre (INSDOC) is a major government science and technology information agency. Established in 1952 as part of CSIR, INSDOC has its main office in New Delhi and regional centers in Bangalore, Calcutta, and Madras. The center provides document delivery, a wide range of on-line database services, directed research and bibliographic services, translation services, training and testing, and other science information services. It also publishes science and technology-related bibliographies, abstracts, library science documentation, conference proceedings, directories, and reference aids, and operates the National Science Library. INSDOC serves government agencies, academia, and public and private organizations and individuals throughout India and South Asia on a partial cost-recovery and partially subsidized basis. Like many government agencies and government-funded organizations, INSDOC in the early 1990s was compelled to recover ever-increasing percentages—upward of 50 percent for some institutes in 1993—of its annual budget from nonappropriated sources.

Industry

Founded in 1942, CSIR is headquartered in New Delhi, but its network of laboratories is spread throughout the nation.

Although heavily involved in science, biotechnology, and information science activities, it also emphasizes industrial research. The president of CSIR is ex officio the prime minister, a situation that gives the council considerable political prestige. CSIR's network of nearly 200 national laboratories has links throughout the nation to another 200 government-sector research and development institutions and about 1,000 research and development units in the industrial sector that are supported by both public and private funds (see Early Policy Developments, this ch.). Beyond pure and applied research, CSIR also has outreach programs such as those under the auspices of the National Institute of Science, Technology, and Development Studies (NISTADS), established in 1974 as a center and raised to institute level in 1981.

CSIR also conducts and funds studies, organizes conferences and training programs, prepares exhibits, and publishes reports on the history and organization of Indian science, resource allocation and planning, analyses of the science and technology community (including behavioral research on scientists), the societal and environmental impact of science and technology, and international cooperation. Part of CSIR's publication program is directed at elementary and secondary school students with the intention of popularizing science at early ages.

The emphasis on industrial research is observable in the organizations supported by CSIR. They include, among others, the Central Electrochemical Research Institute in Karaikudi, Tamil Nadu; the Central Electronics Engineering Institute in Pilani, Rajasthan; the Central Glass and Ceramic Research Institute in Calcutta; the Central Leather Research Institute in Madras; the Indian Institute of Petroleum in Dehra Dun, Uttar Pradesh; the National Metallurgical Laboratory in Jamshedpur, Bihar; and the National Physical Laboratory in New Delhi.

Nuclear Power

The key policy-planning body for India's nuclear energy program is the Atomic Energy Commission, which was founded in 1948 and has offices in New Delhi and Bombay. The chairman of the commission is concurrently the secretary of the Department of Atomic Energy (later the Ministry of Atomic Energy), which was established in 1954 (with Homi Bhabha as is first head) and exercises executive control over nuclear programs and executes India's development and utilization of nuclear energy for peaceful purposes. To carry out its avowed peaceful-use mission, the department has policy bodies involved with regulatory and safety issues; research and development centers, both integral to the department and private concerns that receive government funding; organizations involved with nuclear fuel and heavy water development; and public-sector rare earths and uranium mining and electronics companies (see Energy, this ch.). The department also funds numerous research institute- and university-based projects.

As a far-reaching result of India's 1974 test of a nuclear explosive device, nuclear proliferation problems continue to confront both the department and the commission (see Space and Nuclear Programs, ch. 10). Divisive issues between India and the United States over nuclear-fuel supplies for the Tarapur nuclear power plant (which the United States wants cut off) were compounded in 1993 when the Ministry of Atomic Energy announced it was seeking foreign buyers for surplus heavy water being made by India's seven operating heavy water plants. The plants were developed originally because of the fuel shortage that confronted India after the Treaty on the Non-Proliferation of Nuclear Weapons was signed by most other nuclear nations in 1968. Over time the plants met domestic needs and began to produce an exportable surplus, leading to India-United States friction. The Atomic Energy Commission's January 1994 announcement that it planned to continue its development of fast breeder reactors also was likely to cause international concern.

India also has made a major commitment to the use of nuclear power for the generation of electricity. Major resources have been devoted to research, power station construction, and delivery services.

Space

The space program had its genesis in the Indian National Committee of Space Research, which was established in 1962 as part of the Department of Atomic Energy. In 1972 the Department of Space and the Space Commission were established as the executive and policy wings of the program. The Department of Space operates the Indian Space Research Organisation (ISRO, established in 1969) and four independent projects: the Indian National Satellite Space Segment Project, the Natural Resource Management System, the National Remote Sensing Agency, and the Physical Research Laboratory.

The department also sponsors research in various academic and research institutions. The ISRO is headquartered in Bangalore and has operating units at twenty-two sites throughout the country that deal with space systems, propulsion, communications, telemetry and tracking, research, launches, and other facets of the space program. The major achievements of the space program have been in the area of the domestic design, production, and launching of remote sensing and communications satellites. The primary goal of the space program is to have independent remote sensing and communications satellite systems with launcher autonomy.

In 1992 the ISRO set up the Antrix Corporation to market space and telecommunications products to help recover some of the costs of the annual space budget. That budget increased from Rs3.8 billion in FY 1990 to an estimated Rs7.5 billion in FY 1994. The majority of the FY 1994 expenditures were slated for rocket development (50 percent) and communications and remote sensing satellite operations (26.8 percent).

Space research began with the establishment of the Thumba Equatorial Rocket Launching Station near Thiruvananthapuram, Kerala. From Thumba Indian scientists launched United States-made rockets carrying French satellites to study the upper atmospheric winds over the magnetic equator. From this station, Indian scientists also have carried out original research in electrojet currents over the magnetic equator, vertical profiles of airglow, and cosmic X-ray background radiation. The first Indian experimental satellite was launched in 1975, followed by four others; operational communications and remote sensing satellites have been launched as part of the Indian National Satellite System (Insat). Insat is an interagency project operated by the Department of Space for domestic radio relay, computer network, television, rural telegraph network, and weather, emergency, and other radio communications.

Three satellites operated by Insat were in use in the mid-1990s in cooperation with the International Telecommunication Union's International Telecommunications Satellite (Intelsat) system. The three satellites (the first-generation Insat–1D in June 1990, the second-generation Insat–2A in July 1992, and Insat–2B in July 1993) were indigenously built under the direction of the ISRO and put into geostationary orbit over the Indian Ocean using French rockets launched in French Guiana. Additional and more advanced communications satellites—Insat–2C, Insat–2D, and Insat–2E—were planned for launch in FY 1994, FY 1995, and FY 1996.

Although early Indian satellites were launched by the Soviet Union, the United States, and the European Space Agency, in 1980 India began using domestically produced launch vehicles for its Rohini and Stretched Rohini experimental satellites. The ISRO has launch ranges at Thumba, Sriharikota Island on the east coast of Andhra Pradesh, and Balasore in Orissa.

Foreign observers in 1993 believed that the launch vehicle program was the least developed part of the space program and had fallen behind the satellite program in technological capability. Supporting this belief was the September 1993 launch of India's liquid-and-solid-fuel Polar Satellite Launch Vehicle (PSLV), designed to carry a 1,000-kilogram satellite, at Sriharikota. Although the PSLV–D1 was successfully launched, it malfunctioned before reaching orbit. Despite such setbacks, the national goal of achieving launcher autonomy has been set for 2000.

In May 1994, after several failed launches, India's five-stage, solid-fuel Augmented Satellite Launch Vehicle (ASLV) program, which started its test phase in 1987, succeeded in deploying a 133-kilogram satellite and placing it in a low earth orbit via a solid-fuel launch vehicle, the ASLV–D4. The ASLV–D4 was launched from Sriharikota. In March 1995, the head of the ISRO announced that India would become self-reliant in launcher technology by 1997–98 when the first Geostationary Launch Vehicle (GSLV) flight was planned.

Through international cooperation programs, India also has put a man in space with the Soviet Union, has participated in various French and German space ventures, and has had a payload aboard the United States Space Shuttle. It also provided technical expertise to the Arab Satellite Communication Organization (Arabsat) and entered into a cooperative space research agreement with the Ukrainian National Space Agency.

Indian weather satellites help nations throughout the Indian Ocean littoral by providing weather information and real-time distress alert services. Like the nuclear energy program, the space program has military implications that are contentious international political issues (see Russia; United States, ch. 9).

Other Leading Institutions

Although much of the top executive authority of the science and technology infrastructure resides in New Delhi, some premier science and technology institutions are located elsewhere. Bangalore, the capital of Karnataka, is a center for high-technology industry and a major research and development site. Much of the activity in Bangalore's "Silicon Valley" is carried out through collaborative arrangements with multinational corporations in fields such as aeronautics, communications, electronics, and machine tools. By 1990 there were more than 100,000 people employed by 3,000 companies in the electronics industry alone.

The Tata Institute of Fundamental Research in Bombay conducts fundamental research in astronomy, mathematics, molecular biology, and physics; and applied research in computer science, ion accelerators, material science, and solid state electronics. Organizationally, the institute is a component of the Department of Atomic Energy. When the atomic energy program began in 1948, the Tata Institute provided trained staff, and in 1955, because of the important role it played in nuclear energy research, the institute was recognized as the National Centre of the Government of India for Advanced Study and Fundamental Research in Nuclear Science and Mathematics. In this capacity, the institute became a world-class nuclear research facility, recognized for its discoveries in the field of strange particles.

Research on applied mathematics, astrophysics, deoxyribonucleic acid (DNA), high-power microwaves, stratospheric and underground nuclear physics, theoretical computer science, and other high-technology fields is carried out by the Tata Institute in Bombay and at its facilities in Bangalore and Kolar in Karnataka, Hyderabad in Andhra Pradesh, Pachmarhi in Madhya Pradesh, Pune in Maharashtra, and Udhagamandalam (Ooty) in Tamil Nadu.

Tata Institute scientists designed the first Indian digital computer in the 1960s and since then have contributed directly to the manufacture of microwave components and devices. Joint work has been conducted with foreign laboratories, such as accelerator experiments with Switzerland and the United States. The Tata Institute also provides both formal and informal science education aimed at improving the quality of science education and developing remedial measures for improving scholastic performance.

Prospects in Science and Technology

Some observers of the Indian science and technology community, while acknowledging its strong points, complain that there is a lack of communication and coordination among the numerous science and technology institutes. They also have commented that because of a lack of materials and purpose, the quality of some government laboratories is low and that quality-control research is found primarily in the private sector. Although little movement is being made toward privatization of science and technology research, the government is trying to bring private industry—where there is more innovation and competitiveness—into the research process. In the 1990s, a considerable amount of discussion and experimentation is occurring in the area of technology transfer from fundamental research institutes to the marketplace.

On a more fundamental level, it has been observed that there often is, at best, a tenuous link between major financial investment in research and development and the results enjoyed by India's society and economy. Despite major achievements in such fields as agriculture, telecommunications, health care, and nuclear energy—many of which derived from foreign technology inputs—parts of India's population face malnutrition, depend on bullock carts for transportation, suffer from diseases wiped out in many other nations, and use cow dung and wood for fuel. Although the government has decentralized to some extent, inordinate government control over planning and operation of research institutions continues, and the weak link between the research and industrial sectors persists. However, with its sizable domestic- and foreign-trained base of scientists and engineers and considerable participation in the scientific programs of official international organizations, India has immense potential for self-fulfillment and technological aid to other Asian nations in the early twenty-first century.

In the mid-1990s, the Indian economy appears to be at a crossroads. The economic system established after independence, which was marked by a large public sector, a tightly regulated private sector, and a limited role for foreign trade, is under attack from many quarters. However, the extent to which the government is willing and able to make changes remains unclear, and the opposition of vested interests to liberalization makes it likely that reforms will continue to take place only gradually.

*　　　*　　　*

A good survey of the Indian economy from independence until the mid-1980s is V.N. Balasubramanyam's *The Economy of India.* The various essays in *The Indian Economy: Recent Development and Future Prospects*, edited by Robert E.B. Lucas and Gustav F. Papanek, cover the same period and also evaluate the early stage of the "new economic policy" of the mid-1980s. For more recent developments, the periodical literature is the most useful, especially the articles in *Economic and Political Weekly* [Bombay]. Also helpful are Bimal Jalan's *India's Economic Crisis*, which covers the 1990 balance of payments crisis, and the volume he edited, *The Indian Economy: Problems and Prospects*, which reviews India's economic conditions since 1947. *India in Transition: Freeing the Economy*, by Jagdish Bhagwati, is also an important contribution to the analysis of India's economic reforms.

The most current and easily accessible sources on the economy are two publications of the Economist Intelligence Unit in London: *Country Profile: India, Nepal*, an annual survey of the economy; and *Country Report: India, Nepal*, a quarterly publication that includes the latest economic information. The annual *Economic Survey*, prepared by India's Ministry of Finance, reviews economic developments in each fiscal year. The Ministry of Planning's *Statistical Abstract*, which is published at irregular intervals, provides considerable statistical information, including the most recent released by the government.

There are numerous works on Indian science and technology. A.K. Bag's *Science and Civilization in India*, Abdur Rahman's *Science and Technology in Indian Culture*, and the *Directory of Scientific Research Institutions in India*, published by the Indian National Scientific Documentation Centre, are useful. Also very useful are annual and other reports from various scientific institutions, such as the Indian Institute of Science, and government science agencies, such as the Council of Scientific and Industrial Research and the Indian Space Research Organisation. Several articles by William A. Blanpied are helpful critiques of India's scientific and technology developments. (For further information and complete citations, see Bibliography.)

Chapter 7. Agriculture

A cow drawn in the paper stencil art (sanzi khaka) *style found in parts of Uttar Pradesh and Rajasthan*

AGRICULTURE HAS ALWAYS BEEN INDIA'S most important economic sector. In the mid-1990s, it provides approximately one-third of the gross domestic product (GDP—see Glossary) and employs roughly two-thirds of the population. Since independence in 1947, the share of agriculture in the GDP has declined in comparison to the growth of the industrial and services sectors. However, agriculture still provides the bulk of wage goods required by the nonagricultural sector as well as numerous raw materials for industry. Moreover, the direct share of agricultural and allied sectors in total exports is around 18 percent. When the indirect share of agricultural products in total exports, such as cotton textiles and jute goods, is taken into account, the percentage is much higher.

Dependence on agricultural imports in the early 1960s convinced planners that India's growing population, as well as concerns about national independence, security, and political stability, required self-sufficiency in food production. This perception led to a program of agricultural improvement called the Green Revolution, to a public distribution system, and to price supports for farmers (see The Green Revolution, this ch.). In the 1980s, despite three years of meager rainfall and a drought in the middle of the decade, India managed to get along with very few food imports because of the growth in food-grain production and the development of a large buffer stock against potential agricultural shortfalls. By the early 1990s, India was self-sufficient in food-grain production. Agricultural production has kept pace with the food needs of the growing population as the result of increased yields in almost all crops, but especially in cereals. Food grains and pulses account for two-thirds of agricultural production in the mid-1990s. The growth in food-grain production is a result of concentrated efforts to increase all the Green Revolution inputs needed for higher yields: better seed, more fertilizer, improved irrigation, and education of farmers. Although increased irrigation has helped to lessen year-to-year fluctuations in farm production resulting from the vagaries of the monsoons, it has not eliminated those fluctuations.

Food-grain production increased from 50.8 million tons in fiscal year (FY—see Glossary) 1950 to 176.3 million tons in FY 1990. The compound growth rate from FY 1949 to FY 1987 was

2.7 percent per annum. Overall, wheat was the best performer, with production increasing more than eightfold in forty years. Wheat was followed by rice, which had a production increase of more than 350 percent. Coarse grains had a poorer rate of increase but still doubled in output during those years; production of pulses went up by less than 70 percent. The increase in oilseed production, however, was not enough to fill consumer demands, and India went from being an exporter of oilseeds in the 1950s to a major importer in the 1970s and the early 1980s. The agricultural sector attempted to increase oilseed production in the 1980s and early 1990s. These efforts were successful: oilseed production doubled and the need for imports was reduced. In the early 1990s, India was on the verge of self-sufficiency in oilseed production. After independence in 1947, the cropping pattern became more diversified, and cultivation of commercial crops received a new impetus in line with domestic demands and export requirements. Nontraditional crops, such as summer mung (a variety of lentil, part of the pulse family), soybeans, peanuts, and sunflowers, were gradually gaining importance.

The per capita availability of a number of food items increased significantly in the postindependence period despite a population increase from 361 million in 1951 to 846 million in 1991. Per capita availability of cereals went up from 334 grams per day in 1951 to 470 grams per day in 1990. Availability of edible oils increased significantly, from 3.2 kilograms per year per capita in FY 1960 to 5.4 kilograms in FY 1990. Similarly, the availability of sugar per capita increased from 4.7 to 12.5 kilograms per year during the same period. The one area in which availability decreased was pulses, which went from 60.7 grams per day to 39.4 grams per day. This shortfall presents a serious problem in a country where a large part of the population is vegetarian and pulses are the main source of protein.

There are large disparities among India's states and territories in agricultural performance, only some of which can be attributed to differences in climate or initial endowments of infrastructure such as irrigation. Realizing the importance of agricultural production for economic development, the central government has played an active role in all aspects of agricultural development. Planning is centralized, and plan priorities, policies, and resource allocations are decided at the central level. Food and price policy also are decided by the central government. Thus, although agriculture is constitutionally the responsibility of the states rather than the central government, the latter plays a key role in formulating policy and providing financial resources for agriculture.

Land Use

In FY 1987, field crops were planted on about 45 percent of the total land mass of India. Of this cultivated land, almost 37 million hectares were double-cropped, making the gross sown area equivalent to almost 173 million hectares. About 15 million hectares were permanent pastureland or were planted in various tree crops and groves. Approximately 108 million hectares were either developed for nonagricultural uses, forested, or unsuited for agriculture because of topography. About 29.6 million hectares of the remaining land were classified as cultivable but fallow, and 15.6 million hectares were classified as cultivable wasteland. These 45 million hectares constitute all the land left for expanding the sown area; for various reasons, however, much of it is unsuited for immediate cropping. Expansion in crop production, therefore, has to come almost entirely from increasing yields on lands already in some kind of agricultural use (see table 26; table 27, Appendix).

Topography, soils, rainfall, and the availability of water for irrigation have been major determinants of the crop and livestock patterns characteristic of the three major geographic regions of India—the Himalayas, the Indo-Gangetic Plain, and the Peninsula—and their agro-ecological subregions (see fig. 5; Principal Regions, ch. 2). Government policy as regards irrigation, the introduction of new crops, research and education, and incentives has had some impact on changing the traditional crop and livestock patterns in these subregions. The monsoons, however, play a critical role in determining whether the harvest will be bountiful, average, or poor in any given year. One of the objectives of government policy in the early 1990s was to find methods of reducing this dependence on the monsoons.

Himalayas

The Himalayan region, with some 520,000 square kilometers of land, ranks well behind the other two regions in agricultural importance. Despite generally adequate rainfall, the rugged topography allows less than 10 percent of the land to be used for agriculture. The sandy, loamy soils on the hillsides and the alluvial clays in the region's premier agricultural subregion, the Vale of Kashmir—located in the northwestern part of the state of Jammu and Kashmir—provide fertile land for agricultural use. The main crops are rice, corn, wheat, barley, millet, and potatoes. Most of India's temperate-zone fruits (apples, apricots, cherries, and peaches) and walnuts are grown in the vale. Sericulture and sheepherding also are being undertaken. In the eastern Himalayan subregion, the soils are moderately rich in organic matter and are acidic. Although much of the farming is done on terraced hillsides, there is a significant amount of shifting cultivation, which has resulted in deforestation and soil erosion. Rice, corn, millet, potatoes, and oilseeds were the main crops in the early 1990s. The region also is well known for the tea plantations of the mountainous Darjiling (Darjeeling) area in the northern tip of West Bengal.

Indo-Gangetic Plain

The vast Indo-Gangetic Plain, extending from Punjab to Assam, is the most intensively farmed zone of the country and one of the most intensively farmed in the world. Rainfall, most of which comes with the southwest monsoon, is generally adequate for summer-grown crops, but in some years vast areas are seared by drought. Fortunately, much of the land has access, or potential access, to irrigation waters from wells and rivers, ensuring crops even in years of drought and making possible a winter crop as well as a summer harvest. Wheat is the main crop in the west, rice in the east. Pulses, sorghum, oilseeds, and sugarcane are among other important crops. Mango orchards are common. Other fruits of the subregion include guavas, jackfruit, plums, lemons, oranges, and pomegranates.

In the Great Indian Desert, rainfall is scanty and erratic. About 20 percent of the total area is under cultivation, mostly in Haryana and Gujarat states, and comparatively little in Rajasthan. The Indira Gandhi Canal—begun in 1958 as the Rajasthan Canal—was designed to bring water from the north. Progress was slow, and only the first stage was close to completion by the end of the Seventh Five-Year Plan (FY 1985–89). By then, the canal had substantially increased the area under cultivation in Rajasthan, and a new completion date of 1999 is anticipated (see Development Programs, this ch; Development Planning, ch. 6). The cultivable area is expected to expand further with the development of the canal's second stage during the 1990s. The leading crops of the subregion are millet, sorghum, wheat, and peanuts. Vast expanses of sparse vegetation provide sustenance for sheep and goats. In the late 1980s, dairy farming became important in locations that had sufficient pastureland.

Peninsular India

The east and west coasts, the coastal plains, and the deltaic tracts that extend inland for some 100 to 200 kilometers in Peninsular India benefit from both the June-to-September southwest monsoon and the October-to-November northeast monsoon. Farther inland, as the topography and climate change, so does the pattern of agriculture. The proportion of land under cultivation ranges from about 50 percent along the coastal plain and in the western part of Andhra Pradesh to about 25 percent in eastern Madhya Pradesh. Except in areas of certain developed river valleys, double-cropping is rare. Rice is the predominant crop in high-rainfall areas and sorghum in low-rainfall areas. Other crops of significance along the east coast and in the Central Highlands in the early 1990s were pigeon peas, mustard, peanuts, millet, linseed, castor beans, cotton, and tobacco.

On the Deccan Plateau, deep, alluvial black soils that retain moisture for a long time are the basis for much of the region's output of farm products. However, the region also has many farming areas that are covered by thin, light-textured soils that suffer quickly from drought. Whether a crop is made or lost is, therefore, often dependent on the availability of supplementary water from ponds and streams. About 60 percent of the land in the state of Maharashtra was under cultivation in the early 1990s, less in Madhya Pradesh. About 75 percent of the cropland of the Deccan during this period was planted in food crops, such as millet, sorghum, rice, wheat, and peanuts; most of the remaining cropland was planted in fodder crops.

In the far south of the Peninsula, the area under cultivation varies from about 10 percent in the Western Ghats, to 25 percent in the western coastal tract, to 55 percent on the Karnataka Plateau. Here is the India—the land of spices—that Vasco da Gama and other European navigators came searching for in the fifteenth century. On the Karnataka Plateau, sorghum, millet, pulses, cotton, and oilseeds are the main crops on the 90 percent of the cultivated land that is dry-farmed; rice, sugarcane, and vegetables predominate on the 10 percent that was irrigated in the late 1980s. Coconuts, areca, coffee, pepper, rubber, cashew nuts, tapioca, and cardamom are widely grown on plantations in the Nilgiri Hills and on the western slopes of the Western Ghats.

Land Tenure

Matters concerning the ownership, acquisition, distribution, and taxation of land are, by provision of the constitution, under the jurisdiction of the states (see Local Government, ch. 8). Because of the diverse attitudes and approaches that would result from such freedom if there were no general guidelines, the central government has at times laid down directives dealing with the main problems affecting the ownership and use of land. But it remains for the state governments to implement the central government guidelines. Such implementation has varied widely among the states.

Landholding Categories

India is a land of small farms, of peasants cultivating their ancestral lands mainly by family labor and, despite the spread of tractors in the 1980s, by pairs of bullocks. About 50 percent of all operational holdings in 1980 were less than one hectare in size. About 19 percent fell in the one-to-two hectare range, 16 percent in the two-to-four hectare range, and 11 percent in the four-to-ten hectare range. Only 4 percent of the working farms encompassed ten or more hectares.

Although farms are typically small throughout the country, the average size holding by state ranges from about 0.5 hectare in Kerala and 0.75 hectare in Tamil Nadu to three hectares in Maharashtra and five hectares in Rajasthan. Factors influencing this range include soils, topography, rainfall, rural population density, and thoroughness of land redistribution programs.

Many factors—historical, political, economic, and demographic—have affected the development of the prevailing land-tenure status. The operators of most agricultural holdings possess vested rights in the land they till, whether as full owners or as protected tenants. By the early 1990s, there were tenancy laws in all the states and union territories except Nagaland, Meghalaya, and Mizoram. The laws provide for states to confer ownership on tenants, who can buy the land they farm in return for fair payment; states also oversee provision of security

Indira Gandhi Canal, Rajasthan
Courtesy Indian Ministry of External Affairs

of tenure and the establishing of fair rents. The implementation of these laws has varied among the states. West Bengal, Karnataka, and Kerala, for example, have achieved more success than other states. The land tenure situation is complicated, and it has varied widely from state to state. There is, however, much less variation in the mid-1990s than in the postindependence period.

Independent India inherited a structure of landholding that was characterized by heavy concentration of cultivable areas in the hands of relatively large absentee landowners (zamindars—see Glossary), the excessive fragmentation of small landholdings, an already growing class of landless agricultural workers, and the lack of any generalized system of documentary evidence of landownership or tenancy. Land was important as a status symbol; from one generation to the next, there was a tendency for an original family holding to be progressively subdivided, a situation that continued in the early 1990s. This phenomenon resulted in many landholdings that were too small to provide a livelihood for a family. Borrowing money against land was almost inevitable and frequently resulted in the loss of land to a local moneylender or large landowner, further widening the gap between large and small landholders. Moreover, inasmuch as landowners and moneylenders tended to belong to higher castes and petty owners and tenants to lower castes, land tenure had strong social as well as economic impact (see *Varna*, Caste, and Other Divisions; Settlement and Structure, ch. 5).

By the early 1970s, after extensive legislation, large absentee landowners had, for all practical purposes, been eliminated; their rights had been acquired by the state in exchange for compensation in cash and government bonds. More than 20 million former zamindar-system tenants had acquired occupancy rights to the land they tilled. Whereas previously the landlord collected rent from his tenants and passed on a portion of it as land revenue to the government, starting in the early 1970s, the state collected the rent directly from cultivators who, in effect, had become renters from the state. Most former tenants acquired the right to purchase the land they tilled, and payments to the state were spread out over ten to twenty years. Large landowners were divested not only of their cultivated land but also of ownership of forests, lakes, and barren lands. They were also stripped of various other economic rights, such as collection of taxes on sales of immovable property within their jurisdiction and collection of money for grazing privileges on uncultivated lands and use of river water. These rights also were taken over by state governments in return for compensation. By 1980 more than 6 million hectares of waste, fallow, and other categories of unused land had been vested in state governments and, in turn, distributed to landless agricultural workers.

Land Reform

A major concern in rural India is the huge number of landless or near-landless families, many of whom are wholly dependent on a few weeks of work at the peak planting and harvesting seasons. The number of landless rural families has grown steadily since independence, both in absolute terms and as a proportion of the population. In 1981 there were 195.1 million rural workers: 55.4 million were agricultural laborers who depended primarily on casual farm work for a livelihood. In the early 1990s, the rural work force had grown to 242 million, of whom 73.7 million were classified as agricultural laborers. Approximately 33 percent of the employed rural workers were classified as casual wage laborers.

Because of the large number of landless farmers and the frequent neglect of land by absentee landlords in the early years of independence, the principle that there should be a ceiling on the size of landholdings, depending on the crop planted and the quality of the land, was embodied in the First Five-Year Plan (FY 1951–55). An agricultural census was conducted to provide guidance in setting such ceilings. During the Second Five-Year Plan (FY 1956–60), most states legislated fixed ceilings, but there was little uniformity among the states; ceilings ranged from six to 132 hectares. Certain specialized branches of agriculture, such as horticulture, cattle breeding, and dairy farming, were usually exempted from ceilings.

All the states instituted programs to force landowners to sell their over-the-ceiling holdings to the government at fixed prices; the states, in turn, were to redistribute the land to the landless. But adamant resistance, high costs, sloppy record keeping, and poor administration in general combined to weaken and delay this aspect of land reform. The delays in legislation allowed large landowners to circumvent the intent of the laws by spurious partitioning, sales, gifts to family members, and other methods of evading ceilings. Many exemptions were granted so that there was little surplus land.

To ensure more uniformity in income, to combat evasion of the intent of the laws, and to secure more land for distribution to the landless, the central government in the 1970s pushed for greatly reduced ceilings. For a family of five, the central government guidelines called for not more than 10.9 hectares of good, irrigated land suitable for double-cropping, not more than 10.9 hectares of land suited for one crop annually, and not more than 21.9 hectares for orchards. Exemptions were continued for land used as cocoa, coffee, tea, and rubber plantations; land held by official banks and other government units; and land held by agricultural schools and research organizations. At the option of the states, land held by religious, educational, and charitable trusts also could be exempted. To protect the states from legal challenges to their land reform laws, the constitution was amended in 1974 to include in its Ninth Schedule the state laws that had been enacted in conformance with national guidelines. Land reform laws enacted after 1974 also were included in the amendment.

By the beginning of the 1990s, all states and union territories, except Goa, Arunachal Pradesh, Nagaland, Manipur, Mizoram, and Tripura, had passed ceiling laws to conform to central government guidelines. In Maharashtra, for example, the revised ceiling law that became effective in 1975 set upper limits at perennially irrigated land, 7.2 hectares; seasonally irrigated land, 10.8 hectares; paddy land in an assured rainfall area, 14.6 hectares; and other dry land, 21.9 hectares. By the early 1980s, about 150,000 hectares had been declared surplus under this act, about 100,000 of which had been distributed to 6,500 landless persons. A 1973 land reform amendment in Bihar set a range of ceilings on holdings for a family of five, from six to eighteen hectares depending on land quality, and offered an allowance for each additional family member, subject to a maximum of one-and-one-half times the holding. Within five years, the Bihar government had acquired 94,000 hectares of surplus land and had distributed 53,000 hectares to 138,000 landless families. Success nationwide was limited. Of the 2.9 million hectares of land declared surplus, nearly 1.9 million hectares had been distributed by the end of the seventh plan, leaving 1 million hectares still to be distributed as of early 1993.

By the early 1990s, nearly all the states had enacted legislation aimed at the consolidation of each tiller's landholdings into one contiguous plot. Implementation was patchy and sporadic, however. By the early 1980s, the work had been completed only in Punjab, Haryana, and western Uttar Pradesh and had begun in Orissa and Bihar. In most of the other states, nothing had been accomplished by the early 1990s. The Sixth Five-Year Plan (FY 1980–84) set a goal for the completion of the consolidation of holdings within ten years, which was not achieved.

In order to protect tenants from exorbitant rents (often up to 50 percent of their produce), the states passed legislation to regulate rents. The maximum rate was fixed at levels not exceeding 20 to 25 percent of the gross produce in all states except Andhra Pradesh, Haryana, and Punjab. The states also adopted various other measures for the protection of tenants, including moratoriums on evictions, minimum periods of tenure, and security of tenure subject to eviction on prescribed grounds only.

By the early 1980s, most of the cultivated area had been surveyed and records of rights prepared. In most states, revenue assessment—the tax on land—against farmland had been revised upward in keeping with a rise in farm prices (see Agricultural Taxation, this ch.). In several states, steps were taken to associate village assemblies, or *panchayat* (see Glossary), with the maintenance of land records, the collection of land revenue, and the management of lands belonging to government; the results of these efforts have frequently been unsatisfactory.

Economic Development

Evolution of Policy

The British colonial government of India did not pursue an active policy of agricultural development despite modest efforts to formulate a policy (see The British Raj, 1858–1947, ch. 1). One such effort was the appointment in 1926 of the Royal Commission on Agriculture, which made some recommendations for improving agriculture and promoting the welfare of the rural population. Most of the commission's recommendations were deferred because of the Great Depression of the 1930s. One outcome, however, was the establishment of the Imperial (later Indian) Council of Agricultural Research in 1929. During World War II, disruptions in international trade also led the government to initiate the Grow More Food Campaign. The government adopted its first agricultural policy statement in the wake of famine in Bengal in 1943. The policy objectives included increased production of food grains, use of better methods of production, improved marketing, better prices for the producers, fair wages for agricultural labor, fair distribution of food, increased production of raw materials, and improvements in research and education. This statement was the basis of many of the policies adopted soon after independence, especially in the First Five-Year Plan, when the central government was committed to giving priority to agricultural production to increase the food supply in the country.

The prolonged neglect of agriculture meant that there was almost no growth in the agricultural sector. From 1891 to 1946, output of all crops grew at 0.4 percent a year; the rate for food grains was only 0.1 percent per year. The land tenure system led to exploitative agrarian relations and stagnation (see Land Tenure, this ch.). Farmers had little incentive to invest, and despite great strides in foreign agricultural technology, Indian agricultural technology stagnated. Specifically, there were few improvements in seeds, agricultural implements, machines, or chemical fertilizers.

At the time of independence in 1947, agriculture and allied sectors provided well over 70 percent of the country's employment and more than 50 percent of the gross national product (GNP—see Glossary). Agricultural development was a key to a number of national goals, such as reducing rural poverty, providing an adequate diet for all citizens, supplying agricultural raw materials for the textile industry and other industries, and expanding exports. In the mid-1960s, the goal of self-reliance was added to this list. The central government has played a progressively more important role on the agricultural front by providing overall leadership and coordination, as well as by providing a significant part of the financing for agricultural programs. However, the primary responsibility for the design and implementation of agricultural programs, in accordance with the constitution, remained with the states in the late twentieth century (see The Constitutional Framework, ch. 8).

India's agricultural growth strategy after independence evolved over three distinct phases. In the first phase, roughly covering the period through the Second Five-Year Plan, agricultural growth rested on removing basic socioeconomic constraints through land reform, change in the village power structure, reorganization of the rural poor into cooperatives, and better citizen participation in planning. The initial assumption was that changing the land tenure system by abolishing the zamindar system—a method of revenue collecting and landholding developed during the Mughal and British colonial periods—would stimulate agricultural output (see The Mughal Era; The British Empire in India, ch. 1).

The second phase occurred during the Third Five-Year Plan (FY 1961–65). The continuing shortages of food in the 1960s and the consequent crises convinced planners that raising agricultural output, especially food grains, was essential for political stability and independence from foreign food aid. Self-sufficiency in food-grain production and development of an adequate buffer stock through procurement became clearly defined goals in the mid-1960s. Keeping in mind the variety of socioeconomic and agroclimatic differences, the government adopted an area-specific approach, and emphasized programs such as the Intensive Area Agricultural Programme and the Intensive Agricultural District Programme.

The third phase is identified predominantly as the Green Revolution. This phase relied on better seeds, more water via irrigation, and improved quantity and quality of fertilizer during the Fourth Five-Year Plan (FY 1969–73), the Fifth Five-Year Plan (FY 1974–78), and the Sixth Five-Year Plan (FY 1980–84). The Green Revolution was successful in meeting the goals of self-sufficiency in food-grain production and adequate buffer stocks by the end of the 1970s. Production was more than 100 million tons in 1978 and 1979. Imports were negligible, and the year-end buffer stocks from 1976–79 averaged more than 17 million tons. After 1980 buffer stocks fell below 10 millions tons only once, in 1988.

In the mid-1990s, the major goals of agricultural policy continued to be self-sufficiency in food staples and adequate food supplies at affordable prices for consumers. Expanding cereal production continued to be a major objective because of the population growth rate of almost 2 percent per year. The budgetary share of agriculture, together with irrigation and flood control projects, remained almost constant in the first six plans, varying between 21 percent and 24 percent.

The Eighth Five-Year Plan (FY 1992–96), as conceived in the early 1990s, not only aimed at continued self-sufficiency in food production, but also included plans to generate surpluses of some agricultural commodities for export. It also aimed at spreading the Green Revolution to more regions of the country with an emphasis on dryland farming.

Development Programs

Within the broad framework of policy, the government has undertaken a wide variety of programs in agriculture to build up the physical and information infrastructures necessary for sustained development. There are programs for the betterment of the rural population; research, education, and extension programs; irrigation development schemes; plans to increase the supply of agricultural inputs, such as seeds, fertilizers, and pesticides; plans to change the institutional framework of land ownership; plans to improve agricultural financing; better marketing techniques; and plans to improve technology. These programs are administered, financed, and run by the central government and by the state governments, and both levels encourage private-sector development through direct or indirect programs.

Some of the specialized programs in place in the 1990s were introduced during the Fifth Plan. Among them were the Small Farmers Development Agency, Minimum Needs Programme, Hill Area Development Programme, and Drought-Prone Areas Programme. In 1989 two other programs, the National Rural Employment Programme and the Rural Landless Employment Guarantee Programme, were merged into a single program called the Jawahar Employment Plan (Jawahar Rozgar Yojana; Jawahar in memory of Jawaharlal Nehru [1889–1964], India's first prime minister; *rozgar* means daily employment in Hindi; and *yojana* means project or plan).

The Integrated Rural Development Programme, launched in FY 1978 and extended throughout India by FY 1980, is a self-employment program intended to raise the income-generation capacity of target groups among the poor. The aim is to raise recipients above the poverty line by providing substantial opportunities for self-employment. During the seventh plan, the total expenditure under the program was Rs33.2 million (for value of the rupee—see Glossary), and Rs53.7 million of term credit was mobilized. Some 13 million new families participated, bringing total coverage under the program to more than 18 million families. These development programs have played an important role in increased agricultural production by educating farmers and providing them with financial and other inputs to increase yields. They have also alleviated some problems of the rural poor. However, further success has been limited by the lack of efficient administrative mechanisms, the limitation of resources, the magnitude of the task, and the lack of willingness to change the status quo. Many of the program results appear better on paper than the actual results in the field because of lack of implementation and poor monitoring.

Research, Education, and Extension

The central government's Department of Agricultural Research and Education was established in 1973 in the Ministry of Agriculture and Rural Development (later, the Ministry of Agriculture). The department is responsible for coordinating research and educational facilities in agriculture, animal husbandry, and fisheries. The department also provides support services to the Indian Council of Agricultural Research (see Major Research Organization, ch. 6).

Sowing wheat in central India
Courtesy Doranne Jacobson

Higher education has also seen advances. India has twenty-eight agricultural universities, which include 164 colleges specializing in agriculture, veterinary science, agricultural engineering, home science, fisheries, dairy technology, forestry, horticulture, sericulture, food science, and food-handling technology. They are located through most of the states in India. One of them is a central university that has specialized extension colleges in the seven northeastern states. The undergraduate student enrollment in the early 1990s was around 9,600 and there was a capacity for some 4,500 graduate students (see Colleges and Universities, ch. 2).

Agricultural, animal husbandry, and forestry research is conducted under the auspices of the Indian Council of Agricultural Research, central research institutes, and various commodity committees. The council had forty-six institutes in operation in 1992. India's largest such institute is the Indian

Agricultural Research Institute, established in 1905 at Pusa, Bihar. Because of an earthquake at Pusa, the research institute moved to New Delhi in 1936. The institute was later accorded university status.

In addition to these agricultural research and education institutions, the Indian Council of Agricultural Research also has a large network of organizations to disseminate agricultural technology information. In the mid-1990s, there were national centers used to demonstrate new crop varieties and production technologies in forty-eight districts throughout the country. There also were seventy nationwide coordinated research projects operating at 120 centers to test specific production technologies.

Agricultural Extension

After independence in 1947, the government's first step toward building an agricultural extension system was expansion of the World War II Grow More Food Campaign. Administrators and extension workers were exhorted to convince cultivators of the gains in yields that could be obtained through the use of improved seeds, compost, farmyard manure, and better cultivation practices. Rural agents, often inundated with other assignments, had little or no training for extension work, however. Gains in yields were minimal, and India's leaders came to realize that converting millions of poor farmers to the use of new technologies was a colossal task.

The Community Development Programme was inaugurated in 1952 to implement a systematic, integrated approach to rural development. The nation was divided into development blocks, each consisting of about 100 villages having populations of 60,000 to 70,000 people. By 1962 the entire country was covered by more than 5,000 such blocks. The key person in the program was the village-level worker, who was responsible for transmitting to about ten villages not only farming technology, but also village uplift programs such as cooperation, adult literacy, health, and sanitation. Although each block was staffed with extension workers, the villagers themselves were expected to provide the initiative and much of the needed financial and labor resources, which they were not in a position to do or inclined to do. Although progress had been made by the early 1960s, it was apparent that the program was spread too thin to bring about the hoped-for increase in agricultural production. Criticism of the program led to more specialized development projects, and some of the functions were taken up by local village bodies. There was only a negligible allocation for community development in the sixth plan, however, and the program was phased out in the early 1980s.

The Intensive Agricultural District Programme, launched in five districts in 1960 by the central government in cooperation with the United States-based Ford Foundation, used a distinctly different approach to boosting farm yields. The program operated under the premise that concentrating scarce inputs in the potentially most productive districts would increase farm-crop yield faster than would a wider but less concentrated distribution of resources in less productive districts. Among these inputs were technical staff, fertilizers, improved seeds, and credit. Under the technical guidance of American cooperative specialists, the program placed unusual emphasis on organizational structures and administrative arrangements. For the first time, modern technology was systematically introduced to Indian farmers. Within a decade, the program covered fifteen districts, 28,000 villages, and 1 million inhabitants. The Intensive Agricultural District Programme was thus a significant influence on the forthcoming Green Revolution.

Irrigation

Except in southeastern India, which receives most of its rain from the northeast monsoon in October and November, dryland cultivators place their hopes for a harvest on the southwest monsoon, which usually reaches India in early June and by mid-July has extended to the entire country. There are great variations in the average amount of rainfall received by the various regions—from too much for most crops in the eastern Himalayas to never enough in Rajasthan. Season-to-season variations in rainfall are also great. The consequence is bumper harvests in some seasons, crop-searing drought in others. Therefore, the importance of irrigation cannot be overemphasized.

Irrigation has been a high priority in economic development since 1951; more than 50 percent of all public expenditures on agriculture have been spent on irrigation alone. The land area under irrigation expanded from 22.6 million hectares in FY 1950 to 59 million hectares in FY 1990, an increase of 161 percent in four decades (see table 28, Appendix). This increase was about 33 percent of the estimated potential. The overall strategy has been to concentrate public investments in surface systems, such as large dams, long canals, and other large-scale works requiring huge outlays of capital over a period of years, and in deep-well projects that also involve large capital outlays. Shallow-well schemes and small surface-water projects, mainly ponds (called tanks in India), have been supported by government credit but were otherwise installed and operated by private entrepreneurs. Roughly 42 percent of the net irrigated area in FY 1990 was from surface water sources. Tanks, step wells, and tube wells provided another 51 percent; the rest came from other sources.

Between 1951 and 1990, nearly 1,350 large- and medium-sized irrigation works were started, and about 850 were completed. The most ambitious of these projects was the Indira Gandhi Canal, with an anticipated completion date of close to 1999. When completed, the Indira Gandhi Canal will be the world's longest irrigation canal. Beginning at the Hairke Barrage, a few kilometers below the confluence of the Sutlej and Beas rivers in western Punjab, it will run south-southwest for 650 kilometers, terminating deep in Rajasthan near Jaisalmer, close to the border with Pakistan. A dramatic change already had taken place in this hot and inhospitable wasteland by the late 1980s. As a result, desert dwellers switched from raising goats and sheep to raising wheat, and outsiders flocked in to purchase six-hectare plots for the equivalent of US$3,000.

Progress in irrigation has not been without problems. Large dams and long canals are costly and also highly visible indicators of progress; the political pressure to launch such projects was frequently irresistible. But because funds and technical expertise were in short supply, many projects moved forward at a slow pace. The Indira Gandhi Canal project is a leading example. And the central government's transfer of huge amounts of water from Punjab to Haryana and Rajasthan, frequently cited as a source of grievance by Sikhs in Punjab, contributed to the civil unrest in Punjab during the 1980s and early 1990s (see Political Issues, ch. 8; Insurgent Movements and External Subversion, ch. 10).

Problems also have arisen as ground water supplies used for irrigation face depletion. Drawing water off from one area to irrigate another often leads to increased salinity in the supply area with resultant effects on crop production there. Some areas receiving water through irrigation are poorly managed or inadequately designed; the result often is too much water and water-logged fields incapable of production. To alleviate this problem, more emphasis is being placed on using irrigation water to spray fields rather than allowing it to flow through ditches. Furthermore, charges of corruption and mismanagement have been levied against government-operated facilities. Cases of bribery, maldistribution of water, and carelessness are frequently raised in the media.

Another major problem has been the displacement of thousands of people, usually poor people, by large hydroelectric projects. Critics also claim that the projects are damaging to the ecology. Smaller projects and such traditional methods for irrigation as tanks and wells are seen as having less serious impact. In the late 1980s and early 1990s, the debate between large-scale versus small-scale projects came to the fore because of the US$3 billion Sardar Sarovar project on the Narmada River. Sardar Sarovar, as conceived, was one of the world's largest hydroelectric and irrigation projects. Some 37,000 hectares of land in Madhya Pradesh, Gujarat, and Maharashtra were slated to be submerged following the construction of some 3,000 dams, 75,000 kilometers of canals, and an electric power generating capacity of 1,450 megawatts of power per year. Included among the 3,000 dams was the proposed 160-meter-high Sardar Sarovar Dam. In 1985 the World Bank (see Glossary) agreed to loan US$450 million for the project. Environmentalists in India and abroad, however, argued that the project was ecologically undesirable. In the face of this strong protest, the World Bank appointed a two-member team in 1991 to review the project. Despite a negative review of the environmental impact by the team, World Bank funding and the project continued. By 1993, however, in the face of continued international protest as well as opposition and a call for a satyagraha (passive resistance—see Glossary) by villages in the affected areas, the central government cancelled the dam project loan. Work on the Sardar Sarovar project continues, however, with funds provided by the central government and the governments of the three states involved.

Although India had the second largest irrigated area in the world, the area under assured irrigation or with at least minimal drainage is inadequate. The irrigation potential estimated to have been created by the early 1990s was about 82.8 million hectares. This amount includes the gross irrigated area plus the potential for double cropping provided by irrigation. There was a cumulative gap in irrigated land use of about 8.6

million hectares until FY 1990, by which time the gap had decreased through improved land management.

Seeds

The central government established the National Seeds Corporation in 1963 and the State Farm Corporations of India in 1969 to encourage production and distribution of certified seeds of various crops. Thirteen state seed corporations were established to arrange production and distribution of certified seeds. Production of breeder seed was organized by the Indian Council of Agricultural Research through interested breeders and scientists. The National Seeds Corporation and State Farm Corporations of India also produced breeder seeds. The availability of breeder seeds increased eightfold during the 1980s, from 391.4 tons in FY 1981 to 3,213 tons in FY 1988.

The production and availability of seeds has increased enormously since the late 1970s. The distribution of certified and quality seeds showed an increase from 140,000 tons in FY 1979 to 568,000 tons in FY 1988. A buffer stock of seeds is maintained by the National Seeds Corporation for the northeastern states and by the State Farm Corporations of India for the other states against such unforeseen contingencies as floods, droughts, and diseases.

Fertilizer

The rate of fertilizer consumption increased dramatically after independence, although it was still lower than in most other countries worldwide. India used only sixty-nine kilograms per hectare in 1989, ranking it fifty-sixth worldwide and below all its South Asian neighbors except Nepal. Fertilizer consumption increased from approximately 69,000 tons of nutrients in FY 1950 to 12.6 million tons in FY 1990, and was expected to be about 13.8 million tons in FY 1993. Punjab used the highest amount of fertilizer per hectare followed by Tamil Nadu. The use of fertilizers was high in Punjab and Harayana in the north because of adequate irrigation. In the south, other than in Tamil Nadu, consumption, especially in Andhra Pradesh and Kerala, was higher than the national average. The disparity in the use of fertilizers across states was decreasing, however. Cow dung is an important source of fertilizer—and fuel—in India. Statistics on its usage, however, are not available.

The fertilizer subsidy has been growing since FY 1976. The initial subsidy was a response to the increase in the price of

Women at step well, Rajasthan
Courtesy Janice Hyde

crude oil by the Organization of the Petroleum Exporting Countries (OPEC—see Glossary). The price increase led to a rise in the cost of naphtha, which in turn increased fertilizer prices. The fertilizer subsidy increased from Rs600 million in FY 1976 to Rs32 billion in FY 1988, to nearly Rs44 billion in FY 1990. Further increases are expected as the decade progresses. Plans in 1992 to cut the subsidy by 40 percent were curtailed following heavy political opposition from the major farming states.

Plant Protection and Pesticides

The government has introduced integrated pest management at the central and state levels for purposes of plant protection. Twenty-five central, integrated pest-management centers have been established in twenty-two states and one union territory for pest surveillance and monitoring, promotion of biocontrol methods of conservation, promotion of nonchemical methods of pest control, training of extension workers and farmers, and demonstration farms.

The use of synthetic pesticides has increased steadily because of the spreading use of new high-yielding varieties of seeds and their greater vulnerability to plant pests and diseases. The sale of synthetic pesticides jumped from 8,620 tons in crop year 1960–61 to 65,000 tons in 1982–83 and 85,660 tons in

1989–90. In 1960 only about 6 million hectares received chemical pesticides, but by the early 1980s some 100 million hectares were being treated, and the growth in coverage continues in the 1990s. The rapid rise in the use of plant protection led to the enactment of the Insecticides Act of 1968 to regulate the import, sale, transport, distribution, and use of insecticides.

Technology and Mechanization

Despite the pervasive, large-scale use of draft animals throughout India, agricultural machinery and implements, tractors, in particular, have had an important place in increasing agricultural productivity. The stock of tractors increased from 8,600 in FY 1950 to 518,500 in FY 1982 and continued to grow rapidly throughout the 1980s (see table 29, Appendix). The number and sale of power tillers and combine harvesters produced and sold was small, with 4,678 tillers and 110 harvesters sold in FY 1988. There was a significant increase in the number of electric pumps and oil pump sets for irrigation during the 1980s.

The production and use of machinery are hampered by the small size of many operational holdings. However, a number of improved agricultural implements are available for tilling, seeding and fertilizer application, weeding, harvesting, and threshing. The implements include moldboard plows, disc harrows, cultivators, seed drills (more than 110,000 were sold annually in the early 1990s), and mechanical power threshers. These tools have the potential of increasing yields for all crops, but the adoption rate of improved machinery is low. The Central Institute of Agricultural Engineering at Bhopal, Madhya Pradesh, under the aegis of the Indian Council for Agricultural Research, is responsible for coordinating the manufacture and promotion of technology for small and marginal farmers. The government introduced an incentive scheme in 1990 to subsidize the cost of machinery by up to 50 percent to small and marginal farms. Additionally, farmers' agroservice centers are being established to provide custom service for improved implements and machinery. The eighth plan includes a major thrust for upgrading and adopting proven technology.

In a country with a large and growing labor force, too much mechanization in the short run could create fossil fuel shortages as well as social and economic problems (see Size and Composition of the Work Force, ch. 6). There is, nevertheless, room for improvements in technology. Since FY 1983, there have been attempts to popularize improved animal-drawn agricultural implements and hand tools through demonstrations and subsidies to small and marginal farmers.

Despite these advances in mechanization, most crops are still sown, transplanted, weeded, and harvested through labor-intensive human work. Most grains are harvested by teams of laborers wielding hand-forged iron sickles, binding up sheaves of grain, and carrying loads of sheaves on their heads to bullock carts to be transported to threshing floors. Teams of bullocks are then driven over the sheaves to separate the grains from the stalks, and workers toss basketloads of grain into the air to separate the grain from the chaff. Lentils, a crucial part of the Indian diet, also are harvested through labor-intensive means. Groups of laborers squat down in fields for hours at a time, ripping out lentil plants at the root by hand. Machinery available to lentil farmers has proven difficult to use, and traditional methods are preferred.

Price Policy and Terms of Trade

After independence, India's initial price policy could be characterized as serving the interests of the consumers, particularly where food grains were concerned, and most of all in regard to wheat. Food prices were kept low to provide cheap food for urban consumers under the theory that a cheap and easy supply of wage goods—of which food grains formed the main component—would inhibit inflationary pressures on the economy. This policy, buttressed with imports under the United States Public Law 480 Food for Peace Program, kept prices at a low level during the late 1950s and early 1960s but did not provide incentives for Indian farmers to invest or increase production. The terms of trade vis-à-vis manufacturing were favorable to agriculture in FY 1959 and then on a par with other sectors for three years. Thereafter, when manufacturing prices went up faster than agricultural prices as a result of government policy, terms of trade favored manufacturing and turned against the agricultural sector. This change led to a food crisis in the mid-1960s when agricultural production fell.

From about 1965, the need to guarantee remunerative prices to farmers was stressed to ensure self-sufficiency in food-grain production as soon as possible. The Agricultural Prices Commission—in 1993 called the Commission for Agricultural Costs and Prices—was set up to advise the government on agricultural prices, keeping in view the interests of both the consumer and the producer. Of particular concern were prices for wheat, rice, coarse grains, pulses, sugarcane, oilseeds, cotton, and jute. In the late 1980s and early 1990s, the commission was supplied with cost of production data, compiled through sample surveys, to improve its effectiveness in setting prices. The commission was reasonably successful in providing remunerative prices for farmers. It used the price mechanism to increase the production of commodities in demand, such as oilseeds at the end of the 1980s, and to keep prices at a reasonable level for consumers.

Production

Crop Output

The average rate of output growth since the 1950s has been more than 2.5 percent per year and was greater than 3 percent during the 1980s, compared with less than 1 percent per annum during the period from 1900 to 1950. Most of the growth in aggregate crop output was the result of an increase in yields, rather than an increase in the area under crops. The yield performance of crops has varied widely (see table 30, Appendix).

The national growth rates mask variability in the performance of different states, but in the regions with the greatest increases three categories are discernible. The first category includes states or areas that have an exceptionally high agricultural growth rate—Punjab, Haryana, and western Uttar Pradesh. The second is states or areas that have high growth rates, but not as high as the first category—Andhra Pradesh, Maharashtra, and Jammu and Kashmir. A third category has a lesser growth rate and includes Bihar, Gujarat, Karnataka, Orissa, Rajasthan, Tamil Nadu, eastern Uttar Pradesh, and West Bengal. These eight states, however, comprise 55 percent of the total food-grains area (see fig. 13).

Some observers believe that the increase in productivity has been an important factor explaining the satisfactory growth of food-grain production since the mid-1960s. However, the gains in productivity remain confined to select areas. Between FY 1960 and FY 1980, yields increased by 125.6 percent in North India (Punjab, Haryana, and western Uttar Pradesh). The increase in the other regions was much less: central India, 36 percent; eastern, 22.7 percent; southern, 58.3 percent; and western India, 31.6 percent. The national average was nearly

40.9 percent. Part of this disparity can be explained by the fact that during this period Punjab and Haryana were way ahead of other states in terms of irrigated area, intensity of irrigation, and intensity of cropping. Availability of irrigation is one of the crucial factors governing regional variations.

As a result of a good monsoon during FY 1990, food grain production reached 176 million tons, 3 percent more than in FY 1989. The production of rice and wheat was 74.6 million and 54.5 million tons, respectively. Among the commercial crops, sugarcane and oilseeds reached production levels of 240.3 million tons and 21.8 million tons, respectively. The increased production in FY 1990 was mainly the result of continuing increases in yields for all the main crops—rice, wheat, pulses, and oilseeds. In the case of oilseeds and sugarcane, higher production was also the result of the increased number of hectares planted (see table 31, Appendix).

The growth in food-grain production did not occur in a linear trend, but as a series of spurts depending mostly on the weather, input availability, and price policy. Aggregate growth was composed of an even split between area expansion and yield growth before FY 1964. Since FY 1967, the contribution of growth in yields has become dominant and attests to the vigor with which agriculture has responded to the opportunities opened up by new seed, water, and fertilizer technology.

Food-Grain Production

Food grains include rice, wheat, corn (maize), coarse grains (sorghum and millet), and pulses (beans, dried peas, and lentils). In FY 1990, approximately 127.5 million hectares were sown with food grains, about 75 percent of the total planted area. The total number of hectares increased by 31 percent over the forty-year period from FY 1950 to FY 1990. Most of this increase occurred in the 1950s; there was almost no change in the sown number of hectares through the 1980s. Around 33 percent of cropland was given over to rice, about 29 percent to coarse grains, and the rest evenly divided between wheat and pulses.

Rice, India's preeminent crop, is the staple food of the people of the eastern and southern parts of the country. Production increased from 53.6 million tons in FY 1980 to 74.6 million tons in FY 1990, a 39 percent increase over the decade. By FY 1992, rice production had reached 111 million tons, second in the world only to China with its 182 million tons. Since 1950 the increase has been more than 350 percent. Most of this increase was the result of an increase in yields; the number of hectares increased only 40 percent during this period. Yields increased from 1,336 kilograms per hectare in FY 1980 to 1,751 kilograms per hectare in FY 1990. The per-hectare yield increased more than 262 percent between 1950 and 1992.

Wheat production showed an 843 percent increase, from nearly 6.5 million tons in FY 1950 to 54.5 million tons in FY 1990 to 56.7 million tons in FY 1992. Most of this greater production was the result of an increase in yields that went from 663 kilograms per hectare in FY 1950 to 2,274 kilograms in FY 1990. Along with the excellent performance in yields, improved wheat production resulted from an increase in the area planted from nearly 9.8 million hectares in FY 1950 to 24.0 million hectares in FY 1990.

Sorghum and millet, the principal coarse grains, are dryland crops most frequently grown as staples in central and western India. Corn and barley are staple foods grown mainly near and in the Himalayan region. As the result of increased yields, the production of coarse grains has doubled since 1950; there was hardly any change in the area sown for these grains. The production of pulses did not fare well, increasing by only 68 percent over the four decades. Land devoted to pulses increased by 28 percent, and yields were up by 30 percent. Pulses are an important source of protein in the vegetarian diet; the small improvement in production along with the increase in population meant a reduced availability of pulses per capita.

Before the Green Revolution, coarse grains showed satisfactory rates of growth but afterward lost cultivated areas to wheat and rice, and their growth declined. The area sown with coarse grains increased from FY 1950 to FY 1970 by roughly 20 percent but declined subsequently up to the early 1990s. In FY 1990 the area sown was 3 percent less than in FY 1950 and 20 percent less than in FY 1970. The area sown with two coarse grains, *jowar* (barley) and *bajra* (millet), increased from FY 1950 to FY 1970 and then declined during the 1970s and the 1980s. The area sown with *jowar* increased from 15.6 million hectares in FY 1950 to 17.4 million hectares in FY 1970 and then decreased to 14.5 million hectares in FY 1990. The area sown with *bajra* increased from 9.0 million hectares in FY 1950 to 12.9 million hectares in FY 1970 and stood at 10.4 million hectares in FY 1990. A similar pattern existed for other coarse grains. Overall, India's coarse-grain production increased from

15.4 million tons in 1950 to 29 million tons in 1980 to 33.1 million tons in 1990 and 33.7 million tons in 1993.

Oilseeds

India in the mid-1990s has almost attained self-sufficiency in the production of oilseeds to extract vegetable oil, essential in the Indian diet. Peanuts, grown mainly as a rain-fed crop on part of the semiarid areas of western and southern India, account for the largest source of the nation's production of vegetable oils. The second-ranking source of vegetable oils in the early 1990s was rapeseed. Cottonseed, an important by-product of cotton fiber and once mostly fed to cattle, was another source of vegetable oils. Soybeans and sunflower seeds were relatively new as significant oilseeds, but their production increased rapidly in the 1980s.

The production of oilseeds increased from 5.2 million tons in FY 1950 to 21.8 million tons in FY 1990. Specific information regarding area planted is not available for all oilseeds, but it increased in the 1980s, as did the yields. The growth of production before the mid-1970s was not adequate to meet the needs of the increasing population, and large quantities had to be imported from the 1970s to the mid-1980s, using scarce foreign exchange.

Commercial Crops

India is the largest producer of sugar in the world, harvesting 12 million tons in 1993, followed by Brazil's 9 million tons and China's 7 million tons. Sugar availability per capita increased from 4.7 kilograms per year in FY 1960 to 12.5 kilograms per year in FY 1990, following the more than fourfold increase in production from 57 million tons in FY 1950 to 240 million tons in FY 1990. This increase in production was a result of the doubling of the yield per hectare and a doubling of the area sown with sugar. Imports of sugar were negligible in FY 1992 and FY 1993. However, in the FY 1995 budget presentation to the Lok Sabha in March 1995, Minister of Finance Manmohan Singh said it was necessary to supplement the public distribution system with "necessary imports of sugar."

Raw cotton is the most important nonfood commodity produced on India's farms. Cotton was an important export crop in the 1950s, but thereafter it provided the raw material for India's textile industry, which grew greatly to meet the needs of an expanding population (see Manufacturing, ch. 6). Cotton fabrics found an expanding international market in the 1980s and earned valuable foreign exchange. The foreign exchange earned from raw cotton, cotton yarn, and fabrics of all textile materials increased from US$163 million in FY 1960 to US$1.4 billion in FY 1980 to nearly US$3.9 billion in FY 1990 and US$3.8 billion by FY 1992. Cotton production increased from 600,000 tons in FY 1950 to nearly 1.7 million tons in FY 1990. These improvements largely resulted from increased yields, as there was little increase in the sown area devoted to cotton.

Raw jute is second only to cotton as a farm-produced industrial raw material. Before partition in 1947, India was the world's main supplier of jute and jute goods used as packaging material. As a result of the partition of India and Pakistan, the main jute growing area was in East Pakistan (eastern Bengal, after 1971 the independent nation of Bangladesh), and the factories manufacturing jute goods were in West Bengal, which remained part of India after partition. Jute also had been India's main source of export earnings. As a result, there was a concerted effort to increase raw jute production. The area sown with jute increased from 571,000 hectares in FY 1950 to nearly 1.2 million hectares in FY 1985 but then decreased to 692,000 hectares in FY 1988. Yields increased steadily from 1,040 kilograms per hectare in FY 1950 to 1,803 kilograms per hectare in FY 1990. These two factors combined to more than double jute production from 595 million tons in FY 1950 to 1.4 billion tons in FY 1990, with a maximum production of nearly 2 billion tons in FY 1985. Because technological changes in packaging reduced the worldwide demand for jute, production in the early 1990s was mainly for the domestic market. In FY 1990, jute provided less than 1 percent of export earnings.

The Green Revolution

The introduction of high-yielding varieties of seeds after 1965 and the increased use of fertilizers and irrigation are known collectively as the Green Revolution, which provided the increase in production needed to make India self-sufficient in food grains. The program was started with the help of the United States-based Rockefeller Foundation and was based on high-yielding varieties of wheat, rice, and other grains that had been developed in Mexico and in the Philippines. Of the high-yielding seeds, wheat produced the best results. Production of coarse grains—the staple diet of the poor—and pulses—the

Mechanized threshing, Uttar Pradesh
Courtesy Robert L. Worden

main source of protein—lagged behind, resulting in reduced per capita availability.

The total area under the high-yielding-varieties program was a negligible 1.9 million hectares in FY 1960. Since then growth has been spectacular, increasing to nearly 15.4 million hectares by FY 1970, 43.1 million hectares by FY 1980, and 63.9 million hectares by FY 1990. The rate of growth decreased significantly in the late 1980s, however, as additional suitable land was not available (see table 32, Appendix).

The major benefits of the Green Revolution were experienced mainly in northern and northwestern India between 1965 and the early 1980s; the program resulted in a substantial increase in the production of food grains, mainly wheat and rice. Food-grain yields continued to increase throughout the 1980s, but the dramatic changes in the years between 1965 and 1980 were not duplicated. By FY 1980, almost 75 percent of the total cropped area under wheat was sown with high-yielding varieties. For rice the comparable figure was 45 percent. In the 1980s, the area under high-yielding varieties continued to increase, but the rate of growth overall was slower. The eighth plan aimed at making high-yielding varieties available to the whole country and developing more productive strains of other crops.

The Green Revolution created wide regional and interstate disparities. The plan was implemented only in areas with assured supplies of water and the means to control it, large inputs of fertilizers, and adequate farm credit. These inputs were easily available in at least parts of the states of Punjab, Haryana, and western Uttar Pradesh; thus, yields increased

411

most in these states. In other states, such as Andhra Pradesh and Tamil Nadu, in areas where these inputs were not assured, the results were limited or negligible, leading to considerable variation in crop yields within these states. The Green Revolution also increased income disparities: higher income growth and reduced incidence of poverty were found in the states where yields increased the most and lower income growth and little change in the incidence of poverty in other states.

Livestock and Poultry

A large number of farmers depend on livestock for their livelihood. In addition to supplying milk, meat, eggs, and hides, animals, mainly bullocks, are the major source of power for both farmers and drayers. Thus, animal husbandry plays an important role in the rural economy. The gross value of output from this sector was Rs358 billion in FY 1989, an amount that constituted about 25 percent of the total agricultural output of Rs1.4 trillion.

In FY 1992, India had approximately 25 percent of the world's cattle, with a collective herd of 193 million head. India also had 110 million goats, 75 million water buffalo, 44 million sheep, and 10 million pigs. Milk production in FY 1990 was estimated to have reached 53.5 million tons, and egg production had reached a level of 23.3 billion eggs. Dairy farming provided supplementary employment and an additional source of income to many small and marginal farmers. The National Dairy Development Board was established in 1965 under the auspices of Operation Flood at Anand, in Gujarat, to promote, plan, and organize dairy development through cooperatives; to provide consultations; and to set up dairy plants, which were then turned over to the cooperatives. There were more than 63,000 Anand-style dairy cooperative societies with some 7.5 million members in the early 1990s. The milk produced and sold by these farmers brought Rs320 million a day, or more than Rs10 trillion a year. The increase in milk production permitted India to end imports of powdered milk and milk-related products. In addition, 30,000 tons of powdered milk were exported annually to neighboring countries.

Operation Flood, the world's largest integrated dairy development program, attempted to establish linkages between rural milk producers and urban consumers by organizing farmer-owned and -managed dairy cooperative societies. In the early 1990s, the program was in its third phase and was receiving financial assistance from the World Bank and commodity assistance from the European Economic Community. At that time, India had more than 64,000 dairy cooperative societies, with close to 7.7 million members. These cooperatives established a daily processing capacity of 15.5 million liters of whole milk and 727 tons of milk powder.

Forestry

Some 50 million hectares, about 17 percent of India's land area, were regarded as forestland in the early 1990s. In FY 1987, however, actual forest cover was 64 million hectares. However, because more than 50 percent of this land was barren or brushland, the area under productive forest was actually less than 35 million hectares, or approximately 10 percent of the country's land area. The growing population's high demand for forest resources continued the destruction and degradation of forests through the 1980s, taking a heavy toll on the soil. An estimated 6 billion tons of topsoil were lost annually. However, India's 0.6 percent average annual rate of deforestation for agricultural and nonlumbering land uses in the decade beginning in 1981 was one of the lowest in the world and on a par with Brazil.

Many forests in the mid-1990s are found in high-rainfall, high-altitude regions, areas to which access is difficult. About 20 percent of total forestland is in Madhya Pradesh; other states with significant forests are Orissa, Maharashtra, and Andhra Pradesh (each with about 9 percent of the national total); Arunachal Pradesh (7 percent); and Uttar Pradesh (6 percent). The variety of forest vegetation is large: there are 600 species of hardwoods, *sal* (*Shorea robusta*) and teak being the principal economic species.

Conservation has been an avowed goal of government policy since independence. Afforestation increased from a negligible amount in the first plan to nearly 8.9 million hectares in the seventh plan. The cumulative area afforested during the 1951–91 period was nearly 17.9 million hectares. However, despite large-scale tree planting programs, forestry is one arena in which India has actually regressed since independence. Annual fellings at about four times the growth rate are a major cause. Widespread pilfering by villagers for firewood and fodder also represents a major decrement. In addition, the forested area has been shrinking as a result of land cleared for farming, inundations for irrigation and hydroelectric power projects, and construction of new urban areas, industrial plants, roads, power lines, and schools.

India's long-term strategy for forestry development reflects three major objectives: to reduce soil erosion and flooding; to supply the growing needs of the domestic wood products industries; and to supply the needs of the rural population for fuelwood, fodder, small timber, and miscellaneous forest produce. To achieve these objectives, the National Commission on Agriculture in 1976 recommended the reorganization of state forestry departments and advocated the concept of social forestry. The commission itself worked on the first two objectives, emphasizing traditional forestry and wildlife activities; in pursuit of the third objective, the commission recommended the establishment of a new kind of unit to develop community forests. Following the leads of Gujarat and Uttar Pradesh, a number of other states also established community-based forestry agencies that emphasized programs on farm forestry, timber management, extension forestry, reforestation of degraded forests, and use of forests for recreational purposes.

Such socially responsible forestry was encouraged by state community forestry agencies. They emphasized such projects as planting wood lots on denuded communal cattle-grazing grounds to make villages self-sufficient in fuelwood, to supply timber needed for the construction of village houses, and to provide the wood needed for the repair of farm implements. Both individual farmers and tribal communities were also encouraged to grow trees for profit. For example, in Gujarat, one of the more aggressive states in developing programs of socioeconomic importance, the forestry department distributed 200 million tree seedlings in 1983. The fast-growing eucalyptus is the main species being planted nationwide, followed by pine and poplar.

The role of forests in the national economy and in ecology was further emphasized in the 1988 National Forest Policy, which focused on ensuring environmental stability, restoring the ecological balance, and preserving the remaining forests. Other objectives of the policy were meeting the need for fuelwood, fodder, and small timber for rural and tribal people while recognizing the need to actively involve local people in the management of forest resources. Also in 1988, the Forest Conservation Act of 1980 was amended to facilitate stricter conservation measures. A new target was to increase the forest cover to 33 percent of India's land area from the then-official

*Building a haystack, Uttar
Pradesh
Courtesy Robert L. Worden*

estimate of 23 percent. In June 1990, the central government adopted resolutions that combined forest science with social forestry, that is, taking the sociocultural traditions of the local people into consideration.

Since the early 1970s, as they realized that deforestation threatened not only the ecology but their livelihood in a variety of ways, people have become more interested and involved in conservation. The best known popular activist movement is the Chipko Movement, in which local women decided to fight the government and the vested interests to save trees. The women of Chamoli District, Uttar Pradesh, declared that they would embrace—literally "to stick to" (*chipkna* in Hindi)—trees if a sporting goods manufacturer attempted to cut down ash trees in their district. Since initial activism in 1973, the movement has spread and become an ecological movement leading to similar actions in other forest areas. The movement has slowed down the process of deforestation, exposed vested interests, increased ecological awareness, and demonstrated the viability of people power.

Fishing

Fish production has increased more than fivefold since independence. It rose from only 800,000 tons in FY 1950 to 4.1 million tons in the early 1990s. Special efforts have been made to promote extensive and intensive inland fish farming, modernize coastal fisheries, and encourage deep-sea fishing through joint ventures. These efforts led to a more than fourfold increase in coastal fish production from 520,000 tons in FY 1950 to 2.4 million tons in FY 1990. The increase in inland fish production was even more dramatic, increasing almost eightfold from 218,000 tons in FY 1950 to 1.7 million tons in FY 1990. The value of fish and processed fish exports increased from less than 1 percent of the total value of exports in FY 1960 to 3.6 percent in FY 1993.

The important marine fish in the mid-1990s are mackerel, sardines, Bombay duck, shark, ray, perch, croaker, carangid, sole, ribbonfish, whitebait, tuna, silverbelly, prawn, and cuttlefish. The main freshwater fish are carp and catfish; the main brackish-water fish are *hilsa* (a variety of shad), and mullet.

Great potential exists for expanding the nation's fishing industry. India's exclusive economic zone, stretching 200 nautical miles into the Indian Ocean, encompasses more than 2 million square kilometers. In the mid-1980s, only about 33 percent of that area was being exploited. The potential annual catch from the area has been estimated at 4.5 million tons. In addition to this marine zone, India has about 1.4 million hectares of brackish water available for aquaculture, of which only 60,000 hectares were being farmed in the early 1990s; about 1.6 million hectares of freshwater lakes, ponds, and swamps; and nearly 64,000 kilometers of rivers and streams.

In 1990 there were 1.7 million full-time fishermen, 1.3 million part-time fishermen, and 2.3 million occasional fishermen, many of whom worked as saltmakers, ferrymen, or seamen, or operated boats for hire. In the early 1990s, the fishing fleet consisted of 180,000 traditional craft powered by sails or oars, 26,000 motorized traditional craft, and some 34,000 mechanized boats.

Fisheries research and training institutions are supported by central and state governments that deserve much of the credit for the expansion and improvements in the Indian fishing industry. The principal fisheries research institutions, all of which operate under the Indian Council of Agricultural Research, are the Central Institute of Marine Fisheries Research at Kochi (formerly Cochin), Kerala; the Central Inland Fisheries Institute at Barrackpore, West Bengal; and the Central Institute of Fisheries Technology at Willingdon Island near Kochi. Most fishery training is provided by the Central Institute for Fishery Education in Bombay (or Mumbai in Marathi), which has ancillary institutions in Barrackpore, Agra (Uttar Pradesh), and Hyderabad (Andhra Pradesh). The Central Fisheries Corporation in Calcutta is instrumental in bringing about improvements in fishing methods, ice production, processing, storing, marketing, and constructing and repairing fishing vessels. Operating under a 1972 law, the Marine Products Export Authority, headquartered in Kochi, has made several market surveys abroad and has been instrumental in introducing and enforcing hygiene standards that have gained for Indian fishery export products a reputation for cleanliness and quality.

The implementation of two programs for inland fisheries—establishing fish farmers' development agencies and the National Programme of Fish Seed Development—has led to encouragingly increased production, which reached 1.5 million tons during FY 1990, up from 0.9 million tons in FY 1984. A network of 313 fish farmers' development agencies was functioning in 1992. Under the National Programme of Fish Seed Development, forty fish-seed hatcheries were commissioned. Fish-seed production doubled from 5 billion fry in FY 1983 to 10 billion fry in FY 1989. A new program using organic waste for aquaculture was started in FY 1986. Inland fish production as a percent of total fish production increased from 36 percent in FY 1980 to 40 percent by FY 1990.

Apart from four main fishing harbors—Kochi (Kerala), Madras (Tamil Nadu), Vishakhapatnam (Andhra Pradesh), and Roychowk in Calcutta (West Bengal)—twenty-three minor fishing harbors and ninety-five fish-landing centers are designated to provide landing and berthing facilities to fishing craft. The harbors at Vishakhapatnam, Kochi, and Roychowk were completed by 1980; the one at Madras was completed in the 1980s. A major fishing harbor was under construction at Sassoon Dock in Bombay in the early 1990s, as were thirteen additional minor fishing harbors and eighteen small landing centers. By early 1990, there were 225 deep-sea fishing vessels operating in India's exclusive economic zone. Of these, 165 were owned by Indian shipping companies, and the rest were chartered foreign fishing vessels.

The government provides subsidies to poor fishermen so that they can motorize their traditional craft to increase the range and frequency of operation, with a consequent increase in the catch and earnings. A total of about 26,171 traditional craft had been motorized under the program by 1992.

The banning of trawling by chartered foreign vessels and the speedy motorization of traditional fishing craft in the 1980s led to a quantum jump in marine fish production in the late 1980s. The export of marine products rose from 97,179 tons (Rs531 billion) in FY 1987 to 210,800 tons (Rs17.4 trillion) in FY 1992, making India one of the world's leading seafood exporting nations. This achievement was largely a result of significant advancements in India's freezing facilities since the 1960s, advancements that enabled India's seafood products to meet international standards. Frozen shrimp, a high-value item, has become the dominant seafood export. Other significant export items are frozen frog legs, frozen lobster tails, dried fish, and shark fins, much of which is exported to seafood-loving Japan. During the eighth plan, marine products were identified as having major export potential.

There are several specialized institutes that train fishermen. The Central Institute of Fisheries Nautical and Engineering Training in Kochi instructs operators of deep-sea fishing vessels and technicians for shore establishments. It has facilities in Madras and Vishakhapatnam for about 500 trainees a year. The Integrated Fisheries Project, also headquartered in Kochi, was established for the processing, popularizing, and marketing of unusual fish. Another training organization, the Central Institute of Coastal Engineering for Fisheries in Bangalore, has done techno-economic feasibility studies on locations of fishing harbor sites and brackish-water fish farms.

To improve returns to fishermen and provide better products for consumers, several states have organized marketing cooperatives for fishermen. Nevertheless, most traditional fishermen rely on household members or local fish merchants for the disposal of their catches. In some places, marketing is carried on entirely by fisherwomen who carry small quantities in containers on their heads to nearby places. Good wholesale or retail markets are rare.

Agricultural Credit

Credit institutions serving agricultural-sector needs developed in three phases. In the first phase, which lasted from 1947 to 1969, cooperative agencies were the primary vehicle providing credit. In the second phase, after nationalization of banks in 1969, commercial banks were assigned a role in providing

Fishing boats, Bombay, Maharashtra
Courtesy Bernice Huffman Collection, Library of Congress

agricultural credit but were supplementary to cooperatives (see Fiscal Administration, ch. 6). In the last phase starting in 1975, regional rural banks were established to provide credit. In the 1990s, agricultural credit is provided through a multiagency approach in the form of cooperatives, commercial banks, and regional rural banks. These institutions have gradually ensured that credit reaches the most remote agricultural and rural areas.

Since the inception of central economic planning in 1950, the government has favored cooperative societies as a channel for providing credit and as a means of broadening the experience of villagers in such activities as marketing, community farming, and consumer purchasing. Credit societies were the first to be established and continue to be the most extensive and important group of cooperatives. Of the roughly 250,000 cooperatives in India in 1980, about 100,000 were primarily agricultural credit cooperatives. By the late 1980s, because regional rural banks were doing more lending, the number of agricultural credit cooperatives had decreased to 87,300. By 1988 there were 93,000 primary agricultural credit societies operating in rural areas, with a membership of 89.8 million. The societies aimed for universal membership in order that poorer members of society could join cooperatives and use their services. Total loans advanced by such societies amounted to nearly Rs36.9 billion during FY 1987. These agricultural credit societies had a share capital of about Rs10.1 billion at the end of June 1988.

Cooperatives played a significant role in the production and distribution of agricultural inputs. For example, during FY 1988 nearly 3.5 million tons, representing more than 33 percent of total fertilizer (less cow dung), were distributed through a network of 76,000 cooperative retail outlets. Cooperatives also distributed other inputs, such as seeds, pesticides, and agricultural implements.

The overall control of rural credit for the development of agriculture and the rural sector is under the control of the National Bank for Agriculture and Rural Development, which was established in July 1980. It was chartered to oversee the workings of regional rural banks, and in the mid-1990s was slated to establish a rural infrastructure development fund to provide loans to state governments and state-owned corporations to enable completion of irrigation, soil conservation, watershed management, and other rural infrastructure projects in progress. By June 1991, there were 14,522 regional rural banks in India.

Public-sector banks, including commercial and regional rural banks, increased their activities in the countryside after the nationalization of banks. Many bank branches were opened in rural areas. One indicator of increased availability of credit through public-sector banks was the increase in the number of accounts. The number went from 164,000, with outstanding loans of Rs1.6 billion, to nearly 21.8 million accounts, with an outstanding balance of nearly Rs165.2 billion in March 1990.

In economic terms, the growth in credit supply has been satisfactory, but the growth in deposits has not kept pace with credit supply and there has been a high rate of loan defaults. Field-level rural financial institutions have increased, however, even though there are fewer primary agricultural credit societies. The large increase in the number of branches of commercial banks in the rural areas and the expansion of regional rural banks led to the reduction.

Agricultural Taxation

Agricultural property and some agricultural income were being taxed in the early 1990s, but the revenue from these taxes was negligible. In the early 1950s, however, land revenue agricultural property taxes were a significant form of government income, providing just under 10 percent of the tax revenue of the central, state, and union territory governments. At the end of the 1980s, that proportion was less than 1 percent because land revenue had been fixed. For instance, land revenue was an average of Rs28 per hectare in Kerala and Rs23 per hectare in Uttar Pradesh, the two states with the highest assessment rates. The national average was Rs16.50 per hectare. Agricultural property also was subject to stamp duties and registration fees. (All property transactions have to be made on official, stamped forms, and registration fees have to be paid to register transactions.) No data were available in early 1993 on the proportion of these fees that came from the agricultural sector, but a taxation inquiry committee put it at approximately 20 percent. Between 1950 and 1990, only about 1.5 percent of the total taxes collected by the central, state, and union territory governments came from the agricultural sector. Overall, the impact of tax on agricultural property was negligible but was a likely target for economic reform in the mid-1990s.

Since the 1950s, agricultural income tax has been collected as a federal tax, but it has been levied only on income from plantations. All other agricultural income has been exempt from tax. The total collection from this tax was less than 1 percent of the total taxes collected by the central, state, and union territory governments in FY 1950; in the late 1980s, it had dropped below 0.3 percent.

Marketing, Trade, and Aid

Marketing and Marketing Services

The agricultural marketing system operates primarily according to the forces of supply and demand in the private sector. Government intervention is limited to protecting the interests of producers and consumers and promoting organized marketing of agricultural commodities. In 1991 there were 6,640 regulated markets to which the central government provided assistance in the establishment of infrastructure and in setting up rural warehouses. Various central government organizations are involved in agricultural marketing, including the Commission for Agricultural Costs and Prices, the Food Corporation of India, the Cotton Corporation of India, and the Jute Corporation of India. There also are specialized marketing boards for rubber, coffee, tea, tobacco, spices, coconut, oilseeds, vegetable oil, and horticulture.

A network of cooperatives at the local, state, and national levels assist in agricultural marketing. The major commodities handled are food grains, jute, cotton, sugar, milk, and areca nuts. Established in 1958 as the apex of the state marketing federations, the National Agricultural Cooperative Marketing Federation of India handles much of the domestic and most of the export marketing for its member organizations.

Large enterprises, such as cooperative sugar factories, spinning mills, and solvent-extraction plants mostly handle their own marketing operations independently. Medium- and small-sized enterprises, such as rice mills, oil mills, cotton ginning and pressing units, and jute baling units, mostly are affiliated with cooperative marketing societies.

In the late 1980s, there were some 2,400 agroprocessing units in the cooperative sector. Of all the cooperative agroprocessing industries, cooperative sugar factories achieved the most notable success. The number of licensed or registered units remained at 232, of which 211 had been installed by March 1988. During the October 1987–September 1988 sugar season, 196 cooperative sugar factories were in production. They produced nearly 5.3 million tons of sugar, accounting for about 57.5 percent of the country's total production of 9.2 million tons. The National Federation of Cooperative Sugar Factories rendered advice to member cooperatives on technical improvement, financial management, raw materials development, and inventory control.

In the early 1990s, the cooperative marketing structure comprised 6,777 primary marketing societies: 2,759 general-purpose societies at the *mandi* (wholesale market) level and 4,018 special commodities societies for oilseeds and other such commodities. There were also 161 district or central societies covering nearly all important *mandis* in the country and twenty-nine general-purpose state cooperative marketing federations. The total value of agricultural produce marketed by cooperatives amounted to about Rs54.2 billion in FY 1988, compared with Rs18 billion in FY 1979. The total value of food grains handled by marketing cooperatives increased from Rs5 billion in FY 1979 to about Rs11.3 billion in FY 1986.

The Ministry of Agriculture's Directorate of Marketing and Inspection is responsible for administering federal statutes concerned with the marketing of agricultural produce. Another function is market research. The directorate also works closely with states to provide agricultural marketing services that constitutionally come under state purview.

Under the Agricultural Produce (Grading and Marketing) Act of 1937, more than forty primary commodities are compulsorily graded for export and voluntarily graded for internal consumption. Although the regulation of commodity markets is a function of state government, the Directorate of Marketing and Inspection provides marketing and inspection services and financial aid down to the village level to help set up commodity grading centers in selected markets.

By the 1980s, warehouses for storing agricultural produce and farm supplies played an increasing role in government price support and price control programs and in distributing farm commodities and farm supplies. Because the public warehouses issue a receipt to the owners of stored goods on which loans can be raised, warehouses are also becoming important in agricultural finance. The Central Warehousing Corporation, an entity of the central government, operates warehouses at major points within its jurisdictions, and cooperatives operate warehouses in towns and villages. The growth of the warehousing system has resulted in a decline in weather damage to produce and in loss to rodents and other pests.

Most agricultural produce is sold by farmers in the private sector to moneylenders (to whom the farmer may be indebted) or to village traders. Produce is sold in various ways. It might be sold at a weekly village market in the farmer's own village or in a neighboring village. If these outlets are not available, then produce might be sold at irregularly held markets in a nearby village or town, or in the *mandi*. Farmers also can sell to traders who come to the work site.

The government has adopted various measures to improve agricultural marketing. These steps include establishing regulated markets, constructing warehouses, grading and standardizing produce, standardizing weights and measures, and providing information on agricultural prices over All India

Radio (Akashvani), the national radio network (see Radio, ch. 6; The Media, ch. 8).

The government's objective of providing reasonable prices for basic food commodities is achieved through the Public Distribution System, a network of 350,000 fair-price shops that are monitored by state governments. Channeling basic food commodities through the Public Distribution System serves as a conduit for reaching the truly needy and as a system for keeping general consumer prices in check. More than 80 percent of the supplies of grain to the Public Distribution System is provided by Punjab, Haryana, and western Uttar Pradesh.

The Food Corporation of India was established in 1965 as the public-sector marketing agency responsible for implementing government price policy through procurement and public distribution operations. It was intended to secure for the government a commanding position in the food-grain trade. By 1979 the corporation was operating in all states as the sole agent of the central government in food-grain procurement. The corporation uses the services of state government agencies and cooperatives in its operations.

The Food Corporation of India is the sole repository of food grains reserved for the Public Distribution System. Food grains, primarily wheat and rice, account for between 60 and 75 percent of the corporation's total annual purchases. Food-grain procurement was 8.9 million tons in FY 1971, 13.0 million tons in FY 1981, and 17.8 million tons in FY 1991. Food grains supplied through the Public Distribution System amounted to 7.8 million tons in FY 1971, 13.0 million tons in FY 1981, and 17.0 million tons in FY 1991. The corporation has functioned effectively in providing price supports to farmers through its procurement scheme and in keeping a check on large price increases by providing food grains through the Public Distribution System.

External Trade

Agricultural exports were 44 percent of total exports in FY 1960; they decreased to 32 percent in FY 1970, to 31 percent in FY 1980, to 18.5 percent in FY 1988, and to 15.3 percent in FY 1993. This drop in agriculture's share was somewhat misleading because agricultural products, such as cotton and jute, that were exported in the raw form in the 1950s, have been exported as cotton yarn, fabrics, ready-made garments, coir yarn, and jute manufactures since the 1960s.

Women washing water buffalo, Agra, Uttar Pradesh
Courtesy Sandra Day O'Connor

The composition of agricultural and allied products for export changed mainly because of the continuing growth of demand in the domestic market. This demand cut into the surplus available for export despite a continuing desire, on the part of government, to shore up the constant foreign-exchange shortage (see Foreign-Exchange System, ch. 6). In FY 1960, tea was the principal export by value. Oil cakes, tobacco, cashew kernels, spices, and raw cotton were about equal in value but were only one-eighth of the value of tea exports. By FY 1980, tea was still dominant, but coffee, rice, fish, and fish products came close, followed by oil cakes, cashew kernels, and cotton. In 1992–93 fish and fish products became the primary agricultural export, followed by oil meals, then cereals, and then tea. The share of fish products rose steadily from less than 2 percent of all agricultural exports in FY 1960, to 10 percent in FY 1980, to approximately 15 percent for the three-year period ending in FY 1990, and to 23 percent in FY 1992. The share of tea in agricultural exports fell from 40 percent in FY 1960 to roughly 17 percent in the FY 1988–FY 1990 period, and to only 13 percent by FY 1992.

External Aid

Foreign aid—financial and technical—since the 1950s has made a significant contribution to the agricultural progress in rural India. Aid has come from many sources: the United States government, the Ford Foundation, the Rockefeller Foundation, the World Bank, the Food and Agriculture Organization (FAO—see Glossary) of the United Nations (UN), the European Economic Community, the former Soviet Union, Britain, and Japan, among others (see Aid, ch. 6).

Agricultural aid also has come in many forms. Between 1963 and 1972, for example, under a program of the United States Agency for International Development, some 400 American scientists and scholars served on the faculties of India's agricultural universities, while more than 500 faculty members from Indian institutions received advanced training in the United States and other countries. Several hundred agricultural research projects, financed with funds generated from sales of American farm commodities under the United States Public Law 480 program, fueled technological breakthroughs in Indian agriculture.

Aid to the agricultural sector continued in the late 1980s and the early 1990s; the FAO, the European Union, the World Bank, and the United Nations Development Programme (UNDP) provided the bulk of the assistance. The FAO provided technical assistance in a number of emerging areas; it provided quality control for exports; videos for rural communication and training; and market studies for wool processing, mushroom production, and egg and poultry marketing. Operation Flood—a dairy development program—was jointly sponsored by the European Economic Community, the World Bank, and India's National Dairy Development Board (see Livestock and Poultry, this ch.). The UNDP provided technical assistance by sending foreign experts, consultants, and equipment to India. The World Bank and its affiliates supported agricultural extension, social (community-based) forestry, agricultural credit, dairy development, horticulture, seed development, rain-fed fish farms, storage, marketing, and irrigation.

India has not only been a receiver of aid. Increasingly since independence, India has been sharing its agricultural technology with other developing countries. Numerous foreign scientists have received special and advanced training in India; hundreds of foreign students have attended Indian state agricultural universities. Among other international agricultural endeavors, India has contributed scientists, services, and funds to the work of the International Rice Research Institute, headquartered in the Philippines. In the late 1980s and early 1990s, India provided short- and long-term training courses to hundreds of foreign specialists each year under a variety of programs, including the Technical Cooperation Scheme of the Colombo Plan for Cooperative Economic and Social Development in Asia and the Pacific (Colombo Plan—see Glossary) and the Technical Cooperation Scheme of the Commonwealth of Nations Assistance Program (see Participation in International Organizations, ch. 9).

Impact of Economic Reforms on Agriculture

The serious foreign-exchange crisis in 1990 led to a number of well-publicized economic reforms in the early 1990s dealing with trade, industrial licensing, and privatization. The reforms had an impact on the agricultural sector through the central government's effort to withdraw the fertilizer subsidy and place greater emphasis on agricultural exports. The cut in the fertilizer subsidy was a result of the government's commitment to reduce New Delhi's fiscal deficit by removing grants and subsidies from the budget. The government action led to a reduction in the use of chemical fertilizers and protests by farmers and opposition political parties. The government was forced to continue the subsidies but at a somewhat lower level.

New import and export policies aim at enhancing export capabilities of the agricultural sector by increasing productivity and promoting modernization and competitiveness. The measures to facilitate export growth include allowing the import of capital for the agricultural sector, reducing the list of agricultural products that cannot be exported, and removing the minimum export price from a number of products. Agricultural exports increased by 30 percent in FY 1991 and 14 percent in FY 1992 in terms of rupee value, but declined by 8 percent from FY 1990 to FY 1992 in United States dollar terms because of the devaluation of the rupee in 1991.

In the mid-1990s, it was expected that agriculture would continue to be the most important sector of the economy for the rest of the decade in terms of the proportion of GDP. However, even when it is not the sector providing the largest share of GDP, the importance of agriculture is not likely to diminish because of its critical role in providing food, wage goods, employment, and raw materials to industries. Despite their preoccupation with industrial development, India's planners and policy makers have had to acknowledge the critical role of agriculture in the early 1990s by changing basic policy. The gains in agricultural production should not lead to complacency, however. Continuing increases in productivity, developing allied activities in rural areas, and building infrastructure in rural areas are essential if India is to continue to be self-reliant in food and agricultural products and provide a modest surplus for exports.

*   *   *

There is abundant literature on Indian agriculture, and much of it is highly detailed. A source that brings together a wide variety of useful information is Subhash C. Kashyap's *National Policy Studies*, which provides a good overview of agricultural policy. A critical review of agricultural development and policy is provided by B.M. Bhatia's *Indian Agriculture: A Policy Perspective*. N.S.S. Narayana, K.S. Parikh, and T.N. Srinivasan's *Agriculture, Growth, and Redistribution of Income* is a more rigorous analysis of policy issues that also contains a large amount of descriptive information. The Indian Ministry of Information and Broadcasting's *India: A Reference Annual* is a valuable source. The Ministry of Finance's annual *Economic Survey* gives a detailed account of developments in agriculture. The *Economic and Political Weekly* is India's premier source of news and analysis regarding all issues connected with agriculture. (For further information and complete citations, see Bibliography.)

Chapter 8. Government and Politics

Geometric and floral floor design, Rajasthan

INDIAN POLITICS ENTERED a new era at the beginning of the 1990s. The period of political domination by the Congress (I) branch of the Indian National Congress (see Glossary) came to an end with the party's defeat in the 1989 general elections, and India began a period of intense multiparty political competition. Even though the Congress (I) regained power as a minority government in 1991, its grasp on power was precarious. The Nehruvian socialist ideology that the party had used to fashion India's political agenda had lost much of its popular appeal. The Congress (I) political leadership had lost the mantle of moral integrity inherited from the Indian National Congress's role in the independence movement, and it was widely viewed as corrupt. Support among key social bases of the Congress (I) political coalition was seriously eroding. The main alternative to the Congress (I), the Bharatiya Janata Party (BJP—Indian People's Party), embarked on a campaign to reorganize the Indian electorate in an effort to create a Hindu nationalist majority coalition. Simultaneously, such parties as the Janata Dal (People's Party), the Samajwadi Party (Socialist Party), and the Bahujan Samaj Party (BSP—Party of Society's Majority) attempted to ascend to power on the crest of an alliance of interests uniting Dalits (see Glossary), Backward Classes (see Glossary), Scheduled Tribes (see Glossary), and religious minorities.

The structure of India's federal—or union—system not only creates a strong central government but also has facilitated the concentration of power in the central government in general and in particular in the Office of the Prime Minister. This centralization of power has been a source of considerable controversy and political tension. It is likely to further exacerbate political conflict because of the increasing pluralism of the country's party system and the growing diversity of interest-group representation.

Once viewed as a source of solutions for the country's economic and social problems, the Indian polity is increasingly seen by political observers as the problem. When populist political appeals stir the passions of the masses, government institutions appear less capable than ever before of accommodating conflicts in a society mobilized along competing ethnic and religious lines. In addition, law and order have become increasingly tenuous because of the growing inability of the police to curb criminal activities and quell communal disturbances. Indeed, many observers bemoan the "criminalization" of Indian politics at a time when politicians routinely hire "muscle power" to improve their electoral prospects, and criminals themselves successfully run for public office. These circumstances have led some observers to conclude that India has entered into a growing crisis of governability.

Few analysts would deny the gravity of India's problems, but some contend they have occurred amidst the maturation of civil society and the emergence of new, more democratic political practices. Backward Classes, the Dalits, and tribal peoples increasingly have refused to rest content with the patronage and populism characteristic of the "Congress system." Mobilization of these groups has provided a viable base for the political opposition and unraveled the fabric of the Congress. Since the late 1970s, there has been a proliferation of nongovernmental organizations. These groups made new demands on the political system that required a substantial redistribution of political power, economic resources, and social status.

Whether or not developments in Indian politics exacerbate the continuing problems or give birth to greater democracy broadly hinges on efforts to resolve three key issues. How will India's political system, now more than ever based on egalitarian democratic values, accommodate the changes taking place in its hierarchical social system? How will the state balance the need to recognize the interests of the country's remarkably heterogeneous society with the imperatives of national unity? And, in the face of the declining legitimacy of the Indian state and the continuing development of civil society, can the Indian state regenerate its legitimacy, and if it is to do so, how should it redefine the boundaries between state and society? India has confronted these issues throughout much of its history. These issues, with their intrinsic tensions, will continue to serve as sources of change in the continuing evolution of the Indian polity.

The Constitutional Framework

The constitution of India draws extensively from Western legal traditions in its outline of the principles of liberal democracy. It is distinguished from many Western constitutions, however, in its elaboration of principles reflecting the aspirations to end the inequities of traditional social relations and enhance the social welfare of the population. According to constitutional scholar Granville Austin, probably no other nation's constitution "has provided so much impetus toward changing and rebuilding society for the common good." Since its enactment, the constitution has fostered a steady concentration of power in the central government—especially the Office of the Prime Minister. This centralization has occurred in the face of the increasing assertiveness of an array of ethnic and caste groups across Indian society. Increasingly, the government has responded to the resulting tensions by resorting to the formidable array of authoritarian powers provided by the constitution. Together with the public's perception of pervasive corruption among India's politicians, the state's centralization of authority and increasing resort to coercive power have eroded its legitimacy. However, a new assertiveness shown by the Supreme Court and the Election Commission suggests that the remaining checks and balances among the country's political institutions continue to support the resilience of Indian democracy.

Adopted after some two and one-half years of deliberation by the Constituent Assembly that also acted as India's first legislature, the constitution was put into effect on January 26, 1950. Bhimrao Ramji (B.R.) Ambedkar, a Dalit who earned a law degree from Columbia University, chaired the drafting committee of the constitution and shepherded it through Constituent Assembly debates. Supporters of independent India's founding father, Mohandas Karamchand (Mahatma) Gandhi, backed measures that would form a decentralized polity with strong local administration—known as *panchayat* (pl., *panchayats*—see Glossary)—in a system known as *panchayati raj,* that is rule by *panchayats.* However, the support of more modernist leaders, such as Jawaharlal Nehru, ultimately led to a parliamentary government and a federal system with a strong central government (see Nehru's Legacy, ch. 1). Following a British parliamentary pattern, the constitution embodies the Fundamental Rights, which are similar to the United States Bill of Rights, and a Supreme Court similar to that of the United States. It creates a "sovereign democratic republic" called India, or Bharat (after the legendary king of the *Mahabharata*), which "shall be a Union of States." India is a federal system in which residual powers of legislation remain with the central government, similar to that in Canada. The constitution provides detailed lists dividing up powers between central and state governments as in Australia, and it elaborates a set of Directive Principles of State Policy as does the Irish constitution.

The 395 articles and ten appendixes, known as schedules, in the constitution make it one of the longest and most detailed in the world. Schedules can be added to the constitution by amendment. The ten schedules in force cover the designations of the states and union territories; the emoluments for high-level officials; forms of oaths; allocation of the number of seats in the Rajya Sabha (Council of States—the upper house of Parliament) per state or territory; provisions for the administration and control of Scheduled Areas (see Glossary) and Scheduled Tribes (see Glossary); provisions for the administration of tribal areas in Assam; the union (meaning central government), state, and concurrent (dual) lists of responsibilities; the official languages; land and tenure reforms; and the association of Sikkim with India.

The Indian constitution is also one of the most frequently amended constitutions in the world. The first amendment came only a year after the adoption of the constitution and instituted numerous minor changes. Many more amendments followed, and through June 1995 the constitution had been amended seventy-seven times, a rate of almost two amendments per year since 1950. Most of the constitution can be amended after a quorum of more than half of the members of each house in Parliament passes an amendment with a two-thirds majority vote. Articles pertaining to the distribution of legislative authority between the central and state governments must also be approved by 50 percent of the state legislatures.

Fundamental Rights

The Fundamental Rights embodied in the constitution are guaranteed to all citizens. These civil liberties take precedence over any other law of the land. They include individual rights common to most liberal democracies, such as equality before the law, freedom of speech and expression, freedom of association and peaceful assembly, freedom of religion, and the right to constitutional remedies for the protection of civil rights such as habeas corpus. In addition, the Fundamental Rights are aimed at overturning the inequities of past social practices. They abolish "untouchability"; prohibit discrimination on the grounds of religion, race, caste, sex, or place of birth; and forbid traffic in human beings and forced labor. They go beyond conventional civil liberties in protecting cultural and educational rights of minorities by ensuring that minorities may preserve their distinctive languages and establish and administer their own education institutions. Originally, the right to property was also included in the Fundamental Rights; however, the Forty-fourth Amendment, passed in 1978, revised the status of property rights by stating that "No person shall be deprived of his property save by authority of law." Freedom of speech and expression, generally interpreted to include freedom of the press, can be limited "in the interests of the sovereignty and integrity of India, the security of the State, friendly relations with foreign States, public order, decency or morality, or in relation to contempt of court, defamation or incitement to an offence" (see The Media, this ch.).

Directive Principles of State Policy

An important feature of the constitution is the Directive Principles of State Policy. Although the Directive Principles are asserted to be "fundamental in the governance of the country," they are not legally enforceable. Instead, they are guidelines for creating a social order characterized by social, economic, and political justice, liberty, equality, and fraternity as enunciated in the constitution's preamble.

In some cases, the Directive Principles articulate goals that, however admirable, remain vague platitudes, such as the injunctions that the state "shall direct its policy towards securing . . . that the ownership and control of the material resources of the community are so distributed to subserve the common good" and "endeavor to promote international peace and security." In other areas, the Directive Principles provide more specific policy objectives. They exhort the state to secure work at a living wage for all citizens; take steps to encourage worker participation in industrial management; provide for just and humane conditions of work, including maternity leave; and promote the educational and economic interests of Scheduled Castes, Scheduled Tribes, and other disadvantaged sectors of society. The Directive Principles also charge the state with the responsibility for providing free and compulsory education for children up to age fourteen (see Administration and Funding, ch. 2).

The Directive Principles also urge the nation to develop a uniform civil code and offer free legal aid to all citizens. They urge measures to maintain the separation of the judiciary from the executive and direct the government to organize village *panchayats* to function as units of self-government. This latter objective was advanced by the Seventy-third Amendment and the Seventy-fourth Amendment in December 1992. The Directive Principles also order that India should endeavor to protect and improve the environment and protect monuments and places of historical interest.

The Forty-second Amendment, which came into force in January 1977, attempted to raise the status of the Directive Principles by stating that no law implementing any of the Directive Principles could be declared unconstitutional on the grounds that it violated any of the Fundamental Rights. The amendment simultaneously stated that laws prohibiting "antinational activities" or the formation of "antinational associations" could not be invalidated because they infringed on any of the Fundamental Rights. It added a new section to the constitution on "Fundamental Duties" that enjoined citizens "to promote harmony and the spirit of common brotherhood among all the people of India, transcending religious, linguistic and regional or sectional diversities." However, the amendment reflected a new emphasis in governing circles on order and discipline to counteract what some leaders had come to perceive as the excessively freewheeling style of Indian democracy. After the March 1977 general election ended the control of the Congress (Congress (R) from 1969) over the executive and legislature for the first time since independence in 1947, the new Janata-dominated Parliament passed the Forty-third Amendment (1977) and Forty-fourth Amendment (1978). These amendments revoked the Forty-second Amendment's provision that Directive Principles take precedence over Fundamental Rights and also curbed Parliament's power to legislate against "antinational activities" (see The Legislature, this ch.).

Group Rights

In addition to stressing the right of individuals as citizens, Part XVI of the constitution endeavors to promote social justice by elaborating a series of affirmative-action measures for disadvantaged groups. These "Special Provisions Relating to Certain Classes" include the reservation of seats in the Lok Sabha (House of the People) and in state legislative bodies for members of Scheduled Castes and Scheduled Tribes. The number of seats set aside for them is proportional to their share of

President Shankar Dayal Sharma being driven in a coach to Rashtrapatri Bhavan, the Presidential Palace, after his July 26, 1992, swearing-in ceremony
Courtesy India Abroad News Service

the national and respective state populations. Part XVI also reserves some government appointments for these disadvantaged groups insofar as they do not interfere with administrative efficiency. The section stipulates that a special officer for Scheduled Castes and Scheduled Tribes be appointed by the president to "investigate all matters relating to the safeguards provided" for them, as well as periodic commissions to investigate the conditions of the Backward Classes. The president, in consultation with state governors, designates those groups that meet the criteria of Scheduled Castes and Scheduled Tribes. Similar protections exist for the small Anglo-Indian community.

The framers of the constitution provided that the special provisions would cease twenty years after the promulgation of the constitution, anticipating that the progress of the disadvantaged groups during that time would have removed significant disparities between them and other groups in society. However, in 1969 the Twenty-third Amendment extended the affirmative-action measures until 1980. The Forty-fifth Amendment of 1980 extended them again until 1990, and in 1989 the Sixty-second Amendment extended the provisions until 2000. The Seventy-seventh Amendment of 1995 further strengthened the states' authority to reserve government-service positions for Scheduled Caste and Scheduled Tribe members.

Emergency Provisions and Authoritarian Powers

Part XVIII of the constitution permits the state to suspend various civil liberties and the application of certain federal principles during presidentially proclaimed states of emergency. The constitution provides for three categories of emergencies: a threat by "war or external aggression" or by "internal disturbances"; a "failure of constitutional machinery" in the country or in a state; and a threat to the financial security or credit of the nation or a part of it. Under the first two categories, the Fundamental Rights, with the exception of protection of life and personal liberty, may be suspended, and federal principles may be rendered inoperative. A proclamation of a state of emergency lapses after two months if not approved by both houses of Parliament. The president can issue a proclamation dissolving a state government if it can be determined, upon receipt of a report from a governor, that circumstances prevent the government of that state from maintaining law and order according to the constitution. This action establishes what is known as President's Rule because under such a proclamation the president can assume any or all functions of the state government; transfer the powers of the state legislature to Parliament; or take other measures necessary to achieve the objectives of the proclamation, including suspension, in whole or in part, of the constitution. A proclamation of President's Rule cannot interfere with the exercise of authority by the state's high court. Once approved, President's Rule normally lasts for six months, but it may be extended up to one year if Parliament approves. In exceptional cases, such as the violent revolt in Jammu and Kashmir during the early and mid-1990s, President's Rule has lasted for a period of more than five years.

President's Rule has been imposed frequently, and its use is often politically motivated. During the terms of prime ministers Nehru and Lal Bahadur Shastri, from 1947 to 1966, it was imposed ten times. Under Indira Gandhi's two tenures as prime minister (1966–77 and 1980–84), President's Rule was imposed forty-one times. Despite Mrs. Gandhi's frequent use of President's Rule, she was in office longer (187 months) than any other prime minister except Nehru (201 months). Other prime ministers also have been frequent users: Morarji Desai (eleven times in twenty-eight months), Chaudhury Charan Singh (five times in less than six months), Rajiv Gandhi (eight times in sixty-one months), Vishwanath Pratap (V.P.) Singh (two times in eleven months), Chandra Shekhar (four times in seven months), and P.V. Narasimha Rao (nine times in his first forty-two months in office).

State of emergency proclamations have been issued three times since independence. The first was in 1962 during the border war with China. Another was declared in 1971 when India went to war against Pakistan over the independence of East Pakistan, which became Bangladesh. In 1975 the third Emergency was imposed in response to an alledged threat by "internal disturbances" stemming from the political opposition to Indira Gandhi (see The Rise of Indira Gandhi, ch. 1; National-Level Agencies, ch. 10).

The Indian state has authoritarian powers in addition to the constitution's provisions for proclamations of Emergency Rule and President's Rule. The Preventive Detention Act was passed in 1950 and remained in force until 1970. Shortly after the start of the Emergency in 1962, the government enacted the Defence of India Act. This legislation created the Defence of India Rules, which allow for preventive detention of individuals who have acted or who are likely to act in a manner detrimental to public order and national security. The Defence of India Rules were reimposed during the 1971 war with Pakistan; they remained in effect after the end of the war and were invoked for a variety of uses not intended by their framers, such as the arrests made during a nationwide railroad strike in 1974.

The Maintenance of Internal Security Act promulgated in 1971 also provides for preventive detention. During the 1975–77 Emergency, the act was amended to allow the government to arrest individuals without specifying charges. The government arrested tens of thousands of opposition politicians under the Defence of India Rules and the Maintenance of Internal Security Act, including most of the leaders of the future Janata Party government (see Political Parties, this ch.).

Shortly after the Janata government came to power in 1977, Parliament passed the Forty-fourth Amendment, which revised the domestic circumstances cited in Article 352 as justifying an emergency from "internal disturbance" to "armed rebellion." During Janata rule, Parliament also repealed the Defence of India Rules and the Maintenance of Internal Security Act. However, after the Congress (I) returned to power in 1980, Parliament passed the National Security Act authorizing security forces to arrest individuals without warrant for suspicion of action that subverts national security, public order, and essential economic services. The Essential Services Maintenance Act of 1981 permits the government to prohibit strikes and lockouts in sixteen economic sectors providing critical goods and services. The Fifty-ninth Amendment, passed in 1988, restored "internal disturbance" in place of "armed rebellion" as just cause for the proclamation of an emergency.

The Sikh militant movement that spread through Punjab during the 1980s spurred additional authoritarian legislation (see Insurgent Movements and External Subversion, ch. 10). In 1984 Parliament passed the National Security Amendment Act enabling government security forces to detain prisoners for up to one year. The 1984 Terrorist Affected Areas (Special Courts) Ordinance provided security forces in Punjab with unprecedented powers of detention, and it authorized secret tribunals to try suspected terrorists. The 1985 Terrorist and Disruptive Activities (Prevention) Act imposed the death penalty for anyone convicted of terrorist actions that led to the death of others. It empowered authorities to tap telephones, censor mail, and conduct raids when individuals are alleged to pose a threat to the unity and sovereignty of the nation. The legislation renewing the act in 1987 provided for in camera trials, which may be presided over by any central government officer, and reversed the legal presumption of innocence if the government produces specific evidence linking a suspect to a terrorist act. In March 1988, the Fifty-ninth Amendment increased the period that an emergency can be in effect without legislative approval from six months to three years, and it eliminated the assurance of due process and protection of life and liberty with regard to Punjab found in articles 20 and 21. These rights were restored in 1989 by the Sixty-third Amendment.

By June 30, 1994, more than 76,000 persons throughout India had been arrested under the Terrorist and Disruptive

Activities (Prevention) Act. The act became widely unpopular, and the Rao government allowed the law to lapse in May 1995.

The Structure of Government

The union government, as India's central government is known, is divided into three distinct but interrelated branches: legislative, executive, and judicial (see fig. 14). As in the British parliamentary model, the leadership of the executive is drawn from and responsible to the legislative body. Although Article 50 stipulates the separation of the judiciary from the executive, the executive controls judicial appointments and many of the conditions of work. In addition, one of the more dramatic institutional battles in the Indian polity has been the struggle between elements wanting to assert legislative power to amend the constitution and those favoring the judiciary's efforts to preserve the constitution's basic structure.

The Legislature

Parliament consists of a bicameral legislature, the Lok Sabha (House of the People—the lower house) and the Rajya Sabha (Council of States—the upper house). Parliament's principal function is to pass laws on those matters that the constitution specifies to be within its jurisdiction. Among its constitutional powers are approval and removal of members of the Council of Ministers, amendment of the constitution, approval of central government finances, and delimitation of state and union territory boundaries (see State Governments and Union Territories, this ch.).

The president has a specific authority with respect to the function of the legislative branch (see The Executive, this ch.). The president is authorized to convene Parliament and must give his assent to all parliamentary bills before they become law. The president is empowered to summon Parliament to meet, to address either house or both houses together, and to require attendance of all of its members. The president also may send messages to either house with respect to a pending bill or any other matter. The president addresses the first session of Parliament each year and must give assent to all provisions in bills passed.

Lok Sabha

The Lok Sabha in 1995 constitutionally had 545 seats. For a

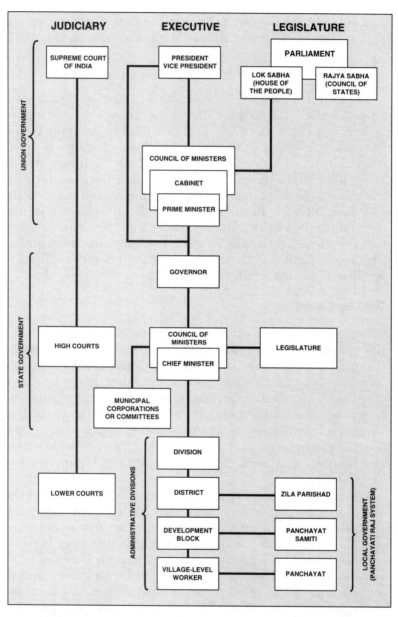

Source: Based on information from India, Ministry of Information and Broadcasting,
Research and Reference Division, *India, 1994: A Reference Annual*, New Delhi,
1995, 28–94.

Figure 14. Structure of the Government, 1995

variety of reasons, elections are sometimes not held in all constitutiencies, leaving some seats vacant and giving the appearance of fewer seats in the lower house. A member must be at least twenty-five years of age. Two members are nominated by the president as representatives of the Anglo-Indian community, and the rest are popularly elected. Elections are held on a one-stage, "first-past-the-post" system, similar to that in the United States. As in the United States, candidates from larger parties are favored because each constituency elects only the candidate winning the most votes. In the context of multiple-candidate elections, most members of Parliament are elected with pluralities of the vote that amount to less than a majority. As a result, political parties can gain commanding positions in the Parliament without winning the support of a majority of the electorate. For instance, Congress has dominated Indian politics without ever winning a majority of votes in parliamentary elections. The best-ever Congress performance in parliamentary elections was in 1984 when Congress (I) won 48 percent of the vote and garnered 76 percent of the parliamentary seats. In the 1991 elections, Congress (I) won 37.6 percent of the vote and 42 percent of the seats.

The usual Lok Sabha term is five years. However, the president may dissolve the house and call for new elections should the government lose its majority in Parliament. Elections must be held within six months after Parliament is dissolved. The prime minister can choose electorally advantageous times to recommend the dissolution of Parliament to the president in an effort to maximize support in the next Parliament. The term of Parliament can be extended in yearly increments if an emergency has been proclaimed. This situation occurred in 1976 when Parliament was extended beyond its five-year term under the Emergency proclaimed the previous year. The constitution stipulates that the Lok Sabha must meet at least twice a year, and no more than six months can pass between sessions. The Lok Sabha customarily meets for three sessions a year. The Council of Ministers is responsible only to the Lok Sabha, and the authority to initiate financial legislation is vested exclusively in the Lok Sabha.

The powers and authority of the Lok Sabha and the Rajya Sabha are not differentiated. The index of the constitution, for example, has a lengthy list of the powers of Parliament but not for each separate house. The key differences between the two houses lie in their disparate authority in the legislative process.

443

Rajya Sabha

The Rajya Sabha has a maximum of 250 members. All but twelve are elected by state and territory legislatures for six-year terms. Members must be at least thirty years old. The president nominates up to twelve members on the basis of their special knowledge or practical experience in fields such as literature, science, art, and social service. No further approval of these nominations is required by Parliament. Elections are staggered so that one-third of the members are elected every two years. The number of seats allocated to each state and territory is determined on the basis of relative population, except that smaller states and territories are awarded a larger share than their population justifies.

The Rajya Sabha meets in continuous session. It is not subject to dissolution as is the Lok Sabha. The Rajya Sabha is designed to provide stability and continuity to the legislative process. Although considered the upper house, its authority in the legislative process is subordinate to that of the Lok Sabha.

Legislative Process

The initiative for substantial legislation comes primarily from the prime minister, cabinet members, and high-level officials. Although all legislation except financial bills can be introduced in either house, most laws originate in the Lok Sabha. A legislative proposal may go through three readings before it is voted on. After a bill has been passed by the originating house, it is sent to the other house, where it is debated and voted on. The second house can accept, reject, or amend the bill. If the bill is amended by the second house, it must be returned to the originating house in its amended form. If a bill is rejected by the second house, if there is disagreement about the proposed amendments, or if the second house fails to act on a bill for six months, the president is authorized to summon a joint session of Parliament to vote on the bill. Disagreements are resolved by a majority vote of the members of both houses present in a joint session. This procedure favors the Lok Sabha because it has more than twice as many members as the Rajya Sabha.

When the bill has been passed by both houses, it is sent to the president, who can refuse assent and send the bill back to Parliament for reconsideration. If both houses pass it again, with or without amendments, it is sent to the president a second time. The president is then obliged to assent to the legislation. After receiving the president's assent, a bill becomes an act on the statute book.

The legislative procedure for bills involving taxing and spending—known as money bills—is different from the procedure for other legislation. Money bills can be introduced only in the Lok Sabha. After the Lok Sabha passes a money bill, it is sent to the Rajya Sabha. The upper house has fourteen days to act on the bill. If the Rajya Sabha fails to act within fourteen days, the bill becomes law. The Rajya Sabha may send an amended version of the bill back to the Lok Sabha, but the latter is not bound to accept these changes. It may pass the original bill again, at which point it will be sent to the president for his signature.

During the 1950s and part of the 1960s, Parliament was often the scene of articulate debate and substantial revisions of legislation. Prime ministers Indira Gandhi, Rajiv Gandhi, and P.V. Narasimha Rao, however, showed little enthusiasm for parliamentary debate. During the 1975–77 Emergency, many members of Parliament from the opposition as well as dissidents within Indira's own party were arrested, and press coverage of legislative proceedings was censored. It is generally agreed that the quality of discourse and the expertise of members of Parliament have declined since the 1960s. An effort to halt the decline of Parliament through a reformed committee system giving Parliament new powers of oversight over the executive branch has had very limited impact.

Under the constitution, the division of powers between the union government and the states is delimited into three lists: the Union List, the State List, and the Concurrent List. Parliament has exclusive authority to legislate on any of the ninety-seven items on the Union List. The list includes banking, communications, defense, foreign affairs, interstate commerce, and transportation. The State List includes sixty-seven items that are under the exclusive jurisdiction of state legislatures, including agriculture, local government, police, public health, public order, and trade and commerce within the state. The central—or union—government and state governments exercise concurrent jurisdiction over forty-four items on the Concurrent List, including criminal law and procedure, economic and social planning, electricity, factories, marriage and divorce, price control, social security and social insurance, and trade unions. The purpose of the Concurrent List is to secure legal and administrative unity throughout the country. Laws passed by Parliament relevant to Concurrent List areas take precedence over laws passed by state legislatures.

The Executive

The executive branch is headed by the president, in whom the constitution vests a formidable array of powers. The president serves as head of state and the supreme commander of the armed forces. The president appoints the prime minister, cabinet members, governors of states and territories, Supreme Court and high court justices, and ambassadors and other diplomatic representatives. The president is also authorized to issue ordinances with the force of acts of Parliament when Parliament is not in session. The president can summon and prorogue Parliament as well as dissolve the Lok Sabha and call for new elections. The president also can dismiss state and territory governments. Exercise of these impressive powers has been restricted by the convention that the president acts on the advice of the prime minister. In 1976 the Forty-second Amendment formally required the president to act according to the advice of the Council of Ministers headed by the prime minister. The spirit of the arrangement is reflected in Ambedkar's statement that the president "is head of the State but not of the Executive. He represents the nation but does not rule the nation." In practice, the president's role is predominantly symbolic and ceremonial, roughly analogous to the president of Germany or the British monarch.

The president is elected for a five-year term by an electoral college consisting of the elected members of both houses of Parliament and the elected members of the legislative assemblies of the states and territories. The participation of state and territory assemblies in the election is designed to ensure that the president is chosen to head the nation and not merely the majority party in Parliament, thereby placing the office above politics and making the incumbent a symbol of national unity.

Despite the strict constraints placed on presidential authority, presidential elections have shaped the course of Indian politics on several occasions, and presidents have exercised important power, especially when no party has a clear parliamentary majority. The presidential election of 1969, for example, turned into a dramatic test of strength for rival factions when Prime Minister Indira Gandhi put up an opponent to the official Congress candidate. The electoral contest contributed to the subsequent split of the Congress. In 1979, after the Ja-

India's Parliament, New Delhi
Courtesy Robert L. Worden

nata Party began to splinter, President Neelam Sanjiva Reddy
(1977–82) first selected Janata member Chaudhury Charan
Singh as prime minister (1979–80) to form a minority government and then dissolved Parliament and called for new elections while ignoring Jagjivan Ram's claim that he could
assemble a stable government and become the country's first
Scheduled Caste prime minister.

Tensions between President Giani Zail Singh (1982–87) and
Prime Minister Rajiv Gandhi (1984–88) also illustrate the
potential power of the president. In 1987 Singh refused to sign
the Indian Post Office (Amendment) Bill, thereby preventing
the government from having the authority to censor personal
mail. Singh's public suggestion that the prime minister had not
treated the office of the president with proper dignity and the
persistent rumors that Singh was plotting the prime minister's
ouster contributed to the erosion of public confidence in Rajiv
Gandhi that ultimately led to his defeat in the 1989 elections.
In November 1990, President Ramaswami Venkataraman
(1987–92) selected Chandra Shekhar as India's eleventh prime
minister, even though Chandra Shekhar's splinter Samajwadi
Janata Dal held only fifty-eight seats in the Lok Sabha. Chandra

Shekhar resigned in June 1991 when the Congress (I) withdrew its support.

In the same manner as the president, the vice president is elected by the electoral college for a five-year term. The vice president is ex officio chairman of the Rajya Sabha and acts as president when the latter is unable to discharge his duties because of absence, illness, or any other reason or until a new president can be elected (within six months of the vacancy) when a vacancy occurs because of death, resignation, or removal. There have been three instances since 1969 of the vice president serving as acting president.

The prime minister is by far the most powerful figure in the government. After being selected by the president, typically from the party that commands the plurality of seats in Parliament, the prime minister selects the Council of Ministers from other members of Parliament who are then appointed by the president. Individuals who are not members of Parliament may be appointed to the Council of Ministers if they become a member of Parliament either through election or appointment within six months of selection. The Council of Ministers is composed of cabinet ministers (numbering seventeen, representing thirty-one portfolios in 1995), ministers of state (forty-five, representing fifty-three portfolios in 1995), and deputy ministers (the number varies). Cabinet members are selected to accommodate different regional groups, castes, and factions within the ruling party or coalition as well as with an eye to their administrative skills and experience. Prime ministers frequently retain key ministerial portfolios for themselves.

Although the Council of Ministers is formally the highest policy-making body in the government, its powers have declined as influence has been increasingly centralized in the Office of the Prime Minister, which is composed of the top-ranking administrative staff. After the Congress split to form the Congress (R)—R for Requisition—and the Congress (O)—O for Organisation—in 1969, Indira Gandhi (who headed the Congress (R)) increasingly concentrated decision-making authority in the Office of the Prime Minister. When Rajiv Gandhi became prime minister in 1984, he promised to delegate more authority to his cabinet members. However, power rapidly shifted back to the Office of the Prime Minister and a small coterie of Rajiv's personal advisers. Rajiv's dissatisfaction with his cabinet ministers became manifest in his incessant reshuffling of his cabinet. During his five years in office, he changed his cabinet thirty-six times, about once every seven weeks. When P.V. Narasimha Rao became prime minister in June 1991, he decentralized power, giving Minister of Finance Manmohan Singh, in particular, a large measure of autonomy to develop a program for economic reform. After a year in office, Rao began again to centralize authority, and by the end of 1994, the Office of the Prime Minister had grown to be as powerful as it ever was under Rao's predecessors. As of August 1995, Rao himself held the portfolios in thirteen ministries, including those of defense, industry, and Kashmir affairs.

The Judiciary

Supreme Court

The Supreme Court is the ultimate interpreter of the constitution and the laws of the land. It has appellate jurisdiction over all civil and criminal proceedings involving substantial issues concerning the interpretation of the constitution. The court has the original and exclusive jurisdiction to resolve disputes between the central government and one or more states and union territories as well as between different states and union territories. And the Supreme Court is also empowered to issue advisory rulings on issues referred to it by the president. The Supreme Court has wide discretionary powers to hear special appeals on any matter from any court except those of the armed services. It also functions as a court of record and supervises every high court.

Twenty-five associate justices and one chief justice serve on the Supreme Court. The president appoints the chief justice. Associate justices are also appointed by the president after consultation with the chief justice and, if the president deems necessary, with other associate justices of the Supreme Court and high court judges in the states. The appointments do not require Parliament's concurrence. Justices may not be removed from office until they reach mandatory retirement at age sixty-five unless each house of Parliament passes, by a vote of two-thirds of the members in attendance and a majority of its total membership, a presidential order charging "proved misbehavior or incapacity."

The contradiction between the principles of parliamentary sovereignty and judicial review that is embedded in India's constitution has been a source of major controversy over the years. After the courts overturned state laws redistributing land from zamindar (see Glossary) estates on the grounds that the laws violated the zamindars' Fundamental Rights, Parliament passed the first (1951), fourth (1955), and seventeenth amendments (1964) to protect its authority to implement land redistribution. The Supreme Court countered these amendments in 1967 when it ruled in the *Golaknath v State of Punjab* case that Parliament did not have the power to abrogate the Fundamental Rights, including the provisions on private property. On February 1, 1970, the Supreme Court invalidated the government-sponsored Bank Nationalization Bill that had been passed by Parliament in August 1969. The Supreme Court also rejected as unconstitutional a presidential order of September 7, 1970, that abolished the titles, privileges, and privy purses of the former rulers of India's old princely states.

In reaction to Supreme Court decisions, in 1971 Parliament passed the Twenty-fourth Amendment empowering it to amend any provision of the constitution, including the Fundamental Rights; the Twenty-fifth Amendment, making legislative decisions concerning proper land compensation nonjusticiable; and the Twenty-sixth Amendment, which added a constitutional article abolishing princely privileges and privy purses. On April 24, 1973, the Supreme Court responded to the parliamentary offensive by ruling in the *Keshavananda Bharati v the State of Kerala* case that although these amendments were constitutional, the court still reserved for itself the discretion to reject any constitutional amendments passed by Parliament by declaring that the amendments cannot change the constitution's "basic structure."

During the 1975–77 Emergency, Parliament passed the Forty-second Amendment in January 1977, which essentially abrogated the *Keshavananda* ruling by preventing the Supreme Court from reviewing any constitutional amendment with the exception of procedural issues concerning ratification. The Forty-second Amendment's fifty-nine clauses stripped the Supreme Court of many of its powers and moved the political system toward parliamentary sovereignty. However, the Forty-third and Forty-fourth amendments, passed by the Janata government after the defeat of Indira Gandhi in March 1977, reversed these changes. In the *Minerva Mills* case of 1980, the Supreme Court reaffirmed its authority to protect the basic structure of the constitution. However, in the *Judges Transfer* case on December 31, 1981, the Supreme Court upheld the

President Shankar Dayal Sharma
Courtesy Embassy of India,
Washington

government's authority to dismiss temporary judges and transfer high court justices without the consent of the chief justice.

The Supreme Court continued to be embroiled in controversy in 1989, when its US$470 million judgment against Union Carbide for the Bhopal catastrophe resulted in public demonstrations protesting the inadequacy of the settlement (see The Growth of Cities, ch. 5). In 1991 the first-ever impeachment motion against a Supreme Court justice was signed by 108 members of Parliament. A year later, a high-profile inquiry found Associate Justice V. Ramaswamy "guilty of willful and gross misuses of office . . . and moral turpitude by using public funds for private purposes and reckless disregard of statutory rules" while serving as chief justice of Punjab and Haryana. Despite this strong indictment, Ramaswamy survived parliamentary impeachment proceedings and remained on the Supreme Court after only 196 members of Parliament, less than the required two-thirds, voted for his ouster.

During 1993 and 1994, the Supreme Court took measures to bolster the integrity of the courts and protect civil liberties in the face of state coercion. In an effort to avoid the appearance of conflict of interest in the judiciary, Chief Justice Manepalli Narayanrao Venkatachaliah initiated a controversial model code of conduct for judges that required the transfer of high court judges having children practicing as attorneys in their courts. Since 1993, the Supreme Court has implemented a policy to compensate the victims of violence while in police custody. On April 27, 1994, the Supreme Court issued a ruling that enhanced the rights of individuals placed under arrest by stipulating elaborate guidelines for arrest, detention, and interrogation.

High Courts

There are eighteen high courts for India's twenty-five states, six union territories, and one national capital territory. Some high courts serve more than one state or union territory. For example, the high court of the union territory of Chandigarh also serves Punjab and Haryana, and the high court in Gauhati (in Meghalaya) serves Assam, Nagaland, Meghalaya, Mizoram, Manipur, Tripura, and Arunachal Pradesh. As part of the judicial system, the high courts are institutionally independent of state legislatures and executives. The president appoints state high court chief justices after consulting with the chief justice of the Supreme Court and the governor of the state. The president also consults with the chief justice of the state high court before he appoints other high court justices. Furthermore, the president may also exercise the right to transfer high court justices without consultation. These personnel matters are becoming more politicized as chief ministers of states endeavor to exert their influence with New Delhi and the prime minister exerts influence over the president to secure politically advantageous appointments.

Each high court is a court of record exercising original and appellate jurisdiction within its respective state or territory. It also has the power to issue appropriate writs in cases involving constitutionally guaranteed Fundamental Rights. The high court supervises all courts within its jurisdiction, except for those dealing with the armed forces, and may transfer constitutional cases to itself from subordinate courts (see Criminal Law and Procedure, ch. 10). The high courts have original jurisdiction on revenue matters. They try original criminal cases by a jury, but not civil cases.

Lower Courts

States are divided into districts (*zillas*), and within each a judge presides as a district judge over civil cases. A sessions judge presides over criminal cases. The judges are appointed

The Supreme Court, New Delhi
Courtesy Robert L. Worden

by the governor in consultation with the state's high court. District courts are subordinate to the authority of their high court.

There is a hierarchy of judicial officials below the district level. Many officials are selected through competitive examination by the state's public service commission. Civil cases at the subdistrict level are filed in *munsif* (subdistrict) courts. Lesser criminal cases are entrusted to the courts of subordinate magistrates functioning under the supervisory authority of a district magistrate. All magistrates are under the supervision of the high court. At the village level, disputes are frequently resolved by *panchayats* or *lok adalats* (people's courts).

The judicial system retains substantial legitimacy in the eyes of many Indians despite its politicization since the 1970s. In fact, as illustrated by the rise of social action litigation in the 1980s and 1990s, many Indians turn to the courts to redress grievances with other social and political institutions. It is frequently observed that Indians are highly litigious, which has contributed to a growing backlog of cases. Indeed, the Supreme Court was reported to have more than 150,000 cases pending in 1990, the high courts had some 2 million cases pending, and the lower courts had a substantially greater backlog. Research findings in the early 1990s show that the backlogs at levels below the Supreme Court are the result of delays in the litigation process and the large number of decisions that are appealed and not the result of an increase in the number of new cases filed. Coupled with public perceptions of politicization, the growing inability of the courts to resolve disputes expeditiously threatens to erode the remaining legitimacy of the judicial system.

Election Commission

Article 324 of the constitution establishes an independent Election Commission to supervise parliamentary and state elections. Supervising elections in the world's largest democracy is by any standard an immense undertaking. Some 521 million people were eligible to vote in 1991. Efforts are made to see that polling booths are situated no more than two kilometers from a voter's place of residence. In 1991, this objective required some 600,000 polling stations for the country's 3,941 state legislative assembly and 543 parliamentary constituencies. To attempt to ensure fair elections, the Election Commission deployed more than 3.5 million officials, most of whom were temporarily seconded from the government bureaucracy, and 2 million police, paramilitary, and military forces.

Over the years, the Election Commission's enforcement of India's remarkably strict election laws grew increasingly lax. As a consequence, candidates flagrantly violated laws limiting campaign expenditures. Elections became increasingly violent (350 persons were killed during the 1991 campaign, including five Lok Sabha and twenty-one state assembly candidates), and voter intimidation and fraud proliferated.

The appointment of T.N. Seshan as chief election commissioner in 1991 reinvigorated the Election Commission and curbed the illegal manipulation of India's electoral system. By cancelling or repolling elections where improprieties had occurred, disciplining errant poll officers, and fighting for the right to deploy paramilitary forces in sensitive areas, Seshan forced candidates to take the Election Commission's code of conduct seriously and strengthened its supervisory machinery. In Uttar Pradesh, where more than 100 persons were killed in the 1991 elections, Seshan succeeded in reducing the number killed to two in the November 1993 assembly elections by enforcing compulsory deposit of all licensed firearms, banning unauthorized vehicular traffic, and supplementing local police with paramilitary units. In state assembly elections in Andhra Pradesh, Goa, Karnataka, and Sikkim, after raising ceilings for campaign expenditures to realistic levels, Seshan succeeded in getting candidates to comply with these limits by deploying 336 audit officers to keep daily accounts of the candidates' election expenditures. Although Seshan has received enthusiastic support from the public, he has stirred great controversy among the country's politicians. In October 1993, the Supreme Court issued a ruling that confirmed the supremacy of the chief election commissioner, thereby deflecting an effort to rein in Seshan by appointing an additional two election commissioners. Congress (I)'s attempt to curb Seshan's powers through a constitutional amendment was foiled after a public outcry weakened its support in Parliament.

State Governments and Territories

India has twenty-five states, six union territories, and one national capital territory, with populations ranging from 406,000 (Sikkim) to 139 million (Uttar Pradesh). Ten states each have more than 40 million people, making them country-like in significance (see Structure and Dynamics, ch. 2). There are eighteen official Scheduled Languages (see Glossary), clearly defined since the reorganization of states along linguistic lines in the 1950s and 1960s (see The Social Context of Languages, ch. 4). Social structures within states vary considerably, and they encompass a great deal of cultural diversity, as those who have watched India's Republic Day (January 26) celebrations will attest (see Larger Kinship Groups, ch. 5).

The constitution provides for a legislature in each state and territory. Most states have unicameral legislatures, but Andhra Pradesh, Bihar, Jammu and Kashmir, Maharashtra, Tamil Nadu, and Uttar Pradesh have bicameral legislatures. The lower house, known as the *vidhan sabha,* or legislative assembly, is the real seat of legislative power. Where an upper house exists, it is known as the *vidhan parishad,* or legislative council; council functions are advisory, and any objections expressed to a bill may be overridden if the assembly passes the bill a second time. Members of the assembly serve five-year terms after being chosen by direct elections from local constituencies. Their numbers vary, from a minimum of sixty to a maximum of 500. Members of the council are selected through a combination of direct election, indirect election, and nomination. Their six-year terms are staggered so that one-third of the membership is renewed every two years. Whether in the upper or lower house, membership in the assembly has come to reflect the predominantly rural demography of most states and the distribution of social power resulting from the state's agrarian and caste structures.

The structure of state governments is similar to that of the central government. In the executive branch, the governor plays a role analogous to that of the president, and the elected chief minister presides over a council of ministers drawn from the legislature in a manner similar to the prime minister. Many of the governor's duties are honorific; however, the governor also has considerable power. Like the president, the governor selects who may attempt to form a government; he may also dismiss a state's government and dissolve its legislative assembly. All bills that the state legislature passes must receive the assent of the governor. The governor may return bills other than money bills to the assembly. The governor may also decide to send a bill for consideration to the president, who has the power to promulgate ordinances. The governor may also recommend to the president that President's Rule be invoked. Governors are appointed to office for a five-year term by the president on the advice of the prime minister, and their conduct is supposed to be above politics.

Since 1967 most state legislatures have come under the control of parties in opposition to the majority in Parliament, and governors have frequently acted as agents of the ruling party in New Delhi. Increasingly, governors are appointed more for their loyalty to the prime minister than for their distinguished achievements and discretion. The politicization of gubernatorial appointments has become such a widespread practice that in 1989, shortly after the National Front government replaced the Congress (I) government, Prime Minister V.P. Singh (1989–90) asked eighteen governors to resign so that he could replace them with his own choices. Governors not only attempt to keep opposition state governments in line, but also, while keeping the state bureaucracy in place, have exercised their power to dismiss the chief minister and his or her council of ministers.

The strength of the central government relative to the states is especially apparent in constitutional provisions for central intervention into state jurisdictions. Article 3 of the constitution authorizes Parliament, by a simple majority vote, to establish or eliminate states and union territories or change their boundaries and names. The emergency powers granted to the central government by the constitution enable it, under certain circumstances, to acquire the powers of a unitary state. The central government can also dismiss a state government through President's Rule. Article 249 of the constitution enables a two-thirds vote of the Rajya Sabha to empower Parliament to pass binding legislation for any of the subjects on the State List. Articles 256 and 257 require states to comply with laws passed by Parliament and with the executive authority of the central government. The articles empower the central government to issue directives instructing states on compliance in these matters. Article 200 also enables a state governor, under certain circumstances, to refuse to give assent to bills passed by the state legislature and instead refer them to the president for review.

The central government exerts control over state governments through the financial resources at its command. The central government distributes taxes and grants-in-aid through the decisions of finance commissions, usually convened every five years as stipulated by Article 275. The central government also distributes substantial grants through its development plans as elaborated by the Planning Commission. The dependence of state governments on grants and disbursements grew throughout the 1980s as states began to run up fiscal deficits and the share of transfers from New Delhi increased. The power and influence of central government finances also can be seen in the substantial funds allocated under the central government's five-year plans to such areas as public health and agriculture that are constitutionally under the State List (see Health Care, ch. 2; Development Programs, ch. 7).

Besides its twenty-five states, India has seven centrally supervised territories. Six are union territories; one is the National Capital Territory of Delhi. Jurisdictions for territories are smaller than states and less populous. The central government administers union territories through either a lieutenant governor or a chief commissioner who is appointed by the president on the advice of the prime minister. Each territory also has a council of ministers, a legislature, and a high court; however, Parliament may also pass legislation on issues in union territories that in the case of states are usually reserved for state assemblies. The Sixty-ninth Amendment, passed in December 1991, made Delhi the national capital territory effective February 1, 1992. Although not having the same status as statehood, Delhi was given the power of direct election of members of its legislative assembly and the power to pass its own laws.

Local Government

The district is the principal subdivision within the state (union territories are not subdivided). There are 476 districts in India; the districts vary in size and population. The average size of a district is approximately 4,300 square kilometers, and the average population numbered nearly 1.8 million in the early 1990s. The district collector, a member of the Indian Administrative Service, is the preeminent official in the district (see The Civil Service, this ch.). During the colonial period, the collector was responsible for collecting revenue and maintaining law and order. In the 1990s, the collector's role in most states is confined to heading the district revenue department and coordinating the efforts of the other departments, such as agriculture, irrigation, public works, forestry, and public health, that are responsible for promoting economic development and social welfare.

Districts are subdivided into *taluqs* or *tehsils*, areas that contain from 200 to 600 villages. The *taluqdar* or *tehsildar*, who serves in much the same capacity as the collector, is the chief member of the *taluq* revenue department and is the preeminent official at this level. Economic development and social welfare departments are also likely to have offices at the *taluq* level. Although the revenue department may have village representatives, generally known as *patwaris* (village record-keepers), to maintain land records, the development and welfare departments generally do not have offices below the *taluq* level.

Article 40 of the constitution directs the government to establish *panchayats* to serve as institutions of local self-government. Most states began implementing this Directive Principle along the lines of the recommendations of the government's Balwantrai Mehta Commission report. According to these recommendations, the popularly elected village council (*gram panchayat*) is the basic unit. Village council chairs, elected by the

The Vidhana Saudha, the seat of the Karnataka state legislature, Bangalore
Courtesy Robert L. Worden

members of the village council, serve as members of the block council (*panchayat samiti*). A block is a large subunit of a district. In some states, blocks are coterminous with *taluqs* or *tehsils*. In other states, *taluqs* or *tehsils* are divided into blocks. The district council (*zilla parishad*) is the top level of the system. Its jurisdiction includes all village and block councils within a district. Its membership includes the block council chairs.

Deficient in funds and authority, the *panchayats* in most states were largely inactive until the late 1970s. However, efforts were then initiated to reinvigorate the *panchayats*. West Bengal led the way by transferring substantial funds and authority over rural development projects to the *panchayats* and then holding popular elections for *panchayat* representatives at all three levels in which political parties were allowed to field candidates for the first time. In the mid-1980s, the state of Karnataka also made important efforts to revive the *panchayats*.

In 1989 Rajiv Gandhi's government took two major initiatives designed to enhance the *panchayats'* role in local government and economic development. It initiated the Jawahar Employment Plan (Jawahar Rozgar Yojana), which provided funding directly to village councils to create jobs for the unem-

459

ployed through public works projects. Rajiv Gandhi's government also proposed the Sixty-fourth Amendment Bill to make it mandatory for all states to establish a three-tiered (village, block, and district) system of *panchayats* in which representatives would be directly elected for five-year terms. *Panchayats* were to be given expanded authority and funding over local development efforts. Despite the popular appeal of transferring power to *panchayats*, the Sixty-fourth Amendment Bill was rejected by the Rajya Sabha. Its hasty introduction in an election year made it appear to be a popular gimmick. Opposition to the bill also arose from those who feared that the transfer of authority from state governments to *panchayats* was designed to reduce the power of state legislatures under opposition control and promote "greater centralization through decentralization" by enabling the central government to establish direct relations with *panchayats*.

On December 22, 1992, the Congress (I) government passed the Seventy-third Amendment, which gave *panchayats* constitutional status (previously *panchayat* matters were considered a state subject). The amendment also institutionalized a three-tiered system of *panchayats* (except for states with a population of less than 2 million), with *panchayats* at the village, block, and district levels. The amendment also stipulated that all *panchayat* members be elected for five-year terms in elections supervised by state election commissions.

The 26 percent of the population living in urban areas are governed by municipal corporations and municipal councils. The municipal corporations governing the larger cities are composed of elected councils and a president or mayor elected from within the council. The state governor appoints a commissioner who acts as the chief executive of the municipal corporation. The municipal councils administering the smaller cities have elected committees or boards. The municipal government is responsible for education, health, sanitation, safety, and maintaining roads and other public facilities. The country's municipal governments have long been troubled, in part because of their limited authority and lack of funds. The frequent intervention of state governments to suspend the activities of municipal administrations has also undermined them. For instance, state or union territory governments suspended the elected bodies of forty-four out of sixty-six municipal corporations in 1986. The Seventy-fourth Amendment was passed in December 1992 in order to revive municipal governments.

Among other things, it mandates that elections for municipal bodies must be held within six months of the date of their dissolution. The amendment also provides for financial review of the municipalities in order to enable recommendations concerning the distribution of proceeds from taxes, duties, tolls, and fees.

The Civil Service

During the colonial period, the British built up the elite Indian Civil Service, often referred to as the "steel frame" of the British Raj. Nehru and other leaders of the independence movement initially viewed the colonial civil service as an instrument of foreign domination, but by 1947 they had come to appreciate the advantages of having a highly qualified institutionalized administration in place, especially at a time when social tensions threatened national unity and public order.

The constitution established the Indian Administrative Service to replace the colonial Indian Civil Service and ensure uniform and impartial standards of administration in selected fields, promote effective coordination in social and economic development, and encourage a national point of view. In the early 1990s, this small elite accounted for fewer than 5,000 of the total 17 million central government employees. Recruits appointed by the Union Public Service Commission are university graduates selected through a rigorous system of written and oral examinations. In 1988 only about 150 out of a candidate pool of approximately 85,000 recruits received appointments in the Indian Administrative Service. Indian Administrative Service officers are primarily from the more affluent and educated classes. However, efforts to recruit women and individuals from the Scheduled Castes and Scheduled Tribes have enhanced the diversity of the civil service.

Recruits are trained as administrative generalists at an academy at Mussoorie (in Uttar Pradesh). After a period of apprenticeship and probation in the central and state governments, an Indian Administrative Service officer is assigned to increasingly more responsible positions, such as a district collector after six or seven years. Approximately 70 percent of all officers serve in state administrations; the rest serve in the central government.

A larger organization, the Central Public Services, staffs a broad variety of administrative bureaus ranging from the Indian Foreign Service to the Audits and Accounts Service and the Postal Service. The states (but not Delhi or the union territories) have independent services within their own jurisdictions that are regulated by local laws and public service commissions. The governor usually appoints members of the state public services upon the recommendation of the state public service commission. To a large extent, states depend upon nationwide bodies, such as the Indian Administrative Service and Indian Police Service, to staff top administrative posts.

Although the elite public services continue to command great prestige, their social status declined in the decades after independence. In the 1990s, India's most capable youths increasingly are attracted to private-sector employment where salaries are substantially higher. Public opinion of civil servants has also been lowered by popular perceptions that bureaucrats are unresponsive to public needs and are corrupt. Although the ranks of the civil service are filled with many dedicated individuals, corruption has been a growing problem as civil servants have become subject to intense political pressures.

The Political Process

The decline of the Congress (I) since the late 1980s has brought an end to the dominant single-party system that had long characterized India's politics. Under the old system, conflict within the Congress was often a more important political dynamic than was conflict between the Congress and the opposition. The Congress had set the political agenda and the opposition responded. A new party system, in which the Congress (I) is merely one of several major participants, was in place by 1989 (see fig. 15). As often as not in the mid-1990s, the Congress (I) seems to respond to the initiatives of other parties rather than set its own political agenda.

Elections

At least once every five years, India's Election Commission supervises one of the largest, most complex exercises of collective action in the world. India's elections in the 1990s involve overseeing an electorate of about 521 million voters who travel to nearly 600,000 polling stations to chose from some 8,950 candidates representing roughly 162 parties. The elections reveal much about Indian society. Candidates span a wide spectrum of backgrounds, including former royalty, cinema superstars, religious holy men, war heroes, and a growing number of

farmers. Campaigns utilize communications technologies ranging from the latest video van with two-way screens to the traditional rumor traveling by word of mouth. Increasing violence
also has come to characterize elections. In 1991, some 350 people, including former Prime Minister Rajiv Gandhi, four other
parliamentary candidates, and twenty-one candidates running
in state legislative assembly elections, were killed in election-
related violence.

Political Parties

India's party system is in the throes of historic change. The
1989 general elections brought the era of Congress dominance
to an end. Even though the Congress (I) regained power in
1991, it was no longer the pivot around which the party system
revolved. Instead, it represented just one strategy for organizing a political majority, and a declining one at that. While the
Congress (I) was encountering growing difficulties in maintaining its coalition of upper-caste elites, Muslims, Scheduled
Castes, and Scheduled Tribes, the BJP was endeavoring to organize a new majority around the appeal of Hindu nationalism.
The Janata Dal and the BSP, among others, were attempting to
fashion a new majority out of the increasingly assertive Backward Classes, Dalits, Scheduled Castes, Scheduled Tribes, and
religious minorities.

The Congress

The Congress has, by any standards, remarkable political
accomplishments to its credit. As the Indian National Congress, its guidance fashioned a nation out of an extraordinarily
heterogeneous ensemble of peoples. The party has played an
important role in establishing the foundations of perhaps the
most durable democratic political system in the developing
world. As scholars Francis Robinson and Paul R. Brass point
out, the Congress constituted one of the few political organizations in the annals of decolonialization to "make the transition
from being sole representative of the nationalist cause to being
just one element of a competitive party system."

The Congress dominated Indian politics from independence until 1967. Prior to 1967, the Congress had never won
less than 73 percent of the seats in Parliament. The party won
every state government election except two—most often exclusively, but also through coalitions—and until 1967 it never won

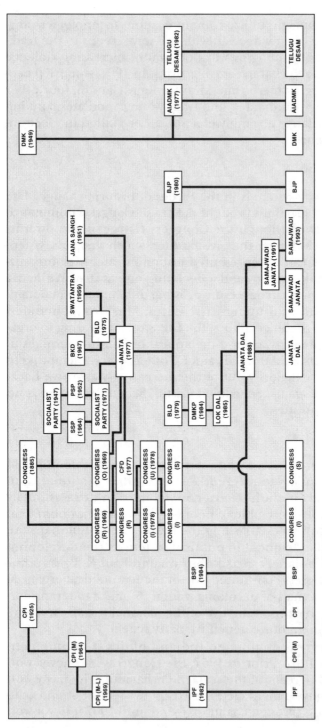

NOTE: For full party names—see Table A.

Source: Based on information from D.S. Lewis and D.J. Sagar, eds., *Political Parties of Asia and the Pacific: A Reference Guide*, Harlow, United Kingdom, 1992, 100–14; and Foreign Broadcast Information Service, *Daily Report: Near East and South Asia*, various dates, 1993–94.

Figure 15. Evolution of Major Political Parties, 1885–1994 (Simplified)

less than 60 percent of all elections for seats in the state legislative assemblies.

There were four factors that accounted for this dominance. First, the party acquired a tremendous amount of good will and political capital from its leadership of the nationalist struggle. Party chiefs gained substantial popular respect for the years in jail and other deprivations that they personally endured. The shared experience of the independence struggle fostered a sense of cohesion, which was important in maintaining unity in the face of the party's internal pluralism.

The second factor was that the Congress was the only party with an organization extending across the nation and down to the village level. The party's federal structure was based on a system of internal democracy that functioned to resolve disputes among its members and maintain party cohesion. Internal party elections also served to legitimate the party leadership, train party workers in the skills of political competition, and create channels of upward mobility that rewarded its most capable members.

A third factor was that the Congress achieved its position of political dominance by creating an organization that adjusted to local circumstances rather than transformed them, often reaching the village through local "big men" (*bare admi*) who controlled village "vote banks." These local elites, who owed their position to their traditional social status and their control over land, formed factions that competed for power within the Congress. The internal party democracy and the Congress's subsequent electoral success ultimately reinforced the local power of these traditional elites and enabled the party to adjust to changes in local balances of power. The nonideological pragmatism of local party leadership made it possible to coopt issues that contributed to opposition party success and even incorporate successful opposition leaders into the party. Intra-party competition served to channel information about local circumstances up the party hierarchy.

Fourth, patronage was the oil that lubricated the party machine. As the state expanded its development role, it accumulated more resources that could be distributed to party members. The growing pool of opportunities and resources facilitated the party's ability to accommodate conflict among its members. The Congress enjoyed the benefits of a "virtuous cycle," in which its electoral success gave it access to economic and political resources that enabled the party to attract new supporters.

The halcyon days of what Indian political scientist Rajni Kothari has called "the Congress system" ended with the general elections in 1967. The party lost seventy-eight seats in the Lok Sabha, retaining a majority of only twenty-three seats. Even more indicative of the Congress setback was its loss of control over six of the sixteen state legislatures that held elections. The proximate causes of the reversal included the failure of the monsoons in 1965 and 1966 and the subsequent hardship throughout northern and eastern India, and the unpopular currency devaluation in 1966. However, profound changes in India's polity also contributed to the decline of the Congress. The rapid growth of the electorate, which increased by 45 percent from 1952 to 1967, brought an influx of new voters less appreciative of the Congress's role in the independence movement. Moreover, the simultaneous spread of democratic values produced a political awakening that mobilized new groups and created a more pluralistic constellation of political interests. The development of new and more-differentiated identities and patterns of political cleavage made it virtually impossible for the Congress to contain the competition of its members within its organization. Dissidence and ultimately defection greatly weakened the Congress's electoral performance.

It was in this context that Indira Gandhi asserted her independence from the leaders of the party organization by attempting to take the party in a more populist direction. She ordered the nationalization of India's fourteen largest banks in 1969, and then she supported former labor leader and Acting President Varahagiri Venkata Giri's candidacy for president despite the fact that the party organization had already nominated the more conservative Neelam Sanjiva Reddy. After Giri's election, the party organization expelled Indira Gandhi from the Congress and ordered the parliamentary party to choose a new prime minister. Instead, 226 of the 291 Congress members of Parliament continued to support Indira Gandhi. The Congress split into two in 1969, the new factions being the Congress (O)—for Organisation—and Mrs. Gandhi's Congress (R)—for Requisition. The Congress (R) continued in power with the support of non-Congress groups, principally the Communist Party of India (CPI) and the Dravida Munnetra Kazhagam (DMK—Dravidian Progressive Federation).

With the Congress (O) controlling most of the party organization, Indira Gandhi adopted a new strategy to mobilize popular support. For the first time ever, she ordered parliamentary elections to be held separately from elections for the state government. This delinking was designed to reduce the power of the Congress (O)'s state-level political machines in national elections. Mrs. Gandhi traveled throughout the country, energetically campaigning on the slogan "*garibi hatao*" (eliminate poverty), thereby bypassing the traditional Congress networks of political support. The strategy proved successful, and the Congress (R) won a dramatic victory. In the 1971 elections for the Lok Sabha, the Congress (R) garnered 44 percent of the vote, earning it 352 seats. The Congress (O) won only sixteen seats and 10 percent of the vote. The next year, after leading India to victory over Pakistan in the war for Bangladesh's independence, Indira Gandhi and the Congress (R) further consolidated their control over the country by winning fourteen of sixteen state assembly elections and victories in 70 percent of all seats contested.

The public expected Indira Gandhi to deliver on her mandate to remove poverty. However, the country experienced a severe drought in 1971 and 1972, leading to food shortages, and the price of food rose 20 percent in the spring of 1973. The decision by the Organization of the Petroleum Exporting Countries (OPEC) to quadruple oil prices in 1973–74 also led to inflation and increased unemployment. Jayaprakash (J.P) Narayan, a socialist leader in the preindependence Indian National Congress who, after 1947, left to conduct social work in the Sarvodaya movement (*sarvodaya* means uplift of all), came out of retirement to lead what eventually became widely known as the "J.P. movement." Under Narayan's leadership, the movement toppled the government of Gujarat and almost brought down the government in Bihar; Narayan advocated a radical regeneration of public morality that he labelled "total revolution."

After the Allahabad High Court ruled that Mrs. Gandhi had committed electoral law violations and Narayan addressed a massive demonstration in New Delhi, at Indira Gandhi's behest, the president proclaimed an Emergency on June 25, 1975. That night, Indira Gandhi ordered the arrest of almost all the leaders of the opposition, including dissidents within the Congress. In all, more than 110,000 persons were detained without trial during the Emergency.

Indira Gandhi's rule during the Emergency alienated her popular support. After postponing elections for a year following the expiration of the five-year term of the Lok Sabha, she called for new elections in March 1977. The major opposition party leaders, many of whom had developed a rapport while they were imprisoned together under the Emergency regime, united under the banner of the Janata Party. By framing the key issue of the election as "democracy versus dictatorship," the Janata Party—the largest opposition party—appealed to the public's democratic values to rout the Congress (R). The vote share of the Congress (R) dropped to 34.5 percent, and the number of its seats in Parliament plunged from 352 to 154. Indira Gandhi lost her seat.

The inability of Janata Party factions to agree proved the party's undoing. Indira Gandhi returned to win the January 1980 elections after forming a new party, the Congress (I—for Indira), in 1978.

The Congress (I) largely succeeded in reconstructing the traditional Congress electoral support base of Brahmans (see Glossary), Muslims, Scheduled Castes, and Scheduled Tribes that had kept Congress in power in New Delhi during the three decades prior to 1977. The Congress (I)'s share of the vote increased by 8.2 percent to 42.7 percent of the total vote, and its number of seats in the Lok Sabha grew to 353, a majority of about two-thirds. This success approximated the levels of support of the Congress dominance from 1947 to 1967. Yet, as political scientist Myron Weiner observed, "The Congress party that won in 1980 was not the Congress party that had governed India in the 1950s and 1960s, or even the early 1970s. The party was organizationally weak and the electoral victory was primarily Mrs. Gandhi's rather than the party's." As a consequence, the Congress's appeal to its supporters was much more tenuous than it had been in previous decades.

Indira Gandhi's dependence on her flamboyant son Sanjay and, after his accidental death in 1980, on her more reserved son Rajiv gives testimony to the personalization and centralization of power within the Congress (I). Having developed a means to mobilize support without a party organization, she paid little attention to maintaining that support. Rather than allowing intraparty elections to resolve conflicts and select party leaders, Indira Gandhi preferred to fill party posts herself with those loyal to her. As a result, party leaders at the state level lost their legitimacy among the rank and file because their

Campaign advertisement for Youth Congress candidate, West Bengal
Courtesy India Abroad News Service

positions depended on the whims of Indira Gandhi rather than on the extent of their popular support. In addition, centralization and the demise of democracy within the party disrupted the flow of information about local circumstances to party leaders and curtailed the ability of the Congress (I) to adjust to social change and incorporate new leaders.

When Rajiv Gandhi took control after his mother's assassination in November 1984, he attempted to breathe new life into the Congress (I) organization. However, the massive electoral victory that the Congress (I) scored under Rajiv's leadership just two months after his mother's assassination gave him neither the skill nor the authority to succeed in this endeavor. Rajiv did, however, attempt to remove the more unsavory elements within the party organization. He denied nominations to one-third of the incumbent members of Parliament during the 1984 Lok Sabha campaign, and he refused to nominate two of every five incumbents in the state legislative assembly elections held in March 1985.

Another of Rajiv's early successes was the passage of the Anti-Defection Bill in January 1985 in an effort to end the bribery that lured legislators to cross partisan lines. Speaking at the Indian National Congress centenary celebrations in Bombay (officially called Mumbai as of 1995), Rajiv launched a vitriolic attack on the "culture of corruption" that had become so pervasive in the Congress (I). However, the old guard showed little enthusiasm for reform. As time passed, Rajiv's position was weakened by the losses that the party suffered in a series of state assembly elections and by his government's involvement in corruption scandals. Ultimately, Rajiv was unable to overcome the resistance within the party to internal elections and reforms. Ironically, as Rajiv's position within the party weakened, he turned for advice to many of the wheelers and dealers of his mother's regime whom he had previously banished.

The frustration of Rajiv Gandhi's promising early initiatives meant that the Congress (I) had no issues on which to campaign as the end of his five-year term approached. On May 15, 1989, just months before its term was to expire, the Congress (I) introduced amendments that proposed to decentralize government authority to *panchayat* and municipal government institutions. Opposition parties, many of whom were on record as favoring decentralization of government power, vehemently resisted the Congress (I) initiative. They charged that the initiative did not truly decentralize power but instead enabled the central government to circumvent state governments (many of which were controlled by the opposition) by transferring authority from state to local government and strengthening the links between central and local governments. After the Congress (I) failed to win the two-thirds vote required to pass the legislation in the Rajya Sabha on October 13, 1989, it called for new parliamentary elections and made *"jana shakti"* (power to the people) its main campaign slogan.

The Congress (I) retained formidable campaign advantages over the opposition. The October 17, 1989, announcement of elections took the opposition parties by surprise and gave them little time to form electoral alliances. The Congress (I) also blatantly used the government-controlled television and radio to promote Rajiv Gandhi. In addition, the Congress (I) campaign once again enjoyed vastly superior financing. It distributed some 100,000 posters and 15,000 banners to each of its 510 candidates. It provided every candidate with six or seven vehicles, and it commissioned advertising agencies to make a total of ten video films to promote its campaign.

The results of the 1989 elections were more of a rebuff to the Congress (I) than a mandate for the opposition. Although the Congress (I) remained the largest party in Parliament with

197 seats, it was unable to form a government. Instead, the Janata Dal, which had 143 seats, united with its National Front allies to form a minority government precariously dependent on the support of the BJP (eighty-five seats) and the communist parties (forty-five seats). Although the Congress (I) lost more than 50 percent of its seats in Parliament, its share of the vote dropped only from 48.1 percent to 39.5 percent of the vote. The Congress (I) share of the vote was still more than double that of the next largest party, the Janata Dal, which received support from 17.8 percent of the electorate. More grave for the long-term future of the Congress (I) was the erosion of vital elements of the traditional coalition of support for the Congress (I) in North India. Alienated by the Congress (I)'s cultivation of Hindu activists, Muslims defected to the Janata Dal in large numbers. The Congress (I) simultaneously lost a substantial share of Scheduled Caste voters to the BSP in Haryana, Madhya Pradesh, and Uttar Pradesh and to the Indian People's Front in Bihar.

To offset these losses, the Congress (I) attempted to play a "Hindu card." On August 14, 1989, the Supreme Court ruled that no parties or groups could disturb the status quo of the Babri Masjid, a sixteenth-century mosque in Ayodhya, Uttar Pradesh. The mosque was controversial because Hindu nationalists claim it was on the site of the birthplace of the Hindu god Ram and that, as such, the use by Muslims was sacrilegious (see Vishnu, ch. 3). Despite the court ruling, in September the Congress (I) entered into an agreement with the Vishwa Hindu Parishad (VHP—World Hindu Council), a conservative religious organization with close ties to Hindu nationalists, to allow the VHP to proceed with a ceremony to lay the foundation for the Ramjanmabhumi (birthplace of Ram) Temple. (The VHP had been working toward this goal since 1984.) In return, the Congress (I) secured the VHP's agreement to perform the ceremony on property adjacent to the Babri Masjid that was not in dispute. By reaching this agreement, the Congress (I) attempted to appeal to Hindu activists while retaining Muslim support. Rajiv Gandhi's decision to kick off his campaign less than six kilometers from the Babri Masjid and his appeal to voters that they vote for the Congress (I) if they wished to bring about "Ram Rajya" (the rule of Ram) were other elements of the Congress (I)'s strategy to attract the Hindu vote (see Political Issues, this ch.)

The 1991 elections returned the Congress (I) to power but did not reverse important trends in the party's decline. The Congress (I) won 227 seats, up from 197 in 1989, but its share of the vote dropped from 39.5 percent in 1989 to 37.6 percent. Greater division within the opposition rather than growing popularity of the Congress (I) was the key element in the party's securing an increased number of seats. Also troubling was the further decline of the Congress (I) in heavily popu- lated Bihar and Uttar Pradesh, which together account for more than 25 percent of all seats in Parliament. In Uttar Pradesh, the number of seats that the Congress (I) was able to win went down from fifteen to two, and its share of the vote dropped from 32 percent to 20 percent. In Bihar the seats won by the Congress (I) fell from four to one, and the Congress (I) share of the vote was reduced from 28 percent to 22 percent. The Congress (I) problems in these states, which until 1989 had been bastions of its strength, were reinforced by the party's poor showing in the November 1993 state elections. These elections were characterized by the further disintegration of the traditional Congress coalition, with Brahmans and other upper castes defecting to the BJP and Scheduled Castes and Muslims defecting to the Janata Dal, the Samajwadi Party (Socialist Party), and the BSP.

Strong evidence indicates that the Congress (I) would have fared significantly worse had it not been for the assassination of Rajiv Gandhi in the middle of the elections. A wave of sympathy similar to that which helped elect Rajiv after the assassination of his mother increased the Congress (I) support. In the round of voting that took place before Rajiv's death, the Congress (I) won only 26 percent of the seats and 33 percent of the vote. In the votes that occurred after Rajiv's death, the Congress (I) won 58 percent of the seats and 40 percent of the popular vote. It may also be that Rajiv's demise ended the "anti-Congressism" that had pervaded the political system as a result of his family's dynastic domination of Indian politics through its control over the Congress.

Rajiv Gandhi was assassinated by a Tamil suicide bomber affiliated with the Sri Lankan Liberation Tigers of Tamil Eelam (LTTE) during a political campaign in May 1991. Only after his assassination did hope for reforming the Congress (I) reap- pear. The end of three generations of Nehru-Gandhi family leadership left Rajiv's coterie of political manipulators in search of a new kingpin. The bankruptcy of the Congress (I) leadership was highlighted by the fact that they initially turned to Sonia Gandhi, Rajiv's Italian-born wife, to lead the party. Sonia's primary qualification was that she was Rajiv's widow. She had never held elected office and, during her early years in India, she had expressed great disdain for political life. However, although she did not assume a leadership role, she continued to be seen as a "kingmaker" in the Congress (I). Her advice was sought after, and she was called on to lead the party in the mid-1990s. An unusual public speech by Sonia Gandhi criticizing the government of P.V. Narasimha Rao in August 1995 further fueled speculation that she was a candidate for political leadership.

Sonia Gandhi's refusal in 1991 to become president of the Congress (I) led the mantle of party leadership to fall on Rao. Rao was a septuagenarian former professor who had retired from politics before the 1991 elections after undergoing heart-bypass surgery. Rao had a conciliatory demeanor and was acceptable to the party's contending factions. Paradoxically, the precariously positioned Rao was able to take more substantial steps in the direction of party reform than his predecessors. First, Rao had to demonstrate that he could mobilize popular support for himself and the party, a vital currency of power for any Congress (I) leader. He did so in the November 15, 1991, by-elections by winning his own seat in Andhra Pradesh unopposed and leading the party to victory in a total of eight of the fifteen parliamentary by-elections. By the end of 1991, Rao had succeeded in initiating the first intraparty elections in the Congress in almost twenty years. Although there was widespread manipulation by local party bosses, the elections enhanced the legitimacy of party leaders and held forth the prospect of a rejuvenated party organization. The process culminated in April 1992 at the All-India Congress (I) Committee at Tirupati, Andhra Pradesh, where elections were held for the ten vacant seats in the Congress Working Committee.

In the wake of the Tirupati session, Rao became less interested in promoting party democracy and more concerned with consolidating his own position. The change was especially apparent in the 1993 All-India Congress (I) Committee session at Surajkund (in Haryana), where Rao's supporters lavishly praised the prime minister and coercively silenced his opponents. However, Rao's image was damaged in July 1993 after Harshad Mehta, a stockbroker under indictment for allegedly playing a leading role in a US$2 billion stock scam in 1992, accused Rao of personally accepting a bribe that he had delivered on November 4, 1991. The extent of the press coverage of the charges and their apparent credibility among the public was evidence of the pervasive public cynicism toward politicians. Rao's stock in the party and Congress (I)'s position within Parliament were greatly weakened. On July 28, 1993, his government barely survived a no-confidence motion in the Lok Sabha. Rao's position was temporarily strengthened at the end of 1993 when he was able to cobble together a parliamentary majority. However, support for Rao and the Congress (I) declined again in 1994. The party was rocked by a scandal relating to the procurement of sugar stocks that cost the government an estimated Rs6.5 billion (US$210 million; for value of the rupee—see Glossary) and by losses in legislative assembly elections in Andhra Pradesh—Rao's home state, where he personally took control over the campaign—and Karnataka. The Congress (I) again lost in three of four major states in elections held in the spring of 1995. The political fallout in New Delhi was an increase in dissident activity within the Congress (I) led by former cabinet members Narain Dutt Tiwari and Arjun Singh and other Rao rivals who sought to split the Congress and form a new party.

Opposition Parties

Opposition to the Congress has always been fragmented. Opposition parties range from Hindu nationalist parties such as the BJP on the right to communist parties on the left (see table 33, Appendix). The divisiveness of the opposition, combined with the "first-past-the-post" electoral system, has enabled the Congress to dominate Indian politics without ever winning a majority of the vote from the national electorate. The extent of electoral alliances among the opposition is an important predictor of its ability to win seats in Parliament. The first two instances when the opposition succeeded in forming a government at the center occurred after it united under the Janata Party banner in 1977 and after the formation of the Janata Dal and the National Front in 1988. In each of these cases, the unity that was facilitated by anti-Congress sentiment prior to the elections collapsed in the face of rivalry and ambition once the opposition came into power.

The Rise and Decline of "Janata Politics"

Prior to 1967, the opposition was divided into an array of

Prime Minister P.V. Narasimha Rao
Courtesy Embassy of India, Washington

small parties. While the Congress garnered between 45 percent
and 48 percent of the vote, no opposition party gained as much
as 11 percent, and during the entire period, only two parties
won 10 percent. Furthermore, in each election, independent
candidates won between 12 percent and 20 percent of the vote.

The opposition's first significant attempt to achieve electoral
unity occurred during the 1967 elections when opposition
party alliances won control of their state governments in Bihar,
Kerala, Orissa, Punjab, and West Bengal. In Rajasthan an opposition coalition prevented the Congress from winning a majority in the state legislature and forced it to recruit independents
to form a government. The Congress electoral debacle encouraged even more dissidence within the party, and in a matter of
weeks after the elections, defections brought down Congress
governments in Haryana, Madhya Pradesh, and Uttar Pradesh.

By July 1967, state governments of two-thirds of the country were under opposition rule. However, opposition rule in many cases was short-lived. The aftermath of the 1967 elections initiated a climate of politics by defection in which the Congress, and to a lesser extent the opposition, attempted to overthrow governments by winning over their state legislators with promises of greater political power and outright bribes. Needless to say, this period seriously undermined the ability of most parties to discipline their members. The increase in opposition-ruled state governments after 1967 also prompted the Congress to use President's Rule to dismiss opposition-led state governments with increasing frequency (see Emergency Provisions and Authoritarian Powers, this ch.).

Although the centrist and right-wing opposition formed a "grand alliance" during the 1971 parliamentary elections, it was not until the general elections of 1977 that opposition efforts culminated in electoral success at the national level. Imprisoned together under the authoritarian measures of the Emergency, India's senior opposition leaders found their personal animosity toward Indira Gandhi and the Congress to be a powerful motivation to overcome their division and rivalry. In January 1977, opposition parties reactivated a pre-Emergency multiparty front, campaigned under the banner of the Janata Party, and won a dramatic electoral victory in March 1977. The Janata Party was made up of the Congress (O), the Jana Sangh, the Bharatiya Lok Dal (Indian People Party), the Samajwadi Party (Socialist Party), a handful of imprisoned Congress dissidents, and the Congress for Democracy—a group led by Scheduled Caste leader Jagjivan Ram that had splintered off from the Congress during the election campaign.

Despite the diversity of this assemblage of parties and the different social strata that they represented, members of the Janata Party achieved surprising ideological and programmatic consensus by passing a program stressing decentralization, development of rural industries, and employment opportunities. It was not ideology, but rather an inability to consolidate partisan organizations and political rivalry among the leadership that led to the demise of the Janata government in 1979. The Janata's three most senior leaders—Morarji Desai, Charan Singh, and Jagjivan Ram—each aspired to be prime minister. The rivalry continued during Desai's tenure (March 1977–July 1979). Desai, Charan Singh, and Ram continually conspired to discredit each other. Their connivances ultimately discredited the Janata Party and allowed the Congress (I) to return to power in 1980.

Just as key defections from the Congress were essential to the Janata electoral success in 1977, so too did V.P. Singh's defection from the Congress (I) in 1987 enable opposition factions from the Janata Party and Bharatiya Lok Dal to unite the Janata Dal in 1988. Regional parties, such as the Telugu Desam Party (Telugu National Party), the DMK, and the Asom Gana Parishad (AGP—Assam People's Assembly), together formed the National Front, led by Janata Dal, which defeated Rajiv Gandhi's Congress (I) in the 1989 parliamentary elections. With V.P. Singh as prime minister, the National Front government earned the appellation of "the crutch government" because it depended on the support of the Communist Party of India (Marxist—CPI (M)) on its left and the BJP on the right.

On August 7, 1990, V.P. Singh suddenly announced that his government would implement the recommendations of the Mandal Commission (see Glossary) to reserve 27 percent of central government jobs for the Backward Classes, defined to include around 52 percent of the population. Although Singh's Janata Dal had pledged to implement the Mandal Commission recommendations as part of its election manifesto, his announcement led to riots throughout North India. Some seventy-five upper-caste youths died after resorting to self-immolation to dramatize their opposition, and almost 200 others were killed in clashes with the police.

BJP president Lal Kishan (L.K.) Advani announced that he would traverse the country on a pilgrimage to Ayodhya where he would lead Hindu activists in the construction of the Ramjanmabhumi Temple on the site of the Babri Masjid. As the pilgrimage progressed, riots between Hindus and Muslims broke out throughout the country. The National Front government decided to end the agitation, and Janata Dal chief minister of Bihar, Laloo Prasad Yadav, arrested Advani on October 23, 1990. On October 30, religious militants attempted to storm the Babri Masjid despite a massive military presence, and as many as twenty-six activists were killed. The BJP's withdrawal of support for the National Front government proved fatal, and V.P. Singh lost a parliamentary vote of confidence on November 7, 1990.

Two days before the vote, Chandra Shekhar, an ambitious Janata Dal rival who had been kept out of the National Front government, joined with Devi Lal, a former deputy prime minister under V.P. Singh, to form the Samajwadi Janata Party—Samajwadi meaning socialist—with a total of sixty Lok Sabha members. The day after the collapse of the National Front government, Chandra Shekhar informed the president that by gaining the backing of the Congress (I) and its electoral allies he enjoyed the support of 280 members of the Lok Sabha, and he demanded the right to constitute a new government. Even though his rump party accounted for only one-ninth of the members of the Lok Sabha, Chandra Shekhar succeeded in forming a new minority government and becoming prime minister (with Devi Lal as deputy prime minister). However, Chandra Shekhar's government fell less than four months later, after the Congress (I) withdrew its support.

The Janata Dal and the Samajwadi Janata Party declined after the fall of the Chandra Shekhar government. In the May-June 1991 parliamentary elections, their share of the vote dropped from 17.8 percent to 15.1 percent, and the number of seats in Parliament that they won fell from 142 to sixty-one. The parties were able to win seats only in Bihar, Orissa, and Uttar Pradesh. The factional rivalry and ineffectiveness that impeded the National Front government's efforts to provide effective government tarnished the Janata Dal image. In the absence of strong national leadership, the party was rendered a confederation of ambitious regional leaders whose rivalry prevented the establishment of a united party organization. The Janata Dal's persistent backing of the Mandal Commission recommendations made the party highly unpopular among high-caste people in the middle and upper classes, creating fund-raising difficulties. Although the Janata Dal won state elections in Karnataka in 1994 and Bihar in the spring of 1995, its poor showing in most other states gave the impression that its support was receding to a few regional bastions.

The Bharatiya Janata Party and the Rise of Hindu Nationalism

The BJP is unique among India's political parties in that neither it nor its political predecessors were ever associated with the Congress. Instead, it grew out of an alternative nationalist organization—the Rashtriya Swayamsevak Sangh (RSS—National Volunteer Organisation). The BJP still is affiliated with the network of organizations popularly referred to as the RSS family. The RSS was founded in 1925 by Keshav Baliram Hedgewar. Until 1928 a member of the Congress with radical nationalist political leanings, Hedgewar had grown increasingly disenchanted with the leadership of Mahatma Gandhi. Hedgewar was particularly critical of Gandhi's emphasis on nonviolence and civil disobedience, which he felt discouraged the forceful political action necessary to gain independence. He established the RSS as an organization that would provide training in martial arts and spiritual matters to rejuvenate the spiritual life of the Hindu community and build its unity.

Hedgewar and his successor, M.S. Golwalkar, scrupulously endeavored to define the RSS's identity as a cultural organization that was not directly involved in politics. However, its rapidly growing membership and the paramilitary-like uniforms and discipline of its activists made the political potential of the RSS apparent to everyone on the political scene. There was considerable sentiment within the Congress that RSS members should be permitted to join, and, in fact, on October 7, 1947, the Congress Working Committee voted to allow in RSS members. But in November 1947, the Congress passed a rule requiring RSS members to give up their affiliation before joining. The RSS was banned in 1948 after Nathuram Godse, a former RSS member, assassinated Mahatma Gandhi. The ban was lifted in 1949 only after the RSS drafted an organizational constitution that was acceptable to the government. Intensely loyal RSS members refused to give up their affiliation to join the Congress and, instead, channeled their political energies to the Jana Sangh (People's Union) after its founding in 1951.

The Jana Sangh grew slowly during the 1950s and 1960s, despite the efforts of RSS members, who quickly took control of the party's organization. Although the Jana Sangh succeeded in displacing the Hindu Mahasabha (a communal party established in 1914 as a counter to Muslim separatists) as the preeminent party of Hindu activists in the Indian political system, it failed to develop into a major rival to the Congress. According to political scientist Bruce Graham, this failure occurred because of the Jana Sangh's inability "to transcend the limitations of its origins," in particular, its identification with the Hindi-speaking, northern heartland and its Brahmanical interpretation of Hinduism rather than the more inclusive and syncretic values of popular Hinduism. However, the experience of the Jana Sangh during the 1970s, especially its increasing resort to populism and agitational tactics, provided essential ingredients for the success of the BJP in the 1980s.

In 1977 the Jana Sangh joined the Janata Party, which defeated Indira Gandhi and the Congress (I) in parliamentary elections and formed a government through the end of 1979. The rapid expansion of the RSS under Janata rule soon brought calls for all members of the RSS family to merge with Janata Party affiliates. Ultimately, intraparty tensions impelled those affiliated with the Jana Sangh to leave the Janata Party and establish a new party—the BJP.

The BJP was formed in April 1980, under the leadership of Atal Behari Vajpayee. Although the party welcomed members of the RSS, the BJP's effort to draw from the legacies of the Janata Party as well as that of the Jana Sangh were suggested by its new name, its choice of a green and saffron flag similar to that of the Janata Party rather than the solid saffron flag of the old Jana Sangh, its adoption of a decentralized organizational structure along the lines of the Janata Party rather than the more centralized model of the Jana Sangh, and its inclusion in its working committee of several non-Jana Sangh individuals, including Sikandar Bakht—a Muslim. The invocation of Gandhian socialism as one of the guiding principles of the BJP rather than the doctrine of "integral humanism" associated with the Jana Sangh was another indication of the impact of the party members' experience in the Janata Party and "J.P. movement."

The new synthesis, however, failed to achieve political success. In 1984 the BJP won only two seats in the parliamentary elections. In the wake of the 1984 elections, the BJP shifted course. Advani replaced Vajpayee as party president. Under Advani's leadership, the BJP appealed to Hindu activists by criticizing measures it construed as pandering to minorities and advocating the repeal of the special status given to the Muslim majority state of Jammu and Kashmir. Simultaneously, it cooperated more closely with other RSS affiliates, particularly the VHP. During the 1980s, the BJP-VHP combine developed into a dynamic political force through its brilliant use of religious symbolism to rouse the passions of the public. The BJP and VHP attained national prominence through their campaign to convert back to Hinduism members of the Scheduled Castes who had converted to Islam. The VHP also agitated to reclaim the Babri Masjid site and encouraged villagers throughout the country to hold religious ceremonies to consecrate bricks made out of their own clay and send them to be used in the construction of the Ramjanmabhumi Temple in Ayodhya.

In the general elections of 1991, the BJP expanded its support more than did any other party. Its number of seats in the

Lok Sabha increased from eighty-five to 119, and its vote share grew from 11.4 percent to 21.0 percent. The party was particularly successful in Uttar Pradesh, where it increased its share of the vote from 7.6 percent (eight seats) in 1989 to 35.3 percent (fifty seats) in 1991, and in Gujarat, where its votes and seats climbed from 30 percent (twelve seats) to 52 percent (twenty seats). In addition, BJP support appeared to be spreading into new areas. In Karnataka, its vote rose from 2.6 percent to 28.1 percent, and in West Bengal the BJP's share of the vote expanded from 1.6 to 12.0 percent. However, the elections also revealed some of the limitations of the BJP juggernaut. Exit polls showed that while the BJP received more upper-caste support than all other parties and made inroads into the constituency of Backward Classes, it did poorly among Scheduled Castes and Scheduled Tribes, constituencies that it had long attempted to cultivate. In Himachal Pradesh, Madhya Pradesh, and Rajasthan, three state governments run by the BJP since 1990, the BJP lost parliamentary seats although its share of the vote increased. In Uttar Pradesh, where the BJP also won control of the state government in 1991, veteran political analyst Paul R. Brass cogently argued that the BJP had reached the limits of its social base of support.

The limits of the BJP's Hindu nationalist strategy were further revealed by its losses in the November 1993 state elections. The party lost control over the state-level governments of Himachal Pradesh, Madhya Pradesh, and Uttar Pradesh while winning power in Gujarat and the National Capital Territory of Delhi. In the aftermath of the Hindu activists' dismantling of the Babri Masjid in December 1992, the evocative symbolism of the Ramjanmabhumi controversy had apparently lost its capacity to mobilize popular support. Nevertheless, the BJP, by giving more emphasis to anticorruption and social issues, achieved unprecedented success in South India, where it won 28 percent of the vote and came in second in elections in Karnataka in November 1994. In the spring of 1995, the BJP won state elections in Gujarat and became the junior partner of a coalition with Shiv Sena (Army of Shivaji—Shivaji Bhonsle was a seventeenth-century Maratha guerrilla leader who kept Mughal armies at bay) in Maharashtra (see The Marathas, ch. 1). In view of the potential demise of the Congress (I), the BJP stands poised to emerge as India's largest party in the 1990s. However, it is likely to have to play down the more divisive aspects of

Hindu nationalism and find other issues to expand its support if it is to win a majority in the Lok Sabha.

Communist Parties

The Communist Party of India (CPI) was founded on December 26, 1925, at an all-India conference held at Kanpur, Uttar Pradesh, in late December 1925 and early January 1926. Communists participated in the independence struggle and, as members of the Congress Socialist Party, became a formidable presence on the socialist wing of the Indian National Congress. They were expelled from the Congress Socialist Party in March 1940, after allegations that the communists had disrupted party activities and were intent on coopting party organizations. Indeed, by the time the communists were expelled, they had gained control over the entire Congress Socialist Party units in what were to become the southern states of Kerala, Tamil Nadu, and Andhra Pradesh. Communists remained members of the Indian National Congress although their support of the British war effort after the German invasion of the Soviet Union and their nationalist policy supporting the right of religious minorities to secede from India were diametrically opposed to Congress policies. As a result, the communists became isolated within the Congress. After independence, communists organized a peasant uprising in the Telangana region in the northern part of what was to become Andhra Pradesh. The uprising was suppressed only after the central government sent in the army. Starting in 1951, the CPI shifted to a more moderate strategy of seeking to bring communism to India within the constraints of Indian democracy. In 1957 the CPI was elected to rule the state government of Kerala only to have the government dismissed and President's Rule declared in 1959.

In 1964, in conjunction with the widening rift between China and the Soviet Union, a large leftist faction of the CPI leadership, based predominantly in Kerala and West Bengal, split from the party to form the Communist Party of India (Marxist), or CPI (M). The CPI (M)-led coalition victory in the 1967 West Bengal state elections spurred dissension within the party because a Maoist faction headed a peasant rebellion in the Naxalbari area of the state, just south of Darjiling (Darjeeling). The suppression of the Naxalbari uprising under the direction of the CPI (M)-controlled Home Ministry of the state government led to denunciations by Maoist revolutionary fac-

A communist campaign rally, Kerala
Courtesy Mary Orr

tions across the country. These groups—commonly referred to
as Naxalites—sparked new uprisings in the Srikakulam region
of Andhra Pradesh, Bihar, and other parts of West Bengal. In
1969 several Naxalite factions joined together to form a new
party—the Communist Party of India (Marxist-Leninist)—CPI
(M-L). However, pursuit of insurrectionary tactics in the face of
harsh repression by the government along with an array of
ideological disputes kept Naxalite factions isolated in their
local bases.

In the 1990s, the CPI (M) enjoys the most political strength
of any communist group. Nationally, its share of the vote has
gradually increased from 4.2 percent in 1967 to 6.7 percent in
1991, but it has largely remained confined to Kerala, Tripura,
and West Bengal. In Kerala the CPI (M) in coalition with other
parties wrested control from the Congress and its allies (fre-

quently including the CPI) in 1967, in 1980, and in 1987. Support for the CPI (M) in Kerala in general elections has ranged from 19 percent to 26 percent, but the party has never won more than nine of Kerala's twenty seats in Parliament. From 1977 to 1989, the CPI (M) dominated Tripura's state government. It won two parliamentary seats in 1971, 1980, and 1984, but it lost all of its seats in 1977, 1989, and 1991. In West Bengal, the CPI (M) has ruled the state government with a coalition of other leftist parties since 1977, and, since that time, the party has also dominated West Bengal's parliamentary delegation.

Support for the CPI is more evenly spread nationwide, but it is weak and in decline. The CPI share of the parliamentary vote has more than halved from 5.2 percent in 1967 to 2.5 percent in 1991.

In 1982 a CPI (M-L) faction entered the parliamentary arena by forming the Indian People's Front. In the 1989 general elections, the front won a parliamentary seat in western Bihar, and in 1990 it won seven seats in the Bihar legislative assembly. However, the Indian People's Front lost its parliamentary seat in the 1991 parliamentary elections when its vote in Bihar declined by some 20 percent.

Regional Parties

Given India's social, cultural, and historical diversity, it is only natural that regional parties play an important role in the country's political life. Because of India's federal system, state assembly votes are held in an electoral arena that often enables regional parties to obtain power by espousing issues of regional concern. Simultaneously, the single-member district, first-past-the-post electoral system has given the advantage to national parties, such as the Congress, which possess a realistic chance of gaining or retaining power at the national level and the opportunity to use central government resources to reward their supporters. Although regional parties have exercised authority at the state level, collectively they receive only from 5 to 10 percent of the national vote in parliamentary elections. Only during the governments of the Janata Party (1977–79) and the National Front (1989–90) have they participated in forming the central government. However, as India's party system becomes more fragmented with the decline of the Congress (I), the regional parties are likely to play an important role at the national level.

Regional political parties have been strongest in Tamil Nadu, where they have dominated state politics since 1967. Regional parties in the state trace their roots to the establishment of the Justice Party by non-Brahman social elites in 1916 and the development of the non-Bhraman Self-Respect Movement, founded in 1925 by E.V. Ramaswamy Naicker. As leader of the Justice Party, in 1944 Ramaswamy renamed the party the Dravida Kazhagam (DK—Dravidian Federation) and demanded the establishment of an independent state called Dravidasthan. In 1949, charismatic film script writer C.N. Annadurai, who was chafing under Ramaswamy's authoritarian leadership, split from the DK to found the DMK in an attempt to achieve the goals of Tamil nationalism through the electoral process. The DMK dropped its demand for Dravidasthan in 1963 but played a prominent role in the agitations that successfully defeated attempts to impose the northern Indian language of Hindi as the official national language in the mid-1960s. The DMK routed the Congress in the 1967 elections in Tamil Nadu and took control of the state government. With the deterioration of Annadurai's health, another screen writer, M. Karunanidhi, became chief minster in 1968 and took control of the party after Annadurai's death in 1969.

Karunanidhi's control over the party was soon challenged by M.G. Ramachandran (best known by his initials, M.G.R.), one of South India's most popular film stars. In 1972 M.G.R. split from the DMK to form the All-India Anna Dravida Munnetra Kazhagam (AIADMK). Under his leadership, the AIADMK dominated Tamil politics at the state level from 1977 through 1989. The importance of personal charisma in Tamil politics was dramatized by the struggle for control over the AIADMK after M.G.R's death in 1988. His widow, Janaki, herself a former film star, vied for control with Jayalalitha, an actress who had played M.G.R.'s leading lady in several films. The rivalry allowed the DMK to gain control over the state government in 1989. The AIADMK, securely under the control of Jayalalitha, who was cast as a "revolutionary leader," recaptured the state government in 1991. However, since 1980, the Congress (I), usually in alliance with the AIADMK, has won a majority of Tamil Nadu's seats in Parliament.

After three decades of Congress rule, the politics of Andhra Pradesh during the 1980s also became dominated by a charismatic film star who stressed regional issues. In 1982 N.T. Rama Rao (popularly known as N.T.R.), an actor who frequently played Hindu deities in Telugu-language films, formed the Telugu Desam. The party ruled the state from 1983 to 1989. It also won thirty of Andhra Pradesh's forty-two parliamentary seats in 1984. With the objective of enhancing Andhra Pradesh's regional autonomy, N.T.R. played a key role in the formation of the National Front coalition government in 1989. However, in the 1989 elections, the Telugu Desam won only two parliamentary seats and lost control over the state government to the Congress (I). It was able to improve its showing to thirteen seats in Parliament in the 1991 elections. The Telugu Desam returned to power in Andhra Pradesh after winning the state legislative assembly elections in November 1994.

The Akali Dal (Eternal Party) claims to represent India's Sikhs, who are concentrated primarily in Punjab. It was first formed in the early 1920s to return control of *gurdwaras* (Sikh places of worship) to the orthodox Sikh religious community. During the 1960s, the Akali Dal played an important role in the struggle for the creation of Punjab as a separate state with a Sikh majority. Even with the majority Sikh population, the Akali Dal's political success has been limited by the Congress's ability to win votes from the Sikh community. The Akali Dal won nine of Punjab's thirteen parliamentary seats in the general elections of 1977 and seven in 1984 but only one in the 1971 and 1980 elections. Similarly, the Akali Dal headed coalition state governments in 1967 and 1977 and formed the state government in 1985, but it lost state government elections to the Congress (R) in 1972, and to Congress (I) in 1980 and in 1992. As the 1980s progressed, the Akali Dal became increasingly factionalized. In 1989 three Akali Dal factions ran in the elections, winning a total of seven seats. The Akali Dal factions boycotted parliamentary and state legislative elections that were held in February 1992. As a result, voter turnout dropped to 21.6 percent, and the Congress (I) won twelve of Punjab's thirteen seats in Parliament and a majority of seats in the legislative assembly (see Twentieth-Century Developments, ch. 3).

The National Conference, based in Jammu and Kashmir, is a regional party, which, despite its overwhelmingly Muslim following, refused to support the All-India Muslim League (Muslim League—see Glossary) during the independence movement; instead it allied itself with the Indian National Congress. The National Conference was closely identified with its leader, Sheikh Mohammed Abdullah, a personal friend of Nehru, and, after Abdullah's death in 1982, with his son,

Farooq Abdullah. Friendship, however, did not prevent Nehru from imprisoning Sheikh Abdullah when he became concerned that the "Lion of Kashmir" was disposed to demand independence for his state. Ultimately, Sheikh Abdullah struck a deal with Indira Gandhi, and in 1975 he became chief minister of Jammu and Kashmir. The National Conference remained Jammu and Kashmir's dominant party through the 1980s and maintained control over the state government for most of the period. In parliamentary elections, it won one of Kashmir's six parliamentary seats in 1967, none in 1971, two in 1977, and three in 1980, 1984, and 1989. However, popular support for the National Conference was badly eroded by allegations of electoral fraud in the 1987 state elections—which were won by the National Conference in alliance with the Congress (I)—and the widespread corruption of the subsequent state government under the leadership of Farooq Abdullah. There was little popular sympathy for Farooq Abdullah and the National Conference even after the government was dissolved and President's Rule declared in 1990. Jammu and Kashmir remained under President's Rule through 1995, and the absence of elections makes it difficult to ascertain the extent of the National Conference's popular support. Nevertheless, it appears that Farooq and the National Conference remain discredited.

During the late 1980s, the AGP rose to power in Assam on the crest of Assamese nationalism. Immigration to Assam—primarily by Muslim Bengalis from neighboring Bangladesh—had aroused concern that the Assamese would become a minority in their own state. By 1979 attention was focused on the controversial issue of determining how many immigrants would be allowed on the state's list of eligible voters. The Congress (I), which gained a substantial share of the immigrants' votes, took a more expansive view of who should be included while the Assamese nationalist organizations demanded a more restrictive position. An attempt to hold state elections in February 1983, and in effect to force the Assamese nationalists to accept the status quo, resulted in a breakdown of law and order and the deaths of more than 3,000 people. The subsequent formation of a Congress (I) government led by Hiteshwar Saikia was widely viewed in Assam as illegitimate, and it was dissolved as part of the terms of the Assam Accord that was signed between Rajiv Gandhi and Assamese nationalists on August 15, 1985. The Assam Accord also included a compromise on the voter eligibility issue, settled the issue of the citizenship status of immigrants, and stipulated that new elections were to be held in December. The AGP was formed by Assamese student leaders after the signing of the accord, and the new party won the December 1985 elections with 35 percent of the vote and sixty-four of 108 seats in the state legislature.

The victory of the AGP did not end the controversy over Assamese nationalism. The AGP was unable to implement the accord's provisions for disenfranchising and expelling illegal aliens, in part because Parliament passed legislation making it more difficult to prove illegal alien status. The AGP's failure to implement the accord along with the general ineffectiveness with which it operated the state government undercut its popular support, and in November 1990 it was dismissed and President's Rule declared. As the AGP floundered, other nationalist groups of agitators flourished. The United Liberation Front of Assam (ULFA) became the primary torchbearer of militant Assamese nationalism while the All Bodo Students' Union (ABSU) and Bodo People's Action Committee (BPAC) led an agitation for a separate homeland for the central plain tribal people of Assam (often called Bodos). By 1990 ULFA militants ran virtually a parallel government in the state, extorting huge sums from businesses in Assam, especially the Assamese tea industry. The ULFA was ultimately subdued through a shrewd combination of ruthless military repression and generous terms of surrender for many of its leaders. The ABSU/BPAC-led mass agitation lasted from March 1987 until February 1993 when the ABSU signed an accord with the state government that had been under the Congress (I) control since 1991. The accord provided for the creation of a Bodoland Autonomous Council with jurisdiction over an area of 5,186 square kilometers and 2.1 million people within Assam. Nevertheless, Bodo agitation continued in the mid-1990s as a result of the demands of many Bodo leaders, who insisted that more territory be included under the Bodoland Autonomous Council.

Caste-Based Parties

One irony of Indian politics is that its modern secular democracy has enhanced rather than reduced the political salience of traditional forms of social identity such as caste. Part of the explanation for this development is that India's political parties have found the caste-based selection of candidates and appeals to the caste-based interests of the Indian

Woman voting, Uttar Pradesh
Courtesy India Abroad News
Service

Muslim woman voting, Delhi
Courtesy India Abroad News
Service

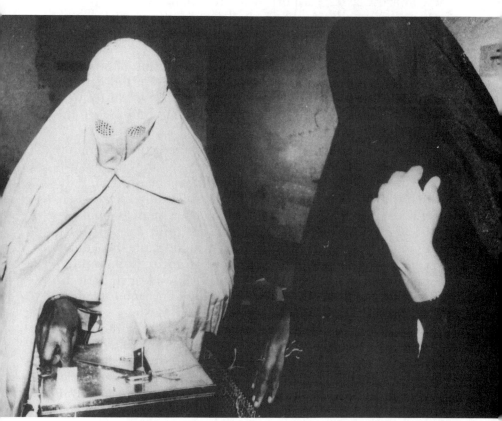

electorate to be an effective way to win popular support. More fundamental has been the economic development and social mobility of those groups officially designated as Backward Classes and Scheduled Castes. Accounting for 52 and 15 percent of the population, respectively, the Backward Classes and Scheduled Castes, or Dalits as they prefer to be called, constitute a diverse range of middle, lower, and outcaste groups who have come to wield substantial power in most states. Indeed, one of the dramas of modern Indian politics has been the Backward Classes and Dalits' jettisoning of their political subordination to upper castes and their assertion of their own interests.

The Backward Classes are such a substantial constituency that almost all parties vie for their support. For instance, the Congress (I) in Maharashtra has long relied on Backward Classes' backing for its political success. The 1990s have seen a growing number of cases where parties, relying primarily on Backward Classes' support, often in alliance with Dalits and Muslims, catapult to power in India's states. Janata Dal governments in Bihar and Karnataka are excellent examples of this strategy. An especially important development is the success of the Samajwadi Party, which under the leadership of Mulayam Singh Yadav won the 1993 assembly elections in India's most populous state, Uttar Pradesh, relying almost exclusively on Backward Classes and Muslim support in a coalition with the Dalit-supported BSP.

The growing support of the BSP also reflects the importance of caste-based politics and the assertiveness of the Dalits in particular. The BSP was founded by Kanshi Ram on April 13, 1984, the birthday of B.R. Ambedkar. Born as a Dalit in Punjab, Kanshi Ram resigned from his position as a government employee in 1964 and, after working in various political positions, founded the All-India Backward, Scheduled Caste, Scheduled Tribe, Other Backward Classes, and Minority Communities Employees Federation (BAMCEF) in 1978. Although both the BAMCEF and BSP pursue strategies of building support among Backward Classes, Scheduled Tribes, and Muslims as well as Dalits, Kanshi Ram has been most successful in building support among the Dalit Chamar (Leatherworker) caste in North India. In the November 1993 Uttar Pradesh state elections, Ram's BSP achieved the best showing of any Dalit-based party by winning sixty-seven seats. At the same time, the BSP increased its representation in the Madhya Pradesh state legislature from two to twelve seats. On June 1, 1995, the BSP withdrew from the state government of Uttar Pradesh and, with the support of the BJP, formed a new government, making its leader, Mayawati, the first Dalit ever to become a chief minister of Uttar Pradesh. The alliance, however, was seen by observers as doomed because of political differences.

Political Issues

Punjab and Jammu and Kashmir

Conflicts in Punjab and Jammu and Kashmir are each the result of centralized power operating in a predominantly heterogeneous society. Although tensions in the two states have important historical roots, they have been fueled by controversy over the policies of India's central government. Opposition is built upon the feeling that political power in New Delhi is inaccessible and unresponsive to local needs. Furthermore, in each case, the Congress (I) leadership has attempted to intervene in the conflicts to advance its partisan interests only to have its intervention backfire and aggravate regional tensions.

The confrontation in Punjab began in 1973 when the Akali Dal issued the Anandpur Sahib Resolution calling for the establishment of a "Sikh Autonomous Region" with its own constitution. It also called for the transfer of Chandigarh, a union territory, to Punjab as the state's capital—promised by the central government in 1970—and demanded that the central government establish a more favorable allocation of river waters used for irrigation. A particular concern was the shared distribution of water from the Beas and Sutlej rivers with neighboring Haryana (see Rivers, ch. 2). The Akali Dal further demanded changes involving greater symbolic recognition of Sikhism. These demands included the recognition of Amritsar, the site of the Sikhs' Golden Temple, as a holy city; exemption from antihijacking regulations to enable Sikhs flying on Indian airlines to wear their *kirpan* (ceremonial saber); and the passage of the All-India Gurdwara Act to place the management of all *gurdwaras* in the country under a single administration (see Early History and Tenets, ch. 3).

Akali Dal members were engaged in a heated competition with the Congress (I) over control of the Punjab assembly. It was in this context that the Congress (I) found it advantageous to encourage Sikh fundamentalism. Giani Zail Singh, who was the Congress (I) chief minister in Punjab from 1972 to 1977 and minister of home affairs in the central government from 1980 to 1982, developed links with the fiery Sikh militant Sant Jarnail Singh Bhindranwale. By encouraging Bhindranwale, the Congress (I) hoped to reap advantage from sowing division in the already fractious Akali Dal. However, what may have been good for the interests of the Congress (I) turned out to be bad for the country. By the spring of 1984, Bhindranwale and his followers had taken over the Akal Takht (Throne of the Eternal God) shrine facing the Golden Temple and transformed it into a headquarters and armory for Sikh militants. Indira Gandhi sent in the army, which, during a bloody three-day siege, almost destroyed the Akal Takht, did some damage to the Golden Temple, and killed Bhindranwale and hundreds of his followers (see Insurgent Movements and External Subversion, ch. 10). The army's action generated widespread resentment among India's Sikhs. The subsequent assassination of Indira Gandhi by Sikh members of her bodyguard on October 31, 1984, unleashed a wave of riots throughout India in which more than 2,700 Sikhs were killed.

Rajiv Gandhi attempted to put an end to the crisis by signing an agreement with Akali Dal moderate Harchand Singh Longowal in August 1985. The Gandhi-Longowal Accord acquiesced to many Akali Dal demands and called for elections to put an end to central government control over the state government through President's Rule, which had been in effect since October 1983. Although the accord was criticized by Sikh activists as being a sellout, it apparently had widespread support, as evidenced by the public's defiance of the militants' call for a boycott of the ensuing elections and the mandate given to Akali Dal moderates to form a new government. Public support for the Akali Dal government, however, was soon undermined by Rajiv Gandhi's failure to fulfill his commitments, such as the transfer of Chandigarh to Punjab, as enunciated in the Gandhi-Longowal Accord. With the failure to implement the accord, the popularity of the Akali Dal state government led by Surjit Singh Barnala declined, and its internal divisions grew. As a result, its efforts to combat the militants' increasing violence became ineffective. In May 1987, the Punjab assembly was dissolved and replaced with President's Rule.

The violence of Sikh militants spread throughout Punjab during the 1980s. In many cases, activist groups became undisciplined or were taken over by criminals. Armed robbery, extortion, and murder became a way of life. Police actions also became more repressive. The residents of Punjab were caught in a vise of indiscriminate militant and police violence. After an unprecedented five years of President's Rule, the central government gambled by holding elections for Parliament and the state legislative assembly in February 1992. Most Akali Dal groups and militants called for a boycott of the poll, and the election turnout was a record low of 20 percent. Not surprisingly, the Congress (I) emerged victorious, winning twelve of thirteen seats in Parliament and control over the state government. After the elections, the police and paramilitary forces under the leadership of K.P.S. Gill scored a series of successes in infiltrating activist groups and capturing or killing their members. Popular participation in the conventional political process increased; voter turnout for municipal elections in September 1992 and *gram panchayats* in January 1993 exceeded 70 percent. Although violence diminished during 1993 and 1994, the sources of many of the tensions remained, and resentments among the Sikhs continue to simmer in the mid-1990s.

Ethnic and regional tensions also raged out of control in the strategically sensitive Jammu and Kashmir. The conflict assumes considerable symbolic as well as strategic importance because, as India's only Muslim-majority state, Jammu and Kashmir validates India's national identity as a religiously and culturally diverse society held together by a common history and cultural heritage. The roots of the Kashmir conflict extend at least as far back as 1947 when Maharaja Hari Singh, the princely state's Hindu ruler, decided to cede his domain with its predominantly Muslim population to the Indian Union at a time when Kashmir was under attack by a Muslim paramilitary force supported by Pakistan. Tensions persisted through the mid-1980s. The National Conference, led by Sheikh Abdullah until his death in 1983, first supported the accession to India and its provisions under Article 370 of the constitution for special autonomy, but later made demands for greater autonomy as popular resentment against India's central government began to spread. The status of Kashmir was the cause of two wars between India and Pakistan, in 1947 and 1965, and was an issue in the third war, in 1971 (see The Experience of Wars, ch. 10).

The Kashmir crisis of the 1990s is reflective of trends occurring throughout the Indian polity: the increasing intervention of the central government in local affairs, the resort to coercion to resolve social conflict and maintain social order, and the increasing political assertiveness of the Indian public. The National Conference government, which had been elected in 1983 under the leadership of Farooq Abdullah, son of Sheikh Abdullah, was brought down in 1984 after leaders of the Congress (I) supported Ghulam Mohammad Shah's split of the National Conference and formation of a separate government. The Congress (I) switched its support back to Farooq in 1986, and the National Conference under Farooq's leadership participated in the 1987 state elections in alliance with the Congress (I). The alliance served to discredit Farooq and the National Conference in the eyes of many Kashmiris, and the coalition faced stiff competition from an alliance of Muslim activists under the banner of the Muslim United Front. The National Conference-Congress (I) coalition won the election, but only after creating a popular perception of widespread election rigging. Farooq's government proved to be inept and corrupt, further alienating the Kashmiri public. The activists, feeling that they had been electorally defrauded, incited an increasing number of demonstrations, strikes, bombings, and assassinations.

The problem reached a climax in December 1989 when militants took as hostage the daughter of Mufti Mohammed Sayeed, the minister of home affairs of the newly formed National Front government. When the militants exchanged their hostage for the release of five jailed militant leaders, a jubilant public showed its support for the militants with massive demonstrations in Srinagar, the capital. It became obvious to all that Farooq's government had lost control over the state, and President's Rule was declared. Insurgency broke out as fighting spread between the Kashmiri militants and paramilitary forces. Reports by human rights groups left little doubt that each side had perpetrated gross atrocities and that victims included large numbers of innocent civilians. The issue was further complicated by charges that the insurgents had received sanctuary and support from Pakistan and from movements like the Ekta Yatra (Unity Pilgrimage—a BJP political pilgrimage from the southern tip of India to Srinagar from December 1991 to January 1992).

The conflict raged through 1994 as the government sent in paramilitary and army troops in an effort to break the back of the resistance and convince the Kashmiri public of the futility of the struggle. By then the militants had fragmented into more than 100 groups. The Jammu and Kashmir Liberation Front, which demands independence from both India and Pakistan, had the widest support, but a number of heavily armed groups, the most prominent being the Hezb-ul Mujahideen, which favored union with Pakistan, also had support. Events offered a glimmer of hope that the crisis might be resolved through negotiation. Earlier, in November 1993, the government had successfully negotiated the settlement of a crisis at the Hazratbal—a Srinagar mosque, which is one of the holiest Muslim shrines in India because it is believed to house a hair of the Prophet Muhammad. The government negotiated the settlement with the All-Party Hurriyat Conference by agreeing to the departure of the occupying militant forces. In April 1994, the leaders of the conference further raised hopes by coming to New Delhi to discuss ways of resolving the conflict with the leaders of non-Muslim communities in Kashmir. The government responded by releasing more moderate activist leaders from prison and beginning preparations for elections. But with tension growing and the destruction in May 1995 by fire of a Sufi mausoleum and mosque in the town of Charar Sharif—each side blamed the other for the conflagration—the central government postponed plans for elections. This event posed new impediments to resolving the conflict.

Hindu-Muslim Tensions

The kindling of Hindu-Muslim tensions during the 1990s was neither a reawakening of ancient hatreds nor a consequence of religious fundamentalism. Rather it occurred because of the interaction between the various socioeconomic developments in India during the 1980s and 1990s and the strategies and tactics of India's politicians.

Rapid urbanization has uprooted individuals from their previous occupations and communities and placed many in competition for new livelihoods. Newcomers who succeed frequently arouse resentment, and many riots have targeted successful Muslim merchants, business owners, and Muslim returnees from the Persian Gulf states, where they often earn incomes many times higher than they would have earned in India. High-caste Hindus, fearing the loss of their social prestige, have provided an important social base for Hindu militancy. Hard-pressed members of these high-caste groups have been an especially receptive constituency for appeals to curtail the "special privileges of pampered minorities." In addition, the economy was unable to provide jobs for all who wanted to enter the labor market, and the 1980s and early 1990s saw an increase in the ranks of the unemployed. Some of the unemployed have become involved in gangs whose strong-arm tactics are used by politicians wishing to intimidate or incite communal tensions. Other unemployed youths join militant religious organizations like the Bajrang Dal (Party of the Adamani [Diamond]-Bodied, a reference to Bajrang, a Hindu god) and Shiv Sena. The militant groups provide security for temples and members of their religion but are also sources of communal violence.

Changes in the nature of India's political process also have contributed to the rise of religious tensions. Analysts from a variety of perspectives have commented on the increasing willingness of India's politicians to exploit religious and ethnic tensions for short-term political gain, regardless of their longer-term social consequences. Political scientist Rajni Kothari, for example, charges that there has been a general decline in the morality of Indian politicians. He alleges that politicians play a "numbers game," in which they appeal to chauvinistic caste and religious sentiments to win elections, despite the longer-term social tensions that their campaigns create. The support of the Congress for Article 370 in the constitution, which provides a special status for the Muslim majority state of Jammu and Kashmir, and the measures taken to provide India's Muslim community with distinctive rights have contributed to the popular resonance of the BJP's charges that the Congress (I) stands for minority appeasement and "pseudo-secularism." The violence of religious militants in Punjab and Jammu and Kashmir has also contributed to sentiment among the Hindu majority that religious minorities employ aggressive tactics to win special concessions from the government.

The 1985 Shah Bano controversy put state-religion relations in the forefront of the political agenda. Shah Bano was a seventy-three-year-old Muslim woman from Madhya Pradesh who filed for alimony after being divorced according to Muslim law by her husband after forty-three years of marriage. The Supreme Court ruled in Shah Bano's favor, creating outrage among sectors of the Muslim community who felt that the sharia (Islamic law), which does not provide for alimony, had been slighted. In apparent capitulation to this important political constituency, Rajiv Gandhi pushed the Muslim Women (Protection of Rights on Divorce) Bill, which removed Muslim divorce cases from India's civil law and recognized the jurisdiction of sharia. The legislation, in turn, enraged large sectors of Hindus, whose personal conduct is judged under India's secular civil code.

Shortly thereafter, in a ploy that Rajiv Gandhi may have misguidedly conceived to placate Hindu militants, the courts ruled that the doors of the Babri Masjid should be opened to Hindu worshipers. The VHP was joined by the BJP in a campaign to reclaim the disputed birthplace of Ram. In 1989 the VHP launched a campaign encouraging Hindu devotees from across India each to bring a brick from their villages to Ayodhya. Outbreaks of violence between Hindus and Muslims spread as the campaign progressed, and the BJP successfully prevailed upon the VHP to withdraw the campaign before the 1989 elections. Tensions heated up again in the summer of 1990 when BJP leader Advani embarked on a 10,000-kilometer tour of the country in a Toyota van decorated to resemble the mythological chariot of Ram. Advani's arrest did not prevent clashes at Ayodhya between paramilitary forces and Hindu activists; the clashes sparked a wave of communal violence and left more than 300 dead.

The Ramjanmabhumi Temple mobilization appeared to pay substantial dividends in terms of the BJP's remarkable growth of support in North India in the 1991 elections, and the VHP and BJP kept the issue alive despite the fact that their actions put tremendous pressure on the newly elected BJP state government in Uttar Pradesh. Its July 1992 *kar sewa* (mass mobilization force work service) to build the temple ended peacefully only through last-minute negotiations with Prime Minister Rao; Rao had been promised by BJP leader L.K. Advani that the December 6, 1992, *kar sewa* would also be peaceful. Despite Advani's promise, thousands of Hindu activists broke through a police cordon and destroyed the Babri Masjid (see Public Worship, ch. 3). This event and the subsequent riots throughout the country left no doubt that tensions between Hindus and Muslims had reached a high pitch.

During the following week, riots spread throughout the countryside, killing some 1,700 people. Riots broke out again in Bombay from January 9 through January 11, killing 500 more people. In March 1993, the Bombay Stock Exchange and other prominent places in the city were shaken, and some 200 people were killed by bombs that the central government alleges were placed by members of India's criminal underworld at the behest of Pakistan's intelligence service. The manipulation of India's religious tensions by militants, criminals, and politicians highlighted the extent to which religious sentiments in India had become an object of exploitation. Religious tensions eased somewhat and incidents of communal violence declined during the remainder of 1993 and through 1994, but the persistence of the social conditions that gave birth to violence and the continued opportunism of India's politicians suggest that the relative peace may be only an interlude.

Corruption and the Anti-Establishment Vote

Corruption not only has become a pervasive aspect of Indian politics but also has become an increasingly important factor in Indian elections. The extensive role of the Indian state in providing services and promoting economic development has always created the opportunity for using public resources for private benefit. As government regulation of business was extended in the 1960s and corporate donations were banned in 1969, trading economic favors for under-the-table contributions to political parties became an increasingly widespread political practice. During the 1980s and 1990s, corruption became associated with the occupants of the highest echelons of India's political system. Rajiv Gandhi's government was rocked by scandals, as was the government of P.V. Narasimha Rao. Politicians have become so closely identified with corruption in the public eye that a *Times of India* poll of 1,554 adults in six metropolitan cities found that 98 percent of the public is convinced that politicians and ministers are corrupt, with 85 percent observing that corruption is on the increase.

The prominence of political corruption in the 1990s is hardly unique to India. Other countries also have experienced corruption that has rocked their political systems. What is remarkable about India is the persistent anti-incumbent sentiment among its electorate. Since Indira's victory in her 1971 "*garibi hatao*" election, only one ruling party has been reelected to power in the central government. In an important sense, the exception proves the rule because the Congress (I) won reelection in 1984 in no small measure because the electorate saw in Rajiv Gandhi a "Mr. Clean" who would lead a new generation of politicians in cleansing the political system. Anti-incumbent sentiment is just as strong at the state level, where the ruling parties of all political persuasions in India's major states lost

*Part of the North Block of the
Secretariat, location of the
ministries of home affairs and
finance, New Delhi
Courtesy Robert L. Worden*

eleven of thirteen legislative assembly elections held from 1991 through spring 1995.

The Media

The Press

Compared with many other developing countries, the Indian press has flourished since independence and exercises a large degree of independence. British colonialism allowed for the development of a tradition of freedom of the press, and many of India's great English-language newspapers and some of its Indian-language press were begun during the nineteenth century. As India became independent, ownership of India's leading English-language newspapers was transferred from British to Indian business groups, and the fact that most English-language newspapers have the backing of large business houses has contributed to their independence from the government. The press has experienced impressive growth since independence. In 1950 there were 214 daily newspapers, with forty-four in English and the rest in Indian languages. By 1990 the number of daily newspapers had grown to 2,856, with 209 in English and 2,647 in indigenous languages. The expansion of literacy and the spread of consumerism during the

1980s fueled the rapid growth of news weeklies and other periodicals. By 1993 India had 35,595 newspapers—of which 3,805 were dailies—and other periodicals. Although the majority of publications are in indigenous languages, the English-language press, which has widespread appeal to the expanding middle class, has a wide multicity circulation throughout India.

There are four major publishing groups in India, each of which controls national and regional English-language and vernacular publications. They are the Times of India Group, the Indian Express Group, the Hindustan Times Group, and the Anandabazar Patrika Group. The *Times of India* is India's largest English-language daily, with a circulation of 656,000 published in six cities. The *Indian Express*, with a daily circulation of 519,000, is published in seventeen cities. There also are seven other daily newspapers with circulations of between 134,000 and 477,000, all in English and all competitive with one another. Indian-language newspapers also enjoy large circulations but usually on a statewide or citywide basis. For example, the Malayalam-language daily *Malayala Manorama* circulates 673,000 copies in Kerala; the Hindi-language *Dainik Jagran* circulates widely in Uttar Pradesh and New Delhi, with 580,000 copies per day; *Punjab Kesari*, also published in Hindi and available throughout Punjab and New Delhi, has a daily circulation of 562,000; and the *Anandabazar Patrika*, published in Calcutta in Bengali, has a daily circulation of 435,000. There are also numerous smaller publications throughout the nation. The combined circulation of India's newspapers and periodicals is in the order of 60 million, published daily in more than ninety languages.

India has more than forty domestic news agencies. The Express News Service, the Press Trust of India, and the United News of India are among the major news agencies. They are headquartered in Delhi, Bombay, and New Delhi, respectively, and employ foreign correspondents.

Although freedom of the press in India is the legal norm—it is constitutionally guaranteed—the scope of this freedom has often been contested by the government. Rigid press censorship was imposed during the Emergency starting in 1975 but quickly retracted in 1977. The government has continued, however, to exercise more indirect controls. Government advertising accounts for as much as 50 percent of all advertisements in Indian newspapers, providing a monetary incentive to limit harsh criticism of the administration. Until 1992, when government regulation of access to newsprint was liberalized, controls on the distribution of newsprint could also be used to reward favored publications and threaten those that fell into disfavor. In 1988, at a time when the Indian press was publishing investigative reports about corruption and abuse of power in government, Parliament passed a tough defamation bill that mandated prison sentences for offending journalists. Vociferous protests from journalists and opposition party leaders ultimately forced the government to withdraw the bill. Since the late 1980s, the independence of India's press has been bolstered by the liberalization of government economic policy and the increase of private-sector advertising provided by the growth of India's private sector and the spread of consumerism.

Broadcast Media

The national television (Doordarshan) and radio (All India Radio, or Akashwani) networks are state-owned and managed by the Ministry of Information and Broadcasting. Their news reporting customarily presents the government's point of view. For example, coverage of the 1989 election campaign blatantly favored the government of Rajiv Gandhi, and autonomy of the electronic media became a political issue. V.P. Singh's National Front government sponsored the Prasar Bharati (Indian Broadcasting) Act, which Parliament considered in 1990, to provide greater autonomy to Doordarshan and All India Radio. The changes that resulted were limited. The bill provided for the establishment of an autonomous corporation to run Doordarshan and All India Radio. The corporation was to operate under a board of governors to be in charge of appointments and policy and a broadcasting council to respond to complaints. However, the legislation required that the corporation prepare and submit its budget within the framework of the central budget and stipulated that the personnel of the new broadcasting corporation be career civil servants to facilitate continued government control. In the early 1990s, increasing competition from television broadcasts transmitted via satellite appeared the most effective manner of limiting the progovernment bias of the government-controlled electronic media (see Telecommunications, ch. 6).

Since the 1980s, India has experienced a rapid proliferation of television broadcasting that has helped shape popular culture and the course of politics. Although the first television program was broadcast in 1959, the expansion of television did not begin in earnest until the extremely popular telecast of the Ninth Asian Games, which were held in New Delhi in 1982. Realizing the popular appeal and consequent influence of television broadcasting, the government undertook an expansion that by 1990 was planned to provide television access to 90 percent of the population. In 1993, about 169 million people were estimated to have watched Indian television each week, and, by 1994, it was reported that there were some 47 million households with televisions. There also is a growing selection of satellite transmission and cable services available (see Television, ch. 6).

Television programming was initially kept tightly under the control of the government, which embarked on a self-conscious effort to construct and propagate a cultural idea of the Indian nation. This goal is especially clear in the broadcasts of such megaseries as the Hindu epics *Ramayana* and *Mahabharata*. In addition to the effort at nation-building, the politicians of India's ruling party have not hesitated to use television to build political support. In fact, the political abuse of Indian television led to demands to increase the autonomy of Doordarshan; these demands ultimately resulted in support for the Prasar Bharati Act.

The 1990s have brought a radical transformation of television in India. Transnational satellite broadcasting made its debut in January 1991, when owners of satellite dishes—initially mostly at major hotels—began receiving Cable News Network (CNN) coverage of the Persian Gulf War. Three months later, Star TV began broadcasting via satellite. Its fare initially included serials such as "The Bold and the Beautiful" and MTV programs. Satellite broadcasting spread rapidly through India's cities as local entrepreneurs erected dishes to receive signals and transmitted them through local cable systems. After its October 1992 launch, Zee TV offered stiff competition to Star TV. However, the future of Star TV was bolstered by billionaire Rupert Murdock, who acquired the network for US$525 million in July 1993. CNN International, part of the Turner Broadcasting System, was slated to start broadcasting entertainment programs, including top Hollywood films, in 1995.

Competition from the satellite stations brought radical change to Doordarshan by cutting its audience and threatening its advertising revenues at a time when the government was pressuring it to pay for expenditures from internal revenues. In response, Doordarshan decided in 1993 to start five new channels in addition to its original National Channel. Programming was radically transformed, and controversial news shows, soap operas, and coverage of high-fashion events proliferated. Of the new Doordarshan channels, however, only the Metro Channel, which carries MTV music videos and other popular shows, has survived in the face of the new trend for talk programs that engage in a potpourri of racy topics.

The Rise of Civil Society

Political participation in India has been transformed in many ways since the 1960s. New social groups have entered the political arena and begun to use their political resources to shape the political process. Scheduled Castes and Scheduled Tribes, previously excluded from politics because of their position at the bottom of India's social hierarchy, have begun to take full advantage of the opportunities presented by India's democracy. Women and environmentalists constitute new political categories that transcend traditional distinctions. The spread of social movements and voluntary organizations has shown that despite the difficulties of India's political parties and state institutions, India's democratic tendency continues to thrive.

An important aspect of the rise of civil society is the proliferation of voluntary or nongovernmental organizations. Estimates of their number ranged from 50,000 to 100,000 in 1993. To some extent, the rise of voluntary organizations has been sponsored by the Indian state. For instance, the central government's Seventh Five-Year Plan of fiscal years (FY—see Glossary) 1985–89 recognized the contributions of voluntary organizations in accelerating development and substantially increased their funding. A 1987 survey of 1,273 voluntary agencies reported that 47 percent received some form of funding from the central government. Voluntary organizations also have thrived on foreign donations, which in 1991–92 contributed more than US$400 million to some 15,000 organizations. Some nongovernmental organizations cooperate with the central government in a manner that augments its capacity to implement public policy, such as poverty alleviation, for example, in a decentralized manner. Other nongovernmental organizations also serve as watchdogs, attempting to pressure government agencies to uphold the spirit of the state's laws and implement policies in accord with their stated objectives. Nongovernmental organizations also endeavor to raise the political consciousness of various social groups, encouraging them to demand their rights and challenge social inequities. Finally, some social groups serve as innovators, experimenting with new approaches to solving social problems.

Beginning in the 1970s, activists began to form broad-based social movements, which proved powerful advocates for interests that they perceived as neglected by the state and political parties. Perhaps the most powerful has been the farmers' movement, which has organized hundreds of thousands of demonstrators in New Delhi and has pressured the government for higher prices on agricultural commodities and more investment in rural areas. Members of Scheduled Castes led by the Dalit Panthers have moved to rearticulate the identity of former Untouchables. Women from an array of diverse organizations now interact in conferences and exchange ideas in order to define and promote women's issues. Simultaneously, an environmental movement has developed that has attempted to compel the government to be more responsive to environmental concerns and has attempted to redefine the concept of "development" to include respect for indigenous cultures and environmental sustainability.

With its highly competitive elections, relatively independent judiciary, boisterous media, and thriving civil society, India continues to possess one of the most democratic political systems of all developing countries. Nevertheless, Indian democracy is under stress. Political power within the Indian state has become increasingly centralized at a time when India's civil society has become mobilized along lines that reflect the country's remarkable social diversity. The country's political parties, which might aggregate the country's diverse social interests in a way that would ensure the responsiveness of state authority, are in crisis. The Congress (I) has been in a state of decline, as reflected in the erosion of its traditional coalition of support and the implication of Congress (I) governments in a series of scandals. The party has failed to generate an enlightened leadership that might rejuvenate it and replace the increasingly discredited Nehruvian socialism with a novel programmatic appeal. The Congress (I)'s split in May 1995 added a new impediment to efforts to reinvigorate the party.

The BJP, although it has a stronger party organization, in 1995 had yet to find a way to transcend the limits of its militant Hindu nationalism and fashion a program that would appeal to diverse social groups and enable it to build a majority coalition in India. The Janata Dal continued to suffer from lack of leadership, inadequate resources, and incessant factionalism. As its bases of power shrink, it stood in danger of being reduced to a party with only a few regional strongholds. As regional groupings and members of the lower echelons of India's caste system become more assertive, regional and caste parties may play a more prominent role in India's political system. At this point, however, it is difficult to envision how they might stabilize India's political system.

The unresponsiveness of India's political parties and government has encouraged the Indian public to mobilize through nongovernmental organizations and social movements. The consequent development of India's civil society has made Indians less confident of the transformative power of the state and more confident of the power of the individual and local community. This development is shifting a larger share of the initiative for resolving India's social problems from the state to society. Fashioning party and state institutions that will accommodate the diverse interests that are now mobilized in Indian society is the major challenge confronting the Indian polity in the 1990s.

*   *   *

Robert L. Hardgrave, Jr., and Stanley A. Kochanek's *India: Government and Politics in a Developing Nation* provides a thorough and insightful overview of Indian politics. The second edition of Paul R. Brass's *The Politics of India since Independence* is a useful account written by a scholar with detailed knowledge of India's grass roots.

Atul Kohli's *Democracy and Discontent* is the definitive study of India's growing crisis of governability, with special emphasis on the decay of Indian political parties. *State Against Democracy* by Rajni Kothari, India's eminent political scientist, is a critique of the Indian state as well as a hopeful analysis of the rise of civil society. Lloyd I. Rudolph and Susanne Hoeber Rudolph's *In Pursuit of Lakshmi* offers an illuminating account of the politics of India's development. *Dominance and State Power in Modern India*, edited by Francine R. Frankel and M.S.A. Rao, is a study of the changing relationship between caste and politics that describes the diversity of politics in India's states and documents the rise of the Backward Classes. Paul R. Brass's *Ethnicity and Nationalism: Theory and Comparison* includes observations about the dynamics of ethnic politics in India. *India Votes,* edited by Harold A. Gould and Sumit Ganguly, offers an account of India's elections in 1989 and 1991. David Butler, Ashok Lahiri, and Prannoy Roy's *India Decides: Elections 1952– 1991* includes copious data about election outcomes.

India Today, India's leading weekly news magazine, offers excellent investigative journalism and news analysis. *Economic and Political Weekly* includes trenchant analyses of India's political economy. *Asian Survey* regularly publishes articles analyzing Indian politics. *Seminar* provides monthly symposia that gather analyses from leading Indian experts on problems confronting Indian society. The "clari.world.asia.india" electronic newsgroup provides releases from Reuters and the Associated Press that are an excellent way to keep up with current events. (For further information and complete citations, see Bibliography.)

Chapter 9. Foreign Relations

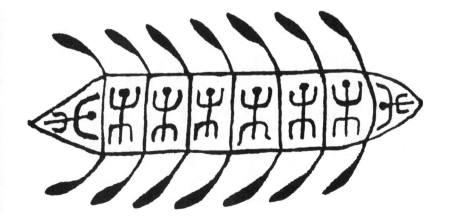

Depiction of a boat from a coastal area of South India

INDIA'S FOREIGN RELATIONS reflect a traditional policy of nonalignment (see Glossary), the exigencies of domestic economic reform and development, and the changing post-Cold War international environment. India's relations with the world have evolved considerably since the British colonial period (1757–1947), when a foreign power monopolized external relations and defense relations. On independence in 1947, few Indians had experience in making or conducting foreign policy. However, the country's oldest political party, the Indian National Congress (the Congress—see Glossary), had established a small foreign department in 1925 to make overseas contacts and to publicize its freedom struggle. From the late 1920s on, Jawaharlal Nehru, who had the most long-standing interest in world affairs among independence leaders, formulated the Congress stance on international issues. As a member of the interim government in 1946, Nehru articulated India's approach to the world.

During Nehru's tenure as prime minister (1947–64), he achieved a domestic consensus on the definition of Indian national interests and foreign policy goals—building a unified and integrated nation-state based on secular, democratic principles; defending Indian territory and protecting its security interests; guaranteeing India's independence internationally through nonalignment; and promoting national economic development unencumbered by overreliance on any country or group of countries. These objectives were closely related to the determinants of India's foreign relations: the historical legacy of South Asia; India's geopolitical position and security requirements; and India's economic needs as a large developing nation. From 1947 until the late 1980s, New Delhi's foreign policy goals enabled it to achieve some successes in carving out an independent international role. Regionally, India was the predominant power because of its size, its population (the world's second-largest after China), and its growing military strength. However, relations with its neighbors, Pakistan in particular, were often tense and fraught with conflict. In addition, globally India's nonaligned stance was not a viable substitute for the political and economic role it wished to play.

India's international influence varied over the years after independence. Indian prestige and moral authority were high in the 1950s and facilitated the acquisition of developmental assistance from both East and West. Although the prestige stemmed from India's nonaligned stance, the nation was unable to prevent Cold War politics from becoming intertwined with interstate relations in South Asia. In the 1960s and 1970s, New Delhi's international position among developed and developing countries faded in the course of wars with China and Pakistan, disputes with other countries in South Asia, and India's attempt to balance Pakistan's support from the United States and China by signing the Treaty of Peace, Friendship, and Cooperation with the Soviet Union in August 1971. Although India obtained substantial Soviet military and economic aid, which helped to strengthen the nation, India's influence was undercut regionally and internationally by the perception that its friendship with the Soviet Union prevented a more forthright condemnation of the Soviet presence in Afghanistan. In the 1980s, New Delhi improved relations with the United States, other developed countries, and China while continuing close ties with the Soviet Union. Relations with its South Asian neighbors, especially Pakistan, Sri Lanka, and Nepal, occupied much of the energies of the Ministry of External Affairs.

In the 1990s, India's economic problems and the demise of the bipolar world political system have forced New Delhi to reassess its foreign policy and to adjust its foreign relations. Previous policies proved inadequate to cope with the serious domestic and international problems facing India. The end of the Cold War gutted the core meaning of nonalignment and left Indian foreign policy without significant direction. The hard, pragmatic considerations of the early 1990s were still viewed within the nonaligned framework of the past, but the disintegration of the Soviet Union removed much of India's international leverage, for which relations with Russia and the other post-Soviet states could not compensate.

Pragmatic security, economic considerations, and domestic political influences have reinforced New Delhi's reliance on the United States and other developed countries; caused New Delhi to abandon its anti-Israeli policy in the Middle East; and resulted in the courtship of the Central Asian republics and the newly industrializing economies of East and Southeast Asia. Although India shares the concerns of Russia, China, and many members of the Nonaligned Movement (see Glossary) about the preeminent position of the United States and other developed countries, different national interests and perceptions make it improbable that India can turn cooperation with these countries to its advantage on most international issues. Furthermore, although Cold War politics have ceased to be a factor in South Asia, the most intractable problems in India's relations with Pakistan—conflict over Kashmir, support for separatists, and nuclear and ballistic missile programs—still face the two countries.

Foreign Policy Formulation

Role of the Prime Minister

Nehru set the pattern for the formation of Indian foreign policy: a strong personal role for the prime minister but a weak institutional structure. Nehru served concurrently as prime minister and minister of external affairs; he made all major foreign policy decisions himself after consulting with his advisers and then entrusted the conduct of international affairs to senior members of the Indian Foreign Service. His successors continued to exercise considerable control over India's international dealings, although they generally appointed separate ministers of external affairs.

India's second prime minister, Lal Bahadur Shastri (1964–66), expanded the Office of Prime Minister (sometimes called the Prime Minister's Secretariat) and enlarged its powers (see The Executive, ch. 8). By the 1970s, the Office of the Prime Minister had become the de facto coordinator and supraministry of the Indian government. The enhanced role of the office strengthened the prime minister's control over foreign policy making at the expense of the Ministry of External Affairs. Advisers in the office provided channels of information and policy recommendations in addition to those offered by the Ministry of External Affairs. A subordinate part of the office—the Research and Analysis Wing—functioned in ways that significantly expanded the information available to the prime minister and his advisers. The Research and Analysis Wing gathered intelligence, provided intelligence analysis to the Office of the Prime Minister, and conducted covert operations abroad.

The prime minister's control and reliance on personal advisers in the Office of the Prime Minister was particularly strong under the tenures of Indira Gandhi (1966–77 and 1980–84) and her son, Rajiv (1984–89), who succeeded her, and weaker during the periods of coalition governments under Morarji Desai (1977–79), Viswanath Pratap (V.P.) Singh (1989–90), Chandra Shekhar (1990–91), and P.V. Narasimha Rao (starting in June 1991). Although observers find it difficult to determine whether the locus of decision-making authority on any particular issue lies with the Ministry of External Affairs, the Council of Ministers, the Office of the Prime Minister, or the prime minister himself, nevertheless in the 1990s India's prime ministers retain their dominance in the conduct of foreign relations.

Ministry of External Affairs

The Ministry of External Affairs is the governmental body most concerned with foreign affairs, with responsibility for some aspects of foreign policy making, actual implementation of policy, and daily conduct of international relations. The ministry's duties include providing timely information and analysis to the prime minister and minister of external affairs, recommending specific measures when necessary, planning policy for the future, and maintaining communications with foreign missions in New Delhi. In 1994 the ministry administered 149 diplomatic missions abroad, which were staffed largely by members of the Indian Foreign Service. The ministry is headed by the minister of external affairs, who holds cabinet rank and is assisted by a deputy minister and a foreign secretary, and secretaries of state from the Indian Foreign Service.

In 1994 the total cadre strength of the Indian Foreign Service numbered 3,490, of which some 1,890 held posts abroad and 1,600 served at the Ministry of External Affairs headquarters in New Delhi. Members of the Indian Foreign Service are recruited through annual written and oral competitive examinations and come from a great variety of regional, economic, and social backgrounds. The Foreign Service Training Institute provides a wide range of courses for foreign service officers, including a basic professional course, a comprehensive course in diplomacy and international relations for foreign service recruits, a refresher course for commercial representatives, and foreign language training.

The Ministry of External Affairs has thirteen territorial divisions, each covering a large area of the world, such as Eastern Europe and the post-Soviet states, or smaller areas on India's periphery, such as Afghanistan, Iran, and Pakistan. The ministry also has functional divisions dealing with external publicity, protocol, consular affairs, Indians abroad, the United Nations

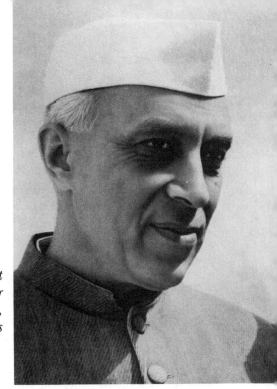

*Jawaharlal Nehru, India's first
prime minister
Courtesy Biographic Collection,
Library of Congress*

(UN) and other international organizations, and international conferences. Two of the eighteen specialized divisions and units of the ministry are of special note. The Policy Planning and Research Division conducts research and prepares briefs and background papers for top policy makers and ministry officials. The briefs cover wide-ranging issues relating to India's foreign policy and role in the changing international environment, and background papers provide information on issues concerning international developments. The Economic Division has the important task of handling foreign economic relations. This division augments its activities to reflect changes in the government's economic policy and the international economic environment (see Liberalization in the Early 1990s, ch. 6). In 1990 the division established the Economic Coordination Unit to assess the impact on India of the Persian Gulf crisis arising from Iraq's invasion of Kuwait, changes in Eastern Europe and the Soviet Union, and formation of a single market in the European Economic Community (after 1993 the European Union), as well as to promote foreign investment. The Economic Division also runs India's foreign aid programs, including the Indian Technical and Economic Cooperation Programme, the Special Commonwealth African Assistance Programme, and aid to individual developing countries in South Asia and elsewhere. The ministry runs the Indian Council for Cultural Relations, which arranges exhibits, visits, and cultural exchanges with other countries and oversees the activities of foreign cultural centers in India.

The Ministry of External Affairs had a budget of Rs8.8 billion (for value of the rupee—see Glossary) for fiscal year (FY—see Glossary) 1994. The largest single expense was the maintenance of missions abroad: Rs3.8 billion, or close to 44 percent of the ministry's expenditures. Foreign aid totaled Rs1.3 billion, or 15.1 percent of the ministry's expenditures. The single largest recipient—as in most previous years—was Bhutan (Rs690 million), whose government operations and development are heavily subsidized by India.

Other Government Organizations

Besides the Office of the Prime Minister and the Ministry of External Affairs, there are other government agencies that have foreign policy-making roles. In theory, the ministers of defence, commerce, and finance provide input to foreign policy decisions discussed in cabinet meetings, but their influence in practical terms is overshadowed by the predominant position of the prime minister and his advisers. The armed forces are removed from policy making and have influence only through the minister of defence, to whom they are subordinate (see Organization and Equipment of the Armed Forces, ch. 10).

Only a limited role in foreign policy making is provided for India's bicameral Parliament (see The Legislature, ch. 8). Negotiated treaties and international agreements become legally binding on the state but are not part of domestic law unless passed by an act of Parliament, which also has no say in the appointment of diplomats and other government representatives dealing with foreign affairs. For the most part, because of the widespread domestic support for India's foreign policy, Parliament has endorsed government actions or sought information. The most important official link between Parliament and the executive in the mid-1990s is the Committee on External Affairs of the Lok Sabha (House of the People), the lower chamber of Parliament. The committee meets regularly and draws its membership from many parties. Usually it has served either as a forum for government briefings or as a deliberative body.

The Role of Political and Interest Groups

Institutional connections between public opinion and foreign policy making are tenuous in the mid-1990s, as they have been since independence. Although international issues receive considerable attention in the media and in academic circles, the views expressed by journalists and scholars in these publications have little impact on foreign policy making. Interest groups concerned with foreign relations exist inside and outside Parliament but are less organized or articulate than in most other democracies. These organizations include such business groups as the Federation of Indian Chambers of Commerce International; religious groups, especially among Muslims; and various friendship or cultural societies promoting closer ties with specific countries. Among the latter are informal groups known as the "Russian" and "American" lobbies.

Opposition political parties often have more effectively articulated differing views regarding foreign policy, but even these views had little impact on policy making until the 1990s. Other than the Congress (I)—(I for Indira), only the communist parties, the Janata Party, and the Jana Sangh and one of its successors, the Bharatiya Janata Party (BJP—Indian People's Party), developed coherent platforms on foreign policy (see Political Parties, ch. 8). After the mid-1950s, the communist parties were broadly supportive of Indian foreign policy. At the beginning of Janata Party rule (1977–79), Prime Minister Desai promised to return to "genuine nonalignment." However, security considerations forced Desai and his minister of external affairs, Jana Sangh stalwart Atal Behari Vajpayee, to adhere to the foreign policy path carved out by the Congress (I)—nonalignment with a pro-Soviet orientation. BJP foreign policy positions differed most strongly from those of the Congress (I). The BJP criticized nonalignment and advocated a more vigorous use of India's power to defend national interests from erosion at the hands of Pakistan and China. The BJP also favored the overt acquisition of nuclear weapons. By the early 1990s, the rising political fortunes of the BJP had an impact on the conduct of foreign policy, forcing the coalition government of V.P. Singh, which depended on BJP support, to take a hard line in the Kashmir crisis in 1990. Pressure from the Congress (I) also had an impact on India's response to the Persian Gulf crisis (see Middle East; Central Asia, this ch.).

Determinants of Foreign Relations

Historical Legacy

During the British colonial period, India was a large political entity bordered by the buffer states of Afghanistan, Nepal, Sikkim, Bhutan, and Tibet to the north and Ceylon (as Sri Lanka was then called) to the south. The withdrawal of the British and partition in 1947, which created India and Pakistan, resulted in geographical boundaries that cut across regional religious, social, ethnic, and linguistic groups, and disrupted economic and cultural ties. A slice of eastern India and the westernmost part of India became the East Wing and West Wing of Pakistan, respectively, and in 1971 the East Wing became Bangladesh.

After independence India's leaders attempted to build a secular state in which national identity would supersede regional, religious, or cultural identities. They regarded the movements for regional autonomy or independence in Punjab, Jammu and Kashmir, Tamil Nadu, and Assam as threats to Indian unity, particularly because Indian leaders believed that their neighbors—Pakistan, later Bangladesh, and Sri Lanka—supported these movements. Furthermore, despite the commitment of Congress (I) leaders to the secular ideal, communal tensions and the rising influence of Hindu political parties pushed the Indian government increasingly to identify Indian greatness with Hinduism. The inability of Indian leaders to restrain anti-Muslim communal violence and the Kashmir policy of the Indian government resulted in continual tensions in relations with its Muslim neighbors. Thus, internal security and domestic political considerations, which stemmed from the perceived goals of building national identity and preserving national unity, permeated India's relations with its neighbors.

Security Perceptions

The British colonial rulers regarded most of South Asia as a strategic unit and endeavored to exclude external powers from the region (see The British Empire in India, ch. 1). In defending this strategic unit, the British established a barrier of buffer states around India, attempting to cut off India from Russia and China, which could threaten from the north, and used naval power to protect India from the south. India's postindependence leaders adapted this concept by defining a position in cultural as well as geographical terms. This view led them to view India as the region's preeminent power whose right to involve itself in its neighbor's affairs was justified in terms of the common ethnicity and common security needs of South Asia.

This geostrategic perception affected India's foreign relations in three ways. First, India endeavored, by treaty, alliance, or threats of force or economic embargo, to overturn any move by its neighbors that it deemed inimical to its own security interests. Of its neighbors, only Pakistan and China have been able to resist or thwart Indian actions. The Indian elite regarded their country as a regional peacekeeper whose moves were entirely defensive, rather than as a regional enforcer who imposed onerous conditions on its neighbors by virtue of its size and military might. Second, India viewed the intrusion of extraregional powers into South Asia as a threat to Indian security and to India's position as the predominant country in the region. India opposed any attempts by powers external to the region, whether by invitation of New Delhi's neighbors or not, to involve themselves or to establish a presence in the region. Therefore India was critical of Pakistan's alliance with China, the Soviet invasion of Afghanistan, and the United States naval presence on Diego Garcia in the central Indian Ocean and its military relations with Pakistan. India also resisted Moscow's entreaties to grant the Soviet navy base rights despite the 1971 friendship treaty with the Soviet Union.

India's program to build the military might necessary to defend its territory and security interests became intertwined in its foreign policy. New Delhi's defense buildup—particularly its covert nuclear weapons program and its drive to develop ballistic missiles—affected relations with Pakistan, China, and the United States. India's refusal to sign the 1968 Treaty on the Non-Proliferation of Nuclear Weapons stemmed as much from Pakistan's similar stance as from India's belief that the treaty discriminated against the development of peaceful nuclear technology by nonnuclear weapons states and failed to prevent the qualitative and quantitative vertical proliferation of nuclear weapons among the nations already possessing nuclear arms. In 1995, when 174 other nations approved an indefinite extension of the treaty, India continued to refuse to sign, denouncing the treaty as "perpetuating nuclear discrimination." In addition, in the early 1990s India's sizable defense expenditures became an issue in New Delhi's attempts to secure assistance from developed countries and multilateral lending bodies (see Defense Spending, ch. 10).

Nonalignment

Nonalignment had its origins in India's colonial experience and the nonviolent independence struggle led by the Congress, which left India determined to be the master of its fate in an international system dominated politically by Cold War alliances and economically by Western capitalism. The principles of nonalignment, as articulated by Nehru and his successors, were preservation of India's freedom of action internationally through refusal to align India with any bloc or alliance, particularly those led by the United States or the Soviet Union; nonviolence and international cooperation as a means of settling international disputes; the Panch Shila (see Glossary), or the five principles of peaceful coexistence, as the basis for relations between states; opposition to colonialism and racism; and international cooperation to alleviate poverty and promote economic development (see Nehru's Legacy, ch. 1). Nonalignment was a consistent feature of Indian foreign policy by the late 1940s and enjoyed strong, almost unquestioning support among the Indian elite.

In the 1950s and 1960s, Nehru's concept of nonalignment brought India considerable international prestige among newly independent states that shared India's concerns about the military confrontation between the superpowers and the influence of the former colonial powers. New Delhi used nonalignment to establish a significant role for itself as a leader of the Third World in such multilateral organizations as the United Nations (UN) and the Nonaligned Movement (see Participation in International Organizations, this ch.). The signing of the Treaty of Peace, Friendship, and Cooperation between India and the Soviet Union in 1971 and India's involvement in the internal affairs of its smaller neighbors in the 1970s and 1980s tarnished New Delhi's image as a nonaligned nation and led some observers to note that in practice, nonalignment applied only to India's relations with countries outside South Asia.

The early 1990s demise of the bipolar world system, which had existed since the end of World War II, shook the underpinnings of India's foreign policy. The Cold War system of alliances had been rendered meaningless by the collapse of the East European communist states, the dissolution of the Warsaw

Treaty Organization (Warsaw Pact), and the demise of the Soviet Union. In the early 1990s, most colonies had become independent, and apartheid in South Africa was being dismantled, diminishing the value of anticolonialism and making it impossible for antiracism to serve as a rallying point for international political action (India and South Africa restored full diplomatic relations in 1993 after a thirty-nine-year lapse). The Panch Shila, peaceful resolution of international disputes, and international cooperation to spur economic development—which was being enhanced by domestic economic reforms—were broad objectives in a changing world. Thus, the 1990s saw India redefining nonalignment and the view of India's place in the world.

Overview of Foreign Relations

South Asia

Pakistan

Relations with Pakistan have demanded a high proportion of India's international energies and undoubtedly will continue to do so. India and Pakistan have divergent national ideologies and have been unable to establish a mutually acceptable power equation in South Asia. The national ideologies of pluralism, democracy, and secularism for India and of Islam for Pakistan grew out of the preindependence struggle between the Congress and the All-India Muslim League (Muslim League—see Glossary), and in the early 1990s the line between domestic and foreign politics in India's relations with Pakistan remained blurred. Because great-power competition—between the United States and the Soviet Union and between the Soviet Union and China—became intertwined with the conflicts between India and Pakistan, India was unable to attain its goal of insulating South Asia from global rivalries. This superpower involvement enabled Pakistan to use external force in the face of India's superior endowments of population and resources.

The most difficult problem in relations between India and Pakistan since partition in August 1947 has been their dispute over Kashmir. Pakistan's leaders did not accept the legality of the Instrument of Accession of Kashmir to India, and undeclared war broke out in October 1947 (see The Experience of Wars, ch. 10). It was the first of three conflicts between the two countries. Pakistan's representatives ever since have argued that the people of Kashmir should be allowed to exercise their right to self-determination through a plebiscite, as promised by Nehru and required by UN Security Council resolutions in 1948 and 1949. The inconclusive fighting led to a UN-arranged cease-fire starting on January 1, 1949. On July 18, 1949, the two sides signed the Karachi Agreement establishing a cease-fire line that was to be supervised by the UN. The demarcation left Srinagar and almost 139,000 square kilometers under Indian control and 83,807 square kilometers under Pakistani control. Of these two areas, China occupied 37,555 square kilometers in India's Ladakh District (part of which is known as Aksai Chin) in 1962 and Pakistan ceded, in effect, 5,180 square kilometers in the Karakoram area to China when the two countries demarcated their common border in 1961–65, leaving India with 101,387 square kilometers and Pakistan with 78,387 square kilometers. Starting in January 1949, and still in place in 1995, the UN Military Observer Group in India and Pakistan was tasked with supervising the cease-fire in Kashmir. The group comprises thirty-eight observers—from Belgium, Chile, Denmark, Finland, Italy, Norway, Sweden, and Uruguay—who rotate their headquarters every six months between Srinagar (summer) and Rawalpindi, Pakistan (winter).

In 1952 the elected and overwhelmingly Muslim Constituent Assembly of Jammu and Kashmir, led by the popular Sheikh Mohammed Abdullah, voted in favor of confirming accession to India. Thereafter, India regarded this vote as an adequate expression of popular will and demurred on holding a plebiscite. After 1953 Jammu and Kashmir was identified as standing for the secular, pluralistic, and democratic principles of the Indian polity. Nehru refused to discuss the subject bilaterally until 1963, when India, under pressure from the United States and Britain, engaged in six rounds of secret talks with Pakistan on "Kashmir and other related issues." These negotiations failed, as did the 1964 attempt at mediation made by Abdullah, who recently had been released from a long detention by the Indian government because of his objections to Indian control.

Armed infiltrators from Pakistan crossed the cease-fire line, and the number of skirmishes between Indian and Pakistani troops increased in the summer of 1965. Starting on August 5, 1965, India alleged, Pakistani forces began to infiltrate the Indian-controlled portion of Jammu and Kashmir. India made a countermove in late August, and by September 1, 1965, the second conflict had fully erupted as Pakistan launched an attack across the international line of control in southwest Jammu and Kashmir. Indian forces retaliated on September 6 in Pakistan's Punjab Province and prevailed over Pakistan's apparent superiority in tanks and aircraft. A cease-fire called by the UN Security Council on September 23 was observed by both sides. At Tashkent, Uzbekistan, in January 1966, the belligerents agreed to restore the status quo ante and to resolve outstanding issues by negotiation.

The third war between India and Pakistan, in December 1971, centered in the east over the secession of East Pakistan (which became Bangladesh), but it also included engagements in Kashmir and elsewhere on the India-West Pakistan front. India's military victory was complete. The independence of Bangladesh was widely interpreted in India—but not in Pakistan—as an ideological victory disproving the "Two Nations Theory" pushed by the Muslim League and that led to partition in 1947. At Shimla (Simla), Himachal Pradesh, on July 2, 1972, Indira Gandhi and Pakistan's President Zulfikar Ali Bhutto signed the Simla Accord by which India would return all personnel and captured territory in the west and the two countries would "settle their differences by peaceful means through bilateral negotiations." External bodies, including the UN, were excluded from the process. The fighting had resulted in the capture of each other's territory at various points along the cease-fire line, but the Simla Accord defined a new line of control that deviated in only minor ways from the 1949 cease-fire line. The two sides agreed not to alter the actual line of control unilaterally and promised to respect it "without prejudice to the recognized position of either side." Both sides further undertook to "refrain from the threat or use of force in violation of the line."

During the late 1970s and early 1980s, Jammu and Kashmir prospered under a virtually autonomous government led first by Sheikh Abdullah and then by his son Farooq Abdullah. In the summer of 1984, differences between Srinagar and New Delhi led to the dismissal of Farooq's government by highly questionable means. Kashmir once again became an irritant in bilateral relations. Indian diplomats consistently accused Pakistan of trying to "internationalize" the Kashmir dispute in violation of the Simla Accord.

In the mid- to late 1980s, the political situation in Kashmir became increasingly unstable. In March 1986, New Delhi invoked President's Rule to remove Farooq's successor, Ghulam

Mohammed Shah, as chief minister, and replace his rule with
that of Governor Jagmohan, who had been appointed by the
central government in 1984. In state elections held in 1987,
Farooq's political party, the National Conference, forged an
alliance with Rajiv Gandhi's Congress (I), which won a majority
in the state elections. Farooq's government failed to deal with
Kashmir's economic problems and the endemic corruption of
its public institutions, providing fertile ground for militant
Kashmiris who demanded either independence or association
with Pakistan.

A rising spiral of unrest, demonstrations, armed attacks by
Kashmiri separatists, and armed suppression by Indian security
forces started in 1988 and was still occurring in the mid-1990s.
New Delhi charged Islamabad (Pakistan's capital) with assisting
insurgents in Jammu and Kashmir, and Prime Minister V.P.
Singh warned that India should be psychologically prepared
for war. In Pakistan Prime Minister Benazir Bhutto stated that
Pakistan was willing to fight a "thousand-year war" for control
of Kashmir. Under pressure from the United States, the Soviet
Union, and China to avoid a military conflict and solve their
dispute under the terms of the Simla Accord, India and Pakistan backed off in May 1990 and engaged in a series of talks on
confidence-building measures for the rest of the year. Tensions
reached new heights in the early and mid-1990s with increasing
internal unrest in Jammu and Kashmir, charges of human
rights abuses, and repeated clashes between Indian paramilitary forces and Kashmiri militants, allegedly armed with Paki-
stani-supplied weapons (see Political Issues, ch. 8; Insurgent
Movements and External Subversion, ch. 10).

A concurrent irritant related to the Kashmir dispute was the
confrontation over the Siachen Glacier near the Karakoram
Pass, which is located in northeast Jammu and Kashmir. In
1984, Indian officials, citing Pakistan's "cartographic aggression" extending the line of control northeast toward the Karakoram Pass, contended that Pakistan intended to occupy the
Siachen Glacier in order to stage an attack into Indian-controlled Kashmir. After New Delhi airlifted troops into the western parts of the Saltoro Mountains, Islamabad deployed troops
opposite them. Both sides maintained 5,000 troops in temperatures averaging –40°C. The estimated cost for India was about
10 percent of the annual defense budget for FY 1992. After several skirmishes between the opposing troops, negotiations to
resolve this confrontation began with five rounds of talks

between 1986 and 1989. After a three-year hiatus because of tensions caused by the other Kashmir conflict, a sixth round of talks was held in November 1992. Some progress was made on the details of an agreement. In March 1994, Indian diplomats garnered enough support at the UN Human Rights Commission to force Pakistan to withdraw a resolution charging India with human rights violations in Jammu and Kashmir. The two sides were encouraged to resolve their dispute through bilateral talks.

After the Soviet Union invaded Afghanistan in December 1979 and Indira Gandhi returned to power in 1980, she quickly dispatched a special emissary to assure Pakistani president General Mohammad Zia ul Haq that he could remove as many divisions as he wished from the Indian border without fear of any advantage being taken by India and suggested talks on reduction of force levels. Indian officials worked hard to prevent Zia from using the Afghan crisis as an opportunity to alter the regional balance of power by acquiring advanced weapons from the United States. In addition, Indira Gandhi attempted to avoid antagonizing the Soviet Union, democratic elements in Pakistan, and the substantial anti-Pakistan lobby within India. These largely secret efforts culminated in the visit of Minister of External Affairs P.V. Narasimha Rao to Pakistan in June 1981, during which time he declared publicly that India was "unequivocally committed to respect Pakistan's national unity, territorial integrity, and sovereign equality" as well as its right to obtain arms for self-defense.

Despite the setback suffered when the United States and Pakistan announced a new security and military assistance program, regular meetings took place between high Indian and Pakistani officials. These meetings were institutionalized in late 1982 in the Indo-Pakistan Joint Commission, which included subcommissions for trade, economics, information, and travel. Indira Gandhi also received Zia on November 1, 1982, in New Delhi, and during their meeting they authorized their foreign ministers and foreign secretaries to proceed with talks leading to the establishment of the South Asian Association for Regional Cooperation (SAARC—see Glossary).

In the mid- and late 1980s, India-Pakistan relations settled into a pattern of ups and downs. Despite the signing of an economic and trade agreement, little progress was made in concluding a comprehensive, long-term economic agreement to have nondiscriminatory bilateral trade. In addition, New Delhi charged Islamabad with arming and training Sikh terrorists in Punjab. The government's 1984 *White Paper on the Punjab Agitation* stated that India's strength, unity, and secularism were targets of attack. The December 1985 visit of Zia to India, during which both sides agreed not to attack each other's nuclear facilities, ushered in a brief phase of cordiality, in which another agreement expanding trade was signed. The cordiality evaporated in early 1986, with further Indian unhappiness over Pakistan's alleged interference in Punjab and the bungled Pakistani handling of the terrorist seizure of a Pan American airliner in which many Indians died. For its part, Pakistan was disturbed by anti-Muslim riots in India, and Zia accused India of assisting the political campaign of Benazir Bhutto.

Between November 1986 and February 1987, first India, then Pakistan, conducted provocative military maneuvers along their border that raised tensions considerably. India's "Operation Brass Tacks" took place in Rajasthan, across from Pakistan's troubled Sindh Province, and Pakistan's maneuvers were located close to India's state of Punjab. The crisis atmosphere was heightened when Pakistan's premier nuclear scientist Abdul Qadir Khan revealed in a March 1987 interview that Pakistan had manufactured a nuclear bomb. Although Khan later retracted his statement, India stated that the disclosure was "forcing us to review our option." The tensions created by the military exercises and the nuclear issue were defused following talks at the foreign secretary level in New Delhi (January 31–February 4) and Islamabad (February 27–March 2), during which the two sides agreed to a phased troop withdrawal to peacetime positions.

The sudden death of Zia in an air crash in August 1988 and the assumption of the prime ministership by Benazir Bhutto in December 1988 after democratic elections provided the two countries with an unexpected opportunity to improve relations. Rajiv Gandhi's attendance at the SAARC summit in Islamabad in December 1988 permitted the two prime ministers to establish a personal rapport and to sign three bilateral agreements, including one proscribing attacks on each other's nuclear facilities. Despite the personal sympathy between the two leaders and Bhutto's initial emphasis on the 1972 Simla Accord as the basis for warmer bilateral ties, domestic political pressures, particularly relating to unrest in Sindh, Punjab, and Kashmir effectively destroyed the chances for improved relations in 1989 and 1990. For her part, Bhutto backed away from

Indira Gandhi, prime minister from 1966 to 1977 and 1980 to 1984
Courtesy Embassy of India, Washington

her comments on the Simla Accord by continuing to press the Kashmir issue internationally, and Indian public opinion forced Rajiv Gandhi and his successor, V.P. Singh, to take a hard line on events relating to Kashmir.

In the early 1990s, Indian-Pakistani relations remained troubled despite bilateral efforts and changes in the international environment. High-level dialogue on a range of bilateral issues took place between foreign ministers and prime ministers at the UN and at other international meetings. However, discussions over confidence-building measures, begun in the summer of 1990 as a response to the Kashmir confrontation, were canceled in June 1992 following mutual expulsions of diplomats for alleged espionage activities. In June 1991, Pakistani prime minister Mian Nawaz Sharif proposed talks by India, Pakistan, the United States, the Soviet Union, and China to consider making South Asia a nuclear-free zone, but the minority governments of Chandra Shekhar and subsequently that of Narasimha Rao declined to participate. Nevertheless, negotiations concerning the Siachen Glacier resumed in November 1992 after a hiatus of three years. By the mid-1990s, little had occurred to improve bilateral relations as unrest in Jammu and Kashmir accelerated and domestic politics in both nations were unsettled.

Bangladesh

Although India played a major role in the establishment of an independent Bangladesh on April 17, 1971, New Delhi's relations with Dhaka, the capital of Bangladesh, were neither close nor free from dispute (see The Rise of Indira Gandhi, ch. 1). In 1975 Bangladesh began to move away from the linguistic nationalism that had marked its liberation struggle and linked it to India's West Bengal state. Instead, Dhaka stressed Islam as the binding force in Bangladeshi nationalism. The new emphasis on Islam, combined with Bangladeshi concern over India's military buildup and bilateral disputes over riparian borders, shared water resources, and illegal immigration of Bangladeshis into West Bengal, made for fluctuations in India-Bangladesh relations.

Relations are generally good, nevertheless; the two countries have maintained a dialogue on a variety of issues and initiated a modest program of joint economic cooperation. In 1977 New Delhi and Dhaka signed an agreement—that is renewed annually—on sharing the waters of the Ganga (Ganges) River during the dry season, but the two sides made little progress in achieving a permanent solution to their other problems. The main item of contention is the Farakka Barrage, where the Ganga divides into two branches and India has built a feeder canal that controls the flow by rechanneling water on the Indian side of the river. The two nations were still at odds, despite high-level talks, in the mid-1990s.

In the mid- and late 1980s, India's plan to erect a fence to prevent cross-border migration from Bangladesh and Bangladesh's desire that Chakma insurgents not receive Indian covert assistance and refuge in India were major irritants in bilateral relations. As agreed eighteen years earlier, in June 1992 India granted a perpetual lease to Bangladesh for the narrow, 1.5-hectare Tin Bigha corridor in the Ganga's delta that had long separated an enclave of Bangladeshis from their homeland. The two countries signed new agreements to enhance economic cooperation. Bangladesh also received Indian developmental assistance, but that aid was minor compared with the amounts India granted to Nepal, Bhutan, Sri Lanka, and Maldives. The year 1991 also witnessed the first-ever visit of an Indian army chief of staff to Dhaka.

Sri Lanka

The two major factors influencing India's relations with Sri

Lanka have been security and the shared ethnicity of Tamils living in southern India and in northern and eastern Sri Lanka. Before 1980 common security perceptions and New Delhi's reluctance to intervene in internal affairs in Sri Lanka's capital of Colombo made for relatively close ties between the two countries' governments. Beginning in the mid-1950s, and coinciding with the withdrawal of Britain's military presence in the Indian Ocean, India and Sri Lanka increasingly came to share regional security interests. In the 1970s, New Delhi and Colombo enjoyed close ties on the strength of the relationship between Indira Gandhi and Sri Lanka's prime minister, Mrs. Sirimavo Ratwatte Dias (S.R.D.) Bandaranaike. India fully approved Sri Lanka's desire to replace the British security umbrella with an Indian one, and both sides pursued a policy of nonalignment and cooperated to minimize Western influence in the Indian Ocean.

In the 1980s, ethnic conflict between Sri Lankan Sinhalese in the south and Sri Lankan Tamils in the north escalated, and Tamil separatists established bases and received funding, weapons, and, reportedly, training in India. The clandestine assistance came from private sources and, according to some observers, the state government of Tamil Nadu, and was tolerated by the central government until 1987. Anti-Tamil violence in Colombo in July 1983 prompted India to intervene in the Tamil-Sinhalese conflict, but mediatory efforts failed to prevent the deterioration of the situation. In May 1987, after the Sri Lankan government attempted to regain control of the Jaffna region, in the extreme northern area of the island, by means of an economic blockade and military action, India supplied food and medicine by air and sea to the region. On July 29, 1987, Indian prime minister Rajiv Gandhi and Sri Lankan president Junius Richard (J.R.) Jayawardene signed an accord designed to settle the conflict by sending the Indian Peace Keeping Force (IPKF) to establish order and disarm Tamil separatists, to establish new administrative bodies and hold elections to accommodate Tamil demands for autonomy, and to repatriate Tamil refugees in India and Sri Lanka. The accord also forbade the military use of Sri Lankan ports or broadcasting facilities by outside powers. The Liberation Tigers of Tamil Eelam (LTTE), the most militant separatist group, refused to disarm, and Indian troops sustained heavy casualties while failing to destroy the LTTE. In June 1989, newly elected Sri Lankan president Ranasinghe Premadasa demanded the withdrawal of the IPKF. Despite the tensions between the two countries created by this request, New Delhi completed the withdrawal in March 1990 (see Peacekeeping Operations, ch. 10).

Bilateral relations improved somewhat in the early 1990s, as the government attempted to expand economic, scientific, and cultural cooperation. India continued to take an interest in the status of Sri Lankan Tamils, but without the direct intervention that characterized the 1980s. The May 1991 assassination of Rajiv Gandhi, allegedly by the LTTE, forced New Delhi to crack down on the LTTE presence in Tamil Nadu and to institute naval patrols in the Palk Strait to interdict LTTE movements to India. In January 1992, repatriation of Tamil refugees to Sri Lanka commenced and was still underway in 1994.

Nepal

Relations between India and Nepal are close yet fraught with difficulties stemming from geography, economics, the problems inherent in big power-small power relations, and common ethnic and linguistic identities that overlap the two countries' borders. In 1950 New Delhi and Kathmandu initiated their intertwined relationship with the Treaty of Peace and Friendship and accompanying letters that defined security relations between the two countries, and an agreement governing both bilateral trade and trade transiting Indian soil. The 1950 treaty and letters stated that "neither government shall tolerate any threat to the security of the other by a foreign aggressor" and obligated both sides "to inform each other of any serious friction or misunderstanding with any neighboring state likely to cause any breach in the friendly relations subsisting between the two governments." These accords cemented a "special relationship" between India and Nepal that granted Nepal preferential economic treatment and provided Nepalese in India the same economic and educational opportunities as Indian citizens.

In the 1950s, Nepal welcomed close relations with India, but as the number of Nepalese living and working in India increased and the involvement of India in Nepal's economy deepened in the 1960s and after, so too did Nepalese discomfort with the special relationship. Tensions came to a head in the mid-1970s, when Nepal pressed for substantial amendments in its favor in the trade and transit treaty and openly criticized India's 1975 annexation of Sikkim as an Indian state. In

*Rajiv Gandhi, prime minister
from 1984 to 1989
Courtesy Embassy of India,
Washington*

1975 King Birendra Bir Bikram Shah Dev proposed that Nepal be recognized internationally as a zone of peace; he received support from China and Pakistan. In New Delhi's view, if the king's proposal did not contradict the 1950 treaty and was merely an extension of nonalignment, it was unnecessary; if it was a repudiation of the special relationship, it represented a possible threat to India's security and could not be endorsed. In 1984 Nepal repeated the proposal, but there was no reaction from India. Nepal continually promoted the proposal in international forums, with Chinese support; by 1990 it had won the support of 112 countries.

In 1978 India agreed to separate trade and transit treaties, satisfying a long-term Nepalese demand. In 1988, when the two treaties were up for renewal, Nepal's refusal to accommodate India's wishes on the transit treaty caused India to call for a single trade and transit treaty. Thereafter, Nepal took a hard-line position that led to a serious crisis in India-Nepal relations. After two extensions, the two treaties expired on March 23, 1989, resulting in a virtual Indian economic blockade of Nepal that lasted until late April 1990. Although economic issues were a major factor in the two countries' confrontation, Indian dissatisfaction with Nepal's 1988 acquisition of Chinese weaponry played an important role. New Delhi perceived the arms purchase as an indication of Kathmandu's intent to build a military relationship with Beijing, in violation of the 1950 treaty and letters exchanged in 1959 and 1965, which included Nepal in India's security zone and precluded arms purchases without India's approval. India linked security with economic relations and insisted on reviewing India-Nepal relations as a whole. Nepal had to back down after worsening economic conditions led to a change in Nepal's political system, in which the king was forced to institute a parliamentary democracy. The new government sought quick restoration of amicable relations with India.

The special security relationship between New Delhi and Kathmandu was reestablished during the June 1990 New Delhi meeting of Nepal's prime minister Krishna Prasad Bhattarai and Indian prime minister V.P. Singh. During the December 1991 visit to India by Nepalese prime minister Girijad Prasad Koirala, the two countries signed new, separate trade and transit treaties and other economic agreements designed to accord Nepal additional economic benefits.

Indian-Nepali relations appeared to be undergoing still more reassessment when Nepal's prime minister Man Mohan Adhikary visited New Delhi in April 1995 and insisted on a major review of the 1950 peace and friendship treaty. In the face of benign statements by his Indian hosts relating to the treaty, Adhikary sought greater economic independence for his landlocked nation while simultaneously striving to improve ties with China.

Bhutan

Despite the long and substantial involvement of India in Bhutan's economic, educational, and military affairs, and India's advisory role in foreign affairs embodied in the August 8, 1949, Treaty of Friendship Between the Government of India and the Government of Bhutan, Thimphu's autonomy has been fully respected by New Delhi. Bhutan's geographic isolation, its distinctive Buddhist culture, and its deliberate restriction on the number and kind of foreigners admitted have helped to protect its separate identity. Furthermore, Bhutan's relationship with China, unlike Nepal's, has not become an issue in relations with India. Bhutanese subjects have the same access to economic and educational opportunities as Indian citizens, and Indian citizens have the right to carry on trade in Bhutan, with some restrictions that protect Bhutanese industries. India also provides Bhutan with developmental assistance and cooperation in infrastructure, telecommunications, industry, energy, medicine, and animal husbandry. Since joining the UN in 1971, Bhutan has increasingly established its international status in a concerted effort to avoid the fate of Sikkim's absorption into India following the reduction of Sikkim's indigenous people to minority status.

Maldives

India and Maldives have enjoyed close and friendly relations since Maldives became independent in 1965. Disputes between the two countries have been few, and both sides amicably settled their maritime boundary in 1976. In November 1988, at the behest of the Maldivian government, Indian paratroopers and naval forces crushed a coup attempt by mercenaries. India's action, viewed by some critics as an indication of Indian ambitions to be a regional police officer, were regarded by the United States, the Soviet Union, Britain, Nepal, and Bangladesh as legitimate assistance to a friendly government and in keeping with India's strategic role in South Asia. In the 1980s and 1990s, Indian and Maldivian leaders maintained regular consultations at the highest levels. New Delhi also has provided developmental assistance to Male (Maldives' capital) and has participated in bilateral cooperation programs in infrastructure development, health and welfare, civil aviation, telecommunications, and labor resources development.

China

Although India and China had relatively little political contact before the 1950s, both countries have had extensive cultural contact since the first century A.D., especially with the transmission of Buddhism from India to China (see Buddhism, ch. 3). Although Nehru based his vision of "resurgent Asia" on friendship between the two largest states of Asia, the two countries had a conflict of interest in Tibet (which later became China's Xizang Autonomous Region), a geographical and political buffer zone where India had inherited special privileges from the British colonial government. At the end of its civil war in 1949, China wanted to reassert control over Tibet and to "liberate" the Tibetan people from Lamaism (Tibetan Buddhism) and feudalism, which it did by force of arms in 1950. To avoid antagonizing China, Nehru informed Chinese leaders that India had neither political nor territorial ambitions, nor did it seek special privileges in Tibet, but that traditional trading rights must continue. With Indian support, Tibetan delegates signed an agreement in May 1951 recognizing Chinese sovereignty and control but guaranteeing that the existing political and social system in Tibet would continue. Direct negotiations between India and China commenced in an atmosphere improved by India's mediatory efforts in ending the Korean War (1950–53).

In April 1954, India and China signed an eight-year agreement on Tibet that set forth the basis of their relationship in the form of the Panch Shila. Although critics called the Panch Shila naive, Nehru calculated that in the absence of either the wherewithal or a policy for defense of the Himalayan region, India's best guarantee of security was to establish a psychological buffer zone in place of the lost physical buffer of Tibet. Thus the catch phrase of India's diplomacy with China in the 1950s was *Hindi-Chini bhai-bhai* (Hindi for "India and China are brothers"). Up to 1959, despite border skirmishes and discrepancies between Indian and Chinese maps, Chinese leaders amicably had assured India that there was no territorial controversy on the border.

When an Indian reconnaissance party discovered a completed Chinese road running through the Aksai Chin region of the Ladakh District of Jammu and Kashmir, border clashes and Indian protests became more frequent and serious. In January 1959, Chinese premier Zhou Enlai wrote to Nehru, rejecting Nehru's contention that the border was based on treaty and custom and pointing out that no government in China had accepted as legal the McMahon Line, which in the 1914 Simla Convention defined the eastern section of the border between India and Tibet. The Dalai Lama—spiritual and temporal head of the Tibetan people—sought sanctuary in Dharmsala, Himachal Pradesh, in March 1959, and thousands of Tibetan refugees settled in northwestern India, particularly in Himachal Pradesh. China accused India of expansionism and imperialism in Tibet and throughout the Himalayan region. China claimed 104,000 square kilometers of territory over which India's maps showed clear sovereignty, and demanded "rectification" of the entire border.

Zhou proposed that China relinquish its claim to most of India's northeast in exchange for India's abandonment of its claim to Aksai Chin. The Indian government, constrained by domestic public opinion, rejected the idea of a settlement based on uncompensated loss of territory as being humiliating and unequal.

Chinese forces attacked India on October 20, 1962. Having pushed the unprepared, ill-equipped, and inadequately led Indian forces to within forty-eight kilometers of the Assam plains in the northeast and having occupied strategic points in Ladakh, China declared a unilateral cease-fire on November 21 and withdrew twenty kilometers behind its new line of control (see The Experience of Wars, ch. 10).

Relations with China worsened during the rest of the 1960s and the early 1970s as Chinese-Pakistani relations improved and Chinese-Soviet relations worsened. China backed Pakistan in its 1965 war with India. Between 1967 and 1971, an all-weather road was built across territory claimed by India, linking China's Xinjiang Uygur Autonomous Region with Pakistan; India could do no more than protest. China continued an active propaganda campaign against India and supplied ideological, financial, and other assistance to dissident groups, especially to tribes in northeastern India. China accused India of assisting the Khampa rebels in Tibet. Diplomatic contact between the two governments was minimal although not formally severed. The flow of cultural and other exchanges that had marked the 1950s ceased entirely. In August 1971, India signed its Treaty of Peace, Friendship, and Cooperation with the Soviet Union, and the United States and China sided with Pakistan in its December 1971 war with India. By this time, Beijing was seated at the UN, where its representatives denounced India as being a "tool of Soviet expansionism."

India and China renewed efforts to improve relations after the Soviet Union invaded Afghanistan in December 1979. China modified its pro-Pakistan stand on Kashmir and appeared willing to remain silent on India's absorption of Sikkim and its special advisory relationship with Bhutan. China's leaders agreed to discuss the boundary issue—India's priority—as the first step to a broadening of relations. The two countries hosted each others' news agencies, and Kailash (Kangrinbogê Feng) and Mansarowar Lake (Mapam Yumco Lake) in Tibet—the mythological home of the Hindu pantheon—were opened to annual pilgrimages from India. In 1981 Chinese minister of foreign affairs Huang Hua was invited to India, where he made complimentary remarks about India's role in South Asia. Chinese premier Zhao Ziyang concurrently toured Pakistan, Nepal, and Bangladesh.

After the Huang visit, India and China held eight rounds of border negotiations between December 1981 and November 1987. These talks initially raised hopes that progress could be made on the border issue. However, in 1985 China stiffened its position on the border and insisted on mutual concessions without defining the exact terms of its "package proposal" or where the actual line of control lay. In 1986 and 1987, the negotiations achieved nothing, given the charges exchanged between the two countries of military encroachment in the Sumdorung Chu valley of the Tawang tract on the eastern sector of the border. China's construction of a military post and helicopter pad in the area in 1986 and India's grant of statehood to Arunachal Pradesh (formerly the North-East Frontier Agency) in February 1987 caused both sides to deploy new troops to the area, raising tensions and fears of a new border war. China relayed warnings that it would "teach India a lesson" if it did not cease "nibbling" at Chinese territory. By the summer of 1987, however, both sides had backed away from conflict and denied that military clashes had taken place.

A warming trend in relations was facilitated by Rajiv Gandhi's visit to China in December 1988. The two sides issued a joint communiqué that stressed the need to restore friendly relations on the basis of the Panch Shila and noted the importance of the first visit by an Indian prime minister to China since Nehru's 1954 visit. India and China agreed to broaden bilateral ties in various areas, working to achieve a "fair and reasonable settlement while seeking a mutually acceptable solution" to the border dispute. The communiqué also expressed China's concern about agitation by Tibetan separatists in India and reiterated China's position that Tibet was an integral part of China and that anti-China political activities by expatriate Tibetans was not to be tolerated. Rajiv Gandhi signed bilateral agreements on science and technology cooperation, on civil aviation to establish direct air links, and on cultural exchanges. The two sides also agreed to hold annual diplomatic consultations between foreign ministers, and to set up a joint ministerial committee on economic and scientific cooperation and a joint working group on the boundary issue. The latter group was to be led by the Indian foreign secretary and the Chinese vice minister of foreign affairs.

As the mid-1990s approached, slow but steady improvement in relations with China was visible. Top-level dialogue continued with the December 1991 visit of Chinese premier Li Peng to India and the May 1992 visit to China of Indian president Ramaswami Venkataraman. Six rounds of talks of the Indian-Chinese Joint Working Group on the Border Issue were held between December 1988 and June 1993. Progress was also made in reducing tensions on the border via confidence-building measures, including mutual troop reductions, regular meetings of local military commanders, and advance notification of military exercises. Border trade resumed in July 1992 after a hiatus of more than thirty years, consulates reopened in Bombay (or Mumbai in the Marathi language) and Shanghai in December 1992, and, in June 1993, the two sides agreed to open an additional border trading post. During Sharad Pawar's July 1992 visit to Beijing, the first ever by an Indian minister of defence, the two defense establishments agreed to develop academic, military, scientific, and technological exchanges and to schedule an Indian port call by a Chinese naval vessel.

Substantial movement in relations continued in 1993. The sixth- round joint working group talks were held in June in New Delhi but resulted in only minor developments. However, as the year progressed the long-standing border dispute was eased as a result of bilateral pledges to reduce troop levels and to respect the cease-fire line along the India-China border. Prime Minister Narasimha Rao and Chinese premier Li Peng signed the border agreement and three other agreements (on cross-border trade, and on increased cooperation on the environment and in radio and television broadcasting) during the former's visit to Beijing in September. A senior-level Chinese military delegation made a six-day goodwill visit to India in December 1993 aimed at "fostering confidence-building measures between the defense forces of the two countries." The visit, however, came at a time when press reports revealed that, as a result of improved relations between China and Burma, China was exporting greater amounts of military matériel to Burma's army, navy, and air force and sending an increasing number of technicians to Burma. Of concern to Indian security officials was the presence of Chinese radar technicians in Burma's Coco Islands, which border India's Union Territory of the Andaman and Nicobar Islands. Nevertheless, movement continued in 1994 on troop reductions along the Himalayan frontier. Moreover, in January 1994 Beijing announced that it not only favored a negotiated solution on Kashmir, but also opposed any form of independence for the region.

Talks were held in New Delhi in February 1994 aimed at confirming established "confidence-building measures" and discussing clarification of the "line of actual control," reduction of armed forces along the line, and prior information about forthcoming military exercises. China's hope for settlement of the boundary issue was reiterated.

The 1993 Chinese military visit to India was reciprocated by Indian army chief of staff General B.C. Joshi. During talks in Beijing in July 1994, the two sides agreed that border problems should be resolved peacefully through "mutual understanding and concessions." The border issue was raised in September 1994 when Chinese minister of national defense Chi Haotian visited New Delhi for extensive talks with high-level Indian trade and defense officials. Further talks in New Delhi in March 1995 by the India-China Expert Group led to an agreement to set up two additional points of contact along the 4,000-kilometer border to facilitate meetings between military personnel. The two sides also were reported as "seriously engaged" in defining the McMahon Line and the line of actual control vis-à-vis military exercises and prevention of air intrusion. Talks in Beijing in July 1995 aimed at better border security and combating cross-border crimes and in New Delhi in August 1995 on additional troop withdrawals from the border made further progress in reducing tensions.

Possibly indicative of the further relaxation of India-China relations—at least there was little notice taken in Beijing—was the April 1995 announcement, after a year of consultation, of the opening of the Taipei Economic and Cultural Center in New Delhi. The center serves as the representative office of Taiwan and is the counterpart of the India-Taipei Association in Taiwan; both institutions have the goal of improving relations between the two sides, which have been strained since New Delhi's recognition of Beijing in 1950.

Southeast Asia

In the 1970s and 1980s, India's close ties with the Soviet Union and its pro-Soviet, pro-Vietnamese policies toward Cambodia precluded development of any constructive relations between India on the one hand and the countries of the Association of Southeast Asian Nations (ASEAN—see Glossary) on the other. Furthermore, India's military buildup, particularly of its naval capabilities and naval installations in the Andaman and Nicobar Islands, worried ASEAN policy makers, who saw

India as a potential threat to regional security. Indian-ASEAN relations improved in the 1990s as the result of the end of the bipolar world system, the UN-brokered peace settlement in Cambodia, and the breakup of the Soviet Union. For its part, New Delhi sought to boost economic and trade ties with the region and to establish closer political and defense ties in order to counteract China's growing influence in Southeast Asia. ASEAN countries grew less concerned with India's regional ambitions after New Delhi's decision to curtail its naval buildup because of financial restraints. In January 1992, ASEAN accepted India's proposal to become a "sectoral dialogue partner" in the areas of trade, technical and labor development, technology, and tourism. India's new role was expected to facilitate economic cooperation. In January 1993, India and Malaysia signed a memorandum of understanding on defense cooperation.

India has had close ties with Cambodia, Laos, and Vietnam as a result of its 1954–73 chairmanship of the International Commissions of Control and Supervision established by the 1954 Geneva Accords on Indochina. These relations were enhanced by India's friendship with the Soviet Union, particularly after 1971 and, in the case of Vietnam, shared perceptions of the threat from China. With regard to Cambodia, India recognized the Vietnamese-installed regime in 1980 and worked to avert censure of the regime in the annual UN General Assembly and triennial Nonaligned Movement summit meetings. In the late 1980s, Indian diplomats attempted to facilitate the search for peace in Cambodia, and India participated in the 1989 Paris Peace Conference on Cambodia and in subsequent efforts to find a solution to the Cambodian situation. New Delhi played a minor but nevertheless constructive role before and after the Agreement on a Comprehensive Political Settlement of the Cambodia Conflict and three other documents were signed in Paris on October 23, 1991. India contributed more than 1,700 civilian, military, and police personnel to the United Nations Advanced Mission in Cambodia and the United Nations Transitional Authority in Cambodia.

Middle East

India has traditionally pursued a pro-Arab policy regarding the Arab-Israeli conflict in order to counteract Pakistani influence in the region and to secure access to Middle East petroleum resources. In the 1950s and early 1960s, this pro-Arab stance did not help India in establishing good relations with all Arab countries but may have served to keep peace with its own Muslim minority. India concentrated on developing a close relationship with Egypt on the strength of Nehru's ties with Egyptian president Gamel Abdul Nasser. But the New Delhi-Cairo friendship was insufficient to counteract Arab sympathy for Pakistan in its dispute with India. Furthermore, Indian-Egyptian ties came at the expense of cultivating relations with such countries as Saudi Arabia and Jordan and thus limited India's influence in the region.

In the late 1960s and in the 1970s, India successfully improved bilateral relations by developing mutually beneficial economic exchanges with a number of Islamic countries, particularly Iran, Iraq, Saudi Arabia, and the other Persian Gulf states. The strength of India's economic ties enabled it to build strong relationships with Iran and Iraq, which helped India weather the displeasure of Islamic countries stemming from India's war with Pakistan in 1971. Indian-Middle Eastern relations were further strengthened by New Delhi's anti-Israeli stance in the Arab-Israeli wars of 1967 and 1973 and by Indian support for the fourfold oil price rise in 1973 by the Organization of the Petroleum Exporting Countries (OPEC). Closer ties with Middle Eastern countries were dictated by India's dependency on petroleum imports. Oil represented 8 percent of India's total imports in 1971; 42 percent in 1981; and 28 percent in 1991. India purchased oil from Iran, Iraq, Saudi Arabia, the United Arab Emirates, and Kuwait and, in return, provided engineering services, manufactured goods, and labor. The 1980–88 Iran-Iraq War forced India to shift its oil purchases from Iran and Iraq to Saudi Arabia and the Persian Gulf states. Saudi Arabia and the Gulf states also have received large numbers of Indian workers and manufactures and have become the regional base for Indian business operations.

Two events in 1978 and 1979—the installation of the Islamic regime under Ayatollah Sayyid Ruhollah Musavi Khomeini in Iran and the Soviet invasion of Afghanistan in support of the pro-Soviet Marxist regime in Kabul—complicated India's relations with Middle East countries. From the Indian perspective, these two events and the Iran-Iraq War changed the balance of power in West Asia by weakening Iran as a regional power and a potential supporter of Pakistan, a situation favorable to India. At the same time, proxy superpower competition in Afghanistan strengthened the hand of India's adversary Pakistan by virtue of the military support Pakistan received from the United States, China, and Arab states led by Saudi Arabia. In the 1980s, India performed a delicate diplomatic balancing act. New Delhi took a position of neutrality in the Iran-Iraq War, maintained warm ties with Baghdad, and built workable political and economic relations with Tehran despite misgivings about the foreign policy goals of the Khomeini regime. India managed to improve relations with Middle Eastern countries that provided support to the Afghan *mujahideen* and Pakistan by redirecting Indian petroleum purchases to Saudi Arabia and the Persian Gulf countries. New Delhi, which traditionally had had close relations with Kabul, condemned the Soviet invasion only in the most perfunctory manner and provided diplomatic, economic, and logistic support for the Marxist regime.

In the early 1990s, India stepped back from its staunch anti-Israeli stance and support for the Palestinian cause. Besides practical economic and security considerations in the post-Cold War world, domestic politics—especially those influenced by Hindu nationalists—played a role in this reversal. In December 1991, India voted with the UN majority to repeal the UN resolution equating Zionism with racism. In 1992, following the example of the Soviet Union and China, India established diplomatic relations with Israel.

During the 1990–91 Persian Gulf War, Indian policy makers were torn between adopting a traditional nonaligned policy sympathetic to Iraq or favoring the coalition of moderate Arab and Western countries that could benefit Indian security and economic interests. India initially adopted an ambivalent approach, condemning both the Iraqi invasion of Kuwait and the intrusion of external forces into the region. When the National Front government led by V.P. Singh was replaced by the Chandra Shekhar minority government in November 1990, the Indian response changed. Wary of incurring the displeasure of the United States and other Western nations on whom India depended to obtain assistance from the International Monetary Fund (IMF—see Glossary), New Delhi voted for the UN resolution authorizing the use of force to expel Iraqi troops from Kuwait and rejected Iraq's linkage of the Kuwaiti and Palestinian problems. In January 1991, India also permitted United States military aircraft to refuel in Bombay. The refueling decision stirred such domestic controversy that the Chandra Shekhar government withdrew the refueling privileges in February 1991 to deflect the criticism of Rajiv Gandhi's

Congress (I), which argued that India's nominal pro-United States tilt betrayed the country's nonaligned principles.

Prime Minister Narasimha Rao's September 1993 visit to Iran was hailed as "successful and useful" by the Indian media and seen as a vehicle for speeding up the improvement of bilateral relations. Key developments included discussions on the construction of a pipeline to supply Iranian natural gas to India and allowing India to develop transit facilities in Iran for Indian products destined for the landlocked Central Asian republics. India also sought to assuage its concerns over a possible Iranian-Central Asian republics nuclear nexus, which some saw as a potential and very serious threat to India should Pakistan also join in an Islamic nuclear front aimed at India and Israel. When Iranian president Hashemi Rafsanjani visited India in April 1995 to sign a major trade accord (the accord also was signed by the minister of foreign affairs of Turkmenistan) and five bilateral agreements, India-Iranian relations could be seen to be on the upswing.

Central Asia

Until large parts of Central Asia were incorporated into the Russian Empire in the mid-nineteenth century, relations between India and Central Asia had been close. During the post-1971 era of close Indian-Soviet relations, cultural exchanges flourished between India and the Central Asian republics. The dissolution of the Soviet Union forced India to construct policies to deal with the new political situation in the Central Asian republics. In 1991 and 1992, India established diplomatic relations with Kazakstan, Kyrgyzstan, Tajikistan, Turkmenistan, and Uzbekistan and worked with these newly independent states to develop frameworks for diplomatic, economic, and cultural cooperation. Besides its long historical connections with this region, India sought good relations for several reasons: to prevent Pakistan from developing an anti-India coalition with the Central Asian states in the dispute over Kashmir, to persuade those states not to provide Pakistan with assistance in its nuclear program, to ensure continued contacts with long-standing commercial and military suppliers, and to provide new opportunities to Indian businesses.

Normal diplomatic and trade relations are an Indian goal in relations with the Central Asian republics. For example, economic and cultural affairs were the focal point of Indian prime minister P.V. Narahimsa Rao's official visit to Uzbekistan and

Kazakstan in May 1993. Security matters also are important as witnessed by a February 1995 visit to India by Kazakstan's defense minister. Adherence to democracy and secularism by these countries also was regarded by India as desirable in order to ensure stability and social progress. The geopolitical competition between India and Pakistan for influence in these countries is likely to be a long-tern factor.

With regard to Afghanistan, India supported the Marxist regime in Kabul until its collapse in the spring of 1992. India then attempted to regain some influence in the country by cooperating with Iran to provide assistance to Dari-speaking and other minorities against the Pashtun groups backed by Pakistan in the ensuing civil war.

Russia

Despite the disintegration of the Soviet Union in 1991, the relationship between India and Russia remains one of considerable importance to both countries. Since the early 1950s, New Delhi and Moscow had built friendly relations on the basis of realpolitik. India's nonalignment enabled it to accept Soviet support in areas of strategic congruence, as in disputes with Pakistan and China, without subscribing to Soviet global policies or proposals for Asian collective security. Close and cooperative ties were forged in particular in the sectors of Indian industrial development and defense production and purchases. But the relationship was circumscribed by wide differences in domestic and social systems and the absence of substantial people-to-people contact—in contrast to India's relations with the United States (see United States, this ch.).

Ties between India and the Soviet Union initially were distant. Nehru had expressed admiration for the Soviet Union's rapid economic transformation, but the Soviet Union regarded India as a "tool of Anglo-American imperialism." After Josef Stalin's death in 1953, the Soviet Union expressed its hopes for "friendly cooperation" with India. This aim was prompted by the Soviet decision to broaden its international contacts and to cultivate the nonaligned and newly independent countries of Asia and Africa. Nehru's state visit to the Soviet Union in June 1955 was the first of its kind for an Indian prime minister. It was followed by the trip of Premier Nikolai Bulganin and General Secretary Nikita Khrushchev to India in November and December 1955. The Soviet leaders endorsed the entire range of Indian foreign policy based on the Panch Shila and supported

India's position against Pakistan on Kashmir. The Soviet Union also supported India's position vis-à-vis Portugal on Goa, which was territorially integrated into India as a union territory by the Indian armed forces in December 1961 (it became a state in May 1987).

The Soviet Union and some East European countries offered India new avenues of trade and economic assistance. By 1965 the Soviet Union was the second largest national contributor to India's development. These new arrangements contributed to India's emergence as a significant industrial power through the construction of plants to produce steel, heavy machinery and equipment, machine tools, and precision instruments, and to generate power and extract and refine petroleum. Soviet investment was in India's public-sector industry, which the World Bank (see Glossary) and Western industrial powers had been unwilling to assist until spurred by Soviet competition. Soviet aid was extended on the basis of long-term, government-to-government programs, which covered successive phases of technical training for Indians, supply of raw materials, progressive use of Indian inputs, and markets for finished products. Bilateral arrangements were made in nonconvertible national currencies, helping to conserve India's scarce foreign exchange. Thus the Soviet contribution to Indian economic development was generally regarded by foreign and domestic observers as positive (see Foreign Economic Relations, ch. 6).

Nehru obtained a Soviet commitment to neutrality on the India-China border dispute and war of 1962. During the India-Pakistan war of 1965, the Soviet Union acted with the United States in the UN Security Council to bring about a cease-fire. Soviet premier Aleksei N. Kosygin went further by offering his good offices for a negotiated settlement, which took place at Tashkent on January 10, 1966. Until 1969 the Soviet Union took an evenhanded position in South Asia and supplied a limited quantity of arms to Pakistan in 1968. From 1959 India had accepted Soviet offers of military sales. Indian acquisition of Soviet military equipment was important because purchases were made against deferred rupee payments, a major concession to India's chronic shortage of foreign exchange. Simultaneous provisions were made for licensed manufacture and modification in India, one criterion of self-reliant defense on which India placed increasing emphasis. In addition, Soviet sales were made without any demands for restricted deployment, adjustments in Indian policies toward other countries, adherence to Soviet global policies, or acceptance of Soviet military advisers. In this way, Indian national autonomy was not compromised.

The most intimate phase in relations between India and the Soviet Union was the period between 1971 and 1976: its highlight was the twenty-year Treaty of Peace, Friendship, and Cooperation of August 1971. Articles 8, 9, and 10 of the treaty committed the parties "to abstain from providing any assistance to any third party that engages in armed conflict with the other" and "in the event of either party being subjected to an attack or threat thereof . . . to immediately enter into mutual consultations." India benefited at the time because the Soviet Union came to support the Indian position on Bangladesh and because the treaty acted as a deterrent to China. New Delhi also received accelerated shipments of Soviet military equipment in the last quarter of 1971. The first state visit of Soviet president Leonid Brezhnev to India in November 1973 was conducted with tremendous fanfare and stressed the theme of economic cooperation. By the late 1970s, the Soviet Union was India's largest trading partner.

The friendship treaty notwithstanding, Indira Gandhi did not alter important principles of Indian foreign policy. She made it clear that the Soviet Union would not receive any special privileges—much less naval base rights—in Indian ports, despite the major Soviet contribution to the construction of shipbuilding and ship-repair facilities at Bombay on the west coast and at Vishakhapatnam on the east coast. India's advocacy of the Indian Ocean as a zone of peace was directed against aggrandizement of the Soviet naval presence as much as that of other extraregional powers. By repeatedly emphasizing the nonexclusive nature of its friendship with the Soviet Union, India kept open the way for normalizing relations with China and improving ties with the West.

After the Soviet intervention in Afghanistan, Indian diplomats avoided condemnatory language and resolutions as useless Cold War exercises that could only antagonize the Soviet Union and postpone political settlement. They called instead for withdrawal of all foreign troops and negotiation among concerned parties. In meetings with Soviet leaders in New Delhi in 1980 and in Moscow in 1982, Indira Gandhi privately pressed harder for the withdrawal of Soviet troops and for the restoration of Afghanistan's traditional nonalignment and independence.

Rajiv Gandhi journeyed to the Soviet Union in 1985, 1986, 1987, and 1989, and Soviet president Mikhail S. Gorbachev traveled to India in 1986 and 1988. These visits and those of other high officials evoked effusive references to the "exemplary" (in Gorbachev's term) friendship between the two countries and also achieved the conclusion of agreements to expand economic, cultural, and scientific and technological cooperation. In 1985 and 1986, and again in 1988, both nations signed pacts to boost bilateral trade and provide Soviet investment and technical assistance for Indian industrial, telecommunications, and transportation projects. In 1985 and 1988, the Soviet Union also extended to India credits of 1 billion rubles and 3 billion rubles, respectively (a total of about US$2.4 billion), for the purchase of Soviet machinery and goods. Protocols for scientific cooperation, signed in 1985 and 1987, provided the framework for joint research and projects in space science and such high-technology areas as biotechnology, computers, and lasers. The flow of advanced Soviet military equipment also continued in the mid- and late 1980s (see The Air Force, ch. 10).

When the Soviet Union disintegrated, India was faced with the difficult task of reorienting its external affairs and forging relations with the fifteen Soviet successor states, of which Russia was the most important (see Central Asia, this ch.). In 1993 New Delhi and Moscow worked to redefine their relationship according to post-Cold War realities. During the January 1993 visit of Russian president Boris Yeltsin to India, the two countries signed agreements that signaled a new emphasis on economic cooperation in bilateral relations. The 1971 treaty was replaced with the new Treaty of Friendship and Cooperation, which dropped security clauses that in the Cold War were directed against the United States and China. Yeltsin stated that Russia would deliver cryogenic engines and space technology for India's space program under a US$350 million deal between the Indian Space Research Organisation (ISRO) and the Russian space agency, Glavkosmos, despite the imposition of sanctions on both organizations by the United States. In addition, Yeltsin expressed strong support for India's stand on Kashmir. A defense cooperation accord aimed at ensuring the continued supply of Russian arms and spare parts to satisfy the requirements of India's military and at promoting the joint production of defense equipment. Bilateral trade, which had fallen drastically during the 1990–92 period, was expected to revive following the resolution of the dispute over New Delhi's debt to Moscow and the May 1992 decision to abandon the 1978 rupee-ruble trade agreement in favor of the use of hard currency.

Pressure from the United States, which believed the engines and technology could be diverted to ballistic missile development, led the Russians to cancel most of the deal in July 1993. Russia did, however, supply rockets to help India to develop the technology to launch geostationary satellites, and, with cryogenic engine plans already in hand, the ISRO was determined to produce its own engines by 1997 (see Space and Nuclear Programs, ch. 10).

Despite Yeltsin's call for a realignment of Russia, India, and China to balance the West, Russia shares interests with the developed countries on nuclear proliferation issues. In November 1991, Moscow voted for a Pakistani-sponsored UN resolution calling for the establishment of a South Asian nuclear-free zone. Russia urged India to support the Treaty on the Non-Proliferation of Nuclear Weapons and decided in March 1992 to apply "full-scope safeguards" to future nuclear supply agreements. Russia also shares interests with the United States in cooling antagonisms between India and Pakistan, particularly with regard to Kashmir, thus making it unlikely that India could count on Russia in a future dispute with Pakistan.

Rao reciprocated Yeltsin's visit in July 1994. The two leaders signed declarations assuring international and bilateral goodwill and continuation of Russian arms and military equipment exports to India. Rao's Moscow visit lacked the controversy that characterized his May 1994 visit to the United States and was deemed an important success because of the various accords, one of which restored the sale of cryogenic engines to India.

Bilateral relations between India and Russia improved as a result of eight agreements signed in December 1994. The agreements cover military and technical cooperation from 1995 to 2000, merchant shipping, and promotion and mutual protection of investments, trade, and outer space cooperation. Political observers saw the visit of Russian prime minister Viktor Chernomyrdin that occasioned the signing of the eight agreements as a sign of a return to the earlier course of warm relations between New Delhi and Moscow. In March 1995, India and Russia signed agreements aimed at suppressing illegal weapons smuggling and drug trafficking. And when Russian nationalist Vladimir V. Zhirinovsky visited India in March 1995, he declared that he would give India large supplies of arms and military hardware if he were elected president of Russia.

United States

With the end of the Cold War and the emergence of India's more outward-looking economic policies, the United States became increasingly important for India. In the mid-1990s, the United States was India's largest trading partner and a major source of technology and investment (see Aid; Trade, ch. 6). Indian students more than ever sought higher education in the United States, especially in the areas of science and engineering. Moreover, the presence of the more than 1 million Indians and Indian Americans residing in the United States was a factor in the relationship. Some foreign policy makers also saw India's strong democratic tradition, although much younger than that of the United States, as an important ingredient in India-United States relations. Despite the asymmetrical relationship that had existed since 1947, the areas of common interest converged in the early 1990s as the benefits of good relations were perceived on both sides. Some Indian observers, however, felt that the United States had a "negative agenda" concerning India with respect to human rights, the nuclear program, and the pace of economic reforms. Furthermore, India's long adherence to the principles of nonalignment has had an inhibiting effect on its evolving relations with the United States. Nevertheless, some opinion makers believed that an India-United States strategic alliance later in the 1990s was a possibility.

Until 1971 nonalignment had a dual effect on United States policies in South Asia. On the one hand, Washington considered Indian economic and political stability necessary to prevent that important regional player from succumbing to communism and Soviet influence; hence the United States gave economic assistance and support to India during its 1962 war with China (see External Aid, ch. 7). On the other hand, India's nonalignment had led the United States in 1954 to ally itself with Pakistan, which appeared to support Western security interests. The United States-Pakistan alliance was renewed in 1959, with accompanying assurances from President Dwight D. Eisenhower to Nehru that the arms supplied to Pakistan would not be used in any aggressive war. When Pakistan and

India went to war in 1965, the United States government refused to support India and suspended military transfers to both countries.

In 1971 the intertwining of the United States-Soviet, Chinese-Soviet, and Indian-Pakistani conflicts dragged India-United States relations to the nadir. That year, while Washington initiated a new relationship with Beijing, New Delhi signed a friendship treaty with Moscow to counteract United States and Chinese influence in South Asia. As the situation in East Pakistan deteriorated, India was unable to convince the United States to cease arms deliveries to Pakistan and persuade Pakistan's leaders to reach a political settlement with East Pakistan's elected representatives. Indira Gandhi's November 1971 visit to Washington failed to alter President Richard M. Nixon's pro-Pakistan stance. When war formally began after Pakistani strikes on Indian airfields in early December 1971, the United States and China voted for a cease-fire in the UN Security Council, but the Soviet Union's veto prevented any resolution from coming into effect. Washington's subsequent deployment of a naval task force to the Bay of Bengal left many in India convinced that the United States was a major security threat.

Relations between India and the United States verged on the antagonistic throughout the 1970s. After Nixon abruptly terminated US$82 million in economic assistance, India closed down a large United States Agency for International Development program. The Indian government also restricted the flow of American scholars and students to India. India's criticisms of United States policies in Vietnam and Cambodia increased, and it upgraded its representation in Hanoi. When the United States expanded its naval base on the island of Diego Garcia and engaged in naval exercises with Pakistan in the Indian Ocean in 1974, India saw its security further threatened. Both governments, however, attempted to limit the damage to bilateral relations. A 1973 agreement defused a dispute over United States rupee holdings by writing off more than 50 percent of the debt and directing use of the remainder to mutually acceptable programs. In 1974 the Indo-United States Joint Commission was established to insulate bilateral dealings in education and culture, economics, and science and technology from political controversy and to provide mechanisms for regular exchanges at high levels of public life.

Hopes for improved relations were expressed in 1977 when Jimmy Carter became president of the United States and the

Janata Party government led by Morarji Desai took over in India (see Political Parties, ch. 8). These expectations came to an abrupt end two years later when the Soviet Union invaded Afghanistan. The promulgation of the Carter Doctrine, establishment of the Rapid Deployment Force (later called the United States Central Command) and an Indian Ocean fleet, planned expansion of the naval base at Diego Garcia, and arrangements to supply Pakistan with US$3.2 billion in military and economic aid over five years all appeared as direct United States intervention in the countries of the Persian Gulf and Indian Ocean. These actions fueled instability in the region and, in India's view, threatened India's security.

The personal rapport between Indira Gandhi and United States president Ronald Reagan, established during a series of meetings in the early 1980s, enabled the two countries gradually to begin improving bilateral relations. The Reagan administration reassessed its policy toward India and decided to expand areas of cooperation, particularly in the economic and scientific realms, as a means of counteracting Soviet influence in the region. Washington also regarded New Delhi's status as the major regional power in South Asia in a more favorable light. For her part, Gandhi realized that India was unable to block United States arms sales to Pakistan, but that improved dialogue with the United States could open other areas of interaction that could benefit Indian interests. Indira Gandhi's highly successful 1982 state visit to the United States was followed by a series of high-level exchanges, including the visits of Vice President George Bush and Secretary of State George Shultz to India. In addition, in 1982 the two sides resolved their dispute concerning supplies of fuel and spare parts for the nuclear power plant at Tarapur. In 1984 the United States decided to expand technology transfers to India.

The warming trend in relations between New Delhi and Washington continued with the 1985 and 1987 visits by Prime Minister Rajiv Gandhi to Washington. Furthermore, as the United States appreciation of India's role as a force for stability in South Asia grew, Washington supported New Delhi's moves in Sri Lanka in 1987 and in Maldives in 1988. In the mid- and late 1980s, visits exchanged by the United States secretary of defense and the Indian minister of defence symbolized a modest but growing program of cooperation in military technology and other defense matters. In 1988 Washington and New Delhi finalized an accord to provide United States technology for

India's light combat aircraft program and also agreed to transfer technology for the F–5 fighter. Cooperation between India and the United States in a variety of scientific fields followed the signing of a bilateral agreement on scientific and technological exchanges in 1985. Nonmilitary technology transfers also accelerated, and in 1987 India purchased a Cray supercomputer for agricultural research and weather forecasting and accepted stringent United States safeguards to preclude military uses. Furthermore, economic liberalization measures paved the way for increased trade and United States investment in India. In 1988 the improved economic climate resulted in the conclusion of a deal for a Pepsi-Cola plant and the signing of a bilateral tax treaty. In 1989 United States investment in India reached US$1 billion.

In the 1980s, the Indian and United States governments had divergent views on a wide range of international issues, including Afghanistan, Cambodia, the Middle East, and Central America. Serious differences also remained over United States policy toward Pakistan and the issue of nuclear proliferation. India was repeatedly incensed in the 1980s when the United States provided advanced military technology and other assistance to Pakistan. New Delhi also found objectionable Washington's unwillingness to cut off military assistance to Islamabad despite United States concerns about Pakistan's covert nuclear program. For its part, Washington continued to urge New Delhi to sign the Treaty on the Non-Proliferation of Nuclear Weapons and, after the successful test launch of the Indian Agni intermediate-range ballistic missile in May 1989, called on New Delhi to refrain from developing a ballistic missile capability by adhering to the restrictions of the Missile Technology Control Regime. India rejected these appeals on the grounds that it had a right to develop such technology and that the Treaty on the Non-Proliferation of Nuclear Weapons and the United States-sponsored Missile Technology Control Regime discriminated against nonnuclear states.

Bureaucratic and private-sector resistance to foreign participation in the economy, infrastructure problems, bureaucratic red tape, and legal problems remained formidable obstacles to significant Indian-United States economic cooperation. In the late 1980s, India had differences with the United States over improving its legal protection of intellectual property rights, opening its markets to American service industries, and liberalizing its foreign investment regulations. In April 1991, the

Office of the United States Trade Representative placed India on Washington's watch list over intellectual property rights issues. Six months later, the United States gave India a three-month grace period before imposing retaliatory sanctions against India's pharmaceutical industry for inadequate patent protection. India resisted United States pressure to adopt a less protectionist stance in the Uruguay Round of negotiations to renew the General Agreement on Tariffs and Trade (GATT).

In the early 1990s, economic reforms permitted a qualitative breakthrough in relations between India and the United States. Washington was instrumental in speeding a US$1.8 billion IMF credit that New Delhi obtained in January 1991 to deal with a severe external-debt-payments crisis. In 1990 India and the United States signed a double taxation pact designed to facilitate American investment in India, further breaking a thirty-year deadlock in economic relations. The United States provided only modest bilateral economic assistance in the form of food aid but was India's largest trading partner and an important source of investments and technology. In December 1990, the United States approved the export of a second Cray supercomputer for the Indian Institute of Science in Bangalore, Karnataka, although the deal fell through two years later because of India's unwillingness to accept safeguards to prevent the computer's diversion to military uses.

The Soviet withdrawal from Afghanistan in 1989 had led Washington to reassess its relationship with Pakistan, with positive ramifications for New Delhi. Without containment of the Soviet Union as the driving factor behind close Pakistani-United States ties, and concerns mounting about Pakistan's nuclear weapons program, the United States suspended military and economic assistance to that country in October 1990. New Delhi appreciated this action and was relieved in summer 1991 when the United States Congress voted not to include India in the Pressler Amendment, which forbade United States assistance to Pakistan if it violated nuclear nonproliferation criteria. Washington also took a more evenhanded approach to the Kashmir problem in 1990, urging both antagonists to resolve their dispute peacefully under the terms of the Simla Accord. Furthermore, the United States began pressuring Pakistan to end its support for Kashmiri and Punjabi Sikh separatists. This pressure was in addition to efforts initiated in the 1980s to prevent assistance to Sikh terrorists from the Sikh expatriate community in the United States (see Rajiv Gandhi, ch. 1). In the wake of terrorist bombings in Bombay in March 1993—widely believed in India to have been instigated by Pakistanis—and stepped-up activities among Kashmiri militants, Indian politicians and the media reveled in the possibility that the United States might declare Pakistan a practitioner of state-sponsored terrorism. Washington's decision in July 1993 not to declare Pakistan a terrorist-supporting state displeased many prominent Indians, and Indian political analysts accused the United States of having a "double standard" in regard to specific states sponsoring terrorism.

Military cooperation also grew. Exchanges of senior military officials became frequent, a high-level bilateral conference on regional security affairs was held, and Minister of Defence Sharad Pawar journeyed to Washington in April 1992 to discuss arms supplies and military technology. Not only did United States navy ships make occasional ports calls in India, but the two navies conducted their first-ever joint exercise in May 1992. Indian officials came to have a greater appreciation of United States interests in maintaining a military presence on Diego Garcia and in the Persian Gulf.

In 1993, India and the United States appeared committed to improve relations and bilateral cooperation despite differences over India's refusal to sign the Treaty on the Non-Proliferation of Nuclear Weapons and to participate in discussions with the United States, Russia, China, and Pakistan on establishing a South Asian nuclear-free zone. Nevertheless, Washington directed its efforts to creating a climate of restraint between New Delhi and Islamabad in order to freeze or roll back their nuclear weapons programs. However, India and the United States remained wary of each other's long-term strategy regionally and globally.

Some Indian political analysts criticize the United States for following a "two-track policy." On the one hand, Washington has supported New Delhi's economic reform and has facilitated international loans to India, but, on the other, it has relentlessly pursued an agenda to force India's accession to United States nonproliferation goals and has used human rights issues to try to force India to meet Washington's political objections. Moreover, many Indians have expressed worries that, with the emergence of the United States as the sole superpower, and as the leader of a Western-dominated coalition after the Persian Gulf War, Washington might attempt to impose its own standards for democratic values, human rights, and free markets. India fears that a United States vision of a new world order not only would hurt the interests of Third World countries economically and politically, but also would damage India's drive to become a leading power in a multipolar system. Washington's decision not to place Pakistan on its list of nations that sponsor terrorism and its successful efforts in getting Russia to cancel the sale of cryogenic engines to India are seen as detrimental to good Indian-United States relations.

In the midst of increasing anti-United States political rhetoric and newspaper headlines, Indian and United States officials have seemed to agree on only one thing, that bilateral relations had reached their lowest point in two decades. Observers in both countries believe that the administration of President William Clinton places a low priority on relations with India despite the fact that the United States has become India's prime trade partner. Against this backdrop, Prime Minister Rao visited the United States in May 1994 for an uneventful round of talks with President Clinton, who encouraged India's economic reforms. Six memorandums of understanding were signed with the intent of expanding official contacts, reviewing and updating a 1984 understanding on high-technology transfer, enhancing defense cooperation, stimulating bilateral ties, and establishing a business partnership initiative.

High-level visits to India in early 1995 portended greater stability in India-United States relations. Secretary of Defense William J. Perry visited New Delhi in January to sign a "landmark agreement" on military cooperation that was seen by some local observers as a convergence in India-United States security perceptions after nearly fifty years of divergent viewpoints (see National Security Challenges, ch. 10). Following the Perry visit was a commercial mission led by Secretary of Commerce Ronald H. Brown that also occurred in January. Agreements signed by Indian and United States businesses during the visit resulted in US$7 billion in contracts and investments in the communications, health care, insurance, finance, and automotive sectors. Some of the deals consummated were intended to build the infrastructure needed by foreign firms to do business in India. In March 1995, Hilary Rodham Clinton, the wife of the United States president, toured India as part of an extensive South Asian goodwill tour. In April, Secretary of the Treasury Robert E. Rubin visited New Delhi to sign a bilateral investment protection treaty reflecting the substantial increases in United States investment in India since 1991 and Washing-

Prime Minister P.V. Narasimha Rao and President William Clinton in
Washington
Courtesy The White House

ton's encouragement to India to apply for Agency for International Development loans.

Britain, Australia, Canada, Western Europe, and Japan

From the late 1940s to the mid-1960s, independent India's most important relationship was with Britain. New Delhi and London had special relations because of common historical ties, political institutions, interest in economic development, high levels of trade between India and Britain, and British investment in India. Despite this special relationship, Nehru's policy of nonalignment was designed, in part, to prevent India from becoming too dependent on Britain and other former colonial powers. In spite of cooperation with Australia, Britain, and Canada in the Commonwealth of Nations—which was established by Britain in 1931—India's nonaligned stance frequently put India at odds with Britain, the United States, and other Western countries on Cold War and anticolonial issues (see Commonwealth of Nations, this ch.). Nevertheless, common democratic principles and the willingness of the developed countries to provide economic assistance prompted India to build modest but constructive relations with these countries.

India's relations with Britain remain important. India has so successfully diversified its economic ties that London's domination is no longer a consideration for New Delhi; British trade, investment, and aid, however, are still significant. A substantial community of people of Indian origin live in Britain, contributing to the business and intellectual life of the country. Economic relations were improving in the early and mid-1990s with the implementation of India's economic reforms. Political differences stemming from India's nonaligned stance tended to dissipate with the end of the Cold War and the collapse of the apartheid system in South Africa.

From the mid-1960s until the early 1980s, the difficulties encountered in conducting trade and investing in India caused countries such as Japan and the Federal Republic of Germany (West Germany) to seek more fruitful commercial opportunities elsewhere in the developing world. In the sphere of international politics, the intricacies of balancing ties with India and Pakistan, India's tilt toward the Soviet Union beginning in 1971, divergent views on nuclear proliferation issues, and the situations in Afghanistan and Cambodia left little room for improvement of relations with Japan and Western Europe. Modest moves taken to liberalize the Indian economy in the early and mid-1980s and increased availability of private investment and official developmental assistance from developed countries, however, provided India with the opportunity to increase trade and obtain aid and investment from Japan and Europe. Indian trade with countries of the European Economic Community rose dramatically, and Japan became India's largest aid donor. By the late 1980s, Indian, West European, and Japanese leaders exchanged regular visits.

In the early 1990s, expanding Indian exports and attracting investment from developed countries became a major priority in India's bilateral relations. India developed closer ties with Berlin—now the capital of a united Germany—Tokyo, and the European Economic Community (later the European Union) to promote Indian economic interests and enhance its diplo-

*Indian naval contingent marching in an Australia Day parade,
Canberra
Courtesy Embassy of India, Washington*

matic maneuverability. Japan remained India's major source of
bilateral assistance, and Berlin was New Delhi's largest trading
partner in the European Economic Community. Nevertheless,
India and the developed countries had differences over security and nuclear issues and the attachment of political criteria
to developmental assistance.

Relations with Australia suffered in 1990 and 1991 as India
expressed its displeasure with Australia's sale of Mirage fighters
to Pakistan. In 1991 the German government announced it was
cutting official aid to India because of "excessive armament,"
while the British, Canadian, and Japanese governments warned
India that future assistance would be cut back if India did not
curtail its high levels of military spending, which the developed
countries contend suppressed economic development. In addition, Britain, France, and Germany also increased pressure on
India to sign the nonproliferation treaty, and France cautioned
India that any future agreements to supply India with nuclear
material and technology must adhere to "full-scope safeguards"
to prevent diversion to nuclear weapons production. Finally,
India remained concerned that developed countries would
impose human rights conditions as criteria for economic aid.

Participation in International Organizations

United Nations

During the Cold War, India's participation in the UN was
notable for its efforts to resist the imposition of superpower dis-

putes on UN General Assembly debates and to focus international attention on the problems of economic development. In the early 1950s, India attempted unsuccessfully to help China join the UN. India's mediatory role in resolving the stalemate over prisoners of war in Korea led to the signing of the armistice ending the Korean War. India chaired the five-member Neutral Nations Repatriation Commission while the Indian Custodian Force supervised the process of interviews and repatriation that followed. The UN entrusted Indian armed forces with subsequent peace missions in the Middle East, Cyprus, and the Congo (since 1971, Zaire). India also served as chair of the three international commissions for supervision and control for Vietnam, Cambodia, and Laos established by the 1954 Geneva Accords on Indochina (see Peacekeeping Operations, ch. 10).

Although not a permanent member of the UN Security Council, India has been elected periodically to fill a nonpermanent seat, and during the 1991–92 period served in that capacity. In the early 1990s, New Delhi supported reform of the UN in the hope of securing a permanent seat on the Security Council. This development would recognize India's position as the second-largest population (possibly the largest in the early twenty-first century) in the world, with an economy projected by some to become the fourth largest, after China, the United States, and Japan, by 2020.

India also has served as a member of many UN bodies—including the Economic and Social Council, the Human Rights Commission, and the Disarmament Commission—and on the board of governors of the International Atomic Energy Agency. In addition, India played a prominent role in articulating the economic concerns of developing countries in such UN-sponsored conferences as the triennial UN Conference on Trade and Development and the 1992 Conference on the Environment and Development in Rio de Janeiro.

Commonwealth of Nations

India is a member of the Commonwealth of Nations, the multinational association of Britain and its former colonies. Although Nehru initially considered withdrawal from this organization, he decided to retain membership to prevent isolation in the bipolar international system, to prevent the Commonwealth from becoming pro-Pakistan, to have access to Western economic assistance and military equipment without excessive

Nehru and Indian delegation at the United Nations, 1960
Courtesy U.S. News and World Report Collection, Library of Congress

dependence on the United States, and to convert the Commonwealth from an extension of the British Empire to a multiracial association of equal states. India actively participates in Commonwealth affairs and has found the organization a useful forum in which to voice its concerns on such matters as apartheid, race relations, and citizenship rights, as well as a source of economic assistance under the Colombo Plan for Cooperative Economic and Social Development in Asia and the Pacific (Colombo Plan—see Glossary). In 1989 the Indian government under Rajiv Gandhi sponsored Pakistan's reapplication for Commonwealth membership under the civilian leadership of Benazir Bhutto. In the early 1990s, with Indian approval, Commonwealth priorities were enlarged to include the importance of democratic institutions and human rights.

Nonaligned Movement

India played an important role in the multilateral movements of colonies and newly independent countries that developed into the Nonaligned Movement. The movement had its origins in the 1947 Asian Relations Meeting in New Delhi and the 1955 Asian-African Conference in Bandung, Indonesia. India also participated in the 1961 Belgrade Conference that officially established the Nonaligned Movement, but Nehru's declining prestige limited his influence. In the 1960s and 1970s, New Delhi concentrated on internal problems and bilateral relations, yet retained membership in an increasingly factionalized and radicalized movement. During the contentious 1979 Havana summit, India worked with moderate nations to reject Cuban president Fidel Castro's proposition that "socialism" (that is, the Soviet Union) was the "natural ally" of nonalignment.

Under Indira Gandhi in the early 1980s, India attempted to reassert its prominent role in the Nonaligned Movement by focusing on the relationship between disarmament and economic development. By appealing to the economic grievances of developing countries, Indira Gandhi and her successors exercised a moderating influence on the Nonaligned Movement, diverting it from some of the Cold War issues that marred the controversial 1979 Havana meeting. Although hosting the 1983 summit boosted Indian prestige within the movement, its close relations with the Soviet Union and its pro-Soviet positions on Afghanistan and Cambodia limited its influence.

The end of the Cold War left the Nonaligned Movement without its original raison d'être, and its membership became deeply divided over international disputes, strategy, and organization. During the 1992 Jakarta summit, India took a middle position between countries favoring confrontation with developed nations on international economic issues, such as Malaysia, and those that favored a more cooperative approach, such as Indonesia. Although New Delhi played a minor role compared with Kuala Lumpur and Jakarta on most issues facing the summit, India formulated the Nonaligned Movement position opposing developed countries' linkage of foreign aid to human rights criteria.

India also is a founding member of the Group of Fifteen (see Glossary), a group of developing nations established at the ninth Nonaligned Movement summit in Belgrade in 1989 to facilitate dialogue with the industrialized countries. India played host to the fourth Group of Fifteen summit in March

1994. At the summit, Prime Minister Rao and other leaders expressed concern over new trade barriers being raised by the industrialized countries despite the conclusion of a new world trade agreement.

South Asian Association for Regional Cooperation

India is a member of SAARC, along with Pakistan, Bangladesh, Nepal, Bhutan, Sri Lanka, and Maldives. SAARC, which slowly emerged out of the initiative of Bangladesh in 1980, was formally inaugurated in 1985. SAARC, which has a permanent secretariat in Kathmandu, is funded by voluntary contributions and operates on the principle of unanimity in decision making. Discussion of contentious bilateral issues is excluded from the SAARC charter at Indian insistence. Instead, SAARC programs exist in the areas of agriculture, rural development, transportation and telecommunications, meteorology, health and population control, postal services, science and technology, culture and sports, women in development, drug trafficking and abuse, and terrorism. By the mid-1990s, SAARC had yet to become an effective regional organization, largely because of mutual distrust between India and its neighbors. India's lukewarm support for SAARC stems from the concern that its neighbors might coalesce against it to the detriment of Indian interests. The reluctance of India and other South Asian countries to turn SAARC into a forum for resolving major regional disputes hampers SAARC's ability to deal with many of South Asia's economic and political problems. Nonetheless, when SAARC's eighth summit was held in New Delhi in May 1995, the conferees declared their nations' commitment to eradicating poverty in South Asia by 2002.

*   *   *

There is an extensive English-language literature on India's foreign relations. Indian government publications—the Ministry of External Affairs's *Annual Report* and the monthly *Foreign Affairs Record*, and the Parliament's *Compendium of Policy Statements Made in the Parliament: External Affairs*—are important official sources of information. The annual edition of *Yearbook on India's Foreign Policy* contains a useful survey of foreign policy trends as well as articles on bilateral relations. The *Economic and Political Weekly* [Bombay] provides a nongovernmental point of view on a wide range of current issues. *Asia Yearbook*, published by the Far Eastern Economic Review in Hong Kong, also includes a review of India's foreign relations for the previous year.

A large number of books and articles are published each year on specific subjects such as nonalignment, foreign aid, nuclear issues, and specific bilateral relations. The speeches and writings of Jawaharlal Nehru offer considerable insight into the rationale and direction of Indian foreign policy during the Cold War period. Norman D. Palmer's *The United States and India*, Selig Harrison and Geoffrey Kemp's *India and America after the Cold War*, Robert C. Horn's *Soviet-Indian Relations*, and Peter J.S. Duncan's *The Soviet Union and India* are good analytical studies of India's relations with the superpowers. Comprehensive surveys of Indian foreign relations before the end of the Cold War are found in Charles Heimseth and Surjit Mansingh's *A Diplomatic History of Modern India* for the period 1911–65, Mansingh's *India's Search for Power: Indira Gandhi's Foreign Policy, 1966–1982*, and Robert W. Bradnock's *India's Foreign Policy since 1971*. Two books that deal with India's foreign policy decision making and the domestic political structure underlying it are Jayant Bandyopadhyaya's *The Making of India's Foreign Policy* and Shashi Tharoor's *Reasons of State*. Articles on the changes in India's foreign policy and foreign relations since the end of the Cold War have appeared in the scholarly and periodical literature, of which *Asian Survey* and *Far Eastern Economic Review* are good sources. Annual editions of the Association for Asian Studies' *Bibliography of Asian Studies* provide comprehensive retrospective source citations. (For further information and complete citations, see Bibliography.)

Chapter 10. National Security

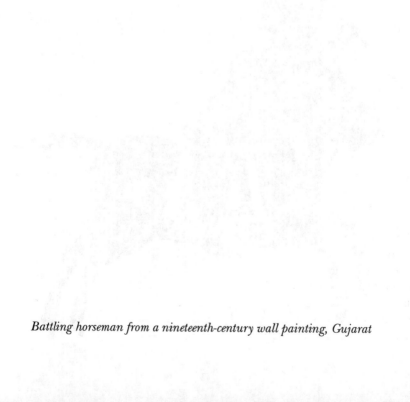

Battling horseman from a nineteenth-century wall painting, Gujarat

THE INDIAN ARMED FORCES have undergone a substantial metamorphosis since the emergence of India and Pakistan from the British Indian Empire in 1947. India's first prime minister, Jawaharlal Nehru (1947–64), had deliberately limited the expansion and modernization of the armed forces. The rationale was twofold: Nehru was acutely concerned about the accelerating costs of defense spending, and he feared that an excessive emphasis on the armed forces would lead to the militarization of society and undermine the nation's fledgling democratic institutions. The disastrous performance of the Indian army during the 1962 border war with China, however, led to a reappraisal of defense strategy and spending. Nehru's legacy eroded rapidly as increasing emphasis was placed on defense needs. The success of the Indian military against Pakistan during their 1971 war contributed to restoring the morale and standing in society of the armed forces. During the rest of the 1970s and in the 1980s, India bolstered its regional preeminence with wide-ranging arms transfers from the Soviet Union. In the late 1980s, in an effort to reduce its dependence on Soviet weaponry, India began to diversify its arms sources. It purchased aircraft, submarines, and long-range artillery pieces from France, the Federal Republic of Germany (West Germany), Sweden, and Britain. Simultaneously, it continued its efforts to expand and strengthen domestic capabilities to manufacture a range of weaponry to maximize self-reliance. The results of these purchases and self-reliance efforts have been mixed.

The 1980s saw not only substantial growth in Indian defense expenditures but also the use of the armed forces in support of larger foreign and security policy goals. Specifically, the army saw action against Pakistani military personnel in disputed areas along the Siachen Glacier in Jammu and Kashmir, deployed at considerable cost as diplomatic efforts failed. All three branches of the armed forces, but particularly the army, were used to pursue India's security and foreign policy objectives in Sri Lanka in the late 1980s (see South Asia, ch. 9). More than 60,000 soldiers were deployed in Sri Lanka as part of the Indian Peace Keeping Force (IPKF) to enforce the terms of the 1987 Indo-Sri Lankan Accord. Designed to serve as a neutral force between contending ethnic forces, the IPKF became enmeshed in operations against the Liberation Tigers of Tamil Eelam (LTTE). In 1989 the new Sri Lankan president, Rana-singhe Premadasa, ended a five-and-a-half-year state of emergency and asked India to withdraw the IPKF. Accordingly, Indian army units returned home with most goals unmet.

In 1988 a smaller, much shorter-lived Indian expedition successfully ended a military coup attempt in Maldives and demonstrated the military's effective use of airborne and naval forces in a joint operation.

India is the preeminent military power in South Asia, but its margin of superiority over Pakistan—its principal South Asian rival—has eroded because the central government of India is faced with severe budgetary constraints. In addition, the armed forces are no longer able to obtain sophisticated weaponry at highly subsidized prices from Russia, and substantial numbers of army units are tied down in various internal security duties. Insurgencies in Assam, Jammu and Kashmir, and Punjab have necessitated the use of the army in "aid-to-the-civil power" when the local police and central paramilitary forces are unable to maintain public order. Increasingly frequent outbreaks of communal violence also have necessitated the use of the army to restore calm.

The increased reliance on the army for internal security duties generated concern among senior officers in the early 1990s. Then chief of army staff General Sunith Francis Rodrigues repeatedly expressed his misgivings about the inordinate use of the army to deal with civil problems because such actions increased the risk of politicizing the armed forces and reduced their battle readiness. Moreover, the very nature of counterinsurgent and counterterrorist operations exposed the army to charges of human rights violations. In 1993, at the insistence of the army, the government agreed to examine this growing problem. Discussions focused on improving the recruitment, training, and organization of the various central paramilitary forces.

The air force and the navy underwent considerable growth and modernization during the 1980s, although their plans for modernization and expansion, like those of the army, were hobbled by financial constraints. Nevertheless, the navy has adequate capabilities for coastal defense as well as the protection of offshore union territories in the Bay of Bengal and the Arabian Sea. The air force is equipped with modern combat aircraft and has moderate airlift capabilities.

Human rights violations in Assam, Jammu and Kashmir, Punjab, and other parts of the country have largely been attributed to the paramilitary forces. The army has willingly acknowledged that some lapses have occurred within its own ranks. It also has court-martialed officers and enlisted personnel charged with breaches of proper discipline and conduct. However, the army has refused to divulge any details about the extent of these problems. The numbers of individuals prosecuted, their ranks, and their names remain outside the public domain. Nevertheless, Amnesty International and Asia Watch have reported on incidents they have been able to document.

Colonial-Era Developments

Company Armies

The roots of the modern Indian army are traced to the forces employed by the English (later British) East India Company, chartered in 1600, and the French East India Company (Compagnie des Indes Orientales), established in 1664. The French, headquartered at Pondicherry (Puduchcheri) by the 1670s, were the first to raise Indian companies and use them in conjunction with European soldiers. Subsequently, in the 1740s, the British started to organize and train Indian units. British units were divided into three armies corresponding to the company's centers of Bengal (headquartered at Fort William in Calcutta), Bombay (or Mumbai in the Marathi language), and Madras (headquartered at Fort Saint George). In 1748 the East India Company armies were brought under the command of Stringer Lawrence, who is regarded by historians as the progenitor of the modern Indian army. Under his guidance, British officers recruited, trained, and deployed these forces. Although formally under a unified command, the three armies in practice exercised considerable autonomy because of the great distances that separated them.

Toward the end of the eighteenth century, the vast majority of the soldiers of each army was composed of Indian troops known as sepoys (from the Hindi *sipahi*, meaning police officer, or, later, soldier). Sepoy units had Indian junior commissioned officers who could exercise only low-level command. British officers held all senior positions. No Indian had any authority over non-Indians. In addition to these all-Indian units, the British deployed some units of the British Army.

The Indian Military under the British Raj

Post-Sepoy Rebellion Reorganization

Shortly after the Sepoy Rebellion of 1857–58, the role of the presidency armies was reevaluated (see The British Raj, 1858–1947, ch. 1). In 1861 the Bengal Army was disbanded, and the total number of sepoys was reduced from 230,000 to 150,000 while the British element was increased from 40,000 to 75,000. Most Indian artillery units were disbanded, and artillery was placed under British control. Under the aegis of the imperial "divide and rule" policy, which had its inception at this time, the British ensured that a sense of nationality would not be allowed to develop among the sepoys. The growth of such feelings, it was feared, would undermine the prospects of imperial control. Accordingly, Indian regiments increasingly were organized on a territorial basis; individual companies—and in some cases entire regiments—were drawn from the same religious, tribal, or caste backgrounds. When companies from several regiments were grouped into battalions, considerable efforts were made to promote cultural and social distinctions among companies of different compositions.

"Martial Races" Theory

By the end of the nineteenth century, recruitment was confined to certain social classes and communities—principally those in the northern border areas and Punjab. The narrowing recruitment base was a response to the Sepoy Rebellion and reflected the needs of prevailing security requirements. The bulk of the rebels in the Bengal Army came from the Indo-Gangetic Plain while those that had remained loyal were mostly from Punjab.

The experience of the mutiny also gave rise to a pseudo-ethnological construction, the concept of "martial races" in South Asia. The popularization of this notion was widely attributed to Frederick Sleigh Roberts, Earl of Kandahar, Pretoria, and Waterford; Roberts was an Indian-born veteran of the British forces that put down the Sepoy Rebellion and the commander in chief of the British Indian Army from 1885 to 1893. Roberts believed that the most martial races were located in northwestern India. He regarded Bengalis, Marathas, and southern ethnic groups as lacking in martial virtues. Their warlike propensities, he contended, had dissipated because of the ease of living and the hot, enervating climate of these regions.

Roberts's views profoundly influenced the composition of the British Indian army in the last decades of the nineteenth century. For example, when the Bengal Army was reestablished in 1885, its new units were drawn from Punjab. In 1892 army policy was changed significantly. Units were no longer raised on a territorial basis but along what was referred to as "class" lines. In effect, regiments admitted only those having similar ethnic, religious, or caste backgrounds. Between 1892 and 1914, recruitment was confined almost entirely to the martial races. These modes of recruitment and organization created a professional force profoundly shaped by caste and regional factors and loyal and responsive to British command. The procedures also perpetuated regional and communal ties and produced an army that was not nationally based.

Administrative Reform and World War I

Administrative reforms in 1895 abolished the presidency armies, and command was centralized under the aegis of a single army headquarters at Delhi. In the early twentieth century, the process of centralization continued; and during this period, the separation between military and civilian spheres of influence and the ultimate primacy of civilian authority gained final acceptance in both civilian and military circles.

During World War I, India's contribution of troops, money, and supplies to the Allied cause was substantial. More than 1 million Indian soldiers were sent abroad, and more than 100,000 were either killed or wounded.

The mobilization for the war effort revealed a number of shortcomings in the military establishment. Officer casualties had a particularly pernicious effect on military formations because only the British officers assigned to a battalion had the authority and standing to exercise overall command. In addition, Indian officers from one company could rarely be transferred to another having a different ethnic, religious, or caste makeup. As a consequence, after the war most battalions were reorganized to ease reinforcement among component companies. Strong pressure from the Indian public also drove the British to begin training a small complement of Indians for commissions as a first step in the Indianization of the officer corps. The Royal Indian Air Force was established in 1932, and a small Indian marine unit was reorganized into the Royal Indian Navy in 1934. Indian artillery batteries were first formed only in 1936. Although the practice of limiting recruitment to the martial races had proved inadequate during World War I and entry had been opened to "nonmartial" groups, the traditional recruitment emphasis on martial races was nonetheless resumed after demobilization.

World War II

The political situation in India underwent a fundamental transformation at the time of Britain's entry into World War II (see Political Impasse and Independence, ch. 1). The viceroy and governor general of India, Victor Alexander John Hope, Marquis of Linlithgow, without consulting Indian political leaders, declared India to be at war with Germany on September 3, 1939. The legislature sustained the viceregal decree and passed the Defence of India Bill without opposition, as the representatives of the Indian National Congress (the Congress—see Glossary) boycotted the session. Between 1939 and mid-1945, the British Indian Army expanded from about 175,000 to more than 2 million troops—entirely through voluntary enlistment. The incipient naval and air forces were also expanded, and the Indian officer corps grew from 600 to more than 14,000. Indian troops were deployed under overall British command in Africa, Italy, the Middle East, and particularly in Burma and Southeast Asia. The great expansion in strength, the overseas service of Indian forces, and the demonstrated soldierly ability of Indians from all groups did much to dispel the martial races theory.

In Asia the Japanese sought to exploit Indian nationalism and anti-British sentiment by forming and supporting the Indian National Army (INA—Azad Hind Fauj), which was composed primarily of 25,000 of the 60,000 Indian troops who had surrendered to the Japanese in Singapore in February 1942. The army was led by Subhas Chandra Bose, a former militant president of the Congress, who also appointed himself head of the Provisional Government of Azad India (Free India). An unusual feature of the INA was an all-woman, intercaste regiment composed of some 1,500 Indian women from Burma, Malaya, and Singapore. Both the women and the 25,000-strong male contingent were organized to fight alongside the Japanese in Burma, but they actually saw little action. Only 8,000 were sent to the front. Japanese and INA troops invaded Manipur in March 1944 and fought and were defeated in battles at Imphal and Kohima (see fig. 1). By May 1945, the INA had disintegrated because of acute logistical problems, defections, and superior British-led forces. It is widely held that Bose was killed in an air crash in Taiwan as he fled at the end of the war. The British court martialed three INA officers. Nationalist-minded lawyers, including Nehru, defended them as national heroes, and the British, feeling intense public pressure, found them guilty but cashiered them without any further punishment. However, after independence Nehru refused to reinstate them into the Indian armed forces, fearing that they might sow discord among the ranks.

Postindependence Developments

The National Forces

Following independence in 1947, important organizational changes strengthened civilian control over the military. The position of commander in chief was abolished in 1955, and the three service chiefs were placed on an equal footing beneath the civilian Ministry of Defence. These changes significantly reduced the influence of the numerically superior army, to which the other services had been subordinate, and limited the service chiefs to advisory roles in the defense decision-making process. The changes reflected the ambiguous feelings of the civilian leadership toward the military. Nehru and other Indian nationalists saw the military as an institution strongly wedded to the colonial past. The heritage of nonviolence (ahimsa) of Mohandas Karamchand Gandhi also was important to the national political leadership (see Mahatma Gandhi, ch. 1).

Independence and the partition from Pakistan imposed significant costs on the Indian defense establishment that took years to redress. The partition of the country had entailed the division of the armed forces personnel and equipment. Predominantly Muslim units went to Pakistan, followed later by individual transfers. Close to two-thirds of all army personnel went to India. As a secular state, India accepted all armed forces personnel without regard to religious affiliation. The division of the navy was based on an estimation of each nation's maritime needs. A combination of religious affiliation and military need was applied to the small air force. As a result of partition, India also received about two-thirds of the matériel and stores. This aspect of the division of assets was complicated by the fact that all sixteen ordnance factories were located in India. India was allowed to retain them with the proviso that it would make a lump sum payment to Pakistan to enable it to develop its own defense production infrastructure.

Independence also resulted in a dramatic reduction of the number of experienced senior personnel available. In 1947 only six Indians had held brigade-level commands, and only one had commanded a division. British officers, out of necessity, were retained for varying periods of time after independence. British chiefs stayed on the longest in the navy and the air force. The navy had a British service chief until 1962 and the air force until 1954. The armed forces also integrated qualified members of the armies of the former princely states that acceded to India (see National Integration, ch. 1). The term *sepoy*, made popular during the colonial era, was dropped about this time, and the word *jawan* (Hindi for able-bodied man) has been used ever since when referring to the Indian soldier.

The Experience of Wars

Pakistan

The first test for the Indian armed forces came shortly after independence with the first Indo-Pakistani conflict (1947–48). The military was called upon to defend the borders of the state of Jammu and Kashmir when tribals—principally Pathans—attacked from the northwest reaches of Kashmir on October 22, 1947. India's 161st Infantry Brigade was deployed and thwarted the advance of the tribal forces. In early November 1947, the 161st counterattacked and successfully broke through the enemy defenses. Despite early successes, the Indian army suffered a setback in December because of logistical problems. The problems enabled the forces of Azad Kashmir (Free Kashmir, as the part of Kashmir under Pakistani control is called) to take the initiative and force the Indian troops to retreat from the border areas. In the spring of 1948, the Indian side mounted another offensive to retake some of the ground that it had lost. No doubt fearing that the war might move into Pakistan proper, regular units of the Pakistani army became more actively involved. As the conflict escalated, the Indian leadership was quick to recognize that the war could not be brought to a close unless Pakistani support for the Azad Kashmir forces could be stopped. Accordingly, on the advice of Governor General Earl Louis Mountbatten (Britain's last viceroy in India in 1947 and governor general of India, 1947–48), the Indian government sought United Nations (UN) mediation of the conflict on December 31, 1947. There was some opposition to this move within the cabinet by those who did not agree with referring the Kashmir dispute to the UN. The UN mediation process brought the war to a close on January 1, 1949. In all, 1,500 soldiers died on each side during the war.

The second Indo-Pakistani conflict (1965) was also fought over Kashmir and started without a formal declaration of war. It is widely accepted that the war began with the infiltration of Pakistani-controlled guerrillas into Indian Kashmir on about August 5, 1965. Skirmishes with Indian forces started as early as August 6 or 7, and the first major engagement between the regular armed forces of the two sides took place on August 14. The next day, Indian forces scored a major victory after a prolonged artillery barrage and captured three important mountain positions in the northern sector. Later in the month, the Pakistanis counterattacked, moving concentrations near Tithwal, Uri, and Punch. Their move, in turn, provoked a powerful Indian thrust into Azad Kashmir. Other Indian forces captured a number of strategic mountain positions and eventually took the key Haji Pir Pass, eight kilometers inside Pakistani territory.

The Indian gains led to a major Pakistani counterattack on September 1 in the southern sector, in Punjab, where Indian forces were caught unprepared and suffered heavy losses. The sheer strength of the Pakistani thrust, which was spearheaded by seventy tanks and two infantry brigades, led Indian commanders to call in air support. Pakistan retaliated on September 2 with its own air strikes in both Kashmir and Punjab. The war was at the point of stalemate when the UN Security Council unanimously passed a resolution on September 20 that called for a cease-fire. New Delhi accepted the cease-fire resolution on September 21 and Islamabad on September 22, and the war ended on September 23. The Indian side lost 3,000 while the Pakistani side suffered 3,800 battlefield deaths. The Soviet-brokered Tashkent Declaration was signed on January 10, 1966. It required that both sides withdraw by February 26, 1966, to positions held prior to August 5, 1965, and observe the cease-fire line agreed to on June 30, 1965.

The origins of the third Indo-Pakistani conflict (1971) were different from the previous conflicts. The Pakistani failure to accommodate demands for autonomy in East Pakistan in 1970 led to secessionist demands in 1971 (see The Rise of Indira Gandhi, ch. 1). In March 1971, Pakistan's armed forces launched a fierce campaign to suppress the resistance movement that had emerged but encountered unexpected mass defections among East Pakistani soldiers and police. The Pakistani forces regrouped and reasserted their authority over most of East Pakistan by May.

As a result of these military actions, thousands of East Pakistanis died at the hands of the Pakistani army. Resistance fighters and nearly 10 million refugees fled to sanctuary in West Bengal, the adjacent Indian state. By midsummer, the Indian leadership, in the absence of a political solution to the East Pakistan crisis, had fashioned a strategy designed to assist the establishment of the independent nation of Bangladesh. As part of this strategy, in August 1971, India signed a twenty-year Treaty of Peace, Friendship, and Cooperation with the Soviet Union. One of the treaty's clauses implied that each nation was expected to come to the assistance of the other in the event of a threat to national security such as that occurring in the 1965 war with Pakistan. Simultaneously, India organized, trained, and provided sanctuary to the Mukti Bahini (meaning Liberation Force in Bengali), the East Pakistani armed resistance fighters.

Unable to deter India's activities in the eastern sector, on December 3, 1971, Pakistan launched an air attack in the western sector on a number of Indian airfields, including Ambala in Haryana, Amritsar in Punjab, and Udhampur in Jammu and Kashmir. The attacks did not succeed in inflicting substantial damage. The Indian air force retaliated the next day and quickly achieved air superiority. On the ground, the strategy in the eastern sector marked a significant departure from previous Indian battle plans and tactics, which had emphasized set-piece battles and slow advances. The strategy adopted was a swift, three-pronged assault of nine infantry divisions with attached armored units and close air support that rapidly converged on Dhaka, the capital of East Pakistan. Lieutenant General Sagat Singh, who commanded the eighth, twenty-third, and fifty-seventh divisions, led the Indian thrust into East Pakistan. As these forces attacked Pakistani formations, the Indian air force rapidly destroyed the small air contingent in East Pakistan and put the Dhaka airfield out of commission. In the meantime, the Indian navy effectively blockaded East Pakistan. Dhaka fell to combined Indian and Mukti Bahini forces on December 16, bringing a quick end to the war.

Indian infantry during the 1962 border war with China Courtesy U.S. News and World Report Collection, Library of Congress

Action in the western sector was divided into four segments, from the cease-fire line in Jammu and Kashmir to the marshes of the Rann of Kutch in northwestern Gujarat. On the evening of December 3, the Pakistani army launched ground operations in Kashmir and Punjab. It also started an armored operation in Rajasthan. In Kashmir, the operations were concentrated on two key points, Punch and Chhamb. The Chhamb area witnessed a particularly intense battle where the Pakistanis forced the Indians to withdraw from their positions. In other parts of Kashmir, the Indians made some small gains along the cease-fire line. The major Indian counteroffensive came in the Sialkot-Shakargarh area south and west of Chhamb. There, two Pakistani tank regiments, equipped with United States-made Patton tanks, confronted the Indian First Armored Corps, which had British Centurion tanks. In what proved to be the largest tank battle of the war, both sides suffered considerable casualties.

Though the Indian conduct of the land war on the western front was somewhat timid, the role of the Indian air force was both extensive and daring. During the fourteen-day war, the air force's Western Command conducted some 4,000 sorties. There was little retaliation by Pakistan's air force, partly because of the paucity of non-Bengali technical personnel.

Additionally, this lack of retaliation reflected the deliberate decision of the Pakistan Air Force headquarters to conserve its forces because of heavy losses incurred in the early days of the war.

China

The Chinese have two major claims on what India deems its own territory. One claim, in the western sector, is on Aksai Chin in the northeastern section of Ladakh District in Jammu and Kashmir. The other claim is in the eastern sector over a region included in the British-designated North-East Frontier Agency, the disputed part of which India renamed Arunachal Pradesh and made a state. In the fight over these areas, the well-trained and well-armed troops of the Chinese People's Liberation Army overpowered the ill-equipped Indian troops, who had not been properly acclimatized to fighting at high altitudes.

Unable to reach political accommodation on disputed territory along the 3,225-kilometer-long Himalayan border, the Chinese attacked India on October 20, 1962. At the time, nine divisions from the eastern and western commands were deployed along the Himalayan border with China. None of these divisions was up to its full troop strength, and all were short of artillery, tanks, equipment, and even adequate articles of clothing.

In Ladakh the Chinese attacked south of the Karakoram Pass at the northwest end of the Aksai Chin Plateau and in the Pangong Lake area about 160 kilometers to the southeast. The defending Indian forces were easily ejected from their posts in the area of the Karakoram Pass and from most posts near Pangong Lake. However, they put up spirited resistance at the key posts of Daulat Beg Oldi (near the entrance to the pass) and Chushul (located immediately south of Pangong Lake and at the head of the vital supply road to Leh, a major town and location of an air force base in Ladakh). Other Chinese forces attacked near Demchok (about 160 kilometers southeast of Chusul) and rapidly overran the Demchok and the Jara La posts.

In the eastern sector, in Assam, the Chinese forces advanced easily despite Indian efforts at resistance. On the first day of the fighting, Indian forces stationed at the Tsang Le post on the northern side of the Namka Chu, the Khinzemane post, and near Dhola were overrun. On the western side of the North-

East Frontier Agency, Tsang Dar fell on October 22, Bum La on October 23, and Tawang, the headquarters of the Seventh Infantry Brigade, on October 24. The Chinese made an offer to negotiate on October 24. The Indian government promptly rejected this offer.

With a lull in the fighting, the Indian military desperately sought to regroup its forces. Specifically, the army attempted to strengthen its defensive positions in the North-East Frontier Agency and Ladakh and to prepare against possible Chinese attacks through Sikkim and Bhutan. Army units were moved from Calcutta, Bihar, Nagaland, and Punjab to guard the northern frontiers of West Bengal and Assam. Three brigades were hastily positioned in the western part of the North-East Frontier Agency, and two other brigades were moved into Sikkim and near the West Bengal border with Bhutan to face the Chinese. Light Stuart tanks were drawn from the Eastern Command headquarters at Calcutta to bolster these deployments.

In the western sector, a divisional organization was established in Leh; several battalions of infantry, a battery of twenty-five-pounder guns, and two troops of AMX light tanks were airlifted into the Chushul area from Punjab. On November 4, the Indian military decided that the post at Daulat Beg Oldi was untenable, and its defenders were withdrawn over the 5,300-meter-high Sasar Brangsa Pass to a more defensible position.

The reinforcements and redeployments in Ladakh proved sufficient to defend the Chushul perimeter despite repeated Chinese attacks. However, the more remote posts at Rezang La and Gurung Hill and the four posts at Spanggur Lake area fell to the Chinese.

In the North-East Frontier Agency, the situation proved to be quite different. Indian forces counterattacked on November 13 and captured a hill northwest of the town of Walong. Concerted Chinese attacks dislodged them from this hard-won position, and the nearby garrison had to retreat down the Lohit Valley.

In another important section of the eastern sector, the Kameng Frontier Division, six Chinese brigades attacked across the Tawang Chu near Jang and advanced some sixteen kilometers to the southeast to attack Indian positions at Nurang, near Se La, on November 17. Despite the Indian attempt to regroup their forces at Se La, the Chinese continued their onslaught, wiping out virtually all Indian resistance in Kameng. By November 18, the Chinese had penetrated close to the outskirts of

Tezpur, Assam, a major frontier town nearly fifty kilometers from the Assam-North-East Frontier Agency border.

The Chinese did not advance farther and on November 21 declared a unilateral cease-fire. They had accomplished all of their territorial objectives, and any attempt to press farther into the plains of Assam would have stretched their logistical capabilities and their lines of communication to a breaking point. By the time the fighting stopped, each side had lost 500 troops.

The fighting war was over, but a new diplomatic war had begun. After more than thirty years of border tension and stalemate, high-level bilateral talks were held in New Delhi starting in February 1994 to foster "confidence-building measures" between the defense forces of India and China, and a new period of better relations began (see China, ch. 9).

Peacekeeping Operations

In addition to the experience gained in wars with Pakistan and China, the Indian army has been involved in two regional peacekeeping operations. The first was in Sri Lanka from 1987 to 1990, the second in Maldives in 1988. In addition, Indian forces have participated in ten UN peacekeeping forces.

Sri Lanka

Since the early 1970s, ethnic conflict has pitted Sri Lanka's Tamil minority against the Sinhalese majority over issues of power sharing and local autonomy. The main combatants are the Sri Lankan army and the secessionist Liberation Tigers of Tamil Eelam. Indian involvement, encouraged by pro-Tamil sentiments in its state of Tamil Nadu, which is close to Sri Lanka, and the Indian government's covert aid to and training of Tamil militants between 1977 and 1987, drew India into the conflict. The Indo-Sri Lankan Accord, signed on July 29, 1987, committed New Delhi to deploying a peacekeeping force on the island, making the Indian government the principal guarantor of a solution to the ethnic violence that had heightened dramatically since 1983. Nearly 60,000 Indian troops drawn from two divisions (one from the Central Command and the other from the Southern Command) were in Sri Lanka as the Indian Peace Keeping Force (IPKF) between 1987 and 1990.

Originally sent to Sri Lanka as a neutral body with a mission to ensure compliance with the accord, the IPKF increasingly became a partisan force fighting against Tamils. The popularity of Indian forces, which was never high, decreased still further amidst charges of rape and murder of civilians. Despite the considerable experience that Indian troops had gained in fighting insurgencies in India's northeast, the IPKF was at a marked disadvantage in Sri Lanka. In fighting Naga and Mizo guerrillas in northeast India, the army had fought on home ground, and the central government could couple the army's efforts with direct political negotiations. In Sri Lanka, the Indian forces did not possess an adequate local intelligence network. Despite the growth of the IPKF to 70,000 strong, the predominantly urban context of northern Sri Lanka imposed constraints on the use of force. It also is widely believed that Sri Lankan forces offered only grudging cooperation. Given the inability of the IPKF to prevent either Sinhalese or Tamil extremist actions, it steadily lost the support of both sides in the conflict.

As the Sri Lankan presidential elections approached in December 1988, both the contending parties, the ruling United National Party led by then Prime Minister Ranasinghe Premadasa, and the three-party United Front led by former Prime Minister Sirimavo Ratwatte Dias Bandaranaike, expressed their reservations about the 1987 accord. Premadasa was elected, and after he was inaugurated, he declared an end to the five-and-a-half-year state of emergency and asked India to withdraw the IPKF. In July 1989, the IPKF started a phased withdrawal of its remaining 45,000 troops, a process that took until March 1990 to complete.

During the three-year involvement, some 1,500 Indian troops were killed and more than 4,500 were wounded during this operation. Another casualty resulting from the Sri Lanka mission was the assassination of former Prime Minister Rajiv Gandhi by a Tamil militant in 1991. As a participant in what began as a peacekeeping mission, the Indian armed forces learned some valuable lessons. These included the realization that better coordination is needed between military and political decision makers for such missions. One of the commanders of the IPKF also noted that training, equipment, and command and control needed improvement.

In 1995, at the request of the Sri Lankan government, Indian naval ships and air force surveillance aircraft established a quarantine zone around the LTTE stronghold in the Jaffna area. The supply of military matériel by Indian sympathizers to the Tamil insurgents in Sri Lanka from Tamil Nadu, just thirty-five kilometers across the Palk Strait, was an ongoing problem that continued to keep India involved in the conflict.

Maldives

In 1988, the Indian Army experienced a small success in squashing an attempted coup in Maldives, 600 kilometers south of India in the Indian Ocean. Maldivian minister of foreign affairs Fathullah Jameel had called Rajiv Gandhi (India's prime minister from 1984 to 1989) at 5:30 a.m. on November 3, 1988 to request India's assistance. By 9:00 a.m. the same morning, India's Cabinet Committee on Political Affairs had been convened. At noon the same day, the committee gave its approval for military support to the regime of President Maumoon Abdul Gayoom. Later in the day, the first Indian troops were airlifted from a military base at Agra, Uttar Pradesh. Some 1,600 Indian troops were dispatched within hours. During the next three days, the mercenaries involved in the attempted coup were rounded up by Indian troops who had parachuted in. The Indian navy also effectively blocked maritime escape routes the coup leaders might have taken. The operation was completed by November 6.

Three important inferences can be made from this successful attempt at force projection. First, it demonstrated that sufficient interservice cooperation existed to allow the armed forces to respond rapidly to political directives. Second, it showed the capability of the armed forces to airlift troops regionally at short notice. And third, it demonstrated the willingness of the Indian political leadership to use its military strength in the region to support a friendly regime.

United Nations Peacekeeping Forces

Indian armed forces personnel have been involved in a variety of UN-sponsored peacekeeping missions and military observer operations, giving them invaluable experience in interacting with the armed forces of other nations. In addition, although it was not a peacekeeping force per se, an Indian airborne field ambulance unit participated in the Korean War (1950–53).

Indian infantry, supply, transportation, and signal units served between 1956 and 1967 with the First United Nations Emergency Force in the Suez Canal, Sinai Peninsula, and Gaza. From 1960 to 1964, Indian infantry, aircraft, and medical personnel, and air dispatch, signal, supply, and postal units served in the Congo (as Zaire was then named). Indian military observers participated in UN observation groups in Lebanon in 1958; Yemen in 1963–64 (where India supplied one of the chiefs of staff); West Irian (which later became Indonesia's Irian Barat Province) in 1962–63; the Iran-Iraq border in 1988–91; Angola in 1989–91; and Costa Rica, El Salvador, Guatemala, Honduras, and Nicaragua in 1989–92. Military observers, police monitors, and election supervisors were sent to Namibia in 1989 and 1990 to help oversee elections.

In the 1990s, more military observers were sent abroad. There was a second observers' mission to Angola (1991–92) as well as missions to El Salvador (starting in 1991), former Yugoslavia (starting in 1992), and Mozambique (starting in 1992). The last was a force of more than 900 administrative, engineering, and logistic personnel. A sappers' contingent charged with clearing landmines and related construction projects participated in the United Nations Transitional Authority in Cambodia in 1992–93. An infantry brigade—including army physicians, nurses, veterinarians, a tank sqaudron, a mechanized battalion, a 120-millimeter mortar battery, an engineer company, and two flights of helicopters—and an air force helicopter detachment, a force totalling nearly 5,000 personnel, were sent to Somalia in 1993–94 to participate in peacekeeping and humanitarian relief efforts.

In an effort to achieve some joint operational understanding with other nations' forces, India has also cooperated in various peacetime joint exercises with Indian Ocean nations and with the United States. In 1992, India and the United States conducted joint naval exercises in the Arabian Sea near Kochi (Cochin), and in 1994 Indian marine commandos and United States Marines conducted joint exercises with little fanfare.

National Security Structure

Civil-Military Relations

The pattern of civil-military relations prevailing in India was created by the staff of Lord Mountbatten as a three-tier system extending from the prime minister to the three service chiefs. At the apex of this structure is the Political Affairs Committee of the Cabinet. The second level is the Defence Minister's Committee of the Cabinet, and the third level is the Chiefs of Staff Committee. Other committees, such as the Joint Intelligence Committee, the Defence Science Advisory Committee, and the

Joint Planning Committee, assist the higher committees. There were proposals in the mid-1990s to establish a joint defense staff for better integration of interservice resources, programs, policies, and operations (see fig. 16).

In the immediate postindependence period, the Defence Minister's Committee of the Cabinet did not play an active role in policy formulation. The higher organization of defense was vested largely with the minister of defence. From 1957 to 1962, this position was held by V.K. Krishna Menon, whose authority far exceeded that usually accorded a minister of defence. A confidante of Nehru's through much of the late preindependence period, Menon functioned as Nehru's alter ego for national security and defense planning. Consequently, the locus of decision making shifted from the cabinet to the Defence Minister's Committee. Menon was in many ways responsible for laying the foundations of India's military-industrial base.

Among other endeavors, Menon was responsible for the development of ordnance facilities to manufacture the Ichapore semiautomatic rifle; a tank manufacturing complex at Avadi, Tamil Nadu; facilities to build frigates at the Mazagon Dock naval shipyard in Bombay; and the licensed manufacture of Soviet-designed MiG–23 fighter aircraft in Nasik, Maharashtra. However, his highly idiosyncratic manners, his high-handed ways, and his involvement in the tactical aspects of military decision making had negative consequences. For example, he quarrelled with the professional military, particularly India's third chief of army staff, General K.S. Thimayya, over Thimayya's attempt to warn Menon and Nehru about the emerging Chinese threat as early as 1959. When Thimayya resigned in protest, Nehru prevailed upon him to withdraw his resignation. Unfortunately, when questioned in the Lok Sabha (House of the People), the lower house of the Parliament, about Thimayya's resignation, Nehru offered a rather weak defense of the general's actions and sought to deflect the criticisms of his minister of defence (see The Legislature, ch. 8). When Thimayya retired as chief of army staff in May 1961, Menon passed over Thimayya's designated successor, Lieutenant General S.P.P. Thorat, and instead appointed a junior officer, Lieutenant General P.N. Thapar. The appointment not only created a rift between the professional military and political leadership but also alienated a number of high-ranking officials in the Ministry of Defence. Menon's actions also demoralized competent personnel in the civilian and military bureaucracies, which led to important gaps in defense preparedness and planning. Menon's dominance of the defense planning process significantly contributed to the military debacle of 1962.

The Indian defeat led to the establishment of a new Emergency Committee of the Cabinet. This committee introduced a system of "morning meetings" with the minister of defence and the three service chiefs. The morning meetings, which are conducted without a predetermined agenda, deal with current defense issues on a regular basis. The meetings are also attended by the cabinet secretary, the defence secretary, and the scientific adviser to the minister of defence. These morning meetings continue to take place.

In the Chiefs of Staff Committee, formal equality prevails among the three service chiefs despite the fact that the army remains the largest of the three branches of the armed services. This formal equality among the three services came about with independence.

To facilitate defense planning, the government established two organizations: the Defence Coordination and Implementation Committee and the Defence Planning Staff. The Defense Coordination and Implementation Committee is chaired by the defence secretary and meets on an ad hoc basis. Its membership includes the three service chiefs, representatives from civilian and military intelligence organizations, and the secretary of defence production. The Defence Planning Staff, a permanent body, was established in 1986. Composed of officers drawn from all three services, it is responsible for developing overall national security strategy. It is also charged with briefing the Chiefs of Staff Committee on long-term threats to national security.

Defense Spending

Until 1962 defense spending was deliberately limited. In the wake of the war with China, defense spending rose from 2.1 percent of the gross national product (GNP—see Glossary) in fiscal year (FY—see Glossary) 1962 to 4.5 percent in FY 1964. In FY 1994, defense spending was slightly less than 5 percent of gross domestic product (GDP—see Glossary). In terms of dollars, FY 1994 total defense services expenditures were projected at US$7.2 billion (but are likely to have been close to US$7.8 billion). Proportionately, based on figures provided by the gov-

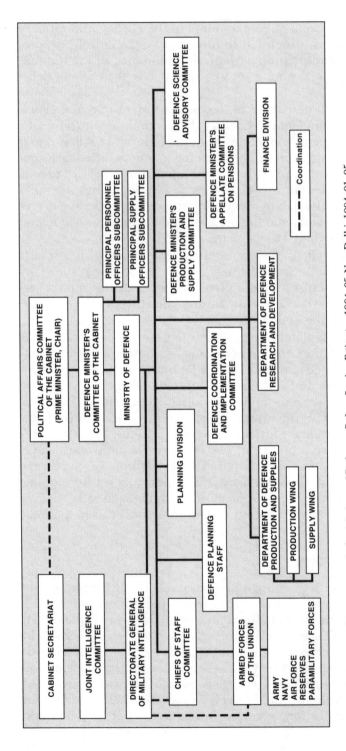

Source: Based on information from India, Ministry of Defence, *Defence Services Estimates, 1994–95*, New Delhi, 1994, 91–95.

Figure 16. National Security Structure, 1995

ernment, 48.4 percent of expenditures were for the army, 15.7 percent for the air force, 5.9 percent for the navy, and 30 percent for capital outlays for defense services and defense ordnance factories. The latter provide matériel to the armed forces through some thirty-nine ordnance factories and eight public-sector enterprises that build ships, aircraft, and major defense items. The defense budget for FY 1994 was 6.5 percent higher than the revised estimate for FY 1993. The allocation increased to 14.9 percent of the total central government budget, up from 13 percent in the previous two fiscal years. Nuclear energy and space research are not fully accounted for in the defense budget, but most paramilitary forces fall within the purview of the Ministry of Defence.

Organization and Equipment of the Armed Forces

The Army

In 1994 the army had approximately 940,000 men and women in its ranks and more than 36,000 in reserve forces. The army is headquartered in New Delhi and is under the direction of the chief of the army staff, always a full general. The chief of the army staff is assisted by a vice chief, two deputy chiefs, a military secretary, and the heads of four main staff divisions: the adjutant general, the quartermaster general, the master general of ordnance, and the engineer in chief.

The army has five tactical area commands: the Northern Command headquartered at Udhampur in Jammu and Kashmir, the Western Command headquartered at Chandimandir in Chandigarh, the Central Command headquartered at Lucknow in Uttar Pradesh, the Eastern Command headquartered at Calcutta, and the Southern Command headquartered at Pune in Maharashtra (see fig. 17). Each command is headed by a lieutenant general. The principal combat formations within the scope of these commands are armored divisions and independent armored brigades, infantry divisions, mountain infantry divisions, independent infantry brigades, airborne/commando brigades, and independent artillery brigades (see table 34, Appendix). These units are organized in twelve corps-level formations.

The army is equipped with some 3,400 main battle tanks. Of these, 1,200 are indigenously manufactured Vijayanta tanks. Additionally, the army has some T–55, T–72, and PT–76 tanks. The Arjun main battle tank has been under development by the Defence Research and Development Organisation (DRDO) since 1983, and, in 1995, limited production was expected to begin in 1996.

To complement indigenous production, however, it was reported in 1994 that Russia had agreed to help India modernize its T–72 tanks and to sell and lease other types of weapons. It is generally understood that about 70 percent of India's military equipment is of Soviet origin. Some army officials continue to favor Russian-made equipment, such as the T–72 tank, over Indian adaptations of the same items, such as the T–72 MI tank developed by the DRDO.

The army also has substantial artillery forces. The best estimate places the army's towed artillery capabilities at more than 4,000 pieces. In addition to the towed artillery, the army has self-propelled artillery. Finally, it has substantial numbers of surface-to-air missile capabilities, the total number being more than 1,200. In 1986 air observation post units were transferred from the air force to the army to form the Army Aviation branch. Using nine helicopter squadrons, Army Aviation has supported ground units in the Siachen Glacier in Jammu and Kashmir and in Sri Lanka, as well as counterinsurgency operations in various parts of the country. Army Aviation has also participated in disaster relief.

Apart from its nine squadrons of helicopters, the army has eight air observation squadrons and six antitank/transport squadrons. It relies on the air force for air support, lift capabilities, and air supply (see table 35, Appendix).

An extensive body of schools and centers supports army operations. The officer corps is largely drawn from the National Defence Academy at Khadakvasla, Maharashtra, a joint services training institution that provides educational equivalents to the bachelor of arts or bachelor of science degrees to cadets for all three service arms. Cadets spend their first three years at the National Defence Academy and then are sent to their respective service academies for further training before being commissioned in the armed forces. A preparatory school, the Rashtriya Indian Military College, at Dehra Dun, Uttar Pradesh, provides education to candidates for the National Defence Academy. After completing their studies at the National Defence Academy, army cadets are sent to the Indian Military Academy at Dehra Dun. Other Indian Military Academy cadets are graduates of the Army Cadet College or are direct-entry students who have qualified by passing the

Union Public Service Commission Examination. They spend between twelve and twenty-four months at the Indian Military Academy before being commissioned in the army as second lieutenants. Still other officer training occurs at the Officers' Training Academy in Madras, Tamil Nadu, where a forty-four-week session is offered to university graduates seeking a short-service commission.

In addition to the Indian Military Academy, the army runs a number of military education establishments. The more prominent ones include the College of Combat at Mhow, Madhya Pradesh; the High Altitude Warfare School at Gulmarg, Jammu and Kashmir; and the Counter-Insurgency and Jungle Warfare School at Vairengte, Mizoram. The army also operates the Defence Services Staff College at Wellington in the Nilgiri Hills in Tamil Nadu, which provides master of science-level joint-service training for mid-level staff appointments and promotes interservice cooperation.

In 1994 it was reported that there were 200 women in the armed forces. In the army, which employs women as physicians and nurses, the participation of women is small but growing. The Indian Military Nursing Service was formed in 1926 and has eight nursing schools (five army, two navy, and one air force) and one nursing college in Pune. Bachelor of science graduates are commissioned as lieutenants in the Medical Nursing Service and attached to the various components of the armed forces. Ranks as high as colonel can be attained by career officers. In the mid-1990s, a small but increasing number of women officers were being assigned to nonmedical services. In 1994, there were fifty women nonmedical army officers and another twenty-five in training. They are university graduates who have been put through rigorous training and are reported to be eager for combat unit assignments.

The Navy

The origins of the modern Indian navy are traced to a maritime force established by the East India Company in the seventeenth century. This force had a variety of names—the Bombay Marine, the Indian Navy, and the Indian Marine. In 1934 the Royal Indian Navy was established, with Indians serving primarily in lower-level positions. After independence the navy was the most neglected of the three services because the national leadership perceived that the bulk of the threats to India were land-based.

The first efforts at naval rearmament emerged in the 1964–69 Defence Plan, which called for the replacement of India's aging fleet and the development of a submarine service. Between 1947 and 1964, fiscal constraints had prevented the implementation of ambitious plans for naval expansion. Consequently, many of the vessels were obsolete and of little operational value. As part of this expansion program, the British helped develop the Mazagon Dock shipyard for the local production of British Leander-class frigates. The Soviets, however, were willing to support all phases of the planned naval expansion. Accordingly, they supplied naval vessels, support systems, and training on extremely favorable terms. By the mid-1960s, they had replaced Britain as India's principal naval supplier (see table 36, Appendix).

During the 1980s, Indian naval power grew significantly. During this period, the naval facilities at Port Blair in the Andaman Islands, in the Nicobar Islands, and in Lakshadweep were significantly upgraded and modernized. A new line of Leander-class frigates was manufactured at Mazagon Dock in collaboration with Vickers and Yarrow of Britain. These frigates, redesignated as the Godavari class, have antisubmarine warfare capabilities and can carry two helicopters. During the 1980s, plans were also finalized for the licensed manufacture of a line of West German Type 1500 submarines (known as the Shishumar class in India). In addition to these developments at Mazagon Dock, the naval air arm also was upgraded. India purchased nearly two squadrons of the vertical and short takeoff and landing (VSTOL) Sea Harriers to replace an earlier generation of Sea Hawks.

In the mid-1990s, India was preparing for a major modernization program that was to include completion of three 5,000-ton Delhi-class destroyers, the building of three 3,700-ton frigates based on Italian Indian Naval Ship (INS)–10 design, and the acquisition of four hydrographic survey ships. Also to be built were an Indian-designed warship called Frigate 2001; six British Upholder-class submarines; an Indian-designed and Indian-built missile-firing nuclear submarine—the Advanced Technology Vessel—based on the Soviet Charlie II class; and an Indian-designed and Indian-built 17,000-ton air defense ship capable of carrying between twelve and fifteen aircraft. The air-defense ship will be, in effect, a replacement for India's two aging British aircraft carriers, the INS *Vikrant*, the keel of which was laid in 1943 but construction of which was not completed

Aircraft on the flight deck of the INS Viraat
Courtesy Embassy of India, Washington

until 1961 and which was slated for decommissioning by 2000, and the INS *Viraat,* which entered service in 1987 and is likely to be decommissioned by 2005. The problems encountered with modernizing these and other foreign-source ships led India to decide against acquiring an ex-Soviet Kiev-class aircraft carrier in 1994.

In the spirit of international military cooperation, India has made moves in the early and mid-1990s to enhance joint-nation interoperability. Indian naval exercises have taken place with ships from the Russian navy and those of Indian Ocean littoral states and other nations, including the United States.

Naval headquarters is located in New Delhi. It is under the command of the chief of naval staff—a full admiral. The chief of naval staff has four principal staff officers: the vice chief of naval staff, the vice chief of personnel, the chief of material, and the deputy chief of naval staff. The total strength of the navy in 1994 was 54,000, including 5,000 naval aviation personnel and 1,000 marines (one regiment, with a second reportedly forming).

Women were inducted into the navy for the first time in 1992, when twenty-two were trained as education, logistics, and law cadres. In 1993 additional women were recruited for air traffic control duties. By 1994 there were thirty-five women naval officers.

The navy is deployed under three area commands, each headed by a flag officer. The Western Naval Command is headquartered in Bombay on the Arabian Sea; the Southern Naval Command in Kochi (Cochin), in Kerala, also on the Arabian Sea; and the Eastern Naval Command in Vishakhapatnam, Andhra Pradesh, on the Bay of Bengal. Additionally, the navy has important bases in Calcutta and Goa.

The Southern Naval Command is responsible for naval officer training, which occurs at the Indian Naval Academy in Goa. Officer candidates are largely drawn from the National Defence Academy. After commissioning, officers are offered specialized training in antisubmarine warfare, aviation, communications, electronic warfare, engineering, hydrography, maritime warfare, missile warfare, navigation, and other naval specialties at various naval training institutions, many of which are collocated with the Training Command headquarters on Willingdon Island, near Kochi.

The Air Force

The air force was established in 1932. In 1994 it had 110,000 personnel and 779 combat aircraft. The air force, which is headquartered in New Delhi, is headed by the chief of air staff, an air chief marshal. He is assisted by six principal staff officers: the vice chief of air staff, the deputy chief of air staff, the air officer in charge of administration, the air officer in charge of personnel, the air officer in charge of maintenance, and the inspector general of flight safety. The air force is deployed into five operational commands: the Western Air Command, headquartered at New Delhi; the Southwestern Air Command, headquartered at Jodhpur, Rajasthan; the Eastern Air Command, headquartered at Shillong, Meghalaya; the Central Air Command, headquartered at Allahabad, Uttar Pradesh; and the Southern Air Command, headquartered at Thiruvananthapuram (Trivandrum), Kerala. Additionally, there are two functional commands: the Training Command at Bangalore,

Karnataka, and the Maintenance Command at Nagpur, Maharashtra.

As of 1994, the air force was equipped with twenty-two squadrons of ground attack fighters. Five of these squadrons had a total of eighty-nine British Jaguar aircraft. Another five squadrons had 120 Soviet-origin MiG–27 aircraft. The air force also fielded twenty fighter squadrons, two of which were equipped with a total of thirty-five French-built Mirage 2000 H/TH aircraft. There were also twelve squadrons of transport aircraft in the inventory (see table 37, Appendix). Because of the large number of Soviet-origin aircraft, the air force is dependent on Russia for spare parts and equipment and weapons upgrades. In March 1995, Russia agreed to upgrade India's MiG–21 aircraft.

Aside from the Training Command at Bangalore, the center for primary flight training is located at the Air Force Academy at Hyderabad, Andhra Pradesh, followed by operational training at various air force schools. Advanced training is also conducted at the Defence Services Staff College; specialized advanced flight training schools are located at Bidar, Karnataka, and Hakimpet, Andhra Pradesh (also the location for helicopter training). Technical schools are found at a number of other locations.

In 1991 the government approved the induction of women into nontechnical air force officer billets, such as administration, logistics, accounting, education, and meteorology. In 1992 opportunities for "pioneer women officers" were opened in the areas of transportation, helicopters, and navigation, and the first group of thirteen women cadets entered the Air Force Academy. During their flight training, they qualified on HPT–32 and Kiran aircraft to earn their air force commissions. After completing ten months' training, five of the seven successful course graduates received further training on various transport aircraft. By 1994, there were fifty-five women officers in the air force.

Recruitment and Training

Under the Indian constitution, as amended in 1977, each citizen has a fundamental duty to "defend the country and render national service when called upon to do so" (see The Constitutional Framework, ch. 8). However, the three services have always been all-volunteer forces, and general conscription has never proved necessary. Military service has long been deemed an attractive option for many in a society where employment opportunities are scarce. The technical branches of the armed forces, however, have experienced problems with recruitment. Since the 1980s, as a result of the growth and diversification of India's industrial base, employment opportunities for individuals with technical training have expanded substantially. Consequently, fewer trained individuals have sought employment opportunities in the armed services.

The army and navy maintain a combined recruitment organization that operates sixty offices in key cities and towns nationwide. The air force has a separate recruiting organization with twelve offices. Army and navy recruitment officers tour rural districts adjacent to their stations and also draw from nearby urban areas. The air force and the navy draw a disproportionate number of their recruits from the urban areas, where educational opportunities are adequate to generate applicants capable of mastering technical skills. The army also recruits outside India, admitting ethnic Gurkhas (also seen as Gorkhas) from Nepal into a Gurkha regiment.

Initial enlistments vary in length, depending on the service and the branch or skill category, but fifteen years is considered the minimum. The tour of duty is generally followed by two to five years of service in a reserve unit. Reenlistment is permitted for those who are qualified, particularly those possessing necessary skills. The minimum age for enlistment is seventeen years; the maximum varies between twenty and twenty-seven, depending on the service and skill category. The compulsory retirement age for officers also varies, ranging from forty-eight for army majors, navy lieutenant commanders, and air force squadron leaders and below, to sixty for army generals, navy admirals, and air force air chief marshals. On occasion a two-year extension is granted on the grounds of exceptional organizational needs or personal ability.

Candidates have to meet minimum physical standards, which differ among the three services and accommodate the various physical traits of particular ethnic groups. Since 1977 recruiting officers have relaxed physical standards slightly when evaluating the only sons of serving or former military personnel—both as a welfare measure and as a means of maintaining a family tradition of military service.

Educational standards for enlisted ranks differ according to service and skill category; the army requirement varies from basic literacy to higher secondary education (see Primary and

Women naval officers
Courtesy Embassy of India, Washington

Secondary Education, ch. 2). The other two services require higher educational levels, reflecting their greater need for technical expertise. The air force requires at least a higher secondary education, and the navy insists on graduation from a secondary school for all except cooks and stewards. Officer candidates have to complete a higher secondary education and pass a competitive qualifying exam for entry into precommission training. All services also accept candidates holding university degrees in such fields as engineering, physics, or medicine for direct entry into the officer corps.

Enlistment was legally opened to all Indians following independence in 1947. In 1949 the government abolished recruitment on an ethnic, linguistic, caste, or religious basis. Exceptions were army infantry regiments raised before World War II, where cohesion and effectiveness were thought to be rooted in long-term attachment to traditions. Some army regiments have a homogeneous composition; other regiments segregate groups only at battalion or company levels. Others are completely mixed throughout. In general, the army has steadily evolved into a more heterogeneous service since 1947. Regiments raised during and after World War II have recruited Indians of almost all categories, and the doubling of the army's size after the 1962 border war with China sped up the process. The armed forces have made a concerted effort to recruit among underrepresented segments of the population and, during the late 1970s and the early 1980s, reformed the recruiting process to eliminate some of the subjectivity in the candidate selection process. Since 1989 the government has sought to apportion recruitment from each state and union territory according to its share of the population. Both the air force and the navy are now almost completely "mixed" services and display considerable heterogeneity in their composition.

Conditions of Service

Pay and allowances for armed forces personnel compare favorably with civilian employment. Monthly salaries vary according to the service, although personnel usually earn similar pay for equivalent duties. Additionally, there is an extensive and complex system of special allowances that depend on conditions and kind of service. Free food for personnel in both field and garrison areas was extended after 1983 to all personnel up to the rank of colonel. All personnel are entitled to annual leaves of varying lengths, and, other than for a few exceptions, the services bear transportation costs for personnel and their families. Commissioned officers and other designated ranks contribute to the Armed Forces Provident Fund, a form of life insurance.

Personnel retiring after twenty years of service as an officer or fifteen years of enlisted service receive pensions based on the rank held at retirement. Retirees without the minimum service requirement receive special one-time bonuses. Additional remuneration accrues to those disabled in the line of service or—in the event of the death of active-duty personnel—to their surviving dependents.

The Soldiers', Sailors', and Airmen's Board, chaired by the minister of defence, is one of the most important organizations dealing with the welfare of active-duty personnel and their dependents. The board works closely with the Directorate of Resettlement in the Ministry of Defence to assist former service personnel and their dependents to find employment on their return to civilian life. The directorate also operates cooperative industrial and agricultural estates and training programs to prepare former service personnel for employment in new fields. Both central and state-level governments reserve a percentage of vacancies in the public sector for former military personnel.

Uniforms, Ranks, and Insignia

Indian military uniforms resemble those in the corresponding British services: olive drab for the army, dark blue for the navy, and sky blue for the air force. More uniform variations exist in the army than in the other services, with certain army regiments preserving traditional accoutrements. Sikhs may wear turbans instead of standard military headgear, for example (see Sikhism, ch. 3).

The rank structure in the three services, especially in the commissioned officer ranks, for the most part follows conventional British practice. The army, however, has the category of junior commissioned officer, for which there is no precise equivalent in the United States or British services. Junior commissioned officers are promoted on a point system from within the enlisted ranks of their regiments, filling most of the junior command slots, such as platoon leaders. The senior junior commissioned officer usually acts as the principal assistant to the commanding officer.

Rank insignia closely follow the British system. Combinations of stars, Lion of Sarnath (the national emblem) badges, crossed sabers, and crossed batons in a wreath show respective army ranks from junior commissioned officer up through field marshal. The latter rank has been granted to only two distinguished Indian officers: K.M. Cariappa, a highly decorated veteran of the 1947–48 war with Pakistan, and S.H.F.J. "Sam" Manekshaw, the strategist of the 1971 war with Pakistan. Arm chevrons worn with the point down indicate enlisted ranks. Naval insignia follow the convention of sleeve stripes for officers and fouled anchor badges for enlisted personnel. The air force uses broad and narrow sleeve stripe combinations for officer ranks and combinations of chevrons, Lion of Sarnath badges, and wing symbols for enlisted ranks (see fig. 18; fig. 19).

INDIAN RANK	2D LIEUTENANT	LIEUTENANT	CAPTAIN	MAJOR	LIEUTENANT COLONEL	COLONEL	BRIGADIER	MAJOR GENERAL	LIEUTENANT GENERAL	GENERAL	FIELD MARSHAL
ARMY 											
U.S. RANK TITLE	2D LIEUTENANT	1ST LIEUTENANT	CAPTAIN	MAJOR	LIEUTENANT COLONEL	COLONEL	BRIGADIER GENERAL	MAJOR GENERAL	LIEUTENANT GENERAL	GENERAL	GENERAL OF THE ARMY
INDIAN RANK	PILOT OFFICER	FLYING OFFICER	FLIGHT LIEUTENANT	SQUADRON LEADER	WING COMMANDER	GROUP CAPTAIN	AIR COMMODORE	AIR VICE MARSHAL	AIR MARSHAL	AIR CHIEF MARSHAL	MARSHAL OF THE AIR FORCE
AIR FORCE 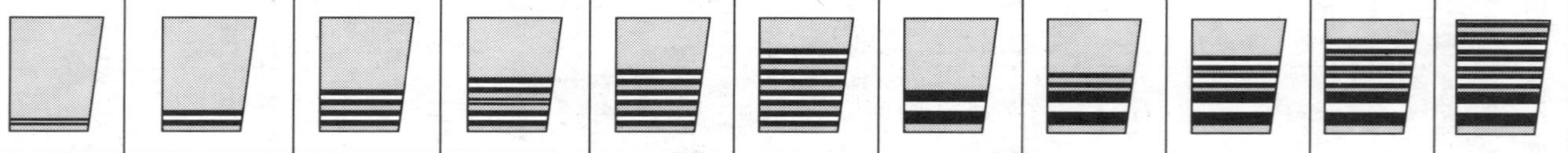											
U.S. RANK TITLE	2D LIEUTENANT	1ST LIEUTENANT	CAPTAIN	MAJOR	LIEUTENANT COLONEL	COLONEL	BRIGADIER GENERAL	MAJOR GENERAL	LIEUTENANT GENERAL	GENERAL	GENERAL OF THE AIR FORCE
INDIAN RANK	ACTING SUB-LIEUTENANT	SUB-LIEUTENANT	LIEUTENANT	LIEUTENANT COMMANDER	COMMANDER	CAPTAIN	COMMODORE	REAR ADMIRAL	VICE ADMIRAL	ADMIRAL	ADMIRAL OF THE FLEET
NAVY 											
U.S. RANK TITLE	ENSIGN	LIEUTENANT JUNIOR GRADE	LIEUTENANT	LIEUTENANT COMMANDER	COMMANDER	CAPTAIN	REAR ADMIRAL LOWER HALF	REAR ADMIRAL UPPER HALF	VICE ADMIRAL	ADMIRAL	FLEET ADMIRAL

Figure 18. Officer Ranks and Insignia, 1995

INDIAN RANK	JAWAN	SEPOY	LANCE NAIK	NAIK	NO RANK	HAVILDAR	COMPANY QUARTERMASTER HAVILDAR	COMPANY HAVILDAR MAJOR	BATTALION QUARTERMASTER HAVILDAR	BATTALION HAVILDAR MAJOR	NAIB SUBEDAR[1]	SUBEDAR[1] / RISALDAR[1]	SUBEDAR MAJOR[1] / RISALDAR MAJOR[1]
ARMY	NO INSIGNIA	NO INSIGNIA 											
U.S. RANK TITLE	BASIC PRIVATE	PRIVATE	PRIVATE 1ST CLASS	CORPORAL/ SPECIALIST	SERGEANT	STAFF SERGEANT	SERGEANT 1ST CLASS	MASTER SERGEANT/ FIRST SERGEANT	SERGEANT MAJOR / COMMAND SERGEANT MAJOR	NO RANK	NO RANK	NO RANK	NO RANK
INDIAN RANK / AIR FORCE	AIRCRAFTMAN	LEADING AIRCRAFTMAN	NO RANK	CORPORAL		SERGEANT	JUNIOR WARRANT OFFICER	WARRANT OFFICER	MASTER WARRANT OFFICER	NO RANK	NO RANK	NO RANK	NO RANK
U.S. RANK TITLE	AIRMAN BASIC	AIRMAN	AIRMAN 1ST CLASS	SENIOR AIRMAN/ SERGEANT	STAFF SERGEANT	TECHNICAL SERGEANT	MASTER SERGEANT	SENIOR MASTER SERGEANT	CHIEF MASTER SERGEANT	NO RANK			
INDIAN RANK / NAVY	NO INSIGNIA	SEAMAN	ABLE SEAMAN	LEADING SEAMAN	NO RANK	PETTY OFFICER	CHIEF PETTY OFFICER[2]	MASTER CHIEF PETTY OFFICER (II)[2]	MASTER CHIEF PETTY OFFICER (I)[2]	NO RANK	NO RANK	NO RANK	NO RANK
U.S. RANK TITLE	SEAMAN RECRUIT	SEAMAN APPRENTICE	SEAMAN	PETTY OFFICER 3D CLASS	PETTY OFFICER 2D CLASS	PETTY OFFICER 1ST CLASS	CHIEF PETTY OFFICER	SENIOR CHIEF PETTY OFFICER	MASTER CHIEF PETTY OFFICER				

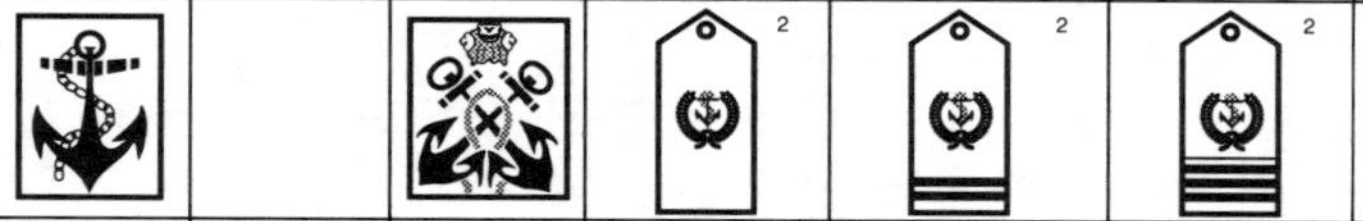

[1] Junior commissioned officer; no United States equivalent. [2] Worn on shoulder.

Figure 19. Enlisted and Junior Noncommissioned Officer Ranks and Insignia, 1995

Paramilitary and Reserve Forces

Paramilitary Forces

In addition to the regular armed forces, India also has paramilitary forces. These forces have grown dramatically since independence. There are twelve paramilitary organizations, which have an authorized strength of around 1.3 million personnel. In 1994, their reported actual strength was 692,500. These organizations include the Coast Guard Organisation and the Defence Security Force, which are subordinate to the Ministry of Defence. Paramilitary forces subordinate to the Ministry of Home Affairs include the Assam Rifles, the Border Security Force, the Central Industrial Security Force, the Central Reserve Police Force, the Indo-Tibetan Border Police, and the Rashtriya Rifles (National Rifles). The National Security Guards, a joint antiterrorist contingency force, are charged with protection of high-level persons (the so-called very very important persons—VVIPs) and are subordinate to the Office of the Prime Minister (also sometimes known as the Prime Minister's Secretariat.) The guards are composed of elements of the armed forces, the Central Reserve Police Force, and the Border Security Force. The Special Frontier Force also is subordinate to the Office of the Prime Minister. The Railway Protection Force is subordinate to the Ministry of Railways. At the local level, there is the Provincial Armed Constabulary, which is controlled by the governments of the states and territories (see State and Other Police Services, this ch.).

During the 1960s, 1970s, and 1980s, local police forces could not deal with the mounting array of sectarian, ethnic, and regional conflicts, and paramilitary forces were increasingly called on for assistance. In addition to security and guard duties, paramilitary organizations assist local and state-level police forces in maintaining public order and shield the army from excessive use in "aid-to-the-civil-power" operations. These operations essentially involve quelling public disorder when local police forces prove inadequate to the task.

The Coast Guard Organisation was constituted as an Armed Force of the Union in 1978 under the administrative control of the Ministry of Defence (although it is funded by the Ministry of Home Affairs), following its 1977 establishment as a temporary navy element. Its principal mission is to protect the country's maritime assets, particularly India's 200-nautical-mile exclusive economic zone and the marine resources contained in the area, which comprises nearly 2.8 million square kilometers. The coast guard is also responsible for the prevention of poaching and smuggling, the control of marine pollution, and carrying out search-and-rescue missions. Under the command of a director general, the coast guard is organized into three national maritime zones: the Western Maritime Zone, headquartered at Bombay; the Eastern Maritime Zone, headquartered at Madras; and the Andaman and Nicobar Maritime Zone, headquartered at Port Blair. The zones are further subdivided into district headquarters, one each for the eight maritime states on the mainland and two in the Andaman and Nicobar Islands. In times of emergency, the coast guard is expected to work with the navy. In the late 1980s, coast guard units from the eastern zone supported Indian peacekeeping efforts in Sri Lanka. The coast guard's equipment includes about fifty ships, nine helicopters, and thirteen fixed-wing aircraft (see table 38, Appendix).

Another Ministry of Defence paramilitary organization has a security mission. The Defence Security Force guards Ministry of Defence facilities throughout India.

The Border Security Force was established in the closing days of the 1965 Indo-Pakistani conflict. Its principal mission involves guarding the Indo-Pakistani line of actual control in Jammu and Kashmir as well as borders with Bangladesh and Burma. It works in internal security and counterinsurgency operations in Assam, Jammu and Kashmir, and Punjab. The border force has also been used to deal with communal rioting.

Another Ministry of Homes Affairs paramilitary force deployed in Jammu and Kashmir is the Rashtriya Rifles. In 1994 it had 5,000 troops, all of whom served in Jammu and Kashmir. Some observers expected the force to grow to thirty battalions, with around 25,000 personnel. In March 1995, Indian television referred to the Delta Force of the "fledgling" Rashtriya Rifles. It was reported that the force was operating against "terrorists" and "foreign mercenaries" in Doda District in south-central Jammu and Kashmir.

Founded in 1939, the Central Reserve Police Force is the country's oldest paramilitary organization. It maintains internal order when local and state-level forces prove inadequate to the task. The Central Reserve Police Force in Assam, Jammu and Kashmir, and Punjab has worked in counterinsurgency operations. This force also was dispatched to Sri Lanka during India's 1987–90 involvement there. The Ministry of Defence's weekly armed forces magazine, *Sainik Samachar,* reported that the Mahila Battalion (Women's Battalion) of the Central Reserve Police Force had "proved its mettle in hot warlike conditions in Sri Lanka," and had established women as "a force to reckon with" in the paramilitary.

Another significant paramilitary organization is the Indo-Tibetan Border Police, established in 1962 in the aftermath of the war with China. It is primarily responsible for the security of the border with China.

The Special Frontier Force, established in 1962 in the aftermath of the war with China, is less well publicized by the government. Apparently it is an elite, parachute-qualified commando unit, nominally subordinate to the army and deployed along sensitive areas of the border with China, and recruited partially from among border-area hill tribes and Tibetan refugees. The Special Frontier Force also appears to have a domestic security role; members of the force were involved in the Golden Temple siege in 1984. In 1994 its reported strength was 3,000, making it one of the smallest paramilitary forces.

Reserve Forces

India's "second line of defense" is composed of several citizen mass organizations. These include the Territorial Army, a voluntary, part-time civilian force that receives military training and serves as a reserve force for the army "to relieve [it] of static duties, to aid the civil power, and to provide units for the regular Army, if and when required." It was raised in 1949 and has been used in times of war and domestic disturbances. Organizationally, Territorial Army personnel are raised from among employees of government agencies and public-sector enterprises and are formed into departmental units. Nondepartmental units are raised from other citizens, including former active-duty military personnel. In the early 1990s, Territorial Army units saw service in Jammu and Kashmir and along the northern and western borders of India and in support of paramilitary units subordinate to the Ministry of Home Affairs.

The National Cadet Corps, which is open to young men and women, was established in 1948 to develop discipline and leadership qualities useful in life and particularly for potential service in the armed forces. The semiautonomous organization receives guidance from the ministries of education and defence at the central level and from state-level governments at the local level. It is organized into army, navy, and air force wings, and its ranks correspond to those in the respective armed forces.

Civil Defence Volunteers are under the leadership of a small paid cadre, who are trained to provide early warning communications at the town level. They also participate in civil works construction projects and natural disaster relief work. Subordination is through the local state or territory government and the Ministry of Home Affairs.

The Home Guards are a voluntary force raised by state and territory governments under the guidance of the Ministry of Home Affairs. Home Guards undergo minimal training and receive pay only when called for duty. They assist the police in crime prevention and detection; undertake watch and patrol duties; and aid in disaster relief, crowd control, and the supervision of elections. The central government reimburses the states and territories at varying rates for expenses incurred in the performance of Home Guard duties.

Space and Nuclear Programs

India detonated its first and only nuclear device at Pokharan in the Rajasthan Desert in May 1974. Subsequently and in all likelihood as a consequence of international pressure, India has chosen not to conduct any further tests. At a formal level, Indian officials and strategists deny that India possesses nuclear weapons and refer to India's position as an "options strategy," which essentially means maintaining the nuclear weapons option and exercising it should regional and international conditions so warrant. In pursuit of this end, India refuses to sign the 1968 Treaty on the Non-Proliferation of Nuclear Weapons. Formally, Indian officials argue that India's refusal to sign the treaty stems from its fundamentally discriminatory character; the treaty places restrictions on the nonnuclear weapons states but does little to curb the modernization and expansion of the nuclear arsenals of the nuclear weapons states.

The Indian ballistic missile program has some elements in common with the nuclear program. Under the aegis of the Integrated Guided Missile Development Programme, India is developing rockets of varying ranges: the Agni, the Prithvi, the Akash, the Trishul, and the Nag. The Agni, which former Prime Minister Rajiv Gandhi referred to as a "technology demonstrator," was first test fired in May 1989 and again in May 1992. In 1995 it was not yet operational, but it has intercontinental ballistic missile potential. The Prithvi—which some sources reported had an operational unit raised in 1995 and deployed along the Pakistani border—is a tactical, short-range surface-to-surface missile designed by the DRDO as part of India's antimissile defense system. Based on the Soviet Scud missile, its 250-kilogram payload can be launched from a mobile launcher. The Trishul is a sea-skimming short-range missile. The Akash is a multitarget surface-to-air missile that was being test fired in 1994 and 1995. The Nag is essentially an antitank missile.

The Indian missile program has been of concern to the United States, which, under the terms of the Missile Technology Control Regime, imposed sanctions against the Indian Space Research Organisation (ISRO) in June 1992. In July 1993, the United States prevailed upon the Russian space agency, Glavkosmos, not to transfer cryogenic rocket engines to India (see Russia; United States, ch. 9). The ISRO decided it would develop the engine on its own by 1997 while continuing to seek purchase of modified versions of the engines from Russia. Seven such cryogenic engines were scheduled for delivery by Glavkosmos between 1996 and 1999. In keeping with its agreement with the United States, Glavkosmos was not going to transfer additional technology for cryogenic engines. However, cryogenic engine technology transfer had begun in 1991, and hence leading ISRO officials were confident about their 1997 projection.

Intelligence Services

The first post-independence military intelligence service was the Intelligence Bureau established in 1947 under the aegis of the Ministry of Home Affairs. Until 1962 the Intelligence Bureau had wide-ranging responsibilities for the collection, collation, and assessment of both domestic and foreign intelligence. The failure of the Intelligence Bureau to assess adequately the nature of the Chinese threat, however, led to a reevaluation of its role and functions in the early 1960s. Military Intelligence, which in the words of one retired Indian general was "little more than a post office," was reactivated and given the task of reporting to the revamped Joint Intelligence Committee. The Joint Intelligence Committee is the key body coordinating and assessing intelligence brought to it by the Intelligence Bureau, Military Intelligence, and the Research and Analysis Wing of the Office of the Prime Minister. Estab-

Navy missile destroyer, INS Rana
Sailors in a ship's operations room
Courtesy Embassy of India, Washington

lished in 1968, the Research and Analysis Wing is primarily responsible for gathering external intelligence. Despite a substantial budget and extensive foreign postings, the wing's efforts to gather intelligence even in South Asia are inadequate according to some foreign analysts (see Role of the Prime Minister, ch. 9).

Each of the armed services has a directorate charged with the collection and dissemination of intelligence. Critics have charged that there is inadequate cooperation and coordination among the service intelligence directorates, the Intelligence Bureau, and the Research and Analysis Wing. There is, however, an interservice Joint Cipher Bureau, which is in charge of cryptology and signals intelligence. The Research and Analysis Wing includes officers from the armed services and also has a chief military intelligence adviser.

Military Justice

The Manual of Military Law and Regulations spells out rules and procedures for the investigation, prosecution, and punishment of military offenses and crimes in the armed forces. Basic authority rests in the constitution, the Army Act of 1954, the Air Force Act of 1950, and the Navy Act of 1957.

The army and air force have three kinds of courts. They are, in descending order of power, the General Court, which conducts general courts-martial; the District Court; and the Summary General Court. Additionally, the army has a fourth kind of court, the Summary Court. Local commanding officers conduct this court with powers similar to nonjudicial punishment in the United States armed forces. The navy uses general courts-martial in addition to the nonjudicial powers established for commanders in the Navy Act.

Courts-martial can be convened by the prime minister, minister of defence, chief of staff of the service concerned, or other officers so designated by the ministry or the chief of staff. There are channels of appeal and stages of judicial review, although procedures differ among the three services.

Members of the armed forces remain subject concurrently to both civilian and military law, and criminal courts with appropriate jurisdictions assume priority over military courts in specific cases. With the approval of the government, a person convicted or acquitted by a court-martial can undergo retrial by a criminal court for the same offense and on the same evidence. Once tried by a civilian court, however, one cannot be tried by a military court for the same offense.

Each of the three services has its own judge advocate general's department, relatively free and independent of the other branches in the discharge of its judicial functions. The various departments have officers among the adjutant general's staff at army headquarters, in the chief of personnel's staff at navy headquarters, and in the administration staff of the air force headquarters.

Public Order and Internal Security

Military Role Expansion

The army has four major roles or functions in the maintenance of public order and internal security. One is to defend India's territorial integrity and to maintain the inviolability of its borders. Another involves dealing with internal security threats stemming from secessionist demands and externally supported insurgencies. The army also is called upon to assist civilian authorities in maintaining civil order when local police forces and the paramilitary prove inadequate to the task. Finally, the army can also be mobilized to deal with natural disasters such as earthquakes and floods, the only domestic function that the army performs with enthusiasm.

Despite the existence of numerous paramilitary forces, the army has had to quell outbreaks of civil violence, primarily in the states of Assam, Jammu and Kashmir, and Punjab (see Paramilitary Forces and Reserve Forces, this ch.). By the early 1990s, army involvement in Assam and Punjab had diminished significantly as insurgencies waned. However, the role of the army in Jammu and Kashmir expanded substantially as both police and paramilitary forces failed to maintain law and order.

In 1993 upper-echelon army officers warned that excessive use of the army to restore civil order might have a number of corrosive effects. First, it might damage the morale of troops who might be distressed at having to shoot civilians. Second, it might have the effect of politicizing the army. The outgoing chief of army staff, General Sunith Francis Rodrigues, publicly articulated his misgivings on this subject. Furthermore, in June 1993, Rodrigues presented a report entitled "Maximizing Effectiveness of Central Police Organizations" to the Committee of Secretaries (composed of a "core group", the secretaries of defence, finance, and home affair, chaired by the cabinet secretary, and meeting on a weekly basis). The report called for the army to take over the training of paramilitary forces.

Civil Liberties, Human Rights, and the Armed Forces

In response to a range of insurgencies since the early 1980s, the central government has enacted an extensive array of legislation that places substantial curbs on civil liberties. The National Security Act of 1980, the National Security Amendment Act of 1984, the Terrorist and Disruptive Activities (Prevention) Act of 1985 (which was renewed in 1987 and suspended in 1995), and the Armed Forces (Jammu and Kashmir) Special Powers Act of 1990 are the most significant laws in force. The ramifications of these four laws are sweeping. Under their aegis, the central government has the right of preventive detention, may seek in-camera trials, may send accused individuals before designated courts, and may destroy property belonging to suspected terrorists. Furthermore, under the terms of the Armed Forces (Jammu and Kashmir) Special Powers Act, members of the armed forces cannot be prosecuted for actions committed in good faith in pursuance of the provisions of this law.

During the 1980s and 1990s, both international and domestic human rights groups asserted that human rights violations are rampant. The principal international organizations making these allegations are the International Commission of Jurists, Amnesty International, and Asia Watch. Two Indian counterparts are the People's Union for Civil Liberties and the People's United Democratic Front. Indian and foreign press reports have alleged that local police and paramilitary forces have engaged in rape, torture, and beatings of suspects in police custody. Numerous "militants" reportedly have simply disappeared in Jammu and Kashmir. On other occasions, especially in Punjab, security forces on various occasions allegedly captured insurgents and then shot them in staged "encounters" or "escapes." The government has either vigorously challenged these allegations or asserted that condign punishment had been meted out against offenders. The government has made efforts to blunt the barrage of domestic and foreign criticism. One such effort was the establishment of the five-member National Human Rights Commission in 1993 composed of senior retired judges. A report released by the commission in November 1993 cited eighty Bombay police officials for "atrocities, ill treatment, collusion, and connivance" and for "being openly on the side of the Hindu aggressors" during the December 1992 Hindu-Muslim riots. The commission's mandate does not extend to violations in Jammu and Kashmir and northeast India, and it must rely on state investigative agencies for its field work.

Insurgent Movements and External Subversion

Kashmir

In the mid-1990s, India was grappling with three separate insurgencies of varying strengths in the states of Assam, Jammu and Kashmir, and Punjab. The insurgency in Jammu and Kashmir has the most serious implications for India. The long-term roots of the Kashmir problem can be traced to the partition of India (see National Integration, ch. 1). The crisis centers on a militant secessionist demand that the Indian state has harshly suppressed. Its proximate causes are located in the central government's attempts to manipulate state-level politics for short-term political ends. Since 1989, approximately 10,000 civilians have died at the hands of security forces or militants. Although the origins of the crisis are quintessentially indigenous, there is widespread agreement among both Indian and foreign observers that the Inter-Services Intelligence Agency of Pakistan has actively aided and abetted some of the insurgent groups, most notably, the radical Islamic Hezb-ul-Mujahideen.

The counterinsurgency strategy that the Indian government has adopted in Jammu and Kashmir was developed in the context of dealing with guerrilla movements in India's northeast in the late 1970s. This strategy involves denying the guerrillas any sanctuaries, sealing the porous Indo-Pakistani border, and using both army and paramilitary forces to conduct house-to-house "cordon-and-search" operations. Whether this strategy will lead eventually to the collapse of the insurgency in Jammu and Kashmir remains an open question; violence has continued to accelerate since 1993, with mounting casualties on both sides and the destruction of an ancient mosque and shrine in 1995 (see Political Issues, ch. 8; South Asia, ch. 9).

Punjab

The insurgency in the state of Punjab originated in the late 1970s. The roots of this insurgency are complex. The Green Revolution, a package of agricultural inputs, transformed the socioeconomic landscape of Punjab (see The Green Revolution, ch. 7). Amidst this new-found prosperity, large numbers of Sikhs started to shed some of the trappings of their faith. This propensity rekindled an age-old fear in the Sikh community—that of being absorbed into the Hindu fold. In turn, many Punjabi Sikhs, who were dispossessed of their land as a consequence of agricultural transformation, found solace in various revivalistic practices. One of the leaders of this revivalistic movement was Sant Jarnail Singh Bhindranwale, a politically ambitious itinerant Sikh preacher. The second factor contributing to the insurgency was the attempt by Indira Gandhi (India's prime minister, 1966–77 and 1980–84), the Congress, and from 1978 Congress (I) to use Bhindranwale to undermine the position of the Akali Dal (Eternal Party), a regional party (see Political Parties, ch. 8). Bhindranwale and his followers were encouraged to verbally intimidate Akali Dal politicians. Although this strategy met with some success, Bhindranwale and his followers became a source of mayhem and disruption in Punjab. Eventually, in June 1984, Gandhi had to order units of the Indian army to flush out Bhindranwale and his followers, who had taken refuge in the Golden Temple complex, Sikhism's most holy shrine, in Amritsar, Punjab (see Sikhism, ch. 3).

This exercise, Operation Bluestar, was, at best, a mixed success. After all efforts at negotiation failed, Indira Gandhi ordered the army to storm the temple. A variety of army units, along with substantial numbers of paramilitary forces, surrounded the temple complex on June 3, 1984. After the demands to surrender peacefully were met with volleys of gunfire from within the confines of the temple, the army was given the order to take the temple by force. Indian intelligence authorities had underestimated the firepower possessed by the militants, however, and the army brought in tanks and heavy artillery to suppress the antitank and machine-gun fire. After a twenty-four-hour firefight, the army successfully took control of the temple. According to Indian government sources, eighty-three army personnel were killed and 249 injured. Insurgent casualties were 493 killed and eighty-six injured. Indian observers assert that the number of Sikh casualties was probably higher.

The attack on the Golden Temple had the effect of inflaming significant segments of the Sikh community. It is widely believed that the two Sikh bodyguards who assassinated Indira Gandhi on October 31, 1984, were driven by their anger over

An Indian Air Force crew prepares for takeoff.
Courtesy Indian Ministry of External Affairs
A Sea Harrier jet, from the Indian Navy's White Tigers Squadron,
on patrol
Courtesy Embassy of India, Washington

the Golden Temple episode. In the wake of Indira Gandhi's assassination, mobs rampaged through the streets of New Delhi and other parts of India over the next few days, killing several thousand Sikhs. The New Delhi police proved to be partisan observers and did little to stop or apprehend the rioters. Only after the deployment of the army, almost three days after the onset of the riots, was order fully restored.

The New Delhi riots had repercussions in Punjab as militants stepped up their activities. Gandhi's son and political successor, Rajiv Gandhi, sought unsuccessfully to bring peace to Punjab with an accord signed with Harchand Singh Longowal, a moderate Sikh leader. Rajiv Gandhi's successors, belonging to the Janata factions, proved to be no more adept at resolving the crisis. In fact, between 1987 and 1991, Punjab was placed under President's Rule and governed directly from New Delhi (see The Executive, ch. 8). Eventually, an election was held in the state in February 1992. Voter turnout, however, was poor; only about 24 percent of the population participated in the elections. Despite its narrow mandate, the newly elected Congress (I) government gave a free hand to the police chief of the state, K.P.S. Gill. His ruthless methods significantly weakened the insurgent movement. Most political observers, however, assert that long-term political stability in Punjab depends on addressing the underlying grievances of segments of the Sikh community.

Assam and the Northeast

The origins of the insurgency in Assam are quite different from those in Kashmir and Punjab. The principal grievance of the radical student movement, the United Liberation Front of Assam, is nativist. Front members are violently opposed to the presence of Bengalis from the neighboring state of West Bengal and waves of illegal immigrants from Bangladesh. Various rounds of negotiations between the United Liberation Front of Assam and two successive central governments resulted in the Assam Accord of August 15, 1985. Under the provisions of this accord, persons who entered the state illegally between January 1966 and March 1971 were allowed to remain but were disenfranchised for ten years, while those who entered after 1971 faced expulsion. A November 1985 amendment to the Indian citizenship law allows noncitizens who entered Assam between 1961 and 1971 to have all the rights of citizenship except the right to vote for a period of ten years.

In 1993 an accord was reached between the Bodo tribe and the central and state governments. The accord established the Bodoland Autonomous Council, which gave the Bodos limited political and administrative autonomy. Nevertheless, violence broke out in 1994: members of the Bodo Security Force, in the wake of demands for a "liberated Bodoland" burned several villages and killed around 100 immigrant villagers. Both local counterinsurgency forces and army units were sent in to engage the Bodo militants.

A number of other insurgencies in the northeast have required extensive use of army and paramilitary forces. Four states in particular have witnessed various insurgent and guerrilla movements. The first and perhaps the most significant insurgency originated in Nagaland in the early 1950s; it was eventually quelled in the early 1980s through a mixture of repression and cooptation. In 1993 Nagaland experienced recrudescent violence as two ethnic groups, the Nagas and the Kukis, engaged in brutal conflict with each other. Adding to India's internal unrest in this region were the links established between the Bodo insurgents in Assam and the National Socialist Council of Nagaland, which, in turn, had links to other active insurgent groups and, reportedly, operatives in Thailand.

In neighboring Manipur, militants organized under the aegis of the People's Liberation Army long fought to unite the Meitei tribes of Burma and Manipur into an independent state. This insurgent movement had been largely suppressed by the mid-1990s.

In Mizoram the Mizo National Front fought a running battle with the Indian security forces throughout the 1960s. As in Nagaland, this insurgency was suppressed in the early 1980s through a mixture of political concessions and harsh military tactics.

In the state of Tripura, tribal peoples organized under the leadership of the Tripura National Front were also responsible for terrorist activity. This movement has, for the most part, also been brought under control by the government.

The central government's success in quelling these insurgencies was not without human and material costs. Although no assessments of these costs exist in the public domain, it is widely believed that the paramilitary forces and the army were given a free hand in suppressing the uprisings. A prominent Indian human rights activist and attorney, Nandita Haksar, has alleged that harsh methods were routinely used, including collective punishment of villagers accused of harboring terrorists in remote areas. Because of the continued level of insurgency by Assamese and other groups, which had bases in neighboring Burma, India and Burma started joint counterinsurgency operations against the rebels in May 1995, the first such operations since the 1980s.

Law Enforcement

National-Level Agencies

The constitution assigns responsibility for maintaining law and order to the states and territories, and almost all routine policing—including apprehension of criminals—is carried out by state-level police forces. The constitution also permits the central government to participate in police operations and organization by authorizing the maintenance of the Indian Police Service. Police officers are recruited by the Union Public Service Commission through a competitive nationwide examination. On completion of a nationwide basic public-service course, police officer candidates attend the National Police Academy at Hyderabad, Andhra Pradesh. They are then assigned to particular state or union territory forces, where they usually remain for the rest of their careers. About 50 percent of the officers are regularly assigned to states or territories other than their own in an effort to promote national integration.

The constitution also authorizes the central government to maintain whatever forces are necessary to safeguard national security. Under the terms of the constitution, paramilitary forces can be legally detailed to assist the states but only if so requested by the state governments. In practice, the central government has largely observed these limits. In isolated instances, the central government has deployed its paramilitary units to protect central government institutions over the protest of a state government. During the Emergency of 1975–77, the constitution was amended (effective February 1, 1976) to permit the central government to dispatch and deploy its paramilitary forces without regard to the wishes of the states (see The Rise of Indira Gandhi, ch. 1). This action proved unpopular, and the use of the paramilitary forces was controversial. After the Emergency was lifted, the constitution was amended in December 1978 to make deployment of central government paramilitary forces once again dependent on the consent of the state government. According to apologists for the central government, this amendment prevented the government from sending in paramilitary forces to protect the Babri Masjid (Babri Mosque) in Ayodhya, Uttar Pradesh, in December 1992 (see Public Worship, ch. 3).

The principal national-level organization concerned with law enforcement is the Ministry of Home Affairs, which supervises a large number of government functions and agencies operated and administered by the central government. The ministry is concerned with all matters pertaining to the maintenance of public peace and order, the staffing and administration of the public services, the delineation of internal boundaries, and the administration of union territories.

In addition to managing the Indian Police Service, the Ministry of Home Affairs maintains several agencies and organizations dealing with police and security. Police in the union territories are the responsibility of the Police Division, which also runs the National Police Academy and the Institute of Criminology and Forensic Science. The Central Bureau of Investigation investigates crimes that might involve public officials or have ramifications for several states. The ministry also is the parent organization of the Border Security Force.

State and Other Police Services

The Police Act of 1861 established the fundamental principles of organization for police forces in India, and, with minor modifications, continues in effect. Consequently, although state-level police forces are separate and may differ in terms of the quality of equipment and resources, their patterns of organization and operation are markedly similar.

An inspector general, answerable to the home secretary of the state, heads each state, union territory, or national capital territory police force. Under the inspector general are a number of police "ranges" composed of three to six districts, headed by deputy inspectors general. District police headquarters are commanded by superintendents. District superintendents have wide discretionary powers and are responsible for overseeing subordinate police stations as well as specialty elements, such as criminal investigation detachments, equipment storehouses and armories, and traffic police. Many large districts also have several assistant district superintendents.

Most preventive police work is carried out by constables assigned to police stations. Depending on the number of stations there, a district may be subdivided and, in some states, further divided into police "circles" to facilitate the supervision from district headquarters. Most of the major metropolitan areas such as New Delhi, Bombay, Calcutta, and Madras have separate municipal forces headed by commissioners. Police in the states and union territories are assisted by units of volunteer Home Guards, maintained under guidelines formulated by the Ministry of Home Affairs.

In most states and territories, police forces are functionally divided into civil (unarmed) police and armed contingents. The former staff police stations, conduct investigations, answer routine complaints, perform traffic duties, and patrol the streets. They usually carry *lathis*—bamboo staffs weighted or tipped with iron.

Contingents of armed police are divided into two groups, the district armed police and the Provincial Armed Constabulary. The district armed police are organized along the lines of an army infantry battalion. They are assigned to police stations and perform guard and escort duties. Those states that maintain distinct armed contingents employ them as a reserve strike force for emergencies. Such units are organized either as a mobile armed force under direct state control or in the case of district armed police (who are not as well equipped) as a force directed by district superintendents and generally used for riot-control duty.

The Provincial Armed Constabulary (Pradeshik) is an armed reserve maintained at key locations in some states and active only on orders from the deputy inspector general and higher-level authorities. Armed constabulary are not usually in contact with the public until they are assigned to VIP duty or assigned to maintain order during fairs, festivals, athletic events, elections, and natural disasters. They may also be sent to quell outbreaks of student or labor unrest, organized crime, and communal riots; to maintain key guard posts; and to participate in antiterrorist operations. Depending on the type of assignment, the Provincial Armed Constabulary may carry only *lathis.*

At all levels, the senior police officers answer to the police chain of command and respond to the general direction and control of designated civilian officials. In the municipal force,

Police officer directing traffic in Bangalore
Courtesy Robert L. Worden

the chain of command runs directly to the state home secretary rather than to the district superintendent or district officials.

Working conditions and pay are poor, especially in the lower echelons of the police forces. Recruits receive only around Rs1,900 per month (about US$64). Opportunities for promotion are limited because of the system of horizontal entry into higher grades. Allegations of bribery, attributable to the low pay and poor working conditions, have been widespread.

Since the late 1980s, women have entered in larger numbers into the higher echelons of the Indian police, mostly through the Indian Police Service system. Women police officers were first used in 1972, and a number of women hold key positions in various state police organizations. However, their absolute numbers, regardless of rank, are small. Uniformed and undercover women police officers have been deployed in New Delhi as the Anti-Eve Teasing Squad, which combats sexual harassment against women ("Eves"). Several women-only police stations have also been established in Tamil Nadu to handle sex crimes against women.

Police uniforms vary widely according to grade, region, and kind of duty performed. Among the armed police, uniforms tend to resemble army dress rather than conventional police uniforms. The khaki uniforms of the Indian Police Service offi-

615

cers are similar in all states, but headgear varies widely, especially among metropolitan areas.

The Criminal Justice System

The criminal justice system descends from the British model. The judiciary and the bar are independent although efforts have been made by some politicians to undermine the autonomy of the judiciary. From about the time of Indira Gandhi's tenure as prime minister, the executive has treated judicial authorities in an arbitrary fashion. Judges who handed down decisions that challenged the regime in office have on occasion been passed over for promotion, for example. Furthermore, unpopular judges have been given less-than-desirable assignments. Because the pay and perquisites of the judiciary have not kept up with salaries and benefits in the private sector, fewer able members of the legal profession have entered the ranks of the senior judiciary.

Despite the decline in the caliber and probity of the judiciary, established procedures for the protection of defendants, except in the case of strife-torn areas, are routinely observed. The penal philosophy embraces the ideals of preventing crime and rehabilitating criminals.

Criminal Law and Procedure

Under the constitution, criminal jurisdiction belongs concurrently to the central government and the states. The prevailing law on crime prevention and punishment is embodied in two principal statutes: the Indian Penal Code and the Code of Criminal Procedure of 1973. These laws take precedence over any state legislation, and the states cannot alter or amend them. Separate legislation enacted by both the states and the central government also has established criminal liability for acts such as smuggling, illegal use of arms and ammunition, and corruption. All legislation, however, remains subordinate to the constitution.

The Indian Penal Code came into force in 1862; as amended, it continued in force in 1993. Based on British criminal law, the code defines basic crimes and punishments, applies to resident foreigners and citizens alike, and recognizes offenses committed abroad by Indian nationals.

The penal code classifies crimes under various categories: crimes against the state, the armed forces, public order, the human body, and property; and crimes relating to elections, religion, marriage, and health, safety, decency, and morals. Crimes are cognizable or noncognizable, comparable to the distinction between felonies and misdemeanors in legal use in the United States. Six categories of punishment include fines, forfeiture of property, simple imprisonment, rigorous imprisonment with hard labor, life imprisonment, and death. An individual can be imprisoned for failure to pay fines, and up to three months' solitary confinement can occur during rare rigorous imprisonment sentences. Commutation is possible for death and life sentences. Executions are by hanging and are rare—there were only three in 1993 and two in 1994—and are usually reserved for crimes such as political assassination and multiple murders.

Courts of law try cases under procedures that resemble the Anglo-American pattern. The machinery for prevention and punishment through the criminal court system rests on the Code of Criminal Procedure of 1973, which came into force on April 1, 1974, replacing a code dating from 1898. The code includes provisions to expedite the judicial process, increase efficiency, prevent abuses, and provide legal relief to the poor. The basic framework of the criminal justice system, however, was left unchanged.

Constitutional guarantees protect the accused, as do various provisions embodied in the 1973 code. Treatment of those arrested under special security legislation can depart from these norms, however. In addition, for all practical purposes, the implementation of these norms varies widely based on the class and social background of the accused. In most cases, police officers have to secure a warrant from a magistrate before instituting searches and seizing evidence. Individuals taken into custody have to be advised of the charges brought against them, have the right to seek counsel, and have to appear before a magistrate within twenty-four hours of arrest. The magistrate has the option to release the accused on bail. During trial a defendant is protected against self-incrimination, and only confessions given before a magistrate are legally valid. Criminal cases usually take place in open trial, although in limited circumstances closed trials occur. Procedures exist for appeal to higher courts.

India has an integrated and relatively independent court system. At the apex is the Supreme Court, which has original, appellate, and advisory jurisdiction (see The Judiciary, ch. 8).

Below it are eighteen high courts that preside over the states and union territories. The high courts have supervisory authority over all subordinate courts within their jurisdictions. In general, these include several district courts headed by district magistrates, who in turn have several subordinate magistrates under their supervision. The Code of Criminal Procedure established three sets of magistrates for the subordinate criminal courts. The first consists of executive magistrates, whose duties include issuing warrants, advising the police, and determining proper procedures to deal with public violence. The second consists of judicial magistrates, who are essentially trial judges. Petty criminal cases are sometimes settled in *panchayat* (see Glossary) courts.

The Penal System

The constitution assigns the custody and correction of criminals to the states and territories. Day-to-day administration of prisoners rests on principles incorporated in the Prisons Act of 1894, the Prisoners Act of 1900, and the Transfer of Prisoners Act of 1950. An inspector general of prisons administers prison affairs in each state and territory.

By the prevailing standards of society, prison conditions are often adequate. Some prison administrators concede that the prevailing conditions of poverty in Indian society contribute to recidivism because a prison sentence guarantees minimal levels of food, clothing, and shelter. Despite this overall view, India's prisons are seriously overcrowded, prisoners are given better or worse treatment according to the nature of their crime and class status, sanitary conditions are poor, and punishments for misbehavior while incarcerated have been known to be particularly onerous.

Prison conditions vary from state to state. The more prosperous states have better facilities and attempt rehabilitation programs; the poorer ones can afford only the most bare and primitive accommodations. Women prisoners are mostly incarcerated in segregated areas of men's prisons. Conditions for holding prisoners also vary according to classification. India retains a system set up during the colonial period that mandates different treatment for different categories of prisoners. Under this system, foreigners, individuals held for political reasons, and prisoners of high caste and class are segregated from lower-class prisoners and given better treatment. This treatment includes larger or less-crowded cells, access to books and

Public security awareness sign in New Delhi
Courtesy Robert L. Worden

newspapers, and more and better food. Despite laws that mandate egalitarian treatment of Dalits (see Glossary), members of Scheduled Tribes (see Glossary), and members of the so-called Backward Classes (see Glossary), a rigid class system that circumvents the spirit of these laws exists within the prison system (see *Varna*, Caste and Other Divisions, ch. 5).

The press and human rights groups periodically raise the subject of prison conditions, including problems of overcrowding, the plight of prisoners detained for long periods while awaiting trial, and the proper treatment of women and juvenile prisoners (children are often incarcerated with their parents). Reports have also surfaced alleging that torture, beatings, rape, sexual abuse, and unexplained suicides occur on many occasions in police stations and prisons. Because of a shortage of mental institutions, numerous "non-criminal lunatics" are imprisoned, often under conditions worse than those afforded criminals. The government concedes that problems exist, but insists that its attempts at prison reform have suffered from a paucity of resources.

National Security Challenges

As the twenty-first century approaches, India faces a number of key challenges to its national security. The vast majority of emergent threats are essentially from within.

Because of increased educational opportunities, greater political awareness, and media exposure, hitherto quiescent ethnic minorities are steadily claiming their rights in the political arena. This form of political assertiveness has generated a backlash from the well-entrenched segments of India's majority population. Much violence has accompanied this process of social change. Increased use of coercion alone, however, is unlikely to contain ethnoreligious violence. Further development of India's political institutions and social policies is also needed.

A related national security problem in the region is linked to the porous borders and cross-national ethnic ties that characterize South Asia. Consequently, Pakistan has found it expedient to support Muslim militants in Jammu and Kashmir and, to a lesser degree, Sikh insurgents in Punjab. India, on occasion, has retaliated in Pakistan's Sindh Province, supporting various movements for Sindhi autonomy. Furthermore, India has also been involved in supporting the Tamil extremists in Sri Lanka. As long as governments in the region yield to these temptations for short-term gains, continued fratricidal violence is inevitable.

The other major source of instability in the region stems from the proliferation of nuclear and ballistic missile capabilities in both India and Pakistan. The long-standing border dispute with China and the memories of the 1962 military debacle have encouraged India's efforts to acquire these capabilities. India's acquisition of weapons of mass destruction may well precipitate a three-way arms race in the region involving India, Pakistan, and China. Such an arms race not only would be strategically destabilizing but also would impose enormous costs on resource-poor societies.

*   *   *

Stephen Philip Cohen's *The Indian Army* is the best work on the historical evolution of the Indian army. One of the earliest and still useful accounts of India's security problems is Lorne J. Kavic's *India's Quest for Security*. Raju G.C. Thomas's *Indian Security Policy* is probably the most comprehensive, although not necessarily the most analytic, treatment of Indian security questions. Basic armed forces information appears in *SP's Military*

Yearbook and the weekly armed forces news magazine *Sainik Samachar* (available in thirteen languages), both published in New Delhi. Analyses of the state of India's armed forces, including its paramilitary forces, periodically appear in the journal *Armed Forces and Society*. Within India the best discussions of security issues are found in the privately produced *Indian Defence Review* and the *Institute of Defence Studies and Analyses Journal*, the house journal of the government-supported think tank, the Institute of Defence Studies and Analyses. Broader discussions of regional security issues can be found in *Survival*, published by the International Institute of Strategic Studies in London.

The various wars that have taken place in the region are well documented. The best analyses are Lionel Protip Sen's *Slender Was the Thread* on the 1947–48 conflict, D.K. Palit's *War in the High Himalaya* and Stephen Hoffmann's *India and The China Crisis* on the 1962 India-China border war, Russell Brines's *The Indo-Pakistani Conflict* on the 1965 war, and Robert Jackson's *South Asian Crisis* and Richard Sisson and Leo E. Rose's *War and Secession* on the 1971 Indo-Pakistani conflict. Sumit Ganguly's *The Origins of War in South Asia* is the only comparative and comprehensive account of the three Indo-Pakistani conflicts. Civil-military relations and defense decision-making issues have been discussed in articles written jointly by Jerrold F. Elkin and W. Andrew Ritezel and by Sumit Ganguly.

An excellent discussion of nuclear proliferation issues is found in Stephen Philip Cohen's *Nuclear Proliferation in South Asia*. Indian nuclear and ballistic missile programs are discussed in some detail in Brahma Chellaney's *Nuclear Proliferation: The U.S.-Indian Conflict*. For an early analysis of the motivations underlying the Indian nuclear program, see Sumit Ganguly's "Why India Joined the Nuclear Club." Another useful analysis of India's nuclear and ballistic missile programs is Raju G.C. Thomas's "India's Nuclear and Space Programs: Defense or Development?" An important discussion of Indian strategic culture and doctrine is George K. Tanham's "Indian Strategic Culture." (For further information and complete citations, see Bibliography.)

Appendix

Table 1. Metric Conversion Coefficients and Factors

When you know	Multiply by	To find
Millimeters........................	0.04	inches
Centimeters.......................	0.39	inches
Meters............................	3.3	feet
Kilometers........................	0.62	miles
Hectares..........................	2.47	acres
Square kilometers	0.39	square miles
Cubic meters	35.3	cubic feet
Liters	0.26	gallons
Kilograms.........................	2.2	pounds
Metric tons.......................	0.98	long tons
....	1.1	short tons
....	2,204.0	pounds
Degrees Celsius (Centigrade)..........	1.8 and add 32	degrees Fahrenheit

Table 2. Annual Climatic Statistics, Selected Stations, 1990

Station	Approximate Precipitation (in millimeters)	Average Temperature Range (in degrees Celsius)	
		Minimum	Maximum
Bangalore.......................	750	14.5	34.7
Bombay	877	19.8	33.2
Calcutta	2,167	14.2	34.5
Darjiling........................	2,783	1.7	21.6
Hyderabad......................	1,596	15.0	38.8
Madras	1,058	19.8	36.1
New Delhi	911	8.3	39.9
Patna...........................	1,011	9.4	36.4
Port Blair	2,257	22.1	31.9
Shillong	2,427	7.1	24.2
Shimla	1,767	4.0	25.3
Srinagar	1,239	–1.7	30.8
Thiruvananthapuram	2,357	22.1	33.6
Vishakhapatnam	2,004	21.0	32.9

Source: Based on information from India, Ministry of Planning, Department of Statistics, Central Statistical Organisation, *Statistical Pocket Book, 1991*, New Delhi, 1992, 225–28.

Table 3. Area, Population, and Population Density by State and Union Territory, 1981 and 1991

State or Union Territory	Area (in square kilometers)	Population (in thousands)		Population Density (persons per square kilometer)	
		1981	1991	1981	1991
Andaman and Nicobar Islands...............	8,249	189	281	23	34
Andhra Pradesh	275,045	53,550	66,508	195	242
Arunachal Pradesh	83,743	632	865	8	10
Assam...................	18,041[1]	22,414	230	286
Bihar	173,877	69,915	86,374	402	497
Chandigarh	114	452	642	3,961	5,632
Dadra and Nagar Haveli	491	104	138	211	282
Daman and Diu...........	112	79	102	705	907
Delhi	1,483	6,220	9,420	4,194	6,352
Goa.....................	3,702	1,008	1,170	272	316
Gujarat..................	196,024	34,086	41,310	174	211
Haryana.................	44,212	12,922	16,464	292	372
Himachal Pradesh.........	55,673	4,281	5,171	77	93
Jammu and Kashmir.......	222,236	5,987	7,719[2]	59	76
Karnataka	191,791	37,136	44,977	194	235
Kerala...................	38,863	25,454	29,098	655	749
Lakshadweep.............	32	40	52	1,258	1,616
Madhya Pradesh	443,446	52,179	66,181	118	149
Maharashtra	307,713	62,784	78,937	204	257
Manipur.................	22,327	1,421	1,837	64	82
Meghalaya	22,249	1,336	1,774	60	79
Mizoram.................	21,081	494	690	23	33
Nagaland	16,579	775	1,210	47	73
Orissa...................	155,707	26,370	31,660	169	203
Pondicherry	492	604	807	1,229	1,642
Punjab	50,362	16,789	20,282	333	403
Rajasthan................	342,239	34,262	44,005	100	129
Sikkim	7,096	316	406	45	57
Tamil Nadu	130,058	48,408	55,859	372	429
Tripura..................	10,486	2,053	2,757	196	263

Table 3. (Continued)   Area, Population, and Population Density by State and Union Territory, 1981 and 1991

State or Union Territory	Area (in square kilometers)	Population (in thousands)		Population Density (persons per square kilometer)	
		1981	1991	1981	1991
Uttar Pradesh.............	294,411	110,863	139,112	377	473
West Bengal..............	88,752	54,581	68,078	615	767
INDIA³.................	3,287,263	683,329	846,303	216	257

[1] The 1981 census was not conducted in Assam. The population figures for 1981 for Assam have been calculated by interpolation by Indian census officials.
[2] The 1991 census was not conducted in Jammu and Kashmir. The population figures for 1991 for Jammu and Kashmir were projected by the Standing Committee of Experts on Population Projections in October 1989. They do not include the population of areas controlled by Pakistan and China.
[3] Numbers may not add to totals because of rounding.

Source: Based on information from India, Ministry of Home Affairs, Registrar General and Census Commissioner, *Census of India 1991: Final Population Totals: Brief Analysis of Primary Census Abstract, Series–1, Paper–2 of 1992*, New Delhi, 1993, 78–97.

627

Table 4. Population and Population Density, Actual and Projected,
Selected Years, 1901–2020

Year	Population[1]	Population Density (persons per square kilometer)
1901	238,396,327	77
1911	252,093,390	82
1921	251,321,213	81
1931	278,977,238	90
1941	318,660,580	103
1951	361,088,090	117
1961	439,234,771	142
1971	548,159,652	177
1981	683,329,097	216
1991	846,302,688	267
1995[2]	936,545,814	284
2000[2]	1,018,105,000	309
2010[2]	1,173,621,000	357
2020[2]	1,320,746,000	401

[1] Data before 1951 include population of prepartition India, which included areas that later became Pakistan and Bangladesh.
[2] Projected by United States Bureau of the Census.

Source: Based on information from India, Ministry of Home Affairs, Registrar General and Census Commissioner, *Census of India 1991, Provisional Population Totals, Series–1, Paper–1 of 1991*, New Delhi, March 1991, 43; India, Ministry of Home Affairs, Registrar General and Census Commissioner, *Census of India 1991, Final Population Totals: Brief Analysis of Primary Census Abstract, Series–1, Paper–2 of 1992*, New Delhi, 1993, 78 and 86; and United States, Bureau of the Census, *World Population Profile: 1994*, Washington, February 1994, A–5.

Table 5. Distribution of Urban Population by Size of City, Selected Years, 1901–91
(in percentages of total urban population)

Size of Urban Center and Number of Inhabitants	1901	1951	1961	1971	1981[1]	1991[1]
Class I (100,000 and above) ...	26.0	44.6	51.4	57.2	60.4	65.2
Class II (50,000 to 99,999)	11.3	10.0	11.2	10.9	11.6	10.9
Class III (20,000 to 49,999)....	15.6	15.7	16.9	16.0	14.3	13.2
Class IV (10,000 to 19,999)....	20.8	13.6	12.8	10.9	9.5	7.8
Class V (5,000 to 9,999)	20.1	13.0	6.9	4.5	3.6	2.6
Class VI (less than 5,000)	6.1	3.1	0.8	0.4	0.5	0.3
Total[2]	100.0	100.0	100.0	100.0	100.0	100.0

[1] Figures for 1981 and 1991 exclude Assam and Jammu and Kashmir.
[2] Figures may not add to totals because of rounding.

Source: Based on information from Tata Services, Department of Economics and Statistics, *Statistical Outline of India, 1994–95*, Bombay, 1994, 48.

Table 6.   *Population and Population Increase in Urban Agglomerates
with More Than 1 Million Persons, 1971–91*

Urban Agglomerate	Population in 1991 (in thousands)	Population Increase, 1971–81 (in percentages)	Population Increase, 1981–91 (in percentages)
Bombay[1]	12,572	42.9	33.4
Calcutta	10,916	23.9	18.7
Delhi	8,375	57.1	46.2
Madras	5,361	35.3	25.0
Hyderabad	4,280	42.7	67.0
Bangalore	4,087	75.6	39.9
Ahmadabad	3,298	45.9	28.9
Pune	2,485	48.6	47.4
Kanpur	2,111	23.5	28.8
Nagpur	1,661	40.8	36.2
Lucknow	1,642	23.8	63.0
Surat	1,517	87.4	64.2
Jaipur	1,514	59.4	49.2
Kochi	1,140	48.8	38.1
Coimbatore	1,136	25.0	23.4
Vadodara	1,115	67.4	42.5
Indore	1,104	47.9	33.1
Patna	1,099	66.7	19.6
Madurai	1,094	27.6	20.5
Bhopal	1,064	74.4	58.5
Vishakhapatnam	1,052	66.1	74.3
Varanasi	1,026	25.5	28.8
Kalyan	1,014	36.7	645.4
Ludhiana	1,012	51.3	66.7

[1] Greater Bombay. The population of the Bombay Municipal Corporation was 9,910,000.

Source: Based on information from Tata Services, Department of Economics and Statistics, *Statistical Outline of India, 1994–95*, Bombay, 1994, 50–52.

Table 7. Infant Mortality, Selected Years, 1911–95

Period	Deaths per 1,000 Live Births
1911–15	204
1916–20	219
1921–25	174
1926–30	178
1931–35	174
1936–40	161
1941–45	161
1946–50	134
1951–61	146
1961–71	129
1975–81	133
1992	91
1994	78
1995 (estimate)	76

Source: Based on information from Sudipto Mundle, "Recent Trends in the Condition of Children in India: A Statistical Profile," *World Development* [London], 12, No. 3, 1984, 301; "World Population Data Sheet of the Population Reference Bureau, Inc.," Washington, 1992; United States, Bureau of the Census, *World Population Profile: 1994*, Washington, February 1994, A–28; and United States, Central Intelligence Agency, *The World Factbook, 1995*, Washington, 1995, 196.

Table 8. Health Care Services, Selected Fiscal Years, 1960–91 (in thousands)

Service	1960	1973	1984	1991
Primary health centers[1]	2.8	5.3	7.3	22.4
Hospitals	4.0	4.0	7.4	11.2
Dispensaries.......................	9.9	10.8	21.9	27.4
Hospital beds[2].....................	186.0	406.0	625.0	811.0
Physicians (registered)	76.0	172.4	297.0	394.0
Nurses (registered)	32.7	94.0	171.0	n.a.[3]

[1] Figures for primary health centers relate to a fiscal year—see Glossary.
[2] Includes beds in dispensaries and other nonhospital health care facilities.
[3] n.a.—not available.

Source: Based on information from Tata Services, Department of Economics and Statistics, *Statistical Outline of India, 1988–89*, Bombay, 1988, 175; and Tata Services, Department of Economics and Statistics, *Statistical Outline of India, 1994–95*, Bombay, 1994, 190.

Table 9. *Enrollment of School Children by Age, Selected School Years,*
1950–91
(in percentages of total population in age-group)

School Year	Primary School (ages 6–11)	Middle School (ages 11–14)	High School (ages 14–17)
1950–51	42.6	12.7	5.3
1955–56	52.8	16.5	7.4
1960–61	62.4	22.5	10.6
1965–66	76.7	30.8	16.2
1970–71	76.4	34.2	n.a.[1]
1975–76	83.8	36.7	18.3
1980–81	80.5	41.9	n.a.
1985–86	93.1	52.0	n.a.
1990–91	100.0	60.1	n.a.

[1] n.a.—not available.

Source: Based on information from Tata Services, Department of Economics and Statistics, *Statistical Outline of India, 1988–89,* Bombay, 1988, 171; and India, Ministry of Information and Broadcasting, Research and Reference Division, *India: A Reference Annual, 1988–89,* New Delhi, December 1989, 73.

Table 10. Number of Schools and Teachers, Selected School Years, 1950–51 to 1986–87

Type	1950–51	1960–61	1970–71	1980–81	1986–87
Schools					
Primary	209,671	330,399	408,378	485,538	530,728
Middle	13,596	49,663	90,600	116,447	n.a.[1]
High.	7,288	17,257	36,700	47,755	206,669[3]
Technical.	1,377	2,738	2,337	8,708	2,627
Universities/ colleges.	27	45	100	132	159
Total schools	231,959	400,102	538,115	658,580	740,183
Teachers					
Primary	537,918	741,515	1,376,176	1,345,376	1,530,938
Middle	85,496	345,228	n.a.	830,649	n.a.
High.	126,504	296,305	948,887[2]	902,332	2,148,239[3]
Technical.	28,283	58,851	33,454	30,055	53,161
University/ college	18,648	41,759	113,037	185,558	277,747
Total teachers.	796,849	1,483,658	2,471,554	3,293,970	4,010,085

[1] n.a.—not available.
[2] Data for middle and high school combined for 1970–71.
[3] Data for middle and high school combined for 1986–87.

Source: Based on information from Tata News Services, *Statistical Outline of India, 1988–89*, Bombay, 1988, 171; India, Ministry of Information and Broadcasting, Research and Reference Division, *India: A Reference Annual, 1988–89*, New Delhi, December 1989, 73; and India, Ministry of Planning, Department of Statistics, Central Statistical Organisation, *Statistical Abstract, 1990*, New Delhi, 1990, 499–500.

Table 11. Enrollment by Education Level, Selected School Years, 1950–51 to 1990–91
(in millions)

School Year	Primary School (Classes I–V)	Middle School (Classes VI–VIII)	High School (Classes IX–XII)
1950–51	19.2	3.1	1.2
1955–56	25.2	4.3	1.9
1960–61	35.0	6.7	2.9
1965–66	50.5	10.5	5.0
1970–71	57.0	13.3	6.6
1975–76	65.7	16.0	7.4
1980–81	73.8	20.7	10.8
1985–86	86.5	28.1	15.1
1990–91[1]	99.1	33.3	20.9

[1] Provisional.

Source: Based on information from Tata Services, Department of Economics and Statistics, *Statistical Outline of India, 1988–89*, Bombay, 1988, 171; Tata Services, Department of Economics and Statistics, *Statistical Outline of India, 1994–95*, Bombay, 1994, 187; and India, Ministry of Information and Broadcasting, Research and Reference Division, *India: A Reference Annual, 1993*, New Delhi, January 1994, 85.

Table 12. Enrollment of School-Age Population by Gender, Selected School Years, 1960–61 to 1986–87
(in percentages)

Level and Gender	1960–61	1975–76	1980–81	1986–87
Primary school	62.4	79.3	80.5	95.9
Males.	82.6	95.7	95.8	111.8
Females.	41.4	62.0	64.1	79.2
Middle school	22.5	35.6	41.9	53.1
Males.	33.2	47.0	54.3	66.5
Females.	11.3	23.3	28.6	38.9
High school.	11.4	18.3	28.2	n.a.[1]
Males.	18.2	25.6	40.8	n.a.
Females.	4.4	10.5	14.3	n.a.

[1] n.a.—not available.

Source: Based on information from United Nations Educational, Scientific, and Cultural Organization, Principal Regional Office for Asia and the Pacific, *National Studies: India*, Bangkok, 1991, 12.

Table 13. *Religious Affiliations, 1991*

Religious Group	Number of Adherents	Percentage of Total Population	Percentage Growth since 1981
Hindus	687,646,721	82.0	22.8
Muslims	101,596,057	12.1	32.8
Christians.......................	19,640,284	2.3	16.9
Sikhs............................	16,259,744	1.9	25.5
Buddhists........................	6,387,500	0.8	35.9
Jains	3,352,706	0.4	4.4
Other religions[1]..................	3,269,355	0.4	13.2
Religion not stated	415,569	0.1	573.5
Total[2]	838,567,936	100.0	n.a.[3]

[1] Sixty-three "other religions" were listed, including animists (1,458), atheists (1,782), Jews (5,271), non-Christians (9,615), pagans (1,711), Zoroastrians (76,382), and unclassified (212,652).
[2] Total tabulated for religious affiliations is different from total tabulated for total national population. (846,302,688), which includes a projected figure for Jammu and Kashmir where the census was not taken in 1991.
[3] n.a.—not applicable.

Source: Based on information from India, Ministry of Home Affairs, Registrar General and Census Commissioner, *Census of India 1991: Religion, Series–1, Paper–1 of 1995*, New Delhi, January 1995, x–xxiii, 18–60.

Table 14. *National Calendar and Government Holidays*

National Calendar

Name of Month	Dates on Gregorian Calendar
Chaitra	March 22–April 20[1]
Vaisakha	April 21–May 21
Jyaistha	May 22–June 21
Ashada	June 22–July 22
Sravana...................	July 23–August 22
Bhadra	August 23–September 22
Asvina...................	September 23–October 22
Kartika	October 23–November 22
Agrahayana	November 23–December 21
Pausa	December 22–January 20
Magha....................	Janaury 21–February 19
Phalguna	February 20–March 21

Table 14. *(Continued)* *National Calendar and Government Holidays*

NOTE: In 1957 the Indian government adopted a uniform, national calendar based on the Gregorian calendar and the Shaka Era (starting in A.D. 78) for civil government purposes. Using this calendar, the year A.D. 1995 is 1917 of the revised Shaka Era. The Shaka calendar has been used at least since the first century A.D. Because the Shaka calendar is based on solar and lunar observations, some of the dates of holidays listed below are subject to change in a given year and from one part of India to another. The dates shown below are from 1993 (Shaka 1915). An unofficial but widely used calendar in North India dates from the ninth century A.D., is based on the Vikrama Era (beginning in 57 B.C.), and starts in Chaitra. The Muslim calendar (starting with A.D. 622) is widely used among the Muslim population. The Buddhist calendar—based on the death of Buddha (483 B.C.)—and the Zoroastrian calendar (starting with 632 B.C.) are also used.

Government Holidays, 1993

Holiday	Significance	Date
Republic Day.............	Commemorates 1950 proclamation of the Republic of India	January 26[2]
Holi	Hindu spring festival	March 8
Id al Fitr.................	Marks end of the month of fasting during Ramadan (Ramzan), the ninth month on the Islamic calendar	March 25
Ramanavami	Commemorates birthday of Ram	April 1
Mahavira Jayanti	Mahavira's birthday	April 5
Good Friday..............	Commemorates death of Christ	April 9
Buddha Purnima...........	Commemorates birth, death, and enlightenment of the Buddha	May 6
Id al Zuha (Bakr Id)	Commemorates Abraham's williness to sacrifice his son Ishmael	June 1
Muharram	Muslim New Year's	July 1
Janmashtami	Birthday of Krishna	August 11
Independence Day	Marks independence from Britain	August 15[2]
Milad-un-Nabi (Id-e-Milad) ...	Prophet Muhammad's birthday	August 31
Mahatma Gandhi's Birthday ..	Commemorates birth of Mohandas K. Gandhi	October 2[2]
Dussehra (Vijaya Dasami)	Commemorates triumph of Ram over Ravana, tenth day of Asvina	October 24
Dipavali (Diwali)	Hindu festival of lights	November 13
Guru Nanak's Birthday.......	Commemorates birth of Sikh leader	November 29
Christmas Day	Commemorates birth of Christ	December 25[2]

[1] Starts on March 21 in leap year.
[2] Fixed date on Gregorian calendar.

Source: Based on information from *Hindustan Year Book and Who's Who, 1994*, Calcutta, 1994, 26–27; India, Ministry of Information and Broadcasting, Directorate of Advertising and Visual Publicity, "List of Government of India Holidays for 1993," New Delhi, 1993; and M.N. Saha and N.C. Lahiri, *History of the Calendar in Different Countries Through the Ages*, New Delhi, 1992, 254, 258.

Table 15. Vernacular Languages with More Than 1 Million Speakers, 1991

Language	Estimated Number of Speakers	States and Union Territories Where Use Is Most Prevalent
HINDI	153,729,062	Andaman and Nicobar Islands, Andhra Pradesh, Bihar, Chandigarh, Delhi, Gujarat, Haryana, Himachal Pradesh, Jammu and Kashmir, Karnataka, Madhya Pradesh, Maharashtra, Orissa, Punjab, Rajasthan, Uttar Pradesh, West Bengal
TELUGU	44,707,697	Andhra Pradesh, Karnataka, Madhya Pradesh, Maharashtra, Orissa, Pondicherry, West Bengal
BENGALI	44,521,533	Andaman and Nicobar Islands, Assam, Bihar, Madhya Pradesh, Meghalaya, Orissa, Tripura, Uttar Pradesh, West Bengal
MARATHI	41,723,893	Andhra Pradesh, Goa, Gujarat, Karnataka, Maharashtra, Madhya Pradesh,
TAMIL	37,592,794	Andaman and Nicobar Islands, Andhra Pradesh, Karnataka, Kerala, Maharashtra, Pondicherry, Tamil Nadu
URDU	28,600,428	Andhra Pradesh, Bihar, Delhi, Gujarat, Haryana, Jammu and Kashmir, Karnataka, Madhya Pradesh, Orissa, Rajasthan, Uttar Pradesh, West Bengal
GUJARATI	25,656,274	Daman and Diu, Gujarat, Maharashtra, Madhya Pradesh
MALAYALAM	21,917,430	Kerala, Lakshadweep, Maharashtra
KANNADA	21,595,019	Andhra Pradesh, Karnataka, Maharashtra, Tamil Nadu,
ORIYA	19,726,745	Andhra Pradesh, Bihar, Madhya Pradesh, Orissa, West Bengal
Bhojpuri	14,340,564	Assam, Bihar, Madhya Pradesh, Uttar Pradesh
PUNJABI	13,900,202	Bihar, Chandigarh, Delhi, Haryana, Himachal Pradesh, Jammu and Kashmir, Madhya Pradesh, Maharashtra, Punjab, Rajasthan, Uttar Pradesh
ASSAMESE	8,958,977	Assam
Chhatisgarhi	6,693,445	Madhya Pradesh
Magadhi	6,638,495	Bihar, West Bengal
Manipuri (Meithei)	6,121,922	Meghalaya
Marwari	4,714,094	Rajasthan
Santali	3,693,558	Assam, Bihar, Orissa, Tripura, West Bengal
KASHMIRI	2,421,760	Jammu and Kashmir
Rajasthani	2,093,557	Rajasthan
Gondi	1,548,070	Andhra Pradesh, Madhya Pradesh, Maharashtra

Table 15. (Continued) Vernacular Languages with More Than 1
Million Speakers, 1991

Language	Estimated Number of Speakers	States and Union Territories Where Use Is Most Prevalent
KONKANI	1,522,684	Karnataka, Goa, Maharashtra,
Dogri-Kangri	1,298,885	Jammu and Kashmir
NEPALI	1,286,824	Sikkim, West Bengal
Garhwali	1,227,151	Jammu and Kashmir, Uttar Pradesh
Pahari	1,269,651	Himachal Pradesh, Jammu and Kashmir
Bhili	1,250,312	Dadra and Nagar Haveli, Haryana, Madhya Pradesh, Maharashtra, Rajasthan
Oraon (Kurukh)	1,240,395	Bihar, Madhya Pradesh, West Bengal
Kumaoni	1,234,939	Assam, Bihar, Delhi, Madhya Pradesh, Uttar Pradesh
SINDHI	1,204,678	Gujarat, Madhya Pradesh, Maharashtra, Rajasthan
Lamani (Lambadi)	1,203,338	Andhra Pradesh, Gujarat, Himachal Pradesh, Karnataka, Madhya Pradesh, Maharashtra, Orissa, Tamil Nadu, West Bengal
Tulu	1,156,950	Karnataka, Kerala
Bagri	1,055,607	Punjab, Rajasthan

Note: Languages shown in UPPER CASE print are Scheduled Languages (see Glossary). The other Scheduled Language—Sanskrit—has an estimated 2,200 speakers. Some observers estimate that more than 28 million people use English as a first, second, or third language with varying degrees of proficiency.

Source: Based on information from *Hindustan Year-Book and Who's Who, 1994*, Calcutta, 1994, Part II, 207–208; Barbara F. Grimes, ed., *Ethnologue: Languages of the World*, Dallas, 1992, 532–65; and Kumar Suresh Singh, ed., *People of India, 11: An Anthropological Atlas*, New Delhi, 1993, 77.

Table 16. Growth of Gross National Product, Fiscal Years 1951–89
(in percentage change from previous year at
constant FY 1980 prices)

Period	GNP[1]	GNP per Capita
1951–55	3.6	1.7
1956–60	3.9	1.9
1961–65	2.3	0.1
1966–68	2.2	–0.1
1969–73	3.3	0.9
1974–79	3.1	2.6
1980–84	5.4	3.2
1985–89	5.5	3.3

[1] GNP—gross national product (see Glossary).

Source: Based on information from Economist Intelligence Unit, *Country Profile: India, Nepal, 1993–94*, London, 1993, 14.

Table 17. Gross Domestic Product by Sector, Selected Fiscal Years, 1987–92
(in percent share)

Sector	1987	1988	1989	1990	1991	1992[1]
Primary (agriculture, forestry, fishing, mining, quarrying)	32.5	34.8	33.8	33.5	32.8	32.3
Secondary (manufacturing, construction, electricity, other)	28.8	26.9	27.0	27.7	27.4	26.9
Trade, transportation, and communications	17.2	17.5	18.5	18.0	18.0	18.3
Real estate and finance	9.4	9.5	9.9	10.7	10.7	10.9
Services, including public administration and defense	12.1	11.3	10.8	11.1	11.1	11.6
TOTAL	100.0	100.0	100.0	100.0	100.0	100.0

[1] Provisional.

Source: Based on information from Economist Intelligence Unit, *Country Profile: India, Nepal, 1994–95*, London, 1995, 21.

Table 18. *Government Income and Expenditure, Fiscal Years 1981,*
1989, and 1992[1]
(in billions of rupees at current prices)[2]

	1981	1989	1992
Direct taxes	44.6	113.5	210.6
Indirect taxes.......................	200.9	668.8	994.3
Profits..............................	−10.5	−23.2	−28.4
Interest receipts	11.1	36.3	64.6
Property receipts....................	9.8	33.8	62.0
Miscellaneous	3.9	18.7	31.4
Total income......................	259.8	847.9	1,334.5
Total outlay	241.8	1,044.3	1,537.2
Savings[3]	17.9	−176.4	−202.7
Savings as percentage of GNP[4]	1.1	−3.9	−2.9

[1] Including administrative departments and departmental enterprises, excluding railroads and telecommunications.
[2] For value of the rupee—see Glossary.
[3] As published.
[4] GNP—gross national product (see Glossary).

Source: Based on information from Tata Services, Department of Economics and Statistics, *Statistical Outline of India, 1992–93*, Bombay, 1992, 20; and Tata Services, Department of Economics and Statistics, *Statistical Outline of India, 1994–95*, Bombay, 1994, 22.

Table 19. Balance of Trade, Selected Fiscal Years, 1980–93
(in billions of rupees)[1]

Year	Imports	Exports[2]	Balance[3]
1980	125.5	67.1	–58.4
1985	196.6	109.0	–87.6
1986	200.9	124.5	–76.4
1987	222.4	156.7	–65.7
1988	282.4	202.3	–80.0
1989	353.3	276.6	–76.7
1990	432.0	325.5	–106.5
1991	478.5	440.4	–38.1
1992	633.8	536.9	–96.9
1993[4]	728.1	695.5	–32.6

[1] For value of the rupee—see Glossary.
[2] Including reexports.
[3] Figures may not add to balances because of rounding.
[4] Provisional figures.

Source: Based on information from Tata Services, Department of Economics and Statistics, *Statistical Outline of India, 1992–93*, Bombay, 1992, 93; and Tata Services, Department of Economics and Statistics, *Statistical Outline of India, 1994–95*, Bombay, 1994, 101.

Table 20. Principal Exports, Fiscal Years 1990–93 (in billions of
United States dollars)

Commodity	1990		1991	
	Value	Percentage	Value	Percentage
Agriculture and allied products				
Cashew kernels.	0.3	1.4	0.3	1.5
Coffee	0.1	0.8	0.1	0.7
Fish and fish products	0.5	2.9	0.6	3.3
Oil meals.	0.3	1.9	0.4	2.1
Raw cotton	0.5	2.6	0.1	0.7
Rice	0.3	1.4	0.3	1.7
Spices	0.1	0.7	0.2	0.8
Sugar.	0.2	0.1	0.1	0.4
Tea and mate	0.6	3.3	0.5	2.7
Tobacco	0.2	0.8	0.2	0.9
Total agriculture and allied products	3.1	15.0	2.5	14.8
Ore and minerals				
Iron ore.	0.6	3.2	0.6	3.3
Other ore and minerals.	0.3	1.4	0.2	1.3
Total ore and minerals	0.8	4.6	0.8	4.6
Manufactured goods				
Chemicals.	1.4	7.8	1.6	8.9
Handicrafts.				
Gems and jewelry	2.9	16.1	2.7	15.3
Other handicrafts	0.5	2.9	0.7	3.7
Total handicrafts	3.4	19.0	3.4	19.0
Industrial machinery.	2.2	11.9	2.2	12.5
Jute manufactures	0.2	0.9	0.2	0.9
Leather and leather products.	1.5	8.0	1.3	7.1
Ready-made garments	2.2	12.3	2.2	12.3
Textiles	1.2	6.5	1.3	7.3
Total manufactured goods.	12.1	66.4	12.2	6.8
Mineral fuels and lubricants				
Petroleum, oil, and lubricants.	0.5	2.9	0.4	2.3
Other mineral fuels and lubricants.	0.0	0.0	0.0	0.1
Total mineral fuels and lubricants	0.5	2.9	0.4	2.4
Other commodities.	0.3	0.2	0.2	10.2
TOTAL[1]	18.1	100.0	17.9	100.0

Table 20. (Continued) Principal Exports, Fiscal Years 1990–93 (in billions of United States dollars)

Commodity	1992		1993	
	Value	Percentage	Value	Percentage
Agriculture and allied products				
Cashew kernels..............	0.3	1.4	0.3	1.5
Coffee	0.1	0.7	0.2	0.8
Fish and fish products	0.6	3.2	0.8	3.6
Oil meals..................	0.5	2.9	0.7	3.3
Raw cotton	0.1	0.3	0.2	0.9
Cereals....................	0.3	1.9	0.4	1.9
Spices.....................	0.1	0.7	0.2	0.8
Fruits and vegetables	0.1	0.6	0.1	0.6
Tea.......................	0.3	1.8	0.3	1.4
Tobacco (unmanufactured) ...	0.1	0.7	0.1	0.5
Total agriculture and allied products	2.5	14.2	3.3	15.3
Ore and minerals				
Iron ore...................	0.4	2.1	0.4	1.9
Processed minerals	0.1	0.8	0.2	0.9
Other ore and minerals.......	0.2	1.0	0.2	1.0
Total ore and minerals	0.7	3.9	0.9	3.8
Manufactured goods				
Drugs, pharmaceuticals, and fine chemicals	0.5	2.9	0.6	2.9
Dyes and coal tar chemicals....	0.3	1.8	0.4	1.6
Electronic goods.............	0.2	1.1	0.3	1.4
Gems and jewelry............	3.1	16.6	4.0	18.0
Handicrafts................	0.9	4.7	0.9	4.2
Iron and steel, primary and semifinished..............	0.2	0.9	0.4	1.9
Leather and leather products (including footwear).......	1.3	6.9	1.3	6.0
Machinery and instruments....	0.5	2.9	0.6	2.9
Metal manufactures	0.6	3.0	0.7	3.1
Ready-made garments	2.4	12.9	2.6	11.6
Textiles, cotton yarns, fabrics...	1.4	7.3	1.5	6.9
Transportation equipment	0.5	2.9	0.6	2.6
Total manufactured goods ..	11.9	13.9	16.8	83.1
Crude oil and petroleum products	0.5	2.6	0.4	1.8
Other commodities............	0.2	0.9	0.1	0.8
TOTAL[1]	18.5	100.0	22.2	100.0

[1] Figures may not add to totals because of rounding.

Source: Based on information from India, Ministry of Finance, Economic Division, *Economic Survey, 1992–93*, New Delhi, 1993, 102; and India, Ministry of Finance, Economic Division, *Economic Survey, 1994–95*, New Delhi, 1994, 95–96.

Table 21. Principal Imports, Fiscal Years 1990–93 (in billions of
United States dollars)

Commodity	1990		1991	
	Value	Percentage	Value	Percentage
Bulk imports				
Food and allied products				
Cereals...................	0.1	0.4	0.1	0.4
Edible oils	0.2	0.8	0.1	0.5
Pulses...................	0.3	1.1	0.1	0.5
Total food and allied products.............	0.6	2.3	0.3	1.4
Fuels				
Petroleum, oil, and lubri- cants	6.0	25.1	5.4	27.6
Coal	0.5	1.8	0.4	2.2
Total Fuels	6.5	26.9	5.8	29.8
Ore and minerals				
Iron and steel	1.2	4.9	0.8	4.1
Nonferrous metals	0.6	2.5	0.3	1.8
Ores and metal scrap	0.9	3.5	0.5	2.4
Total ore and minerals....	2.7	10.9	1.6	8.3
Fertilizers	1.0	4.1	1.0	4.9
Paper, board, and pulp	0.5	2.1	0.3	1.7
Total bulk imports.....	11.2	46.3	9.0	46.1
Nonbulk imports				
Capital goods	5.8	24.2	4.2	21.8
Export-related imports				
Pearls and precious stones ...	2.1	8.7	2.0	10.1
Chemicals	1.3	5.3	1.4	7.1
Textile yarn, fabric, and other	0.3	1.0	0.1	0.7
Cashew nuts..............	0.1	0.3	0.1	0.6
Total export-related imports.............	3.8	15.3	3.6	18.5
Other nonbulk items				
Professional instruments and other	0.6	2.5	0.4	2.1
Chemicals	0.5	2.1	0.4	2.2
Plastics and resins	0.6	2.5	0.6	2.9
Nonmetallic minerals	0.1	0.5	0.1	0.5
Total other nonbulk items...............	1.8	7.6	1.5	7.7
Total nonbulk imports	11.3	47.1	9.3	47.9
Other imports..................	1.6	6.5	1.2	5.9
TOTAL[1]......................	24.2	100.0	19.5	100.0

Table 21. (Continued) Principal Imports, Fiscal Years 1990–93 (in billions of United States dollars)

Commodity	1992		1993	
	Value	Percentage	Value	Percentage
Food and allied products				
Cashew nuts	0.1	0.6	0.2	0.7
Cereals....................	0.3	1.5	0.1	0.4
Edible oils	0.1	0.6	0.1	0.7
Pulses.....................	0.1	0.5	0.2	0.8
Total food and allied products	0.7	3.2	0.6	2.4
Fuels				
Petroleum, oil, and lubri- cants...................	5.9	27.0	5.8	24.7
Coal......................	0.5	2.2	0.5	2.0
Total Fuels	6.4	29.2	6.3	26.7
Fertilizers....................	1.0	4.5	0.8	3.6
Paper board, paper manufactures, and newsprint..............	0.2	0.8	0.2	1.0
Capital goods				
Machinery (except for electrical machine tools)...........	1.7	7.6	2.2	9.4
Electrical machinery	0.8	3.8	0.8	3.4
Transportation equipment	0.5	2.1	1.3	5.4
Project goods	1.3	5.8	1.4	6.0
Total capital goods.........	4.3	19.3	5.7	24.2
Other items				
Pearls, precious stones, and semi- precious stones	2.4	11.2	2.6	11.3
Professional instruments, opti- cal goods, and other	0.5	2.3	0.5	2.1
Chemicals	2.0	9.2	2.0	8.5
Iron and steel	0.7	3.3	0.8	3.4
Nonferrous metals	0.4	1.8	0.5	2.0
Total other items	6.0	27.8	6.4	27.3
Other unclassified imports.......	3.0	13.8	3.1	13.1
TOTAL[1]	21.6	100.0	23.3	100.0

[1] Figures may not add to totals because of rounding.

Source: Based on information from India, Ministry of Finance, Economic Division, *Economic Survey, 1992–93*, New Delhi, 1993, 100; India, Ministry of Finance, Economic Division, *Economic Survey, 1994–95*, New Delhi, 1994, 97–98.

Table 22. *Major Trading Partners, Fiscal Years 1990–93* (in billions of United States dollars)

Destination or Source	1990				1991			
	Exports		Imports		Exports		Imports	
	Value	Percentage	Value	Percentage	Value	Percentage	Value	Percentage
Britain	1.2	6.5	1.2	6.7	1.5	6.4	1.2	6.2
France............	1.4	7.8	1.4	8.0	1.7	7.1	1.6	8.0
Other EC[1]	2.4	13.2	2.6	14.7	3.3	13.5	2.9	15.0
United States	2.7	14.7	2.2	12.1	3.9	16.4	1.9	10.3
Japan	1.7	9.3	1.3	7.5	2.2	9.2	1.4	7.1
Other OECD[2]	0.4	2.0	0.9	5.0	1.3	5.2	1.5	7.7
Soviet Union	2.9	16.1	1.1	5.9	2.2	9.2	0.7	3.8
Eastern Europe	0.3	1.8	0.3	1.9	0.4	1.8	0.3	1.4
OPEC[3]	1.0	5.6	2.9	16.3	2.1	8.7	3.8	19.7
Developing countries (other than OPEC)........	3.0	16.8	3.3	18.4	3.9	16.1	3.0	15.5
Other.............	1.1	6.2	0.6	3.5	1.5	6.3	1.1	5.5
TOTAL[4]	18.1	100.0	17.8	100.0	24.0	100.0	19.4	100.0

Table 22. (Continued) Major Trading Partners, Fiscal Years 1990–93 (in billions of United States dollars)

Destination or Source	1992 Exports		1992 Imports		1993 Exports		1993 Imports	
	Value	Percentage	Value	Percentage	Value	Percentage	Value	Percentage
Britain..........	1.2	6.5	1.4	6.5	1.3	6.2	1.5	6.6
Germany..........	1.4	7.7	1.7	7.6	1.5	6.9	1.7	7.7
Other EU[5]..........	2.6	14.1	3.5	16.1	2.8	12.9	3.6	15.7
United States..........	3.5	19.0	2.1	9.8	3.9	18.0	2.7	11.7
Japan..........	1.4	7.7	1.4	6.5	1.7	7.8	1.5	6.6
Russia..........	0.6	3.3	0.3	1.2	0.6	2.9	0.2	1.1
Eastern Europe..........	0.2	1.1	0.3	1.4	1.9	0.9	1.1	0.5
OPEC[3]..........	1.8	9.6	4.7	21.6	2.3	10.7	5.2	22.4
Developing countries (other than OPEC)..........	3.8	20.8	3.3	15.2	5.3	24.1	3.5	15.3
Other..........	1.9	10.1	3.1	14.2	2.1	9.7	2.8	12.4
TOTAL[4]..........	18.4	100.0	21.8	100.0	23.4	100.0	23.8	100.0

[1] European Community.
[2] Organisation for Economic Co-operation and Development.
[3] Organisation of the Petroleum Exporting Countries.
[4] Figures may not add to totals because of rounding.
[5] European Union, the successor to the European Community as of November 1, 1993.

Source: Based on information from India, Ministry of Finance, Economic Division, *Economic Survey, 1992–93*, New Delhi, 1993, 102, 105; and India, Ministry of Finance, Economic Division, *Economic Survey, 1994–95*, New Delhi, 1994, 98–99.

Table 23. Balance of Payments, Fiscal Years 1988–93[1]
(in billions of United States dollars)

	1988	1989	1990[2]	1991[2]	1992	1993[3]
Current Account						
Exports f.o.b.[4]	14.3	17.0	18.5	18.3	18.9	22.70
Imports c.i.f.[5]	23.6	24.4	27.9	21.1	23.2	23.99
Trade balance	–9.4	–7.5	–9.4	–2.8	–4.4	–1.29
Invisibles (net)[6]	1.4	0.6	–0.2	1.6	0.8	0.97
Current account balance...........	–8.0	–6.8	–9.7	–1.2	–3.5	–0.32
Capital account						
External aid (net)	2.2	1.9	2.2	3.0	1.9	1.70
Commercial borrowings (net).............	1.9	1.8	2.2	1.5[7]	–0.4	0.84
Nonresident deposits (net).............	2.5	2.4	1.5	0.3	2.0	0.94
Other capital flows[8]	1.4	0.9	2.3	0.3	–0.2	2.15
Capital account balance...........	8.1	7.0	8.4	4.8	4.3	9.18
IMF[9] borrowings (net)	–1.8	–0.9	1.2	0.8	1.3	0.19
Official reserves[10]	+1.0	+0.7	+1.3	–3.6	–0.7	–8.87

[1] Figures may not add to totals because of rounding.
[2] Provisional data.
[3] "Quick estimates."
[4] Free on board.
[5] Cargo, insurance, and freight.
[6] Includes nonfactor services, investment income, private transfers, and grants.
[7] Includes India Development Bonds.
[8] Includes delayed export receipts, errors and omissions, and, for FY 1992, errors and omissions arising out of dual exchange rates.
[9] International Monetary Fund—see Glossary.
[10] Minus means increase, plus means decrease.

Source: Based on information from India, Ministry of Finance, Economic Division, *Economic Survey, 1992–93*, New Delhi, 1993, 96; and India, Ministry of Finance, Economic Division, *Economic Survey, 1994–95*, New Delhi, 1994, 87.

Table 24. *Share of Public and Private Sectors in Gross Domestic*
Product (GDP)[1], Fiscal Years 1981 and 1992
(in trillions of rupees at current prices)[2]

Sector	1981		1992[3]	
	Value	Percentage	Value	Percentage
GDP (at factor cost)				
Public sector	0.3	20.8	1.7	27.2
Private sector.	1.1	79.2	4.6	72.8
Total GDP (at factor cost)	1.4	100.0	6.3	100.0
Gross domestic savings				
Public sector	0.1	21.7	0.2	9.5
Private sector.	0.3	78.3	1.4	90.5
Total gross domestic savings[3]	0.3	100.0	1.6	100.0
Gross domestic capital				
Public sector	0.2	41.9	0.7	41.4
Private sector.	0.2	58.1	1.0	58.6
Total gross domestic capital[4]	0.4	100.0	1.8	100.0

[1] GDP—see Glossary.
[2] For value of the rupee—see Glossary.
[3] Provisional figures.
[4] Figures may not add to totals because of rounding.

Source: Based on information from Tata Services, Department of Economics and Sta-
tistics, *Statistical Outline of India, 1992–93*, Bombay, 1992, 20; and Tata Services,
Department of Economics and Statistics, *Statistical Outline of India, 1994–95*,
Bombay, 1994, 22.

Table 25. Production of Selected Industrial Products, Selected Fiscal Years, 1970–92

Product	Unit	1970	1980	1990	1992
Air conditioners (room)	thousands of units	11.0	28.0	39.2	35.1
Aluminum	thousands of tons	169.0	199.0	449.0	483.0
Aluminum conductors	-do-	64.2	86.0	67.6	24.1
Cars, jeeps, and Land Rovers	thousands of vehicles	46.7	49.4	220.8	198.1
Caustic soda..........	thousands of tons	371.0	578.0	981.0	1,079.0
Cement	millions of tons	14.3	18.6	48.8	54.3
Commercial vehicles....	thousands of vehicles	41.2	71.7	145.5	132.6
Copper (blister)	thousands of tons	9.3	25.3	40.6	45.3
Cotton cloth	billions of square meters	7.8	9.6	17.8	19.0
Diesel engines (stationary).........	thousands of units	65.0	174.0	158.0	165.0
Finished steel..........	millions of tons	4.6	6.8	13.5	15.2
Jute textiles	-do-	1.1	1.4	1.4	1.3
Machinery for cement plants	billions of rupees[1]	0.0	0.3	2.8	1.8
Machinery for cotton textiles............	-do-	0.3	3.0	9.5	10.1
Machinery for sugar mills..............	-do-	0.1	0.2	0.9	1.0
Machine tools	-do-	0.4	1.7	7.9	9.7
Paper and board.......	millions of tons	0.8	1.1	2.1	2.2
Pig iron	-do-	7.0	9.6	12.1	13.2
Power transformers.....	millions of kilovolt-amperes	8.1	19.5	36.6	34.1
Refrigerators (domestic)	thousands of units	0.1	0.3	1.3	1.0
Soda ash.............	millions of tons	0.4	0.6	1.4	1.39
Steel ingots	-do-	6.1	10.3	13.5	15.2

[1] For value of the rupee—see Glossary.

Source: Based on information from Tata Services, Department of Economics and Statistics, *Statistical Outline of India, 1992–93*, Bombay, 1992, 71–73; and Tata Services, Department of Economics and Statistics, *Statistical Outline of India, 1994–95*, Bombay, 1994, 79–81.

Table 26. Area Planted in Principal Crops, Selected Fiscal Years,
1950–90
(in thousands of hectares)

Crop	1950	1960	1970	1980	1990[1]
Food grains					
Cereals					
Rice..............	30,810	34,128	37,592	40,152	42,687
Wheat............	9,746	12,927	18,241	22,279	24,167
Coarse grains......	37,674	44,963	45,950	41,779	36,319
Total cereals	78,230	92,018	101,783	104,210	103,173
Pulses..............	19,091	23,563	22,534	22,457	24,662
Total food grains ...	97,321	115,581	124,317	126,667	127,835
Percent change	n.a.[2]	19	8	2	1
Oilseeds					
Peanuts	4,494	6,463	7,326	6,801	8,309
Rapeseed and mustard seed..............	2,071	2,883	3,323	4,113	5,700
Cottonseed	—[3]	—	—	7,823	7,355
Sesame..............	2,204	2,169	2,450	2,472	2,595
Soybeans	—	—	—	392	2,365
Sunflower	—	—	—	119	1,642
Other oilseeds........	1,958	2,255	2,336	4,072	1,977
Total oilseeds......	10,727	13,770	15,435	25,792	29,943
Sugarcane..............	1,707	2,415	2,615	2,667	3,686
Cotton	5,882	7,610	7,605	7,823	7,440
Jute..................	571	629	749	941	778

[1] Preliminary.
[2] n.a.—not available.
[3] —means negligible.

Source: Based on information from United States, Embassy in New Delhi, *Annual Commodity Report, Oilseeds and Products, 1992*, New Delhi, 1992, 2, 13, 18, 21, 24, 32–33; India, Ministry of Finance, Economic Division, *Economic Survey, 1991–92, 2: Sectoral Developments*, New Delhi, 1992, S17–S19; India, Ministry of Planning, Department of Statistics, Central Statistical Organisation, *Statistical Abstract 1990, India*, New Delhi, 1991, 49; and India, Ministry of Information and Broadcasting, Research and Reference Division, *India 1993: A Reference Annual*, New Delhi, 1994, 398–99.

Table 27. Land Use, Selected Fiscal Years, 1970–87
(in millions of hectares)

Category	1970	1980	1985	1987	Percentage of Area Classified, 1987
Forest......................	63.9	67.4	67.0	66.9	19.6
Not available for cultivation					
Nonagricultural uses	n.a.[1]	n.a.	20.5	20.8	6.1
Barren and uncultivable	n.a.	n.a.	20.2	20.4	6.0
Total not available for cultivation	44.6	39.6	40.7	41.2	12.1
Other uncultivated land					
Permanent pastures and grazing lands...................	13.3	12.0	12.0	11.9	3.5
Tree crops and groves	4.3	3.5	3.5	3.5	1.0
Cultivable wasteland	17.5	16.7	15.7	15.6	4.6
Fallow land................	19.4	24.6	24.9	29.6	8.7
Total other uncultivated land.................	54.5	56.8	56.1	60.6	17.8
Cropped area					
Net area sown..............	140.8	140.0	140.9	136.2	39.9
Area sown more than once per year....................	25.0	32.6	37.0	36.7	10.7
Total cropped area	165.8	172.6	177.9	172.9	50.6
Total area classified	328.8	336.4	341.7	341.6	100.0

[1] n.a.—not available.

Source: Based on information from United States, Embassy in New Delhi, *India: Agricultural Situation, Annual Report, 1992*, Washington, 1992, table 11; India, Ministry of Planning, Central Statistical Organization, Department of Statistics, *Statistical Abstract 1990, India*, New Delhi, 1991, 46–47; and Tata Services, Department of Economics and Statistics, *Statistical Outline of India, 1992–93*, Bombay, 1992, 56.

Table 28. Harvested and Irrigated Areas, Selected Fiscal Years, 1970–90
(in millions of hectares)

Area	1970	1980	1987	1990
Harvested area				
Gross	165.8	172.6	172.9	182.5
Net..............................	140.1	140.0	136.2	143.0
Cropping intensity (percentage)[1]	118.4	123.3	127.0	127.6
Irrigated area				
Gross	38.2	49.8	56.2	59.0
Net..............................	31.1	38.7	43.1	47.0
Irrigation intensity (percentage)[2]	23.0	29.0	33.0	32.3

[1] Gross area harvested divided by net area harvested.
[2] Gross irrigated area divided by gross harvested area.

Source: Based on information from United States, Embassy in New Delhi, *India: Agricultural Situation, Annual Report, 1992*, Washington, 1992, table 10; and Tata Services, Department of Economics and Statistics, *Statistical Outline of India, 1992–93*, Bombay, 1992, 56–57.

Table 29. Production and Sale of Selected Mechanized Agricultural Equipment, Selected Fiscal Years, 1986–91
(in number of units)

Equipment	1986	1987	1988	1991
Tractors				
Produced..................	80,004	92,092	109,987	151,759
Sold	78,823	93,157	110,323	150,582
Power tillers				
Produced..................	3,325	3,005	4,798	7,580
Sold	3,209	3,097	4,678	7,528
Combine harvesters				
Produced..................	57	149	109	187
Sold	57	144	110	189

Source: Based on information from *Hindustan Year Book and Who's Who, 1994*, New Delhi, 1994, 236; and India, Ministry of Agriculture, Department of Agriculture and Co-operation, *Annual Report, 1994–95*, New Delhi, 1994, 67.

Table 30. *Yield of Principal Crops, Selected Fiscal Years, 1950–90* (in kilograms per hectare)

Crop	1950	1960	1970	1980	1990[1]
Food grains					
Cereals					
Rice	668	1,013	1,123	1,336	1,751
Wheat..............	663	851	1,306	1,630	2,274
Coarse grains.........	408	528	665	695	n.a.[2]
All cereals[3]	542	693	949	1,142	1,573
Pulses	441	539	524	473	576
All food grains[3] ..	522	710	872	1,023	1,382
Oilseeds					
Peanuts...............	775	744	834	736	919
Rapeseed and mustard seed	368	467	594	560	900
Sesame	202	147	232	180	n.a.
Soybeans..............	n.a.	n.a.	n.a.	1,128	1,022
Sunflower	n.a.	n.a.	n.a.	555	540
Other oilseeds	470	505	604	305	n.a.
All oilseeds[3]..........	481	507	579	532	769
Sugarcane	33,421	46,133	48,324	57,836	65,000
Cotton	88	125	106	152	224
Jute.....................	1,040	1,180	1,186	1,245	1,803

[1] Preliminary.
[2] n.a.—not available.
[3] Numbers in this row represent weighted averages rather than totals.

Source: Based on information from India, Ministry of Finance, Economic Division, *Economic Survey, 1991–92, 2: Sectoral Developments*, New Delhi, 1992, 5–18; and United States, Embassy in New Delhi, *Annual Commodity Report, Oilseeds and Products, 1992*, New Delhi, 1992, 22, 25.

Table 31. Production of Principal Crops, Selected Fiscal Years,
1950–90
(in thousands of tons)

Crop	1950	1960	1970	1980	1990[1]
Food grains					
Cereals					
Rice.............	20,576	34,574	42,225	53,631	74,600
Wheat...........	6,462	10,997	23,832	36,313	54,500
Coarse grains.....	15,376	23,743	30,547	29,018	33,100
Total cereals ...	42,414	69,314	96,604	118,962	162,200
Pulses	8,411	12,704	11,818	10,627	14,100
Total food grains.........	50,825	82,018	108,422	129,589	176,300
Oilseeds					
Peanuts	3,481	4,812	6,111	5,005	7,600
Rapeseed and mustard seed.........	762	1,347	1,976	2,002	5,200
Cottonseed	—[2]	—	—	2,700	3,900
Sesame.............	445	318	568	446	810
Soybeans...........	—	—	—	442	2,400
Sunflower	—	—	—	66	889
Other oilseeds.......	470	505	604	1,242	1,001
Total oilseeds.....	5,158	6,982	9,259	11,903	21,800
Sugarcane.............	57,050	111,410	126,368	154,248	240,300
Cotton	600	1,004	809	1,326	1,666
Jute.................	595,000	744,000	882,000	1,170,000	1,404,000

[1] Preliminary.
[2] —means negligible.

Source: Based on information from India, Ministry of Finance, Economics Division, *Economic Survey, 1991–92, 2: Sectoral Developments*, New Delhi, 1992, S16; and United States, Embassy in New Delhi, *India: Agriculture Situation, Annual Report, 1992*, Washington, 1992, table 19.

Table 32. *Area under High-Yielding Varieties, Selected Fiscal Years, 1950–90*

Category	1960	1970	1980	1990[1]
Area sown with high-yielding varieties (millions of hectares)	1.9	15.4	43.1	63.9
Seeds				
Production, breeder seeds (millions of kilograms)	n.a.[2]	n.a.	527	n.a.
Fertilizer consumption				
Total (millions of tons)	0.3	2.2	5.5	12.6
Per hectare (units)	1.9	13.1	31.8	68.8
Cooperative credit (billions of rupees)	214.4	678.8	2,216.3	3,187.0
Area sown in rice (millions of hectares)	n.a.	5.6	18.2	28.1
Percentage of area sown in rice	n.a.	14.9	45.3	65.9
Area sown in wheat (millions of hectares)	n.a.	6.5	13.5	20.4
Percentage of area sown in wheat	n.a.	35.6	60.6	85.0
Area sown for coarse grains (millions of hectares)	n.a.	3.3	8.8	15.4
Percentage of area sown in coarse grains	n.a.	7.2	21.0	42.2

[1] Preliminary.
[2] n.a.—not available.

Source: Based on information from India, Ministry of Information and Broadcasting, Research and Reference Division, *India 1993: A Reference Annual,* New Delhi, January 1994, 392; and India, Ministry of Finance, Economic Division, *Economic Survey, 1991–92, 2: Sectoral Developments,* New Delhi, 1992, S22.

Table 33. Lok Sabha Elections, 1952–91 (in numbers of seats and percentages of total votes)

Party	1952	1957	1962	1967	1971	1977	1980	1984	1989	1991
Congress (Congress (I) after 1978)	364 (45.0)	371 (47.8)	361 (46.0)	283 (40.7)	352 (43.7)	154 (34.5)	353 (42.7)	415 (48.1)	197 (39.5)	227 (37.6)
Communist Party of India	16 (3.3)	27 (8.9)	29 (10.0)	23 (5.2)	23 (4.7)	7 (2.8)	11 (2.6)	6 (2.7)	12 (2.6)	14 (2.5)
Jana Sangh	3 (3.1)	4 (5.9)	14 (6.4)	35 (9.4)	22 (7.4)	—[1]	—	—	—	—
Republican Party	2 (2.4)	4 (1.5)	3 (2.8)	1 (2.5)	—	—	—	—	—	—
Hindu Mahasabha	4 (1.0)	1 (0.9)	1 (0.4)	—	—	—	—	—	—	—
Ram Rajya Parishad	3 (2.0)	0 (0.4)	2 (0.6)	—	—	—	—	—	—	—
Socialist Party	12 (10.6)	—	6 (2.5)	—	—	—	—	—	—	—
Kisan Mazdoor Praja Party	9 (5.8)	—	—	—	—	—	—	—	—	—
Praja Socialist Party	—	19 (10.4)	12 (6.8)	13 (3.1)	2 (1.0)	—	—	—	—	—
Swatantra	—	—	18 (6.8)	44 (8.7)	8 (3.1)	—	—	—	—	—
DMK[2]	—	—	7 (2.0)	25 (3.9)	23 (3.8)	1 (1.7)	16 (2.1)	—	—	—
Communist Party of India (Marxist)	—	—	—	19 (4.2)	25 (5.1)	22 (4.3)	36 (6.1)	22 (5.7)	33 (6.5)	35 (6.7)

Table 33. (Continued) Lok Sabha Elections, 1952–91 (in numbers of seats and percentages of total votes)

Party	1952	1957	1962	1967	1971	1977	1980	1984	1989	1991
Samyukta Socialist Party	—	—	—	23 (4.9)	3 (2.4)	—	—	—	—	—
Congress (O)	—	—	—	—	16 (10.4)	—	—	—	—	—
Janata Party	—	—	—	—	—	298 (43.0)	31 (19.0)	10 (6.7)	—	—
AIDDMK[3]	—	—	—	—	—	19 (3.0)	2 (2.4)	12 (1.6)	11 (1.5)	11 (2.3)
Congress (U)	—	—	—	—	—	—	13 (5.3)	—	—	—
Lok Dal (DMKP[4] in 1984)	—	—	—	—	—	—	41 (9.4)	3 (5.6)	—	—
Congress (S)	—	—	—	—	—	—	—	5 (1.7)	—	—
AGP[5]	—	—	—	—	—	—	—	7 (1.0)	—	—
BJP[6]	—	—	—	—	—	—	—	2 (7.4)	85 (11.4)	119 (21.0)
Telegu Desam	—	—	—	—	—	—	—	30 (4.1)	2 (3.3)	13 (3.0)
Janata Dal	—	—	—	—	—	—	—	—	143 (17.8)	56 (11.6)
Samajwadi Janata Party	—	—	—	—	—	—	—	—	—	5 (3.5)

Table 33. (*Continued*) *Lok Sabha Elections, 1952–91* (in numbers of seats and percentages of total votes)

Party	1952	1957	1962	1967	1971	1977	1980	1984	1989	1991
Shiv Sena..............	—	—	—	—	—	—	—	—	—	4 (0.8)
Other parties..........	35 (11.1)	29 (4.8)	14 (4.3)	19 (3.7)	30 (10.)	32 (5.2)	17 (4.0)	24 (7.3)	33 (12.2)	26 (6.3)
Independents..........	41 (15.8)	39 (19.4)	27 (12.3)	35 (13.8)	14 (8.4)	9 (5.5)	9 (6.4)	5 (8.1)	12 (5.2)	1 (4.7)
Electorate (in millions)	173.2	193.7	217.7	250.6	274.1	321.2	363.9	400.1	498.1	501.0
Turnout (in percentage)........	45.7	47.7	55.4	61.3	55.3	60.5	57.0	64.1	61.9	51.1
Total seats[7] authorized........	489	494	494	520	518	542	542	542	543	537

[1] —means did not participate in election.
[2] DMK—Dravida Munnetra Kazhagam (Dravidian Progressive Federation).
[3] AIADMK—All-India Anna Dravida Munnetra Kazhagam (All-India Anna Dravidian Progressive Federation).
[4] DMKP—Dalit Mazdoor Kisan Party (Oppressed Workers' and Peasants' Party).
[5] AGP—Asom Gana Parishad (Assam People's Party).
[6] BJP—Bharatiya Janata Party (Indian People's Party).
[7] The number of seats won by political parties may not add to total seats authorized; because of unsettled conditions, elections may not be held in all constituencies, thus occasionally leaving some seats vacant.

Source: Based on information from Robert L. Hardgrave and Stanley A. Kochanek, *India: Government and Politics in a Developing Nation*, Forth Worth, 1993, 314, 319–20, 347.

Table 34. Order of Battle for the Armed Forces, 1994

Branch and Units	Personnel or Unit
Army	
Personnel	940,000
Regional commands	5
Corps	12
Armored divisions	2
Tank regiments	55
Mechanized divisions	1
Infantry divisions	22
Battalions	355
Mountain infantry divisions	10
Independent brigades	14
Airborne/commando	1
Armored	5
Artillery	3
Regiments	290
Infantry	7
Mountain	1
Surface-to-surface missile brigade	1
Air defense brigades	6
Engineer brigades	3
Army aviation	
Air observation squadrons	8
Antitank/transport squadrons	6
Navy	
Personnel	
Line and staff	48,000
Naval air force	5,000
Marines	1,000
Total navy personnel	54,000
Commands	3
Fleets	2
Naval bases	9
Air Force	
Personnel	110,000
Air commands	5
Reserve forces personnel	
Territorial Army	36,456
National Cadet Corps	1,120,000
Civil Defence Volunteers	336,000
Home Guards	472,098
Total reserve forces personnel	1,964,554

Table 34. (Continued) Order of Battle for the Armed Forces, 1994

Branch and Units	Personnel or Unit
Paramilitary forces personnel	
Assam Rifles	40,000
Border Security Force	90,000
Coast Guard Organisation.............................	3,173
Central Industrial Security Force	83,781
Central Reserve Police Force............................	90,000
Defence Security Force	30,000
Indo-Tibetan Border Police............................	14,000
Rashtriya Rifles......................................	5,000
National Security Guards..............................	83,781
Provincial Armed Constabulary	250,000
Railway Protection Force	70,000
Special Frontier Force	3,000
Total paramilitary forces personnel....................	762,735

Source: Based on information from *The Military Balance, 1994–1995*, London, 1994, 153–56; and *SP's Military Yearbook, 1993–94*, ed., J. Baranwal, New Delhi, 1993, 291, 305, 319, 358, and 363.

Table 35. Major Army Equipment, 1994

Type and Description	Country of Origin	Number in Inventory
Armored vehicles		
Tanks		
Arjun MBT–90 main battle...............	India	—[1]
Vijayanta main battle	-do-	1,200
T–55 main battle......................	-do-	800
T–72/M1 main battle	-do-	1,400
PT–76 light amphibious.................	-do-	100
Reconnaissance and personnel		
BRDM–2 reconnaissance vehicles	-do-	n.a.[2]
Ferret (IS) reconnaissance vehicles........	Britain	n.a.
BMP–1, BMP–2 armored infantry fighting vehicles (Sarath)	India	900
OT–62, OT–64 armored personnel carriers...........................	-do-	157
BTR–50, BTR–60, BTR–152 armored personnel carriers	-do-	100
FV432 armored personnel carriers	Britain	n.a.
Recovery		
Vijayanta	India	n.a.
Artillery		
Towed		
75mm 75/24 mountain howitzers	India	900
76mm M–48 mountain guns	Yugoslavia	215
85mm D–48 antitank guns	Soviet Union	n.a.
25-pounder field guns..................	Britain	n.a.
100mm M–1944 towed howitzers..........	Soviet Union	185
105mm (including M–56 pack) howitzers...	India, Italy	50
105mm IFG Mk I/Mk II howitzers........	India	1,200
105mm light field guns.................	-do-	533
130mm M–46 towed howitzers............	Soviet Union	550
5.5-inch medium howitzers	Britain	n.a.
155mm FH–77B howitzers	Sweden	410
180mm S–23 howitzers.................	Soviet Union	n.a.
Self-propelled		
25-pounder howitzers...................	Britain	n.a.
105mm Abbott howitzers	India	80
155mm howitzers	n.a.	—[3]
130mm M–46 Catapult howitzers..........	India	100
Multiple rocket launchers		
122mm BM–21	-do-	80
122mm BM–24	-do-	n.a.

Table 35. (Continued) Major Army Equipment, 1994

Type and Description	Country of Origin	Number in Inventory
Mortars		
81mm E–1	India	n.a.
120mm E–1	-do-	n.a.
120mm M–43.........................	Soviet Union	1,000
120mm Brandt AM–50, E–1	Netherlands	500
160mm M–160.......................	Soviet Union	200
Antitank and guided weapons		
57mm M–18 recoilless rifles	Brazil	n.a.
84mm Carl Gustav recoilless rifles	Sweden	n.a.
106mm M–40A1 recoilless rifles...........	United States	1,000
MILAN.............................	India[4]	n.a.
Nag................................	-do-	n.a.[5]
AT–3 Sagger.........................	Soviet Union	n.a.
AT–4 Spigot	-do-	n.a.
AT–5 Spandrel.......................	-do-	n.a.
ENTAC.............................	France	n.a.
Mines, antipersonnel		
M14...............................	India	n.a.
M16A	-do-	n.a.
Mines, antitank		
M1A	-do-	n.a.
M3A	-do-	n.a.
Antiaircraft weapons		
20mm Oerlikon, towed.................	Switzerland	n.a.
23mm ZU 32/2 air defense guns	Soviet Union	140
23mm ZSU 23 air defense guns	-do-	n.a.
23mm ZSU 23/4 self-propelled air defense guns.........................	-do-	75
30mm 2S6 self-propelled air defense guns.............................	-do-	8
40mm L40/60 air defense guns	Sweden	1,245
40mm L40/70 automatic guns............	-do-	1,000
Surface-to-air missiles		
SA–2 Guideline.........................	Soviet Union	n.a.
SA–3 Goa.............................	-do-	n.a.
SA–6 Gainful..........................	-do-	100
SA–7 Grail............................	-do-	620
SA–8A and SA–8B Gecko..................	-do-	48
SA–9 Gaskin	-do-	200
SA–11 Gadfly..........................	-do-	50
SA–13 Gopher..........................	-do-	45
SA–16...............................	-do-	200
Trishul...............................	India	n.a.[5]

Table 35. (Continued) Major Army Equipment, 1994

Type and Description	Country of Origin	Number in Inventory
Agni.................................	-do-	n.a.[5]
Akash	-do-	n.a.[5]
Surface-to-surface missiles		
Prithvi...............................	-do-	15
Helicopters		
Cheetah SA–315........................	India	40
Chetak SA–319.........................	-do-	50
HAL advanced light helicopter..............	-do-	1[6]

[1] Prototype; developed since 1974; completed trials in 1993; no production as of June 1994; production expected to start 1996.
[2] n.a.—not available.
[3] 120 sought from foreign source, 1994; 480 to be produced under license in India.
[4] Under contract with France.
[5] Under development.
[6] Prototype, shared with Air Force.

Source: Based on information from *The Military Balance, 1994–1995*, London, 1994, 154; *Jane's Infantry Weapons, 1994–95*, Coulsdon, United Kingdom, 1994, 389–90; *Jane's Armour and Artillery, 1994–95*, Coulsdon, United Kingdom, 1994, 61–63, 154, 351–52, 543, 614–15, 692, 773; and *Jane's Military Vehicles and Logistics, 1994–95*, Coulsdon, United Kingdom, 1994, 34, 199–200.

Table 36. *Major Naval Equipment, 1994*

Type and Description	Country of Origin	Number in Inventory
Navy Ships		
Submarines		
Sindhugosh class . . . . (Soviet Kilo (Type 877EM) class)	Soviet Union	8
Kursura class . . . . (Soviet Foxtrot (Type 641) class)	-do-	6
Shishumar class . . . . (German 209 class, Type HDW 1500)	Germany, India	4[1]
Carriers		
INS *Viraat* (Hermes class) . . . . with 12 Sea Harriers FRS Mk 51, 7 Sea Kings, Mk 42B/C, 1 Ka–27 helicopter	Britain	1
INS *Vikrant* (Majestic class) . . . . with 6 Sea Harriers FRS Mk 51, 9 Sea Kings Mk 42, 1 Chetak SAR	-do-	1
Destroyers		
Rajput class. . . . . (Soviet Kashin II class) with Goa surface-to-air missiles, Styx surface-to-surface missiles, 533mm torpedo tubes, antisubmarine rocket launchers, and Ka–28 helicopter	Soviet Union	5
Delhi class . . . . with SS–N–22 Sunburn and SA–N–7 missiles; 324mm torpedo tubes; 2 Sea King Mk42B or HAL advanced light helicopters	India	2[2]
Frigates		
Godavari class . . . . with Sea King helicopters, antisubmarine torpedo tubes, and Styx surface-to-surface missiles	-do-	3[3]
Nilgiri class. . . . . (British Leander class) with antisubmarine torpedo tubes, Limbo antisubmarine warfare mortars, Chetak and Sea King helicopters, antisubmarine warfare rocket launchers, and 114mm guns	-do-	6
Kamorta class. . . . . (Soviet Petya II class) with antisubmarine rocket launchers, 533mm torpedo tubes, and minelaying capabilities	Soviet Union	5
Corvettes		
Khukri class . . . . (antisubmarine warfare) with Styx surface-to-surface missiles and helicopter deck	India	5[4]
Durg class. . . . . (Soviet Nanuchka II class) with Styx surface-to-surface missiles	Soviet Union	3

Table 36. (Continued) Major Naval Equipment, 1994

Type and Description	Country of Origin	Number in Inventory
Veer class . . . . (Soviet Tarantul I class) with Styx surface- to-surface missiles	Soviet Union, India	9[5]
Abhay class. . . . . (Soviet Pauk II class) with antisubmarine torpedo tubes and antisubmarine mortars	-do-	4
Patrol forces ships		
Vidyut class . . . . (Soviet Osa II class) with Styx surface-to- surface missiles	Soviet Union	8
Sukanya patrol ship, offshore. . . . . with 1 Oerlikon 20mm gun, 1 Chetak heli- copter	South Korea, India	8[6]
SDB Mk 2 patrol ship, inshore	India	5
SDB Mk 3 patrol ship, inshore	-do-	7
Mine warfare and countermeasure ships		
Pondicherry minesweeper, ocean . . . . (Soviet Natya I class) with minelaying capabilities	Soviet Union	12
Mahé minesweeper, inshore. . . . . (Soviet Yevgenya class)	-do-	6
Bulsar minesweeper, inshore . . . . (British Ham class)	Britain, India	4[7]
Amphibious ships		
Magar class . . . . landing ship, tank, 200 troops, 12 tanks, 1 helicopter	India	2[8]
Vasco da Gama class (Mk 3) . . . . landing ship, utility, 287 troops	-do-	7
Ghorpad class . . . . landing ship, medium (Soviet Polnocny C and D), 140 troops, 6 tanks	Soviet Union	8
Naval Air Force		
Attack aircraft		
Sea Harrier FRS Mk 51	Britain	23
HAL Jaguar (Shamsher)	India	8
Antisubmarine helicopters		
Chetak	-do-	26
HAL advanced light helicopter	-do-	1[9]
Ka–25 Hormone	Soviet Union	7
Ka–28 Helix.	-do-	10
Sea King Mk 4	Britain	12
Sea King Mk 4A/4B	-do-	32
Marine reconnaissance and antisubmarine war- fare aircraft		
PBN–2B Defender (utility)	-do-	13
Il–38 May	Soviet Union	5
Tu–142M Bear F	-do-	10

Table 36. (Continued) Major Naval Equipment, 1994

Type and Description	Country of Origin	Number in Inventory
HAL Dornier–228–201	India[10]	10[11]
Communications aircraft		
BN–2 Islander	Britain	5
HAL Dornier–228	India	2
Chetak helicopters.	-do-	3
Search and rescue helicopters		
Sea King Mk 42C	Britain	6
Training aircraft		
Sea Harrier T–Mk 60 (training)	-do-	3
Kiran HJT–16.	India	6
Deepak HPT–32	-do-	8
Training helicopters		
Chetak	-do-	2
MD Hughes 300.	United States	4
Missiles		
Air-to-air		
R–550 Magic I and II	France	45
Antisubmarine		
Sea Eagle.	Britain	n.a.[12]
Sea Skua	-do-	n.a.

[1] Two built in Germany, two built in India; one other under construction; one more planned in India.
[2] Two launched but not yet commissioned; one other under construction.
[3] Two more under construction; one more planned.
[4] One more under construction; two more planned.
[5] Five built in Soviet Union, four built in India; two more planned.
[6] Three built in South Korea, five built in India; one more planned.
[7] Two built in Britain, two built in India.
[8] One more under construction.
[9] Prototype.
[10] Under license with Germany.
[11] Seventeen more planned or in production.
[12] n.a.—not available.

Source: Based on information from *The Military Balance, 1994–1995*, London, 1994, 154–55; *Jane's Fighting Ships, 1994–95*, Coulsdon, United Kingdom, 1994, 279–93; and *Jane's All the World's Aircraft, 1994–95*, Coulsdon, United Kingdom, 1994, 119, 121–23.

Table 37. Major Air Force Equipment, 1994

Type and Description	Country of Origin	Number in Inventory
Fighters, ground-attack		
MiG–21MF/PFMA......................	Soviet Union	144
MiG–23 BN/UM	-do-	54
Shamsher (Jaguar)......................	Britain, India	89[1]
Babhadur (MiG–27)	India[2]	120
Fighters		
HAL light combat aircraft.................	-do-	n.a.[3]
MiG–21 FL/U...........................	Soviet Union	74
MiG–21 bis/U	-do-	170
MiG–23 MF/UM	-do-	26
MiG–29 UB.............................	-do-	59
Mirage 2000H/TH.......................	France	35
Electric countermeasures		
Canberra B(I) 58	Britain	5
Airborne surveillance warning and control system (ASWACS)		
HS–758...............................	India[4]	4
Maritime attack		
Jaguar with Sea Eagle....................	Britain	8
Helicopters, attack		
Mi–25	Soviet Union	18
Mi–35	-do-	18
HAL advanced light helicopter.............	India	1[5]
Reconnaissance aircraft		
Canberra PR–57.........................	Britain	6
Camberra PR–67	-do-	2
Andover HS–728	-do-	4
MiG–23R..............................	Soviet Union	6
MiG–23U	-do-	2
Maritime reconnaissance/survey aircraft		
Gulfstream IV SRA......................	United States	2
Learjet 29	-do-	2
Transport aircraft		
An–32 Sutlej...........................	Soviet Union	105
Il–76 Gajraj............................	-do-	24
BAe–748	Britain	33
Dornier–228...........................	Germany	30
Transport helicopters		
Mi–8	Soviet Union	80
Mi–17	-do-	50
Mi–26	-do-	10

Table 37. (Continued) Major Air Force Equipment, 1994

Type and Description	Country of Origin	Number in Inventory
VIP aircraft		
Boeing 707–337C	United States	2
Boeing 737	-do-	3
BAe–748	Britain	7
Liaison aircraft		
BAe–748	-do-	16
Training aircraft		
BAe–748	-do-	28
Hunter F–56	-do-	20
Hunter T–66..........................	-do-	18
Canberra T–54	-do-	2
Canberra TT–18.......................	-do-	5
Jaguar IB	France, Britain	15
Kiran I..............................	India	120
Kiran II	-do-	56
Deepak HPT–32........................	-do-	88
HT–2................................	-do-	60
HTT–35..............................	-do-	n.a.[6]
MiG–29 UB	Soviet Union	5
Iskara TS–11 ac.......................	Poland	44
Training helicopters		
Chetak...............................	India	20
Mi–24...............................	Soviet Union	2
Mi–35...............................	-do-	2
Missiles		
Air-to-surface		
Akash	India	n.a.
AM–39 Exocet	France	n.a.
AS–7 Kerry..........................	Soviet Union	n.a.
AS–10 Karen.........................	-do-	n.a.
AS–11B.............................	France	n.a.
AS–30	-do-	n.a.
FAB–500............................	Soviet Union	n.a.
FAB–750............................	-do-	n.a.
FAB–1000...........................	-do-	n.a.
Sea Eagle	Britain	n.a.
Air-to-air		
AA–2 Atoll	Soviet Union	n.a.
AA–7 Apex..........................	-do-	n.a.
AA–8 Aphid	-do-	n.a.
AA–10 Alamo........................	-do-	n.a.
AA–11 Archer........................	-do-	n.a.

Table 37. (Continued) Major Air Force Equipment, 1994

Type and Description	Country of Origin	Number in Inventory
R–550 Magic	France	n.a.
Super 530D	-do-	n.a.
Surface-to-air		
Divina V75SM/VK (SA–2, SA–3, and SA–5)	Soviet Union	280

[1] Some assembled in India; additional inventory to be manufactured in India under license with Britain.
[2] Under license with Soviet Union and Russia.
[3] n.a.—not available.
[4] Prototype; first flights expected in 1995 and 1996; initial operational capability in 2002; up to 200 units.
[5] With India, French, and German equipment.
[6] Prototype, shared with army.

Source: Based on information from *The Military Balance, 1994–1995*, London, 1994, 155; *Jane's All the World's Aircraft, 1994–95*, Coulsdon, United Kingdom, 1994, 117, 119–21, 123; and *Jane's Radar and Electronic Warfare Systems, 1994–95*, Coulsdon, United Kingdom, 1994, 242.

Table 38. Major Coast Guard Equipment, 1994

Type and Description	Country of Origin	Number in Inventory
Patrol forces		
Offshore		
Samar.............................	India	3
Vikram (Type P–957)	-do-	9
Inshore		
Jija Bai (Type 956)	-do-	7
Raj (SDB Mk 2).......................	-do-	5
32-ton patrol craft.....................	South Korea	8
Jija Bai (Mod 1).......................	Singapore, India	11
49-ton patrol craft.....................	India	7
Aircraft		
HAL Dornier–228 maritime surveillance......	Germany, India	11[1]
Chetak helicopter	India	9
F–27 maritime	Netherlands	2

[1] Three built in Germany, eight built in India; twenty-two more on order.

Source: Based on information from Kailish Kohli, "Aviation in Indian Coast Guard," *Sainik Samachar* [New Delhi], 41, No. 5, January 30, 1994, 11; *Jane's Fighting Ships, 1994–95*, Coulsdon, United Kingdom, 1994, 294–95; and *Jane's All the World's Aircraft, 1994–95*, Coulsdon, United Kingdom, 1994, 123.

Bibliography

Chapter 1

Adas, Michael. *Machines as the Measure of Men: Science, Technology, and Ideologies of Western Dominance.* Ithaca: Cornell University Press, 1989.

Adas, Michael. "Twentieth Century Approaches to the Indian Mutiny of 1857–58," *Journal of Asian History* [Wiesbaden], 5, No. 1, 1971, 1–19.

Ahmad, Imtiaz. *State and Foreign Policy: India's Role in South Asia.* New Delhi: Vikas, 1993.

Ali, M. Athar. "The Mughal Policy—A Critique of Revisionist Approaches," *Modern Asian Studies* [London], 27, Pt. 4, October 1993, 699–710.

Ali, Tariq. *An Indian Dynasty: The Story of the Nehru-Gandhi Family.* New York: Putnam, 1985.

Altekar, A.S. *Rastrakutas and Their Times.* 2d ed., rev. Pune: Oriental Book Agency, 1967.

Asher, Catherine Ella Blanshard. *The New Cambridge History of India, I.4: Architecture in Mughal India.* Cambridge: Cambridge University Press, 1992.

Ashton, S.R. *British Policy Towards the Indian States, 1905–1939.* London Studies on South Asia, No. 2. London: Curzon, 1982.

Austin, Granville. *The Indian Constitution: Cornerstone of a Nation.* Oxford: Clarendon Press, 1966.

Baird, Robert. *Religion in Modern India.* New Delhi: Manohar, 1981.

Baker, Christopher J. *An Indian Rural Economy: The Tamiland Countryside.* Oxford: Clarendon Press, 1984.

Baker, Christopher J. *The Politics of South India, 1920–1937.* Cambridge: Cambridge University Press, 1976.

Baker, David. "Colonial Beginnings and the Indian Response: The Revolt of 1857–58 in Madhya Pradesh," *Modern Asian Studies* [London], 25, Pt. 3, July 1991, 511–43.

Bakshi, S.R. *Morarji Desai.* New Delhi: Amol, 1991.

Banerjee, Hiranmay. *The House of the Tagores.* 3d ed. Calcutta: Rabiondra Bharati University, 1968.

Barker, A.J. *Bastard War: The Mesopotamian Campaign of 1914–1918.* New York: Dial, 1967.

Barraclough, Geoffrey, and Geoffrey Parker, eds. *The Times Atlas of World History.* 4th ed. Maplewood, New Jersey: Hammond, 1993.

Barrier, N. Gerald. *India and America: American Publishing on India, 1930–1985.* New Delhi: American Institute of Indian Studies, 1986.

Basham, A.L. *The Origin and Development of Classical Hinduism.* Ed. and completed by Kenneth G. Zysk. New York: Oxford University Press, 1989.

Basham, A.L. *The Wonder That Was India, 1: A Survey of the History and Culture of the Indian Sub-Continent Before the Coming of the Muslims.* 3d ed., rev. London: Sidgwick and Jackson, 1967.

Basham, A.L., ed. *A Cultural History of India.* Oxford: Clarendon Press, 1975.

Bayly, C.A. *The New Cambridge History of India, II.1: Indian Society and the Making of the British Empire.* Cambridge: Cambridge University Press, 1987.

Bayly, C.A. *Rulers, Townsmen, and Bazaars: North Indian Society in the Age of British Expansion, 1770–1870.* Cambridge: Cambridge University Press, 1983.

Beach, Milo Cleveland. *The New Cambridge History of India, I.3: Mughal and Rajput Painting.* Cambridge: Cambridge University Press, 1992.

Beaumont, Roger. *Sword of the Raj: The British Army in India, 1747–1947.* Indianapolis: Bobbs-Merrill, 1977.

Begley, Vimala, and Richard Daniel DePuma, eds. *Rome and India: The Ancient Sea Trade.* Madison: University of Wisconsin Press, 1992.

Bhattacharjee, Arun. *Rajiv Gandhi: Life and Message.* New Delhi: Ashish, 1992.

Blake, Stephen P. *Shahjahanabad: The Sovereign City in Mughal India.* Cambridge: Cambridge University Press, 1991.

Bondurant, Joan V. *The Conquest of Violence: The Gandhian Philosophy of Conflict.* Princeton: Princeton University Press, 1958.

Bose, Subhas Chandra. *Netaji Subhas Chandra Bose: Correspondence and Selected Documents, 1930–1942.* Ed., Ravindra Kumar. New Delhi: Inter-India, 1992.

Bose, Sugata. *The New Cambridge History of India, III.2: Peasant Labour and Colonial Capital: Rural Bengal since 1770.* Cambridge: Cambridge University Press, 1993.

Brass, Paul R. *The New Cambridge History of India, IV.1: The Politics of India since Independence.* 2d ed. Cambridge: Cambridge University Press, 1994.

Brecher, Michael. *Nehru: A Political Biography.* London: Oxford University Press, 1959.

Brecher, Michael. *The Politics of Succession in India.* Westport, Connecticut: Greenwood, 1976.

Brown, Judith M. *Gandhi and Civil Disobedience.* London: Cambridge University Press, 1977.

Brown, Judith M. *Modern India: The Origins of an Asian Democracy.* New Delhi: Oxford University Press, 1985.

Buchanan, R.A. "The Diaspora of British Engineering," *Technology and Culture*, 27, No. 3. July 1986, 501–24.

Carras, Mary C. *Indira Gandhi in the Crucible of Leadership.* Boston: Beacon Press, 1979.

Carson, Penelope. "An Imperial Dilemma: The Propagation of Christianity in Early Colonial India," *Journal of Imperial and Commonwealth History* [London], 18, No. 2, 1990, 169–90.

Chanchreek, K.L., and Saroj Prasad, eds. *Crisis in India.* Delhi: H.K. Publishers, 1993.

Chandra, Bipan. *Essays on Contemporary India.* New Delhi: Har-Anand, 1993.

Chandra, Bipan. *Modern India.* New Delhi: National Council of Educational Research and Training, 1971.

Chandra, Satish. *Medieval India: A Textbook for Classes XI–XII.* 2 vols. New Delhi: National Council of Educational Research and Training, 1978.

Chattopadhyaya, B.D. "Origins of the Rajputs: The Political, Economic, and Social Progress in Early Medieval Rajasthan," *Indian Historical Review* [Delhi], 3, No. 1, March 1976, 59–82.

Chaudhury, K.N. *The Trading World of Asia and the English East India Company, 1660–1760.* Cambridge: Cambridge University Press, 1978.

Chellaney, Brahma. *Nuclear Proliferation: The U.S.-Indian Conflict.* New Delhi: Orient Longman, 1993.

Chopra, Pran, ed. *Contemporary Pakistan: New Aims and Images.* New Delhi: Vikas, 1983.

Collins, Larry, and Dominique Lapierre. *Freedom at Midnight.* New York: Simon and Schuster, 1975.

Crawford, S. Cromwell. *Ram Mohan Roy.* New York: Paragon, 1987.

Cunningham, Joseph Davey. *History of the Sikhs, From the Origins of the Nation to the Battles of the Sutlej.* Delhi: Sultan Chand, 1955.

Damodaran, A.K., and Bajpai, U.S., eds. *Indian Foreign Policy: The Indira Gandhi Years.* New Delhi: Radiant, 1990.

Das, Arvind. *India Invented.* New Delhi: Manohar, 1992.

Das, Kamal Kishore. *Economic History of Moghul India: An Annotated Bibliography, 1526–1875.* Calcutta: Santiniketan, 1991.

Das, M.N. *India under Morley and Minto: Politics Behind Revolution, Repression, and Reforms.* London: Allen and Unwin, 1964.

Das, Veena. *Mirrors of Violence: Communities, Riots, and Survivors in South Asia.* New Delhi: Oxford University Press, 1992.

Dasgupta, A. "Indian Merchants and the Trade in the Indian Ocean." Pages 407–33 in Tapan Raychaudhuri and Irfan Habib, eds., *The Cambridge Economic History of India, 1: c.1200–c.1750.* Cambridge: Cambridge University Press, 1982.

Datta, V.N. *Sati: Widow Burning in India.* New Delhi: Manohar, 1990.

Davies, C. Collin. *An Historical Atlas of the Indian Peninsula.* London: Oxford University Press, 1959.

Derrett, J. Duncan. *Religion, Law, and the State in India.* London: Faber, 1968.

Desai, Morarji. *The Story of My Life.* 3 vols. New Delhi: Pergamon, 1979.

Dhanagare, D.N. *Peasant Movements in India, 1920–1950.* New Delhi: Oxford University Press, 1983.

Digby, Simon. "The Maritime Trade of India." Pages 125–62 in Tapan Raychaudhuri and Irfan Habib, eds., *The Cambridge Economic History of India, 1: c.1200–c.1750.* Cambridge: Cambridge University Press, 1982.

Dikshit, D.P. *Political History of the Chalukyas of Badami.* New Delhi: Abhinav, 1980.

Dixit, Prabla. *Communalism: A Struggle for Power.* New Delhi: Orient Longman, 1981.

Doniger, Wendy, trans. *Laws of Manu.* New York: Penguin, 1992.

Doshi, Saryu, ed. *India and Greece.* New Delhi: Marg, 1985.

Dunn, Rose E. *The Adventures of Ibn Battuta.* London: Croom Helm, 1986.

Dutt, Ashok K., and Allen G. Noble. "The Culture of India in a Spatial Perspective: An Introduction." Pages 1–28 in Allen G. Noble and Ashok K. Dutt, eds., *India: Cultural Patterns and Processes.* Boulder, Colorado: Westview Press, 1982.

Eaton, Richard M. *The Rise of Islam and the Bengal Frontier, 1204–1760.* Comparative Studies on Muslim Societies, No. 17. Berkeley: University of California Press, 1993.

Eaton, Richard M. *Sufis of Bijapur, 1300–1700: Social Roles of Sufis in Medieval India.* Princeton: Princeton University Press, 1978.

Eldridge, P.J. *The Politics of Foreign Aid in India.* New York: Schocken, 1970.

Ellinwood, DeWitt C., and S.P. Pradhan. *India and World War I.* New Delhi: Manohar, 1978.

Embree, Ainslie T. *1857 in India: Mutiny or War of Independence.* Lexington, Massachusetts: Heath, 1963.

Embree, Ainslie T., ed. *Alberuni's India.* New York: Norton, 1971.

Embree, Ainslie T., ed. *Encyclopedia of Asian History.* 4 vols. The Asia Society. New York: Scribner's, 1988.

Embree, Ainslie T., ed. *Sources of Indian Tradition, 1: From the Beginning to 1800.* 2d ed. Introduction to Oriental Civilization Series. New York: Columbia University Press, 1988.

Erickson, Erik H. *Gandhi's Truth: On the Origins of Militant Nonviolence.* New York: Norton, 1970.

Fairservis, Walter A. *The Roots of Ancient India: The Archaeology of Early Indian Civilization.* New York: Macmillan, 1971.

Farmer, Edward L., Gavin R.G. Hambly, David Kopf, Byron K. Marshall, and Romeyn Taylor. *Comparative History of Civilizations in Asia.* 2 vols. Reading, Massachusetts: Addison-Wesley, 1977.

Featherstone, Donald F. *Victorian Colonial Warfare, India: From the Conquest of Sind to the Indian Mutiny.* London: Cassell, 1992.

Fischer, Louis. *The Life of Mahatma Gandhi.* New York: Harper, 1950.

Fisher, Michael. *A Clash of Cultures: Awadh, the British, and the Mughals.* New Delhi: Manohar, 1987.

Fisher, Michael. *Indirect Rule in India: Residents and the Residency System, 1764–1857.* New Delhi: Oxford University Press, 1991.

Frykenberg, Robert E. *Guntur District 1788–1848: A History of Local Influence and Central Authority in South India.* Oxford: Oxford University Press, 1965.

Frykenberg, Robert E. "The Impact of Conversion and Social Reform upon Society in South India During the Late Company Period: Questions Concerning Hindu-Christian Encounters, with Special Reference to Tinnevelly." Pages 187–243 in C.H. Philips and Mary Doreen Wainwright, eds., *Indian Society and the Beginnings of Modernization, c. 1830–1850.* London: School of Oriental and Arican Studies, 1976.

Gandhi, Mahatma. *An Autobiography: The Story of My Experiments with Truth.* Trans., Mahadev Desai. Boston: Beacon Press, 1957. Reprint. Boston: Beacon Press, 1993.

Gandhi, Mahatma. *Essential Writings of Mahatma Gandhi.* Ed., Raghavan Iyer. New Delhi: Oxford University Press, 1991.

Gandhi, Mahatma. *The Gandhi Reader: A Sourcebook of His Life and Writings.* Ed., Homer A. Jack. Grove Press Eastern Philosophy and Literature Studies. New York: Grove Press, 1961.

Gandhi, Mahatma. *Non-Violent Resistance.* Comp. and ed., Bharatan Kumanappa. New York: Schocken, 1951.

Ganguly, D.K. *Ancient India: History and Archaeology.* New Delhi: Abhinav, 1994.

Gascoigne, Bamber. *The Great Moghuls.* London: Cape, 1971.

Ghose, S.K. *Politics of Violence: Dawn of a Dangerous Era.* Springfield, Virginia: Nataraj, 1992.

Glazer, Sulochana Raghavan, and Nathan Glazer, eds. *Conflicting Images: India and the United States.* Glenn Dale, Maryland: Riverdale, 1990.

Goalen, Paul. *India: From Mughal Empire to British Raj.* Cambridge: Cambridge University Press, 1993.

Gokkhale, B.C. "Buddhism in the Gupta Age." Pages 129–56 in Bardwell L. Smith, ed., *Essays on Gupta Culture.* New Delhi: Motilal Banarsidass, 1983.

Gopal, Sarvepalli. *Jawaharlal Nehru: An Anthology.* New Delhi: Oxford University Press, 1980.

Gopal, Sarvepalli. *Jawaharlal Nehru: A Biography.* 3 vols. London: Cape, 1975–84.

Gopal, Sarvepalli. *Jawaharlal Nehru: A Biography.* Abridged ed. New Delhi: Oxford University Press, 1993.

Gopal, Sarvepalli, ed. *Anatomy of a Confrontation: The Babri Masjid-Ramjanmabhumi Issue.* New Delhi: Viking, 1991.

Goradia, Nayana. *Lord Curzon: The Last of the British Moghuls.* New Delhi: Oxford University Press, 1993.

Gordon, Stewart. *The New Cambridge History of India, II.4: The Marathas, 1600–1818.* Cambridge: Cambridge University Press, 1993.

Gorman, Mel. "Sir William O'Shaughnessy, Lord Dalhousie, and the Establishment of the Telegraph System in India," *Technology and Culture,* 12, No. 4, October 1971, 581–601.

Goyal, Shankar. *Aspects of Ancient Indian History and Historiography.* New Delhi: Harnam, 1993.

Guha, Ranajit, and Gayatri Chakravorty, eds. *Subaltern Studies: Writings on South Asian History and Society.* 5 vols. New York: Oxford University Press, 1982–87.

Gupte, Pranay. *Mother India: A Political Biography of Indira Gandhi.* New York: Scribner's, 1992.

Gupte, Pranay. *Vengeance: India after the Assassination of Indira Gandhi.* New York: Norton, 1985.

Habib, Irfan. *The Agrarian System of Mughal India, 1556–1707.* New York: Asia, 1963.

Habib, Irfan. *An Atlas of the Mughal Empire.* Delhi: Oxford University Press, 1982.

Habib, Irfan. "Mughal India." Pages 214–25 in Tapan Raychaudhuri and Irfan Habib, eds., *The Cambridge Economic History of India, 2: c.1200–c.1750.* Cambridge: Cambridge University Press, 1982.

Habib, Irfan, ed. *Medieval India, 1: Researchers in the History of India, 1200–1750.* New Delhi: Oxford University Press, 1992.

Hadi Hussain, Muhammed. *Syed Ahmed Khan: Pioneer of Muslim Resurgence.* Lahore: Institute of Islamic Culture, 1970.

Halbfass, Wilhelm. *India and Europe: An Essay in Understanding.* Albany: State University of New York Press, 1988.

Hamilton, J.R. *Alexander the Great.* Oxford: Clarendon Press, 1965.

Hardgrave, Robert L., Jr., and Stanley A. Kochanek. *India: Government and Politics in a Developing Nation.* 5th ed. Fort Worth, Texas: Harcourt Brace Jovanovich, 1993.

Harrison, Mark. "Tropical Medicine in Nineteenth-Century India," *British Journal for the History of Science* [Cambridge], 25, Pt. 3, No. 86, September 1992, 299–318.

Hart, Henry C., ed. *Indira Gandhi's India: A Political System Reappraised.* Boulder, Colorado: Westview Press, 1976.

Haynes, Douglas E. *Rhetoric and Ritual in Colonial India: The Shaping of a Public Culture in Surat City, 1852–1928.* Berkeley: University of California Press, 1991.

Heinsath, Charles. *Indian Nationalism and Hindu Social Reform.* Princeton: Princeton University Press, 1964.

Hill, John L., ed. *The Congress and Indian Nationalism: Historical Perspectives.* Westwood, Massachusetts: Riverdale, 1991.

Hindustan Year Book and Who's Who, 1992. 60th ed. Ed., S. Sarkar. Calcutta: M.C. Sarkar, 1992.

Hindustan Year Book and Who's Who, 1994. 62d ed. Ed., S. Sarkar. Calcutta: M.C. Sarkar, 1994.

Hiro, Dilip. *Inside India Today.* London: Routledge and Kegan Paul, 1976.

Hirschman, Edwin. *White Mutiny: The Ilbert Bill Crisis in India and the Genesis of the Indian National Congress.* New Delhi: Heritage, 1980.

Hossain, Hameeda. *The Company Weavers of Bengal: The East India Company and the Organization of Textile Production in Bengal, 1750–1813.* New Delhi: Oxford University Press, 1988.

Humbers, Philippe. *The Rajiv Gandhi Years: Sunshine and Shadows.* New Delhi: Vimot, 1992.

Hutchins, Francis. *The Illusion of Permanence: British Imperialism in India.* Princeton: Princeton University Press, 1967.

Hutchins, Francis. *Spontaneous Revolution: The Quit India Movement.* New Delhi: Manohar, 1971.

Ilankovatikal. *The Cilappatikaram of Ilano Atikal: An Epic of South India.* Trans., R. Parthasarathy. Translations from the Asian Classics. New York: Columbia University Press, 1993.

Inden, Ronald. *Imagining India.* Oxford: Oxford University Press, 1990.

Inder Singh, Anita. "Decolonization in India: The Statement of February 20, 1947," *International History Review* [Toronto], 6, No. 2, May 1984, 191–209.

Inder Singh, Anita. "Imperial Defence and the Transfer of Power in India, 1946–1947," *International History Review* [Toronto], 4, No. 4, November 1982, 568–88.

India Handbook, 1996. 5th ed. Ed., Robert W. Bradnock. Bath, United Kingdom: Trade and Travel, 1995.

Irschich, Eugene F. *Politics and Social Conflict in South India: The Non-Brahman Movement and Tamil Separatism.* Berkeley: University of California Press, 1969.

Irschich, Eugene F. *Tamil Revivalism in the 1930s.* New Delhi: Manohar, 1986.

Jain, C.K., ed. *Rajiv Gandhi and Parliament.* New Delhi: CBS, 1992.

Jain, M.P. *Outlines of Indian Legal History.* 2d ed. Bombay: Tripathi, 1966.

Jalal, Ayesha. *The Sole Spokesman: Jinnah, the Muslim League, and the Demand for Pakistan.* Cambridge: Cambridge University Press, 1985.

Jayakar, Pupul. *Indira Gandhi: A Biography.* New Delhi: Penguin, 1992.

Jeffery, Roger. "Recognizing India's Doctors: The Institutionalization of Medical Dependency, 1918–39," *Modern Asian Studies* [London], 13, Pt. 2, April 1979, 302–26.

Jeffrey, Robin, ed. *People, Princes, and Paramount Power: Society and Politics in Indian Princely States.* New Delhi: Oxford University Press, 1978.

Jones, Kenneth W. *Arya Dharm: Hindu Consciousness in 19th Century Punjab.* Berkeley: University of California Press, 1976.

Jones, Kenneth W. *The New Cambridge History of India, III.1: Socio-Religious Reform Movements in British India.* Cambridge: Cambridge University Press, 1989.

Kandaswamy, S.N. *Buddhism as Expounded in Manimekalai (The Jewelled Belt).* Annamalainagar: Annamalai University, 1978.

Kapur, Rajiv. *Sikh Separatism: The Politics of Faith.* New Delhi: Vikas, 1987.

Karashima, Noboru. *Towards a New Formation: South Indian Society under Vijayanagar Rule.* New Delhi: Oxford University Press, 1992.

Kashvap, Subhash. *The Politics of Defection.* Delhi: National, 1969.

Keay, John. *Democracy and Discontent: India's Growing Crisis of Governability.* Cambridge: Cambridge University Press, 1992.

Keay, John. *The Honourable Company: A History of the English East India Company.* London: Harper Collins, 1991.

Kopf, David. *The Brahmo Samaj and the Shaping of the Modern Indian Mind.* Princeton: Princeton University Press, 1979.

Kopf, David. *British Orientalism and the Bengal Renaissance: The Dynamics of Indian Modernization, 1773–1835.* Berkeley: University of California Press, 1969.

Kosambi, D.D. *Myth and Reality: Studies in the Formation of Indian Culture.* Bombay: Popular Prakashan, 1962.

Kothari, Rajni. *Politics in India.* Boston: Little, Brown, 1970.

Kreisberg, Paul H. "Gandhi at Midterm," *Foreign Affairs,* 65, No. 5, Summer 1987, 1055–76.

Krishna Murari. *The Calukyas of Kalyani, from circa 973 A.D. to 1200 A.D.* Delhi: Concept, 1977.

Kulke, Hermann, ed. *The State in India, 1000–1700.* Oxford in India Readings, Themes in Indian History. Delhi: Oxford University Press, 1995.

Kulke, Hermann, and Dietmar Rothermund. *A History of India.* Rev., updated ed. London: Routledge, 1990.

Kumar, Deepak, ed. *Science and Empire: Essays in Indian Context, 1700–1947.* Delhi: Anamika Prakashan, 1991.

Kumar, Dharma, and Meghnad Desai, eds. *The Cambridge Economic History of India, 2: c.1757–c.1970.* Cambridge: Cambridge University Press, 1983.

Kumar, Ravinder. *The Social History of Modern India.* New Delhi: Oxford University Press, 1983.

Lelyveld, David. *Aligarh's First Generation.* Princeton: Princeton University Press, 1977.

Lewis, Martin D. *The British in India: Imperialism or Trusteeship.* Lexington, Massachusetts: Heath, 1962.

Lingat, R. *The Classical Law of India.* Trans., J.D.M. Derrett. Berkeley: University of California Press, 1973.

Ludden, David. *Peasant History in South India.* Princeton: Princeton University Press, 1985.

McLane, John R. *Indian Nationalism and the Early Congress.* Princeton: Princeton University Press, 1977.

MacLeod, Roy M. "Scientific Advice for British India: Imperial Perceptions and Administrative Goals, 1898–1923," *Modern Asian Studies* [London], 9, Pt. 3, July 1975, 343–84.

Mahajan, Jagmohan. *The Raj Landscape: British Views of Indian Cities.* New Delhi: Spantech, 1988.

Mahalingam, T.V. *Administration and Social Life under Vijayanagar.* 2 vols. Madras: University of Madras, 1969–75.

Mahalingam, T.V. *Readings in South Indian History.* Delhi: B.R. Publishing, 1977.

Mahalingam, T.V. *South Indian Polity.* 2d ed., rev. Madras: University of Madras, 1967.

Malik, Hafeez. *Sir Sayyid Ahamd Khan and Muslim Modernization in India and Pakistan.* New York: Columbia University Press, 1980.

Mansingh, Surjit. *Historical Dictionary of India.* Asian Historical Dictionaries, No. 20. Lanham, Maryland: Scarecrow, 1996.

Marshall, John Hubert. *Taxila: An Illustrated Account of the Archaeological Excavations Carried Out at Taxila under the Orders of the Government of India Between the Years, 1913 and 1934.* 3 vols. Varanasi: Bhartiya, 1975.

Marshall, P.J. *The New Cambridge History of India, II.2: Bengal: The British Bridgehead: Eastern India, 1740–1828.* Cambridge: Cambridge University Press, 1987.

Marshall, P.J. *Problems of Empire: Britain and India, 1757–1813.* New York: Barnes and Noble, 1968.

Masani, Zaheer. *Indira Gandhi: A Biography.* Farmington, New York: Brown, 1976.

Mayer, Adrian C. "Rulership and Divinity: The Case of the Modern Hindu Princes and Beyond," *Modern Asian Studies* [London], 25, Pt. 4, October 1991, 765–90.

Mehra, Parshotam. *A Dictionary of Modern Indian History, 1707–1947.* New Delhi: Oxford University Press, 1985.

Mehta, Ved. *Portrait of India.* New Haven: Yale University Press, 1993.

Menezes, S.L. *Fidelity and Honour: The Indian Army from the Seventeenth to the Twenty-first Century.* New Delhi: Penguin, 1993.

Menon, Vapal Pangunni. *The Story of the Integration of the Indian States.* Madras: Orient Longman, 1956. Reprint. Madras: Orient Longman, 1985.

Menon, Vapal Pangunni. *The Transfer of Power in India.* Princeton: Princeton University Press, 1957.

Metcalf, Thomas R. *The Aftermath of the Revolt: India, 1857–1870.* Princeton: Princeton University, 1964.

Metcalf, Thomas R. *An Imperial Vision: Indian Architecture and .Britain's Raj.* Berkeley: University of California Press, 1989.

Metcalf, Thomas R. *Modern India: An Interpretive Anthology.* London: Macmillan, 1971.

Metcalf, Thomas R. *The New Cambridge History of India, IV.3: Ideologies of the Raj.* Cambridge: Cambridge University Press, 1994.

Michell, George. *The New Cambridge History of India, VI.1: Architecture and Art of Southern India: Vijayanagara and the Successor States, 1350–1750.* Cambridge: Cambridge University Press, 1995.

Miller, Barbara Stoler. "Presidential Address: Contending Narratives—The Political Life of the Indian Epics," *Journal of Asian Studies,* 50, No. 4, November 1991, 783–92.

Minakshi, C. *Administration and Social Life under the Pallavas.* Madras: University of Madras, 1977.

Minault, Gail. *The Khilafat Movement: Religious Symbolism and Political Mobilization in India.* Studies in Oriental Culture, No. 16. New York: Columbia University Press, 1982.

Mishra, Jayashri. *Social and Economic Conditions under the Imperial Rashtrakutas.* New Delhi: Commonwealth, 1992.

Misra, Satya Swarup. *The Aryan Problem: A Linguistic Approach.* New Delhi: Munshiram Manoharlal, 1992.

Moon, Penderel. *The British Conquest and Dominion of India.* London: Duckworth, 1989.

Moon, Penderel. *Divide and Quit.* London: Chatto and Windus, 1961.

Moore, R.J. *Crisis of Indian Unity, 1917–1940.* London: Oxford University Press, 1974.

Moraes, Dom. *Indira Gandhi.* Boston: Little, Brown, 1980.

Moreland, W.H. *India at the Death of Akbar, 1: An Economic Study.* N.p.: 1920. Reprint. Delhi: Atma Ram, 1962.

Morris-Jones, W.H. *The Government and Politics of India.* London: Hutchinson, 1971.

Mukhia, Harbans. *Perspectives on Medieval History.* New Delhi: Vikas, 1993.

Nanda, B.R. *The Indo-Greeks.* Oxford: Clarendon Press, 1957.

Nanda, B.R. "The Kushana State: A Preliminary Study." Pages 251–74 in Henri J. Claessen and Peter Skalnik, eds., *The Study of the State.* The Hague: Mouton, 1981.

Nanda, B.R. *Mahatma Gandhi.* Boston: Beacon Press, 1958.

Nanda, B.R. "Religious Policy and Toleration in Ancient India." Pages 17–52 in Bardwell L. Smith, ed., *Essays on Gupta Culture.* Delhi: Motilal Banarsidass, 1983.

Narain, Harsh. *The Ayodhya Temple Mosque Dispute.* New Delhi: Penman, 1993.

Narashimhan, C.R. *Rajagopalachar: A Biography.* New Delhi: Radiant, 1993.

Nayar, Kuldip, and Kushwant Singh. *Tragedy of Punjab: Operation Bluestar and After.* New Delhi: Vision Books, 1984.

Nehru, Jawaharlal. *Jawaharlal Nehru's Speeches.* 5 vols. New Delhi: Publications Division, Ministry of Information and Broadcasting, 1958–68.

Nehru, Jawaharlal. *Selected Works of Jawaharlal Nehru.* 2d Series. 16 vols. New Delhi: Jawaharlal Memorial Fund, 1988–92.

Nehru, Jawaharlal. *Towards Freedom: An Autobiography.* New York: Day, 1941.

Nelson, David N. *Bibliography of South Asia.* Scarecrow Area Bibliographies, No. 4. Metuchen, New Jersey: Scarecrow, 1994.

Nilakanta Sastri, Killidaikurchi Aiyah Aiyar. *The Colas.* 2d ed., rev. University of Madras Historical Series, No. 9. Madras: University of Madras, 1975.

Nilakanta Sastri, Kallidaikurchi Aiyah Aiyar. *History of South India from Prehistoric Times to the Fall of Vijayanagar.* 4th ed. Madras: Oxford University Press, 1976.

Noble, Allen G., and Ashok K. Dutt, eds. *India: Cultural Patterns and Processes.* Boulder, Colorado: Westview Press, 1982.

Nugent, Nicholas. *Rajiv Gandhi: Son of a Dynasty.* New Delhi: UBS, 1991.

Page, David. *Prelude to Partition: The Indian Muslims and the Imperial System of Control, 1920–1932.* Delhi: Oxford University Press, 1982.

Pandey, B.N. *The Break Up of British India.* London: Macmillan, 1969.

Panikkar, K.M. *Asia and Western Dominance.* 2d ed. New York: Collier, 1969.

Park, Richard L., and Bruce Bueno de Mesquita. *India's Political System.* Englewood Cliffs, New Jersey: Prentice-Hall, 1979.

Patnaik, Naveen. *A Second Paradise: Indian Courtly Life, 1590–1947.* Garden City, New Jersey: Doubleday, 1985.

Patterson, Maureen L.P., in collaboration with William J. Alspaugh. *South Asian Civilizations: A Bibliographic Synthesis.* Chicago: University of Chicago Press, 1981.

Paul, John J. *The Legal Profession in Colonial South India.* Bombay: Oxford University Press, 1991.

Paul, John J. "Religion and Medicine in South India: The Scudder Medical Missionaries and the Christian Medical College and Hospital, Vellore," *Fides et Historia,* 22, No. 3, Fall 1990, 16–29.

Pearson, M.N. *Before Colonialism: Theories of Asian-European Relations, 1500–1750.* New Delhi: Oxford University Press, 1988.

Pearson, M.N. *The New Cambridge History of India, I.1: The Portuguese in India.* Cambridge: Cambridge University Press, 1987.

Piggott, Stuart. *Prehistoric India to 1000 B.C.* London: Penguin, 1952.

Possehl, Gregory L., ed. *The Harappan Civilization.* London: Aris and Phillips, 1982.

Possehl, Gregory L., ed. *South Asian Archaeology Studies.* New Delhi: Oxford University Press, 1992.

Powell, Avril Ann. *Muslims and Missionaries in Pre-Mutiny India.* London: Curzon, 1993.

Prasad, Rajeshwar. *Days with Lal Bahadur Shastri.* New Delhi: Allied, 1991.

Qureshi, I.H. *The Muslim Community of the Indo-Pakistan Subcontinent, 1610–1947.* The Hague: Mouton, 1962.

Ramusack, Barbara N. *The Princes of India in the Twilight of Empire: Dissolution of a Patron-Client System, 1914–1939.* Columbus: Ohio State University Press, 1978.

Rangarajan, L.N., trans. and ed. *Kautilya: The Arthasastra.* New York: Penguin, 1992.

Raychaudhuri, Tapan, and Irfan Habib, eds. *The Cambridge Economic History of India, 1: c.1200–c.1750.* Cambridge: Cambridge University Press, 1982.

Richards, J.F. "The Islamic Frontier in the East: Expansion into South Asia," *South Asia* [Nedlands, Australia], No. 4, October 1974, 91–109.

Richards, John F. *The New Cambridge History of India, II.5: The Mughal Empire.* Cambridge: Cambridge University Press, 1993.

Rizvi, S.A.A. *The Wonder That Was India, 2: A Survey of the History and Culture of the Indian Sub-Continent from the Coming of the Muslims to the British Conquest, 1200–1700.* London: Sidgwick and Jackson, 1987.

Robb, Peter G. *The Evolution of British Policy Towards Indian Politics, 1880–1920.* Westwood, Massachusetts: Riverdale, 1992.

Robinson, Francis. *Separatism among Indian Muslims: The Politics of the United Provinces' Muslims, 1860–1932.* Cambridge: Cambridge University Press, 1974.

Robinson, Francis, ed. *The Cambridge Encyclopedia of India, Pakistan, Bangladesh, Sri Lanka, Nepal, Bhutan, and the Maldives.* Cambridge: Cambridge University Press, 1989.

Roy, Asim. "The Politics of India's Partition: The Revisionist Perspective," *Modern Asian Studies* [London], 24, Pt. 2, April 1990, 385–415.

Rudner, David W. *Caste and Colonialism in Colonial India: The Nattukkottai Chettiars.* Berkeley: University of California Press, 1994.

Rustomji, Nari. *Imperilled Frontiers: India's North-Eastern Borderlands.* New Delhi: Oxford University Press, 1983.

Sahasrabuddhe, P.G., and Manik Chandra Vajpayee. *The People Versus Emergency: A Saga of Struggle.* Trans., Sudhakar Raje. New Delhi: Suruchi Prakashan, 1991.

Saksena, N.S. *India: Towards Anarchy, 1967–1992.* New Delhi: Abhinav, 1993.

Sangwan, Satpal. "Science Education in India under Colonial Constraints, 1792–1857," *Oxford Review of Education* [Oxford], 16, No. 1, 1990, 81–95.

Sangwan, Satpal. *Science, Technology, and Colonisation: An Indian Experience, 1757–1857.* New Delhi: Anmika Prakashan, 1991.

Sankaia, H.D. *Aspects of Indian History and Archeology.* Delhi: B.R. Publishing, 1977.

SarDesai, D.R., and Anand Mohan, eds. *The Legacy of Nehru: A Centennial Assessment.* New Delhi: Promilla, 1992.

Sarkar, Jadhunath. *Fall of the Mughal Empire.* 4 vols. Bombay: Orient Longman, 1964–72.

Sarkar, Sumit. *Modern India, 1885–1947.* Delhi: Macmillan, 1983.

Schuhmacher, Stephan, and Gert Woerner, eds. *The Encyclopedia of Eastern Philosophy and Religion.* Boston: Shambhala, 1989.

Schwartzberg, Joseph E., ed. *A Historical Atlas of South Asia.* 2d impression. Reference Series of Association for Asian Studies, No. 2. New York: Oxford University Press, 1992.

Seal, Anil. *The Emergence of Indian Nationalism: Competition and Collaboration in the Late Nineteenth Century.* London: Cambridge University Press, 1968.

Sen Gupta, Bhabani. *Communism in Indian Politics.* New York: Columbia University Press, 1972.

Sen, S.P., ed. *Dictionary of National Biography.* 4 vols. Calcutta: Institute of Historical Studies, 1975.

Sen, S.P., ed. *Sources of the History of India.* Calcutta: Institute of Historical Studies, 1978.

Seshan, N.K. *With Three Prime Ministers: Nehru, Indira, and Rajiv.* New Delhi: Wiley-Eastern, 1993.

Sewell, Robert. *A Forgotten Empire: Vijayanagar.* London: Sonnenschein, 1900.

Sharma, Kususm. *Ambedkar and Indian Constitution.* New Delhi: Ashish, 1992.

Sharma, Ram Sharman. *Ancient India.* New Delhi: National Council of Educational Research and Training, 1977.

Sharma, Ram Sharman. *Aspects of Political Ideas and Institutions in Ancient India.* 2d ed. Delhi: Motilal Banarsidass, 1968.

Sharma, Ram Sharman. *Indian Feudalism: c. 300–1200.* Calcutta: University of Calcutta Press, 1965.

Sharma, Ram Sharman. *Light on Early Indian Society and Economy.* Bombay: Manaktalas, 1966.

Sharma, Ram Sharman, ed. *Land Revenue in Ancient India: Historical Studies.* Delhi: Motilal Banarsidass, 1971.

Sharma, Ramesh Chandra, Atul Kumar Singh, Sugam Anand, Gyaneshwar Chaturvedi, and Jayati Chaturvedi. *Historiography and Historians in India since Independence.* Agra: M.G. Publishers, 1991.

Shourie, Arun. *Indian Controversies: Essays on Religion in Politics.* New Delhi: Manohar, 1993.

Shourie, Arun. *Symptoms of Fascism.* New Delhi: Vikas, 1978.

Singh, Birendra Kumar. *Early Chalukyas of Vatapi, circa A.D. 500 to 757.* Delhi: Eastern Book Linkers, 1991.

Singh, Gopal. *A History of the Sikh People, 1469–1978.* New Delhi: World Sikh University Press, 1979.

Singh, Harbans. *The Heritage of the Sikhs.* Columbia, Missouri: South Asia Books, 1983.

Singh, Mahendra Prasad, ed. *Lok Sabha Elections 1989: Indian Politics in 1990's.* New Delhi: Kalinga, 1992.

Singh, Patwant, and Harji Malik, eds. *Punjab: The Fatal Miscalculation.* New Delhi: Patwant Singh, 1985.

Singh, Surinder Nihal. *Rocky Road of Indian Democracy: Nehru to Narasimha Rao.* New Delhi: Sterling, 1993.

Sisson, Richard, and Stanley Wolpert, eds. *Congress and Indian Nationalism: The Pre-Independence Phase.* Berkeley: University of California Press, 1988.

Sitaramayya, B. Pattabhi. *History of the Indian National Congress.* 2 vols. Bombay: Padma, 1947.

Smith, Bardwell L., ed. *Essays on Gupta Culture.* Delhi: Motilal Banarsidass, 1983.

Smith, Donald E. *India as a Secular State.* Princeton: Princeton University Press, 1963.

Smith, Vincent, ed. *The Oxford History of India.* 4th ed. New Delhi: Oxford University Press, 1981.

South Asian Handbook: India and the Indian Sub-Continent, 1993. 2d ed. Ed., Robert W. Bradnock. Bath, United Kingdom: Trade and Travel, 1992.

Spate, O.H.K., A.T.A. Learmonth, A.M. Learmonth, and B.H. Farmer. *India and Pakistan: A General and Regional Geography with a Chapter on Ceylon.* 3d ed., rev. London: Methuen, 1967.

Spear, Thomas George Percival. *A History of India, 2.* Baltimore: Penguin, 1965.

Spear, Thomas George Percival, ed. *The Oxford History of Modern India, 1740–1975.* 2d ed. New Delhi: Oxford University Press, 1978.

Spencer, George W. "The Politics of Plunder: The Cholas in Eleventh Century Ceylon," *Journal of Asian Studies,* 35, No. 3, August 1976, 405–19.

Srivastava, Ramesh Chandra. *Judicial System in India.* Lucknow: Print House (India), 1992.

Stein, Burton. *The New Cambridge History of India, I. 2: Vijayanagara.* Cambridge: Cambridge University Press, 1989.

Stein, Burton, ed. *Essays on South India.* Honolulu: University Press of Hawaii, 1975.

Stein, Burton, ed. *Peasant, State, and Society in Medieval South India.* New Delhi: Oxford University Press, 1980.

Stein, Burton, ed. *Thomas Munro: The Origins of the Colonial State and His Vision of Empire.* New Delhi: Oxford University Press, 1989.

Stern, Robert W. *Changing India: Bourgeois Revolution on the Subcontinent.* New York: Cambridge University Press, 1993.

Subrahmanyam, Sanjay. *The Political Economy of Commerce: Southern India, 1500–1650.* Cambridge: Cambridge University Press, 1990.

Subramaniam, Chitra. *Bofors: The Story Behind the News.* New Delhi: Viking, 1993.

Tahseen, Rana. *Education and Modernisation of Muslims in India.* New Delhi: Deep and Deep, 1993.

Talwar, S.N. *Under the Banyan Tree: The Communist Movement in India, 1920–1964.* New Delhi: Allied, 1985.

Tambiah, Stanley J. "Presidential Address: Reflections on Communal Violence in South Asia," *Journal of Asian Studies,* 49, No. 4, November 1990, 741–60.

Tandon, Prakash. *Punjabi Century, 1857–1947.* Berkeley: University of California Press, 1968.

Tarn, W.W. *The Greeks in Bactria and India.* Cambridge: Cambridge University Press, 1951.

Taylor, Jay. *The Dragon and the Wild Goose: China and India, with New Epilogue.* New York: Praeger, 1991.

Taylor, P.J.O. *Chronicles of the Mutiny and Other Historical Sketches.* New Delhi: Indus, 1992.

Thapar, Romesh. *These Troubled Times.* Bombay: Popular Prakashan, 1986.

Thapar, Romila. *Ashoka and the Decline of the Mauryas.* London: Oxford University Press, 1961.

Thapar, Romila. *From Lineage to State: Social Formations in the Mid-First Millennium B.C. in the Ganga Valley.* New Delhi: Oxford University Press, 1984.

Thapar, Romila. *A History of India, 1.* Baltimore: Penguin, 1965.

Thapar, Romila. *Indian Tales.* New Delhi: Puffin Books, 1991.

Thapar, Romila. *Interpreting Early India.* New Delhi: Oxford University Press, 1992.

Thapar, Romila. "The State as Empire." Pages 409–28 in Henry J. Claessen and Peter Skalnik, eds., *The Study of the State.* The Hague: Mouton, 1981.

Thompson, Edward. *The Making of the Indian Princes.* London: Oxford University Press, 1943. Reprint. Columbia, Missouri: South Asia Books, 1980.

Thurston, Edgar. *Caste and Tribes of Southern India.* 7 vols. Madras: Government Press, 1909.

Tolkappiyar. *Tolkappiam.* Trans., E.S. Varadaraja Iyer. 2d ed. Annamalainagar: Annamalai University, 1987.

Tomlinson, B.R. *The New Cambridge History of India, III.3: The Economy of Modern India, 1860–1970.* Cambridge: Cambridge University Press, 1993.

Trautmann, Thomas R. *Dravidian Kinship.* Cambridge Studies in Social Anthropology. New York: Cambridge University Press, 1981.

Trautmann, Thomas R. *Kautilya and the Arthasastra: A Statistical Study.* Leiden: Brill, 1971.

Trevelyan, Raleigh. *The Golden Oriole: A 200-year History of an English Family in India.* A Touchstone Book. New York: Simon and Schuster, 1988.

Tully, Mark. *India: Forty Years of Independence.* New York: Braziller, 1988.

Tully, Mark, and Satish Jacob. *Amritsar: Mrs. Gandhi's Last Battle.* London: Cape, 1985.

United Nations. Legal Department. *Statement of Treaties and International Agreements Registered or Filed and Recorded with the Secretariat, 548.* New York: 1965.

United Nations. Legal Department. *Statement of Treaties and International Agreements Registered or Filed and Recorded with the Secretariat, 560.* New York: 1966.

Venkataramanayya, N. *The Eastern Calukyas of Vengi.* Madras: Vedam Venkataray Sastry, 1950.

Vincent, Rose, ed. *The French in India: From Diamond Traders to Sanskrit Scholars.* Trans., Latika Padgaonkar. Bombay: Popular Prakashan, 1990.

Washbrook, David A. *The Emergence of Provincial Politics: The Madras Presidency, 1870–1920.* Cambridge: Cambridge University Press, 1976.

Washbrook, David A. "South Asia, The World System, and World Capitalism," *Journal of Asian Studies,* 49, No. 3, August 1990, 479–508.

Wheeler, Robert Eric Mortimer. *Civilization of the Indus Valley and Beyond.* New York: McGraw-Hill, 1966.

Wheeler, Robert Eric Mortimer. *Early India and Pakistan: To Ashoka.* Rev. ed. Ancient Peoples and Places, No. 12. New York: Praeger, 1968.

Who Are the Guilty? Report of a Joint Inquiry into the Causes and Impact of the Riots in Delhi from 31 October to 10 November, 1984. 2d ed. New Delhi: People's Union for Democratic Rights and People's Union for Civil Liberties, 1984.

Wink, André. *Al-Hind, the Making of the Indo-Islamic World, 1: Early Medieval India and the Expansion of Islam, 7th–11th Centuries.* 2d. ed., rev. Leiden: Brill, 1991.

Wolpert, Stanley. *India.* Berkeley: University of California Press, 1991.

Wolpert, Stanley. *Jinnah of Pakistan.* New York: Oxford University Press, 1984.

Wolpert, Stanley. *Nehru: A Tryst with Destiny.* New York: Oxford University Press, 1996.

Wolpert, Stanley. *A New History of India.* 4th ed. New York: Oxford University Press, 1992.

Wolpert, Stanley. *Tilak and Gokhale: Revolution and Reform in the Making of Modern India.* Cambridge: Cambridge University, 1962. Reprint. Delhi: Oxford University Press, 1989.

Woodruff, Philip (pseud.). *The Men Who Ruled India, 2: The Founders.* London: Cape, 1963.

Zimmer, Heinrich. *The Art of Indian Asia.* New York: Pantheon, 1955.

Chapter 2

Aggarwal, J.C. *Census of India, 1991: Historical and World Perspective.* New Delhi: Sultan Chand, 1991.

Aggarwal, J.C. *National Policy on Education: Agenda for India 2001.* New Delhi: Concept, 1989.

Aggarwal, J.C., and Sarita Aggarwal. *Education in India: A Comparative Study of States and Union Territories.* New Delhi: Concept, 1990.

Association of Commonwealth Universities. *Commonwealth Universities Yearbook, 1990, 3.* London: 1990.

Baxi, Upendra, and Bhikhu Parekh, eds. *Crisis and Change in Contemporary India.* New Delhi: Sage, in association with The Book Review Literary Trust, New Delhi, 1995.

Bhambhri, C.P. "Constitutional, Educational, and Inherited Social Imbalances." Pages 1–9 in Sheel C. Nuna, ed., *Regional Disparity in Educational Development.* New Delhi: National Institute of Educational Planning and Administration, 1993.

Blaustein, Albert P., ed. "India Supplement," *Constitutions of the Countries of the World, 10.* Dobbs Ferry, New York: Oceana, April 1989.

Blaustein, Albert P., and Gisbert Flanz, eds. "India," *Constitutions of the Countries of the World, 10.* Dobbs Ferry, New York: Oceana, October 1990.

Bos, Eduard, Patience W. Stephens, My T. Vu, and Rodolfo A. Bulatao. *Asia Region Population Projections, 1990–91 Edition.* Working Paper Series, No. 599. Washington: Population and Human Resources Department, World Bank, February 1991.

Bos, Eduard, My T. Vu, Ann Levin, and Rodolfo A. Bulatao. *World Population Projections, 1992–93 Edition.* Baltimore: Johns Hopkins University Press, 1992, for the World Bank.

Bose, Ashish. *India's Urban Population. 1991 Census Data: States, Districts, Cities, and Towns.* New Delhi: Wheeler, 1994.

Bose, Ashish. *Population of India: 1991 Census Results and Methodology.* Delhi: B.R. Publishing, 1991.

Caldwell, John C., Pat Caldwell, and P.H. Reddy. *The Causes of Demographic Change: Experimental Research in South Asia.* Madison: University of Wisconsin Press, 1988.

Central Board for the Prevention and Control of Water Pollution. *River Basin Atlas of India.* Calcutta: Center for Study of Man and Environment, Department of Geology, President College, 1985.

Chapman, Graham P. "Change in the South Asian Core: Patterns of Growth and Stagnation in India." Pages 10–43 in Graham P. Chapman and Kathleen M. Baker, eds., *The Changing Geography of Asia.*London: Routledge, 1992.

Durvasula, Ramesh. "Occupational Health Information Systems in India." Pages 103–34 in Michael R. Reich and Toshiteru Okubo, eds., *Protecting Workers' Health in the Third World: National and International Strategies.* 4th Takemi Symposium on International Health, 1990. New York: Auburn House, 1992.

Dwivedi, O.P., and Renu Khator. "India's Environmental Policy, Programs, and Politics." Pages 47–69 in O.P. Dwivedi and Dhirendra K. Vajpeyi, eds., *Environmental Policies of the Third World: A Comparative Analysis.* Contributions in Political Science, No. 350. Westport, Connecticut: Greenwood, 1995.

Eaton, David J., ed. *The Ganges-Brahmaputra Basin: Water Resource Cooperation Between Nepal, India, and Bangladesh.* Austin: Lyndon B. Johnson School of Public Affairs, University of Texas at Austin, 1992.

Fisher, William C., ed. *Working Toward Sustainable Development: The Narmada Dam Project.* Armonk, New York: Sharpe, 1994.

Gadgil, Madhav, and Ramachandra Guha. *This Fissured Land: An Ecological History of India.* Berkeley: University of California Press, 1993.

Ghosh, Suresh Chandra. *Education Policy in India since Warren Hastings.* Calcutta: Naya Prokash, 1989.

Gillespie, Stuart, and Geraldine McNeill. *Food, Health, and Survival in India and Developing Countries.* Delhi: Oxford University Press, 1992.

Griffin, Charles C. *Health Care in Asia: A Comparative Study of Cost and Financing.* World Bank Regional and Sectoral Studies. Washington: World Bank, 1992.

Hindustan Year Book and Who's Who, 1992. 60th ed. Ed., S. Sarkar. Calcutta: M.C. Sarkar, 1992.

Hindustan Year Book and Who's Who, 1994. 62d ed. Ed., S. Sarkar. Calcutta: M.C. Sarkar, 1994.

India. Meteorological Department. *Climatological Atlas of India.* New Delhi: 1981.

India. Ministry of Home Affairs. Registrar General and Census Commissioner. *Census of India, 1991: Final Population Totals: Brief Analysis of Primary Census Abstract, Series–1, Paper–2 of 1992.* New Delhi: 1993.

India. Ministry of Home Affairs. Registrar General and Census Commissioner. *Census of India, 1991: Final Population Totals, Series–1, Paper–1 of 1992, 1.* New Delhi: 1993.

India. Ministry of Home Affairs. Registrar General and Census Commissioner. *Census of India, 1991: Final Population Totals, Series–1, Paper–1 of 1992, 2.* New Delhi: 1993.

India. Ministry of Home Affairs. Registrar General and Census Commissioner. *Census of India, 1991: Provisional Population Totals: Workers and Their Distribution, Series–1, Paper–3 of 1991.* New Delhi: November 1991.

India. Ministry of Home Affairs. Registrar General and Census Commissioner. *Census of India, 1991: Provisional Population Totals, Series–1, Paper–1 of 1991.* New Delhi: March 1991.

India. Ministry of Home Affairs. Registrar General and Census Commissioner. *Census of India, 1991: Provisional Population Totals: Rural-Urban Distribution, Series–1, Paper–2 of 1991.* New Delhi: August 1991.

India. Ministry of Home Affairs. Registrar General and Census Commissioner. *Census of India, 1991: Religion, Series–1, Paper–1 of 1995.* New Delhi: January 1995.

India. Ministry of Information and Broadcasting. Research and Reference Division. *India: A Reference Annual, 1988–89.* New Delhi: December 1989.

India. Ministry of Information and Broadcasting. Research and Reference Division. *India 1992: A Reference Annual.* New Delhi: February 1993.

India. Ministry of Information and Broadcasting. Research and Reference Division. *India 1993: A Reference Annual.* New Delhi: January 1994.

India. Ministry of Planning. Department of Statistics. Central Statistical Organisation. *Statistical Abstract 1990, India.* New Delhi: 1990.

India. Ministry of Planning. Department of Statistics. Central Statistical Organisation. *Statistical Pocket Book, 1990.* New Delhi: 1991.

India. Ministry of Planning, Department of Statistics. Central Statistical Organisation. *Statistical Pocket Book, 1991.* New Delhi: 1992.

"India." Pages 294–356 in *The Far East and Australasia, 1995.* 26th ed. London: Europa, 1995.

Jeffery, Roger. *The Politics of Health in India.* Comparative Studies of Health Systems and Medical Care, No. 21. Los Angeles: University of California Press, 1988.

Kaifi, Abdul Khaliq. *Socio-Economic Determinants of Health Systems in India under the Aspect of Colonial Structures.* Frankfurt: R.G. Fischer Verlag, 1991.

Katiyar, V.S. *The Indian Monsoon and Its Frontiers.* New Delhi: Inter-India, 1990.

Kohli, Shanta. *Family Planning in India: A Descriptive Analysis.* New Delhi: Indian Institute of Public Administration, 1977.

Kuriyan, George. *India: A General Survey.* New Delhi: National Book Trust, India, 1990.

Ledbetter, Rosanna. "Thirty Years of Family Planning in India," *Asian Survey,* 24, No. 7, July 1984, 736–58.

Livernash, Robert. "The Future of Populous Economies: China and India Shape Their Destinies," *Environment,* 37, No. 6, July–August 1995, 6–11, 25–34.

Mamoria, C.B. *Geography of India.* Agra: Shiva Lal Agarwala, 1975.

Mathur, V.S. *Studies in Indian Education.* New Delhi: Arya Book Depot, 1968.

Mehta, Jayshree P. "The Health Scenario in India." Pages 280–94 in Upendra Baxi and Bhikhu Parekh, eds., *Crisis and Change in Contemporary India.* New Delhi: Sage, 1995.

Misra, Bhaskar D., Ali Ashraf, Ruth S. Simmons, and George B. Simmons. *Organization for Change: A Systems Analysis of Family Planning in Rural India.* New Delhi: Family Planning Association, 1982.

Mukherjee, Dilip. "The Struggle for Literacy in Asia," *UNESCO Features* [Paris], No. 764, 1981, 20–23.

Mukherjee, Sudhansu Bhusan. *The Age Distribution of the Indian Population: A Reconstruction for the States and Territories, 1881–1961.* Honolulu: East-West Population Institute, East-West Center, 1976.

Mundle, Sudipto. "Recent Trends in the Condition of Children in India: A Statistical Profile," *World Development* [London], 12, No. 3, 1984, 297–308.

Muthiah, S., ed. *A Social and Economic Atlas of India.* Oxford: Oxford, University Press, 1987.

Narayana, G., and Kantner, J.F. *Doing the Needful: The Dilemma of India's Population Policy.* Boulder, Colorado: Westview Press, 1992.

National Council of Educational Research and Training. *Fifth All-India Educational Survey.* 2 vols. New Delhi: March 1992.

National Institute of Educational Planning and Administration. *Education for All by 2000: Indian Perspective.* New Delhi: March 1990.

Ngapal, Smita. "Demographic Situation in India in 1991," *Asian Profile* [Hong Kong], 22, No. 2, April 1994, 161–74.

Parry, Clive, ed. and annotator. *The Consolidated Treaty Series, 220: 1914–1915.* Dobbs Ferry, New York: Oceana, 1980.

Platt, Raye R., ed. *India: A Compendium.* New York: American Geographical Society, 1962.

Population Reference Bureau. *1992 World Population Data Sheet of the Population Reference Bureau, Inc.: Demographic Data and Estimates for Countries and Regions of the World.* Washington: 1992.

Pravin, Anand, and Albert P. Blaustein, eds. "India Supplement," *Constitutions of the Countries of the World, 10.* Dobbs Ferry, New York: Oceana, January 1992.

Premi, Mahendra K. *India's Population: Heading Towards a Billion.* Delhi: B.R. Publishing, 1991.

Prescott, John Robert Victor. *Map of Mainland Asia by Treaty.* Carlton: Melbourne University Press, 1975.

Raina, B.L. *Population Policy.* Delhi: B.R. Publishing, 1988.

Ramakrishna, Rao D.V.L.N., and R.C. Sharma, eds. *India's Borders, Ecology, and Security Perspectives.* New Delhi: Scholars' Publishing Forum, 1991.

Reich, Michael R., and Toshiteru Okuba, eds. *Protecting Workers' Health in the Third World: National and International Strategies.* New York: Auburn House, 1992.

Robinson, Francis, ed. *The Cambridge Encyclopedia of India, Pakistan, Bangladesh, Sri Lanka, Nepal, Bhutan, and the Maldives.* Cambridge: Cambridge University Press, 1989.

Rouyer, Alwyn R. "The Political System and the Determinants of Family Planning Program Performance and Fertility Decline in India." Paper presented at the Annual Meeting of the American Political Science Association, Washington, D.C., September 1984.

Roy, S. Guha. "Demographic Trends in China and India," *China Report* [New Delhi], 30, No. 1, January–March 1994, 1–18.

Saroj Prashant. *Drug Abuse and Society.* New Delhi: Ashish, 1993.

Scalisi, Philip, and David Cook. *Classic Mineral Localities of the World: Asia and Australia.* New York: Van Nostrand Reinhold, 1983.

Schwartzberg, Joseph E. "An American Perspective II," *Asian Affairs*, 22, No. 1, Spring 1995, 71–87.

Schwartzberg, Joseph E., ed. *A Historical Atlas of South Asia.* 2d impression. Reference Series of Association for Asian Studies, No. 2. New York: Oxford University Press, 1992.

Singh, Gopal. *A Geography of India.* Delhi: Atma Ram, 1976.

Singhvi, A.K., and Amal Kar, eds. *Thar Desert in Rajasthan: Land, Man, and Environment.* Bangalore: Geological Society of India, 1991.

Tan, Jee-pang, and Alain Mingat. *Education in Asia: A Comparative Study of Cost and Financing.* World Bank Regional and Sectoral Studies. Washington: World Bank, 1992.

Tata Services. Department of Economics and Statistics. *Statistical Outline of India, 1988–89.* 16th ed. Ed., B.S. Gupta. Bombay: 1988.

Tata Services. Department of Economics and Statistics. *Statistical Outline of India, 1992–93.* 20th ed. Ed., B.S. Gupta. Bombay: 1992.

Tata Services. Department of Economics and Statistics. *Statistical Outline of India, 1994–95.* 21st ed. Ed., B.S. Gupta. Bombay: 1994.

Tirtha, Ranjit, and Gopal Krishan. *Emerging India: A Geographical Introduction.* 2d ed. Ann Arbor: Conpub, 1992.

Tyagi, P.N. *Education for All: A Graphic Presentation.* New Delhi: National Institute of Educational Planning and Administration, August 1991.

United Nations. Department of International Economic and Social Affairs, Statistical Office. *1990 Demographic Yearbook.* 42d ed. New York: 1992.

United Nations. Department of International Economic and Social Affairs. *World Population Monitoring 1991: With Special Emphasis on Age Structure.* Population Studies, No. 126. ST/ESA/SER.A/126. New York: 1992.

United Nations. Economic and Social Commission for Asia and the Pacific. Population Division. "1993 ESCAP Population Data Sheet." Bangkok: 1993.

United Nations Educational, Scientific, and Cultural Organization. Principal Regional Office for Asia and the Pacific. *National Studies: India.* Asia-Pacific Program of Education for All Series. Bangkok: 1991.

United Nations Educational, Scientific, and Cultural Organization. Principal Regional Office for Asia and the Pacific. *Simultaneous Education for Women and Girls: Report of a Project.* Asia-Pacific Program of Education for All Series. Bangkok: 1989.

United States. Bureau of the Census. *World Population Profile: 1994.* Washington: February 1994.

United States. Central Intelligence Agency. *Handbook of International Economic Statistics.* CPAS 94–1001. Washington: September 1994.

United States. Central Intelligence Agency. *World Factbook, 1995.* Washington: 1995.

United States. Congress. 102d, 1st Session. House of Representatives. International AIDS Task Force. *Report to the Speaker of the House of Representatives: The AIDS Epidemic in Asia.* Washington: GPO, 1991.

United States. Department of Commerce. Economics and Statistics Administration. Bureau of the Census. "Global Aging: Comparative Indicators and Future Trends." (Chart) Washington: September 1991.

United States. Department of Commerce. Economics and Statistics Administration. Bureau of the Census. *World Demographic Data: 1994.* WP/94–DD. Washington: February 1994.

United States. Department of Commerce. Economics and Statistics Administration. Bureau of the Census. *World Population Profile: 1994*. Comps., Ellen Jamison and Frank Hobbs. WP/94. Washington: February 1994.

United States. Department of State. *Country Reports on Human Rights Practices for 1993*. Report submitted to United States Congress, 103d, 2d Session, House of Representatives, Committee on Foreign Affairs, and Senate, Committee on Foreign Relations. Washington: GPO, February 1994.

Uplekar, Mukund. "Private Doctors and Occupational Health in India." Pages 134–54 in Michael R. Reich and Toshiteru Okubo, eds., *Protecting Workers' Health in the Third World: National and International Strategies*. 4th Takemi Symposium on International Health, 1990. New York: Auburn House, 1992.

Verghese, B.G. *Integrated Water Resources Development and Regional Cooperation Within the Himalayan-Ganga-Brahmaputra-Barak Basin*. New Delhi: Oxford University Press and IBH, 1990.

Verghese, B.G., and Ramaswamy R. Iyer, eds. *Harnessing the Eastern Himalayan Rivers: Regional Cooperation in South Asia*. New Delhi: Centre for Policy Research, 1993.

Vittal Rao, Y. *Education and Learning in Andhra under the East India Company*. Secunderabad: M. Vidyaranya Swamy, 1979.

Weiner, Myron. *The Child and the State in India: Child Labor and Education Policy in Comparative Perspective*. Princeton: Princeton University Press, 1991.

World Bank. Population and Human Resources Division. South Asia Country Department II. *India: Policy and Finance Strategies for Strengthening Primary Health Care Services*. Report No. 10342–IN. Washington: May 15, 1995.

The World of Learning, 1995. 45th ed. London: Europa, 1994.

"World Population Data Sheet of the Population Reference Bureau, Inc." Washington: 1992.

Yadava, Surendar S., and James G. Chadney. "Female Education, Modernity, and Fertility in India," *Journal of Asian and Africa Studies* [Leiden], 29, Nos. 1–2, January–April 1994, 110–19.

Zachariah, Matthew. "The Durability of Academic Secondary Education in India," *Comparative Education Review*, 14, No. 2, June 1970, 152–61.

(Various issues of the following publications also were used in the preparation of this chapter: *Asiaweek* [Hong Kong], 1993; *Far Eastern Economic Review* [Hong Kong], 1993–94; Foreign Broadcast Information Service, *Daily Report: Near East and South Asia*, 1993–94; *Man and Development* [Chandigarh], 1993; *Nature*, 1993; *New Scientist* [London], 1991; *New York Times*, 1994; and *Washington Post*, 1994.)

Chapter 3

Agrawal, S.P., and J.C. Aggarwal, eds. *Information India: 1991– 92, Global View.* Concepts in Communication, Informatics, and Librarianship, No. 47. New Delhi: Concept, 1993.

Agwani, Mohammed S. "God's Government: Jama'at-i-Islami of India." Pages 259–77 in Hussin Mutalib and Taj ul-Islam Hashmi, eds., *Islam, Muslims, and the Modern State: Case Studies of Muslims in Thirteen Countries.* New York: St. Martin's Press, 1994.

Agwani, Mohammed S. *Islamic Fundamentalism in India.* Chandigarh: Twenty-First Century India Society, 1986.

Ahir, D.C. *Buddhism in Modern India.* Delhi: Sri Satguru, 1991.

Ahmad, Aijuzuddin. *Muslims in India: Their Educational, Demographic, and Socio-Economic Status with Inter-Community Comparisons Based on Field Survey Conducted in 1991.* New Delhi: Inter-India, 1993.

Alston, A.J. *The Devotional Poems of Mirabai.* Delhi: Motilal Banarsidass, 1980.

Anand, Balwant Singh. *Guru Tegh Bahadur: A Biography.* New Delhi: Sterling, 1979.

Andersen, Walter K., and Shridhar D. Damle. *The Brotherhood in Saffron: The Rashtriya Swayamsevak Sangh and Hindu Revivalism.* Boulder, Colorado: Westview Press, 1987.

Aprem, Mar. *Indian Christian Directory.* Bangalore: Bangalore Parish Church of the East, 1984.

Babb, Lawrence A. *The Divine Hierarchy: Popular Hinduism in Central India.* New York: Columbia University Press, 1975.

Babb, Lawrence A. *Redemptive Encounters: Three Modern Styles in Hindu Tradition.* Berkeley: University of California Press, 1986.

Banu, Zenab. *Politics of Communalism.* Bombay: Popular Prakashan, 1989.

Basham, A.L. *The Origin and Development of Classical Hinduism.* Ed. and completed by Kenneth G. Zysk. New York: Oxford University Press, 1989.

Baxi, Upendra, and Bhikhu Parekh, eds. *Crisis and Change in Contemporary India.* New Delhi: Sage, in association with The Book Review Literary Trust, New Delhi, 1995.

Bharati, Agehananda. *The Ochre Robe.* London: Allen and Unwin, 1961.

Bharati, Agehananda. *The Tantric Tradition.* London: Rider, 1965.

Bhardwaj, Surinder Mohan. *Hindu Places of Pilgrimage in India: A Study in Cultural Geography.* Berkeley: University of California Press, 1973.

Bhargava, Rajeev. "Religious and Secular Identities." Pages 317–49 in Upendra Baxi and Bhikhu Parekh, eds., *Crisis and Change in Contemporary India.* New Delhi: Sage, 1995.

Bloomfield, Maurice, ed. and trans. *Hymns of the Atharva-Veda.* London: Clarendon Press, 1897. Reprint. London: Oxford University Press, 1978.

Brandt, Michael. "A New Hindu Goddess," *Hemisphere* [Woden, Australia], 26, No. 6, May–June 1982, 380–84.

Brockington, J.L. *The Sacred Thread: Hinduism in Its Continuity and Diversity.* Edinburgh: Edinburgh University Press, 1981.

Caplan, Lionel. *Class and Culture in Urban India: Fundamentalism in a Christian Community.* New York: Oxford University Press, 1987.

Carrithers, Michael, and Caroline Humphrey, eds. *The Assembly of Listeners: Jains in Society.* Cambridge: Cambridge University Press, 1991.

Catholic Bishops' Conference of India. *The Catholic Directory of India, 1990.* New Delhi: 1990.

Cenkner, William. *A Tradition of Teachers: Sankara and the Jagadgurus Today.* Delhi: Motilal Banarsidass, 1983.

Champakalakshmi, R. *Vaisnava Iconography in the Tamil Country.* New Delhi: Orient Longman, 1981.

Chopra, V.D., R.K. Mishra, and Nirmal Singh. *Agony of Punjab.* New Delhi: Patriot, 1984.

Cole, W. Owen, and Piara Singh Sambhi. *The Sikhs: Their Religious Beliefs and Practices.* London: Routledge and Kegan Paul, 1978.

Contursi, Janet A. "Political Theology: Text and Practice in a Dalit Panther Community," *Journal of Asian Studies,* 52, No. 2, May 1993, 320–39.

Courtright, Paul. *Ganesa: Lord of Obstacles, Lord of Beginnings.* New York: Oxford University Press, 1985.

Das, Veena. "Shakti Versus Sati: A Reading of the Santoshi Ma Cult," *Manushi* [Delhi], No. 49, November–December 1988, 26–30.

Davids, Thomas William Rhys, trans. *Buddhist Suttas.* Oxford: Clarendon Press, 1881. Reprint. Sacred Books of the East, No. 11. Delhi: Motilal Banarsidass, 1965.

Davis, Richard H. "Indian Art Objects As Loot," *Journal of Asian Studies,* 52, No. 1, February 1993, 22–48.

Desai, Kalpana S. *Iconography of Visnu.* New Delhi: Abhinav, 1973.

Dimmitt, Cornelle, and J.A. van Buttenen, ed. and trans. *Classical Hindu Mythology: A Reader in the Sanskrit Puranas.* Philadelphia: Temple University Press, 1978.

Doniger, Wendy. *Textual Sources for the Study of Hinduism.* Totowa, New Jersey: Barnes and Noble, 1988.

Downs, Frederick S. *Christianity in North East India.* Delhi: Indian Society for Promoting Christian Knowledge, 1983.

Dundas, Paul. *The Jains.* Library of Religious Beliefs and Practices. New York: Routledge, 1992.

Dutt, Sukumar. *Buddhist Monks and Monasteries of India.* London: Allen and Unwin, 1962.

Eaton, Richard M. *The Rise of Islam and the Bengal Frontier, 1204–1760.* Comparative Studies on Muslim Societies, No. 17. Berkeley: University of California Press, 1993.

Eaton, Richard M. *Sufis of Bijapur, 1300–1700: Social Roles of Sufis in Medieval India.* Princeton: Princeton University Press, 1978.

Eck, Diana. *Banares: City of Light.* New York: Knopf, 1982.

Embree, Ainslie T. *Utopias in Conflict: Religion and Nationalism in Modern India.* Comparative Studies in Religion and Society. Berkeley: University of California Press, 1990.

Engineer, Ashgar Ali, ed. *Communal Riots in Post-Independence India.* Hyderabad: Sangam, 1984.

Foster, Georgana M. "A Popular North Indian Pilgrimage Site: The Shrine of Vaishno Devi in Jammu." Paper presented at the Conference on Pilgrimage, Pittsburgh, May 1991.

Frith, Nigel. *The Legend of Krishna.* New York: Schocken Books, 1976.

Fürer-Haimendorf, Christoph von. *Tribal Populations and Cultures of the Indian Subcontinent.* Handbuch der Orientalistik. Zweite Abteilung, Indien; 7. Bd. Leiden: Brill, 1985.

Fuller, Christopher J. *Servants of the Goddess: The Priests of a South Indian Temple.* Cambridge: Cambridge University Press, 1984.

Gibb, H.A.R., and J.H. Kramers, eds. *Shorter Encyclopaedia of Islam.* Leiden: Brill, 1974.

Goldman, Robert P., trans. *The Ramayana of Valmiki: An Epic of Ancient India.* Princeton: Princeton University Press, 1984.

Gonda, Jan. *Aspects of Early Visnuism.* Delhi: Motilal Banarsidass, 1969.

Gopal, Sarvepalli, ed. *Anatomy of a Confrontation: The Babri Masjid-Ramjanmabhumi Issue.* New Delhi: Viking, 1991.

Grewel, J.S. *The New Cambridge History of India, II.3: The Sikhs of the Punjab.* Cambridge: Cambridge University Press, 1990.

Gupta, Giri Raj, ed. *Religion in Modern India.* Main Currents in Indian Sociology, No. 5. New Delhi: Vikas, 1983.

Gupta, Sanjukta, Dirk Jan Hoens, and Teun Goudrianan. *Hindu Tantrism.* Leiden: Brill, 1979.

Hanson, James A. *India: Recent Developments and Medium-Term Issues.* A World Bank Country Study. Washington: World Bank, 1989.

Harman, William. *The Sacred Marriage of a Hindu Goddess.* Bloomington: Indiana University Press, 1989.

Harvey, Peter. *An Introduction to Buddhism: Teachings, History, and Practices.* Cambridge: Cambridge University Press, 1990.

Hasnain, Nadeem, and Sheikh Abrar Husain. *Shias and Shia Islam in India: A Study in Society and Culture.* New Delhi: Harnam, 1988.

Hawley, John Stratton. *Krishna, the Butter Thief.* Princeton: Princeton University Press, 1983.

Hawley, John Stratton. *Songs of the Saints of India.* New York: Oxford University Press, 1988.

Hay, Stephen, ed. *Sources of Indian Tradition, 2: Modern India and Pakistan.* 2d ed. Introduction to Oriental Civilizations. New York: Columbia University Press, 1988.

Hembram, P.C. *Sari-Sarna (Santhal Religion).* Delhi: Mittal, 1988.

Hiltebeitel, Alf. *Criminal Gods and Demon Devotees: Essays on the Guardians of Popular Hinduism.* Albany: State University of New York, 1989.

Hiltebeitel, Alf. *The Cult of Draupadi.* Chicago: University of Chicago Press, 1988.

Hiltebeitel, Alf. *The Ritual of Battle: Krishna in the Mahabharata.* Albany: State University of New York Press, 1990.

Hindustan Year Book and Who's Who, 1994. 62d ed. Ed., S. Sarker. Calcutta: M.C. Sarkar, 1994.

Hluna, John V. *Church and Political Upheaval in Mizoram: A Study of the Impact of Christianity on the Political Development in Mizoram.* Aisawl: Mizo History Association, 1985.

Hopkins, Thomas J. *The Hindu Religious Tradition.* Encino, California: Dickenson, 1971.

Hume, Robert Ernest, trans. *The Thirteen Principle Upanishads.* 2d ed., rev. London: Oxford University Press, 1971.

Huntington, Susan L. *The Arts of Ancient India: Buddhist, Hindu, and Jain.* New York: Weatherhill, 1985.

India. Ministry of Home Affairs. Registrar General and Census Commissioner. *Census of India, 1991: Religion, Series–1, Paper–1 of 1995,* New Delhi: January 1995.

Isenberg, Shirley Berry. *India's Bene-Israel: A Comprehensive Inquiry and Sourcebook.* Berkeley: Judah L. Magnes Museum, 1988.

Israel, Benjamin J. *The Bene-Israel of India: Some Studies.* Bombay: Orient Longman, 1984.

Israel, Benjamin J. *The Jews of India.* New Delhi: Centre for Jewish and Inter-Faith Studies, Jewish Welfare Association, 1982.

Jackson, Paul, ed. *The Muslims of India: Beliefs and Practices.* Bangalore: Theological Publications in India, 1988.

Jain, Satish Kumar, and Kamal Chand Sognai. *Perspectives on Jain Philosophy and Culture.* New Delhi: Abhinav, 1985.

Jaini, Padmanabh S. *The Jaina Path of Purification.* Berkeley: University of California Press, 1979.

Jayatilleke, Kulatissa Nanda. *The Message of the Buddha.* New York: Free Press, 1974.

Jha, Prem Shankar. *India: A Political Economy of Stagnation.* Bombay, Oxford University Press, 1980.

Keith, Arthur Berriedale. *The Religion and Philosophy of the Veda and Upanishads.* 2 vols. Cambridge: Harvard University Press, 1925. Reprint. Westport, Connecticut: Greenwood, 1971.

Khare, Ravindra S. *The Hindu Hearth and Home.* Durham, North Carolina: Carolina Academic, 1976.

Kinsley, David R. *Hindu Goddesses: Visions of the Divine Feminine in the Hindu Religious Tradition.* Berkeley: University of California Press, 1988.

Kinsley, David R. *Hinduism: A Cultural Perspective.* Englewood Cliffs, New Jersey: Prentice-Hall, 1982.

Kinsley, David R. *The Sword and the Flute: Kali and Krsna, Dark Visions of the Terrible and the Sublime in Hindu Mythology.* Hermeneutic Studies in the History of Religion, No. 3. Berkeley: University of California Press, 1975.

Knipe, David M. *Hinduism: Experiments in the Sacred.* San Francisco: Harper, 1991.

Kramrisch, Stella. *Manifestations of Shiva.* Philadelphia: Philadelphia Museum of Art, 1981.

Kulke, Eckehard. *The Parsees in India: A Minority as Agent of Social Change.* Munich: Weltforum Verlag, 1974.

Kumar, Akhilesh. *Communal Riots in India: Study of Social and Economic Aspects.* New Delhi: Commonwealth, 1991.

LaMotte, Étienne. *History of Indian Buddhism: From the Origins to the Saka Era.* Trans., Sara Wenn-Boin. Publications de l'institut orientaliste de Louvain, No. 36. Louvain-la-Neuve: Institut orientaliste, Université Catholique de Louvain, 1988.

Ling, Trevor. *Buddhist Revival in India: Aspects of the Sociology of Buddhism.* New York: St. Martin's Press, 1980.

McLeod, W.H. *The Evolution of the Sikh Community.* Delhi: Oxford University Press, 1975.

McLeod, W.H. *Guru Nanak and the Sikh Religion.* Oxford: Clarendon Press, 1968.

McLeod, W.H. *The Sikhs: History, Religion, and Society.* New York: Columbia University Press, 1989.

Madan, T.N. "Whither Indian Secularism?" *Modern Asian Studies* [London], 27, Pt. 3, July 1993, 667–97.

Mallik, Madhusudan. *Introduction to Parsee Religion, Customs, and Ceremonies*. Santiniketan: Visva-Bharati Research Publications Committee, 1980.

Mann, R.S., and Vijoy S. Sahay. *Nature-Man-Spirit Complex in Tribal India*. New Delhi: Concept, 1982.

Metcalf, Barbara D. "Presidential Address: Too Little Too Much: Reflections on Muslims in the History of India," *Journal of Asian Studies*, 54, No. 4, November 1995, 951–67.

Miller, Barbara Stoler, trans. *The Bhagavad-Gita: Krishna's Counsel in Time of War*. New York: Bantam, 1986.

Michell, George. *The Hindu Temple: An Introduction to Its Meaning and Forms*. New Delhi: B.I. Publications, 1977.

Mokashi, D.B. *Palkhi: An Indian Pilgrimage*. Trans., Philip C. Engblom and Eleanor Zelliot. Albany: State University of New York Press, 1987.

Mujib, Muhammad. *The Indian Muslims*. Montreal: McGill University Press, 1967.

Murthy, R. Krishna. *A Study of Tirumala-Tirupati Devasthanams Educational Institutions (Higher Education)*. Tirupati: Tirupati-Tirumala Devasthanam, 1984.

Narasimhan, C.V. *The Mahabharata: An English Version Based on Selected Verses*. New York: Columbia University Press, 1965.

Nayar, Kuldip, and Kushwant Singh. *Tragedy of Punjab: Operation Bluestar and After*. New Delhi: Vision Books, 1984.

Netton, Ian Richard. *A Popular Dictionary of Islam*. Atlantic Highlands, New Jersey: Humanities Press, 1992.

O'Connel, Joseph T., Milton Israel, and Willard G. Oxtoby, eds. *Sikh History and Religion in the Twentieth Century*. New Delhi: Manohar, 1990.

O'Flaherty, Wendy Doniger, ed. and trans. *Hindu Myths: A Sourcebook Translated from the Sanskrit*. Baltimore: Penguin, 1975.

O'Flaherty, Wendy Doniger, ed. and trans. *The Rig Veda: An Anthology*. New York: Penguin, 1981.

Pangborn, Cyrus R. *Zoroastrianism: A Beleaguered Faith*. New Delhi: Vikas, 1982.

Parasuram, T.V. *India's Jewish Heritage*. New Delhi: Sagar, 1982.

Patterson, Maureen L.P., in collaboration with William J. Alspaugh. *South Asian Civilizations: A Bibliographic Synthesis.* Chicago: University of Chicago Press, 1981.

Peterson, Indira Viswanathan. *Poems to Siva: The Hymns of the Tamil Saints.* Princeton: Princeton University Press, 1989.

Prebish, Charles S. *Historical Dictionary of Buddhism.* Metuchen, New Jersey: Scarecrow, 1993.

Raj, A.R. Victor. *The Hindu Connection: Roots of the New Age.* Concordia Scholarship Today Series. St. Louis: Concordia, 1995.

Raj, V. Manuel. *A Santal Theology of Liberation.* New Delhi: Uppal, 1990.

Ramanujan, A.K, trans. *Hymns for the Drowning: Poems for Visnu of Nammalvar.* Princeton: Princeton University Press, 1981.

Religions of India: Hinduism, Jainism, Buddhism, Sikhism, Zorastrianism, Christianity, Islam, and Judaism. New Delhi: Clarion, 1983.

Robinson, Francis, ed. *The Cambridge Encyclopedia of India, Pakistan, Bangladesh, Sri Lanka, Nepal, Bhutan, and the Maldives.* Cambridge: Cambridge University Press, 1989.

Robinson, Richard H., and Willard J. Johnson. *The Buddhist Religion: A Historical Introduction.* Belmont, California: Wadsworth, 1977.

Saha, M.N., and N.C. Lahiri. *History of the Calendar in Different Countries Through the Ages.* New Delhi: Council of Scientific and Industrial Research, 1992.

Sangave, Vilas Adinath. *Jaina Community: A Social Survey.* 2d ed., rev. Bombay: Popular Prakashan, 1980.

Sarma, D.S., trans. *The Upanishads: An Anthology.* Bombay: Bharatiya Vidya Bhavan, 1964.

Schimmel, Annemarie. *Islam in the Indian Subcontinent.* Leiden: Brill, 1980.

Schuhmacher, Stephan, and Gert Woerner, eds. *The Encyclopedia of Eastern Philosophy and Religion.* Boston: Shambhala, 1989.

Sen, Makhan Lal, trans. *The Ramayana of Valmiki.* New Delhi: Munshiram Manoharlal, 1978.

Sethi, V.K. *Kabir: The Weaver of God's Name.* Amritsar: Radha Soami Satsang Beas, 1984.

Shearer, Alistair, and Peter Russell, trans. *The Upanishads*. New York: Harper and Row, 1978. Reprint. Boston: Unwin Paperbacks, 1989.

Shulman, David, trans. *Songs of the Harsh Devotee: The Tevaram of Cuntaramurttinayanar*. Philadelphia: Department of South Asia Regional Studies, University of Pennsylvania, 1990.

Singh, Gopal, trans. *Sri Guru Granth Sahib: An Anthology*. Calcutta: M.P. Birla Foundation, 1989.

Sinha, Abdesh Prasad. *Religious Life in Tribal India: A Case-Study of Dugh Kharia*. New Delhi: Classical, 1989.

Sivaramamurti, C. *Sri Lakshmi in Indian Art and Thought*. New Delhi: Kanak, 1982.

Srivastava, Sushil. *The Disputed Mosque: A Historical Inquiry*. New Delhi: Vistar, 1991.

Stevenson, Margaret Sinclair. *The Rites of the Twice-Born*. London: Oxford University Press, 1920.

Thomas, Edward J. *The Life of Buddha as Legend and History*. London: Routledge and Kegan Paul, 1927.

Timberg, Thomas A., ed. *Jews in India*. New Delhi: Vikas, 1986.

Tisserant, Eugene Cardinal. *Eastern Christianity in India: A History of the Syro-Malabar Church from the Earliest Time to the Present Day*. Trans., E.R. Hambye. London: Longmans, Green, 1957.

Torwesten, Hans. *Vedanta: Heart of Hinduism*. New York: Grove Weidenfeld, 1985.

Troisi, J. *Tribal Religion: Religious Beliefs and Practices among the Santals*. New Delhi: Manohar, 1978.

Troll, Christian W., ed. *Muslim Shrines in India: Their Character, History, and Significance*. Delhi: Oxford University Press, 1989.

Van der Veer, Peter. *Gods on Earth: The Management of Religious Experience and Identity in a North Indian Pilgrimage Center*. Atlantic Highlands, New Jersey: Athlone, 1988.

Van der Veer, Peter. "Playing or Praying: A Sufi Saint's Day in Surat," *Journal of Asian Studies*, 51, No. 3, August 1992, 545–64.

Van der Veer, Peter. *Religious Nationalism: Hindus and Muslims in India*. Berkeley: University of California Press, 1994.

Viswanathan, Lakshmi. *Bharatanatyam: The Tamil Heritage*. Madras: Sri Kala Chakra Trust, 1984.

Waghorne, Joanne Punzo, and Norman Cutler, eds. *Gods of Flesh, Gods of Stone: The Embodiment of Divinity in India.* Chambersburg, Pennsylvania: Anima, 1985.

Worthington, Vivian. *A History of Yoga.* London: Routledge and Kegan Paul, 1982.

Zaehner, Robert Charles. *Hinduism.* 2d ed. New York: Oxford University Press, 1966.

Zvelebil, Kamil V. *The Smile of Murugan: On Tamil Literature of South India.* Leiden: Brill, 1973.

(Various issues of the following publications also were used in the preparation of this chapter: *Far Eastern Economic Review* [Hong Kong], 1993; Foreign Broadcast Information Service, *Daily Report: Near East and South Asia,* 1995; *India Today* [New Delhi], 1992; and *Washington Post,* 1994.)

Chapter 4

Abel, Evelyn. *The Anglo-Indian Community: Survival in India.* Delhi: Chanakya, 1988.

Abraham, Margaret. "Ethnic Identity and Marginality among Indian Jews in Contemporary India," *Ethnic Groups,* 9, No. 1, 1991, 33–60.

Aggarwal, J.C., and Sarita Aggarwal. *Education in India: A Comparative Study of States and Union Territories.* New Delhi: Concept, 1990.

Aggarwal, Santosh. *Three Language Formula: An Educational Problem.* New Delhi: Sian, 1991.

Agnihotri, R. K., and A. L. Khanna. *Second Language Acquisition: Socio-Cultural and Linguistic Aspects of English in India, 1: Research in Applied Linguistics.* New Delhi: Sage, 1994.

Akbar, M.J. *The Siege Within: Challenges to a Nation's Unity.* London: Penguin, 1985.

Andronov, M.S. *Dravidian Languages.* Trans., D.M. Segal. Moscow: Nauka, 1970.

Annamalai, A. "Bilingualism Through Schooling in India," *Indian Journal of Applied Linguistics* [New Delhi], 11, No. 2, June 1985, 65–78.

Annamalai, E., ed. *Bilingualism and Achievement in School.* Mysore: Central Institute of Indian Languages, 1980.

Arnold, Adiss, ed. *Crisis in North East India.* Madras: Gurukul Lutheran Theological College and Research Institute, 1981.

Arslan, Mehdi, and Janaki Rajan, eds. *Communalism in India: Challenge and Response.* New Delhi: Manohar, 1994.

Ashraf, Ali, ed. *Ethnic Identity and National Integration.* New Delhi: Concept, 1994.

Axelrod, Paul. "Cultural and Historical Factors in the Population Decline of the Parsis of India," *Population Studies* [London], 44, No. 2, November 1990, 401–19.

Banakar, Mahadev. *Safeguards for Linguistic Minorities in India: Karnataka Sets a Model.* Bangalore: Anubhava Mantapa Prakashan, 1982.

Basu, Sajal. *Jharkhand Movement: Ethnicity and Culture of Silence.* Shimla: Indian Institute of Advanced Study, 1994.

Basu, Sajal. *Regional Movements: Politics of Language, Ethnicity-Identity.* Monograph No. 76. Shimla: Indian Institute of Advanced Study; New Delhi: Manohar, 1992.

Baxi, Upendra, and Bhikhu Parekh, eds. *Crisis and Change in Contemporary India.* New Delhi: Sage, in association with The Book Review Literary Trust, New Delhi, 1995.

Bhatnagar, Satyavan, and Pradeep Kumar, eds. *Regional Political Parties in India.* Panjab University D.C.C. Publications, No. 4. New Delhi: Ess, 1988.

Bloch, Jules. *The Grammatical Structure of Dravidian Languages.* Pune: Decan College Post-graduate and Research Institute, 1954.

Brass, Paul R. "Ethnic Groups and the State." Pages 1–56 in Paul R. Brass, ed., *Ethnic Groups and the State.* Totowa, New Jersey: Barnes and Noble, 1985.

Brass, Paul R. *Language, Religion, and Politics in North India.* London: Cambridge University Press, 1974.

Brass, Paul R. *The New Cambridge History of India, IV.1: The Politics of India since Independence.* 2d ed. Cambridge: Cambridge University Press, 1994.

Breton, Ronald J.L. *Atlas géographique des langues et des ethnies de l'Inde et du subcontinent: Bangladesh, Pakistan, Sri Lanka, Nepal, Bhoutan, et Sikkim.* Quebec: Presses de l'université Laval, 1976.

Breton, Ronald J.L. *Geolinguistics: Language Dynamics and Ethno-linguistic Geography.* Trans. and expanded, Harold F. Schiff-man. Ottawa: University of Ottawa Press, 1991.

Bright, William. *Language Variation in South Asia.* New York: Oxford University Press, 1990.

Cabinetmaker, Perin H. *Parsis and Marriage.* Bombay: 1991.

Cappieri, Mario. *The Andamanese: Cultural Elements, Elements of Demogenetics, Physical Anthropology, and Radiology.* Miami: Field Research Projects, 1974.

Carmel, J. *With the Scattered in the East.* Trans., Charles Weis. Jerusalem: Israel Publishing Institute, 1960.

Chaklader, Snehamoy. *Linguistic Minority as a Cohesive Force in Indian Federal Process.* New Delhi: Associated, 1981.

Chaklader, Snehamoy. *Sociolinguistics: A Guide to Language Problems in India.* New Delhi: Mittal, 1990.

Chatterji, Suniti Kumar. *Select Papers (Angla-nibandhachyana.).* 3 vols. New Delhi: People's, 1972–83.

Chaturvedi, M.G. *Third All-India Education Survey: Languages and Media of Instruction in Indian Schools.* New Delhi: National Council of Educational Research and Training, 1981.

Chaudhuri, A.B. "The Jharkhand Movement: A Study," *Indian Defence Review* [New Delhi], 10, No. 4, October–December 1995, 47–55.

Chauhan, R.R.S. *Africans in India: From Slavery to Royalty.* New Delhi: Asian Publication Services, 1995.

Cohn, Bernard S. *An Anthropologist among the Historians and Other Essays.* Delhi: Oxford University Press, 1987.

Cohn, Bernard S. *India: The Social Anthropology of a Civilization.* Englewood Cliffs, New Jersey: Prentice-Hall, 1971.

Comrie, Bernard, ed. *The Major Languages of South Asia, the Middle East, and Africa.* London: Routledge, 1990.

Crane, Robert I., ed. *Regions and Regionalism in South Asian Studies: An Exploratory Study; Papers Presented at a Symposium held at Duke University, April 7–9, 1966.* Durham, North Carolina: Program in Comparative Studies on Southern Asia, Duke University, 1967.

Das, Victor. *Jharkhand: Caste over the Graves.* Tribal Studies of India Series, No. 155. New Delhi: Inter-India, 1992.

Das Gupta, Jyotirindra. *Language Conflict and National Development: Group Politics and National Language Policy in India.* Berkeley: University of California Press, 1970.

Das Gupta, Jyotirindra, and John J. Bumperz. "Language Communication and Control in North India." Pages 151–66 in Joshua A. Fishman, Charles A. Ferguson, and Jyotirindra Das Gupta, eds., *Language Problems of Developing Nations.* New York: Wiley, 1968.

Datta, Prabhat Kumar. *Regionalism of Indian Politics.* New Delhi: Sterling, 1993.

Davidson, T.T.L. "Indian Bilingualism and the Evidence of the Census of 1961," *Lingua* [Amsterdam], 22, Nos. 2–3, April 1969, 176–96.

Deshpande, C.D. *India: A Regional Interpretation.* New Delhi: Indian Council of Social Science Research and Northern Book Centre, 1992.

Deutsch, Karl Wolfgang. *Nationalism and Social Communication: An Inquiry into the Foundations of Nationality.* Cambridge: Technology Press of the Massachusetts Institute of Technology; and New York: Wiley, 1953.

Devalle, Susana B.C. *Discourses of Ethnicity: Culture and Protest in Jharkhand.* New Delhi: Sage, 1992.

Dhamothara, Ayyadurai, ed. *Word-Borrowing and Word-Making in Modern South Asian Languages.* Heidelberg: South Asia Institute, University of Heidelberg, 1978.

Dhar, Pannalal. *India and Her Domestic Problems: Religion, State, and Secularism.* Calcutta: Punthi-Pustak, 1993.

Dharwadker, Vinay. "Dalit Poetry in Maharashtra," *World Literature Today,* 68, No. 2, Spring 1994, 319–24.

Dhoundiyal, N.C., Vijaya R. Dhoundiyal, and S.K. Sharma, eds. *The Separate Hill State, 2: English.* Almora: Shree Almora Book Depot, 1993.

Drury, David. *The Iron Schoolmaster: Education, Employment, and the Family in India.* Delhi: Hindustani, 1993.

Dua, Hans Raj. *Linguistic Repertoire, Communication, and Interaction Networks in Industry.* Mysore: Central Institute of Indian Languages, 1986.

Dutta, Pratap C. *The Great Andamanese: Past and Present.* Calcutta: Anthropological Survey of India, 1978.

Eapen, K.E. "Daily Newspapers in India: Their Status and Problems," *Journalism Quarterly*, 44, No. 3, Autumn 1967, 520–32.

Emeneau, Murray B. *Dravidian Linguistics; Ethnology and Folktales: Collected Papers*. Annamalainagar: Annamalai University, 1976.

Emeneau, Murray B. *Language and Linguistic Area: Essays*. Language Science and National Development Series. Stanford: Stanford University Press, 1980.

Ezra, Esmond David. *Turning Back the Pages: A Chronicle of Calcutta Jewry*. 2 vols. and 1 sound cassette. London: Brookside Press, 1986.

Fishman, Joshua A., Charles A. Ferguson, and Jyotirindra Das Gupta, eds. *Language Problems of Developing Nations*. New York: Wiley, 1968.

Fishman, Rich. "Manipravalam: Threading the Necklace of a Language for Kerala," *Abstracts of the Annual Meeting of the Association for Asian Studies, Inc*. Ann Arbor: Association for Asian Studies, 1995, 177.

Fox, Richard G. "Hindu Nationalism in the Making, or the Rise of the Hindian." Pages 63–80 in Richard G. Fox, ed., *Nationalist Ideologies and the Production of National Cultures*. American Ethnological Society Monograph Series, No. 2. Washington: American Anthropological Association, 1990.

Fürer-Haimendorf, Christoph von. *Tribal Populations and Cultures of the Indian Subcontinent*. Handbuch der Orientalistik. Zweite Abteilung; 7. Bd. Leiden: Brill, 1985.

Fürer-Haimendorf, Christoph von. *Tribes of India: The Struggle for Survival*. Berkeley: University of California Press, 1982.

Gaeffke, Peter. *Hindi Literature in the Twentieth Century*. History of Indian Literature, 8: Modern Indo-Aryan Literatures (fasc. 5). Wiesbaden: Harrasowitz, 1978.

Galanter, Marc. *Competing Equalities: Law and the Backward Classes in India*. Berkeley: University of California Press, 1984.

Gangadharan, K.K., ed. *Indian National Consciousness: Growth and Development*. New Delhi: Kalamkar Prakashan, 1972.

George, Sudhir Jacob. "The Bodo Movement in Assam: Unrest to Accord," *Asian Survey*, 34, No. 10, October 1994, 878–92.

Grimes, Barbara F., ed. *Ethnologue: Languages of the World*. 12th ed. Dallas: Summer Institute of Linguistics, 1992.

Hart, George Luzerne. *The Relation Between Tamil and Classical Sanskrit Literature.* History of Indian Literature, 10: Dravidian Literature (fasc. 2). Wiesbaden: Harrasowitz, 1976.

Hindustan Year Book and Who's Who, 1994. 62d ed. Ed., S. Sarkar. Calcutta: M.C. Sarkar, 1994.

India. Commissioner for Linguistic Minorities in India. *Report of the Commissioner for Linguistic Minorities in India.* New Delhi: 1957–58.

India. Committee of Parliament on Official Language. *Report.* New Delhi: 1986.

India. Group on Minorities Education. *Report of the Group on Minorities Education.* New Delhi: Government of India Press, 1991.

India. Linguistic Survey. *Linguistic Survey of India.* 12 vols. Ed., George Grierson. Calcutta: Office of the Superintendent of Printing, India, 1903–23. Reprint. Delhi: Motilal Banarsidass, 1968.

India. Ministry of Home Affairs. Registrar General and Census Commissioner. *Census of India, 1981: Series–1. Paper 4 of 1984. Household Population by Religion of Head of Household.* New Delhi: 1984.

India. Ministry of Home Affairs. Registrar General and Census Commissioner. *Census of India, 1981: Series–1, Part IV B(i): Population by Language/Mother-Tongue (Table C–7).* New Delhi: May 1991.

India. Ministry of Home Affairs. Registrar General and Census Commissioner. *Census of India, 1991: Final Population Totals: Brief Analysis of Primary Census Abstract, Series–1, Paper–2 of 1992.* New Delhi: 1993.

India. Ministry of Home Affairs. Registrar General and Census Commissioner. *Census of India, 1991: Final Population Totals, Series–1, Paper–1 of 1992, 2.* New Delhi: 1993.

India. Ministry of Home Affairs. Registrar General and Census Commissioner. *Census of India, 1991: Union Primary Census Abstract for Scheduled Castes and Scheduled Tribes. India-State Level. Series–1, Paper–1 of 1993.* New Delhi: 1993.

India. Ministry of Human Resources Development. Committee for Promotion of Urdu. *Report of the Committee for Promotion of Urdu, 1975.* 3d ed. New Delhi: 1990.

India. West Bengal. Director of Information. *Gorkhaland Agitation: Facts and Issues: Information Document II.* Calcutta: 1987.

India. West Bengal. Director of Information. *Gorkhaland Agitation: The Issues: An Information Document.* Calcutta: 1986.

International Conference on Language and National Development. *The Case of India. Souvenir, Department of Linguistics, Osmania University, 25 Years. Silver Jubilee Year, 1962–1987.* Hyderabad: Organizing Committee, ICLAND (India), 1987.

Isenberg, Shirley Berry. *India's Bene-Israel: A Comprehensive Inquiry and Sourcebook.* Berkeley: Judah L. Magnes Museum, 1988.

Jayadas, Edwin. *Tribals in our Global Village: Agenda for the Third Millenium.* Bangalore: Pan Media, 1992.

Jebasingh, Ananthi. *Script for Tribal Languages for the Promotion of Literacy.* Delhi: Amar Prakashan, 1990.

Kachru, Braj B. *The Indianization of English: The English Language in India.* Delhi: Oxford University Press, 1983.

Kachru, Braj B., and S.N. Sridhar, eds. *Aspects of Sociolinguistics in South Asia.* International Journal of the Sociology of Language, No. 16. The Hague: Mouton, 1978.

Kakar, Sudhir. *The Colors of Violence: Cultural Identities, Religion, and Conflict.* Chicago: University of Chicago Press, 1996.

Karat, Prakash. *Language and Nationality Politics in India.* Bombay: Orient Longman, 1973.

Katz, Nathan, and Ellen S. Goldberg. *The Last Jews of Cochin: Jewish Identity in Hindu India.* Columbia: University of South Carolina Press, 1993.

Kesavan, B.S. *History of Printing and Publishing in India: A Story of Cultural Re-awakening.* 2 vols. New Delhi: National Book Trust, 1984–85.

Khan, Vahiduddin. *Indian Muslims: The Need for a Positive Outlook.* New Delhi: Al-Risala, 1994.

Khubchandani, Lachman Mulchand. *Language, Culture, and Nation-Building: Challenges of Modernisation.* New Delhi: Indian Institute of Advanced Study, in association with Manohar Publications, Shimla, 1991.

Khubchandani, Lachman Mulchand. *Language Demography: Collected Papers.* Mimeograph Series: Studies in Linguistics, No. 3. Pune: Centre for Communication Studies, 1981.

Khubchandani, Lachman Mulchand. *Language Planning: Miscellaneous Papers*. Pune: Centre for Communication Studies, 1981.

Khubchandani, Lachman Mulchand. *Plural Languages, Plural Cultures: Communication, Identity, and Sociopolitical Change in Contemporary India*. Honolulu: University of Hawaii Press for the East-West Center, 1983.

Kliuev, Boris I. *India, National and Language Problem*. New Delhi: Jullundur; and Bangalore: Sterling, 1981.

Krishnamurti, Bh., ed. *South Asian Language: Structure, Convergence, and Diglossia*. MLBD Series in Linguistics, No. 3. Delhi: Motilal Banarsidass, 1986.

Kumar, Purushottam. *History and Administration of Tribal Chotanagpur*. Delhi: Atma Ram, 1994.

Labru, G. L. *Indian Newspaper English*. Delhi: B.R. Publishing, 1984.

Lahiri-dutt, Kuntala. *In Search of a Homeland: Anglo-Indians and McCluskiegunge*. Calcutta: Minerva, 1990.

Lelyveld, David. "Colonial Knowledge and the Fate of Hindustani," *Comparative Studies in Society and History* [Cambridge], 25, No. 4, October 1993, 665–82.

Leshnik, Lawrence Saadia, and Günther-Dietz Sontheimer, eds. *Pastoralists and Nomads in South Asia*. Schriftenreihe des Südasien-Instituts der Universität Heidelberg. Wiesbaden: Harrasowitz, 1975.

Limaye, Madhu. *Religious Bigotry: A Threat to Ordered State*. Delhi: Ajanta, 1994.

McDonald, Ellen E. "The Growth of Regional Consciousness in Maharashtra," *Indian Economic and Social History Review* [Delhi], 5, No. 3, September 1968, 223–43.

McGregor, Ronald Stuart. *Hindi Literature of the Nineteenth and Early Twentieth Centuries*. History of Indian Literature, 8, Pt. 1: Modern Indo-Aryan Literatures (fasc. 2). Wiesbaden: Harrasowitz, 1974.

Madan, T.N. "Whither Indian Secularism?" *Modern Asian Studies*, [London], 27, Pt. 3, July 1993, 667–97.

Mahmood, Tahir, ed. *Minorities and State at the Indian Law: An Anthology*. New Delhi: Institute of Objective Studies, 1991.

Maloney, Clarence, ed. *Language and Civilization Change in South Asia.* Contributions to Asian Studies, No. 11. Leiden: Brill, 1978.

Mandelbaum, David G. *Society in India: Continuity and Change.* 2 vols. Berkeley: University of California Press, 1970.

Mann, Rann Singh. Culture and Integration of Indian Tribes. New Delhi: M.D. Publications, 1993.

Manoharan S. *A Descriptive and Comparative Study of Andamanese Language.* Calcutta: Anthropological Survey of India for Ministry of Human Resource Development, 1989.

Marriott, McKim. "Changing Channels of Cultural Transmission in Indian Civilization." Pages 66–74 in Verne F. Ray, ed., *Intermediate Societies, Social Mobility, and Communication: Proceedings of the 1959 Annual Spring Meeting of the American Ethnological Society.* Seattle: 1959.

Masica, Colin P. *Defining a Linguistic Area: South Asia.* Chicago: University of Chicago Press, 1976.

Masica, Colin P. *The Indo-Aryan Languages.* New York: Cambridge University Press, 1991.

Misra, Dipti. "Konkani: Language-Dialect Controversy," *International Journal of Dravidian Linguistics* [Thiruvananthapuram], 16, No. 1, January 1987, 108–19.

Misra, Kamal Kant. *Tribal Elites and Social Transformation.* New Delhi: Inter-India, 1994.

Misra, P.K., and K.C. Malhotra, eds. *Nomads in India: Proceedings of the National Seminar.* Calcutta: Anthropological Survey of India, 1982.

Misra, Satya Swarup. *Aryan Problem: A Linguistic Approach.* New Delhi: Munshiram Manoharlal, 1992.

Mitra, Roma. *Caste Polarization and Politics.* Patna: Syndicate Publication (India), 1992.

Mitra, Subrata K. "Crowds and Power: Democracy and the Crisis of 'Governability' in India." Pages 216–45 in Upendra Baxi and Bhikhu Parekh, eds., *Crisis and Change in Contemporary India.* New Delhi: Sage, in association with The Book Review Literary Trust, New Delhi, 1995.

Moore, Gloria Jean. *The Anglo-Indian Vision.* Delhi: B.R. Publishing, 1987.

Moseley, Christopher, and R. E. Asher, eds. *Atlas of the World's Languages.* New York: Routledge, 1994.

Munda, Ramdayal. *The Jharkhand Movement: Retrospect and Prospect: A Report Submitted to Home Minister, Buta Singh.* Ranchi: Jharkhand Co-ordination Committee, 1990.

Muthiah, S., ed. *A Social and Economic Atlas of India.* Delhi: Oxford University Press, 1990.

Naidu, K. Munirathna, ed. *Peasant Movements in India.* New Delhi: Reliance, 1994.

Naik. T.B., and G.P. Pandya. *The Sidis of Gujurat: A Socio-Economic Study and Development Plan.* Tribal Research and Training Institute Publication, No. 32. Ahmedabad: Tribal Research and Training Institute, 1993.

Naim, C.M. "The Situation of the Urdu Writer: A Letter from Bara Banki, December 1993/February 1994," *World Literature Today,* 68, No. 2, Spring 1994, 246–46.

Nanavutty, Piloo. *The Parsis.* New Delhi: National Book Trust, 1977.

National Council of Educational Research and Training. *Fifth All-India Educational Survey.* 2 vols. New Delhi: March 1992.

Nigosian, S.A. *The Zoroastrian Faith: Tradition and Modern Research.* Montreal: McGill-Queen's University Press, 1993.

O'Barr, William O., and Jean F. O'Barr. *Language and Politics.* The Hague: Mouton, 1976.

Pakem, B. *Regionalism in India: With Special Reference to North-East India.* Delhi: Har-Anand, 1993.

Pandian, Jacob. *The Making of India and Indian Traditions.* Englewood Cliffs, New Jersey: Prentice-Hall, 1995.

Pandit, Prabodh Bechardas. *India as a Sociolinguistic Area.* Pune: University of Pune, 1972.

Pandit, Prabodh Bechardas. *Language in a Plural Society.* Delhi: Motilal Banarsidass; and Shimla: Indian Institute of Advanced Study, 1988.

Pangborn, Cyrus R. *Zoroastrianism: A Beleaguered Faith.* New Delhi: Vikas, 1982.

Paolucci, Henry. "Italian and English 'Models' for the Modern Vernacular Literatures of India." Pages 209–31 in Aldo Scaglione, ed., *The Emergence of National Languages.* Speculum artium, No. 11. Ravenna, Italy: Longo Editore, 1984.

Parthasarathy, R. "Tamil Literature," *World Literature Today,* 68, No. 2, Spring 1994, 253–59.

Patel, M.L. *Development Dualism of Primitive Tribes: Constraints, Restraints, and Fallacies.* New Delhi: M.D. Publications, 1994.

Pattanayak, D.P. *Language, Education, and Culture.* CIIL Occasional Monograph Series, No. 46. Mysore: Central Institute of Indian Languages, 1991.

Pattanayak, D.P. *Multilingualism and Mother-Tongue Education.* Delhi: Oxford University Press, 1981.

Pattanayak, D.P. *Papers in Indian Sociolinguistics.* Mysore: Central Institute of Indian Languages, 1978.

Pattanayak, D.P., ed. *Multilingualism in India.* Philadelphia: Multilingual Matters, 1990.

Pawte, Ishtalingapappa Siddharamappa. *The Structure of the Ashtadhyayi.* Hubli: 1934.

Peacock, Olive. *Minorities and National Integration in India.* Jaipur: Arihand, 1991.

Perry, John Oliver. "Contemporary Indian Poetry in English," *World Literature Today,* 68, No. 2, Spring 1994, 261–71.

Pescatello, Ann M. "The African Presence in Portuguese India, *Journal of Asian History* [Wiesbaden], 11, No. 1, 1977, 26–48.

Pollock, Sheldon. "Three Local Cultures in the Sanskrit Cosmopolis (AD 300–1300)," *Abstracts of the Annual Meeting of the Association for Asian Studies, Inc.* Ann Arbor: Association for Asian Studies, 1995, 176–77.

Rai, Amrit. *A House Divided: The Origin and Development of Hindi-Urdu.* New York: Oxford University Press, 1991.

Ramaswamy, Sumathi. "Engendering Language: The Poetics of Tamil Identity," *Comparative Studies in Society and History* [Cambridge], 25, No. 4, October 1993, 683–725.

Ramaswamy, Sumathi. "In Praise of Tamil: Ideologies of Language Before the Nation," *Abstracts of the Annual Meeting of the Association for Asian Studies, Inc.* Ann Arbor: Association for Asian Studies, 1995, 177–78.

Ram Reddy, G., and B.A.V. Sharma. *Regionalism in India: A Study of Telangana.* New Delhi: Concept, 1979.

Rao, G.R.S. *Regionalism in India: A Case Study of the Telangana Issue.* New Delhi: Institute of Constitutional and Parliamentary Studies, 1975.

Rao, Narayana. "Style Wars: Sanskrit and Telugu in Medieval Andhra," *Abstracts of the Annual Meeting of the Association for*

Asian Studies, Inc. Ann Arbor: Association for Asian Studies, 1995, 177.

Rastogi, P.N. *Ethno-Social Conflict and National Integration.* New Delhi: Gyan, 1993.

Ray, Punya Sloka. *Language Standardization: Studies in Prescriptive Linguistics.* The Hague: Mouton, 1963.

Raza, Moonis, and Aijazuddin Ahmad. *An Atlas of Tribal India: with Computed Tables of District-Level Data and Its Geographical Interpretation.* New Delhi: Concept, 1989.

Rekhi, Upjit Singh. *Jharkhand Movement in Bihar.* New Delhi: Nunes, 1988.

Rice, Frank A., ed. *Study of the Role of Second Languages in Asia, Africa, and Latin America.* Washington: Center for Applied Linguistics of the Modern Language Association of America, 1962.

Robinson, Francis, ed. *The Cambridge Encyclopedia of India, Pakistan, Bangladesh, Sri Lanka, Nepal, Bhutan, and the Maldives.* Cambridge: Cambridge University Press, 1989.

Roland, Joan G. *Jews in British India: Identity in a Colonial Era.* Tauber Institute for the Study of European Jewry Series, No. 9. Hanover: University Press of New England for Brandeis University Press, 1989.

Roy, S.B., and Asok K. Ghosh, eds. *People of India: Bio-Cultural Dimensions: A K.S. Singh Festschrift.* New Delhi: Inter-India, 1993.

Ruhlen, Merritt. *The Origin of Language: Tracing the Evolution of the Mother Tongue.* New York: Wiley, 1994.

Sadiq Ali, Shanti. *India and Africa Through the Ages.* Delhi: National Book Trust, 1987.

Sarang, Vilas. "Confessions of a Marathi Writer," *World Literature Today,* 68, No. 2, Spring 1994, 309–12.

Sarkar, Ajeya. *Regionalism, State, and the Emerging Political Pattern in India: A New Approach.* Calcutta: Firma KLM, 1990.

Sarkar, Sumit. *Modern India, 1885–1947.* New York: St. Martin's Press, 1989.

Sarma, Satyendra Nath. *Assamese Literature.* A History of Indian Literature, 9: Modern Indo-Aryan Literatures (fasc. 2). Wiesbaden: Harrasowitz, 1976.

Schermerhorn, R.A. *Ethnic Plurality in India.* Tucson: University of Arizona Press, 1978.

Schimmel, Annemarie. *Classical Urdu Literature from the Beginning to Iqbal.* A History of Indian Literature, 8: Modern Indo-Aryan Literatures (fasc. 3). Wiesbaden: Harrasowitz, 1975.

Schimmel, Annemarie. *Islamic Literatures of India.* A History of Indian Literature, 7: Modern Indo-Iranian Literatures (fasc. 1). Wiesbaden: Harrasowitz, 1973.

Schimmel, Annemarie. *Sindhi Literature.* A History of Indian Literature, 8: Modern Indo-Aryan Literatures (fasc. 2). Wiesbaden: Harrasowitz, 1974.

Schwartzberg, Joseph E., ed. *A Historical Atlas of South Asia.* 2d impression. Reference Series of Association for Asian Studies, No. 2. New York: Oxford University Press, 1992.

Sebeok, Thomas A., ed. *Linguistics in South Asia.* Current Trends in Linguistics, 5. The Hague: Mouton, 1969.

Segal, J.B. *A History of the Jews of Cochin.* London: Vallentine Mitchell, 1993.

Sengupta, Nirmal, ed. *Fourth World Dynamics, Jharkhand.* Delhi: Authors Guild, 1982.

Shackle, Christopher, and Rupert Snell. *Hindi and Urdu since 1800: A Common Reader.* New Delhi: Heritage, 1990.

Shah, Beena. *Tribal Education, Perspectives and Prospects.* Calcutta: Naya Prokash, 1992.

Shapiro, Michael C., and Harold Schiffmann. *Language and Society in South Asia.* Delhi: Motilal Banarsidass, 1981.

Sharma, B.N. *Medium of Instruction in India: A Backgrounder Based on Official Documents of the Government of India.* New Delhi: Central Secretariat Library, Department of Culture, 1985.

Sharma, K.L., ed. *Caste and Class in India.* Jaipur: Rawat, 1994.

Sharma, P. Gopal, and Suresh Kumar, eds. *Indian Bilingualism: Proceedings of the Symposium Held under the Joint Auspices of Kendriya Hindi Sansthan and Jawaharlal Nehru University, February 1976.* Agra: Kendriya Hindi Sansthan, 1977.

Sheth, D.L. "The Great Language Debate: Politics of Metropolitan Versus Vernacular India." Pages 187–215 in Upendra Baxi and Bhikhu Parekh, eds., *Crisis and Change in Contemporary India.* New Delhi: Sage, in association with The Book Review Literary Trust, New Delhi, 1995.

Singh, Bhawani, ed. *Regionalism and Politics of Separatism in India.* Jaipur: Printwell, 1993.

Singh, Inderjit. *The Great Ascent: The Rural Poor in South Asia.* Baltimore: Johns Hopkins University Press for the World Bank, 1990.

Singh, Kumar Suresh, ed. *People of India, 3: The Scheduled Tribes.* Calcutta: Anthropological Survey of India, 1992.

Singh, Kumar Suresh, ed. *People of India, 9: Languages and Scripts.* Delhi: Anthropological Survey of India, 1992.

Singh, Kumar Suresh, ed. *People of India, 11: An Anthropological Atlas.* Delhi: Anthropological Survey of India, 1993.

Singh, Kumar Suresh, ed. *People of India, 12: Andaman and Nicobar Islands.* Madras: Anthropological Survey of India, 1994.

Singh, Nancy, and Ram Singh, eds. *The Sugar in the Milk: The Parsis in India.* Delhi: Indian Society for Promoting Christian Knowledge for the Institute for Development Education, 1986.

Singh, Navjyoti. "Foundations of Logic in Ancient India: Linguistics and Mathematics." Pages 79–106 in A. Rahman, ed., *Science and Technology in Indian Culture.* New Delhi: National Institute of Science, Technology, and Development Studies, 1984.

Spate, O.H.K., A.T.A. Learmonth, A.M. Learmonth, and B.H. Farmer. *India and Pakistan: A General and Regional Geography with a Chapter on Ceylon.* 3d ed., rev. London: Methuen, 1967.

Sridhar, Kamal K. *English in Indian Bilingualism.* New Delhi: Manohar, 1989.

Stern, Robert W. *Changing India: Bourgeois Revolution on the Subcontinent.* New York: Cambridge University Press, 1993.

Subba, Tanka B. *Ethnicity, State, and Development: A Case Study of the Gorkhaland Movement in Darjeeling.* New Delhi: Har-Anand, in association with Vikas, 1992.

Taylor, David, and Malcolm Yapp, eds. *Political Identity in South Asia.* London: Curzon, 1979.

Timberg, Thomas A., ed. *Jews in India.* New Delhi: Vikas, 1986.

Tulsi Ram. *Trading in Language: The Story of English in India.* Delhi: GDK, 1983.

Tyagi, P.N. *Education for All: A Graphic Presentation.* New Delhi: National Institute of Educational Planning and Administration, August 1991.

United States. Central Intelligence Agency. *World Factbook, 1995.* Washington: 1995.

Varma, Siddheshwar. *G.A. Grierson's Linguistic Survey of India: A Summary*. 3 vols. Hoshiarpur: Vishweshvaranand Institute, Panjab University, 1972–76.

Verma, Ramesh Kumar. *Regionalism and Sub-regionalism in State Politics: Social, Economic, and Political Bases*. New Delhi: Deep and Deep, 1994.

Wolpert, Stanley. *A New History of India*. 4th ed. New York: Oxford University Press, 1992.

Writer, Rashna. *Contemporary Zoroastrians: An Unstructured Nation.* Lanham: University Press of America, 1994.

Yaquin, Anwarul. *Constitutional Protection of Minority Educational Institutions in India*. New Delhi: Deep and Deep, 1982.

Younger, Coralie. *Anglo-Indians, Neglected Children of the Raj*. Delhi: B.R. Publishing, 1987.

Zide, Normal. "A Bibliographical Introduction to Andamanese Linguistics," *Journal of the American Oriental Society,* 109, No. 4, October–December 1989, 639–51.

Zograf, Georgii Aleksandrovich. *Languages of South Asia: A Guide*. London: Routledge and Kegan Paul, 1982.

Zvabitel, Dusan. *Bengali Literature*. A History of Indian Literature, 9: Modern Indo-Aryan Literatures (fasc. 3). Wiesbaden: Harrasowitz, 1976.

Zvelebil, Kamil V. *Companion Studies to the History of Tamil Literature*. Handbuch der Orientalistik. Zweite Abteilung, Indien. Bd., Ergänzungsband 5. Leiden: Brill, 1992.

Zvelebil, Kamil V. *Tamil Literature*. A History of Indian Literature, 10: Dravidian Literatures (fasc. 1). Wiesbaden: Harrasowitz, 1974.

(Various issues of the following publications were also used in the preparation of this chapter: *Economic and Political Weekly* [Bombay], 1984–86, 1994; *Economist* [London], 1988; *Far Eastern Economic Review* [Hong Kong], 1984–93; *Frontline* [Madras], 1994–95; *Panchayati Raj Update* [New Delhi], 1994–95; *Seminar* [Delhi], 1992; and *Times of India* [New Delhi], 1995.)

Chapter 5

Agrawal, Bina. "Women, Poverty, and Agricultural Growth in India," *Journal of Peasant Studies* [London], 13, No. 4, July 1986, 165–220.

Ahmad, Imtiaz, ed. *Caste and Social Stratification among Muslims in India.* New Delhi: Manohar, 1978.

Ahmad, Imtiaz, ed. *Family, Kinship, and Marriage among Muslims in India.* New Delhi: Manohar, 1976.

Bagwe, Anjali. *Of Woman Caste: The Experience of Gender in Rural India.* New York: Zed, 1995.

Ballhatchet, Kenneth, and John Harrison, eds. *The City in South Asia: Pre-Modern and Modern.* Atlantic Highland, New Jersey: Humanities Press, 1981.

Basham, A.L. *The Wonder That Was India: A Survey of the History and Culture of the Indian Sub-Continent Before the Coming of the Muslims.* 3d ed., rev. London: Sidgwick and Jackson, 1967.

Bedi, Rajeh, and Ramesh Bedi. *Sadhus: The Holy Men of India.* Delhi: Brijbasi, 1961.

Bennett, Lynn. *Women, Poverty, and Productivity in India.* EDI Seminar Paper, No. 43. Washington: Economic Development Institute, World Bank, 1991.

Berreman, Gerald D. *Caste and Other Inequities: Essays on Inequality.* Meerut: Folklore Institute, 1979.

Berreman, Gerald D. *Hindus of the Himalayas.* Berkeley: University of California Press, 1963.

Beteille, Andre. *Caste, Class, and Power: Changing Patterns of Stratification in a Tanjore Village.* Berkeley: University of California Press, 1965.

Boserup, Ester. *Women's Role in Economic Development.* London: Allen and Unwin, 1970.

Brouwer, Jan. *The Makers of the World: Caste, Craft, and Mind of South Indian Artisans.* Delhi: Oxford University Press, 1995.

Bumiller, Elisabeth. *May You Be the Mother of a Hundred Sons: A Journey among the Women of India.* New York: Fawcett Columbine, 1990.

Calman, Leslie J. *Toward Empowerment: Women and Politics in India.* Boulder, Colorado: Westview Press, 1992.

Carstairs, G. Morris. *The Twice Born: A Study of a Community of High-Caste Hindus.* Bloomington: University of Indiana Press, 1967.

Chanchreek, K.L., and Saroj Prasad, eds. *Mandal Commission Report. Myth and Reality: A National Viewpoint.* Delhi: H.K. Publishers, 1991.

Chatterjee, Meera. *Indian Women: Their Health and Economic Productivity.* World Bank Discussion Papers, No. 109. Washington: World Bank, 1990.

Chitkara, M.G. *Bureacracy and Social Change.* New Delhi: Ashish, 1994.

Chopra, J.K. *Women in the Indian Parliament: A Critical Study of Their Role.* New Delhi: Mittal, 1993.

Clark, Alice W., ed. *Gender and Political Economy: Explorations of South Asian Systems.* Delhi: Oxford University Press, 1993.

Cohen, Myron L., ed. *Asia: Case Studies in the Social Sciences: A Guide for Teaching.* Armonk, New York: Sharpe, 1992.

Cohn, Bernard S. *India: The Social Anthropology of a Civilization.* Englewood Cliffs, New Jersey: Prentice-Hall, 1971.

Crane, Robert I., ed. *Aspects of Political Mobilization in South Asia.* Foreign and Comparative Studies/South Asia Series, No. 1. Syracuse: Maxwell School of Citizenship and Public Affairs, Syracuse University, 1976.

Crane, Robert I., ed. *Nations and Regionalism in South Asian Studies: An Exploratory Study.* Duke University Monographs and Occasional Papers Series, Monograph No. 5. Durham: Duke University Press, 1967.

Das, Veena. "Indian Women: Work, Power, and Status." Pages 129–45 in B.R. Nanda, ed., *Indian Women: From Purdah to Modernity.* New Delhi: Vikas, 1976.

Das Gupta, Monica. "Death Clustering, Mothers' Education, and the Determinants of Child Mortality in Rural Punjab," *Population Studies* [London], 44, No. 3, November 1990, 489–505.

Das Gupta, Monica. "Selective Discrimination Against Female Children in Rural Punjab, India," *Population and Development Review,* 13, No. 1, March 1987, 77–100.

Das Gupta, Monica. "Women's Life Cycles, Status, and Demographic Outcomes." Paper presented at the Conference on South Asia, Madison, Wisconsin, 1993.

Day, Richard H., and Inderjit Singh. *Economic Development As an Adaptive Process: The Green Revolution in the Indian Punjab.* New York: Cambridge University Press, 1977.

de Souza, Alfred, ed. *Women in Contemporary India: Traditional Images and Changing Roles.* New Delhi: Manohar, 1975.

Derne, Steve. *Cultures in Action: Family, Life, Emotions, and Male Dominance in Banaras, India.* Albany: State University of New York Press, 1995.

Desai, Sonalde, and Devaki Jain. "Maternal Employment and Changes in Family Dynamics: The Social Context of Women's Work in Rural South India," *Population and Development Review,* 20, No. 1, March 1994, 115–36.

Dickemann, Mildred. "Female Infanticide, Reproductive Strategies, and Social Stratification: A Preliminary Model." Pages 321–37 in Napoleon A. Chagnon and William Irons, eds., *Evolutionary Biology and Human Social Behavior: An Anthropological Perspective.* North Scituate, Massachusetts: Ducksbury, 1979.

Dickemann, Mildred. "Paternal Confidence and Dowry Competition: A Biocultural Analysis of Purdah." Pages 417–38 in Richard A. Alexander and Donald W. Tinkle, eds., *Natural Selection and Social Behavior: Recent Research and New Theory.* New York: Chiron, 1981.

Dubey, Suman. "The Middle Class." Pages 137–64 in Leonard A. Gordon and Philip Oldenburg, eds., *India Briefing, 1992.* Boulder, Colorado: Westview Press, in cooperation with The Asia Society, 1992.

Dumont, Louis. *Homo Hierarchicus: The Caste System and Its Implications.* Trans., Mark Sainsbury, et al. Rev. ed. Chicago: University of Chicago Press, 1980.

Dyson, Tim, and Mick Moore. "On Kinship Structure, Female Autonomy, and Demographic Behavior in India," *Population and Development Review,* 9, No. 1, March 1983, 35–39.

Elwin, Verrier. *The Kingdom of the Young, Abridged from The Muria and Their Ghotul.* Bombay: Oxford University Press, 1968.

Elwin, Verrier. *The Muria and Their Ghotul.* Bombay: Oxford University Press, 1947. Reprint. New Delhi: Oxford University Press, 1991.

Embree, Ainslie T. *Utopias in Conflict: Religion and Nationalism in Modern India.* Comparative Studies in Religion and Society. Berkeley: University of California Press, 1990.

Engineer, Ashgar Ali, ed. *Mandal Commission Controversy.* Delhi: Ajanta, 1991.

Freed, Ruth S., and Stanley A. Freed. "Beliefs and Practices Resulting in Female Deaths and Fewer Females than Males in India," *Population and Environment,* 10, No. 3, Fall 1989, 144–61.

Freed, Ruth S., and Stanley A. Freed. *Ghosts: Life and Death in North India.* Anthropological Papers, No. 72. New York: American Museum of Natural History, 1993.

Freed, Ruth S., and Stanley A. Freed. *The Psychomedical Case History of a Low-Caste Woman of North India.* Anthropological Papers, No. 60, Pt. 2. New York: American Museum of Natural History, 1985.

Freed, Stanley A., and Ruth S. Freed. *Shanti Nagar: The Effects of Urbanization in a Village in North India, 1: Social Organization.* Anthropological Papers, No. 53, Pt. 1. New York: American Museum of Natural History, 1976.

Fuller, Christopher J. "Misconceiving the Grain Heap: A Critique of the Concept of the Indian Jajmani System." Pages 33–63 in J. Parry and M. Blich, eds., *Money and the Morality of Exchange.* Cambridge: Cambridge University Press, 1989.

Gallin, Rita S., and Anne Ferguson, eds. *The Women and Development Annual Review, 2.* Boulder, Colorado: Westview Press, 1991.

Goody, Jack. *Production and Reproduction: A Comparative Study of the Domestic Domain.* Cambridge Studies in Social Anthropology, No. 17. Cambridge: Cambridge University Press, 1976.

Gould, Harold A. "The Adaptive Functions of Caste in Contemporary Indian Society," *Asian Survey,* 13, No. 9, September 1973, 427–38.

Gould, Harold A. "Political Economy and Emergence of a Modern Class System in India." Pages 155–86 in Yogendra K. Malik, ed., *Boeings and Bullock-Carts: Studies in Change and Continuity in Indian Civilization: Essays in Honour of K. Ishwaran, 1: India: Culture and Society.* Delhi: Chanakya, 1990.

Gregory, Robert G. *South Asians in East Africa: An Economic and Social History, 1890–1980.* Boulder, Colorado: Westview Press, 1993.

Gross, Susan Hill. *Wasted Resources, Diminished Lives: The Impact of Boy Preference on the Lives of Girls and Women.* St. Louis Park, Minnesota: Upper Midwest Women's History Center, 1992.

Gupta, Giri Raj. *Cohesion and Conflict in Modern India.* Main Currents in Indian Sociology, No. 3. Durham, North Carolina: Carolina Academic Press, 1978.

Gupta, Giri Raj. *Contemporary India: Some Sociological Perspectives.* Main Currents in Indian Sociology, No. 1. Durham, North Carolina: Carolina Academic Press, 1976.

Gupta, Giri Raj. *Family and Social Change in Modern India.* Main Currents in Indian Sociology, No. 2. Durham, North Carolina: Carolina Academic Press, 1971.

Hanchett, Suzanne. *Coloured Rice: Symbolic Structure in Hindu Family Festivals.* Delhi: Hindustan, 1988.

Harris, Marvin. "The Cultural Ecology of India's Sacred Cattle," *Current Anthropology* [Utrecht], 7, No. 1, February 1966, 51–66.

Hiro, Dilip. *The Untouchables of India.* Rev. ed. MRG Report, No. 26. London: Minority Rights Working Group on Untouchables, 1982.

India. Ministry of Education and Social Welfare. Committee on the Status of Women in India. *Towards Equality: Report of the Committee on the Status of Women in India.* New Delhi: 1974.

India. Ministry of Home Affairs. Registrar General and Census Commissioner. *Census of India, 1991: Final Population Totals: Brief Analysis of Primary Census Abstract, Series–1, Paper–2 of 1992,* New Delhi: 1993.

India. Ministry of Planning. Department of Statistics. Central Statistical Organisation. *Statistical Abstract 1990, India.* New Delhi: 1990.

Indian Social Institute. *Dalit Organisations, A Directory: Programme for Scheduled Castes.* 2d ed. New Delhi: 1994.

Jacobson, Doranne. "Flexibility in Central Indian Kinship and Residence." Pages 263–83 in K. Dacid, ed., *The New Wind: Changing Identities in South Asia.* World Anthropology Series. The Hague: Mouton, 1977.

Jacobson, Doranne. "Gender Relations: Changing Patterns in India." Pages 119–39 in Myron L. Cohen, ed., *Asia. Case Studies in the Social Sciences: A Guide for Teaching.* Armonk, New York: Sharpe, 1992.

Jacobson, Doranne. "Hidden Faces: Hindu and Muslim Purdah in a Central Indian Village." Ph.D. dissertation. New York: Columbia University, 1970.

Jacobson, Doranne. "Indian Women in Processes of Development," *Journal of International Affairs,* 30, No. 2, Winter 1976–77, 211–42.

Jacobson, Doranne. "Purdah and the Hindu Family in Central India." Pages 81–109 in Hanna Papanek and Gail Minault, eds., *Separate Worlds: Studies of Purdah in South Asia.* Columbia, Missouri: South Asia Books; and New Delhi: Chanakya, 1982.

Jacobson, Doranne. "Purdah in India: Life Behind the Veil," *National Geographic,* 152, No. 2, August 1977, 270–86.

Jacobson, Doranne. "Separate Spheres: Differential Modernization in Rural Central India." Pages 179–238 in Helen E. Ullrich, ed., *Competition and Modernization in South Asia.* New Delhi: Abhinav, 1975.

Jacobson, Doranne. "The Veil of Virtue: Purdah and the Muslim Family in the Bhopal Region of Central India." Pages 169–215 in Imtiaz Ahmad, ed., *Family, Kinship, and Marriage among Muslims in India.* New Delhi: Manohar, 1976.

Jacobson, Doranne. *Women and Work in South Asia: An Audiovisual Presentation.* Women and Development Issues in Three World Areas. St. Louis Park, Minnesota: Upper Midwest Women's History Center Collection, 1989.

Jacobson, Doranne, and Susan S. Wadley. *Women in India: Two Perspectives.* 3d ed. Columbia, Missouri: South Asia Books; and New Delhi: Manohar, 1994.

Jeffery, Patricia, Roger Jeffery, and Andrew Lyon. *Labour Pains and Labour Power: Women and Childbearing in India.* London: Zed, 1989.

Joshi, Barbara R. "Whose Law, Whose Order: Untouchables, Social Violence, and the State in India," *Asian Survey,* 22, No. 7, July 1982, 676–87.

Kakar, Sudhir. *The Inner World: A Psychoanalytic Study of Childhood and Society in India.* New Delhi: Oxford University Press, 1978.

Karve, Irawati. *Kinship Organization in India.* 3d ed. London: Asia Publishing House, 1968.

Kinsley, David. *Hindu Goddesses: Visions of the Divine Feminine in the Hindu Religious Tradition.* Berkeley: University of California Press, 1988.

Klass, Morton. *Caste: The Emergence of the South Asian Social System.* Philadelphia: Institute for the Study of Human Issues, 1980.

Kolenda, Pauline M. *Caste in Contemporary India: Beyond Organic Solidarity.* Menlo Park, California: Cummings, 1978.

Kolenda, Pauline M. "Region, Caste, and Family Structure: A Comparative Study of the Indian 'Joint' Family." Pages 339–96 in Milton Singer and Bernard S. Cohn, eds., *Structure and Change in Indian Society.* Viking Fund Publications in Anthropology, No. 47. Chicago: Aldine, 1968.

Kolenda, Pauline M. "Regional Differences in Indian Family Structure." Pages 147–226 in Robert I. Crane, ed., *Regions and Regionalism in South Asian Studies: An Exploratory Study.* Duke University Monograph and Occasional Papers Series, Monograph No. 5. Durham: Duke University Press, 1967.

Kshirasagara, Ramacandra. *Dalit Movement in India and Its Leaders, 1857–1956.* New Delhi: M.D. Publications, 1994.

Lapierre, Dominique. *The City of Joy.* Trans., Kathryn Spink. Garden City, New York: Doubleday, 1985.

Lateef, Shahida. *Muslim Women in India: Political and Private Realities: 1890s–1980s.* London: Zed, 1990.

Lebra, Joyce, J. Paulson, and J. Everett, eds. *Women and Work in India: Continuity and Change.* New Delhi: Promilla, 1984.

Lewis, Oscar. *Village Life in Northern India: Studies in a Delhi Village.* Urbana, University of Illinois Press, 1958. Reprint. New York: Random House, 1965.

Liddle, Joanna, and Rama Joshi. *Daughters of Independence: Gender, Caste, and Class in India.* London: Zed, 1986.

Luschinsky, Mildred Stroop. "The Impact of Some Recent Indian Government Legislation on the Women of an Indian Village," *Asian Survey,* 3, No. 12, December 1963, 573–83.

Lynch, Owen M. *The Politics of Untouchability.* New York: Columbia University Press, 1969.

Lynch, Owen M. "Potter, Plotters, Prodders in a Bombay Slum: Marx and Meaning or Meaning Versus Marx," *Urban Anthropology,* 8, No. 1, Spring 1979, 1–27.

Lynch, Owen M. "Some Aspects of Political Mobilization among Adi-Dravidas in Bombay City." Pages 7–33 in Robert I. Crane, ed., *Aspects of Political Mobilization in South Asia.* Foreign and Comparative Studies/South Asia Series, No. 1. Syracuse: Maxwell School of Citizenship and Public Affairs, Syracuse University, 1976.

Lynch, Owen M. "Stratification, Inequality, Caste System: India." Pages 67–80 in Myron L. Cohen, ed., *Asia: Case Studies in the Social Sciences: A Guide for Teaching.* Armonk, New York: Sharpe, 1992.

Lynch, Owen M., ed. *Divine Passions: The Social Construction of Emotion in India.* Berkeley: University of California Press, 1990.

Mahar, J. Michael, ed. *The Untouchables in Contemporary India.* Tucson: University of Arizona Press, 1972.

Malik, Yogendra K., ed. *Boeings and Bullock-Carts: Studies in Change and Continuity in Indian Civilization: Essays in Honour of K. Ishwaran.* 5 vols. Delhi: Chanakya, 1990.

Maloney, Clarence. *Peoples of South Asia.* New York: Holt, Rinehart and Winston, 1974.

Mandelbaum, David G. *Society in India: Continuity and Change.* 2 vols. Berkeley: University of California Press, 1970.

Mandelbaum, David G. *Women's Seclusion and Men's Honor: Sex Roles in North India, Bangladesh, and Pakistan.* Tucson: University of Arizona Press, 1988.

Marshall, John F. "What Does Family Planning Mean to an Indian Villager?" Paper presented at the Annual Meeting of the American Anthropological Association, New York, 1971.

Martin, M. Kay, and Barbara Voorhies. *Female of the Species.* New York: Columbia University Press, 1975.

Massey, James. *A Concise History of Dalits.* Delhi: Indian Society for Promoting Christian Knowledge, 1994.

Massey, James, ed. *Indigenous People. Dalits: Dalit Issues in Today's Theological Debate.* ISPCK Contextual Theological Education Series, No. 5. Delhi: Indian Society for Promoting Christian Knowledge, 1994.

Mayer, Adrian C. *Caste and Kinship in Central India.* London: Routledge and Kegan Paul, 1960.

Mencher, Joan P. "The Caste System Upside Down, or the Not-So-Mysterious East," *Current Anthropology,* 15, No. 4, December 1974, 469–78.

Mencher, Joan P. *Female Cultivators and Agricultural Laborers: Who They Are and What They Do.* Michigan State University Working Papers on Women in International Development, No. 192. East Lansing: November 1989.

Miller, Barbara D. *The Endangered Sex: Neglect of Female Children in Rural North India.* Ithaca: Cornell University Press, 1981.

Miller, Barbara D. "Son Preference, the Household, and a Public Health Programme in North India." Pages 191–208 in Maithreyi Krishnaraj and Karuna Chanana, eds., *Gender and the Household Domain: Social and Cultural Dimensions.* Women and the Household in Asia, No. 4. New Delhi: Sage, 1989.

Mitter, Sara. *Dharma's Daughters: Contemporary Indian Women and Hindu Culture.* New York: Penguin, 1991.

Mukhopadhyay, Carol Chapnick, and Susan Seymour, eds. *Women, Education, and Family Structure in India.* Boulder, Colorado: Westview Press, 1994.

Naipaul, V.S. *India: A Million Mutinies Now.* New York: Penguin, 1990.

Nanda, Serena. *Neither Man Nor Woman: The Hijras of India.* Belmont, California: Wadsworth, 1990.

Nuckolls, Charles W., ed. *Siblings in South Asia: Brothers and Sisters in Cultural Context.* New York: Guilford, 1993.

Omvedt, Gail. *Dalits and the Democratic Revolution: Dr. Ambedkar and the Dalit Movement in Colonial India.* New Delhi: Sage, 1993.

Omvedt, Gail. "'Patriarchy': The Analysis of Women's Oppression," *Insurgent Sociologist,* 13, No. 3, 1986, 30–50.

Omvedt, Gail. *Reinventing Revolution: New Social Movements and the Socialist Tradition in India.* Armonk, New York: Sharpe, 1993.

Ostor, Akos, Lina Fruzetti, and Steve Barnett, eds. *Concepts of Person: Kinship, Caste, and Marriage in India.* Cambridge: Harvard University Press, 1982.

Papanek, Hanna, and Gail Minault, eds. *Separate Worlds: Studies of Purdah in South Asia.* Columbia, Missouri: South Asia Books; and New Delhi: Chanakya, 1982.

Patterson, Maureen L.P., in collaboration with William J. Alspaugh. *South Asian Civilizations: A Bibliographic Synthesis.* Chicago: University of Chicago Press, 1981.

Pollock, Sheldon. "Ramayana and Political Imagination in India," *Journal of Asian Studies,* 52, No. 2, May 1993, 261–97.

Quale, G. Robina. *Families in Context: A World History of Population.* New York: Greenwood, 1992.

Raheja, Gloria Goodwin. "Crying When She's Born, and Crying When She Goes Away: Marriage and the Idiom of the Gift in Pahansu Song Performance." Pages 19–59 in Lindsey Harlan and Paul Courtright, eds., *From the Margins of Hindu Marriage: Essays on Gender, Religion, and Culture.* New York: Oxford University Press, 1995.

Raheja, Gloria Goodwin. *The Poison in the Gift: Ritual, Prestation, and the Dominant Caste in a North Indian Village.* Chicago: University of Chicago Press, 1988.

Raheja, Gloria Goodwin, and Ann Grodzins Gold. *Listen to the Heron's Words: Reimagining Gender and Kinship in North India.* Berkeley: University of California Press, 1994.

Rao, Bhuvana. "Gender Ideology, Illness Perception, and Decision Making: Cultural Issues in Women's Health Care." Paper presented at Conference on South Asia, Madison, Wisconsin, 1993.

Reynolds, Holly Baker. "The Auspicious Married Woman." Pages 35–60 in Susan S. Wadley, ed., *The Powers of Tamil Women.* Foreign and Comparative Studies/South Asian Series, No. 6. Syracuse: Maxwell School of Citizenship and Public Affairs, Syracuse University, 1980.

Robb, Peter G. *Dalit Movements and the Meanings of Labour in India.* SOAS Studies on South Asia. Delhi: Oxford University Press, 1993.

Robinson, Francis, ed. *The Cambridge Encyclopedia of India, Pakistan, Bangladesh, Sri Lanka, Nepal, Bhutan, and the Maldives.* Cambridge: Cambridge University Press, 1989.

Roland, Alan. *In Search of Self in India and Japan: Toward a Cross-Cultural Psychology.* Princeton: Princeton University Press, 1988.

Routledge, Paul. *Terrains of Resistance: Nonviolent Social Movements and the Contestation of Place in India.* Westport, Connecticut: Praeger, 1993.

Roy, Manisha. *Bengali Women.* Chicago: University of Chicago Press, 1975.

Sakala, Carol. *Women of South Asia: A Guide to Resources.* Millwood, New York: Kraus, 1980.

Saraswathi, T.S., and Baljit Kaur, eds. *Human Development and Family Studies in India: An Agenda for Research and Policy.* New Delhi: Sage, 1993.

Shah, A.M., and I.P. Desai. *Division and Hierarchy: An Overview of Caste in Gujarat.* Delhi: Hindustan, 1988.

Sharma, Miriam. "Caste, Class, and Gender: Production and Reproduction in North India," *Journal of Peasant Studies* [London], 12, No. 4, July 1985, 57–88.

Sharma, Miriam. *The Politics of Inequality: Competition and Control in an Indian Village.* 2d ed. Honolulu: University of Hawaii Press, 1984.

Sharma, Miriam. "(Re)creating Tradition: Transformation of Marriage Practices in Rural North India." Paper presented at the Ninth Biennial Conference of the Asian Studies Association of Australia, University of New England, Armidale, 1991.

Sharma, Ursula. *Women and Property in Northwest India.* London: Tavistock, 1980.

Sims, Holly. "Malthusian Nightmare or Richest in Human Resources?" Pages 103–36 in Leonard Gordon and Philip Oldenburg, eds., *India Briefing, 1992.* Boulder, Colorado: Westview Press, in cooperation with The Asia Society, 1992.

Singer, Milton. *When a Great Tradition Modernizes: An Anthropological Approach to Indian Civilization.* New York: Praeger, 1972.

Singh, Kumar Suresh, ed. *People of India, 2: The Scheduled Castes.* Calcutta: Anthropological Survey of India, 1992.

Singh, Kumar Suresh, ed. *People of India, 3: The Scheduled Tribes.* Calcutta: Anthropological Survey of India, 1992.

Smart, Ninian, and Shivesh Thakur, eds. *Ethical and Political Dilemmas of Modern India.* New York: St. Martin's Press, 1993.

Srinivas, M.N. *Social Change in Modern India.* Berkeley: University of California Press, 1966.

Stern, Robert W. *Changing India: Bourgeois Revolution on the Subcontinent.* New York: Cambridge University Press, 1993.

Tana, Pradumna, and Rosalba Tana. *Traditional Stencil Designs from India.* Dover Pictorial Archives Series. New York: Dover, 1986.

Vatuk, Sylvia. "Authority, Power, and Autonomy in the Life Cycle of North Indian Women." Pages 23–44 in Paul Hockings, ed., *Dimensions of Social Life: Essays in Honor of David G. Mandelbaum.* Berlin: Mouton de Gruyter, 1987.

Vatuk, Sylvia, ed. *American Studies in the Anthropology of India.* New Delhi: Manohar, 1978.

Venkatachalam, R., and Viji Srinivasan. *Female Infanticide.* New Delhi: Har-Anand, 1993.

Wadley, Susan S. "Family Composition Strategies in Rural North India," *Social Science and Medicine* [Oxford], 37, No. 11, November 1993, 1367–76.

Wadley, Susan S. "Female Life Changes in Rural India," *Cultural Survival Quarterly,* 13, No. 2, 1989, 35–39.

Wadley, Susan S. *Struggling with Destiny: Karimpur Lives, 1925–1984.* Berkeley: University of California Press, 1994.

Wadley, Susan S., ed. *The Powers of Tamil Women.* Foreign and Comparative Studies/South Asian Series, No. 6. Syracuse: Maxwell School of Citizenship and Public Affairs, Syracuse University, 1980.

Weiner, Myron. *The Child and the State in India: Child Labor and Education Policy in Comparative Perspective.* Princeton: Princeton University Press, 1991.

Wolpert, Stanley. *India.* Berkeley: University of California Press, 1991.

Yadava, Surendar S., and James G. Chadney. "Female Education, Modernity, and Fertility in India," *Journal of Asian and Africa Studies* [Leiden], 29, Nos. 1–2, January–April 1994, 110–19.

(Various issues of the following publications also were used in the preparation of this chapter: *Economic and Political Weekly* [Bombay], 1992–93; *Hindustan Times* [New Delhi], 1987–95; *India Today* [New Delhi], 1986–94; *New York Review of Books,* 1990; *New York Times,* 1993, and *Washington Post,* 1994.)

Chapter 6

Acharya, Shankar. "India's Fiscal Policy." Pages 287–318 in Robert E.B. Lucas and Gustav F. Papanek, eds., *The Indian Economy: Recent Development and Future Prospects.* Boulder, Colorado: Westview Press, 1988.

Adiseshiah, Malcolm S., ed. *Seventh Plan Perspectives.* New Delhi: Lancer International, 1985.

Agarwal, Manmohan. "A Comparative Analysis of India's Export Performance, 1965–80," *Indian Economic Review* [Delhi], 23, No. 2, July–December 1988, 231–61.

Aggarwal, J.C. *Indian Economy: Crisis and Reforms.* New Delhi: Shipra, 1991.

Ahluwalia, Isher Judge. *Industrial Growth in India: Stagnation since the Mid-Sixties.* Delhi: Oxford University Press, 1985.

Ahluwalia, Montek S. "India's Economic Performance, Policies, and Prospects. Pages 345–60 in Robert E.B. Lucas and Gustav F. Papanek, eds., *The Indian Economy: Recent Development and Future Prospects.* Boulder, Colorado: Westview Press, 1988.

Alagh, Yoginder K. "Growth Performance of the Indian Economy, 1950–89: Problems of Employment and Poverty," *Developing Economies* [Tokyo], 30, No. 2, June 1992, 97–116.

Andersen, Walter K. "India in 1994: Economics to the Fore," *Asian Survey,* 35, No. 2, February 1995, 127–39.

Asher, Catherine Ella Blanshard. *The New Cambridge History of India, I.4: Architecture in Mughal India.* Cambridge University Press, 1992.

Automotive Component Manufacturers Association of India. *Automotive Industry of India: Facts and Figures, 1990–91.* 24th ed. New Delhi: 1991.

Awasthi, Aruna. *History and Development of Railways in India.* New Delhi: Deep and Deep, 1994.

Awasthi, Dipesh. *Regional Patterns of Industrial Growth in India.* New Delhi: Concept, 1991.

Bag, A.K. *Science and Civilization in India.* New Delhi: Navrang, 1985.

Balasubramanyam, V.N. *The Economy of India.* London: Weidenfeld and Nicolson, 1984.

Banerji, Arun Kumar, ed. *The Gulf War and the Energy Crisis in India.* Calcutta: School of International Relations and Strategic Studies, Jadavpur University, 1993.

Bansal, N.K., ed. *Decentralised Energy: Options and Technology.* New Delhi: Omega Scientific, 1993.

Bardhan, Pranab K. *The Political Economy of Development in India.* Delhi: Oxford University Press, 1984.

Beberoglu, Berch, ed. *Class, State, and Development in India.* New Delhi: Sage, 1992.

Behari, Madhuri, and B. Behari. *Indian Economy since Independence: Chronology of Events.* Delhi: D.K. Publications, 1983.

Bhagwati, Jagdish, ed. *India in Transition: Freeing the Economy.* Oxford: Clarendon Press, 1993.

Bhargava, P.K. "Transfers from the Center to the States of India," *Asian Survey,* 24, No. 6, June 1984, 665–87.

Bhatt, V.V. *Two Decades of Development: The Indian Experience.* Bombay: Vora, 1973.

Bhavsar, Praful D. "The Indian Space Program." Pages 596–601 in Frank N. Magill, ed., *Magill's Survey of Science, 2: Space Exploration Series.* Pasadena, California: Salem, 1989.

Blanpied, William A. "The Astronomical Program of Raja Sawai Jai Singh II and Its Historical Context," *Japanese Studies in the History of Science* [Tokyo], No. 13, 1974, 87–126.

Blanpied, William A. "India's Scientific Development," *Pacific Affairs* [Vancouver], 50, No. 1, Spring 1977, 91–99.

Blanpied, William A. "Pioneer Scientists in Pre-Independence India," *Physics Today,* 39, No. 5, May 1986, 36–44.

Blanpied, William A. "Science in India," *Journal for the History of Astronomy* [Chalfont St. Giles, United Kingdom], 6, Pt. 2, No. 16, June 1975, 135–37.

Blanpied, William A. "Science, Technology, and India's Aspirations." Pages 129–60 in Marshall M. Bouton and Philip Oldenburg, eds., *India Briefing, 1988.* Boulder, Colorado: Westview Press, in cooperation with The Asia Society, 1988.

Bookman, Milica Zarkovic. *The Political Economy of Discontinuous Development: Regional Disparities and Inter-regional Conflict.* New York: Praeger, 1991.

Bose, D.M., S.N. Sen, and B.V. Subbarayappa. *A Concise History of Science in India.* New Delhi: Indian National Science Academy, 1971.

Bradnock, Robert W., ed. *India Handbook, 1996.* 5th ed. Bath, United Kingdom: Trade and Travel, 1995.

Byrd, William A. "Planning in India: Lessons from Four Decades of Development Experience," *Journal of Comparative Economics,* 14, No. 4, December 1990, 713–35.

Byres, Terence J., ed. *The State and Development Planning in India.* Delhi: Oxford University Press, 1994.

Chadwick, John. "Amlohri Gears Up," *Mining Magazine* [London], September 1993, 127–34.

Chakravarty, Shubhra. *Atomic Energy in India.* New Delhi: Batra, 1992.

Chakravarty, Sukhamoy. *Development Planning: The Indian Experience.* Oxford: Clarendon Press, 1987.

Chandhok, H.L. *India Database. The Economy: Annual Time Series Data.* New Delhi: Living Media India, 1990.

Chattopadhyaya, Debiprasad, ed. *History of Science and Technology in Ancient India.* 2 vols. Calcutta: Firma KLM, 1986–91.

Chaturvedi, Prem Sagar. *Technology in Vedic Literature.* New Delhi: Books and Books, 1993.

Chaudhuri, Pramit. *The Indian Economy: Poverty and Development.* New York, St. Martin's Press, 1979.

Choy, Jon. "Japan and South Asia: Obstacles and Opportunities," *JEI Report,* No. 48A, December 23, 1994, 1–18.

Dasgupta, Ajit K. *A History of Indian Economic Thought.* Routledge History of Economic Thought Series. London: Routledge, 1993.

Dedrick, Jason, and Kenneth L. Kraemer. "Information Technology in India: Quest for Self-Reliance," *Asian Survey,* 33, No. 5, May 1993, 463–92.

Devinder Singh. *Akali Politics in Punjab, 1964–1985.* New Delhi: National Book Organisation, 1993.

Dhar, Pannalal N. "The Indian Economy: Past Performance and Current Issues." Pages 3–22 in Robert E.B. Lucas and Gustav F. Papanek, eds., *The Indian Economy: Recent Development and Future Prospects.* Westview Special Studies on South and Southeast Asia. Boulder, Colorado: Westview Press, 1988.

Dhingra, Ishwar C. *The Indian Economy: Resources, Planning, Development, and Problems.* Delhi: Sultan Chand, 1983.

Echeverri-Gent, John. "Between State and Market: The Dynamics of Formulating Effective Technology Policy." Paper presented at the Annual Meeting of the American Political Science Association, Washington, 1993.

Economist Intelligence Unit. *Country Profile: India, Nepal, 1992–93.* London: 1992.

Economist Intelligence Unit. *Country Profile: India, Nepal, 1993–94.* London: 1993.

Economist Intelligence Unit. *Country Report: India, Nepal* [London], No. 2, 1993.

Economist Intelligence Unit. *India to 1990: How Far Will Reform Go?* London: 1986.

Frank, Brian. "Satellites and Plowshares: The Potential Demise of the Indian Space Program," *Harvard International Review*, 15, No. 3, Spring 1993, 54–55, 69–70.

Fujita, Natsuki. "Liberalization Policies and Productivity in India," *Developing Economies* [Tokyo], 32, No. 4, December 1994, 509–24.

Gandhi, P. Jegadish, ed. *Economic Development and Policies in India.* New Delhi: Har-Anand, 1994.

Ghosh, Arun, K.K. Subrahmanian, Mridul Eapen, and Haseeb A. Drabu, eds. *Indian Industrialization: Structure and Policy Issues.* Delhi: Oxford University Press, 1992.

Goldsmith, Raymond W. *The Financial Development of India, 1860–1977.* New Haven: Yale University Press, 1983.

Graziano, Milena. *India's Motor Industry: Outlook to 2000.* Special Report No. 2013. London: Economist Intelligence Unit, 1989.

Guhan, S. *The World Bank's Lending in South Asia.* Brookings Occasional Papers. Washington: Brookings Institution, 1995.

Gupta, S.P. *Indian Science in the Eighties and After.* Delhi: Ajanta, 1990.

Gupta, Suraj B. *Black Income in India.* New Delhi: Sage, 1992.

Gupta, Suraj B. *Monetary Planning in India.* London: Oxford University Press, 1979.

Hanson, James A., and Samuel S. Lieberman. *India: Poverty, Employment, and Social Services.* A World Bank Country Study. Washington: World Bank, 1989.

Heitzman, James. "Information Systems and Urbanization in South Asia," *Contemporary South Asia* [Abingdon, United Kingdom], 1, No. 3, 1992, 363–80.

Henderson, P.D. *India: The Energy Sector.* London: Oxford University Press, 1975.

Hindustan Year Book and Who's Who, 1992. 60th ed. Ed., S. Sarkar. Calcutta: M.C. Sarkar, 1992.

Hindustan Year Book and Who's Who, 1994. 62d ed. Ed., S. Sarkar. Calcutta: M.C. Sarkar, 1994.

India. Council of Industrial and Scientific Research. Indian National Scientific Documentation Centre. *Directory of Scientific Research Institutions in India.* New Delhi: 1969.

India. Council of Scientific and Industrial Research. Indian National Scientific Documentation Centre. *Directory of Scientific Research Institutions in India.* New Delhi: 1989.

India. Council of Scientific and Industrial Research. Indian National Documentation Centre. "INSDOC." (Brochure.) New Delhi: n.d.

India. Council of Scientific and Industrial Research. Indian National Documentation Centre. "INSDOC: 40 Years, 1952–1992." (Brochure.) New Delhi: n.d.

India. Council of Scientific and Industrial Research. National Institute of Science, Technology, and Development Studies. *Annual Report, 1990–91.* Publication No. NISTADS-AR–1991. New Delhi: 1991.

India. Council of Scientific and Industrial Research. National Institute of Science, Technology, and Development Studies. *NISTADS.* New Delhi: n.d.

India. Council of Scientific and Industrial Research. Publications and Information Directorate. *Status Report on Science and Technology in India.* New Delhi: 1992.

India. Department of Space. *Annual Report, 1992–93.* Bangalore: 1993.

India. Department of Space. Indian Space Research Organisation. "India in Space." (Pamphlet.) Bangalore: 1992.

India. Director General of Civil Aviation. *Annual Report of the Civil Aviation Department, 1988.* New Delhi: 1989.

India. Ministry of Finance. Economic Division. *Economic Survey, 1990–91.* New Delhi: 1991.

India. Ministry of Finance. Economic Division. *Economic Survey, 1992–93.* New Delhi: 1993.

India. Ministry of Finance. Economic Division. *Economic Survey, 1994–95.* New Delhi: 1994.

India. Ministry of Home Affairs. Registrar General and Census Commissioner. *Census of India, 1991: Final Population Totals: Brief Analysis of Primary Census Abstract, Series–1, Paper–2 of 1992.* New Delhi: 1993.

India. Ministry of Information and Broadcasting. Directorate of Advertising and Visual Publicity. *Indian Economy: Prospects in the Power Sector.* No. 2/33/92 PPI. New Delhi: March 1993.

India. Ministry of Information and Broadcasting. Directorate of Advertising and Visual Publicity. *Indian Economy: Telecom*

Sector Poised for a Big Leap. No. 2/35/92 PPI. New Delhi: April 1993.

India. Ministry of Information and Broadcasting. Directorate of Advertising and Visual Publicity. *Union Budget, 1993–94: Imparting a New Dynamism to the Indian Economy.* No. 2/39/92 PPI. New Delhi: March 1993.

India. Ministry of Information and Broadcasting. Research and Reference Division. *India 1992: A Reference Annual.* New Delhi: February 1993.

India. Ministry of Information and Broadcasting. Research and Reference Division. *India 1993: A Reference Annual.* New Delhi: January 1994.

India. Ministry of Planning. Department of Statistics. Central Statistical Organisation. *Statistical Abstract 1990, India.* New Delhi: 1991.

India. Ministry of Railways. Railway Board. *Indian Railways Year Book, 1991–92.* New Delhi: 1992.

India. Ministry of Science and Technology. Department of Science and Technology. *Research and Development in Industry, 1992–93.* New Delhi: 1994.

India. Planning Commission. *Eighth Five Year Plan, 1992–97, 2: Sectoral Programmes of Development.* New Delhi: 1992.

India. Reserve Bank. Department of Economic Analysis and Policy. *India's Balance of Payments, 1948–49 to 1988–89.* Bombay: July 1993.

Indian Academy of Sciences. *Indian Academy of Sciences: The First Fifty Years.* Bangalore: 1984.

Indian Academy of Sciences. *Year Book, 1993.* Bangalore: 1993.

Indian Institute of Science. *Hand Book, 1992–93.* Bangalore: 1992.

Indian Institute of Science. Centre for Scientific and Industrial Consultancy. *CSIC—A Profile.* Bangalore: January 1991.

Inoue, Kyoko. *Industrial Development Policy of India.* I.D.E. Occasional Papers Series, No. 27. Tokyo: Institute of Developing Economies, 1992.

Ishiguro, Masayasu, and Takamasa Akiyama. *Energy Demand in Five Major Asian Developing Countries: Structure and Prospects.* World Bank Discussion Papers, No. 277. Washington: World Bank, 1995.

Jain, Ashok, and V.P. Kharbanda. *Status of Science and Technology in India.* Country paper presented at the SAARC Workshop on Science Policy. New Delhi: National Institute of Science, Technology, and Development Studies, 1988.

Jain, Nem Kumar. *Science and Scientists in India (Vedic to Modern).* Delhi: Indian Book Gallery, 1982.

Jalan, Bimal, ed. *The Indian Economy: Problems and Prospects.* New Delhi: Viking, 1992.

Jalan, Bimal. *India's Economic Crisis: The Way Ahead.* Delhi: Oxford University Press, 1991.

Jane's International ABC Aerospace Directory, 1994. 43d ed. Ed., Stephen Adams. Coulsdon, United Kingdom: Jane's Information Group, 1994.

Jane's International ABC Aerospace Directory, 1995. 44th ed. Ed., Ian Tandy. Coulsdon, United Kingdom: Jane's Information Group, 1995.

Jane's Space Directory, 1994–94. 10th ed. Ed., Andrew Wilson. Coulsdon, United Kingdom: Jane's Information Group, 1994.

Jane's Urban Transport Systems, 1994–95. 13th ed. Ed., Chris Bushell. Coulsdon, United Kingdom: Jane's Information Group, 1994.

Jane's World Railways, 1994–95. 36th ed. Ed., James Abbott. Coulsdon, United Kingdom: Jane's Information Group, 1994.

Johnson, B.L.C. *Development in South Asia.* Harmondsworth, United Kingdom: Penguin, 1983.

Joshi, Vijay, and I.M.D. Little. *India: Macroeconomics and Political Economy, 1964–1991.* World Bank Macroeconomic Series. Washington: World Bank, 1994.

Kamath, Shyman J. "Foreign Aid and India: Financing the Leviathan State," *Policy Analysis,* No. 170, May 6, 1992, 1–26.

Khatkhate, Deena. "Productivity in Manufacturing as a Determinant of Growth: The India Case," *World Development,* 21, No. 9, September 1993, 1441–45.

Kochanek, Stanley A. "The Politics of Regulation: Rajiv's New Mantras," *Journal of Commonwealth and Comparative Politics* [London], 23, No. 3, November 1985, 189–211.

Kohli, Rajan. *Structural Change in Indian Industries.* New Delhi: Capital Foundation Society, 1994.

Krishna, Raj. "The Economic Development of India," *Scientific American*, 243, No. 3, September 1980, 166–77.

Krishnaswamy, K.S., ed. *Poverty and Income Distribution.* Bombay: Oxford University Press, 1990.

Kumar, Dharma, and Meghnad Desai, eds. *The Cambridge Economic History of India, 2: c.1757–c.1970.* Cambridge: Cambridge University Press, 1983.

Kuppuram, G., and K. Kumudamani, eds. *History of Science and Technology in India.* 12 vols. Delhi: Sundeep Prakashan, 1990.

Lall, Sanjaya. "India," *World Development* [Oxford], 12, Nos. 5–6, May–June 1984, 535–65.

Lipton, Michael, and John Toye. *Does Aid Work in India? A Country Study of the Impact of Official Development Assistance.* London: Routledge, 1990.

Lucas, Robert E.B. "India's Industrial Policy," Pages 185–202 in Robert E.B. Lucas and Gustav F. Papanek, eds., *The Indian Economy: Recent Development and Future Prospects.* Westview Special Studies on South and Southeast Asia. Boulder, Colorado: Westview Press, 1988.

Lucas, Robert E.B., and Gustav F. Papanek, eds. *The Indian Economy: Recent Development and Future Prospects.* Boulder, Colorado: Westview Press, 1988.

Maddox, John, and K.S. Jayaraman. "Science in India," *Nature* [London], 366, No. 6456, December 16, 1993, 611–26.

Mandal, S.K. *Regional Disparities and Imbalances in India's Planned Economic Development.* New Delhi: Deep and Deep, 1987.

Mehta, Fredie A. "Growth, Controls, and the Private Sector." Pages 203–13 in Robert E.B. Lucas and Gustav F. Papanek, eds., *The Indian Economy: Recent Development and Future Prospects.* Boulder, Colorado: Westview Press, 1988.

Mohan, R., and V. Aggarwal. "Comments and Controls: Planning for Indian Industrial Development," *Journal of Comparative Economics*, 14, No. 4, December 1990, 681–712.

Mongia, J.N. *India's Economic Development Strategies, 1951–2000 A.D.* New Delhi: Allied, 1986.

Morehouse, Ward. *Science in India: Institution-Building and the Organizational System for Research and Development.* Bombay: Popular Prakashan, 1971.

Mukerjee, Swati. "The Impact of Liberalizing Imports: India, a Case Study," *Journal of Developing Areas*, 28, No. 4, July 1994, 521–33.

Mukerji, S.K., and B.V. Subbarayappa, eds. *Science in India: A Changing Profile*. New Delhi: Indian National Science Academy, 1984.

Mydral, Gunnar. *Asian Drama: An Inquiry into the Poverty of Nations*. 3 vols. New York: Pantheon, 1968.

Nehru, Jawaharlal. *The Discovery of India*. New York: Day, 1946. Reprint. Ed., Robert I. Crane. Garden City, New York: Anchor, 1960.

Papanek, Gustav F. "Poverty in India." Pages 121–41 in Robert E.B. Lucas and Gustav F. Papanek, eds., *The Indian Economy: Recent Development and Future Prospects*. Boulder, Colorado: Westview Press, 1988.

Patel, I.G. "On Taking India into the Twenty-First Century (New Economic Policy in India)," *Modern Asian Studies* [London], 21, Pt. 2, April 1987, 209–31.

Percy, Charles H. "South Asia's Take-Off," *Foreign Affairs*, 72, No. 5, Winter 1992–93, 166–74.

Petroleum Economist. "Energy Map of India." (Map.) London: October 1993.

Rahman, A. "Indian Muslims: A Historical Perspective." Pages 5–18 in Ratna Sahai, ed., *Muslims in India*. New Delhi: Ministry of External Affairs, 1989.

Rahman, Abdur, ed. *Science and Technology in Indian Culture: A Historical Perspective*. New Delhi: National Institute of Science, Technology and Development Studies, 1984.

Raj, K.N. *New Economic Policy*. Delhi: Oxford University Press, 1986.

Ramaseshan, Sivaraj. "The Problems of Growing Science in India and Other Developing Countries: The Role of Academics," *Annals of the New York Academy of Sciences*, 610, October 31, 1990, 141–49.

Ramaseshan, Sivaraj, and C. Ramachandra Rao, comps. *C.V. Rama: A Pictorial Biography*. Bangalore: Indian Academy of Sciences, 1988.

Ranganathan, V. "Electricity Privatization: The Case of India," *Energy Policy*, 21, No. 8, August 1993, 875–80.

Rangarajan, C. "India's Foreign Borrowing." Pages 253–70 in Robert E.B. Lucas and Gustav F. Papanek, eds., *The Indian Economy: Recent Development and Future Prospects*. Boulder, Colorado: Westview Press, 1988.

Rashid, Aneesa Ismail. "Trade, Growth, and Liberalization: The Indian Experience, 1977–1989," *Journal of Developing Areas*, 29, No. 3, April 1995, 355–70.

Ray, Animesh. *Maritime India: Ports and Shipping*. Calcutta: Pearl, 1993.

Ray, Rajat Kanta. *Entrepreneurship and Industry in India, 1800–1947*. Oxford in India Readings: Themes in Indian History. New Delhi: Oxford University Press, 1992.

Ray, S.K. *Indian Economy*. New Delhi: Prentice-Hall, 1987.

Robinson, E.A.G., and Michael Kidron. *Economic Development in South Asia: Proceedings of a Conference Held by the International Economic Association at Kandy, Ceylon*. London: Macmilan, 1970.

Robinson, Francis, ed. *The Cambridge Encyclopedia of India, Pakistan, Bangladesh, Sri Lanka, Nepal, Bhutan, and the Maldives*. Cambridge: Cambridge University Press, 1989.

Rosen, George. *Contrasting Styles of Industrial Reform: China and India in the 1980s*. Chicago: University of Chicago Press, 1992.

Rothermund, Dietmar. *An Economic History of India from Pre-colonial Times to 1986*. London: Croom Helm, 1988.

Sangwan, Satpal. "Science Education in India under Colonial Constraints, 1792–1857," *Oxford Review of Education* [Oxford], 16, No. 1, 1990, 81–95.

Sato, Hiroshi. "The Political Economy of Central Budgetary Transfers to States in India, 1972–82," *Developing Economies* [Tokyo], 30, No. 4, December 1992, 347–76.

Schiff, Maurice. "The Impact of Two-Tier Producer and Consumer Food Pricing in India," *World Bank Economic Review*, 8, No. 1, January 1994, 103–25.

Sen, Amartya Kumar. "Indian Development: Lessons and Non-Lessons," *Daedalus*, 18, No. 4, Fall 1989, 369–92.

Shanti Jagannathan. *EC and India in the 1990s: Towards Corporate Synergy*. New Delhi: Indian Council for Research on International Economic Relations, 1993.

Singh, Navjyoti. "Foundations of Logic in Ancient India: Linguistics and Mathematics." Pages 79–106 in A. Rahman, ed., *Science and Technology in Indian Culture*. New Delhi: National Institute of Science, Technology, and Development Studies, 1984.

Singh, Prahlad. *Jantar-Mantars of India (Stone Observatories)*. Jaipur: Holiday Publications, 1986.

Singh, Virendra. "Tata Institute of Fundamental Research." (Unpublished text of lecture.) Bombay: n.d.

Sinha, Ajit Kumar, ed. *New Economic Policy of India: Restructuring and Liberalizing the Economy for the 21st Century*. New Delhi: Deep and Deep, 1994.

Sinha, R.K., ed. *Economic Development since Independence*. New Delhi: Deep and Deep, 1988.

Sinha, R.K., ed. *The Great Ascent: The Rural Poor in South Asia*. Baltimore: Johns Hopkins University Press, 1990.

Sinha, R.K., ed. *Planning and Development in India*. New Delhi: Har-Anand, 1994.

Society of Indian Aerospace Technologies and Industries. *Directory of Indian Aerospace, 1993*. Bangalore: Interline, 1993.

Sondhi, Sunil. *Science, Technology, and India's Foreign Policy*. Delhi: Anamika Prakashan, 1994.

South Asian Handbook: India and the Indian Sub-Continent, 1994. 2d ed. Ed., Robert W. Bradnock. Bath, United Kingdom: Trade and Travel, 1993.

Sridharan, E. "Economic Liberalism and India's Political Economy: Towards a Paradigm Synthesis," *Journal of Commonwealth and Comparative Politics* [London], 31, No. 3, November 1993, 1–31.

Sridharan, E. "Leadership Time Horizons in India: The Impact on Economic Restructuring," *Asian Survey*, 31, No. 12, December 1991, 1200–13.

Streeten, Paul, and Michael Lipton, eds. *The Crisis of Indian Planning: Economic Planning in the 1960s*. London: Oxford University Press, 1968.

Subbarayappa, B.V. *In Pursuit of Excellence: A History of the Indian Institute of Science*. New Delhi: Tata McGraw-Hill, 1992.

Tata Institute of Fundamental Research. *Annual Report, 1991–92*. Ed., S.K. Mitra. Bombay: 1992.

Tata Services. Department of Economics and Statistics. *Statistical Outline of India, 1988–89.* 16th ed. Ed., B.S. Gupta. Bombay: 1989.

Tata Services. Department of Economics and Statistics. *Statistical Outline of India, 1992–93.* 20th ed. Ed., B.S. Gupta. Bombay: 1992.

Tata Services. Department of Economics and Statistics. *Statistical Outline of India, 1994–95.* 21st ed. Ed., B.S. Gupta. Bombay: 1994.

Thomas, Richard. *India's Emergence as an Industrial Power: Middle Eastern Contracts.* Hamden, Connecticut: Archon, 1982.

Tytler, Jagdish. "India's Transportation Opportunities," *Leaders,* 17, No. 4, December 1994, 217.

United Nations. Development Programme. *Human Development Report, 1993.* New York: Oxford University Press, 1993.

United Nations. Industrial Development Organization. *New Dimensions of Industrial Growth.* Oxford: Basil Blackwell, 1990.

United States. Central Intelligence Agency. Directorate of Intelligence. *Handbook of International Economic Statistics.* CPAS 94–1001. Washington: September 1994.

United States. National Science Foundation. *Human Resources for Science and Technology: The Asian Region.* Surveys of Science Resources Series, NSF 93–303. Washington: 1993.

United States. Trade and Development Agency. "The Trade and Development Agency in India." (Brochure.) Washington: September 1993.

Vaidyanathan, A. "The Indian Economy since Independence, 1947–1970." Pages 947–95 in Dharma Kumar and Meghnad Desai, eds., *Cambridge Economic History of India,* 2: *c.1757–c.1970.* Cambridge: Cambridge University Press, 1983.

Verma, R.K., and Anupama Verma. *Evaluation and Impact of Jawahar Rozgar Yojana.* New Delhi: Mohit, 1994.

Wallich, Christine, Raja J. Chelliah, and Narain Sinha, eds. *State Finances in India.* 3 vols. World Bank Staff Working Paper, No. 523. Washington: World Bank, 1982.

West, Jim, ed. *International Petroleum Encyclopedia.* Tulsa, Oklahoma: PennWell, 1992.

World Bank. *Economic Developments in India: Achievements and Challenges.* World Bank Country Study. Washington: 1995

World Bank. *India: Recent Economic Developments and Prospects.* A World Bank Country Study. Washington: 1995.

World Bank. Country Operations Industry and Finance Division. *India: Country Economic Memorandum: Recent Developments: Achievements and Challenges.* Report No. 14402–IN. Washington: May 30, 1995.

World Bank. Operations Evaluation Department. *World Bank Support for Industrialization in Korea, India, and Indonesia.* World Bank Operations Evaluation Study. Washington: 1992.

The World of Learning, 1995. 45th ed. London: Europa, 1994.

World Radio TV Handbook, 1995. 49th ed. Ed., Andrew G. Sennitt. Amsterdam: Billboard, 1995.

(Various issues of the following publications also were used in the preparation of this chapter: *Asian Wall Street Journal* [Hong Kong], 1992–93; *Asiaweek* [Hong Kong], 1993–94; *Defense News*, 1993; *Economic and Political Weekly* [Bombay], 1984–92; *Far Eastern Economic Review* [Hong Kong], 1993–95; *Financial Times* [London], 1994; Foreign Broadcast Information Service, *Daily Report: Near East and South Asia*, 1993–95; *International Railway Journal and Rapid Transit Review* [Falmouth], 1993–94; *New York Times*, 1994; *Sainik Samachar* [New Delhi], 1994; and *Washington Post*, 1994–95.)

Chapter 7

Acharya, K.C.S. *Food Security System of India: Evolution of the Buffer Stocking Policy and Its Evaluation.* New Delhi: Concept, 1983.

Alderman, Harold, George Mergos, and Roger Slade. *Cooperatives and the Commercialization of Milk Production in India: A Literature Review.* Washington: International Food Policy Research Institute, 1987.

Ansari, Nasim, ed. *Agrarian Structure, Land Reform, and Agricultural Growth in India.* Delhi: Tata McGraw-Hill, 1991.

Attwood, D.W., and B.S. Baviskar, eds. *Who Shares? Co-operatives and Rural Development.* New Delhi: Oxford University Press, 1988.

Bagchi, Kathkali S. *Drought-Prone India: Problems and Perspectives.* 2 vols. New Delhi: Agricole, 1991.

Bahuguna, Vinod Kumar, Vinay Luthra, and Brij McMan Singh Rathor. "Collective Forest Management in India," *Ambio* [Stockholm], 23, No. 4–5, July 1994, 269–73.

Baral, Lok Raj. "India-Nepal Relations: Continuity and Change," *Asian Survey*, 32, No. 9, September 1992, 815–29.

Bardhan, Pranab K. "Demographic Effects on Agricultural Proletarianization: The Evidence from India." Pages 175–83 in Ronald D. Lee, W. Brian Arthur, Allen C. Kelley, Gerry Rodgers, and T.N. Srinivasan, eds., *Population, Food, and Rural Development*. International Studies in Demography. Oxford: Clarendon Press, 1988.

Bardhan, Pranab K. *Land, Labor, and Rural Poverty: Essays in Development Economics*. New Delhi: Oxford University Press, 1984.

Baxi, Upendra, and Bhikhu Parekh, eds. *Crisis and Change in Contemporary India*. New Delhi: Sage, 1995.

Bhalla, A.S., and A.K.N. Reddy, eds. *The Technological Transformation of Rural India*. New York: St. Martin's Press, 1994.

Bhalla, G.S, and Y.K. Alagh. *Performance of Indian Agriculture: A Districtwide Study*. New Delhi: Sterling, 1979.

Bhalla, G.S., and D.S. Tyagi. *Patterns in Indian Agricultural Development: A District Level Study*. New York: Institute for Studies in Industrial Development, 1989.

Bhatia, B.M. *Indian Agriculture: A Policy Perspective*. New Delhi: Sage, 1988.

Bhatta, Sitesh. *Agricultural Price Policy and Production in India*. Delhi: Konark, 1991.

Bhuleshkar, Ashok Vasant, ed. *Indian Economy in the World Setting*. Bombay: Himalaya, 1988.

Blyn, George. *Agricultural Trends in India, 1891–1947: Output, Availability, and Productivity*. Philadelphia: University of Pennsylvania Press, 1966.

Brass, Paul, ed. "New Farmers' Movements in India," *Journal of Peasant Studies* [London], 21, Nos. 3–4, April–July 1994, 1–286.

Dahiya, L.N. *Dynamics of Economic Life in Rural India*. Delhi: Gian, 1991.

Dantwala, M.L., et al. *Indian Agricultural Development since Independence: A Collection of Essays*. New Delhi: Oxford University Press and IBH, 1986.

de Janury, Alain, and K. Subbarao. *Agricultural Price Policy and Income Distribution in India.* New Delhi: Oxford University Press, 1986.

Desai, Vasant. *A Study of Rural Economics: A Systems Approach.* Bombay: Himalaya, 1983.

Dhawan, B.D. *The Big Dams: Claims and Counter Claims.* New Delhi: Commonwealth, 1981.

Dhawan, B.D. "Water Resource Management in India," *Indian Journal of Agricultural Economics* [Bombay], 44, No. 3, July–September 1989, 233–41.

Diwakar, D.M. *Agriculture and Industry: Dynamics of Imbalances in India.* New Delhi: Manak, 1991.

Doornbos, Martin, Frank Van Borsten, Manoshi Mitra, and Piet Terhal. *Dairy Aid and Development: India's Operation Flood.* New Delhi: Sage, 1990.

Ghosh, Ambica. *Emerging Capitalism in Indian Agriculture, 1: The Historical Roots of Its Uneven Development.* New Delhi: People's, 1988.

Gillespie, Stuart, and Geraldine McNeill. *Food, Health, and Survival in India and Developing Countries.* New Delhi: Oxford University Press, 1992.

Goyal, S.K. *Agricultural Prices and Its Impact on the Indian Economy: A Case Study of Haryana.* New Delhi: Classical, 1992.

Hazell, Peter B.R., and C. Ramasamy. *The Green Revolution Reconsidered: The Impact of High-Yielding Rice Varieties in South India.* Baltimore: Johns Hopkins University Press, 1991.

Hindustan Year Book and Who's Who, 1994. 62d ed. Ed., S. Sarkar. Calcutta: M.C. Sarkar, 1994.

India. Ministry of Agriculture. *Department of Agricultural Research and Education Report, 1988–89.* New Delhi: 1992.

India. Ministry of Agriculture. Department of Agriculture and Co-operation. *Annual Report, 1991–92.* New Delhi: 1992.

India. Ministry of Agriculture. Department of Agriculture and Co-operation. *Annual Report, 1994–95.* New Delhi: 1994.

India. Ministry of Agriculture. Department of Agriculture and Co-operation. Directorate of Economics and Statistics. *Agricultural Situation in India.* New Delhi: 1991.

India. Ministry of Agriculture. Fisheries Division. *Hand Book of Fisheries Statistics, 1991.* New Delhi: 1992.

India. Ministry of Finance. Economic Division. *Economic Survey, 1991–92, 2: Sectoral Developments.* New Delhi: 1992.

India. Ministry of Finance. Economic Division. *Economic Survey, 1993–94.* New Delhi: 1994.

India. Ministry of Information and Broadcasting. Research and Reference Division. *India 1992: A Reference Annual.* New Delhi: February 1993.

India. Ministry of Information and Broadcasting. Research and Reference Division. *India 1993: A Reference Annual.* New Delhi: January 1994.

India. Ministry of Planning. Department of Statistics. Central Statistical Organisation. *Statistical Abstract 1990, India.* New Delhi: 1991.

India. Planning Commission. *Eighth Five Year Plan, 1992–97, 1: Objectives, Perspectives, Macro Dimensions, Policy Framework, and Resources.* New Delhi: 1992.

India. Planning Commission. *Eighth Five Year Plan, 1992–97, 2: Sectoral Programmes of Development.* New Delhi: 1992.

India. Planning Commission. *Sixth Five Year Plan, 1980–85.* New Delhi: 1992.

Jakhade, M., and H.B. Shivamaggi. "Inter-District Comparisons of Agricultural Development and Spread of Banking Facilities in Rural Areas," *Reserve Bank of India Bulletin* [Bombay], 23, No. 10, October 1969, 1559–1615.

Jannuzi, F. Tomasson. *India's Persistent Dilemma: The Political Economy of Agrarian Reform.* Boulder: Colorado: Westview Press, 1994.

Jha, P.R. *Agriculture and Economic Development.* New Delhi: Ashish, 1988.

Kapila, Uma, ed. *Indian Economy since Independence: Different Aspects of Agricultural Development.* Delhi: Academic Foundation, 1990.

Kashyap, Subhash C., ed. *National Policy Studies.* New Delhi: Tata McGraw-Hill for the Lok Sabha Secretariat, 1990.

Lele, Uma, and A.A. Goldsmith. "The Development of National Agricultural Research Capacity: India's Experience with the Rockefeller Foundation and Its Significance for Africa," *Economic Development and Cultural Change,* 37, No. 2, January 1989, 305–43.

Maheshwari, Shriram. *Rural Development in India: A Public Policy Approach.* 2d ed. New Delhi: Sage, 1995.

Mandal, Gobinda. *Technology, Growth, and Welfare in Indian Agriculture.* New Delhi: Agricole, 1989.

Mellor, John W., and Gunvant M. Desai. *Agricultural Change and Rural Poverty: Variations on a Theme by Dharm Narain.* Delhi: Oxford University Press, 1986.

Narain, Dharm. *Impact of Price Movements on Areas under Selected Crops in India, 1900–1939.* Cambridge: Cambridge University Press, 1957.

Narain, Dharm. "Growth and Imbalances in Indian Agriculture," *Journal of the Indian Society of Agricultural Statistics* [New Delhi], 24, No. 1, June 1972, 9–20.

Narain, Dharm. *Studies on Indian Agriculture.* Eds., K.N. Raj, Amratya Sen, and C.H. Hanumantha Rao. Delhi: Oxford University Press, 1988.

Narayana, N.S.S., K.S. Parikh, and T.N. Srinivasan. *Agriculture, Growth, and Redistribution of Income: Policy Analysis with a General Equilibirum Model of India.* Amsterdam: Elsevier Science, 1991.

"NGO-Government Interaction in India." Pages 91–188 in John Farrington and David J. Lewis, eds., *Non-Governmental Organizations and the State in Asia: Rethinking Roles in Sustainable Agricultural Development.* Non-Governmental Organizations Series. London: Routledge, 1993.

Raghuram, Parvati. "Invisible Female Agricultural Labour in India." Pages 109–19 in Janet Henshall Momsen and Vivian Kinnaird, eds., *Different Places, Different Voices: Gender and Development in Africa, Asia, and Latin America.* International Studies of Women and Place. London: Routledge, 1993.

Ravindranath, N.H., and D.O. Hall. "Indian Forest Conservation and Tropical Deforestation," *Ambio* [Stockholm], 23, No. 8, December 1994, 521–23.

Robinson, Francis, ed. *The Cambridge Encyclopedia of India, Pakistan, Bangladesh, Sri Lanka, Nepal, Bhutan, and the Maldives.* Cambridge: Cambridge University Press, 1989.

Sehgal, J.L., D.K. Mondal, C. Mondal, and S. Vadivelo. *Agro-Ecological Regions of India.* Technical Bulletin, NBSS Publication, No. 24. Nagpur: National Bureau of Soil Survey and Land

Use Planning, Indian Council of Agricultural Research, 1990.

Sharma, Rita, and Thomas T. Poleman. *The New Economics of India's Green Revolution: Income and Employment Diffusion in Uttar Pradesh.* Ithaca: Cornell University Press, 1993.

Sheth, Pravin N. "The Sardar Sarovar Project: Ecopolitics of Development," Pages 400–31 in Upendra Baxi and Bhikhu Parekh, eds., *Crisis and Change in Contemporary India.* New Delhi: Sage, 1995.

Shome, K.B., and S.P. Raychaudhri. "Rating Soils of India," *Proceedings of the National Institute of Sciences of India* [New Delhi], 26, Part A, Supplement 1, December 1960, 260–89.

Srinivasan, T.N., ed. *Agriculture and Trade in China and India: Policy and Performance since 1950.* San Francisco: International Center for Economic Growth, 1994.

Subrahmanya, Susheela, and I. Satya Sundaram, eds. *Growth of Agriculture and Rural Development in India.* New Delhi: Deep and Deep, 1987.

Tata Services. Department of Economics and Statistics. *Statistical Outline of India, 1988–89.* 16th ed. Ed., B.S. Gupta. Bombay: 1989.

Tata Services. Department of Economics and Statistics. *Statistical Outline of India, 1992–93.* 20th ed. Ed., B.S. Gupta. Bombay: 1992.

Tata Services. Department of Economics and Statistics. *Statistical Outline of India, 1994–95.* 21st ed. Ed., B.S. Gupta. Bombay: 1994.

Thornton, Thomas P. "India Adrift: The Search for Moorings in a New World Order," *Asian Survey,* 32, No. 12, December 1992, 1063–77.

United Nations. Department of Economic and Social Information and Policy Analysis. Statistical Division. *Statistical Yearbook, 1992.* 39th ed. New York: 1994.

United States. Central Intelligence Agency. Directorate of Intelligence. *Handbook of International Economic Statistics.* CPAS 94–1001. Washington: September 1994.

United States. Department of Agriculture. Foreign Agricultural Service. *Foreign Agriculture, 1990–91.* Washington: August 1991.

United States. Department of Agriculture. Foreign Agricultural Service. *Foreign Agriculture, 1992.* Washington: December 1992.

United States. Embassy in New Delhi. *Annual Commodity Report, Oilseeds and Products, 1992.* New Delhi: 1992.

United States. Embassy in New Delhi. *India: Agricultural Situation, Annual Report, 1992.* CERP Series, No. IN–2023. Washington: United States Department of Agriculture, 1992.

Varma, Rameswari. "Assessing Rural Development Programmes in India from a Gender Perspective." Pages 120–30 in Janet Henshall Momsen and Vivian Kinnaird, eds., *Different Places, Different Voices: Gender and Development in Africa, Asia, and Latin America.* International Studies of Women and Place. London: Routledge, 1993.

Washbrook, David A. "The Commercialization of Agriculture in Colonial India: Production, Subsistence, and Reproduction in the 'Dry South', c. 1870–1930," *Modern Asian Studies* [London], 28, Pt. 1, February 1994, 129–64.

(Various issues of the following publications also were used in the preparation of this chapter: *Economic and Political Weekly* [Bombay], 1987–95; *New York Times,* 1993; and *Times of India* [New Delhi], 1993.)

Chapter 8

Agrawal, Suren. *Government and Politics in India: A Bibliographical Study of Contemporary Scenario Chronicling Rajiv Gandhi Era.* New Delhi: Concept, 1993.

Ahuja, Gurdas M. *BJP and the Indian Politics: Politics and Programmes of the Bharatiya Janata Party.* New Delhi: Ram, 1994.

Akbar, M.J. *Kashmir: Behind the Vale.* New Delhi: Viking, 1991.

Akbar, M.J. *The Siege Within: Challenges to a Nation's Unity.* London: Penguin, 1985.

Alexander, K.C. "Caste Mobilization and Class Consciousness: The Emergence of Agrarian Movements in Kerala and Tamil Nadu." Pages 362–413 in Francine R. Frankel and M.S.A. Rao, eds., *Dominance and State Power in Modern India: Decline of a Social Order, 1.* Delhi: Oxford University Press, 1989.

Amin, Shahid. "Gandhi as Mahatma: Gorakhpur District, Eastern UP, 1921–2." Pages 1–61 in Ranajit Guha, ed., *Subaltern Studies, 3.* Delhi: Oxford University Press, 1984.

Anand, C.L., and H.N. Seth. *Constitutional Law and History of Government of India, Government of India Act, 1935, and the Constitution of India.* 7th ed. Allahabad: University Book Agency, 1992.

Andersen, Walter K. "India in 1994: Economics to the Fore," *Asian Survey,* 35, No. 2, February 1995, 127–39.

Andersen, Walter K. "India's 1991 Elections: The Uncertain Verdict," *Asian Survey,* 31, No. 10, October 1991, 976–89.

Andersen, Walter K., and Shridhar D. Damle. *The Brotherhood in Saffron: The Rashtriya Swayamsevak Sangh and Hindu Revivalism.* Boulder, Colorado: Westview Press, 1987.

Austin, Dennis. *Democracy and Violence in India and Sri Lanka.* Chatham House Papers. London: Royal Institute of International Affairs, 1995.

Austin, Granville. *The Indian Constitution: Cornerstone of a Nation.* Oxford: Clarendon Press, 1966.

Baar, Carl. "Social Action Litigation in India: The Operation and Limitations of the World's Most Active Judiciary," *Policy Studies Journal,* 19, No. 1, September 1990, 140–50.

Bajpai, K. Shankar. "India in 1991: New Beginnings," *Asian Survey,* 32, No. 2, February 1992, 207–16.

Balaram, Nhalileveettil Edapalath. *A Short History of the Communist Party of India.* Trivandrum: Prabhath, 1967.

Barnett, Marguerite Ross. *The Politics of Cultural Natonalism in South India.* Princeton: Princeton University Press, 1976.

Baruah, Sanjib. "The State and Separatist Militancy in Assam: Winning a Battle or Losing the War?" *Asian Survey,* 34, No. 10, October 1994, 863–77.

Basu, Amrita. *Two Faces of Protest: Contrasting Modes of Women's Activism in India.* Berkeley: University of California Press, 1992.

Baxi, Upendra. *Courage, Craft, and Contentions: The Indian Supreme Court in the Eighties.* Bombay: Tripathi, 1985.

Baxi, Upendra. *The Crisis of the Indian Legal System.* New Delhi: Vikas, 1982.

Baxi, Upendra, and Bhikhu Parekh, eds. *Crisis and Change in Contemporary India.* New Delhi: Sage, 1995.

Baxter, Craig, Yogendra K. Malik, Charles H. Kennedy, and Robert C. Oberst. *Government and Politics in South Asia.* 3d ed. Boulder, Colorado: Westview Press, 1993.

Bhargava, P.K. "Transfers from the Center to the States of India," *Asian Survey,* 24, No. 6, June 1984, 665–87.

Blaustein, Albert P., ed. "India Supplement," *Constitutions of the Countries of the World, 10.* Dobbs Ferry, New York: Oceana, April 1989.

Blaustein, Albert P., and Gisbert Flanz, eds. "India," *Constitutions of the Countries of the World, 10.* Dobbs Ferry, New York: Oceana, October 1990.

Brass, Paul R. *Ethnicity and Nationalism: Theory and Comparison.* New Delhi: Sage, 1991.

Brass, Paul R. *Factional Politics in an Indian State: The Congress Party in Uttar Pradesh.* Berkeley: University of California Press, 1966.

Brass, Paul R. *The New Cambridge History of India, IV.1: The Politics of India since Independence.* 2d ed. Cambridge: Cambridge University Press, 1994.

Brass, Paul R. "The Punjab Crisis and the Unity of India." Pages 169–213 in Atul Kohli, ed., *India's Democracy: An Analysis of Changing State-Society Relations.* Princeton: Princeton University Press, 1988.

Brass, Paul R. "The Rise of the BJP and the Future of Party Politics in Uttar Pradesh." Pages 255–92 in Harold A. Gould and Sumit Ganguly, eds., *India Votes: Alliance Politics and Minority Governments in the Ninth and Tenth General Elections.* Boulder, Colorado: Westview Press, 1993.

Butler, David, Ashok Lahiri, and Prannoy Roy. *India Decides: Elections 1952–1991.* 2d ed. New Delhi: Living Media India, 1991.

Calman, Leslie J. *Toward Empowerment: Women and Politics in India.* Boulder, Colorado: Westview Press, 1992.

Chatterjee, Partha. "Gandhi and the Critique of Civil Society." Pages 153–95 in Ranajit Guha, and Gayatri Chatravorty, eds., *Subaltern Studies: Writings on South Asian History and Society, 3.* Delhi: Oxford University Press, 1984.

Chaudhuri, Joyotpaul. "Federalism and the Siamese Twins: Diversity and Entropy in India's Domestic and Foreign Policy," *International Journal* [Toronto], 48, No. 3, Summer 1993, 448–69.

Chopra, J.K. *Women in the Indian Parliament: A Critical Study of Their Role.* New Delhi: Mittal, 1993.

Clive, John. *Macaulay: The Shaping of the Historian.* New York: Knopf, 1973.

Clive, John, and Thomas Pinney, eds. *Thomas Babington Macaulay: Selected Writings.* Chicago: University of Chicago Press, 1972.

Cohn, Bernard S. "History and Anthropology: The State of Play," *Comparative Studies in Society and History* [Cambridge], 22, No. 2, April 1980, 198–221.

Crossette, Barbara. *India: Facing the Twenty-First Century.* The Essential Asia Series. Bloomington: Indiana University Press, 1993.

Das Gupta, Joyotirindra. "India 1979: The Prize Chair and the People's Share—Electoral Diversion and Economic Rehearsal," *Asian Survey*, 20, No. 2, February 1980, 176–87.

Dhar, Pannanlal N. *Preventive Detention under Indian Constitution.* New Delhi: Deep and Deep, 1986.

Dhavan, Rajeev. *Litigation Explosion in India.* Bombay: Tripathi, 1986.

Dirks, Nicholas S. *The Hollow Crown.* Cambridge: Cambridge University Press, 1987.

Dua, Bhagwan D. "Federalism or Patrimonialism: The Making and Unmaking of Chief Ministers in India," *Asian Survey*, 25, No. 8, August 1985, 793–804.

Echeverri-Gent, John. *The State and The Poor: Public Policy and Political Development in India and the United States.* Berkeley: University of California Press, 1993.

Eisenstadt, S.N. "Dissent, Heterodoxy, and Civilization Dynamics: Some Analytical and Comparative Implications." Pages 1–10 in S.N. Eisenstadt, Reuven Kahane, and David Shulman, eds., *Orthodoxy, Heterodoxy, and Dissent in India.* Religion and Society, No. 23. New York: Mouton, 1984.

Engineer, Asghar Ali. *Communalism and Communal Violence in India: An Analytical Approach to Hindu Muslim Conflict.* Delhi: Ajanta, 1989.

Engineer, Ashghar Ali, and Pradeep Nayak, eds. *Communalisation of Politics and 10th Lok Sabha Elections.* Delhi: Ajanta, 1993.

Estava, Gustavo, and Madhu Suri Prakash. "Grassroots Resistance to Sustainable Development: Lessons from the Banks of the Narmada," *Ecologist,* 22, No. 2, March–April 1992, 45–51.

Farmer, Victoria L. "Politics and Airways: The Evolution of Television in India." Paper presented at the Annual Meeting of the Association for Asian Studies, Boston, March 23–27, 1994.

Fickett, Lewis P., Jr. "The Rise and Decline of the Janata Dal," *Asian Survey,* 33, No. 12, December 1993, 1151–62.

Frankel, Francine R. "Conclusion: Decline of a Social Order." Pages 382–417 in Francine R. Frankel and M.S.A. Rao, eds., *Dominance and State Power in Modern India: Decline of a Social Order,* 2. Delhi: Oxford University Press, 1990.

Frankel, Francine R. "India's Democracy in Transition," *World Policy Journal,* 7, No. 4, Summer 1990, 521–55.

Frankel, Francine R. *India's Political Economy, 1947–1977.* Princeton: Princeton University Press, 1978.

Frankel, Francine R., and M.S.A. Rao, eds. *Dominance and State Power in Modern India: Decline of a Social Order.* 2 vols. Delhi: Oxford University Press, 1989–90.

Gadgil, Madhav, and Ramachandra Guha. *This Fissured Land: An Ecological History of India.* Berkeley: University of California Press, 1993.

Ganguly, Sumit. "Avoiding War in Kashmir," *Foreign Affairs,* 69, No. 5, Winter 1990–1991, 57–73.

Ganguly, Sumit, and Kanti Bajpai. "India and the Crisis in Kashmir," *Asian Survey,* 34, No. 5, May 1994, 401–16.

George, Sudhir Jacob. "Bodo Movement in Assam: Unrest to Accord," *Asian Survey,* 34, No. 10, October 1994, 878–92.

Ghosh, Partha S. "Foreign Policy and Electoral Politics in India: Inconsequential Connection," *Asian Survey,* 34, No. 9, September 1994, 807–17.

Goswami, B. *The Indian Parliamentary Scene.* Jaipur: Pointer, 1994.

Gould, Harold A. "Modern Politics in an Indian District: 'Natural Selection' and 'Selective Co-optation'." Pages 217–48 in

Richard Sisson and Ramashray Roy, eds., *Diversity and Dominance in Indian Politics.* New Delhi: Sage, 1990.

Gould, Harold A., and Sumit Ganguly, eds. *India Votes: Alliance Politics and Minority Governments in the Ninth and Tenth General Elections.* Boulder, Colorado: Westview Press, 1992.

Goyel, Purushottam. *Delhi's March Towards Statehood.* New Delhi: UBS, 1993.

Graham, B.D. *Hindu Nationalism and Indian Politics: The Origins and Development of the Bharatiya Jana Sangh.* Cambridge: Cambridge University Press, 1990.

Grover, Verinder, and Ranjana Arora, eds. *Development of Politics and Government in India.* New Delhi: Deep and Deep, 1994.

Gupta, Akhil, and James Ferguson. "Beyond `Culture:' Space Identity and the Politics of Difference," *Cultural Anthropology*, 7, No. 1, February 1992, 6–23.

Hachten, William A. *The Growth of Media in the Third World.* Ames: Iowa State University Press, 1993.

Hardgrave, Robert L., Jr. *Under Pressure: Prospects for Political Stability.* Boulder, Colorado: Westview Press, 1984.

Hardgrave, Robert L., Jr., and Stanley A. Kochanek. *India: Government and Politics in a Developing Nation.* 5th ed. Fort Worth: Harcourt Brace Jovanovich, 1993.

Hauser, Walter. "Violence, Agrarian Radicalism, and the Audibility of Dissent: Electoral Politics and the Indian People's Front." Pages 341–79 in Harold A. Gould and Sumit Ganguly, eds., *India Votes: Alliance Politics and Minority Governments in the Ninth and Tenth General Elections.* Boulder, Colorado: Westview Press, 1993.

Hauser, Walter, and Wendy Singer. "The Democratic Rite: Celebration and Participation in the Indian Elections," *Asian Survey*, 26, No. 9, September 1986, 941–58.

Hewitt, Vernon. "Undoing the Centre? The Sarkaria Commission and the National Front Government in India." Pages 183–96 in Subrata K. Mitra and James Chiriyankandath, eds., *Electoral Politics in India: A Changing Landscape.* New Delhi: Segment 1992.

India. Backward Classes Commission. *Report of the Backward Classes Commission, Government of India.* 3 vols. Delhi: 1982–83.

India. Ministry of Agriculture and Irrigation. *Report of the Committee on Panchayat Raj Institutions.* New Delhi: 1978.

India. Ministry of Information and Broadcasting. Research and Reference Division. *India, 1994: A Reference Annual.* New Delhi: 1995.

India. Planning Commission. *Report of the Committee for the Study of Community Projects and National Extension Service.* (Chair, Balwantrai Mehta.) New Delhi: 1957.

India. Planning Commission. *Seventh Five Year Plan, 1985–1990.* New Delhi: 1985.

"India." Pages 294–356 in *The Far East and Australasia, 1995.* 26th ed. London: Europa, 1995.

Jagmohan. *My Frozen Turbulence in Kashmir.* New Delhi: Allied, 1991.

Jones, Kenneth W. *The New Cambridge History of India, III. 1: Socio-Religious Reform Movements in British India.* Cambridge: Cambridge University Press, 1989.

Joshi, Shashi. *Struggle for Hegemony in India, 1920–47: The Colonial State, the Left, and the National Movement.* 3 vols. New Delhi: Sage, 1991.

Khator, Renu. *Environment, Development, and Politics in India.* Lanham, Maryland: University Press of America, 1991.

Kishwar, Madhu, and Ruth Vanita. "Indian Women: A Decade of New Ferment." Pages 131–52 in Marshall M. Bouton and Philip Oldenberg, eds., *India Briefing, 1989.* Boulder, Colorado: Westview Press, in cooperation with the Asia Society, 1989.

Kochanek, Stanley A. "Briefcase Politics in India: The Congress Party and the Business Elite," *Asian Survey,* 27, No. 12, December 1987, 1279–1301.

Kochanek, Stanley A. *The Congress Party of India.* Princeton: Princeton University Press, 1968.

Kochanek, Stanley A. "Mrs. Gandhi's Pyramid." Pages 93–124 in Henry C. Hart, ed., *Indira Gandhi's India: A Political System Reappraised.* Boulder, Colorado: Westview Press, 1976.

Kohli, A.B. *First Citizens of India: Dr. Rajendra Prasad to Dr. Shanker Dayal Sharma: Profile and Bibliography.* New Delhi: Reliance, 1995.

Kohli, Atul. *Democracy and Discontent: India's Growing Crisis of Governability.* Cambridge: Cambridge University Press, 1990.

Kohli, Atul. "From Elite Activism to Democratic Consolidation: The Rise of Reform Communism in West Bengal." Pages 367–415 in Francine R. Frankel and M.S.A. Rao, eds., *Dominance and State Power in Modern India: Decline of a Social Order,* 2. Delhi: Oxford University Press, 1990.

Kohli, Atul. "The NTR Phenomenon in Andhra Pradesh: Political Change in a South Indian State," *Asian Survey,* 28, No. 10, October 1988, 991–1017.

Kohli, Atul. *The State and Poverty in India.* Cambridge: Cambridge University Press, 1987.

Kopf, David. *The Brahmo Samaj and the Shaping of the Modern Indian Mind.* Princeton: Princeton University Press, 1979.

Kothari, Rajni. "The Congress 'System' in India," *Asian Survey,* 4, No. 12, December 1964, 1161–73.

Kothari, Rajni. "Continuity and Change in the Indian Party System," *Asian Survey,* 10, No. 11, November 1970, 937–48.

Kothari, Rajni. *Politics in India.* Boston: Little, Brown, 1970.

Kothari, Rajni. *State Against Democracy: In Search of Humane Governance.* Delhi: Ajanta, 1988.

Kothari, Smitu. "Social Movements and the Redefinition of Democracy." Pages 131–62 in Philip Oldenburg, ed., *India Briefing, 1993.* Boulder, Colorado: Westview Press, in cooperation with The Asia Society, 1993.

Krishen, Pradip. "Cinema and Television." Pages 159–79 in Harold A. Gould and Sumit Ganguly, eds., *India Votes: Alliance Politics and Minority Governments in the Ninth and Tenth General Elections.* Boulder, Colorado: Westview Press, 1992.

Kumar, Dharma. "The Affirmative Action Debate in India," *Asian Survey,* 33, No. 3, March 1992, 290–302.

Lawson, Edward, ed. *Encyclopedia of Human Rights.* New York: Taylor and Francis, 1989.

Lewis, D.S., and D.J. Sagar, eds. *Political Parties of Asia and the Pacific: A Reference Guide.* Harlow, United Kingdom: Gale Research, 1992.

Limaye, Madhu. *Janata Party Experiment.* Delhi: B.R. Publishing, 1994.

Maheshwari, Shriram. *Indian Administrative System.* New Delhi: Jawahar, for the Centre for Political and Administrative Studies, 1994.

Maheshwari, Shriram. *The Mandal Commission and Mandalisation: A Critique.* New Delhi: Concept, 1991.

Malik, Yogendra K., and Jesse F. Marquette. *Political Mercenaries and Citizen Soldiers: A Profile of North Indian Party Activities.* Delhi: Chanakya, 1990.

Malik, Yogendra K., and V.B. Singh. "Bharatiya Janata Party: An Alternative to the Congress (I) to Govern?" *Asian Survey,* 32, No. 4, April 1992, 318–36.

Mallick, Ross. *Indian Communism: Opposition, Collaboration, and Institutionalization.* Delhi: Oxford University Press, 1994.

Mangal Deo, Jai. "Voluntary Agencies vis-à-vis Government," *Yojana* [New Delhi], 31, No. 4, March 1–15, 1987, 11–13.

Manor, James. "How and Why Liberal and Representative Politics Emerged in India," *Political Studies* [Oxford], 38, No. 1, March 1990, 20–38.

Manor, James. "Innovative Leadership in Modern India: M.K. Gandhi, Nehru, and I. Gandhi." Pages 187–214 in Gabriel Sheffer, ed., *Innovative Leaders in International Politics.* SUNY Series in Leadership Studies. Albany: State University of New York Press, 1993.

Manor, James. "Parties and the Party System." Pages 62–98 in Atul Kohli, ed., *India's Democracy: An Analysis of Changing State-Society Relations.* Princeton: Princeton University Press, 1988.

Manor, James. "Party Decay and Political Crisis in India," *Washington Quarterly,* 4, No. 3, Summer 1981, 25–40.

Mathur, Kuldeep. "The State and the Use of Coercive Power in India," *Asian Survey,* 32, No. 4, April 1992, 337–49.

Mathur, Kuldeep, and J.W. Bjorkman. *Top Policy Makers in India (Cabinet Ministers and Their Civil Service Advisers).* New Delhi: Concept, 1994.

Matthew, George, ed. *Panchayati Raj in Karnataka Today.* New Delhi: Institute of Social Sciences and Concept, 1986.

Mehrotra. N.C. *The Socialist Movement in India.* New Delhi: Radiant, 1995.

Meyer, Ralph C., and David S. Malcolm. "Voting in India: Effects of Economic Change and New Party Formation," *Asian Survey,* 33, No. 5, May 1993, 507–19.

Misra, B.B. *The Indian Middle Classes: Their Growth in Modern Times.* New Delhi: Oxford University Press, 1961.

Mitra, Subrata K. *Power, Protest, and Participation: Local Elites and Development in India.* New York: Routledge, 1992.

Moog, Robert. "Indian Litigiousness and the Litigation Explosion: Challenging the Legend," *Asian Survey,* 33, No. 12, December 1993, 1136–50.

Morris-Jones, W.H. *Politics Mainly Indian.* Madras: Orient Longman, 1978.

Mukherjee, Bimal Chandra. *Administration in Changing India.* New Delhi: Blaze, 1994.

Mundle, Sudipto, and M. Govinda Rao. "Issues in Fiscal Policy." Pages 228–45 in Bimal Jalan, ed., *The Indian Economy: Problems and Prospects.* New Delhi: Viking, 1992.

Myrdal, Jan. *India Waits.* Trans., Alan Bernstein. Chicago: Lake View Press, 1986.

Nadkarni, M.V. *Farmers' Movement in India.* Ahmedabad: Allied, 1987.

Nicholas, Nugent. "Rajiv Gandhi and the Congress Party—The Road to Defeat." Pages 43–52 in Subrata K. Mitra and James Chiriyankandath, eds., *Electoral Politics in India: A Changing Landscape.* New Delhi: Segment, 1992.

Nossiter, T.J. *Marxist State Governments in India.* London: Pinter, 1988.

Oldenburg, Philip. "Politics: How Threatening a Crisis?" Pages 1–9 in Philip Oldenburg, ed., *India Briefing, 1991.* Boulder, Colorado: Westview Press, in cooperation with The Asia Society, 1991.

Omvedt, Gail. "Kanshi Ram and the Bahujan Smaj Party." Pages 153–69 in K.L. Sharma, ed., *Caste and Class in India.* Jaipur: Rawat, 1994.

Omvedt, Gail. *Reinventing Revolution: New Social Movements and the Socialist Tradition in India.* Armonk, New York: Sharpe, 1993.

Overstreet, Gene D., and Marshall Windmiller. *Communism in India.* 2d ed. Bombay: Perennial, 1960.

Peritore, N. Patrick. "Environmental Attitudes of Indian Elites: Challenging Western Postmodernist Models," *Asian Survey,* 33, No. 8, August 1993, 804–18.

Pravin, Anand, and Albert P. Blaustein, eds. "India Supplement,"*Constitutions of the Countries of the World, 10.* Dobbs Ferry, New York: Oceana, January 1992.

Press Trust of India. *The Tenth Round: Story of Indian Elections 1991.* Calcutta: Rupa, 1991.

Rajagopal, Arvind. "The Rise of National Programming: The Case of Indian Television, Media," *Media, Culture, and Society* [London], 15, No. 1, January 1993, 91–111.

Rao, Hemlata. "Financial Relations," *Seminar* [New Delhi], No. 357, May 1989, 31–35.

Ray, Ashwini. "Towards the Concepts of a Post-Colonial Democracy." Pages 127–49 in Zoya Hasan, S.N. Jha, and Rasheeduddin Khan, eds., *The State Political Processes and Identity: Reflections on Modern India.* New Delhi: Sage, 1988.

Robinson, Francis, ed. *The Cambridge Encyclopedia of India, Pakistan, Bangladesh, Sri Lanka, Nepal, Bhutan, and the Maldives.* Cambridge: Cambridge University Press, 1989.

Robinson, Francis, and Paul R. Brass. "Introduction: The Development of the Indian National Congress." Pages 1–57 in Paul R. Brass and Francis Robinson, eds., *The Indian National Congress and Indian Society, 1885–1985.* Delhi: Chanakya, 1987.

Roy, Ramashray. "India in 1992: Search for Safety," *Asian Survey,* 33, No. 2, February 1993, 119–28.

Rubin, Barnett R. "The Civil Liberties Movement in India: New Approaches to the State and Social Change," *Asian Survey,* 27, No. 3, March 1987, 371–92.

Rubinoff, Arthur G. "India at the Crossroads," *Journal of Asian and Africa Studies* [Leiden], 28, Nos. 3–4, July–October 1993, 198–216.

Rudolph, Lloyd I. "The Faltering Novitiate: Rajiv at Home and Abroad in 1988." Pages 1–33 in Marshall M. Bouton and Philip Oldenburg, eds., *India Briefing, 1989.* Boulder, Colorado: Westview Press, in cooperation with the Asia Society, 1989.

Rudolph, Lloyd I. "The Media and Cultural Politics." Pages 159–79 in Harold A. Gould and Sumit Ganguly, eds., *India Votes: Alliance Politics and Minority Governments in the Ninth and Tenth General Elections.* Boulder, Colorado: Westview Press, 1993.

Rudolph, Lloyd I. "The Subcontinental Empire and the Regional Kingdom in Indian State Formation." (Unpublished manuscript.) University of Chicago: 1990.

Rudolph, Lloyd I. "Why Rajiv Gandhi's Death Saved the Congress: How an Event Affected the Outcome of the 1991 Election." Pages 436–47 in Harold A. Gould and Sumit Ganguly, eds., *India Votes: Alliance Politics and Minority Governments in the Ninth and Tenth General Elections.* Boulder, Colorado: Westview Press, 1993.

Rudolph, Lloyd I., and Susanne Hoeber Rudolph. *The Modernity of Tradition: Political Development in India.* Chicago: University of Chicago Press, 1967.

Rudolph, Lloyd I., and Susanne Hoeber Rudolph. *In Pursuit of Lakshmi: The Political Economy of the Indian State.* Chicago: University of Chicago Press, 1987.

Rudolph, Lloyd I., and Susanne Hoeber Rudolph. "Organisational Adaptation of the Congress under Rajiv Gandhi's Leadership." Pages 85–102 in Richard Sisson and Ramashray Roy, eds., *Diversity and Dominance in Indian Politics, 1: Changing Bases of Congress Support.* New Delhi: Sage, 1990.

Rudolph, Susan Hoeber. "Comparative Perspectives on the History of State Formation in India." Pages 15–29 in Subrata K. Mitra and James Chiriyankandath, eds., *Electoral Politics in India: A Changing Landscape.* New Delhi: Segment, 1992.

Sarkar, Sumit. *Modern India, 1885–1947.* Madras: Macmillan, 1983.

Sathe, S.P. *Constitutional Amendments in India, 1950–1988: Law and Politics.* Bombay: Tripathi, 1989.

Saxena, Rekha. *Indian Politics in Transition: From Dominance to Chaos.* New Delhi: Deep and Deep, 1994.

Sen Gupta, Bhabani. *Communism in Indian Politics.* New York: Columbia University Press, 1972.

Sethi, Harsh,and Smitu Kothari, eds. *The Non-Party Process: Uncertain Alternatives.* Delhi: Lokayan/UNRISD, 1985.

Sharma, K.L., ed. *Caste and Class in India.* Jaipur: Rawat, 1994.

Sharma, P.D., and Ramesh Kumar. "Legislators in an Indian State: A Study in Social Characteristics," *Asian Survey,* 32, No. 11, November 1992, 1000–11.

Shehth, D.L., and Harsh Sethi. "The NGO Sector in India: Historical Context and Current Discourse," *Voluntas: International Journal of Voluntary and Non-Profit Organizations* [Manchester], 2, No. 2, November 1991, 49–68.

Singh, Gurharpal. "The Punjab Elections 1992: Breakthrough or Breakdown?" *Asian Survey*, 32, No. 11, November 1992, 988–99.

Singh, Gurharpal. "Understanding the 'Punjab Problem '," *Asian Survey*, 27, No. 12, December 1987, 1268–77.

Singh, Hoshiar. "Constitutional Base for Panchayati Raj in India: The 73rd Amendment Act," *Asian Survey*, 34, No. 9, September 1994, 818–27.

Singh, Mahendra Prasad. "The Dilemma of the New Indian Party System: To Govern or Not to Govern?" *Asian Survey*, 32, No. 4, April 1992, 303–17.

Singh, Prakash. *The Naxalite Movement in India.* New Delhi: Rupa, 1995.

Singhal, Arvind, and Everett M. Rogers. *India's Information Revolution.* Newbury Park, California: Sage, 1989.

Sinha, Dipankar. "B.P. Singh, Chandra Shekhar, and 'Nowhere Politics' in India," *Asian Survey*, 31, No. 7, July 1991, 598–612.

Smith, Chris. *The Diffusion of Small Arms and Light Weapons in Pakistan and Northern India.* London: Center for Defence Studies, 1994.

Som, Reba. "Jawaharlal Nehru and the Hindu Code: A Victory of Symbol over Substance?" *Modern Asian Studies* [London], 28, Pt. 1, February 1994, 164–94.

Telford, Hamish. "The Political Economy of Punjab: Creating Space for Sikh Militancy," *Asian Survey*, 32, No. 11, November 1992, 969–87.

Tewary, I.N. *People, Panchayat, and Parliament.* New Delhi: Print Media, 1994.

Thakur, Devendra, ed. *District Planning and Panchayat Raj.* New Delhi: Deep and Deep, 1991.

Thakur, Ramesh Chandra. *Government and Politics of India.* New York: St. Martin's Press, 1995.

Thomas, Raju G.C., ed. *Perspectives on Kashmir: The Roots of Conflict in South Asia.* Boulder, Colorado: Westview Press, 1992.

Tully, Mark, and Satish Jacob. *Amritsar: Mrs. Gandhi's Last Battle.* London: Cape, 1985.

Tummala, Krishna K. "Democracy Triumphant: The Case of Andhra Pradesh," *Asian Survey*, 26, No. 3, March 1989, 378–95.

Tummala, Krishna K. "India's Federalism under Stress," *Asian Survey,* 32, No. 6, June 1992, 538–53.

United States. Central Intelligence Agency. Directorate of Intelligence. *Chiefs of State and Cabinet Members of Foreign Governments.* DI CS 95–004. Washington: April 1995.

Varshney, Ashutosh. "Battling the Past, Forging a Future? Ayodhya and Beyond." Pages 9–42 in Philip Oldenburg, ed., *India Briefing, 1993.* Boulder, Colorado: Westview Press, in cooperation with The Asia Society, 1993.

Varshney, Ashutosh. *Democracy, Development, and the Countryside: Urban-Rural Struggles in India.* Cambridge: Cambridge University Press, 1995.

Varshney, Ashutosh. "India, Pakistan, and Kashmir: Antinomies of Nationalism," *Asian Survey,* 31, No. 11, November 1991, 997–1019.

Verney, Douglas V. "From Executive to Legislative Federalism? The Transformation of the Political System in Canada and India," *Review of Politics,* 51, No. 2, Spring 1989, 241–63.

Verney, Douglas V. "The Role of the Governor in India's Administrative Federalism," *Indian Journal of Public Administration* [New Delhi], 31, No. 4, October–December 1985, 1243–68.

Wade, Robert. "The Market for Public Office: Why the Indian State Is Not Better at Development," *World Development,* 13, No. 4, April 1985, 467–97.

Wade, Robert. "The System of Administrative and Political Corruption: Canal Irrigation in South India," *Journal of Development Studies,* 18, No. 3, April 1982, 287–328.

Wallace, Paul. "Religious and Ethnic Politics: Political Mobilization in the Punjab." Pages 416–81 in Francine R. Frankel and M.S.A. Rao, eds., *Dominance and State Power in Modern India: Decline of a Social Order,* 2. Delhi: Oxford University Press, 1990.

Washbrook, David A. "Caste, Class, and Dominance in Modern Tamil Nadu: Non-Brahmanism, Dravidianism, and Tamil Nationalism." Pages 204–64 in Francine R. Frankel and M.S.A. Rao, eds., *Dominance and State Power in Modern India: Decline of a Social Order,* 1. New Delhi: Oxford University Press, 1989.

Weiner, Myron. *India at the Polls, 1980*. Washington: American Enterprise Institute, 1983.

Weiner, Myron. *Party Building in a New Nation: The Indian National Congress*. Chicago: University of Chicago Press, 1967.

Who Are the Guilty? Report of a Joint Inquiry into the Causes and Impact of the Riots in Delhi from 31 October to 10 November. New Delhi: People's Union for Democratic Rights and People's Union for Civil Liberties, 1984.

Wood, John R. "India's Narmada River Dams: Sardar Sarovar under Siege," *Asian Survey*, 33, No. 10, October 1993, 968–84.

(Various issues of the following publications also were used in the preparation of this chapter: "clari.world.asia.india" [electronic newsgroup], 1994–95; *Economic and Political Weekly* [Bombay], 1991; *Far Eastern Economic Review* [Hong Kong], 1994–95; Foreign Broadcast Information Service, *Daily Report: Near East and South Asia*, 1994–95; *Frontline* [Madras], 1995; *Guardian* [Manchester], 1989; *India Abroad*, 1994; *India Today* [New Delhi], 1987–95; *Keesing's Record of World Events* [London], 1994–95; *New Republic*, 1993; *New York Times*, 1989–94; and *Seminar* [New Delhi], 1989.)

Chapter 9

Ahmad, Imtiaz. *State and Foreign Policy: India's Role in South Asia*. New Delhi: Vikas, 1993.

Anderson, Ewan W. *An Atlas of World Political Flashpoints: A Sourcebook of Geopolitical Crisis*. New York: Facts on File, 1993.

Asia Yearbook. Annuals 1990 through 1995. Hong Kong: Far Eastern Economic Review, 1990–95.

Ayoob, Mohammed. *India and Southeast Asia: Indian Perceptions and Policies*. New York: Institute of Southeast Asian Studies; and Singapore: Routledge, 1990.

Ayoob, Mohammed. "India in South Asia: The Quest for Regional Predominance," *World Policy Journal*, 7, No. 1, Winter 1989–90, 107–33.

Babbage, Ross, and Sandy Gordon, eds. *India's Strategic Future: Regional State or Global Power?* New York: St. Martin's Press, 1992.

Bandyopadhyaya, Jayant. *The Making of India's Foreign Policy.* New Delhi: Allied, 1980.

Banerji, Arun Kumar. "India and West Asia: Changing Images Reflect Shifts in the Regional Balance of Power," *Round Table* [London], No. 305, 1988, 26–38.

Baral, J.K., and J.N. Mahanty. "India and the Gulf Crisis: The Response of a Minority Government," *Pacific Affairs* [Vancouver], 65, No. 3, Fall 1992, 368–84.

Baral, Lok Raj. "India-Nepal Relations: Continuity and Change," *Asian Survey,* 32, No. 9, September 1992, 815–29.

Batersky, M.V., and S.I. Lunyov. "India at the End of the Century: Transformation into an Asian Regional Power," *Asian Survey,* 30, No. 10, October 1990, 927–42.

Baxter, Craig, Yogendra K. Malik, Charles H. Kennedy, and Robert C. Oberst. *Government and Politics in South Asia.* 3d ed. Boulder, Colorado: Westview Press, 1993.

Bradnock, Robert W. *India's Foreign Policy since 1971.* London: Royal Institute of International Affairs; and New York: Council on Foreign Relations Press, 1990.

Brar, Bhupinder, ed. *Collapse of the Soviet Union: Lessons for India.* Delhi: Ajanta, 1993.

Buszynski, Leszek. "ASEAN Security Dilemmas," *Survival* [London], 34, No. 4, 1992–93, 90–107.

Chand, Khub. "India and the Federal Republic of Germany: Partners in Progress." Pages 163–74 in Satish Kumar, ed., *Yearbook on India's Foreign Policy, 1988–89.* New Delhi: Sage, 1989.

Chaudhuri, Joyotpaul. "Federalism and the Siamese Twins: Diversity and Entropy in India's Domestic and Foreign Policy," *International Journal* [Toronto], 48, No. 3, Summer 1993, 448–69.

Chellaney, Brahma. "Non-proliferation: An Indian Critique of U.S. Export Controls," *Orbis,* 38, No. 3, Summer 1994, 439–56.

Chellaney, Brahma. "South Asia's Passage to Nuclear Power," *International Security,* 16, No. 1, Summer 1991, 43–72.

Clad, James C. "India: Crisis and Transition," *Washington Quarterly,* 15, No. 1, Winter 1992, 91–104.

Cohen, Stephen Philip. "The Regional Impact of a Reforming India," *Adelphi Paper* [London], No. 276, April 1993, 83–93.

Cohen, Stephen Philip. "The Soviet Union and South Asia." Pages 201–26 in Edward A. Kolodziej and Roger E. Kaned, eds., *The Limits of Soviet Power in the Developing World.* Baltimore: Johns Hopkins University Press, 1989.

Cohen, Stephen Philip, ed. *Nuclear Proliferation in South Asia: The Prospects for Arms Control.* Boulder, Colorado: Westview Press, 1991.

Cohen, Stephen Philip, ed. *The Security of South Asia: American and Asian Perspectives.* Urbana: University of Illinois Press, 1987.

DeSilva, Kingsley. *India in Sri Lanka, 1983–1991.* Occasional Paper, No. 25. Washington: Asia Program, Woodrow Wilson Center, 1992.

Dhar, Pannalal N. *India, Her Neighbours and Foreign Policy.* New Delhi: Deep and Deep, 1991.

Duncan, Peter J.S. *The Soviet Union and India.* London: The Royal Institute of International Affairs; and New York: Council on Foreign Relations Press, 1989.

Fischer, Stephanie. "Israel and India: Forming a New Partnership," *Near East Report,* 36, No. 39, 1992, 182.

Gaan, N. "Hopes and Realities in Indo-US Relations: From a Cold War to a Post-Cold War Perspective," *India Quarterly* [New Delhi], 48, No. 4, October–December 1992, 1–22.

Ganguly, Sumit. "Avoiding War in Kashmir," *Foreign Affairs,* 69, No. 5, Winter 1990–1991, 57–73.

Ganguly, Sumit. "India: Charting a New Course?" *Current History,* 92, No. 578, December 1993, 426–30.

Ganguly, Sumit. "The Sino-Indian Border Talks, 1981–1989: A View from New Delhi," *Asian Survey,* 29, No. 12, December 1989, 1123–35.

Ganguly, Sumit. *Slouching Towards a Settlement: Sino-Indian Relations, 1962–1993.* Occasional Paper, No. 60. Washington: Asia Program, Woodrow Wilson Center, 1994.

Ganguly, Sumit, and Kanti Bajpai. "India and the Crisis in Kashmir," *Asian Survey,* 34, No. 5, May 1994, 401–16.

Ghosh, Partha S. "Foreign Policy and Electoral Politics in India: Inconsequential Connection," *Asian Survey,* 34, No. 9, September 1994, 807–17.

Gordon, A.D.D. *India's Security Policy: Desire and Necessity in a Changing World.* Working Paper No. 236. Canberra: Strategic and Defence Studies Centre, Australian National University, 1991.

Gould, Harold A., and Sumit Ganguly, eds. *The Hope and the Reality: U.S.-Indian Relations from Roosevelt to Reagan.* Boulder, Colorado: Westview Press, 1992.

Grover, Verinder, ed. *International Relations and Foreign Policy of India.* 10 vols. New Delhi: Deep and Deep, 1992.

Hagerty, Devin T. "India's Regional Security Doctrine," *Asian Survey,* 31, No. 4, April 1991, 351–63.

Harrison, Selig S. "South Asia and the United States: A Chance for a Fresh Start," *Current History,* 91, No. 563, March 1992, 97–105.

Harrison, Selig S., and Geoffrey Kemp. *India and America after the Cold War: Report of the Carnegie Endowment Study Group on U.S.-Indian Relations in a Changing International Environment.* Washington: Carnegie Endowment for International Peace, 1993.

Heimsath, Charles, and Surjit Mansingh. *A Diplomatic History of Modern India.* New Delhi: Allied, 1971.

Hennayake, Shantha K. "The Peace Accord and the Tamils in Sri Lanka," *Asian Survey,* 29, No. 4, April 1989, 401–15.

Horn, Robert C. *Soviet-Indian Relations: Issues and Influence.* New York: Praeger, 1982.

Imhasly, Bernard. "India's Cautious Approach to the USA," *Swiss Review of World Affairs* [Zurich], 41, No. 1, April 1991, 27–28.

India. Ministry of External Affairs. *Annual Report, 1991–92.* New Delhi: 1992.

India. Ministry of External Affairs. *Annual Report, 1992–93.* New Delhi: 1993.

India. Ministry of External Affairs. *Annual Report, 1994–95.* New Delhi: 1995.

India. Ministry of Home Affairs. Registrar General and Census Commissioner. *Census of India, 1991: Final Population Totals: Brief Analysis of Primary Census Abstract, Series–1, Paper–2 of 1992,* New Delhi: 1993.

India. Parliament. Parliamentary News and Views Service. *Compendium of Policy Statements Made in the Parliament: External Affairs.* New Delhi: various dates.

Jha, Nalini Kant. "Reviving U.S.-India Friendship in a Changing International Order," *Asian Survey*, 34, No. 12, December 1994, 1035–46.

Johal, Sarbjit. "India's Search for Capital Abroad: The U.S. Relationship," *Asian Survey*, 29, No. 10, October 1989, 971–82.

Jones, Rodney W. "Old Quarrels and New Realities: Security in Southern Asia after the Cold War," *Washington Quarterly*, 15, No. 1, 1992, 105–28.

Josh, Harcharan Singh, ed. *India's Foreign Policy: Nehru to Rao.* I.C.W.A. Seminar Publication Series. New Delhi: Indian Council of World Affairs, 1994.

Kapur, Ashok. "The Indian Subcontinent: The Contemporary Structure of Power and the Development of Power Relations," *Asian Survey*, 28, No. 7, July 1988, 693–710.

Kapur, Harish. *India's Foreign Policy, 1947–92: Shadows and Substance.* New Delhi: Sage, 1994.

Kolodziej, Edward A., and Roger E. Kanet, eds. *The Limits of Soviet Power in the Developing World.* Baltimore: Johns Hopkins University Press, 1989.

Kreisberg, Paul H. "The United States, South Asia, and American Interests," *Journal of International Affairs*, 43, No. 1, Summer–Fall 1989, 83–95.

Kumar, Satish. "Foreign Policy Trends." Pages 11–15 in Satish Kumar, ed., *Yearbook on India's Foreign Policy, 1987–88.* New Delhi: Sage, 1988.

Kumar, Satish. "Foreign Policy Trends." Pages 12–16 in Satish Kumar, ed., *Yearbook on India's Foreign Policy, 1989.* New Delhi: Sage, 1990.

Kumar, Satish. "Foreign Policy Trends." Pages 1–11 in Satish Kumar, ed., *Yearbook on India's Foreign Policy, 1990–91.* New Delhi: Tata McGraw-Hill, 1991.

Levin, André. "L'Inde a-t-elle encore les moyens de ses ambitions?" *Stratégique* [Paris], 50, No. 2, 1991, 171–81.

Liu, Xuecheng. *The Sino-India Border Dispute and Sino-India Relations.* Lanham, Maryland: University Press of America, 1994.

Lockwood, David E., and Barbara Leitch LePoer. "Kashmir: Conflict and Crisis." Major Issues Systems, IB90087. Washington: Congressional Research Service, Library of Congress, July 3, 1990.

Makeig, Douglas C. "War, No War, and the India-Pakistan Nego-
tiating Process," *Pacific Affairs* [Vancouver], 60, No. 3, 1987,
271–94.

Malik, J. Mohan. "India Copes with the Kremlin's Fall," *Orbis*,
37, No. 1, Winter 1993, 69–87.

Malik, J. Mohan. "India's Response to the Gulf Crisis: Implications for Indian Foreign Policy," *Asian Survey*, 31, No. 9, September 1991, 847–61.

Mansingh, Surjit. "India-China Relations in the Post-Cold War
Era," *Asian Survey*, 34, No. 3, March 1994, 285–300.

Mansingh, Surjit. *India's Search for Power: Indira Gandhi's Foreign
Policy, 1966–82.* New Delhi: Sage, 1984.

Mansingh, Surjit, and Steven I. Levine. "China and India: Moving Beyond Confrontation," *Problems of Communism*, 38, Nos.
2–3, March–June 1989, 30–49.

Mehra, Parshotam. *An 'Agreed' Frontier: Ladakh and India's
Northernmost Borders, 1846–1947.* Delhi: Oxford University
Press, 1992.

Mehrotra, Santosh. *India and the Soviet Union: Trade and Technology Transfer.* Soviet and East European Studies, No. 73. New
York: Cambridge University Press, 1990.

Menon, Rajan, and Henri J. Barkey. "The Transformation of
Central Asia: Implications for Regional and International
Security," *Survival* [London], 34, No. 4, 1992–93, 68–69.

Mudiam, Prithvi Ram. *India and the Middle East.* London: British Academic Press, 1994.

Muni, S.D. "India and the Post-Cold War World: Opportunities
and Challenges," *Asian Survey*, 31, No. 9, September 1991,
862–74.

Murthy, P.A. Narasimha. "Trends in India-Japan Relations."
Pages 137–50 in Satish Kumar, ed., *Yearbook on India's Foreign
Policy, 1989.* New Delhi: Sage, 1989.

Nehru, Jawaharlal. *Jawaharlal Nehru's Speeches.* 5 vols. New
Delhi: Publications Division, Ministry of Information and
Broadcasting, 1958–68.

Nehru, Jawaharlal. *Selected Works of Jawaharlal Nehru.* 16 vols. 2d
Series. New Delhi: Jawaharlal Memorial Fund, 1988–92.

Nehru, Jawaharlal. *Towards Freedom: An Autobiography.* New
York: Day, 1941.

Nester, William R. *Japan and the Third World: Patterns, Power, Prospects.* New York: St. Martin's Press, 1992.

Ollapally, Deepa, and Raja Ramanna. "U.S.-India Tensions: Misperceptions on Nuclear Proliferation," *Foreign Affairs,* 74, No. 1, January–February 1995, 13–18.

Palmer, Norman D. *The United States and India: The Dimensions of Influence.* New York: Praeger, 1984.

Panya, Amit. "Kashmir: The Way Forward," *Journal of Asian and African Affairs* [New Delhi], 2, No. 1, July 1990, 1–6.

Rais, Rasul B. "Afghanistan and Regional Security after the Cold War," *Problems of Communism,* 41, No. 3, 1992, 82–94.

Ranganathan, C.V. "China, The 'Asian Miracle' and India-China Relations," *Indian Defence Review* [New Delhi], 9, No. 4, October–December 1994, 9–18.

Rao, P. Venkateshwar. "Ethnic Conflict in Sri Lanka: India's Role and Perception," *Asian Survey,* 28, No. 4, April 1988, 419–36.

Razvi, S.M. Mujtaba. "India and the Security of the Indian Ocean/South Asia," *Round Table* [London], No. 311, July 1989, 317–22.

Rizvi, Hasan-Askari. *Pakistan and the Geostrategic Environment: A Study of Foreign Policy.* New York: St. Martin's Press, 1993.

Robinson, Francis, ed. *The Cambridge Encyclopedia of India, Pakistan, Bangladesh, Sri Lanka, Nepal, Bhutan, and the Maldives.* Cambridge: Cambridge University Press, 1989.

Rose, Leo E., and Eric Gonsalves, eds. *Towards a New World Order: Adjusting India-U.S. Relations.* Research Papers and Policy Studies, No. 38. Berkeley: Institute of East Asian Studies, University of California, 1992.

Rubinoff, Arthur G. "Commonalities and Dissimilarities in American and Canadian Approaches Towards the Indian Subcontinent," *Contemporary South Asia* [Abingdon, United Kingdom], 1, No. 3, 1992, 393–405.

Rubinoff, Arthur G. "The Multilateral Imperative in India's Foreign Policy," *Round Table* [London], No. 319, July 1991, 313–34.

Rubinoff, Arthur G. "Political Integration in Goa," *Journal of Developing Societies* [Leiden], 11, No. 1, June 1995, 36–50.

Saikal, Amin. "The Future of India and Southwest Asia." Pages 122–43 in Ross Babbage and Sandy Gordon, eds., *India's*

Strategic Future: Regional State or Global Power? New York: St. Martin's Press, 1992.

Saikal, Amin. *India in Southwest Asia.* Working Paper No. 1990/ 4. Canberra: Research School of Pacific Studies, Australian National University, 1990.

Shah, Sayed Mehtab Ali. "Anatomy of Indo-Pak Discord," *Journal of Asian and African Affairs* [New Delhi], 1, No. 1, July 1989, 35–47.

Shaumian, Tatyana L. "India's Foreign Policy: Interaction of Global and Regional Aspects," *Asian Survey,* 28, No. 11, November 1988, 1161–69.

Shukul, H.C. *India's Foreign Policy: The Strategy of Nonalignment.* Delhi: Chanakya, 1993.

Singh, Jasjit, ed. *Indo-US Relations in a Changing World: Proceedings of the Indo-US Strategic Symposium.* New Delhi: Lancer, in association with Institute for Defence Studies and Analyses, 1992.

Sismanidis, Roxane D.V. "China's International Security Policy," *Problems of Communism,* 40, No. 4, July–August 1991, 49–62.

Sreedhar, John Kaniyalil, comp. *Indo-Pak Relations: A Documentary Study.* New Delhi: ABC, 1993.

Sudhakar, E. *SAARC: Origin, Growth, and Future.* New Delhi: Gyan, 1994.

Tanham, George K. "Indian Strategic Culture," *Washington Quarterly,* 15, No. 1, Winter 1992, 129–42.

Taylor, Jay. *The Dragon and the Wild Goose: China and India. With New Epilogue.* New York: Praeger, 1991.

Thakur, Ramesh. "India and the Soviet Union: Conjunctions and Disjunctions of Interests," *Asian Survey,* 31, No. 9, September 1991, 826–46.

Thakur, Ramesh Chandra. "Normalizing Sino-Indian Relations," *Pacific Review* [London], 4, No. 1, 1991, 5–18.

Thakur, Ramesh, and Carlyle A. Thayer. *Soviet Relations with India and Vietnam.* New York: St. Martin's Press, 1992.

Tharoor, Shashi. *Reasons of State: Political Development and India's Foreign Policy under Indira Gandhi, 1966–1977.* New Delhi: Vikas, 1982.

Thomas, Raju G.C. "The Security and Economy of a Reforming India," *Adelphi Paper* [London], No. 276, April 1993, 62–82.

Thomas, Raju G.C., ed. *Perspectives on Kashmir: The Roots of Conflict in South Asia.* Boulder, Colorado: Westview Press, 1992.

United Nations. Department of Public Information. *Peace-Keeping Information Notes, 1993: Update No. 1.* New York: March 1993.

Untawale, Mukund G. "India and the World," *Conflict,* 11, No. 2, April–June 1991, 113–30.

Varshney, Ashutosh. "India, Pakistan, and Kashmir: Antinomies of Nationalism," *Asian Survey,* 31, No. 11, November 1991, 997–1019.

Viswam, S. "South-east and East Asia," *World Focus* [New Delhi], 12, Nos. 11–12, November–December 1991, 52–54.

Wang Hongyu. "Sino-Indian Relations: Present and Future," *Asian Survey,* 35, No. 6, June 1995, 546–54.

Ward, Richard Edmund. *India's Pro-Arab Policy: A Study in Continuity.* New York: Praeger, 1992.

Wariavwalla, Bharat. "India in 1987: Democracy on Trial," *Asian Survey,* 28, No. 2, February 1988, 119–25.

Wariavwalla, Bharat. "India in 1988: Drift, Disarray, or Patterns?" *Asian Survey,* 29, No. 2, February 1989, 189–98.

Yadav, R.S. "India and the Indian Ocean in the 1990s," *Asian Profile* [Hong Kong], 20, No. 5, October 1992, 415–25.

Yadav, R.S., ed. *India's Foreign Policy Towards 2000 A.D.* New Delhi: Deep and Deep, 1993.

Yearbook on India's Foreign Policy, 1987–88. Ed., Satish Kumar. New Delhi: Sage, 1988.

Yearbook on India's Foreign Policy, 1989. Ed., Satish Kumar. New Delhi: Sage, 1989.

Yearbook on India's Foreign Policy, 1990–91. Ed., Satish Kumar. New Delhi: Tata McGraw-Hill, 1991.

Zheng Ruixiang. "Shifting Obstacles in Sino-Indian Relations," *Pacific Review* [London], 6, No. 1, 1993, 63–70.

(Various issues of the following publications also were used in the preparation of this chapter: *Asiaweek* [Hong Kong], 1992; *Beijing Review* [Beijing], 1994; *Christian Science Monitor,* 1992; *Economic and Political Weekly* [Bombay], 1980–91; *Far Eastern Economic Review* [Hong Kong], 1987–94; Far Eastern Economic Review, *Asia Yearbook* [Hong Kong], 1985–92; *Foreign Affairs Record* [New Delhi], 1990–94; Foreign Broadcast Information Service, *Daily Report: China,* 1994–95; Foreign Broadcast

Information Service, *Daily Report: Near East and South Asia,* 1993–95; *India Today* [New Delhi], 1991–92; *Indian Express* [New Delhi], 1992; *Nation,* 1992; *New York Times,* 1992–95; *Sainik Samachar* [New Delhi], 1994; *Strategic Analysis* [New Delhi], 1989–91; *Times of India* [New Delhi], 1993; *Washington Post,* 1993–95; and *Washington Times,* 1992.)

Chapter 10

Akbar, M.J. *The Siege Within: Challenges to a Nation's Unity.* London: Penguin, 1985.

Ali, S. Mahmud. *The Fearful State: Power, People, and Internal War in South Asia.* London: Zed, 1993.

Amnesty International. *India: Torture, Rape, and Deaths in Custody.* London: 1992.

Amnesty International USA. *Amnesty International Report, 1994.* New York: 1994.

Amnesty International USA. *Amnesty International Report, 1995.* New York: 1995.

Amnesty International USA. *India: Torture and Deaths in Custody in Jammu and Kashmir.* New York: January 1995.

Andrade, John. *World Police and Paramilitary Forces.* Basingstoke, United Kingdom: Macmillan, 1985.

Asia Society. Contemporary Affairs Department. Study Group. *Preventing Nuclear Proliferation in South Asia.* New York: 1995.

Asia Watch/Physicians for Human Rights. *A Pattern of Impunity.* New York: Human Rights Watch, 1993.

Bain, William W. "Sino-Indian Military Modernization: The Potential for Destabilization," *Asian Affairs,* 21, No. 3, Fall 1994, 131–47.

Bajpai, Kanti P., and Harish C. Shukul, eds. *Interpreting World Politics: Essays for A.P. Rana.* New Delhi: Sage, 1995.

Baruah, Sanjib. "Immigration, Ethnic Conflict, and Political Turmoil—Assam 1979–1985," *Asian Survey,* 26, No. 11, November 1986, 1184–1206.

Brar, K.S. *Operation Blue Star: The True Story.* New Delhi: UBS, 1993.

Brass, Paul R. *The New Cambridge History of India, IV, 1: The Politics of India since Independence.* Cambridge: Cambridge University Press, 1990.

Brines, Russell. *The Indo-Pakistani Conflict.* New York: Pall Mall, 1968.

Bristow, Damon. *India's New Armament Strategy: A Return to Self-Sufficiency?* RUSI Whitehall Paper Series, 1995. London: Royal United Services Institute for Defence Studies, 1995.

Chattopadhyay, Rupak. "Indian Maritime Security: Case for a Blue Water Fleet," *Indian Defence Review* [New Delhi], 9, No. 3, July 1994, 79–85.

Chellaney, Brahma. *Nuclear Proliferation: The U.S.-Indian Conflict.* New Delhi: Orient Longman, 1993.

Chopra, S.C. "India's Maritime Security Concerns." Pages 92–108 in Jasjit Singh, ed., *Maritime Security.* New Delhi: Institute for Defence Studies and Analyses, 1993.

Cohen, Stephen Philip. *The Indian Army: Its Contributions to the Development of a Nation.* Berkeley: University of California Press, 1971.

Cohen, Stephen Philip, ed. *Nuclear Proliferation in South Asia: The Prospects for Arms Control.* Boulder, Colorado: Westview Press, 1991.

Das, Samir Kumar. *UFLA: United Liberation Front of Assam—A Political Analysis.* Delhi: Ajanta, 1994.

Datta, Prabhat Kumar. *Regionalism of Indian Politics.* New Delhi: Sterling, 1993.

Dixit, Aabha. "Indian Defence Industry Programmes: Current Stand and Cooperation Projects," *Military Technology* [Bonn], 38, No. 12, December 1994, 16–23.

Elkin, Jerrold F., and W. Andrew Ritezel. "The Debate on Restructuring India's Higher Defense Organization," *Asian Survey,* 24, No. 10, October 1984, 1069–85.

Elkin, Jerrold F., and W. Andrew Ritezel. "Military Role Expansion in India," *Armed Forces and Society,* 11, No. 4, Summer 1985, 489–504.

Encyclopedia of Police in India. 2 vols. Eds., S.K. Ghosh and K.F. Rustamji. New Delhi: Ashish, 1993–94.

Fay, Peter Ward. *The Forgotten Army: India's Armed Struggle for Independence, 1942–45.* Ann Arbor: University of Michigan Press, 1993.

Ganguly, Sumit. "Avoiding War in Kashmir," *Foreign Affairs,* 69, No. 5, Winter 1990–91, 57–73.

Ganguly, Sumit. "Ethno-Religious Conflict in South Asia," *Survival,* [London], 35, No. 2, Summer 1993, 88–109.

Ganguly, Sumit. "From the Defense of the Nation to Aid to the Civil: The Army in Contemporary India." Pages 11–26 in Charles H. Kennedy and David J. Louscher, eds., *Civil-Military Interaction in Asia and Africa.* Leiden: Brill, 1991.

Ganguly, Sumit. "From the Defence of the Nation to Aid to the Civil: The Army in Contemporary India," *Journal of Asian and African Studies* [Leiden], 26, Nos. 1–2, January–April 1991, 11–26.

Ganguly, Sumit. *The Origins of War in South Asia: The Indo-Pakistani Conflicts since 1947.* 2d ed. Boulder, Colorado: Westview Press, 1994.

Ganguly, Sumit. "Why India Joined the Nuclear Club," *Bulletin to the Atomic Scientists,* 39, No. 4, April 1983, 30–33.

Ganguly, Sumit, and Kanti Bajpai. "India and the Crisis in Kashmir," *Asian Survey,* 34, No. 5, May 1994, 401–16.

Garver, John W. "China-India Rivalry in Nepal: The Clash over Chinese Arms Sales," *Asian Survey,* 31, No. 10, October 1991, 956–75.

Ghosh, Partha S. *Conflict and Cooperation in South Asia.* New Delhi: Manohar, 1989.

Ghosh, Partha S. "Nuclear Rivalry in South Asia: Strategic Imperatives and National Pride," *Conflict Studies* [London], No. 274, September 1994, 1–22.

Ghosh, S.K. *Women and Crime.* New Delhi: Ashish, 1993.

Goldston, James A., and Patricia Gossman. *Human Rights in India: Kashmir under Siege.* An Asia Watch Report. New York: Human Rights Watch, May 1991.

Gordon, Sandy. "Economic Growth Dissipated on Regional Arms Race," *Asia-Pacific Defence Reporter* [Prahan], 21, Nos. 6–7, December 1994–January 1995, 46–49.

Gordon, Sandy. *India's Rise to Power in the Twentieth Century and Beyond.* New York: St. Martin's Press, 1995.

Gordon, Sandy. "Indian Defense Spending: Treading Water in the Fiscal Deep," *Asian Survey,* 32, No. 10, October 1992, 934–50.

Gould, Harold A. "The Utopian Side of the 1857 Uprising." Pages 86–116 in David Plath, ed., *Aware of Utopia.* Urbana: University of Illinois Press, 1971.

Handa, Tejinder. "Reorganisation of Indian Armed Forces," *Combat Journal* [Mhow], 20, No. 2, August 1993, 23–31.

Heehs, Peter. "The World at War: India's Divided Loyalties?" *History Today*, 45, No. 7, July 1995, 16–23.

Hills, Carol, and Daniel C. Silverman. "Nationalism and Feminism in Late Colonial India: The Rani of Jhansi Regiment, 1943–1945," *Modern Asian Studies* [London], 27, Pt. 4, October 1993, 741–60.

Hoffmann, Steven. *India and the China Crisis.* Berkeley: University of California Press, 1990.

Horn, Robert C. *Soviet-Indian Relations: Issues and Influence.* New York: Praeger, 1982.

Inder Singh, Anita. "India's Relations with Russia and Central Asia," *International Affairs*, 71, No. 1, January 1995, 69–81.

India. Ministry of Defence. *Annual Report, 1992–93.* New Delhi: 1993.

India. Ministry of Defence. *Defence Services Estimates, 1993–94.* New Delhi: 1993.

India. Ministry of Defence. *Defence Services Estimates, 1994–95.* New Delhi: 1994.

India. Ministry of Home Affairs. *Amnesty International Report. India: Torture, Rape, and Deaths in Custody: Allegations and Facts.* New Delhi: n.d. [ca. 1993].

India. Ministry of Home Affairs. *Legal Provisions for Protection of Human Rights.* New Delhi: n.d.

India. Ministry of Home Affairs. *Profile of Terrorist Violence in Jammu and Kashmir.* New Delhi: n.d. [ca. 1993].

India. Ministry of Information and Broadcasting. Directorate of Advertising and Visual Publicity. *Union Budget, 1993–94: Imparting a New Dynamism to the Indian Economy.* No. 2/39/92 PPI. New Delhi: March 1993.

India. Ministry of Information and Broadcasting. Research and Reference Division. *India 1992: A Reference Annual.* New Delhi: February 1993.

India. Ministry of Information and Broadcasting. Research and Reference Division. *India 1993: A Reference Annual.* New Delhi: January 1994.

Ispahani, Mahnaz. "India's Role in Sri Lanka's Ethnic Conflict." Pages 209–39 in Ariel E. Levite, Bruce W. Jentleson, and Larry Berman, eds., *Foreign Military Intervention: The Dynam-*

ics of Protracted Conflict. New York: Columbia University Press, 1992.

Jackson, Robert. *South Asian Crisis: India, Pakistan, Bangla Desh.* Studies in International Security, No. 17. London: Institute for Strategic Studies, 1975.

Jane's All the World's Aircraft, 1994–95. 85th ed. Ed., Mark Lambert. Coulsdon, United Kingdom: Jane's Information Group, 1994.

Jane's Armour and Artillery, 1994–95. 15th ed. Ed., Christopher F. Foss. Coulsdon, United Kingdom: Jane's Information Group, 1994.

Jane's Fighting Ships, 1994–95. 97th ed. Ed., Richard Sharpe. Coulsdon, United Kingdom: Jane's Information Group, 1994.

Jane's Infantry Weapons, 1994–95. 20th ed. Ed., Ivan V. Hogg. Coulsdon, United Kingdom: Jane's Information Group, 1994.

Jane's Land-Based Air Defence, 1994–95. 7th ed. Eds., Tony Cullen and Christopher F. Foss. Coulsdon, United Kingdom: Jane's Information Group, 1994.

Jane's Military Vehicles and Logistics, 1994–95. 15th ed. Eds., Christopher F. Foss, and Terry J. Gander. Coulsdon, United Kingdom: Jane's Information Group, 1994.

Jane's Radar and Electronic Warfare Systems, 1994–95. 6th ed. Ed., Bernard Blake. Coulsdon, United Kingdom: Jane's Information Group, 1994.

Jogindar Singh. *Behind the Scene: An Analysis of India's Military Operations, 1947–1971.* New Delhi: Lancer International, 1993.

Joshi, Manoj. *Combating Terrorism in Punjab.* Conflict Studies, No. 261. London: Research Institute for the Study of Conflict and Terrorism, May 1993.

Joshi, Manoj. "India's Nuclear Submarine Plans," *Asia-Pacific Defence Reporter* [Prahan], 21, Nos. 6–7, March–April 1995, 52.

Kadian, Rajesh. *India and Its Army.* New Delhi: Vision Books, 1990.

Kadian, Rajesh. *The Kashmir Tangle.* Boulder, Colorado: Westview Press, 1993.

Kapur, Rajiv A. *Sikh Separatism: The Politics of Faith.* London: Allen and Unwin, 1986.

Karnad, Bharat. *Future Imperilled: India's Security in the 1990s and Beyond.* New Delhi: Viking, 1994.

Kasturi, Bhashyam. "Military Intelligence in India: An Analysis," *Indian Defence Review* [New Delhi], 9, No. 1, January 1994, 71–74.

Kavic, Lorne J. *India's Quest for Security.* Berkeley: University of California Press, 1967.

Khanna, D.D., and P.N. Mehrotra. *Defence Versus Development: A Case Study of India.* New Delhi: Indus, 1993.

Kohli, Kailash. "Aviation in Indian Coast Guard," *Sainik Samachar* [New Delhi], 41, No. 5, January 30, 1994, 9–11.

Kolff, Dirk H. *Naukar, Rajput and Sepoy: The Ethnohistory of the Military Labour Market in Hindustan, 1450–1859.* Cambridge: Cambridge University Press, 1990.

Kukreja, Veena. *Civil-Military Relations in South Asia: Pakistan, Bangladesh, and India.* New Delhi: Sage, 1991.

Kundu, Apurba. "The Indian Armed Forces' Sikh and Non-Sikh Officers' Opinions of Operation Blue Star," *Pacific Affairs* [Vancouver], 67, No. 1, Spring 1994, 46–69.

Longer, V. *Red Coats to Live Green: A History of the Indian Army, 1600–1974.* New Delhi: Allied, 1993.

Makeig, Douglas C. "'Aid-To-Civil': Indian Army and Paramilitary Involvement in Domestic Peacekeeping." Washington: Federal Research Division, Library of Congress, 1984.

Makeig, Douglas C. "National Security." Pages 203–46 in James Heitzman and Robert L. Worden, eds., *Bangladesh: A Country Study.* 2d ed. DA Pam 550–175. Washington: GPO, 1989.

Mama, Hormuz. "India and Pakistan Retreat from the Brink," *International Defense Review* [Geneva], 23, No. 8, 1990, 851–52.

Manwani, Ranjna. *Indigenisation of Defence.* New Delhi: Associated Chambers of Commerce and Industry of India, May 1990.

Mathur, Kuldeep. "The State and the Use of Coercive Power in India," *Asian Survey*, 32, No. 4, April 1992, 337–49.

Maxwell, Neville. *India's China War.* New York: Doubleday, 1972.

Menezes, S.L. *Fidelity and Honour: The Indian Army from the Seventeenth to the Twenty-first Century.* New Delhi: Penguin, 1993.

The Military Balance: 1992–1993. London: International Institute for Strategic Studies, 1992.

The Military Balance: 1994–1995. London: International Institute for Strategic Studies, 1994.

The Military Yearbook, 1991–92. 23d ed. Ed., J. Baranwal. New Delhi: Guide, 1991.

Mishra, Rashmi, and Samarendra Mohanty. *Police and Social Change in India.* New Delhi: Asish, 1992.

Mohan Ram. *Sri Lanka: The Fractured Island.* New Delhi: Penguin, 1989.

Mukerjee, Dilip. "U.S. Weaponry for India," *Asian Survey,* 27, No. 6, June 1987, 595–614.

Nanda, Ravi. *India's Security in New World Order.* New Delhi: Lancer, 1994.

Narain, Partap. *Indian Arms Bazaar.* Delhi: Shipra, 1994.

Neier, Aryeh, and David Rothman. *Prison Conditions in India.* An Asia Watch Report. New York: Human Rights Watch, April 1991.

Nirmal, Anjali. *Role and Functioning of Central Police Organisations.* New Delhi: Uppal, 1992.

Palit, D.K. *War in the High Himalaya.* London: Hurst, 1991.

Parmar, Leena. *Society, Culture, and Military System.* Indian Sociological Studies. Jaipur: Rawat, 1994.

Pettigrew, Joyce J. M. *The Sikhs of the Punjab: Unheard Voices of State and Guerrilla Violence.* Atlantic Highlands, New Jersey: Zed, 1995.

Preston, Antony. "World Navies in Review," *U.S. Naval Institute Proceedings,* 121, No. 3, March 1995, 96–116.

Racioppi, Linda. *Soviet Policy Towards South Asia since 1970.* Cambridge: Cambridge University Press, 1994.

Robinson, Francis, ed. *The Cambridge Encyclopedia of India, Pakistan, Bangladesh, Sri Lanka, Nepal, Bhutan, and the Maldives.* Cambridge: Cambridge University Press, 1989.

Rodrigues, Sunith Francis. *Maximizing Effectiveness of Central Police Organisations.* New Delhi: June 1993.

Schwartzberg, Joseph E. "An American Perspective II," *Asian Affairs,* 22, No. 1, Spring 1995, 71–87.

Schwartzberg, Joseph E., ed. *A Historical Atlas of South Asia.* 2d impression. Reference Series of Association for Asian Studies, No. 2. New York: Oxford University Press, 1992.

Sehgal, B.P. Singh, ed. *Law, Judiciary, and Justice in India.* New Delhi: Deep and Deep, 1993.

Sen, Lionel Protip. *Slender Was the Thread: Kashmir Confrontation, 1947–48.* Bombay: Orient Longman, 1969.

Shah, Giriraj. *Elite Forces of India.* 2 vols. New Delhi: Cosmo, 1994.

Shah, Giriraj. *Image Makers: An Attitudinal Study of Indian Police.* New Delhi: Abhinav, 1993.

Sharma, R. "Indian Peacekeeping Contingent in Somalia," *Indian Defence Review* [New Delhi], 10, No. 2, April–June 1995, 41–44.

Singh, Depinder. *The IPKF in Sri Lanka.* Delhi: Trishul, 1991.

Singh, Jagjit. *Indian Gunners at War: The Western Front, 1971.* New Delhi: Lancer International, 1994.

Singh, Jasjit, ed. *Indo-US Relations in a Changing World: Proceedings of the Indo-US Strategic Symposium.* New Delhi: Lancer, in association with Institute for Defence Studies and Analyses, 1992.

Singh, Jasjit, ed. *Maritime Security.* New Delhi: Institute for Defence Studies and Analyses, 1993.

Singh, Surinder Nihal. "Why India Goes to Moscow for Arms," *Asian Survey,* 24, No. 7, July 1984, 707–20.

Sisson, Richard, and Leo E. Rose. *War and Secession: Pakistan, India, and the Creation of Bangladesh.* Berkeley: University of California Press, 1990.

Smith, Chris. *India's Ad Hoc Arsenal: Arms Procurement in Historical Perspective.* Oxford: Oxford University Press, 1994.

Society of Indian Aerospace Technologies and Industries. *Directory of Indian Aerospace, 1993.* Bangalore: Interline, 1993.

SP's Military Yearbook, 1992–93. 24th ed. Ed., J. Baranwal. New Delhi: Guide, 1992.

SP's Military Yearbook, 1993–94. 25th ed. Ed., J. Baranwal. New Delhi: Guide, 1993.

Srivasata, H.K. "UN Peace Support Operations (PSOs) and India: The Need for a New Approach," *Combat Journal* [Mhow], 21, No. 3, December 1994, 33–39.

Subramanian, K.S. "Police Organization in India: A Historical and Contemporary Assessment," *Indian Defence Review* [New Delhi], 10, No. 1, January–March 1995, 35–40.

Tanham, George K. "Indian Strategic Culture," *Washington Quarterly*, 15, No. 1, Winter 1992, 129–42.

Tanham, George K. *Indian Strategic Thought: An Interpretive Essay.* Santa Monica, California: Rand, 1992.

Thomas, Raju G.C. *The Defence of India: A Budgetary Perspective of Strategy and Politics.* New Delhi: Macmillan, 1978.

Thomas, Raju G.C. *Democracy, Security, and Development in India.* New York: St. Martin's Press, 1996.

Thomas, Raju G.C. *Indian Security Policy.* Princeton: Princeton University Press, 1986.

Thomas, Raju G.C. "India's Nuclear and Space Programs: Defense or Development?" *World Politics*, 38, No. 2, January 1986, 315–42.

Thomas, Raju G.C. "South Asian Security in the 1990s," *Adelphi Paper* [London], No. 278, July 1993, 3–86.

Thomas, Raju G.C., ed. *Perspectives on Kashmir: The Roots of Conflict in South Asia.* Boulder, Colorado: Westview Press, 1992.

Tully, Mark, and Satish Jacob. *Amritsar: Mrs. Gandhi's Last Battle.* London: Cape, 1985.

United Nations. Department of Public Information. *The Blue Helmets: A Review of United Nations Peace-keeping.* United Nations Publication No. E.90.I.18. New York: August 1990.

United Nations. Department of Public Information. *Peace-Keeping Information Notes, 1993: Update No. 1.* New York: March 1993.

United States. Department of State. *Country Reports on Human Rights Practices for 1993.* Report submitted to United States Congress, 103d, 2d Session, House of Representatives, Committee on Foreign Affairs, and Senate, Committee on Foreign Relations. Washington: GPO, February 1994.

Vaughn, Bruce. "The Use and Abuse of Intelligence Services in India," *Intelligence and National Security*, 8, No. 1, January 1993, 1–22.

Wirsing, Robert G. *India, Pakistan, and the Kashmir Dispute: On Regional Conflict and Its Resolution.* New York: St. Martin's Press, 1994.

Wolpert, Stanley. *A New History of India*. 4th ed. New York: Oxford University Press, 1992.

"World Defence Almanac, 1993–94: India," *Military Technology* [Bonn], 28, No. 1, January 1994, 222, 224–25.

Wulf, H. "India: The Unfulfilled Quest for Self-Sufficiency." Pages 125–45 in Michael Brzoska and Thomas Ohlson, eds., *Arms Production in the Third World*. London: Taylor and Francis for Stockholm International Peace Research Institute, 1986.

(Various issues of the following publications also were used in the preparation of this chapter: *Asiaweek* [Hong Kong], 1994; *Christian Science Monitor*, 1988; *Defense News*, 1994; *Far Eastern Economic Review* [Hong Kong], 1994–95; Foreign Broadcast Information Service, *Daily Report: China*, 1994; Foreign Broadcast Information Service, *Daily Report: Near East and South Asia*, 1993–95; *India Today* [New Delhi], 1990; *Jane's Defence Weekly* [Coulsdon, United Kingdom], 1995; *New York Times*, 1994–95; *Sainik Samachar* [New Delhi], 1993–94; *U.S. Naval Institute Proceedings*, 1994; and *Washington Post*, 1994–95.)

Glossary

All-India Muslim League (Muslim League)—Founded in 1906 in Dacca (Dhaka), in what then was the province of Eastern Bengal and Assam, by Muslim representatives from throughout India and Burma as a counterpoise to the Indian National Congress (*q.v.*).

Association of Southeast Asian Nations (ASEAN)—Founded in 1967 for the purpose of promoting regional stability, economic development, and cultural exchange. ASEAN's membership includes Brunei, Indonesia, Malaysia, the Philippines, Singapore, Thailand, and Vietnam. India is a "dialogue partner" along with Austria, Canada, China, Japan, New Zealand, the Republic of Korea (South Korea), Russia, and the United States.

Backward Classes—Citizens of India otherwise defined as members of Scheduled Castes (*q.v.*), Scheduled Tribes (*q.v.*), and other low-ranking and disadvantaged groups (sometimes referred to as Other Backward Classes). Discrimination against the Backward Classes is prohibited by Article 15 of the Indian constitution. The Backward Classes reportedly constitute an estimated 52 percent of India's population. The Mandal Commission (*q.v.*) identified 3,743 Backward Classes.

Brahman(s)—From the Sanskrit *brahmana*, one of four major caste groups (*varna*) or social classes. Brahmans are the highest caste group, traditionally made up of priests, philosophers, scholars, and religious leaders. Not to be confused with *brahman* (*q.v.*, the Absolute Reality).

brahman—The Absolute Reality, the eternal, supreme, or ultimate principle. A state of pure transcendence. In some Vedantic schools of Hindu thought, a Supreme Being who is the cause of the universe, with theistic attributes. Not to be confused with Brahman (*q.v.*, the priestly caste group).

British Raj (1858–1947)—The period of direct rule of India by the British government. The period began with the demise of the Mughal Empire and of East India Company rule and ended with the achievement of independence by India and Pakistan. During this time, the British crown was represented in India by a viceroy.

Colombo Plan for Cooperative Economic and Social Development in Asia and the Pacific (Colombo Plan)—Founded in 1950 to coordinate and aid development among newly independent countries. Members include nations throughout the Asia-Pacific region. Donor countries include Australia, Britain, Canada, India, Japan, New Zealand, and the United States. The headquarters are in Colombo, Sri Lanka.

Congress—See Indian National Congress.

crore—A unit of measure equal to 10 million (or 100 lakh, *q.v.*).

Dalit(s)—Sanskrit word meaning burst, split, broken, crushed, or destroyed but, since the nineteenth century, often taken to mean downtrodden; used in reference to Untouchables (Harijans, *q.v.*), outcastes, Scheduled Castes (*q.v.*), and others living in a reduced social state.

Devanagari—Literally, "the script of the city of the gods." Script used in the written forms of Hindi, Marathi, Nepali, Tibetan, Sanskrit, and in some forms of Konkani. In use in North India throughout the second millennium A.D.

dharma—A divinely ordained code of proper conduct.

fiscal year (FY)—April 1 to March 31. The fiscal year from April 1, 1995 through March 31, 1996, for example, is designated FY 1995.

Food and Agriculture Organization (FAO)—A United Nations specialized agency established in 1945 to raise living standards and increase the availability of agricultural products.

gross domestic product (GDP)—A value measure of the flow of domestic goods and services produced by an economy over a period of time, such as a year. Only output values of goods for final consumption and intermediate production are assumed to be included in the final prices. GDP is sometimes aggregated and shown at market prices, meaning that indirect taxes and subsidies are included; when these indirect taxes and subsidies have been eliminated, the result is GDP at factor cost. The word *gross* indicates that deductions for depreciation of physical assets have not been made. *See also* gross national product.

gross national product (GNP)—Gross domestic product (*q.v.*) plus net income or loss stemming from transactions with foreign countries, including income received from abroad by residents and subtracting payments remitted abroad to nonresidents. GNP is the broadest measurement of the output of goods and services by an economy. It can be calculated at market prices, which include indirect taxes and subsidies. Because indirect taxes and subsidies are only transfer payments, GNP is often calculated at factor cost by removing indirect taxes and subsidies.

Group of Fifteen (G–15)—Group of Third World countries that participated in the Conference on International Economic Cooperation held in several sessions between December 1975 and June 1977. At the Ninth Nonaligned Movement Summit in Belgrade in May 1989, the G–15 was designated a "Summit Level Group of South-South Consultation and Cooperation" and charged with opening a dialogue with the industrialized nations, specifically the members of the Group of Seven (Canada, France, Germany, Italy, Japan, Britain, and the United States). G–15 summits were held in Kuala Lumpur (June 1990), Caracas (November 1991), Dakar (November 1992), and New Delhi (March 1994). The group includes Algeria, Argentina, Brazil, Egypt, India, Indonesia, Jamaica, Malaysia, Mexico, Nigeria, Peru, Senegal, Venezuela, Yugoslavia, and Zimbabwe.

guru—In the Sikh faith, one of ten spiritual leaders and teachers, the first of whom was Nanak Dev, the last being Gobind Singh. In Hinduism, a religious teacher or guide.

Harijans—Term introduced by Mahatma Gandhi for Untouchables. Literal meaning is children of God. Militant members of this group prefer to be called Dalit (*q.v.*) in self-recognition of their historical oppression.

imam(s)—In general use and lower-cased, imam means the leader of congregational prayers; as such it implies no ordination or special spiritual powers beyond sufficient education to carry out this function. Imam is also used figuratively by many Sunni (*q.v.*) Muslims to mean the leader of the Islamic community. Among Shia (*q.v.*) Muslims, the word is usually upper-cased and takes on many complex and controversial meanings; in general, however, it indicates that particular descendant of the House of Ali who is believed to have been God's designated repository of the spiritual authority inherent in that line. The identity of this individual and the means of ascertaining his identity have been the major issues causing divisions among Shias.

Indian National Congress—Founded in 1885; before and after 1947, popularly called Congress or the Congress. A major force in the independence movement, the Congress has been dominant in Parliament and formed governments from 1947 to 1977, 1980 to 1985, and 1991 to 1996. In 1969 the Congress split, and the ruling party under Indira Gandhi became known as Congress (R)—R for Requisition—while the faction opposed to her was called Congress (O)—O for Organisation. In 1978 she renamed her party Congress (I)—I for Indira. There also have been Congress (S)—S for Socialist or Secular—and Congress (U)—for Urs, named after its founder Devanaj Urs—splinter groups.

International Monetary Fund (IMF)—Established along with the World Bank (*q.v.*) in 1945, the IMF is a specialized agency affiliated with the United Nations and is responsible for stabilizing international exchange rates and payments. The main business of the IMF is the provision of loans to its members (including industrialized and developing countries) when they experience balance of payments difficulties. These loans frequently carry conditions that require substantial internal economic adjustments by the recipients, most of which are developing countries.

jati—Literally, birth group. Basic endogamous unit of the caste system. There are approximately 3,000 *jatis* in contemporary society. The word *jati* is also sometimes used for ethnic, religious, or linguistic groups.

karma—Literally, action. Spiritual merit or demerit that a being acquired in a previous incarnation and is acquiring in present existence.

lakh—A unit of measure equal to 100,000. Also see crore (*q.v.*).

Mandal Commission—A government-appointed commission, officially the Second Backwards Classes Commission, chaired by former member of Parliament Bindhyeshwari Prasad Mandal from December 1978 to December 1980. Of the five members, four were from Backward Classes (*q.v.*) and one was from a Scheduled Caste (*q.v.*). The commission's controversial December 1980 report (the *Mandal Commission Report of the Backward Classes Commission*) called for reserving 27 percent of all services and public-sector undertakings under the central government and 27 percent of all admissions to institutions of higher education (except in states that have reserved higher percentages) for Backward Class members and Dalits (*q.v.*). In August 1990, Prime Minister Vishwanath Pratap Singh announced his support for the radical affirmative-action 1980 proposals. The First Backward Classes Commission existed from January 1950 to March 1955.

Muslim League—See All-India Muslim League.

Nonaligned Movement—Established in September 1961 with the aim of promoting the concept of political and military nonalignment (*q.v.*) apart from the traditional East and West blocs. India was among the original members. The Nonaligned Movement in 1995 included 107 members plus the Palestine Liberation Organization, twenty-one observer nations and organizations, and twenty-one "guest" nations.

nonalignment—The ideological basis of Indian foreign policy, first articulated by Jawaharlal Nehru: refusal to align India with any bloc or alliance, peaceful settlement of international disputes, the Panch Shila (*q.v.*), anticolonialism, antiracism, and international cooperation to promote economic development.

Organization of the Petroleum Exporting Countries (OPEC)—Established on September 14, 1960, with the aim of coordinating the members' petroleum policies and prices. Members include Algeria, Gabon, Indonesia, Iran, Iraq, Kuwait, Libya, Nigeria, Qatar, Saudi Arabia, United Arab Emirates, and Venezuela.

Panch Shila—Literally, five principles of foreign policy: mutual respect for territorial integrity and sovereignty, mutual nonaggression, mutual noninterference in internal affairs, equality and mutual benefit, and peaceful coexistence. The Panch Shila were enunciated by Jawaharlal Nehru in April 1954 in a trade agreement with China and adopted as a keystone of relations among nations at the Asian-African Conference (the Bandung Conference) held in Bandung, Indonesia, in 1955.

panchayat—A council of five or more. Found both in villages and in *jatis* (*q.v.*). Also refers to an administrative grouping of villages under constitutionally mandated elected councils.

pandit(s)—Honorific for erudite individual, sometimes taken as personal or family name. Various Brahmans (*q.v*) (such as the family of Jawaharlal Nehru) were known as pandits. Sometimes transliterated as pundit.

Punjab—State in India (and a province in adjacent Pakistan). Term *the Punjab* usually refers to either the pre-1947 state of British India or the geographic region centered on the five major rivers, whence its name, *panch ab*, meaning five waters, or rivers.

rupee (Rp; Rs—plural)—Basic unit of currency consisting of 100 paise. From September 1949 to June 1966, the official value of the rupee was Rs4.76 per US$1. From June 1966 through mid-December 1971, the official value was Rs7.50 per US$1, and from mid-December 1971 to late June 1972, the value was Rs7.28 per US$1. Thereafter, the official value of the rupee as compared with the United States dollar began to fall, from Rs7.44 in 1971–72 to Rs 8.08 in 1979–80 to Rs12.24 in 1985–86 to Rs14.48 in 1988–89, Rs16.66 in 1989–90, Rs17.95 in 1990–91, Rs24.52 in 1991–92, and Rs26.41 in 1992–93. A dual exchange-rate system was established in March 1992, and, starting in March 1993, the exchange rate was reunified at the free-market rate. As of July 1996, US$1 was worth Rs35.67. Aluminum-magnesium, stainless steel, and cupro-nickel coins are minted at the Calcutta and Bombay mints for circulation in five, ten, twenty, twenty-five, and fifty paise and Rs1 and Rs2 denominations. Bank notes issued by the Reserve Bank of India are issued in denominations of Rs1, Rs2, Rs5, Rs10, Rs20, Rs50, Rs100, and Rs500.

satyagraha—Method employed by Mahatma Gandhi and his followers to secure sociopolitical reform by nonviolent, passive resistance and noncooperation; the individual following the method is called a satyagrahi.

Scheduled Areas—Article 244 of the Indian constitution allows the government to compile a schedule (list) of areas of the country occupied by Scheduled Tribes (*q.v.*). The Sixth and Ninth Schedules of the constitution list the Scheduled Areas.

Scheduled Castes—Article 341 of the Indian constitution allows thegovernment to compile a schedule (list) of castes, races, or tribes or parts of groups within castes, races, or tribes that are economically and socially disadvantaged and are therefore entitled to protection and specified benefits under the constitution. Untouchables, also known as Harijans (*q.v.*) or Dalits (*q.v.*), constitute the bulk of Scheduled Castes. See also Scheduled Tribes (*q.v.*). The 1991 census tabulated 138 million Scheduled Caste members throughout India, representing about 16 percent of the total population. The largest numbers were in Uttar Pradesh, West Bengal, Bihar, Andhra Pradesh, and Tamil

Nadu. The schedule in the constitution does not list the Scheduled Castes by name.

Scheduled Languages—Article 351 of the Indian constitution allows the government to compile a schedule (list) of languages recognized by the government for use in state legislatures. The Eighth Schedule, written in 1950, lists Assamese, Bengali, Gujarati, Hindi, Kannada, Kashmiri, Malayalam, Marathi, Oriya, Punjabi, Sanskrit, Tamil, Telugu, and Urdu. Sindhi was added to the schedule in 1967, and Konkani, Manipuri, and Nepali were added in 1992. Article 343 of the constitution designates Hindi written in Devanagari (*q.v.*) as the official language of India. Even though it was supposed to be phased out by 1965, English continues as India's other official language for use in Parliament, the Supreme Court, and the high courts unless otherwise authorized by the president.

Scheduled Tribes—Article 342 of the Indian constitution includes a schedule (list) of tribes or tribal communities that are economically and socially disadvantaged and are entitled to specified benefits. The tribes are listed in the Fifth Schedule. The 1991 census tabulated 67.8 million members of Scheduled Tribes throughout India, representing about 8 percent of the total population. The largest numbers are in Maharashtra, Orissa, and West Bengal. See also Scheduled Castes (*q.v.*).

Shia (from Shiat Ali, the Party of Ali)—A member of the smaller of the two great divisions of Islam. The Shia supported the claims of Ali and his line to presumptive right to the caliphate and leadership of the Muslim community, and on this issue they divided from the Sunnis (*q.v.*) in the major schism of Islam. Later schisms have produced further divisions among the Shia over the identity and number of imams (*q.v.*). Most Shia revere twelve Imams, the last of whom is believed to be hidden from view.

South Asian Association for Regional Cooperation (SAARC)—Comprises the seven nations of South Asia: Bangladesh, Bhutan, India, Maldives, Nepal, Pakistan, and Sri Lanka; founded as the South Asia Regional Cooperation (SARC) organization at a meeting of foreign ministers in New Delhi on August 1–2, 1983. A second organizational meeting of foreign ministers was held in Thimphu in May 1985, followed by the inaugural meeting of heads of state and government in Dhaka on December 7–8, 1985. SAARC's

goal is to effect economic, technical, and cultural cooperation and to provide a forum for discussions of South Asian
political problems.

Sufi(s)—Comes from *suf,* the Arabic word for "wool." The term
derives from the practice of wearing a woolen robe, a sign
of dedicating oneself to the mystical life, known in Islam as
becoming a Sufi. Sufis seek mystical union with God and
have been condemned by some Sunni (*q.v.*) legal schools.

Sunni—Comes from *sunna,* meaning "custom," with connota-
tions of orthodoxy. One of the two great divisions of Islam,
the Sunnis supported the traditional method of election to
the caliphate and accepted the Umayyad line. On this
issue, they divided from the Shia (*q.v.*) belief in the first
great schism within Islam.

swadeshi—Literally, of one's own country. A preindependence
movement to further the use of Indian-made items, particularly cottage-industry products, such as hand-loomed
cloth, and to oppose British-made goods.

tribal—In addition to its use as an adjective—tribal land or
tribal customs—the word is also used as a noun to describe
a tribesperson, tribesman, or tribeswoman.

twice-born—Referring to *jatis* (*q.v.*) claiming membership in
one of the three upper *varnas* (*q.v.*), that is, Brahman
(*q.v.*), Kshatriya, and Vaishya. Male member's natural birth
is followed by a sprititual rebirth in a rite involving investiture with a sacred thread.

varna—Literally, color. One of the four large caste groups
(Brahman (*q.v.*) Kshatriya, Vaishya, and Sudra) from
which most *jatis* (*q.v.*) are believed to derive.

World Bank—Informal name used to designate a group of four
affiliated international institutions: the International Bank
for Reconstruction and Development (IBRD), the International Development Association (IDA), the International
Finance Corporation (IFC), and the Multilateral Investment Guarantee Agency (MIGA). The IBRD, established
in 1945, has the primary purpose of providing loans at
market-related rates of interest to developing countries at
more advanced stages of development. The IDA, a legally
separate loan fund but administered by the staff of the
IBRD, was set up in 1960 to furnish credits to the poorest
developing countries on much easier terms than those of
conventional IBRD loans. The IFC, founded in 1956, sup-
plements the activities of the IBRD through loans and

assistance designed specifically to encourage the growth of productive private enterprises in the less-developed countries. The MIGA, founded in 1988, insures private foreign investment in developing countries against various noncommercial risks. The president and certain officers of the IBRD hold the same positions in the IFC. The four institutions are owned by the governments of the countries that subscribe their capital. To participate in the World Bank group, member states must first belong to the International Monetary Fund (*q.v.*).

zamindar(s)—Landlord, but particularly the group of landlords and the zamindar system that emerged after the British Permanent Settlement (Landlease) Act of 1793. In essence, the former revenue collectors of the Mughal period (1526–1858) became landlords under the British.

Index

Abdullah, Farooq, li, 487, 494, 521; corruption under, 494; dismissed, 521

Abdullah, Sheikh Mohammed, 486, 493, 494; accession to India under, 520; arrested, 487; as chief minister of Jammu and Kashmir, 487

abortion, 254; of female fetuses, 93, 252, 253, 291

Abu Bakr, 156

Achaemenid Empire, 9

acharyas, 132–33

acquired immune deficiency syndrome (AIDS), 64; and blood supply, 99; and HIV infection, 97, 98, 98–99; discrimination against people with, 98; spread of, 98, 99; suspected cases of, 97, 98

Adhikary, Man Mohan, 530

Adi Granth (Original Book), 164

Advani, Lal Krishna, l; arrested, 477, 497; in BJP, 480; Ramjanmabhumi Temple pilgrimage of, 477, 497

Afghanistan: border with, 516; relations with, 541; Soviet invasion of, xlviii, 55, 517, 523, 538–39, 543–44, 548; Soviet withdrawal from, 551

Africans, 213–14; under British, 213–14; geographic distribution of, 214; under Mughals, 213–14; religion of, 214

aghoris, 280

Agni, 121

AGP. *See* Asom Gana Parishad

Agra, 23

Agreement on a Comprehensive Political Settlement of the Cambodia Conflict, 537

agricultural cooperatives, 392, 412; agricultural processing in, 422; credit from, 418, 419–20; dairy, 412–13; inputs from, 420; marketing by, 422, 423; value of produce marketed by, 422–23

agricultural credit, 317, 418–21; from banks, 418–19; from cooperatives, 418, 419–20; support for, 426

agricultural development, 391–404;

under British, 391; goals of, 392; government role in, 382–83, 392; policy, 391–93

agricultural development programs, 393–404; administration of, 393–94; education, 393, 394–96; extension, 393, 394–97; finance, 393; in five-year plans, 394; marketing, 393, 423; research, 393, 394–96; technology, 393, 402–3; types of, 393

agricultural growth, 299; rates, 404–7

agricultural inputs, 393, 400–2, 397; distribution of, 420; fertilizer, xxxviii, 305, 400–1, 407; machinery, 402–3; pesticides, 401–2; production of, 420; seeds, xxxviii, 310, 400, 407, 410, 426

agricultural marketing, 421–24; cooperatives for, 422; government control of, 421–22, 423–24; support for, 426

agricultural policy: goals of, 393

agricultural prices, 403–4; policy for, 403–4; supports for, 381

Agricultural Prices Commission, 403

Agricultural Produce (Grading and Marketing) Act (1937), 423

agricultural production, 402, 404–12; decreases in, 403; increases in, 394; limitations on, 394

agricultural products *(see also under individual crops)*: barley, 384; commercial crops, 382, 407, 409–10; corn, 384, 407; cotton, 298, 303, 305, 331, 368, 381, 385, 404, 409–10, 422, 425; crop failures of 1972–73, 54; fodder crops, 385; fruit, 384; grading of, 423; grain, 4, 300, 305, 307–8, 310, 381–82, 391, 392–93, 403, 404, 407–9, 411, 422, 423, 424; inspection of, 423; jute, 297, 298, 368, 381, 404, 409, 410, 422; millet, 384, 385, 407, 408; nontraditional crops, 382; nuts, 384, 386; oilseeds, 303, 368, 382, 384, 385, 404, 407, 409; output, 404–10; potatoes, 384; pulses, 381, 382, 384, 385, 403, 404, 407, 408, 410–11; rice, 75, 368, 382, 384, 385,

ments in, 64, 106–7; of Jains, 128; languages of instruction in, 34, 108, 184, 193–94, 195, 207, 212; of linguistic minorities, 184, 195; in mathematics, 361; middle, 103; of middle class, xl, 107; of Muslims, 39; nonformal, 64, 112, 113; as percentage of gross national product, 105; policy, 104; primary, 103, 105–8; programs, 104–5; in rural areas, 104–5, 285, 308; in science, 361, 369–70, 372; secondary, 103, 105–8; and society, 110; in technology, 361, 369–70; of tribal people, 207–9; in urban areas, 104–5; of women, 113

educational development, 222

EEC. *See* European Economic Community

Egypt: relations with, 538

Einstein, Albert, 362

Eisenhower, Dwight D., 546

Ekta Yatra (Unity Pilgrimage), 494

Election Commission, 454–55; assertiveness of, 433; functions of, 462

election laws, 454–55; enforcement of, 454–55

elections (*see also* voting), 462–63; corruption in, 498; killings in, 454, 455, 463; of 1937, 45; of 1952, 215; of 1967, 52, 466, 475; of 1969, 446; of 1971, 52–53, 467; of 1972, 467; of 1977, 54, 476; of 1981, 55; of 1983, 217; of 1989, 58, 470–71; of 1991, 472, 473, 478, 480–81, 497; of 1992, 486; of 1993, 481; of 1995, 227; of 1996, l; *panchayat,* 225–26; parliamentary, 443, 470; violence in, 454

electric power (*see also* energy), 339–40; capacity, 339; consumption of, 339; under five-year plans, 309, 310; generation, 300, 307, 309, 339; hydro, 76, 222, 339, 340; investment in, 299, 312; nuclear, 339, 373; in rural areas, 339; shortages, 286, 339, 340; thermal, 339; transmission, 339; in urban areas, 340

electronics industry, xxxix, 332; employment in, 376; growth of, 332; investment in, 57; research in, 372, 373

elite class, xxxvii, xl; backlash by, 620; conspicuous consumption by, 306; employment in, 251; Parsis as, 171, 172; as percentage of population, xl;

279; political affiliation of, 463, 481; political activities of, 495; and pollution and purity practices, 239–40; population of, 301; women, 251

Elliot, Gilbert John, 39

El Salvador: peacekeeping forces in, 579

EL TV, 357

employment: affirmative action in, 302; in agriculture, 297, 381, 392; of Anglo-Indians, 212, 213; of children, 105–6, 112, 255, 325; in cities, 288; of college graduates, 109; in construction, 335; in electronics industry, 376; in fishing, 297, 416; under five-year plans, 311; in forestry, 297; and job creation, 76, 306, 328; of people with technical training, 592; of poor people, 308; in private sector, 325; in public sector, 302, 325; in railroads, 212, 345; requirements, 329; in rural areas, 311; in textiles industry, 331; of women, 251

energy (*see also* electricity; *see also under* individual energy sources), 335–41; commercial, 335, 336; consumption, 335; under five-year plans, 311; government control of, 330; investment in, 306; noncommercial, 335–36; nuclear, 300; production, 335; sources of, 335

English, 187–88, 192–94; broadcasts in, 356; knowledge of, 192, 198; as language of instruction, 34, 194–94, 207, 212; as official language, 182, 183, 187–88, 195; publications in, 194, 499, 500; teaching of, 193, 194

Enron Corporation, 307

environment: under constitution, 436; and forestry, 414; as political issue, 503, 504; protection programs, 320, 414; quality of, 76

environmental problems: motor vehicle emissions, 350; radiation leaks, 340; scientific and technical support for, 358

Essential Commodities Act (1955), 304–5

Essential Services Maintenance Act (1981), 440

Eternal Party. *See* Akali Dal

ethnic diversity, 233

ethnic minorities, 199–214

297, 305; of fertilizer, 330; of foreign exchange, 304, 305, 321, 323; of imports, 297, 305; of industry, xxxix, 297, 329; of investment, 305; of iron and steel, xxxix, 304, 330; of land tenure, 386; of metals, 330; of mining, xxxix, 304; of newspapers, 500–1; of oil, 330; of prices, 304, 305; of production, 304; of railroads, xxxix, 304; of services, 304; of shipbuilding, 304, 330; of state governments, 457; of taxes, 457; of telecommunications, xxxix, 297, 304, 330, 355, 356, 501; of territories, 457–58; of trade, 302, 321; of transportation, 297, 342

government finance: reorganized, 37

Government of India Act (1919), 41; satyagraha against, 42

Government of India Act (1935), 44; goals of, 44–45

government spending: on education, 105; on health care, 100–101; on nongovernmental organizations, 503; on research and development, 50, 358, 363–68

governors, 456–57; appointment of, 456

Graham, Bruce, 479

grain (*see also* food grains): area sown in, 407; availability of, 382; harvesting methods for, 403; prices, 404; production, 408–9, 410–11; supplies, 307–8

Great Depression: agriculture during, 391

Greater Himalayan Range, 69

Great Indian Desert, 67, 384–85; agriculture in, 384; climate of, 78, 384

Greece: influence of, 9, 10; and mathematics, 359

Green Revolution, xxxviii–xxxix, 362, 381, 393, 410–12; area sown under, 411; benefits of, 411; criteria for, 411; growth of, 411; socioeconomic impact of, 275, 412, 607–8; support for, 410

Grierson, George, 182

gross domestic product (GDP): growth rate, 303, 311; agriculture, 297, 299–300, 381; budget deficit, 312; communications, 300; construction, 300, 335; exports, 321; finance, 300; fishing, 297, 299–300; forestry, 297, 299–300; health care, 100; imports, 321; industry, 300; informal economy, 300;

investment, 299; manufacturing, 297, 300; mining and quarrying, 299–300, 341; real estate, 300; research and development, 365; services sector, 300; taxes, 315; textile industry, 297; trade, 300; transportation, 300; utilities, 300

gross national product (GNP), 49; agriculture as a percentage of, 392; defense spending as a percentage of, 581; education spending as a percentage of, 105; health care spending as a percentage of, 100

Group of Fifteen, 558–59

Grow More Food Campaign, 391

Guatemala: peacekeeping forces in, 579

guest workers: in Middle East, 326; in Persian Gulf, 302, 326; remittances from, 283, 302, 326

Gujarat: Africans in, 214; agricultural growth in, 404; elections in, 481; forestry agency in, 414; Jains in, 127, 128; hydroelectric projects in, 399; irrigation projects in, 399; nuclear power plant in, 340; oil in, 337, 338; Parsis in, 171; personal names in, 246–47; political parties in, 481; under President's Rule, 54; rural population of, 88; teachers in, 107; tribes in, 200; urbanization in, 86, 87

Gujarati language, 182; native speakers of, 182

Gupta Empire (320–550), 12–14; disintegration of, 14; education in, 13; medicine in, 13–14; religion in, 13

gurdwaras, 166, 167, 486, 491

Guru Granth Sahib (Holy Book of the Gurus), 164, 165

gurus, 125, 279; role of, 164–65; Sikh, 163, 164–65

Haksar, Nandita, 611–12

Hanuman, 136

Harappa, 4

Harappan culture (Indus Valley culture), xxxv, 4–5; cities in, 4; decline in, 5; discoveries in, 359; economy of, 4–5; languages in, 5

Hardwar: pilgrimage to, 152

Hargobind, Guru, 163

Harihara I, 19

Harijans. *See* Dalits

Harsha Vardhana (606–647), 13
hartal (general strike): of 1919, 41
Haryana (state), xliv; agricultural growth
in, 404; elections in, 475; fertilizer
consumption in, 400; Green Revolution in, 411–12; Hindi in, 191; irrigation in, 407; land reform in, 390;
poverty in, 301; roads in, 349; sex ratio
in, 253; Sikh shrines in, 166
Haryana Plain, 67, 68; irrigation of, 68;
urban areas in, 86
Hastings, Warren, 32
Hazratbal mosque, 495
health, 94–99; influences on, 94; SAARC
program for, 559; research in, 366
health, public, 99; vaccine production,
368–69
health care, 99–103; *ayurvedic*, 103; discoveries in, 359; in Gupta Empire, 13–
14; impact of, on population growth,
82; for poor people, 308; role of government in, 99–100; *unani*, 103
health care professionals, 101, 103; number of, 101, 103, 366; training of, 103,
361
health facilities, 63, 101–3; adversarial
role of, 102; dispensaries, 102; equipment in, 102–3; family planning programs in, 90, 102; geographic
distribution of, 102; hospitals, 102,
286; number of, 101, 102; primary
health centers, 101–2; problems in,
102; rural, 102; urban, 286
health problems, xl, 64; AIDS, 97–99;
attempts to control, 94–95; blindness,
96; cancer, 97; cardiovascular disease,
97; diarrheal diseases, 96; disease, 94–
97; filaria, 95; goiter, 96; HIV infection, 97; leprosy, 95–96; malaria, 95;
malnutrition, 94, 96; pneumonic
plague, 96; smallpox, 143; tuberculosis, 96
heavy water, 373
Hedgewar, Keshav Baliram, 175, 478–79
Hezb-ul Mujahideen, 495, 607
hierarchy, 234–35, 292; academic, 235;
in business, 235; of caste, 267; of clans,
244; in families, 235, 247, 254–55; of
hijras, 280; in Islam, 234–35; of judges,
453; and language, 183–85; marriage
up in, 261; of renunciants, 280; of
sadhus, 280; by sex, 247

High Altitude Warfare School, 587
hijras (transvestite-eunuchs), 279, 280–
81; hierarchy of, 281; living arrangements of, 281; population of, 280;
powers of; worship by, 280
Hill Area Development Programme, 394
Hillmen's Association, 223–24; origins
of, 224
Himachal Pradesh (state), xliv; Buddhists in, 131; development of, 222;
elections in, 481; Hindi in, 191; political parties in, 481; poverty in, 301; refugees in, 532; rural population of, 88;
Sikh shrines in, 166; tribes in, 199
Himalayas, 63, 64, 68–70; agriculture in,
384; area of, 383; climate of, 78; crop
and livestock patterns in, 383; extent
of, 68; formation of, 68; land use in,
383–84; livestock in, 384; population
density in, 87; soil in, 384; tea plantations in, 384; tribes in, 169, 206
Hindi language (*see also* Urdu), 182,
187–92; in British Raj, 188; broadcasts
in, 356; cinema, 191; demonstrations
against, 51, 195, 485; dominance of,
188–91; geographic distribution of,
191; as language of instruction, 207; as
lingua franca, 191; literary forms of,
188, 191; mutual intelligibility of, with
Punjabi and Urdu, 184, 191; native
speakers of, 182; as official language,
182, 183 187–88, 195, 485; origins of,
188; publications in, 500; script, 188;
spread of, 188; standard, 188–91
Hindu: charity, 146; enlightened masters, 132–33; gurus, 125; inheritance
laws of, 248; influence, 210; life-cycle
rituals, 146–48; monastic communities, 132–33; pilgrimages, 149–53; pilgrims, 144, 152; refugees, 46;
traditions, 5–6
Hindu festivals, 153–54; Dipavali, 23,
142, 154; Dussehra, 136; Ganesh
Chaturthi, 154; Holi, 138, 154; Janmashtami, 154; Mahashivaratri, 154;
parades in, 153; participation in, 128;
plays in, 153; Pongal, 154; Ramanavami, 154
Hindu goddesses, 141–43; blood sacrifice to, 143; local, 143; of smallpox,
143
Hindu gods, 121, 122; hymns of, 134; as

linguistic states, 184, 194–95; organization of, 195
Linguistic Survey of India (Grierson), 182
Lion of Kashmir. *See* Abdullah, Sheikh Mohammed
Li Peng, 534–35
literacy: in English, 193
literacy rate, 106; in Bihar, 106; campaigns to improve, 106, 312; of Christians, 244; female, 106, 113; in Kerala, 106, 244; in Khasi tribe, 244; male, 106, 113
literature: Tamil, 12; tribal, 171
livestock, 412–13; ancient, 4; cattle, 412; education, 394, 395; in Himalayas, 384; in Indo-Gangetic Plain, 385; landholdings for, 389; patterns, 383; percentage of work force in, 325; research, 368, 394, 395; as source of energy, 412
Lodi, Ibrahim (1517–26), 20
Lodi Dynasty (1451–1526), 16
Lok Sabha, 441–44; Committee on External Affairs, 514; foreign affairs under, 514; functions of, 441; government budget under, 313; members of, 443; money bills in, 445; number of seats in, 441; powers of, 441; reserved seats in, 436–37, 443; sessions of, 443; term in, 443
Longowal, Harchand Singh, 492, 610
LTTE. *See* Liberation Tigers of Tamil Eelam
Lucknow: education in, 113
Lucknow Pact (1li), 40
Lucknow University, 109
Lutheran Church: number members of, 171

Madras, 290; airport, 354; as British presidency, 29, 32; fishing in, 417; IIT campus in, 370; population of, 285; port of, 350, 351; public transportation in, 349, 350
Madras (state) (*see also* Tamil Nadu): demonstrations in, 51; political representation in, 52
Madhya Pradesh: agriculture in, 385; coal in, 336; education in, 112; elections in, 475, 481; family structure in, 258–59; forests in, 413; Hindi in, 191;

hydroelectric projects in, 399; irrigation projects in, 399; Jains in, 128; political parties in, 481, 490–91; poverty in, 301; Scheduled Tribes in, 88; tribes in, 200; urbanization in, 86
Magadha Kingdom, 8, 9–10
Magadhi language, 192
Mahabharata (Great Battle of the Descendants of Bharata), xxxv, 9, 136–37, 142; broadcast of, 502
Mahabodhi Society (Society of Great Enlightenment), 130–31
Mahanadi River, 67, 75
Mahanagar Telephone Nigam, 355
Maharashtra: Africans in, 214; agriculture in, 385, 404; Buddhists in, 131; farms in, 386; forests in, 413; hydroelectric projects in, 399; irrigation projects in, 399; land distribution in, 390; landholding ceiling in, 390; legislature of, 455; Jains in, 127, 128; nuclear power plant in, 340; Parsis in, 171; population growth rate in, 93; rural population of, 88; Scheduled Tribes in, 88; tribes in, 200; urbanization in, 86
Mahars: conversion of, to Buddhism, 177
Mahashivaratri festival, 154
Mahavira, Vardamana, xxxvii, 125–26
Mahmud of Ghazni, 16
Maintenance of Internal Security Act (1971), 439; politicians arrested under, 439; repealed, 440
Maithili language, 191, 192
Malabar Coast, 64
Malayala Manorama, 500
Malayalam language, 15, 182, 186; in Christian churches, 170; native speakers of, 182; publications in, 500
Malaysia: military cooperation with, 537
Maldives: aid to, 526, 531; border with, 74, 531; coup attempt in, xlviii, 531, 548, 564, 578; membership of, in SAARC, 559; military assistance to, xlviii, 531, 548, 564, 578
Malwa Plateau, 67
Mamluk Dynasty (1206–90), 16
Manasarowar Lake, 74
Mandal Commission report: opposition to, 222–23, 274–75, 477; support for, 478
Manekshaw, S.H.F.J. (Sam), 595

Contributors

Ashok Bhargava is Professor of Economics at the University of Wisconsin-Whitewater, Whitewater, Wisconsin.

John Echeverri-Gent is Associate Professor of Government and Foreign Affairs at the University of Virginia.

Sumit Ganguly is Professor of Political Science, Hunter College, and the Graduate School of the City University of New York.

James Heitzman is Associate Professor of Information Science at Cazenovia College, Syracuse, New York.

Doranne Jacobson is a South Asian area research consultant and Director of International Images, Springfield, Illinois.

John J. Paul is Associate Professor of History, Fitchburg State College, Fitchburg, Massachusetts.

John D. Rogers is Lecturer on Social Studies, Harvard University, Cambridge, Massachusetts.

Karl E. Ryavec, formerly an analyst at the Defense Mapping Agency, is a doctoral candidate, Department of Geography, University of Hawaii, Honolulu.

Roxane D.V. Sismanidis is an Asian area consultant and a Program Officer with the United States Institute of Peace, Washington, D.C.

Allen W. Thrasher is Senior Reference Librarian, Southern Asian Section, Asian Division, Library of Congress, Washington, D.C.

Robert L. Worden is head of the Regional Section, Federal Research Division, Library of Congress, Washington, D.C.

Published Country Studies

(Area Handbook Series)

550–65	Afghanistan	550–36	Dominican Republic
550–98	Albania		and Haiti
550–44	Algeria	550–52	Ecuador
550–59	Angola	550–43	Egypt
550–73	Argentina	550–150	El Salvador
550–111	Armenia, Azerbaijan, and Georgia	550-113	Estonia, Latvia, and Lithuania
550–169	Australia	550–28	Ethiopia
550–176	Austria	550–167	Finland
550–175	Bangladesh	550–173	Germany, East
550–112	Belarus and Moldova	550–155	Germany, Fed. Rep. of
550–170	Belgium	550–153	Ghana
550–66	Bolivia	550–87	Greece
550–20	Brazil	550–78	Guatemala
550–168	Bulgaria	550–174	Guinea
550–61	Burma	550–82	Guyana and Belize
550–50	Cambodia	550–151	Honduras
550–166	Cameroon	550–165	Hungary
550–159	Chad	550–21	India
550–77	Chile	550–154	Indian Ocean
550–60	China	550–39	Indonesia
550–26	Colombia	550–68	Iran
550–33	Commonwealth Caribbean, Islands of the	550–31	Iraq
		550–25	Israel
550–91	Congo	550–182	Italy
550–90	Costa Rica	550–30	Japan
550–69	Côte d'Ivoire (Ivory Coast)	550–34	Jordan
		550–56	Kenya
550–152	Cuba	550–81	Korea, North
550–22	Cyprus	550–41	Korea, South
550–158	Czechoslovakia	550–58	Laos

550–24	Lebanon	550–70	Senegal
550–38	Liberia	550–180	Sierra Leone
550–85	Libya	550–184	Singapore
550–172	Malawi	550–86	Somalia
550–45	Malaysia	550–93	South Africa
550–161	Mauritania	550–95	Soviet Union
550–79	Mexico	550–179	Spain
550–76	Mongolia	550–96	Sri Lanka
550–49	Morocco	550–27	Sudan
550–64	Mozambique	550–47	Syria
550–35	Nepal and Bhutan	550–62	Tanzania
550–88	Nicaragua	550–53	Thailand
550–157	Nigeria	550–89	Tunisia
550–94	Oceania	550–80	Turkey
550–48	Pakistan	550–74	Uganda
550–46	Panama	550–97	Uruguay
550–156	Paraguay	550–71	Venezuela
550–185	Persian Gulf States	550–32	Vietnam
550–42	Peru	550–183	Yemens, The
550–72	Philippines	550–99	Yugoslavia
550–162	Poland	550–67	Zaire
550–181	Portugal	550–75	Zambia
550–160	Romania	550–171	Zimbabwe
550–37	Rwanda and Burundi		
550–51	Saudi Arabia		